PATRIOTIC BETRAYAL

PATRIOTIC BETRAYAL

The Inside Story of the CIA's

Secret Campaign to Enroll American Students

in the Crusade Against Communism

KAREN M. PAGET

Yale UNIVERSITY PRESS/NEW HAVEN & LONDON

Published with assistance from the foundation established in memory
of Amasa Stone Mather of the Class of 1907, Yale College.

Yale University Press books may be purchased in quantity for educational, business,
or promotional use. For information, please e-mail sales.press@yale.edu
(U.S. office) or sales@yaleup.co.uk (U.K. office).

Designed by Mary Valencia.
Set in Janson O.S., Friz Quadrata, and Birch types by Tseng Information Systems, Inc.
Printed in the United States of America.

Library of Congress Cataloging-in-Publication Data
Paget, Karen M.
Patriotic betrayal : the inside story of the CIA's secret campaign to enroll
American students in the crusade against communism / Karen M. Paget.
pages cm
Includes bibliographical references and index.
ISBN 978-0-300-20508-4
1. United States. Central Intelligence Agency—History—20th century.
2. United States National Student Association. 3. Anti-communist movements—
United States—History—20th century. I. Title.
JK468.16P27 2015
327.1273—dc23
2014021916

A catalogue record for this book is available from the British Library.

This paper meets the requirements of ANSI/NISO z39.48-1992 (Permanence of Paper).

10 9 8 7 6 5 4 3 2 1

Dedicated to my late parents,

Robert (2011) and Maxine (2013) Eggert,

whose unconditional love and support

made everything possible

CONTENTS

CONTENTS

PREFACE

FROM 1950 TO 1967, the Central Intelligence Agency ran a series of international covert operations through the U.S. National Student Association (NSA)—most of whose members had no idea they were "working" for the U.S. government. The operation came to a halt in 1967, when *Ramparts* magazine published an exposé of the covert relationship.

In 1965–66, my then-husband served on the NSA International Commission staff and was among those who knew about the CIA. As his wife, I also had been sworn to secrecy by agents of the U.S. government. Even after the *Ramparts* exposé, we kept quiet, cowed by the threat of prison terms if we divulged information. I remember thinking then that someday someone would tell the whole story. Years passed, but no one did.

One day in 1982 or 1983, two young Washington lawyers approached me in my role as a foundation director on behalf of the United States Student Association, the successor to the NSA, to request a grant to obtain documents under the Freedom of Information Act. Unaware of my background, they were surprised when I immediately awarded them the funds. I also helped them search for someone to write a history of the NSA-CIA relationship. Several people expressed interest, but the timing was not right for them. A friend from NSA days finally said to me, "Why don't you do it—you know more than all of us put together." A seed was planted. Decades later, it has blossomed.

Readers of this book will find a tension between the need to establish a solid historical record that scholars can mine in the future and rendering a good yarn. Since the NSA-CIA operation spanned continents and countries, often painful narrative choices had to be made. I decided to focus on well-known episodes of the Cold War, such as the Hungarian uprising, to reduce the need for background information. The perspective is American-centric, since the NSA is the prism through which this history is told. It is my hope that scholars from affected countries can build on this work and deepen the understanding of how the American operation influenced international student politics.

Since the sine qua non of *Patriotic Betrayal* is detail, the voluminous notes in the original manuscript posed a special problem, threatening to overwhelm the story. A happy compromise was reached: notes were pared to source identifications in this book, and a Web site was established (patrioticbetrayal.com) for those who want to delve deeper into the evidence or pursue the scholarly literature.

Creating a historical record has not been easy; wrenching protected information from the U.S. government requires sustained effort. I expected this problem. I did not expect the CIA to *reclassify* in 2001 documents pertinent to the NSA that were fifty and sixty years old and had been declassified under the twenty-five-year rule. Had I requested these documents earlier, they would have been available in the National Archives and Records Administration. A request in 2003 for two 1949-vintage reclassified reports took nine years to process. The re-declassified documents contained no bombshells or even revelatory information. To paraphrase an adage, "Justice delayed is justice denied," accountability delayed is no accountability at all.

Despite these obstacles, *Patriotic Betrayal* is drawn almost entirely from original sources. The international papers of the NSA, long rumored to have been burned or carted off in the middle of the night, reside at the Hoover Institution at Stanford University, beautifully archived and immune to CIA purges. Since CIA–private sector relationships were unique in that organizations had to bury them in public agendas, the NSA international papers amount to a blueprint, a guide to the architecture of the operation.

I also conducted extensive interviews, more than 150, which provided a constant check on the interpretation of the documents. Former NSA and CIA officials agreed to go on the record, perhaps because they had finally come to terms with their role, or perhaps, more simply, because someone finally asked them to. Surprisingly, these participants proved to be among the toughest critics of their own actions. This was true even of those who spent five or more years with the NSA-CIA operation or who became career CIA officers. Their reflections, offered on the record, correct a major weakness in the scant literature on the CIA's private-sector operations.

Finally, this research yielded unexpected insight into a contemporary issue. It offers a cautionary tale to those who urge a return to Cold War strategies to fight new enemies. Such advocates see parallels between fighting international communism and radical Islam, a position most explicitly laid out in a Rand Corporation study of 2007. Whether in pursuit of moderate Muslims or Western-friendly future leaders, advocates—and the wider public—would do well to ponder the lessons offered here by veterans of Cold War covert action.

PATRIOTIC BETRAYAL

PROLOGUE

ONE EVENING AFTER DARK, sometime in mid-October 1965, I took a
car ride that led me into uncharted territory. Two men, who over dinner earlier that evening had introduced themselves as former U.S. National Student Association (NSA) officials, drove my husband and me
to a house somewhere in northwest Washington, D.C. The moment we
entered the house, the phone rang. One of the men said he had to run
an "urgent errand" and asked my husband to accompany him. I was left
alone with the other man, who ushered me into a sunroom and took a
chair opposite me.

Until that moment, my husband and I had been excited by our involvement with the NSA. Both from small towns, we had met at the
University of Colorado and married in 1964. In August of that year,
along with thousands of students from across the nation, we traveled
to the University of Minnesota for the annual NSA Congress. I volunteered to type and run off stencils that contained the hundreds of reports, resolutions, and amendments debated by the delegates. After a
week or so of committee meetings, students gathered in a large hall for
sessions that often lasted into the early hours of the morning. By then,
I had proved a reliable volunteer and was asked to sit onstage and take
notes, a backup record in case the tape recorder failed.

Seated behind the podium at a table with other note takers, I had
a full view of the large hall, its long rows of tables crammed on each
side with delegates. Tall signs marked off the different regions. NSA
Congresses mimicked political party conventions, which I had seen only
on television. August in the Midwest is hot and steamy, and everyone
smoked. My eyes smarted from the heat and tobacco haze that hung over
the hall, but I was riveted by the political speeches; some delegates were
funny, a few droned, but many were gifted orators. I had never seen or
heard anything like it. I had grown up more devoted to cheerleading and
baton twirling than political or intellectual pursuits. If I read a newspaper at all it was for the local sports section.

Some months after the Minnesota Congress, in the spring of 1965, an NSA official came to Boulder and encouraged my husband to apply for the association's prestigious international summer seminar to be held at Haverford College, just outside NSA headquarters in Philadelphia. I embraced the idea, eager to taste more of the astonishing world I had first relished in Minnesota. He was accepted, and I was hired to type material for the seminar; the NSA even gave us an extra dorm room for our five-month-old baby. We joined eleven remarkable men and one woman: most were college newspaper editors or student body presidents; others were graduate students who specialized in African, Asian, or Latin American area studies. Whenever my work was caught up or the baby asleep, I was permitted to sit in on the formal sessions and absorb lectures about African or Latin American student politics.

On one occasion we traveled as a group from Philadelphia to Washington to visit the State Department, where we watched a film on John F. Kennedy called *Years of Lightning, Day of Drums*. The movie was intended for overseas audiences, and we felt privileged at being allowed to see it. And weepy. Kennedy's assassination in November 1963 was still fresh for all of us, and no one emerged from the film with a dry eye.

In the final days of the seminar, the NSA offered my husband a salaried post on the international staff. This meant postponing law school and moving to Washington, D.C., where the NSA headquarters was relocating. Again with my enthusiastic support, he accepted.

Before the move, we once more attended the annual NSA Congress in late August, a requirement for all seminar participants. We drove through the night to reach Madison, Wisconsin, stopping for a brief time in Chicago. This time, I worked as paid staff in the secretariat that churned out convention material. Not yet aware of the women's movement, I was thrilled when the NSA president decided that a woman should sit onstage during a speech by Vice President Hubert H. Humphrey lest he need a drink of water. The war in Vietnam was a huge issue, and Humphrey was coming to defend President Lyndon B. Johnson's policy. As I sat onstage taking notes, I understood more of the debate and watched the votes with an avidity I had lacked the summer before. On the spur of the moment, my husband ran for national affairs vice president and lost by one vote.

Despite his loss, the international job offer remained secure, and after we moved to Washington, I enrolled at George Washington University as a junior, having taken a year out of college for the birth of our son. The new NSA headquarters, four-story twin townhouses off S Street near Dupont Circle, hummed with excitement. It was posh in comparison with the ramshackle Philadelphia office that previously housed the NSA: the international staff had two whole floors at the top. Our new life seemed almost magical. Then came the evening with the NSA veterans.

Once I was seated in the sunroom, the man sitting across from me asked whether I had noticed the strong bond among former NSA members. I nodded, remembering the older men I had seen at the NSA Congress in Madison, looking oddly out of place among the hundreds of undergraduates. He then told me that my husband was "doing work of great importance to the United States government," and handed me a document to sign.

My husband had tried to prepare me. He had undergone a similar ritual with the same two men a few weeks earlier and realized that I might not appreciate his abrupt departure, especially since I was still recovering from a bout of pneumonia. So I knew that the phone call had been a pretext to leave me alone with one of the men. Still feverish, I sat on the edge of an overstuffed chair, my eyes burning and my ears ringing, and tried not to look too frightened. I pretended to read the document, but lingering fever blurred my vision, and anxiety made the words jump off the page. To this day, I have no idea what was in the small print, and I never again saw the document. I knew only that I was never to reveal what I was about to learn. As an apolitical twenty-year-old from a small town in Iowa, I had no reason to distrust the U.S. government. I signed.

My host then revealed that he worked for the Central Intelligence Agency, that the CIA funded the NSA international program, and that he was my husband's case officer (with the unlikely code name "Aunt Alice"). I caught key phrases: "the United States had to support France in its war with Algeria, because France and the U.S. were allies . . . but . . . we all knew that the nationalists would win . . . it behooves the United States to get to know . . . student leaders . . . future rulers." I knew nothing about the Algerian war for independence or U.S. foreign policy, and I hadn't a clue why the United States couldn't have supported the Algerians. But the word *behooves* left an indelible mark. For years afterward, whenever I heard someone say "behooves," the hair on the back of my neck would stand up.

Our dinner companions that night, Robert Kiley and Matthew Iverson, did have bona-fide credentials as former NSA officials, but they were also the director and deputy director, respectively, of CIA Covert Action, Branch Five: Youth and Students (Covert Action 5). In CIA-speak, my husband and I had been made "witting"—inducted into the secret knowledge that the CIA funded and ran the international program of the United States National Student Association. The document I had signed was a security oath under the Espionage Act. I don't recall whether Iverson used the terms *felony* or *prison* when he talked to me that night, but I soon understood that revealing what he'd told me was a crime punishable by up to twenty years in prison.

Beyond keeping silent, my burden was minimal, since I didn't work for the NSA. But my husband had reporting requirements. Part of his salary came secretly from the CIA, deposited directly into our bank account.

Like so many student leaders before him, my husband trusted the officials who asked him to sign the security oath. He, like me, trusted the U.S. government. As student body president at the University of Colorado, he had been to Selma, Alabama, for the civil rights march and thought of federal action as key to ending segregation. But he had never imagined that the CIA was involved in the NSA—something he learned only after he signed the oath.

He was deeply shaken by the revelation, which turned our time in Washington from a period of elation to one of confusion and, later, fear. We took the oath literally and seriously. We told no one. We sought no counsel. Aged twenty (me) and twenty-two (my husband), we felt isolated. And we kept asking ourselves: How could this have happened?

IN LATE AUTUMN 1966, reporters on the small San Francisco–based *Ramparts* magazine got a tip that the CIA was involved with the U.S. National Student Association. The editors were flummoxed. The NSA was a liberal organization. It supported the civil rights movement, raised bail money for jailed activists, condemned the anticommunist witch hunts of the House Committee on Un-American Activities, and at its last Congress had debated supporting civil disobedience against the draft and the Vietnam War. Most *Ramparts* journalists, part of an emerging radical culture that did not take the communist threat seriously, viewed the CIA, as the investigative reporter Judith Coburn put it, as "right-wing assassins." Any connection between the CIA and a liberal organization made no sense.

Coburn later reflected that she, like many of her *Ramparts* colleagues, had no understanding of liberal anticommunism. By the 1960s, many people associated the fight against communism with Senator Joseph McCarthy, congressional committees that hunted down suspected communists, new conservatives who called themselves Goldwaterites and condemned Richard Nixon for being soft on the Soviets, and the far-right John Birch Society, which advocated the impeachment of liberal Supreme Court justice Earl Warren. "Liberal anticommunism" sounded like an oxymoron.

But it was not only the liberal politics of the NSA that befuddled the young journalists. They asked why the CIA would be involved with kids who played at "sandbox politics."

The *Ramparts* team shared the peculiarly American conceit that students were not significant political actors but teenagers preoccupied with football and fraternities or caught up in the emerging culture of sex, drugs, and rock and roll. Elsewhere in the world, students took to the streets, toppled governments, overthrew dictators, or at the very least shaped educational policy. Street protests would soon come to the United States over the Vietnam War, but in 1966 protest had been largely confined to "teach-ins," extended debates over American foreign policy that fell squarely within the academic tradition. While political awareness was growing on the nation's campuses, the wider public did not take students seriously.

These two features of the National Student Association, its liberalism and its youthful constituency, not only puzzled the *Ramparts* journalists; they help explain how the CIA was able to camouflage its relationship with the organization for nearly two decades. The latter, in particular, also helped the CIA deflect the charges after *Ramparts* broke the story the following year, citing names of foundations that operated as CIA conduits, witting officers of the NSA, and details of some covert operations.

In the wake of the *Ramparts* disclosures, the CIA maintained that its role had been minimal: the agency had merely awarded a few travel grants for NSA members to attend international meetings. Nothing could be farther from the truth. The CIA ran an *operation* through the NSA, global in scope, which disguised and protected the hand of the U.S. government—the very definition of covert action. The *Ramparts* investigators had caught glimpses of this global reach but were overwhelmed by its breadth, hampered as they were by limited resources and the sphinxlike silence that met them whenever they questioned anyone who knew anything. Thus, even after *Ramparts* created a firestorm in 1967 with its charges, the public was left wondering what the students had actually done for the CIA and what the CIA had gotten in return.

The answers are by no means simple, and they change over time. What began as a straightforward operation to thwart Soviet influence at home and abroad grew, multiplied, and divided like a vast spider plant. Intelligence gathering and espionage—despite subsequent CIA denials—were integral to its nature. In its later stages, the NSA funneled support to a wide variety of revolutionaries: Algerians, anti-Batista Cubans, Angolan and Mozambique liberationists, and anti-Shah Iranian activists. The NSA also pushed the Palestinian cause in the Middle East until American Jewish groups caught wind of its activities. It meddled in the internal politics of foreign student bodies, its work occasionally eased by suitcases of CIA cash. But because the NSA was both liberal and a student organization, virtually no one suspected its importance to the CIA.

In fact, following the *Ramparts* story, in 1967 the CIA orchestrated a successful cover-up to prevent the public from peering into its extensive private-sector operations. The White House, the U.S. Congress, and the State Department helped keep the shroud intact. Witting NSA participants kept silent, honoring their security oaths or bowing to Agency pressure (and a few threats) to reveal no details, a tactic known informally as a *non-denial denial*, something that acknowledged the CIA presence (non-denial) but withheld its significance (denial). (The phrase suggests that the CIA understood well the power of the old adage "the devil is in the details.")

How did a liberal student organization become, effectively, an arm of a covert government organization? The answer lies in the very origins of the NSA, founded in 1947 to represent American students, and in the actions of prewar progenitors—Roosevelt liberals, prominent educators, youth professionals, and U.S. government officials—committed to a noncommunist student organization at home and the projection of

American student leadership overseas. After World War II, the number of individuals and institutions concerned with keeping the student movement free from communist penetration would expand to include the Catholic Church and U.S. intelligence agencies. This informal coalition existed largely behind the scenes, its actions neither nefarious nor clandestine. But during and after the war, the various members built the networks and relationships that allowed the CIA to see operational opportunities in the new student organization.

PART ONE

COOPERATION OR COMBAT

1

A FIGHTING FAITH

FIRST LADY ELEANOR ROOSEVELT felt betrayed. In the late 1930s, she had put the prestige of the White House behind the American Student Union (ASU), a coalition that included liberal, socialist, and communist groups. She had seen in the left-liberal coalition a youthful constituency broadly in support of her husband's New Deal policies and one that could carry on his legacy. The ASU and its sister organization, the American Youth Congress, shared a commitment to racial equality, labor rights, and peace. Despite the presence of communist students, Roosevelt defended the coalition against charges of subversion. When in December 1939 the ASU general secretary, Joseph Lash—a socialist rather than a communist—was summoned to testify before the congressional House Committee on Un-American Activities, she had signaled her support by sitting behind the witness table, knitting quietly. After the hearing, she had invited Lash, who became her close friend and eventual biographer, and other leaders to the White House. Sometimes she had dipped into her own purse to finance their activities. On one occasion, she had confronted several young leaders and asked whether they belonged to the Communist Party, and they had denied any affiliation. She later learned they had lied to her.[1]

It wasn't only that the students had lied to her that made Eleanor Roosevelt feel the sting of betrayal. A single event in 1939 had revealed the influence of the Soviet Union in the ASU coalition and shattered liberals' faith in it. Once committed to fighting the fascists in Franco's Spain, Hitler's Germany, and Mussolini's Italy, the ASU suddenly switched its position.

On August 23, 1939, Stalinist Russia had stunned the world by signing a nonaggression pact with Nazi Germany, and communists around the world, heretofore opposed to Adolf Hitler, had thrown their support behind it. At an ASU meeting in December, delegates, who had defended Russia's invasion of Finland on November 30, implicitly supported the pact. In the United States, socialists like Lash and New Deal liberals like Roosevelt watched in horror as their coalition partners justified Stalin's deal with the devil. The twin blows—that Stalin could ally himself with Hitler and that Moscow's foreign policy could dictate the agenda of a U.S. student organization—tore the left-liberal coalition apart.[2] The consequences of the pact ripped through labor, civic, religious, and youth coalitions as liberals searched for evidence of Moscow-directed communist influence.

According to Lash, after Roosevelt's experiences with popular front organizations, she refused to work in coalition with communists; they were untrustworthy partners. She argued that Party allegiance, when kept secret, made communists resistant to persuasion, one of the essential elements of democracy. But as late as 1941 the First Lady made it clear that she distinguished between tolerance for ideas—she would debate any proposition—and secrecy. "I don't care if a young person is a Communist—if he's frank about it," she told *PM's Weekly*.[3] Not every liberal displayed such broad-mindedness, and hers would diminish as her experience with communist deception grew. By 1949, she was openly opposed to negotiating or compromising with communists.[4]

The Stalin-Hitler Pact became a cautionary tale that defined a generation of liberals. "It was 1939, not 1946 or 1947," concluded one historian, "that marked the inauguration of the ideological cold war between those who still saw the communist movement as an integral part of the American progressive tradition and those whose hostility to the communists was fundamental and implacable."[5] Not all liberals took a firm position against communism this early, but those who did were the precursors to a bitter fight within the Democratic Party, a battle that gradually forced out left-wing activists and drove Communist Party members underground.

The emergence of a liberal anticommunist doctrine between 1939 and 1946 reshaped the American political landscape. It caused Democratic president Harry S. Truman to fire his secretary of commerce, Henry Wallace, formerly Franklin Roosevelt's vice president, for advocating cooperation with the Soviet Union. It created a generation of leaders dedicated to purging communist influence in liberal organizations. It swelled the ranks of Cold Warriors willing to combat the Soviet Union by any means necessary. It put nongovernmental organizations in the service of U.S. national security objectives, and would find its fullest expression during the presidency of John F. Kennedy—ironically, since prominent liberals, including Eleanor Roosevelt, were none too sure of his political bona fides. When, later, a younger generation of liberals judged their elders harshly for elevating ends over means and compromising civil liberties, and accused them of betraying democracy—the very thing they had sought to protect—liberal anticommunist defenders responded that fighting evil sometimes required a tempering of idealism. They justified their actions by invoking patriotism, placing loyalty to the United States above more democratic values.

Had Eleanor Roosevelt been a more traditional First Lady, we might not have so clear a picture of how she and other veterans of 1930s student politics wrestled with the Stalin-Hitler Pact, of their sense of betrayal, or of how they subsequently sought to marry their liberal ideals to a hard-nosed anticommunism. But Roosevelt was an activist. In 1940, she joined the U.S. Committee of the International Student Service, a group of like-minded educators and New Deal colleagues, to mobilize American youth, and ensure that the American Student Union experience was not repeated. And in 1941, she offered her family's thirty-one-room summer cottage on Campobello Island, in New Brunswick, Canada, to train a new generation on the danger of communist tactics. The record of this group's actions, available in rarely perused archives, reveals important continuities with postwar developments that are usually ignored, if for no other reason than the tendency to divide history into distinct eras.

The group Eleanor Roosevelt joined had ambitious goals: to restructure the American student movement, train a new generation of leaders, and form a national student organization free of communist influence. Had they succeeded—and they nearly did—America might have emerged from World War II with a strong national union of students. Despite organizational failures, the legacy of the Roosevelt group influenced the founding of the postwar U.S. National Student Association, shaped its relationship with the government, and, most important, determined its first international activities.

The U.S. Committee was an affiliate of the International Student

Service (ISS), based in Geneva. Formed in 1920 after World War I to mobilize relief to students, the ISS was largely Protestant but prided itself on religious ecumenism, including in its membership both Catholic and Jewish groups. Fiercely nonpartisan, the ISS worked with war refugees regardless of country, combatant status, or political affiliation. In the United States, ISS committee members included prominent college presidents (from Smith, Hunter, and Brooklyn Colleges, the New School for Social Research, and Rockefeller Institute) and prestigious professors, dubbed by a younger board member "the Heavyweights of Education."[6] But the inclusion of the word *student* in the organization's name is misleading. Adults in Geneva and the United States ran the ISS, a practice common in the first half of the twentieth century, when few student-controlled organizations existed.

The fear that communists might fill the organizational vacuum left by the collapse over the next year of the American Student Union gave urgency to the U.S. agenda. In September 1940, Eleanor Roosevelt and committee member Archibald MacLeish, a poet and the Librarian of Congress, headlined a major conference on students and the future of democracy at International House near Columbia University in New York. The conference, attended by more than three hundred students from ninety-two colleges, marked the public launch of a campaign to revamp the American student movement.[7]

During the conference, longtime U.S. ISS Committee board member Clyde Eagleton, an expert in international law at Columbia, approached Joseph Lash, and asked whether Lash would be interested in staffing the committee. Lash had evolved politically from a socialist skeptical of the New Deal to an ardent Roosevelt supporter, and now was working for the president's reelection. After some consideration (and the offer of a munificent salary of $4,000), Lash accepted.[8]

That Lash was thirty-two years old and had no student status and few ties to American campuses apparently concerned no one. With his popular-front experience, he was ideally suited to spot and combat communist tactics, an overriding objective of the U.S. Committee. Lash suggested that the Committee also hire his socialist colleague from ASU days, Molly Yard (known to a later generation of feminists as the head of the National Organization for Women). Paradoxically, the fact that Lash and Yard had socialist backgrounds fueled charges in the United States that the ISS had turned pink if not red; the public rarely understood the deep antagonism between communists and socialists and more often equated the two.[9]

Eleanor Roosevelt's address to the conference drew a derisive response from *Time* magazine, whose editors described the First Lady as a "friend & guardian of the Communist-riven American Youth Congress," who had taken "time off from early Christmas shopping to help launch another youth movement." *Time* patronizingly dismissed the conference as "an attempt to wean youth from passing angry resolutions to sober discussion."[10]

Although written in flippant *Time*-ese, the article accurately captured the U.S. Committee's aversion to the protest tactics that had characterized the 1930s. In 1940, mass mobilizations, demonstrations, and campus strikes carried worrisome echoes of Nazi youth rallies. The Committee soon abandoned large conferences as too difficult to control, a view solidified by a postmortem of the September event and Lash's contention that his former colleagues had tried to take it over.[11]

The ISS sought instead to screen, select, and train students who had the backing of campus bigwigs: presidents, provosts, and deans. This top-down approach, prevalent until the 1960s, created a subtle conservative bias in picking leaders. The students' need to acquire the imprimatur of powerful elites meant striving to please those in authority, tempering rebellious tendencies, and staying within prescribed boundaries. During the formative stages of the NSA-CIA relationship, such habits of deference, especially among undergraduates, helped camouflage CIA interest.

At the time, it seemed possible that a group of elite (mostly) men without strong ties to American students could achieve the Committee's sweeping goals. Roosevelt, who often hosted meetings in her 65th Street home in New York City, wrote the foreword to a widely circulated pamphlet outlining the omnibus ISS program in the United States, which included conferences, seminars, a Washington office, a newspaper, and leadership training institutes. The Committee also looked ahead to a postwar world and the international role American students could play in it, even though in 1940 the United States had not even entered World War II.[12]

Key to the ISS agenda was a six-week leadership institute, first held in the summer of 1941 at the Roosevelts' summer home in Campobello. The U.S. Committee took care in its choice of students, enlisting the anthropologist Margaret Mead to devise a two-page questionnaire to screen applicants.[13] Once the list was winnowed, finalists underwent personal interviews. They were asked to elaborate on statements such as "The course of history is fixed and it is beyond the power of any individual to change it" and "The last generation got us into this mess, and we can't do anything about it," as well as more provocative questions like "Are there appeasers in the State Department?" Thirty out of eighty students made the cut, many of them from East Coast colleges.[14] The ISS provided scholarships to those who couldn't afford the room and board.

Getting to Campobello took almost as much commitment as meeting the goals of the Committee. Located near the Maine-Canada border, the isolated island was accessible only by ferry (once the fog had lifted), following a long journey by bus, train, or car. In July 1941, Roosevelt drove herself from New York, being careful to go slowly, as she noted in her "My Day" syndicated newspaper column, because her mother-in-law was along.[15] Despite its natural beauty, Campobello lacked modern amenities like electricity and indoor toilets. Former Smith College president William Allan Neilson, then seventy-two, endured these hardships for the entire session, surely a measure of his devotion to the enterprise.

Many prominent New Dealers ferried out to Campobello Island that summer. Supreme Court justice Felix Frankfurter lectured on the role of law in civilized society. Treasury secretary Henry Morgenthau schooled the students in international finance. Other guests included Roosevelt stalwarts such as White House adviser Lauchlin Currie and Archibald MacLeish. Students also heard from Louis Fischer, a journalist who later wrote a seminal essay about his years covering the Russian Revolution and living in the Soviet Union.[16] The listeners included his son George Fischer, a future founder of the U.S. National Student Association and perhaps the only American student who was once a member of the Soviet Young Pioneers.[17] Other academics who made the trek included U.S. ISS Committee members Clyde Eagleton and Austrian émigré Walter Kotschnig, from Smith, who stepped off the ferry too soon and splashed down, suitcase and all, in the Bay of Fundy.[18]

But the curriculum consisted of more than lectures. The second half of the course, "The Student as Student," distilled the lessons of the

American Student Union. The Campobello students held mock conventions in order to develop skills for combating such communist tactics as noisy floor demonstrations and microphone grabs. Lash schooled the younger students on why communists, often the minority in organizations, wielded disproportionate influence: communist cadres were indefatigable, came to meetings early, stayed late, and never lost focus. He argued the need for liberal cadres, "capable of coping with the 'professional revolutionists' who staffed the communist-inspired and -directed groups in the United States."[19]

The students hammered out principles to guide a new national student organization: its membership base must be comprised of student governments, not national groups like the YMCA that might have chapters on campus. It must focus on "student" (that is, educational) issues and avoid politics and ideology. It must be structured regionally to dilute the influence of big cities that produced left-wing agitators. After days of discussion, George Fischer and Louis Harris (of the University of North Carolina, the future pioneering pollster), among others, turned the discussion into a written statement of principles. After the war, the new U.S. National Student Association would adopt these principles of nonpartisanship, student government affiliation, a focus on student issues, and a regional structure.

The thorniest question for the Campobello students was whether to ban communists from their future organizations. It was an issue, Lash later wrote, that "the group never fully came to terms with."[20] Exclusionary provisions flew in the face of the liberal commitment to civil liberties. Shifting alliances also affected the debate. A few weeks earlier, the Nazis had violated the nonaggression pact by invading the Soviet Union, and Stalin's allegiance had shifted once again. While the reversal brought about a new level of disgust for American communists who followed Moscow's changing line, the Soviet Union was now an official U.S. ally, which tended to undercut the rationale for a ban.

Lash struggled with an alternative to outright bans. Since fascists and communists were investing substantial resources in young people, he returned to the idea of cadres, who would be "just as committed and dedicated to liberal principles as the Communists were to Soviet doctrine."[21] A few students questioned the wisdom of such fervor. Lash remembered an objection from Alice Kahn of Smith College: "I think a crusading spirit is incompatible with the democratic temper which is one of open-mindedness and tolerance of conflicting views. Democracy cannot strive for singleness of purpose. Its essence is diversity."[22]

Few students shared Kahn's skepticism, however, and the phrase heard frequently at Campobello, "a fighting faith for democracy," became a liberal rallying cry after the war, popularized by the New Deal stalwart Arthur Schlesinger, Jr., in his *The Vital Center*.[23] After the summer institute ended, *Time* took note of the students' new political enthusiasms: "Last week they packed up and whooped off home, full of schemes to give their contemporaries a 'fighting faith.'" The article depicted the students as youngsters on a frolic. "Trainees . . . put salt in the sugar bowl, sucked lollipops handed out by Mrs. Roosevelt, satirized their lecturers in songs, played tennis, danced, picknicked."[24]

While the Campobello debates offer an important glimpse into the development of liberal anticommunism, and its dilemmas, the course had other themes as well, including the importance of international cooperation. Most U.S. ISS Committee members were passionate Wilsonians, advocates of Woodrow Wilson's vision of a peaceful world and supporters of the League of Nations. Eminent sponsors of the committee, such as the diplomats James Shotwell and Quincy Wright, had witnessed the signing of the Versailles Treaty after World War I that created the League. It was axiomatic among Committee members that America's failure to join the League of Nations had resulted in the League's weakness and failure to prevent a new war; they were determined that history not be repeated after World War II.[25]

Individual Committee members had already begun to work for a replacement to the League before the United States entered the war. Their ideas for postwar international cooperation gave them a further stake in the next generation. Since extreme nationalism, in their view, led to war, young people needed to be schooled in the virtue of ceding a little national sovereignty to world organizations in return for world peace.

Most ISS educators believed equally, as MacLeish would put it in his opening sentence to the preamble of the 1945 UNESCO constitution, that "since wars begin in the minds of men, it is in the minds of men that the defenses of peace must be constructed." Cultural exchange programs to build friendship across national boundaries, for example, were seen as a cornerstone to cooperation. While cynics might dismiss international cultural exchange as harmless hands-across-the-sea altruism, the U.S. ISS Committee understood its ideological promise. Projecting a positive view of American democracy overseas could counter the lure (and falsehoods) of communism. This blend of liberalism, anticommunism, and internationalism infused the U.S. Committee's agenda for American students, as it would animate the future U.S. National Student Association.

After the Japanese attacked Pearl Harbor on December 7, 1941, the United States entered the war, and most members of the U.S. ISS Committee joined the Roosevelt war effort. Over the next few years, these educator-activists forged new relations: between the private sector and government, between the nation's campuses and the military, between intelligence and diplomatic agendas. The national mobilization was unprecedented and had lasting consequences. It created institutions and informal networks that later eased the transition from hot to cold war.

Committee member Arnold Wolfers, for example, a Swiss émigré and Yale professor of international relations, served as an adviser to the new civilian intelligence agency, the Office of Strategic Services (OSS). This relationship anticipated his postwar career as a prolific campus recruiter for the CIA. Kotschnig, George Shuster, and Harry D. Gideonse, presidents, respectively of Smith, Hunter, and Brooklyn Colleges, were advisers on postwar exchange programs for the tiny new Division of Cultural Relations in the State Department.[26] Others headed new civic organizations in support of the war, some of which had covert ties to the federal government; their success later suggested models for concealing government involvement.

Wartime objectives reshaped the immediate U.S. Committee agenda. After two years of intensive work between 1940 and 1942, including the establishment of a Washington office, the launch of a student newspaper, *Threshold*, and plans for a new national student organization, the U.S. ISS Committee eagerly accepted backing from the Roosevelt administration for an international student conference. Kotschnig wrote a friend, "I don't think I am giving away a secret by stating that Mr. Roosevelt will use this Assembly as a sounding board for an appeal to the youth of the world."[27] It seemed logical and consistent with ISS objectives to cultivate generational solidarity across national boundaries; no one foresaw that this decision would shatter the Committee or that entanglement with government objectives might offer as potent a cautionary tale to student organizations as the Stalin-Hitler Pact.

On September 2, 1942, three hundred delegates from fifty-six countries convened at American University in Washington—an unprecedented wartime event, when travel, especially foreign travel, was difficult. Some delegates represented occupied countries like France and Poland; others appeared in military uniform. Some were already working directly with the War Department: an Italian refugee, Bruno Luzzatto, for example, helped the U.S military identify bombing targets. Joseph Lash took pride in including the Soviet delegation. He believed it undercut his old enemies in ASU by demonstrating that a nonpartisan group could have friendly relations with the Soviet Union without marching in ideological lockstep.[28]

The Soviets stole the show by sending Lyudmila Pavlichenko, a trained sniper with more than three hundred kills under her belt, to address the assembly. In a gesture toward the new U.S.-Soviet alliance, Eleanor Roosevelt entertained Pavlichenko at the White House. The First Lady met individually with other foreign delegations, even driving the four British representatives one night to see the Lincoln Memorial, which she judged more impressive when illuminated.[29]

The second day of the conference, delegates trooped into a large auditorium in the Commerce Building to hear a radio address by President Roosevelt, which was also piped abroad to thirty-two countries in seven languages. "But now," the president told the assembly, "the world knows that the Nazis, the Fascists and Militarists of Japan have nothing to offer to youth—except death." He flattered them as the postwar face of the United Nations. (Throughout the war, President Roosevelt deliberately referred to U.S. allies as "the United Nations." According to Lash one of FDR's major objectives was to build support for a postwar institution of the same name.) The delegates from the "twenty-nine United Nations . . . represent, in spirit at least, the younger generation of many other nations who, though they are not now actively at war on our side, are with us heart and soul in aspiration for a secure and peaceful world." The president told them that, as students, they had a right to speak for themselves.[30]

When Campobello graduate Louis Harris strode across the stage on behalf of the United States delegation to sign the Credo of Youth, which read, "We affirm our united determination to fight on to the complete rout of fascism," the assembly erupted with applause and shouts of "Forward to Victory, Forward to Victory."[31] The lengthy credo emphasized unity of purpose on the battlefield and for peace. In 1942, this powerful rallying cry of unity served U.S aims. The Office of Wartime Information (founded by Archibald MacLeish) packaged material from the conference, including Roosevelt's speech, and beamed it by short-wave radio into occupied territories. Individual delegates gave radio interviews to reach similar audiences. The Youth Credo was printed on tiny cards and distributed overseas via underground networks. Louise Morley, a young aide to Eleanor Roosevelt, took a six-week leave of absence and with funding received from the Office of War Information went to London to foster solidarity between British and American students.[32]

Initially, it seemed that the American delegation, led by Lash, Trude Pratt, Molly Yard, Louis Harris, and others, had succeeded beyond anyone's dreams. The conference established a new International Assembly of Students, and, despite some grumbling from foreign delegates, the United States won the right to host the first postwar conference.[33] The president of the Harvard Student Council, Thomas Matters, was elected interim chair and offered the council's assistance in planning a future conference.[34]

Just when success seemed at hand, with American students positioned to play major international leadership roles after the war, the U.S. ISS Committee fractured over political differences, personality conflicts, and its relationship to Geneva.[35] Some of the long-time committee members had grown increasingly fearful of Lash's passion for politics, which conflicted with the nonpartisan orientation of the ISS in Geneva. In turn, Lash and other staff resented their lack of autonomy and had supported resolutions at the assembly that defied the ISS policy on political positions. They had supported India's independence from Great Britain, a controversial move that threatened relationships with both ISS Geneva and the ISS committee in England. Clyde Eagleton feared they were headed for a rift that could destroy the U.S. ISS Committee and be fatal to their overall purpose, for, as he told his colleagues, "If they [students] are not under our guidance, they may fall into left-wing hands."[36]

The conflict erupted just as long-delayed plans for a new national student organization were coming to fruition. A constitutional convention to establish a United States Student Assembly was planned for spring, its name chosen to signify a relationship with the new International Student Assembly. After months of stalemate, on January 13, 1943, the acting director of the U.S. ISS Committee staff, Trude Pratt (who later married Joseph Lash), submitted her resignation. A few weeks later, the staff declared their independence as officers of the freestanding United States Student Assembly (USSA). Eleanor Roosevelt backed Lash, Pratt, and the other activist Campobello liberals who chafed at the insistence on neutrality.[37]

A few Committee members tried to keep in with both camps to guard against communist infiltration, the one issue that united all members. Harry D. Gideonse, one of the committee's most ardent anticommunists, drafted the new USSA constitution, which explicitly excluded communist (as well as fascist) members.[38] George Shuster and Clyde Eagleton agreed to serve as advisers. In May 1943, the United States Student Assembly held a constitutional convention. A letterhead was quickly printed that reinforced the connection between the USSA and the International Student Assembly. With so many men mobilized and overseas—Lash himself was in the army—women took over the leadership. Campobello-trained Mary Louise Munts won the presidency.

The major benefactors of the U.S. ISS Committee, who were committed to ISS nonpartisanship and wary of student autonomy, retaliated by withdrawing financial support. A handful of prominent women had supported the ISS agenda through personal donations and fundraising, among them Dorothy Hearst Paley, wife of the CBS chief and philanthropist William Paley, and Adele Levy, daughter of Julius Rosenwald, the founder of Sears Roebuck and one of the wealthiest men in the country.[39]

Absent financial resources and with the defection of prominent educators, the USSA floundered. In 1943, Munts suspended activities for the duration of the war, mindful, she said later, of the fate of the American Student Union. "It was Molly [Yard]'s tutelage about these events, together with that of my Swarthmore mentors, that made me so wary of a repeat performance."[40]

The conflict ended the U.S. ISS Committee as constituted. A handful of members, including Wolfers, Kotschnig, Gideonse, and Shuster, continued to meet. In February 1943, they had incorporated as the Student Service of America, Inc. (SSA), with Gideonse as general secretary.[41] This nomenclature caused no end of confusion with Geneva, especially since the U.S. ISS Committee sponsored a fundraising arm with a similar name, the World Student Service Fund.[42]

Unknown to all but a few elites, the smaller group of educators who formed the SSA were in discreet but not secret coordination with officials from the U.S. State Department. With the SSA, they crafted the nucleus of an international program that would later be adopted by the National Student Association.[43] It is not an exaggeration to argue that the NSA's international program predated the organization's formation.

Prior to the conflict, program discussions with the State Department had been under way.[44] The U.S. ISS Committee had obtained funds for a small program to assist European student refugees. The SSA kept the grant, with Kotschnig arguing, "It could serve as the nucleus around which other programs can be built up."[45] The projects devised under the Student Service of America designation lacked, in terminology common to wartime planners, an instrument to administer them. It was a phenomenon unique to the war years, albeit a common one, which upended the traditional order of creating an organization before adopting a program.

In the short term, the U.S. ISS Committee debacle proved fateful. Americans lost the initiative they had seized in 1940, and the International Student Assembly died a quiet death. The United States Student Assembly was revived in 1945 but remained weak; in 1947, Eleanor Roosevelt, Joseph Lash, and other prominent liberals gave it a new identity as the student chapter (Students for Democratic Action) of the newly founded Americans for Democratic Action, which had anticommunism as a central tenet. For these liberals, the debate over whether to cooperate with communists at home or abroad had long been settled.

The full cost of the conflict became apparent before the war's end. On January 1, 1945, the London-based World Youth Council, formed in November 1943, invited hundreds of youth groups from more than sixty countries to a World Youth Conference in London. The invitation renewed fears in government, diplomatic, and educational circles that young communists would fill organizational vacuums in the United States and abroad. Diplomatic cables from England fed these fears. The American Embassy in London warned the State Department that the conference was being organized by "politically-minded young adults and not by the recognized educational and character building groups."[46]

Soviet watchers grew further alarmed when they learned that the New York–based American Youth for a Free World would choose the American delegation. This patriotic-sounding organization was closely aligned with the former Young Communist League, which itself had changed its name to American Youth for Democracy. Diplomats and professional youth leaders on both sides of the Atlantic faced the same dilemma the Campobello students had failed to resolve: in 1945, the continuing alliance with the Soviet Union made it difficult to openly attack groups friendly to it, regardless of what they called themselves.

In the spring of 1945, Roosevelt liberals in the State Department made one last attempt to create a noncommunist national student association in the United States. The plan, as conveyed to Frank Graham, president of the University of North Carolina, involved the founding of eight separate regional organizations that could later unite. Graham, who served as an adviser to the then-moribund USSA and moved in ISS circles, agreed to host the first meeting. The resulting Conference of Southern Students was under way on the North Carolina campus when on April 13 news arrived of President Roosevelt's fatal heart attack at his Warm Springs retreat in Georgia. The end of the Roosevelt administration prevented further regional conferences, although two officers of the new organization would reappear as founders of the National Student Association.[47]

In November 1945, just as anticommunists feared, the London conference culminated in the new World Federation of Democratic Youth (WFDY). The pageantry and emotion at the Royal Albert Hall created a powerful bond among those present. As delegations carried their national flags down the aisle, spectators hung over the crowded balconies to see which friends had survived the war. Moments of joy alternated with tears as the names of martyrs were read aloud. The ceremony gave calls for unity and peace a ghostly specificity.[48]

Those who followed Moscow politics pointed to the simultaneous creation of several other federations—the World Federation of Trade Unions (October) and the World Federation of Democratic Women (November)—as evidence that the Soviet Union was again building popular fronts and disguising its hand. When Czech and British leaders announced a World Student Congress during the summer of 1946 in Prague, students appeared to be next on Moscow's agenda.

In 1946, the specter of a resurgent American Student Union seemed closer, not farther away, than it had when Eleanor Roosevelt and prominent educators acted to fill the vacuum in student activism left by its demise. The prospect of a communist-led World Student Congress mobilized powerful forces in the United States. These included one of the

Kremlin's oldest and most implacable foes—the Catholic Church. The ensuing alliance between anticommunist liberal student leaders and doctrinaire Catholics, uneasy at first, provided a powerful check on those who had not yet joined the anticommunist chorus. Catholics brought to the alliance their own set of relationships with several agencies of the U.S. government, among them the FBI, equally determined to prevent communist infiltration into American student and youth organizations.

2

APOSTOLIC CATHOLICS

IF LIBERALS WERE UNCERTAIN about how far to go in opposing communism without violating principles of tolerance, pluralism, and civil liberties, Catholics had no such ambivalence. Catholic anticommunism was grounded in papal encyclicals that dated back to the nineteenth century.[1] The American Catholic Church worked openly during the 1930s to destroy the American Student Union. But it worked alone, as suspicious of secular influence and interfaith cooperation as of communist penetration.

In the spring of 1946, the Catholic Church in the United States made the unprecedented decision to let Catholic students join the largely secular American delegation (later known as the Prague 25) to the World Student Congress in Czechoslovakia. The consequences of this move were far-reaching. Their loyalties shaped more by religious doctrine than liberal agendas, the Catholic students in the American delegation constituted a disciplined bloc of anticommunists—the committed cadres Joseph Lash had envisioned. But their participation also brought the Vatican directly into American student politics, though not everyone involved realized it at the time.

The change in church policy was heralded by Father John Courtney Murray, a leading Jesuit and the religion editor of the prominent Catholic journal *America*, who sounded the Vatican's alarm over the forthcoming student gathering in Czechoslovakia. On April 13, Murray wrote that the Soviets had begun a campaign to influence the world's youth. The Soviet Union, he said, "is consciously enlisting the aid of youth in furthering its own purposes, whose sinister character is ably concealed beneath the aura of idealism that youth finds so seductive." He then expressed the pope's desire for counter-mobilization. "Pius XII wants the Catholic international student movement to be a strong ally in the mission upon which he has focused the eyes of the universal church." The pope wished for "the intellectual penetration of the university milieu — the winning of the universities, professors and students, for the ideas that underlie peace and Christian world order."[2]

The worldly Murray, described by a Protestant theologian as a backroom man with a penchant for dry martinis, offered details.[3] "What the Holy See wants in confronting the Soviet threat is an 'Operation University.'" A "group of twelve students" would be "selected, carefully and intensively trained and sent over to the Prague meeting . . . with the quite sober and entirely feasible intent of 'taking it over.'" They would not be alone but would have help from their Catholic European allies. Murray issued a plea for financial support.[4] Archbishop Richard J. Cushing of Boston, who had just taken over supervision of the bishops conference youth department, responded by pledging a thousand dollars.[5]

By the time Murray had published his public exhortation to American Catholics, a U.S. delegation to the World Student Congress was already being formed. Muriel Jacobson, a professional staff member of the Young Women's Christian Association headquartered on Madison Avenue, had seized the initiative to assemble an American delegation. The YWCA and its counterpart, the Young Men's Christian Association, together constituted the largest and most important youth group in the country. The YWCA had belonged to the American Student Union, and the matronly looking Jacobson was a veteran of 1930s student politics.[6] After the founding of the World Federation of Democratic Youth in London in November 1945, Jacobson had attended a smaller meeting of students at Bedford College and had listened as Josef Grohman, head of the Czechoslovakia Union of Students, invited participants to Prague the following summer for the World Student Congress.

A small and slender man and a self-proclaimed member of the Communist Party, Grohman embodied the moral authority of a wartime resistance leader. He stood before the group at Bedford College, emaciated and tubercular from his years in a German prison camp. (After he was freed, friends had sneaked him into Prague wrapped in a sheet and disguised as a hospital patient in time for the liberation of the city.)

Grohman received an enthusiastic response to his invitation, and when he asked for volunteer assistance with the planning Jacobson put her hand up.

Two other women who had traveled with her to London aboard the *Queen Mary* also volunteered: Alice Horton, the new head of the revived United States Student Assembly, then trying to find its postwar footing, and Mollie Lieber from American Youth for Democracy, formerly the Young Communist League. (Lieber, however, chose not to go from London to Prague for a planning session but rather visited the gravesite of her husband in southern France, suggesting she was not under party discipline.)[7] Upon Jacobson's return to the United States, she leveraged her volunteer position and stature as a YWCA official to assemble the twenty-five-person American delegation, hosting the first meeting in January 1946, and hiring Horton as her assistant.[8]

Behind the scenes, Jacobson took several steps that indicate continuity with the defunct U.S. ISS Committee board members, and the committee's successor, the Student Service of America, Inc. She asked several educators to sponsor an American Preparatory Commission. She incorporated as delegates the two elected leaders of the Conference of Southern Students, the organization founded in 1945 at the behest of the State Department, although neither student, Charles Proctor, an African American from Fisk University in Tennessee, and Jimmy Wallace from the University of North Carolina, was identified as an officer. Rather, both were identified as campus representatives.[9]

Jacobson also adopted principles hammered out at Campobello to shape the delegation. To minimize the influence of national organizations, she allocated the largest block of delegates (fifteen) to American colleges and universities. Ironically, the one person later suspected of hiding Communist Party credentials, Russell Austin from the University of Chicago, won his position in a campus-wide election. If Austin was a communist, his election suggests that principles of decentralization were not always an effective screen.

Although alert to communist influence, Jacobson believed that excluding left-wing students was a dubious strategy, one that would drive the dissidents underground and make them difficult to identify.[10] She awarded a single delegate to Mollie Lieber's group of young communists. The group with the largest representation was the National Intercollegiate Christian Council (NICC), the umbrella organization dominated by the YW-YMCA. It originally expected to send eight delegates, among them nonstudent Jacobson.[11] Instead, Jacobson and her YMCA counterpart, its director, the Rev. R. H. Edwin Espy, decided to share their slots with American Catholics.

Two days after Father Murray's article appeared, Alice Horton took the train to Washington to confer with Murray protégé Edward Kirchner, the thirty-four-year-old head of the North American chapter of Pax Romana. This officially sanctioned Vatican international student movement had begun to experiment with interfaith cooperation.[12] In 1939, it had joined with the ISS in Geneva and the World Student Christian Federation to form European Student War Relief. In 1942, when the project became known as World Student Relief, Pax Romana continued as a member.[13] Kirchner was well versed on events in Europe, and had observed the London youth conference and attended the Bedford College students meeting that followed.

Kirchner also had experience with the ISS educators who formed the Student Service of America. Toward the end of the war, he had worked actively with the group on war relief and reconstruction projects.[14] It is not recorded who brought Jacobson and Kirchner together, but it was probably someone from ISS/SSA circles. Although Horton acted as Jacobson's emissary, she said in a subsequent interview that "higher-ups" made all major decisions.[15]

Kirchner appeared interested in joining the American delegation. Before a final decision was made, Father Murray commissioned former FBI agents to investigate the sponsors of the Jacobson-led preparatory commission.[16] These overly zealous former agents are legendary in the annals of right-wing anticommunism; their organization later published *Counterattack*, a newsletter in which hundreds of innocent people were accused of communist subversion. Even before Murray deployed the former G-men, nervous Catholic bishops' staff had been seeking guidance from U.S. government officials.[17] Letters and internal memoranda in the National Catholic Welfare Council (NCWC) archive indicate consultations with the State Department began before the World Student Congress and continued after it.

The investigators must have been satisfied with the results of their inquiries, since the Catholics accepted the invitation to participate. Before the American delegation assembled in July 1946, Catholic students spent two weeks in specialized training. From June 6 to June 16, they gathered at the Ridgely Manor estate of philanthropist Mrs. Francis H. Leggett in the Hudson Valley north of New York City.[18] The dozen or so students were bound for a number of meetings in Europe, not just the World Student Congress. Eight experts in communist tactics taught the Catholics how to spot and fight communists.

The chief trainer at Ridgely Manor, Ruth (Elfriede Eisler) Fischer, was notorious in anticommunist circles. Once the secretary general of the German Communist Party, she had broken with the party and migrated to the United States. She typified former communists who later devoted their lives to destroying the party: in 1947 she testified against her own brother, Gerhard Eisler, before the House Committee on Un-American Activities, identifying him as an agent for the Comintern, the Soviet entity that directed Communist Party activity abroad.[19]

The Catholic activists at Ridgely Manor wrestled with the same question that Campobello students had debated: "Why are the Communists so successful?" Their answer was similar. Communists, like Catholics, were apostolic: that is, dedicated communists put their beliefs into action.[20] The analysis reinforced the belief that Catholics should stop shielding themselves from secular influences, enter the fray, and adopt their own apostolic mission, in Father Murray's words, "to wrest the initiative from those who have for their goal the destruction of Christian civilization."[21]

The training was not all theoretical or theological. Kirchner later described Fischer's emphasis on the role of alcohol in the communists' manipulation of unsuspecting students. The Russians, she explained, line the stomach with cheeses and fats to cope with banquets that would require many Vodka toasts. They also "served their Vodka in tiny jigger size glasses that can be carefully concealed in the hand and then discretely emptied into a nearby plant." Russians were tricky, she told the participants, often using "two teams of students, one to drink and fall to the floor, another one to go to bed and be ready early the next morning to cast votes." Fischer instructed the Catholics that they could spot non-Russian communists by looking for "dedicated and hard-working individuals who would scrupulously attend all sessions, working late in the evenings and early in the mornings." Kirchner characterized the group that left Ridgely Manor as ready to fight evil.[22]

On July 9, a hot, steamy night in New York City, the Catholics entered the lion's den at the Hotel Diplomat for their first introduction to the rest of the American delegation. It was not an easy fit. As a whole, the Catholics were older.[23] Twenty-eight-year-old Martin McLaughlin, a Ph.D. candidate from Notre Dame, was the diplomat of the group; a tall, handsome, well-spoken man and a masterful tactician, he had the capacity to tone down political differences without altering his own position. McLaughlin would later join the CIA and cap his government career as deputy assistant secretary of state for educational and cultural affairs.[24] Vince Hogan, the youngest Catholic delegate, graduated from Notre Dame in 1942, and was then overseas completing his Ph.D. dissertation. Kirchner, who joined the delegation when it arrived in Prague, was thirty-four. Twenty-four-year-old Henry Briefs, a 1943 graduate of the Georgetown School of Foreign Service, was the most conservative and pugnacious of the four. If McLaughlin smoothed over political differences, Briefs exacerbated them. One Protestant delegate recalled him as a "little Jesuit tough."[25]

Both McLaughlin and Briefs kept their intelligence service credentials hidden from the non-Catholic delegates. McLaughlin had served in the army air force as an intelligence officer, with stints in India and North Africa, Briefs in army intelligence in Europe.[26] Briefs's father, Goetz, a Rhinelander who fled Germany in 1934 and became a Georgetown University economics professor, was a close friend of Father Murray's. During the war, the senior Briefs had been an adviser to the Office of Strategic Services. Despite the Catholics' discretion, the delegate from North Carolina, Jimmy Wallace, later told Richard Cummings, Allard Lowenstein's biographer, that the men traveled on diplomatic passports and made reports to the State Department. (No record of those reports has been found.)[27] One Prague-bound woman stated simply, "They were men with agendas and I didn't like them."[28]

Despite their strong anticommunism, the Catholic delegates were not conservative in the traditional political sense. They would not have been comfortable listening to the right-wing radio priest Father Coughlin, who in the 1930s filled the airwaves with anticommunist and anti-Semitic venom and denounced President Roosevelt as a tool of the bankers. Rather, they were Democrats and in some cases activists for social justice. At Notre Dame, McLaughlin had joined a "cell group" of Catholic Action, a new international movement that emphasized workers' rights and justice for the poor.[29] The social reformer Dorothy Day, who worked with the homeless and the hungry, exemplified the principles of

Catholic Action, whose slogan "Observe, Judge, Act" formed the basis for apostolic missions.

At the same time, Catholics like McLaughlin would not have called themselves liberal, since the word raised thorny theological issues, especially the implied freedom of religion associated with liberalism.[30] In the context of the American delegation, given its overriding liberal orientation, the Catholics seemed conservative and were identified as such.

A *Harvard Crimson* reporter who endured two weeks of sweltering heat and intense debates described the atmosphere at the Hotel Diplomat as "bitter" and "bombastic."[31] The delegates covered a range of issues, from the atomic bomb to federal aid to education, the new International Monetary Fund, the World Bank, and the need for a universal language.

The rancorous debates also brought to light tensions among liberals. In 1946, not all liberals had adopted a fighting faith or a hostile attitude toward communism. That summer the debate over the proper attitude to take toward both American communists and the Soviet Union raged in the pages of the *New Republic*, the *Nation*, and other liberal magazines.[32] For those who were not already on the anticommunist bandwagon, it was still a time of hope that the U.S.-Soviet alliance could bring peace to a war-weary world. Catholics condemned this attitude as a dangerous illusion.

The Catholics' reports to the NCWC Youth Department paint their fellow delegates with a broad brush as "non-Communist and pro-Soviet, liberal, susceptible to Soviet propaganda, and either unable or unwilling to perceive the Communist party line when it was presented."[33] But the Catholics reserved their harshest judgment for naive liberals—those who did not understand the significance of communist tactics and unwittingly facilitated the designs of a dedicated minority whose real aim was power. They quickly identified the delegate from Harvard University, S. Douglass Cater, as a prototypical naive liberal. His influence within the American delegation made him their target.[34]

The first thing that people remembered after meeting Douglass Cater was his southern drawl and booming voice. Born and raised in Alabama, Cater nonetheless was at home in the largely northern delegation. He had graduated in 1942 from Philips Exeter Academy, one of New England's most elite boarding schools, and afterward entered Harvard. During the war, he had served in the Office of Strategic Services Russian section.[35] In the fall of 1946, he enrolled in a newly created masters program at Harvard in international administration, specializing in Slavic and Russian studies.[36] As editorial chairman of the *Harvard Crimson*, he commanded a journalistic platform from which to disseminate his views. His folksy manner concealed a keen intelligence, which later took him to the Lyndon Johnson White House. Cater disliked hysterical anticommunism and identified the Catholics as its standard-bearers.

The sharp-elbowed political differences between Cater and the Catholics have further significance. After the *Ramparts* disclosures in 1967, rumors circulated that the CIA had created the NSA. Anyone looking for evidence of this must take into account two facts: the Central Intelligence Agency did not yet exist and the delegates who had intelligence experience, far from engaging in coordinated effort, loathed one another.[37]

At the same time, the delegates' wartime experience in intelligence was not irrelevant. McLaughlin, Briefs, and Cater all tapped into networks of civilian and military intelligence officials that provided numerous avenues for informal conversation. The younger postwar veterans also began to create new networks among their peers. New military reserve units fostered contact and often encouraged a desire to fight the Soviets. But as to whether any of the Prague 25 had a formal relationship with U.S. intelligence—there are tantalizing hints but no firm evidence—the need to jockey for position within the delegation suggests the absence of central direction.

AFTER A WEEK of discussions at the Hotel Diplomat, Cater and six others disrupted the schedule by leaving early for Europe. They had learned that the World Federation of Democratic Youth was going to meet in Paris, and wanted to observe the meeting at firsthand.[38] Rumors abounded that the World Student Congress would create a new international student organization and affiliate with the WFDY. If the WFDY was communist dominated, as Soviet watchers charged, mainstream American students would be skittish about joining. The remaining eighteen delegates sailed to Europe on July 26 aboard the S.S. *George Washington*.

For delegates who had never traveled outside the United States, the trip was both exciting and sobering, as travelers from Paris to Prague caught glimpses of war-ravaged Europe. The train was blacked out for part of the way as it chugged through Germany, but most peeked under the dark window screens and stared at cities reduced to rubble. Once in Prague, they lodged at the Masaryk student hostel and gawked at bullet holes that remained in the walls of Charles University from the Nazis' massacre of students on November 17, 1939.

One young woman found herself overcome with guilt. Miriam Haskell, a junior at Smith College, originally from Brookline, Massachusetts, wangled credentials from the *Boston Globe* and became an honorary member of the American delegation. She later described her feelings as a Jewish woman and an American: "I felt horrified that fate had handed me such good fortune." It was obvious, said Haskell, which delegates had spent the war years in concentration camps.[39] She was not alone in her feelings. A sense of privilege affected many in the American delegation as they realized how insulated the United States had been from the devastation of the war, and how healthy and well fed they were compared to so many other delegates.

But not all differences between European and U.S. students stemmed from the war. Long-established European student unions wielded influence unheard of in America. Their leaders were sophisticates who shaped education policy in their home countries and were often fluent in several languages: Josef Grohman welcomed the delegates to Prague in Czech, English, Russian, and French, never once using an interpreter. "We felt keenly the gulf that has existed between American and European students and wondered whether it could ever be bridged," Cater lamented afterward.[40]

After an opening session on August 18 at the House of Arts and Music, the Neo-Renaissance building known as the Rudolfinum, three hundred students from thirty-eight countries ignored food and sleep as they wrestled with the task of creating a new international student organization. As leaders of a new generation, survivors of a terrible war, they sought a vehicle for peace. Calls for unity evoked intense emotions, just as they had in 1942 at the International Student Assembly, and again in 1945 at the London World Youth Conference. Unity had won the war against fascism. Unity could now win the peace.

Catholics saw malevolent intent behind the constant chants for unity. What McLaughlin found "most distressing of all was the blatant appeal to emotions; all the techniques of mass psychology were used to advantage."[41] As anticipated, American Catholics formed a bloc with Catholics from Canada, France, Belgium, and other countries, but they were jarringly out of sync with the spirit of the conference. The American delegate from NICC, William (Bill) Ellis, an African American who had been substituted at the last minute for a YMCA adult professional and usually avoided making critical remarks about his colleagues, told the delegation organizers, Muriel Jacobson and Reverend Espy, that he found it "difficult to work with the Catholics as a block." They were so driven by "uncompromising hostility to communism," he explained, that they were "blind to the specific situation" in Prague, their actions "a violation of the spirit of peace and friendship."[42]

The Catholics scrutinized every word or clause in the constitution, bylaws, and resolutions proposed for the new International Union of Students (IUS), provoking many of the congress's most contentious moments. The constant exhortations to fight fascism led Henry Briefs to demand that the delegates define fascism and spell out democratic norms. They refused. Ellis also struggled with the intense emotion unleashed by the word *fascism* for Europeans. Somewhat warily, he speculated that given what they had lived through, "anti-fascism may have some very positive values which we as American students do not fully realize."[43]

Catholics challenged the requirement that member student unions could be suspended or expelled if they did not carry out the mandates of the IUS, claiming that it smacked of totalitarianism. Briefs offered an amendment to permit member autonomy, but delegates rejected his argument, 196 to 71.[44] The Vatican's gambit to take over the congress, so ably articulated by Father Murray, failed from the outset. The Catholics did not have enough allies. Undaunted, Catholic students met outside the formal meetings and pledged themselves to work for an alternative to the new IUS.[45]

In the IUS elections, Josef Grohman won the presidency, defeating Thomas Madden, a left-wing pre-med student from Great Britain whose powers of persuasion later earned him the sobriquet "Golden Tongue."[46] Madden became secretary general, making him and Grohman the two most powerful people in the Prague-based secretariat. But the Americans were not without influence. Six Americans—Douglass Cater, Martin McLaughlin, Jimmy Wallace, Walter Wallace (representing Youth Builders), and Lee Marsh (American Youth for Democracy)—won seats on the larger IUS Council that planned to meet twice a year.

Bill Ellis was elected as one of several vice presidents and invited to work in the secretariat. With characteristic modesty, he wrote his parents, "It is a little difficult to explain how I was elected, for I had done very little that was exceptional." He accepted because the organization "may have a great future" and because "my convictions—what I regard as right—and my personal advantage point out this way for me."[47] He emphasized the opportunity the position provided for fully subsidized travel around Europe, an early hint of how personal advantage and lofty ideals would later blend together for witting students. After a few weeks in the secretariat, Ellis returned to the United States for several months, then headed back to Prague.[48]

Delegates rejected a proposal to affiliate the new International Union of Students with the left-wing World Federation of Democratic Youth, based in Paris, which meant one less hurdle if Americans decided to join the IUS. According to Madden, who today emphasizes the independence of the IUS from Moscow during this period, the decision not to affiliate infuriated the Soviets. He remembered hearing after the congress that Stalin summoned the returning Russian delegates to the Kremlin and berated them for their failure. Madden said neither he nor Grohman could stand the "holier than thou" types who led the WFDY, although he emphasized that neither of them would have voiced this criticism in public.[49]

No evidence appears in any archival reports or declassified U.S. government documents, including those of American embassy officials in Prague, that communists shouted down the American delegates during the congress. Yet this charge, developed long after the Prague meeting concluded, has become the standard CIA explanation—former CIA director Richard Helms even repeated it in his 2003 memoir—of why the American association founded in the wake of the Prague congress eventually refused to become a member of the IUS.[50] At the time, it was the absence of conflict that drew officialdom's concern.

The U.S. ambassador to Czechoslovakia, Laurence Steinhardt, criticized the American delegation for being too deferential to the Soviets and not introducing "any resolution which might offend the sensibilities of the USSR delegation or those from other countries of Eastern

Europe."[51] Before the congress opened, Steinhardt tried his best to push the American delegation to be aggressive. He invited several delegates to an elegant dinner at the embassy and exhorted them to oppose the Russians at every turn. This "war is here" attitude left several of the American students aghast, among them Bernard Lown, who represented an organization called American Internists and Medical Students. That night is etched in Lown's memory; he left the embassy horrified, and devoted the rest of his life to peace, winning the Nobel Peace Prize in 1985 as a founder of the International Physicians for the Prevention of Nuclear War.[52]

When they left Prague, and regardless of their political beliefs and ideologies, the Prague 25 agreed on one point: if U.S. students were to join the IUS, the groups represented in the delegation needed to cooperate and create a new national organization. No existing organization dared claim to speak for all American students.

NO ONE COULD PREDICT what political faction might dominate a nationwide student meeting, and all parties proceeded with caution. Adopting a two-step process to determine interest before holding a founding convention, the Prague 25 called an initial meeting to be held over Christmas vacation at the University of Chicago. In the run-up to the meeting, the Prague veterans vied with one another to control the interpretation of the World Student Congress and organize delegates. In this endeavor the Catholics, able to draw on hundreds of small Catholic colleges spread across the United States, out-organized everyone else. The Catholics' numerical strength—they constituted nearly a third of all delegates—created a bloc of disciplined students, thoroughly anticommunist, whose deference to ecclesiastic direction enabled them to wield considerable influence in Chicago on both foreign policy questions and election outcomes.

The man behind this success was the military intelligence veteran Martin McLaughlin, who took a leave of absence from his graduate work at Notre Dame.[53] Two months before the Chicago meeting, on October 13, McLaughlin and Henry Briefs invited two Catholic students, army veterans John Simons from Fordham University, a Ridgely Manor trainee, and Philip DesMarais from the University of Minnesota, to a meeting at the National Catholic Welfare Conference headquarters. Under the watchful eyes of Fathers Murray and Charles Bermingham (of the NCWC Youth Department), and the Rev. Louis J. Putz of Notre Dame, the foursome created—in their terminology—an instrument to prepare for Chicago.[54]

The resulting Joint Committee for Student Action (JCSA), led by McLaughlin and Briefs, nominally consisted of the Newman Club Federation, which ministered to Catholics on non-Catholic campuses and was now led by DesMarais, and the National Federation of Catholic College Students, now led by Simons. Endowed with a generous budget from an unidentified trust fund, the committee divided the country into thirty regions and smaller cell groups, each overseen by regional desk officers.[55]

At all levels—local, regional, and national—clergy provided supervision to JCSA groups, a fact kept hidden from non-Catholics. As Father Bermingham informed Chicago's archbishop, Cardinal Stritch: "It is not deemed wise . . . to convey the impression of a direct link between ecclesiastical authorities and the students."[56] Bermingham assured the archbishop of the reliability of the committee members: "Those students already comprising the nucleus of this joint committee are keen, loyal, and zealous. Many of them are former soldiers and some of them were Intelligence Officers with considerable background and prudence."[57]

Unable to anticipate the intensity of anti-Catholic prejudice among delegates to the Chicago meeting, JCSA leaders opted for a soft approach to recruiting delegates. Their aim, McLaughlin wrote, was "not a mass movement with mass demonstrations and appeals to the mass-minded," nor was it to organize "soul-stirring meetings." Rather, the JCSA wished to find "a couple of hundred carefully selected students with tested interest [and] aptitude."[58] McLaughlin made the point more bluntly in *America*: "We are not looking for rabble-rousers and Red-baiters."[59]

At this time most Americans had no contact with Catholics, who generally kept to themselves in self-described ghettos. Catholics read Catholic newspapers and magazines, educated their children in parochial schools, joined Catholic civic groups, and eschewed even recreational contact with non-Catholics.[60] Many of these barriers had been broken down in the armed services, where immigrant Catholics, often Irish, saw an opportunity to prove themselves patriotic Americans. But even before the war some Catholic intellectuals had argued that it was time to move into the mainstream.[61] The decision to recruit Catholics to join a national student organization was part of this broader assimilationist movement.[62]

Behind the scenes, Catholics resorted to tougher measures. They ran a special operation against Russell Austin, head of the Prague 25 delegation, whom they, armed with FBI information, suspected of hiding communist credentials. According to an account written by a Jesuit priest, a Loyola University student had used an alias to attend meetings of the American Youth for Democracy, where, posing as an insider, the so-called sleeper had circulated rumors to discredit Austin.[63] Whether or not the clandestine operation was responsible for it, Austin did not win a leadership position in Chicago and subsequently disappeared from student politics.

While AYD leaders were probably unaware of the scheme to discredit Austin, they nonetheless aimed their pre-Chicago fury at the Catholics. They believed that the JCSA had teamed up with their old enemies, renegade liberals and socialists, like Joseph Lash, from the American Student Union, to wage a "fear-inspiring, red-baiting attack on AYD." When the *New Leader*, a magazine created by social democrats and disillusioned former Communist Party members, gave print space to JCSA leader John Simons, their suspicions seemed confirmed.[64]

For circulation among Catholic clergy and prospective Catholic delegates, McLaughlin analyzed the Prague outcomes in a report named after Murray's original article, "Operation University." He argued that twelve of the seventeen IUS executive committee members, a majority, were communists or communist sympathizers. To buttress his case, McLaughlin included a meticulous count of communists and Soviet allies within each of the seventy foreign delegations, individuals who "took their voting cue from the speech of the Russian delegate."[65] The apparent mathematical precision of the report enabled Catholic students to claim that the IUS had begun life under communist domination without resorting to fiery rhetoric that might alienate non-Catholics at the Chicago meeting.

In fact, the Catholics stood alone in their assessment—which made their soft approach strategy difficult to execute. NICC delegates Bill Ellis and Joyce Pembroke argued that the number of Soviet allies on the executive committee was eight, not twelve, making them a minority.[66] In *Harvard Crimson* articles, Douglass Cater ridiculed the whole exercise. He assured his audience that "the will of the majority stood behind all [the congress's] decisions." He argued that American affiliation in the IUS was essential if American students were "to participate in the international exchange of students and other international student activities."[67]

Liberal members of the Prague 25 also organized for Chicago, though far more casually than the Catholics. Throughout the fall, Bill Ellis toured campus chapters of the YM-YWCA. Douglass Cater stumped in New England.[68] In another of those barely visible instances of continuity with wartime ISS activities, Cater was chosen as a Chicago delegate by a committee that included Thomas Matters, chair of the short-lived International Student Assembly.[69] Before Chicago, Cater tried to build regional cohesion by hosting a meeting of prospective New England delegates.

On December 21, the *Harvard Crimson* published an inside report on the meeting, describing how the group shifted position on important issues, such as whether to permit national groups, such as the YMCA, to join a new U.S. organization. New England students arrived at the Harvard session in favor of inclusion and left opposed, adopting the view that the new organization should be campus based. Such feats suggested that deft leadership could reroute errant student sentiment. [70]

The day before the meeting of New England schools, the simmering tension between Cater and the Catholics spilled onto the front pages of the *Crimson*. William Y. Elliott, a Harvard professor of government and a conservative hard-liner, attacked Harvard students for wanting to join the IUS.[71] Using materials supplied by the Catholics, he labeled those who urged affiliation—implicitly Cater—naive.[72]

Cater counterattacked the next day. If Elliott had been paying attention, Cater told the *Crimson*, he would have known that "our paramount effort has been to make certain that delegates to the Chicago conference be elected by their student bodies, and not by non-representative campus organizations." If the IUS became a propaganda arm of Moscow, students would withdraw, "but only if at the beginning we participate vigorously and offer our best leadership and our best ideas, can we be absolved from blame should this great post-war experiment in internationalism prove a failure."[73]

In responding this way, Cater revealed that a clear-headed calculus underpinned his liberalism. From the beginning, the Americans' drive to affiliate with the IUS contained a more complicated mixture of motivations than was acknowledged then or today. At the time, liberals emphasized their earnest desire to cooperate for world peace. But Cater's response to Elliott shows that a strategic judgment also buttressed this position: Americans must *appear* to cooperate in order to avoid blame for shattering international student unity. Unbeknownst to Cater, the Catholics operated under a similar strategy. Father Bermingham had advised cooperation so that the communists could not claim that "Americans and Catholics have no interest in international student collaboration."[74]

Personal animosities between Cater and the JCSA leaders tended to disguise key points of agreement. The 750 delegates and observers from around the country who streamed into the University of Chicago's Reynold's Club Auditorium after Christmas overwhelmingly adopted the Campobello principles backed by both factions. They chose to create a loose federation of thirty regions to avoid centralization of power. They chose an equally large executive committee of regional representatives to thwart infiltration by organizations that would target small but powerful decision-making bodies. As an additional filter, they required regional representatives to prove student government affiliation in order to stand for regional election. Finally, they adopted term limits to prevent the rise of professional students, who could amass expertise and influence through longevity. They established a temporary committee to draft a constitution and schedule a constitutional convention for what would become the United States National Student Association for the beginning of the 1947 fall semester.[75]

On the crucial issue of IUS affiliation, Martin McLaughlin had shown that he could be as deft as Cater in rerouting student opinion. A straw vote favored affiliation. McLaughlin offered a resolution that favored affiliation in principle but put off a final decision in order to investigate key questions.[76] He argued that a national student organization would not officially exist until after it held its constitutional convention; therefore, technically, delegates could not affiliate with any other organization. When his argument won the day, Catholics were jubilant. Henry Briefs's brother Godfrey informed Professor Elliott that "IUS affiliation was circumvented by referring the whole thing to committee."[77]

The Catholics scored other victories. According to Chaplain Charles Marhoefer, who oversaw the Chicago cell, the thirty regions had been gerrymandered to the advantage of Catholics, although he does not say how.[78] Catholic strength was dispersed throughout the nation, thereby increasing the odds of Catholics winning regional elections and serving on the executive committee even without their tampering with regional boundary lines.

Catholics had enough delegates to elect John Simons treasurer of the National Continuations Committee, the interim body that would plan a constitutional convention in the fall. The army veteran dropped out of his first year at Fordham Law School to devote full time to student activities. In various capacities, Simons would be continuously involved with the NSA for the next twenty years, most of them as a CIA career officer. It is tempting to conclude that he had already become involved in secret intelligence work. But it is equally likely that his high profile in student politics over the next few years made him a logical CIA recruit.

Somewhat improbably, given the political tensions before Chicago, everyone left the meeting pleased with its outcome. Chaplain Marhoefer reported proudly that the Catholics had acquitted themselves so well that "the student organization is in their hands for the immediate future."[79]

Liberals were euphoric. The Harvard delegate Selig Harrison wrote in the *Harvard Crimson*, "You cannot bait the new student organization now, for it produced a leadership which represents a cross-section of the American students in the strictest sense." With a nod to the American Student Union and the ill-fated Roosevelt effort, he praised students for escaping "from the shadow of past failures."[80]

Even the AYD was pleased. The Communist Party's *Daily Worker* praised the diverse Chicago attendance, "from Catholics to Communists." Correspondent Ruby Cooper offered no objections to McLaughlin's motion on the International Union of Students. She heralded it as a step toward affiliation.[81]

The largely undergraduate students who came to Chicago from as far away as Washington State, California, Louisiana, and Maine had every reason to believe they, and they alone, would determine the fate of the national organization they were in the process of creating. After all, they held the power of votes. They had no way of knowing how many watchful eyes were upon them or the power that resided behind some of the observers.

3

BEHIND THE SCENES

IN THE NINE MONTHS between the Chicago meeting to test the sentiment for a new national student organization and the constitutional convention in September 1947 in Madison, Wisconsin, American attitudes toward the Soviet Union hardened. In March, President Truman issued an ultimatum: henceforth, he told Congress, the United States would oppose any Soviet move to bring Greece and Turkey into its sphere. In the summer of 1947, the Soviet Union refused to participate in the Marshall Plan for the reconstruction of Europe, a rejection made inevitable, perhaps, by the inclusion of unacceptable demands, but a decision that heightened East-West tensions. In another omen of communist influence, Czechoslovakia, whose leaders had heralded the country's role as a bridge between East and West, followed Russia's example and refused to participate in the Plan.[1]

The prospect that an American student organization might affiliate with the Prague-based International Union of Students captured the attention of the FBI, the Vatican, the American Catholic hierarchy, and U.S. Department of State officials, most of whom shared the view that the IUS was a Moscow-directed front organization.

FBI director J. Edgar Hoover had ordered his agents to infiltrate all sessions of the Chicago meeting. Afterward, Hoover distributed the name of every delegate, alternate, and observer to his field offices for further investigation.[2] Since Hoover obtained the lists *before* the Chicago meeting, we can reasonably infer that someone inside the planning apparatus supplied them. After Chicago, FBI agents debriefed professional youth leaders from the National Intercollegiate Christian Council and others, including Douglass Cater's bête noire at Harvard, Profes-

43

sor William Y. Elliott.[3] Someone from the YWCA, most likely Muriel Jacobson, praised the Catholics for supplying the force that prevented communists from wielding influence in Chicago.[4]

These FBI reports, declassified decades later with heavy redactions, hint that other still-protected sources monitored the Prague and Chicago meetings. A YMCA Student Division official, most likely Edwin Espy, told FBI agents that he kept abreast of developments "by virtue of his position in [redacted]." In addition to exhaustive information on students from regional and state FBI bureaus, Hoover also received reports on American students traveling overseas from his legal attachés to American embassies in Europe.[5]

The U.S. government quietly stepped up its efforts to monitor Soviet initiatives aimed at students, youth, labor, and other constituencies. While the Central Intelligence Agency did not officially exist until September 1947—the same month the NSA held its constitutional convention—the United States had other watchdogs at home and abroad. These included intelligence units in the Departments of War and State, an interim Central Intelligence Group, a special office based in Germany known as EUR/X, dedicated to fighting international communism, and several ad hoc coordinating committees. Special intelligence panels reviewed reports and coordinated raw intelligence.[6]

In addition, many intelligence officers in the civilian Office of Strategic Services formed a new State Department Bureau of Intelligence and Research. On April 1, 1947, the Bureau initiated a sweeping study of communist influence in the World Federation of Democratic Youth, including an analysis of national chapters and individual members. Louis Nemzer, a Soviet propaganda specialist who headed the Social and Cultural Affairs Branch and served as an informal adviser to the bishops' conference and Catholic student leaders, oversaw the study.[7]

Some NSA founders depict the State Department as uninterested in their activities, but that was not the case. In addition to intelligence collection, the State Department had its own observer in Chicago, a man with a long history of involvement in international student politics. Kenneth Holland, the assistant director of the Office of International Information and Cultural Affairs, was once a staff director of the U.S. ISS Committee (1934); he subsequently joined the board. During the war, Holland had facilitated funding for a prospective ISS-sponsored

Pan-American student conference to build solidarity in the Western Hemisphere.[8] Holland secured financing from his boss, Nelson Rocke feller, director of the wartime Inter-American Agency, a temporary organization responsible for activities in Central and South America, including intelligence, under White House guidance. When the U.S. ISS Committee imploded in 1943, the successor group of educators retained the funds even though the conference was canceled.

Holland understood the political stakes of the Chicago meeting, especially the danger of left-wing influence. But he also recognized the potential of strong, noncommunist student leadership to represent American democracy abroad. His office, for example, secured former troop ships to make student travel to Europe affordable during the summer of 1947. On June 30, Holland saw off the *Marine Tiger*, a converted troop ship, from the New York harbor, and told the students, "You are fighting another phase of the same war your brothers fought by force of arms." He bid them be ambassadors for democracy.[9] Like Nemzer, Holland was fully informed on the IUS affiliation question.

There were other discreet relationships between the wartime educators and the Prague 25 delegation. Douglass Cater, the recently retired OSS officer, declined in Chicago to accept the presidency of the interim National Continuations Committee, but he did not leave the stage.[10] A few weeks before the gathering, he had established the Harvard International Activities Committee (HIACOM), a subcommittee of the Student Council, to serve as a clearinghouse for student projects in the international field pending the birth of the new national student organization.[11] The "temporary" body would last nearly eight years and become an entry point for CIA covert operations. Its establishment and role, therefore, must be added to the list of forces that shaped the NSA international program months before the organization formally existed.

After the Chicago meeting, HIACOM expanded its activities. On February 6, 1947, the *Harvard Crimson* carried an announcement that the subcommittee would publish an international activities bulletin to inform students about "exchange, travel, relief, and rehabilitation of students all over the globe." Content would come from "information provided by the embassies of various nations and such world-wide organizations as American Friends Service Committee, the World Student Service Fund, and the Unitarian Service Committee."[12] The bulletin would be sent to all delegates and observers who had been in Chicago to keep them informed of international developments prior to the constitutional convention.[13]

The announcements for the various HIACOM programs proposed over the next year match almost word for word proposed programs crafted by the ISS educators who in 1943 incorporated as the Student Service of America. In October 1945, General Secretary Harry D. Gideonse had called for an urgent resumption of activities.[14] Clyde Eagleton, George N. Shuster, and Arnold Wolfers, among others, had met and voted to expand the board, inviting college presidents and educators to join them. They also brought in several OSS officials, thereby creating another tie with intelligence veterans.[15]

On March 19, 1946, nearly four months *before* the Prague 25 sailed for Europe, Gideonse convened another meeting in his office at Brooklyn College. The expanded board adopted an omnibus program of "international student conferences (local, regional, national and international), travel, relief activities (Europe and Asia), and student exchange programs."[16] Retiring assistant secretary of state for public affairs and former ISS committee member Archibald MacLeish informed the group that he had passed the proposals on to his successor, William A. Benton. A former advertising legend, Benton, like MacLeish, sat atop a growing bureaucracy of information and cultural exchange programs that included Kenneth Holland's division.

The March 1946 minutes of the SSA indicate that the omnibus program had been submitted to several foundations, including the Rockefeller, Rockefeller Brothers, Marshall Field, and Carnegie Corporation. Discussions had been held with top-level officials, including the president of the Rockefeller Foundation, Raymond Fosdick, and his assistant John Marshall. The SSA board considered whether to give their plans publicity, then decided, according to the minutes, that "on the general form of its activities, and its special projects, no publicity shall at this moment be given."[17]

The minutes also indicate that the educators anticipated spearheading the resumption of international student activities. But the prospect of a new American national student organization altered their plans. Subsequently, the Gideonse group transferred its activities to the World Student Service Fund in New York.[18] While there was nothing clandestine or nefarious about these activities, the frequent changes of identity (from ISS to SSA to WSSF) and the men's desire to work quietly behind the scenes have obscured their role in creating a postwar student international program.

The World Student Service Fund served as a common denominator in all HIACOM's international projects, even though each project appeared to have a different origin, sponsors, and funders. On February 21, 1947, two months after the Chicago meeting, Cater announced a Seminar on American Civilization, to be held in Salzburg.[19] He heralded the project as "entirely student-run," despite a faculty of renowned academics, several of whom served in the OSS, including Margaret Mead.[20] Other projects in the WSSF portfolio included the Foreign Students Summer Seminar at the Massachusetts Institute of Technology, which brought aspiring engineers and scientists from Europe to the United States, and the Program of American Studies at Yale University for Foreign Students.

Sponsoring programs was an entirely new role for the small fund. Previously, the World Student Service Fund had conducted war relief drives among American high school and college students, and sent the proceeds to ISS headquarters in Geneva. Despite its name, an adult, Wilmer Kitchen, a pipe-smoking young Protestant minister who had long been active in the New England Christian Movement, directed the fund.[21]

In such a circuitous fashion, the New York–based fund provided the basis for the future NSA to describe itself as an "information agent" for the Salzburg Seminar, the MIT program, and others, giving it an instant international portfolio without actual financial or administrative responsibility.[22] George Shuster, a veteran of both the ISS and the SSA, became the new WSSF president.[23] Its budget soared to $600,000—an astronomical figure in 1947, and twice as high as its wartime budgets when the impulse to contribute war relief funds ran high. Since its financial statements usually identify income sources by category, such as "Foundations," it is difficult to reconstruct precisely where the money for different projects came from, although large grant awards are traceable through the Rockefeller and other foundation archives.

The WSSF also played a behind-the-scenes role in encouraging the Chicago meeting. According to Kitchen's correspondence, the fund financially supported Prague 25 delegate Bill Ellis in making the rounds of "some of the larger colleges in the mid-west."[24] At the Chicago meeting, Kitchen announced a program of student travel to Europe aboard the former troop ships secured by Kenneth Holland's office. Few students were aware of Kitchen's relationship to the Department of State or that he had acceded to State Department demands to screen all student travelers for communist affiliations.[25] After the Chicago meeting, Kitchen financed at least one, if not all three, issues of the *International Information Bulletin* announced by Cater.[26]

Between May and September 1947, Kitchen sought to remedy the dearth of student participation in WSSF. He invited half a dozen American student organizations to become sponsors of the fund. These included Cater's HIACOM, Hillel, the NICC, the National Federation of Catholic College Students, and the National Newman Club Federation, along with the future National Student Association. The arrangement enabled older activists like the Ridgley Manor–trained Catholic John Simons to build influence in student circles. It blurred the lines between student leaders and adult professional youth leaders, such as Muriel Jacobson and Edwin Espy, who remained active participants. Its intricate series of committees, subcommittees, and ad hoc committees kept control in adult hands. All these arrangements defied bureaucratic charting; they were chaotic, eternally changing, and rarely understood by anyone but a handful of insiders.

Years later, one former CIA officer claimed that the WSSF had served as the Agency's first funding conduit. If that is the case, and scant evidence supports it, the WSSF role must be distinguished from that of a later period, when funds came to the NSA from the CIA covert action office, a unit that was not established until September 1, 1948. More likely, educational elites, State Department officials, intelligence veterans, and major philanthropists who had forged common goals during World War II continued their informal cooperation. Similar networks would later facilitate an almost seamless transition to covert action.

These relationships should dispel the notion that government officials were uninterested in the formation of the NSA. The government even discreetly approached some of the leading Prague 25 figures. According to State Department records, in August 1947 Acting Secretary of State Robert A. Lovett assured the American embassy in Prague that Bill Ellis, who had been elected to the IUS Secretariat, had "favorably impressed Dept concerning desired cooperation Dept and his loyalty."[27] Earlier, FBI officials reported that they had received a twelve-page report from Ellis on the February 1947 IUS Council meeting in Prague, although it is unclear whether Ellis or someone else supplied it.[28]

Informal cooperation, even report sharing, is not the same thing as covert action, and should be distinguished from it. Nevertheless, lines of influence were being forged between key players and government agencies long before the constitutional convention formally created the Unites States National Student Association.

AS THE CLOCK TICKED toward the Madison convention, the Catholic activists faced unexpected pressure from the Vatican. In January 1946, shortly after the World Federation of Democratic Youth was formed, the Vatican had issued orders prohibiting Catholic participation in it. Martin McLaughlin had traveled from Prague to Rome after the World Student Congress to urge the Vatican's cardinal secretary of state, Monsignor Giovanni Battista Montini (later Pope Paul VI) to delay judgment on the new International Union of Students.[29] McLaughlin argued that a premature condemnation by the Vatican would weaken minority forces (mainly Catholics) in the anticipated IUS and in any new American student union.

Three weeks before the Madison convention, the Vatican acted. The apostolic delegate in Washington conveyed a confidential document to the American bishops' staff that read: "I have received a confidential communication from the Holy See stating that according to information reaching the Holy See communistic elements are working actively in order to have the National Congress of American Students, to be held probably next September, affiliate with the International Student Union [*sic*]. Since this Union is nothing other than a communistic organization it seems advisable that some action be taken [in Madison] to prevent the sought for affiliation."[30] If anyone noted the irony of an outside power trying to dictate the agenda of an American organization, the very thing that destroyed the American Student Union, it is not recorded.

What is recorded is the dilemma the papal communiqué created for McLaughlin and others. If, as expected, sentiment to join the IUS remained high at the convention, the minority Catholics would be hard pressed to stop it. If Catholics fought openly against world student unity and IUS affiliation, their chances of coalescing with non-Catholics on other issues, especially the election of officers, could be damaged.

49

Faced with these difficulties, the Catholics chose subterfuge. They adopted a strategy identified by Father Bermingham as originating in "confidential memoranda from the across the sea."[31] An unidentified author advised the Catholics to appear supportive of IUS affiliation but to use delaying tactics to stop immediate action. The "kicker," a term used by Father Bermingham to explain the strategy to his superiors, would be to invoke the IUS constitutional provision that required members to conform to its policies, argue that the provision was undemocratic, and demand repeal as a condition of American affiliation.

While this memo might have come from the Vatican, it could also have come from Sally Cassidy, one of the Ridgely Manor–trained Catholics. Shortly before the group departed for Europe in the summer of 1946, Bishop John Wright, the private secretary to Archbishop Cushing, had approached Cassidy and asked if she would like to remain in Europe to report on student developments. Cassidy, who held a Ph.D. from Fordham University, portrays herself today as a sophisticate, well-versed in Marxism: "I read Trotsky when I was twelve," she sniffs. She dismissed the Ridgely Manor training as simplistic, disparaging Ruth Fischer as "a kind of batwoman." But eager to get away from her controlling mother, Cassidy said yes to the bishop and accepted his check for $2,000.[32]

Based in Paris, Cassidy filed regular reports to Martin McLaughlin and personally briefed Vatican officials. During her interview, Cassidy said that she used a military APO address for McLaughlin, which again raises the question of whether he was on active military duty, and, if so, whether he formally reported to U.S. government authorities.[33] On several occasions, Cassidy traveled to Rome, as McLaughlin had done, to brief the cardinal secretary of state. Presumably, she discussed future courses of action.[34] The author of the advisory memo to American Catholics, either Cassidy or a Vatican official, argued that the IUS would never amend its constitution because "other national student organizations in other countries would demand the same autonomy of action." If the ploy to keep the NSA out of the IUS worked, the author concluded, Catholics could "defeat the whole Communist strategy."[35]

To pursue this goal, the Joint Committee for Student Action put out a twice-monthly newsletter and tightened regional ecclesiastical supervision over Catholic delegates, while vowing to do a better job of keeping priestly intervention hidden from view. Once the constitutional convention began, JCSA leaders met nightly to plot tactics.[36]

NEITHER THE CATHOLICS nor the Harvard liberals, albeit for different reasons, wanted an open fight over communism that would risk tearing the Madison convention apart. The Catholics wanted to prevent IUS affiliation without having to say they did; liberals wanted to avoid blame for precipitating an East-West split. Both Catholics and liberals debated the central question of IUS affiliation in a kind of code. Rather than call the IUS communist dominated, they said it engaged in *partisan political activity*. Rather than argue against the IUS mandate to debate social and political issues, they called for a focus on *students as students*, the language of Campobello, meant to restrict debate to issues such as tuition costs, housing, or course curricula.

An occasional voice at the convention urged a broader focus. The American Youth for Democracy delegate Lee Marsh, who in a later interview described himself as a scrawny kid from Brooklyn who had once traveled as a young communist organizer with folk singer Pete Seeger, made the case for engaging with social and political issues. Students in colonial countries, he argued, "feel as strongly about anti-imperialism and anti-colonialism as we do [about] democracy."[37] But few American undergraduates identified with students who lived under the thumb of a colonial power, and they readily adopted the restriction.

In the end, undergraduates deferred to the Prague 25 and a few Campobello graduates to decide key issues. Press and FBI reports identify the leaders of the IUS debate as Martin McLaughlin, Douglass Cater, navy veteran Frank Fisher (Cater's second-in-command on the Harvard committee), and Campobello graduate George Fischer, now at Harvard. The convention voted overwhelmingly in favor of affiliation with the IUS (429–35), but, happily for the Catholics, the delegates attached conditions to the vote that postponed a final decision for at least a year.[38] The conditions included daunting procedural obstacles such as referring the final decision on IUS membership to the member campuses, and requiring a yea vote from "one-half of the member colleges containing two-thirds of the member students."[39] The convention also agreed to send an NSA team to Prague the following summer to determine whether the IUS met democratic standards.

However pleased the American Catholics might be with their tactical success,—and they were ecstatic—the Vatican did not share their sense of triumph. Following the convention, in January 1948, the apostolic delegate to the United States, A. G. Cicognani, notified the American bishops that the report on the NSA constitutional convention had been "submitted to the Holy Father and carefully examined."[40] The Vatican was displeased with "the compromise resolution" that left the door open to IUS affiliation. Still, the Catholics had bought a whole year's delay. McLaughlin and others drafted a response to the Vatican pledging that there would be no affiliation with the IUS and promising other actions on behalf of the NSA that would have shocked the Madison delegates: "NSA intends, however, to do more than merely not join IUS; it intends to destroy the present IUS and replace it with a genuine world student confederation."[41] In fact, the Madison delegates had enthusiastically opted for cooperation with the IUS while awaiting formal affiliation. It would not be the last time that Catholics would cite their own agenda as if it were NSA policy, even though they did so in this case to placate ecclesiastic superiors. Such actions reflected their apostolic mission—to destroy the IUS and create an alternative.

Whether the NSA would adhere to the Congress's mandate for co-operation with the IUS rested on the shoulders of the officers who were elected at the Madison convention, especially the vice president in charge of the international program (the International Commission). The decision made in Chicago to exclude national organizations from the NSA limited the field of candidates to campus delegates, includ-ing graduate students, so long as they remained officially enrolled at a college or university.[42] Several Prague 25 veterans, among them Curtis Farrar of Yale and Douglass Cater, constructed a slate of talented stu-dents with balanced representation in terms of race, sex, religion, and geography for all offices, except—notably—the crucial position of inter-national affairs vice president.

None of the candidates for president, treasurer, vice president for educational affairs, and secretary came to Madison with the intention of running for office. The future president, William (Bill) Welsh, from liberal Berea College in Kentucky described his recruitment in later conversations. He was awakened one evening by loud knocks on his dor-mitory door. Someone, he thinks perhaps Curtis Farrar, intoned, "Wake up and run for president."[43] Sleepy and aware that a University of Chi-cago delegate, William Birenbaum, had thrown his hat into the ring, Welsh asked, "What's wrong with him?" But he finally agreed to run. While Birenbaum had Catholic support and opposed affiliation with the IUS, the more liberal Welsh favored affiliation and won, 312 to 244.[44]

The other officers included a female (Secretary, Janice Tremper, Rockford College), an African American (Treasurer, Lee Jones, Buffalo State University), and a Catholic (National Affairs Vice President, Ralph Dungan, St. Joseph's College).[45]

By contrast, the candidate to fill the international position had not been left to chance. The old ISS/SSA committee had positioned a student from Yale. In the fall of 1946, Arnold Wolfers had hired Wallace Doerr, a former OSS officer and Central European expert, as staff director for the ISS/SSA. Doerr, in turn, helped select Robert Solwin (Bob) Smith, a U.S. Navy veteran and Yale senior, to attend the Chicago meeting that December.[46] Wolfers and Doerr also tapped Smith to be a delegate for the ISS General Assembly, scheduled to meet in the summer of 1947 in Arhus, Denmark. One of Smith's tasks was to clear up confusion over who represented the United States in the ISS after the collapse of the U.S. Committee.

When Smith boarded the *Marine Tiger*, carrying students to Europe on June 30, he had two senior advisers in tow, Doerr and Douglass Cater.[47] There is no evidence that these two former OSS officials still worked for U.S. intelligence, although the possibility must remain. Most likely, they acted as talent scouts, seeking to find and groom a politically reliable student for a crucial leadership position.

Smith, a New Yorker with an upscale address on Fifth Avenue across from the Metropolitan Museum of Art who summered in the Hamptons, later described his life before the European trip: "I used to be a pretty average sort of a guy—Yale, white shoe, party weekends."[48] The summer sojourn in Denmark transformed the future diplomat's interests and aspirations. His itinerary expanded to include a tour of the country, trips to Paris and Geneva, attendance at the World Youth Festival sponsored by the WFDY and IUS in Prague, and an introduction to IUS politics.

By the time Smith and Cater arrived in Prague, American embassy officials were beside themselves over the behavior of the American delegation. The State Department had ignored pleas from the Czechoslovak foreign minister, Jan Masaryk, to send a representative delegation, leaving the way clear for left-wing students to go instead.[49] The final straw for the embassy was the delegation's display of a poster that featured the lynching of an African American placed next to a fifteen-foot-high illuminated statue of Stalin.[50]

Smith and Cater joined a handful of other Americans in Prague who were deemed "competent observers" by U.S. intelligence officials to run a last-minute self-described guerrilla operation against the offending left-wing delegation.[51] The group worked out of the hotel room of Spurgeon M. Keeny, Jr., a recent graduate of Columbia University's new program in Russian Affairs.[52] As part of his summer learning intensive, Smith saw firsthand the increasingly bitter divide between American liberals and the far left, a division that would soon affect him personally.

Smith and Cater had expected to confer with Bill Ellis at an IUS Council meeting scheduled for after the festival, but in June, Ellis had taken ill. He was subsequently diagnosed with paratyphoid, and was recuperating in a Swiss sanitarium. Cater exercised Ellis's proxy on the IUS Council, and passed it occasionally to Smith, an act that later gave rise to conservative charges that the NSA flirted with international communism. Before he left Prague, Smith promised the U.S. cultural attaché, Paul Lewand, a full report on his summer experiences.[53]

Unknown to Smith, his performance during the IUS Council meeting was closely monitored by Sally Cassidy, who had come from Paris to cast a proxy vote for Martin McLaughlin. Fortunately for Smith's future career, Cassidy found him "the only one of the American delegation who was neither a fellow traveler nor an opportunist."[54] She shared the Catholics' disdain for the liberal Cater—more than five decades later, she bristled upon hearing his name: "I wouldn't be caught dead in the same room with him."[55] Cassidy's favorable evaluation later helped Smith win Catholic votes in Madison.

In order to get to Wisconsin in time for the constitutional convention, Cater and Smith took a transatlantic flight back to the United States, an expensive rarity in those days. In Madison, Smith learned that he would chair the Sub-Commission on International Affairs, through which all resolutions on the IUS would pass.[56] Armed with the latest information on the ISS Assembly, the World Youth Festival, and the politics of the IUS, Smith established himself as an international expert, one of the few delegates whose authority could match that of the Prague 25, many of whom were no longer students. He also had backup: Wallace Doerr remained at his elbow, as he had at Arhus, serving in small committee sessions as a technical expert.[57]

During the larger plenary session, delegates suspended the rules in order to listen to a report about Smith's experiences in Europe. Thanks to this deft positioning, he became the sole candidate for international affairs vice president.[58] Doerr left Yale soon afterward, his whereabouts a mystery to many who had worked with him.[59]

Then came a move that cleaved the new NSA in half and made oversight of the International Commission nearly impossible. Delegates had deliberately chosen a midwestern location for their headquarters, to be accessible to more students but also, and more important, to avoid the intense political environment that characterized urban campuses, especially on the East Coast. But Smith refused to work in Madison; rather, he insisted on setting up the international office in Cambridge, where he was beginning graduate school at Harvard. (Years later, Bill Welsh remembered Smith's intransigence: "he was absolutely adamant.")[60] The two offices, more than eleven hundred miles apart, were forced to communicate by mail, since the students' spartan budget permitted few long-distance phone calls.

But Smith's move wasn't the only thing that obscured the lines of authority between Cambridge and Madison. Convention delegates asked the Cater-created Harvard International Activities Committee of the Student Council to continue working *under mandate* to the new NSA. Thus, Harvard University was home to not one but two NSA international offices. Smith set up an office in Hillel House on the edge of campus, while the HIACOM students worked out of the Phillips Brooks House on campus. Relations between the two offices in Cambridge varied from year to year, sometimes cordial, sometimes tense, but their actions were almost always opaque to NSA headquarters in Madison.

The geographical distance permitted Smith considerable discretion in what to share with the Madison-based National Commission staff, including funding. After the constitutional convention, Smith had stopped in New York City to see Wilmer Kitchen at WSSF and confer with John Simons. He never told his Madison colleagues, who were scraping by on meager NSA salaries, sharing meals, and shooing rats out of a ramshackle office, that he had obtained another source of funds. WSSF records indicate that Smith was hired as a publicity director for a period of one year beginning October 1, 1947.[61] While no salary figure is cited in the minutes, it is possible that Kitchen viewed the formal designation as a way to make travel funds available to Smith. In later years, the CIA secretly subsidized the salaries of individual NSA students, but it must be noted that from the beginning, outside funding was available for the international programs. The WSSF subsidy to Bob Smith lasted nearly two years, until April 1949, only ceasing long after his one-year term of office had expired.[62]

Meanwhile, Smith immediately began pressing Bill Welsh for authority to seek outside funding.[63] When Welsh was slow to answer, Smith raised the issue several more times, referring to unspecified "people up here who can get funds."[64] In November, he informed Welsh in a hope-you-don't-mind letter about a proposed mailing to Canadian students, "I am going to try and get outside funds from one of the educational foundations."[65] Welsh finally responded that he preferred to defer the decision about external funds to the December executive committee.[66]

WITHIN WEEKS OF THE Madison convention, the pending IUS question threatened the fragile existence of the new association. A prominent conservative Detroit banker, Allen Crow, one of many self-appointed watchdogs keeping an eye out for any hint that the American Student Union had been resurrected, charged that the NSA consorted with international communism.[67] Throughout September and early October, Crow bombarded the Madison office with letters and phone calls.[68] He sent a seven-page missive to college presidents, deans of students, and State Department officials. When Crow learned of Bob Smith's appearance at the IUS Council meeting, he saw evidence that the NSA served "two masters," implying that one of them was Moscow.[69]

Campus newspapers headlined Crow's charges. Students at Northwestern University refused to join the NSA. Even the University of Texas, which had had representatives among the Prague 25, voted not to affiliate with the NSA. The dean of students at the University of Georgia told Welsh "not to come on the campus or meet with any students." The climate on southern campuses was so hostile to liberals, Welsh remembered, that a Louisiana University student hid his copy of the *New Republic* under his bed. The possibility of IUS affiliation kept the issue alive. "There wasn't a campus in the United States that we didn't have to deal with this problem."[70]

On October 7, Welsh accepted Crow's invitation to speak at the Detroit Economic Club, and gave a self-described "flag-waving speech," but the attacks did not stop.[71] By then, Welsh recalled, the staff was "really desperate for a nod from the federal government for protection from the right-wing nuts."[72]

The nod came. On October 14 a telegram from the U.S. Department of State arrived at NSA headquarters. Welsh cabled its substance to Smith in Cambridge: "You appointed NSA member UNESCO."[73] Welsh remembered waving the State Department cable joyously around the office and shouting, "Look, look, we're legitimate."[74] He also remembered it as coming out of the blue. In fact, the appointment had been approved months earlier. Henry D. Gideonse served on the U.S. National Commission for UNESCO and chaired the subcommittee that recommended the appointment of three student and youth representatives.[75] The decision had been made in March 1947, but State Department officials felt obliged to delay the official appointment until after the NSA's constitutional convention.[76]

The effect of the government imprimatur cannot be overstated. The men and women who served on the bipartisan U.S. National Commission for UNESCO were establishment figures, top diplomats, and university presidents whose credentials placed them, in 1947, beyond political attack. The UNESCO appointment signaled that the NSA had no connection to the defunct American Student Union. College presidents pointed to it as a way of reassuring concerned parents and wary boards of regents.[77] Without the appointment, Crow's attack on the new organization's political identity might have destroyed it.

U.S. Attorney General Tom Clark used the UNESCO appointment to answer public inquiries about communist penetration of the NSA. At the same time, he privately asked J. Edgar Hoover to open an FBI investigation to confirm that the NSA had no communist ties, unaware that Hoover had been on the case since 1946.[78]

As the Crow campaign subsided, the NSA leadership fell prey to an internal witch hunt over the question of IUS affiliation, spurred on by external forces, including the Catholic Church. The battle mirrored the political war that was then consuming the wider public: advocates of cooperation with the Soviet Union were not only losing ground to those who wanted to fight the Soviets, but the very act of advocating cooperation was being seen as political heresy.

Henry A. Wallace, Roosevelt's vice president, became the symbol of the change in attitude. After Truman fired Wallace from the Cabinet over his position regarding the Soviet Union in September 1946, Wallace formed the Progressive Party and ran for president in 1948, accusing Truman of ushering in a "century of fear."[79] Eleanor Roosevelt and other liberals led the opposition to Wallace, charging him with the "corruption of American liberalism." Others called him Stalin's candidate. But though there were few Wallace supporters in the top echelons of the NSA, a major exception was James W. (Jim) Smith, a Prague 25 member, who had been appointed to substitute for the ailing Bill Ellis in the IUS secretariat.

Smith, a former student body president at the University of Texas, had a droll sense of humor and a well-established reputation as a civil liberties advocate. When the Texas Board of Regents had fired President Homer Rainey for alleged communist tendencies in 1944—he had permitted John Dos Passos's *USA* to be adopted as a textbook—Smith led demonstrations in support of Rainey.[80] In December 1946, at the Chicago meeting, Smith had been elected president of the National Continuations Committee. He subsequently joined the Wallace-led Progressive Citizens of America. In Madison, his lack of student status kept him from running for office, but in the chaotic aftermath of an exhausting convention, the new NSA executive committee appointed him temporary replacement for the stricken Ellis.

Suspicion soon attached to every act Jim Smith took or failed to take. His early letters from Prague, intended to reassure the NSA that all was going well, had the opposite effect. Smith wrote that the secretariat was "quite elated over the statement that NSA will cooperate in IUS activities this year."[81] This was a statement of fact, but the implied enthusiasm rang alarm bells for Bob Smith in Cambridge. On December 13, he wrote to the Madison staff: "I don't mean to sound like an old maid about it, but we've got to slow him down a little, for his own good and for that of NSA. There is nothing that IUS hdqtrs would like more than to 'pull him over to their side' in some of our difficulties."[82]

If Bob Smith was apprehensive, Catholics were in open revolt. Rumors spread that Jim Smith had belonged to the Communist Party in the 1930s. Stories circulated about his summer work for the steelworkers union in Texas. He carried a lunch pail, which affluent Ivy Leaguers had thought merely odd, but which now offered ominous hints of working-class sympathies.[83]

At a late-December meeting of the NSA executive committee, the regional chairs voted 19 to 1 to strip Jim Smith of his authority and his right to interpret NSA policy.[84] Some chairs expressed regret over their hasty vote to send him to Prague; others said that they felt they had been duped.[85] The committee voted to place all authority on the IUS question in the hands of the annual Congress. This unexpected move astonished the other NSA officers. President Welsh noted later that he sensed forces outside the NSA in play, but he could not identify what they were.[86] He had no inkling of the Vatican's involvement or of how much Catholics feared that the NSA would affiliate with the IUS.

Jim Smith's situation in Prague was further complicated by the fact that technically neither he nor Ellis represented the NSA. Illness had prevented Ellis from resigning as an NICC representative, as planned, and being reappointed by the NSA. Thus, Jim Smith's status at IUS was ambiguous. In February, Muriel Jacobson seized on this technicality and informed the NSA that Smith was not an acceptable replacement for Ellis.[87] Before that formal notice, someone outside the NSA, possibly Jacobson, suggested that Spurgeon M. Keeny, whose hotel room in Prague had been the site of the campaign against left-wing Americans, might travel to Prague and observe Smith at an upcoming IUS Executive Committee meeting. Bob Smith agreed and informed the Madison staff.[88]

When Keeny arrived in Prague for the January 18 meeting, he checked in with the American Embassy before contacting Jim Smith. Ironically, Smith, unaware of Keeny's purpose in Prague, was waging a successful fight to keep the IUS Executive Committee meeting open to observers. Once the issue was settled, Keeny was admitted and took verbatim notes of the marathon meetings, which began at 9:30 A.M. and lasted into the night. After traveling to Switzerland and conferring with Ellis, Keeny turned his notes into a twenty-eight-page single-spaced confidential report with one overriding conclusion: "One must accept the clear and obvious fact that IUS is at present a Communist controlled 'front.'"[89]

While Keeny recognized the difficulty of Jim Smith's position, he damned him with faint praise. Yes, Smith had tried to represent the positions of the NSA fairly, but "I could not help feeling that he was always disassociating himself from these opinions and apologizing for rather than defending the attitude of the NSA and American students." In Keeny's judgment, Smith lacked the requisite backbone to deal with communists: "He compromised too far and too easily for a person in his position."[90] Keeny found no objection to anything Jim Smith actually did—he simply sensed a lack of ardor in his arguments. Keeny, by contrast, was described by Bob Smith as a gung-ho anticommunist, an "'action man' on this student politics . . . business—feels that we should get in and fight IUS tooth and nail."[91]

Unknown to either Keeny or the NSA, Jim Smith had already told relatives in early February that he planned to quit. He felt that the NSA had moved to the right, while the IUS had moved to the left.[92] The attack by the Catholics deepened his disillusionment. He wrote to his family that Catholic leaders "spread the word that Jim Smith is a Communist, from one end of the country to the other." He told his family that he would resign as of March 1, 1948.

Jim Smith did resign but not before events in Czechoslovakia took the matter out of his hands. The same events would bring the NSA closer to clandestine intelligence operations. But long before then, the external institutions and agencies that had developed a stake in the NSA's political character and foreign policy made sure that the question of IUS affiliation would not be left to chance or the whims of American undergraduates.

4

ENTER THE CIA

HAD THE INTERNATIONAL UNION of Students been headquartered somewhere other than Eastern Europe, its history over the next few years might have been different. The choice of Prague originally linked the IUS with Czechoslovakia's earlier student wartime resistance: Charles University was where the students had been massacred by the Nazis in 1939. But when Czech communists staged a government coup on February 25, 1948, they brought the country firmly into the Eastern bloc and under Soviet domination, and restricted IUS autonomy. The Czech coup constitutes a defining moment in the Cold War: it forced countries and institutions to choose sides, made advocacy of East-West cooperation increasingly unpopular, boosted the fortunes of supporters of covert government action in the United States, reshaped the NSA's foreign policy agenda, and escalated CIA interest in the NSA.

On February 24, 1948, Jim Smith, still in Prague, walked past a bulletin board in a Charles University dormitory and noticed a flyer announcing a student rally the next day in Wenceslas Square.[1] The political climate in Czechoslovakia that winter had been tense. The Communist Party had won enough seats in the 1946 election to become the most powerful partner in the coalition government, and in the intervening months communist cabinet ministers gradually purged noncommunists from their ranks. Ministers from the National Socialist Party, which had established democracy in Czechoslovakia, resigned in protest. Although President Edvard Beneš refused to accept their resignations, his stand heightened tensions among government officials.

When the communists widened their purges of noncommunists in government ministries, schools, and universities, the crisis worsened.

What was left of the Beneš government teetered on the brink. If it fell, Czechoslovakia would join Poland, Romania, Bulgaria, and Yugoslavia behind the Iron Curtain.[2] Such an event would also put Jim Smith in an untenable position as the de facto NSA representative in the IUS secretariat.

On February 25, Smith joined thousands of students in the courtyard of Technical High School near Wenceslas Square. Antonin Navratil, chair of the Prague Union of Students, announced that President Beneš had agreed to meet with a student delegation. Accompanied by four other students, Navratil began walking across Charles Bridge toward Hradčany Castle, where Beneš and Foreign Minister Jan Masaryk were in session.

Before they set off, Navratil urged the assembled students to remain peaceful, not to engage in shouting or singing. If the police blocked their procession, he urged, the students should quietly disperse. Navratil had good reason to be cautious. He had not obtained the required permit for a public gathering, believing it would be denied.[3] Growing throngs of students pushed their way up Prague's narrow cobblestone streets toward the castle. Those who had assembled at other locations joined the demonstration, and the crowd swelled — most estimates put the number at ten thousand.

Smith edged his way up to the front of the crowd, where he had a clear view. He later described what he saw. "The students . . . proceeded into a narrow street leading to the President's Castle, and when it was about one third of the way along a squad of about twenty policemen, armed with pistols, rifles, and machine guns, formed up across the road. . . . The five member delegation was escorted to the Castle by two police officers and for the next twenty minutes the students faced the police at a distance of about seventy five yards."[4] Then came the police order to disperse.

"The students stood their ground for several minutes, after which the police formed a line across the road with their rifles held across their bodies, and began to press the students back. . . . Some of the students began to cry 17th November, comparing the incident to the massacre of 1939. . . . This comparison with the attack of the German Gestapo upon the student movement naturally angered the members of the police who began to drive the students more quickly down the hill."[5]

What happened next is disputed. Smith heard rumors that four students had been shot. He saw one student collapsed in the street. He never heard the police give an order to fire on the crowd, although he thought that the rumors of shootings might be true because the atmosphere had been so charged. While "the students were defiant, and very slow to move," Smith observed, "the narrowness of the street may have added to the difficulty."[6] As rumors spread, casualty estimates grew.

That afternoon, Prime Minister Klement Gottwald appeared on a balcony in Wenceslas Square and announced the formation of a communist-led government. A few days later, Masaryk, one of the government's few remaining noncommunists, fell from his office window to his death in the courtyard below. Few in the West believed the official verdict of suicide.[7]

The IUS leaders refused to condemn either the coup or the continuing purges. From his sanitarium in Leysin, Switzerland, Bill Ellis demanded that Jim Smith resign in protest. Smith complied. On March 1, in Madison, Wisconsin, Bill Welsh opened a cable from Ellis that began with the dramatic phrase "Students Fired Upon," and contained news of Ellis and Smith's resignations from the IUS.[8]

After reading the telegram, Welsh concluded that the four-person negotiating team mandated by the constitutional convention and chosen by the NSA executive committee in December no longer had a purpose. The resignations made the issue of affiliation with IUS moot. Accordingly, he issued a press release to announce the resignations and the termination of the negotiating team.[9] Welsh did not consult beforehand with his international vice president, Bob Smith.

Bob Smith was in New York at a meeting of the World Student Service Fund when Muriel Jacobson circulated a copy of Ellis's cable. The next day, back at Harvard, Smith conferred with Douglass Cater and others. A few days later, Smith berated Welsh by letter for acting precipitously and usurping Smith's authority. In the future, Smith commanded, "I must control all correspondence on the IUS subject." He cited his superior expertise, his "full understanding" of events, thanks to the Keeny report on the IUS—which the Madison office had not seen—and "long talks with Doug [Cater], Sally Cassidy and Frank Fisher."[10]

Smith had already informed Welsh that he had learned during the WSSF meeting that "something new might take place." The group had discussed "a Canadian proposal for a new world organization, which is to be consistent with the principles for which we stand."[11]

Welsh's press release canceling the negotiation team temporarily fore-stalled plans by Catholics to use the summer trip to discreetly explore the possibility of a new international organization. Martin McLaughlin had been one of four students chosen the previous December by the NSA executive committee to serve on the team. It was clear in Catholic circles that McLaughlin intended to use his position to explore an alternative to the IUS, despite the fact that the executive committee had explicitly forbidden any discussion of an alternative. Team members were going to be briefed by the State Department before departure, a fact that Bob Smith asked the foursome not to discuss, assuring them that they were "not beholden to the department in any way that would limit our activities."[12]

But even before the coup, Bob Smith had been drawn into discussions about the IUS and alternatives with State Department and intelligence officials. While in Washington for a UNESCO Commission meeting in late January, Smith had joined Catholic leaders John Simons and Philip DesMarais at Henry Briefs's spacious home in Bethesda for a social event that included Louis Nemzer from State Department intelligence and Don Cook from the International Exchange of Persons office. Nemzer, who had been advising the Catholics for some months, was overseeing an omnibus study of the World Federation of Democratic Youth, and kept track of IUS developments. He argued that the students' situation in the IUS was roughly equivalent to that of American labor in the World Federation of Trade Unions, also dominated by communists, where an initiative was under way to create a pro-West rival. Smith reported the gist of these conversations to the Madison staff but omitted any mention of Nemzer's presence.[13]

The coup in Czechoslovakia preempted all discussions. It ushered in a period of uncertainty and disappointment. Bob Smith reported Douglass Cater as saying, "There goes two years' work shot to hell."[14] Smith himself wrestled with whether things could have turned out differently.[15] If American students had organized earlier, joined the IUS sooner, or played a stronger leadership role in Prague, he mused, perhaps the situation could have been avoided. But after considering the question further, he decided, it probably couldn't. He told his colleagues, "The circumstances in the higher echelons of social and political life appear to be not such as to permit too great a contrast between that which students do and the games of their elders."[16] His tone is matter-of-fact, not rebellious, merely a recognition that the NSA's international fortunes were tied to decisions made by men in power.

The events in Czechoslovakia also galvanized advocates of covert government action. When the CIA was formed in September 1947, former military and civilian intelligence officials, among them Allen Dulles (OSS Switzerland) and Frank Wisner (OSS Romania), pushed hard for it to have a covert action arm. Both the CIA and the State Department resisted. The first CIA general counsel argued that the Agency's charter didn't permit covert action, while State Department diplomats feared secret activities not under their control, which carried the risk of exposure and damage to American foreign policy.[17] Dulles therefore advised his good friend Wisner to join the State Department, burrow in, and wait for the time to be ripe.[18]

Three months later, in December, the National Security Council had authorized covert psychological warfare activities, understood as the rough equivalent of propaganda designed to undermine the morale of the enemy.[19] While psychological warfare strategies were prevalent during World War II, diplomats and American citizens alike feared government-sponsored propaganda. To accommodate public sensibilities, psychological warfare activities were publicly rechristened *information activities.*

After the communists took over in Czechoslovakia, qualms about covert action evaporated. In June 1948, National Security Council directive 10/2 broadened the authorized covert activities to include political warfare and subversion so that the government's hand in such activities could be disguised or plausibly denied. In September 1948, Wisner became head of the Office of Policy Coordination (OPC), an obscurely named office buried in the State Department that oversaw covert activities.[20] Funds, but not overall direction, came from the CIA. The ambiguous status of the OPC gave Wisner a free hand—too free in the judgment of many, for he was accountable to no one. Wisner soon staked a claim on a portion of Marshall Plan moneys designed to rehabilitate the European economy, which added millions to his stash of unvouchered funds, nicknamed "candy," or "catnip" by some American labor union recipients.[21]

Armed with these funds, Wisner mobilized quickly to fight Soviet-backed international organizations, placing an initial priority on labor and youth. The OPC secretly passed money to American labor organizations to build opposition to the World Federation of Trade Unions.[22] Nemzer and the U.S. intelligence analysts had completed their exhaustive study of communist influence in the World Federation of Democratic Youth, its national affiliates, and individual youth leaders by April 1, 1948, and concluded that the organization was under communist domination.[23]

By then, planning for an alternative international youth group had already begun. Since 1945, professional youth staff, among them YM-YWCA officials, had worked with their British counterparts, who were upset over the formation of WFDY and its claim to represent all young people. The London launch of the WFDY had also motivated British government officials to seize the initiative.[24] In the United States, government officials encouraged an existing, adult-led Association of Youth Serving Organizations, under the auspices of the National Social Welfare Assembly, to reorganize into the Young Adult Council, and anticipate the creation of something new.[25] In 1946, Bill Ellis and Muriel Jacobson initially represented the YW-YMCA in this group before it was renamed, and until Ellis asked to be relieved of his duties to join the Prague 25.[26] In August 1948, six months after the Czech coup, a pro-West alternative, the World Assembly of Youth (WAY), held its first meeting in London and included American delegates from the Young Adult Council.[27] Despite all this activity in youth and labor arenas, a student counteroffensive against the International Union of Students lagged behind. In October 1947, Raymond Murphy, the head of EUR/X and preoccupied with the study of the World Federation of Democratic Youth, lamented that lack of time had prevented an equally comprehensive study of the IUS and its members.[28]

The lack of adequate intelligence was not the only deterrent to a student counteroffensive to the IUS. To the surprise of NSA leaders, European student unions did not defect en masse after the coup in Czechoslovakia. In a contemporary interview, Paul Bouchet, a French resistance leader in World War II, cited wartime resistance movements to explain his sanguine view of communists in the IUS. "We knew these people. We worked with these people."[29] For many European students, communists were fellow students battling for their beliefs, not automatons spouting Soviet lines. Even if individual European student leaders wanted to disaffiliate, and only the most conservative did, overturning existing policies in their respective national organizations required time and debate.

In addition, IUS leaders vigorously defended their actions in the wake of the coup. General Secretary Thomas Madden campaigned effectively throughout the spring to retain European members. A report written by British National Union of Students president W. Bonney Rust, who was not a communist, examined the charges that Czech students had been fired upon during the march to the castle. He found a single incident during which two students grappled with a policeman and a rifle went off, wounding one student in the foot.[30] Rust publicly urged Bill Ellis and Jim Smith to reconsider their resignations.

Rust's attitude underscored the difficulty of organizing an American-led initiative against the IUS. If the British were not ready to be allies, who would be? Nor could NSA leaders afford to articulate a clear policy until the August 1948 NSA Congress when delegates would decide to reject affiliating with the IUS. In addition, the young NSA leaders were often stunned by the hostility they encountered from European student leaders. In September 1948, Bob Smith would observe an IUS council meeting in Paris and find widespread suspicion of the Americans' motives. He reported that even NSA friends, "those who shared our anxieties [about] partisanship in the I.U.S.[,] had tended to write us off as too headstrong and tactless, and therefore unwelcome allies."[31]

State Department officials, by contrast, had decided months earlier that the IUS issue was settled: the secretary of state informed overseas American embassies in March that the NSA would take "no further action toward affiliation or [have] contact with IUS."[32] In similar cables he took for granted that the NSA would back a pro-Western alternative organization, discussed the obstacles a new organization would confront, and predicted outcomes.[33] Not surprisingly, the Catholic activists vigorously supported this position, having pledged themselves to work for an alternative to the IUS as early as 1946. Not long after the Czech coup, Vincent J. Flynn, president of St. Thomas College in Saint Paul, Minnesota, and a Catholic adviser to the NSA, was informed confidentially that John Simons "knows a great deal about these plans," and referred to "the possibility of establishing a new, and Western nation, Union of Students."[34]

When the NSA Congress met seven months after the events in

Czechoslovakia, the undergraduates who determined NSA policy—or thought they did—begged to differ. Nearly a thousand students and observers packed Memorial Union Building at the University of Wisconsin for the first annual NSA Congress. Outgoing vice president Bob Smith set the stage for the IUS debate. He described his hope for a junior United Nations that would prove "we were not going to be isolationistic." He praised Czechoslovakia as "a bridge-country between the East and West." He then blamed the communist coup and the failure of the IUS to condemn the coup for dashing American hopes, telling the delegates that "the parallel between documents of the IUS and the Cominform is too sharp to ignore."[35]

Smith's rejection of the IUS diverged from his earlier views. The previous February, after receiving Spurgeon Keeny's report, Smith had left the door open to cooperation. He observed to the Madison staff, "We can't sit back behind the 'iron curtain' and hurl invectives if there is any door open through which we might travel."[36] By August, he regarded the door as shut tight.

Three of the four members of the NSA team chosen in December had traveled in Europe over the summer, and returned divided on the IUS question. Two (Lawrence Jaffa of Harvard Divinity School and William Birenbaum of the University of Chicago) took a hard line: they urged delegates to break off all contact.[37] By contrast, Robert (Rob) West, a self-possessed Nebraskan with a Yale degree, fought for cooperation. West argued that the NSA could participate in IUS travel, educational, and cultural activities without becoming a full member. In his mind, refusing to cooperate constituted an active step toward a new war. As he had told Bob Smith when he learned of Ellis and Jim Smith's resignations, "I guess I'd better re-reconvert my uniform," a reference to his previous wartime service.[38] The fourth team member, Martin McLaughlin, had resigned from the team.

The Congress delegates agreed with West and refused to close the door on cooperation. They voted to suspend, rather than terminate, negotiations with the IUS and to cooperate with individual IUS departments. The young delegates went a step farther and forbade NSA officers to try to establish a rival organization.[39]

Despite West's view on cooperation with the IUS, the Harvard group and Bob Smith, as part of a slate-making deal with Catholic delegates, backed him to head the NSA international office. But West's ability to implement NSA policy was hampered by the fact that the slate also included for president a Catholic, who would not be able to escape Vatican and American hierarchy pressure to hold the line against cooperation with the IUS. The delegates constrained West, perhaps inadvertently, by renewing the mandate of the Harvard International Activities Committee, continuing its influence over the NSA International Commission. Pressure also came from NSA founders who remained active in international student affairs. Bob Smith, John Simons, and Bill Ellis (after he returned to the United States), among others, continued to serve on World Student Service Fund committees. Not bound by NSA Congress policy, they pushed for a Western rival to the IUS.

The Catholic president-elect, James T. (Ted) Harris, was an African American from La Salle College in Pennsylvania. Harris had refused to campaign for the top position but accepted a draft after the coalition of liberals and Catholics cleared the field of other candidates. Judging from archival correspondence, the pressure on Harris over the next year must have been searing. Catholics constantly pressured him to rein in Rob West. They scrutinized West's every utterance, once attacking him for using the word *dogma* in an NSA newsletter, convinced it was a deliberate slur on Catholics, even though West used it in a non-Catholic context. The bishops' conference Youth Department director, Joseph Scheider, who had replaced Father Bermingham, called West's use of the word a "malicious, filthy insult to any Catholic."[40]

West stirred up a more serious ruckus in the spring of 1949. He learned that IUS leaders Josef Grohman and Thomas Madden planned to tour the United States, and offered NSA hospitality. Archbishop Cushing initially demanded that all Catholic colleges withdraw from the NSA immediately.[41] Catholic advisers, including Father Flynn, disagreed, believing that the church's investment in the NSA was too great to begin anew. If they had not prevailed, the NSA would have collapsed: it could not have withstood the loss of a third of its members. The hospitality issue became moot when U.S. government officials denied Grohman a visa. But the Catholic Church had made a point: it could act as effectively as sentries to police desired boundaries, even if this meant overriding NSA policy and overruling the actions of elected officials.

While the Catholics kept West in check, the Harvard group continued to pursue its own agenda. Over the next two years, a handful of intelligence war veterans tied the NSA's international agenda to Frank Wisner's new CIA-funded covert action unit and its Cold War agenda.

Neither West nor his successor as international affairs vice president, Erskine Childers, seemed to have suspected the CIA's interest in the NSA.[42] Both men fought to preserve NSA autonomy from the U.S. government. Neither was a leftist. Both were liberal Democrats. Cold Warriors often argue that it is unfair for a younger generation of liberals to condemn their actions by applying the values and standards of a different era to the immediate postwar period. Yet West and Childers belonged to the same generation as the Cold Warriors, and both placed democratic process and self-determination over compliance with U.S. government objectives, whether openly stated or discreetly whispered.[43]

West realized late in his term that the HIACOM members were sometimes excluding him from important decisions while regularly supplying men with stellar credentials to direct NSA projects. During West's term, a third-year law student at Harvard, Thomas Farmer, took over an anticipated project involving German students. Farmer, a World War II veteran who was fluent in German—his father taught in Berlin until 1933—moved in elite circles; he was on a first-name basis with publishers, journalists, and diplomats, including former secretary of war John J. McCloy and the U.S. ambassador to England, Lewis Douglass.[44] West readily accepted Farmer's application, especially since Farmer hinted that he could pay his own way to Germany.[45]

Farmer had another credential of greater significance: he was a former intelligence officer (1942–45) attached to the War Department's general staff; and in 1949 he had joined a military intelligence reserve unit in Boston. In a later interview, Farmer implied that others who worked under HIACOM auspices belonged to the same unit, but declined to identify them.[46] His admission helps explain the perfect match over the next few years between individual projects and the older war veterans who directed them.

In Farmer's case, the German project was initiated by American military authorities eager to end the isolation of German students. While the U.S. occupation government had sanctioned the formation of a German student union, officials remained wary of the political views of young people. Over the summer of 1949, with funds from the U.S. government and the Rockefeller Foundation, Farmer led a six-person team from three countries—the United States, Sweden, and Great Britain—to survey the attitudes of German students, looking carefully at arenas where Nazism or fascism might still flourish.[47]

Farmer would parlay his NSA experience into a full-time position with the CIA in 1951, overseeing youth and student operations, initially as Allen Dulles's assistant. "I knew very little about the NSA," he said in an interview, recalling his early experience. "I mean I just knew that I needed some sort of legitimacy for this German project. I never thought beyond that." Then he amended his statement to say he was grateful to the NSA because it led him to Olof Palme, the future prime minister of Sweden, then in charge of foreign relations for the Swedish Student Federation, and Farmer's Swedish partner in the German project.[48]

Farmer credits Palme with educating him about the danger of the IUS. Palme had warned him that the IUS "was having a major political impact in Western Europe and other countries." Farmer recalled, correctly, that Palme was so angered by the coup in Czechoslovakia that he married a Czech national for the sole purpose of helping the woman leave the country. In general, Farmer identified the 1948 coup as "a watershed, the thing that really woke us up." Before this event, he said, as a liberal Democrat, he had been "reluctant about the Cold War."[49]

With Palme's conversations in mind, at the end of the summer of 1949, Farmer went to Bad Nauheim to finish writing his report and spend time with his old friend John J. McCloy, the new high commissioner for Germany. During this visit, Farmer said later, he dreamed up a second phase for the project. He hashed over the details with McCloy and his assistant Shepard Stone, described by one CIA officer as a "little Wisner," a phrase meant to portray Stone as a covert action entrepreneur.[50] Farmer's idea was to convene a summer seminar in Germany that emphasized democratic student self-government, hosted by student leaders from Europe, the United States, and Great Britain.

The proposal meshed with McCloy's desire to end the isolation of German students and imbue them with democratic norms. But the seminar, despite being called a summer seminar, was a year-round project, one that provided an arena for networking, discussion, and alliance-building among Europeans concerning IUS strategy. (In 1952, the seminar, now funded by the CIA, was renamed the International Student Seminar, and continued to serve as a European student caucus, enabling the NSA to spot early signs of trouble in the U.S.-European alliance.)[51]

Although Rob West had been excited by the German project, he soon came to realize how little influence he had over it. While in Bad Nauheim, Farmer intercepted a letter that West wrote to Palme, in which West worried that the NSA was now working for the American government. Apparently not embarrassed by reading mail intended for someone else, Farmer shot back a response calling West's concern "silly. . . . I can understand your worries about us deteriorating into becoming mere employees of Harry S. Truman. But I think I can assure you that these worries are unjustified. Hell, we didn't even have to sign an anticommunist affidavit, which[,] I guess, is the best assurance that we are still solidly entrenched in the lofty spheres of student self-government."[52]

If West felt excluded by Farmer and others, his successor, Erskine Childers from Stanford University, encountered active opposition. The Irish-born Childers, a pale, often sickly student, was a political sophisticate with an unusual heritage. He was the grandson of the famed Irish patriot and novelist Robert Erskine Childers, who fought for independence and was martyred.[53] Childers agonized over whether to run for NSA office. He would have to become a U.S. citizen, thus ending the Childers legacy in Ireland, a prospect he found heart-breaking. But Childers made up for his delicate constitution with a formidable commitment to peace. Why did he decide to run? "A principle and an attitude," he explained at the time, "before the tragedy of a world divided on both sides."[54]

It was during Childers's campaign for the international affairs vice presidency at the 1949 Congress in Madison that the CIA made its first (though perhaps its clumsiest) attempt to intervene in NSA elections. Dismayed at the prospective election of an advocate of cooperation with the IUS, the CIA tried to find an alternative to Childers. Around nine o'clock on Sunday morning, Norman Holmes, a delegate from the University of Wisconsin, heard a knock on his door. He opened it to CIA agent Craig Colgate. Holmes had met Colgate the year before when he and a friend, Roy Voegeli, had been NSA observers at a Brussels meeting of dissident student unions and the IUS Council. Colgate had subsequently debriefed the two in Paris. (Voegeli later spent two years working for the CIA.)[55] Now Colgate urged Holmes to run for office.[56] Holmes declined, although he was a vocal opponent of any form of cooperation with the IUS, calling it in plenary debate "an instrument of Soviet foreign policy."[57]

Presumably Childers knew nothing of the CIA's intervention, but he felt keenly the campaign tactics used against him. "The tricks, the deliberate attempts to distort and to confuse, the foul personal talk behind hands and doors—all this in an effort to have NSA tell the world that we had forgotten the most fundamental of inspirations. . . hope and faith in men and their destiny!" But he could withstand the attacks, he wrote. As a child he had been "kicked by English boys" and called a traitor.[58] As disappointing as NSA electoral politics were turning out to be, they did not match the brutality of his former political world. Childers handily beat his opponent, William Holbrook of the University of Minnesota, 212–124.[59]

The 1949 Congress policy outcomes did nothing to allay the internal tensions of the previous year. Once again, delegates affirmed their desire for limited cooperation with the IUS. Yet once again they elected a Catholic, Robert Kelly of St. Peter's College in New Jersey, as president. Kelly had demonstrated his fealty to the Catholic hierarchy the year before. As a member of the NSA executive committee, Kelly had initially supported West's offer of hospitality to Grohman and Madden on their U.S. tour, but changed his mind after it caused an uproar among Catholic clergy.[60] Kelly could be counted upon to hold the line against any gestures of cooperation Childers might make.

Over the next year, Childers encountered situations that left him puzzled, dismayed, and ultimately furious. Like West, he soon realized that he shared the stage with a growing cadre of former NSA officers and older Harvard men who were united in their ambition to create a rival to the IUS. When Childers attended his first WSSF meeting in New York, he was appalled at the members' eagerness to create a rift with the IUS. Afterward he wrote, "I do not believe for one moment that the strategy to use with communism is either to back away from it, or to present so adamantly converse a front as to make any working relationship [with the IUS] almost impossible."[61] He stopped attending the WSSF meetings and designated a proxy, Elmer Brock, who later reported to Childers that there were no real students involved.[62]

Childers also joined West in his concern over the German seminar. He was unsure whether the NSA should participate with anything so closely aligned with the U.S. government. He questioned the promotion of Shepard Stone, a former newsman, not because he knew about Stone's involvement with covert action but because Stone stressed a public relations approach to German education, which Childers interpreted as superficial and lacking in serious pedagogy. Then, in the spring of 1950, Childers made a proposal that galvanized his opponents. He suggested that a large NSA delegation, perhaps twelve students, attend the Second World Student Congress in Prague. Their observations and report, he reasoned, might resolve the IUS membership issue once and for all. Philip DesMarais, who had worked with Martin McLaughlin and John Simons since 1946, quickly alerted NSA adviser Father Vincent Flynn to "this serious and dangerous project."[63]

The CIA saw Childers's proposal differently. With a little stage-managing, Childers's observers could be turned into a global intelligence-gathering unit to test foreign student opinion on the IUS and an alternative organization. This plan required a more direct intervention in the NSA. Whether or not Frederick Delano Houghteling, a Harvard student active in the NSA and HIACOM since 1947, arrived at Madison headquarters as a witting CIA participant, he left as one.[64]

Many years later, after the NSA/CIA disclosures, Houghteling told a reporter the story of how he became witting. Late one night he and an unnamed "friend from Washington" drove to the outskirts of Madison, where they stopped beside a cornfield on a deserted road and blinked their headlights. Headlights from a second car blinked back. Houghteling and his friend walked over to the second car, where a man gave Houghteling a document to sign pledging him to secrecy and outlined a plan to finance the delegation's summer travel.[65]

Since Houghteling was pledged to secrecy, injecting covert funds into the NSA headquarters budget required an elaborate ruse and the help of an unwitting accomplice. The man chosen was Craig Wilson, editor of *NSA News* in the Madison office. When Wilson first heard about the plan to send twelve students abroad as ambassadors during the summer of 1950, he figured it was a pipe dream; the NSA did not have that kind of money. Then one day, while they were lounging around the office, Wilson said, Houghteling announced that he could raise $12,000. "My father has friends who are interested in our plans. We need to make a formal presentation to a couple of key people . . . a man in Chicago . . . the other in Wilmington, Delaware." Houghteling invited Wilson to come along.[66]

Wilson describes himself today as a working-class kid from Detroit more at home driving a taxicab than pitching to wealthy donors. He found Houghteling's invitation peculiar. After all, Houghteling had the Harvard pedigree, the family connections—he was related to the Roosevelts on the Delano side—and the ease to deal with the wealthy. But Wilson was up for the adventure and said yes.[67]

The first leg of the trip took the two from Madison to the downtown Loop of Chicago. Wilson later described the visit. "The Chicago contact turned out to be an attorney . . . [who] listened attentively . . . and commended us for our good intentions." When the attorney seemed uninterested in the NSA and preferred reminiscing about "the good times he had canoeing with his girl on Lake Mendota," Wilson concluded that their pitch—given by Houghteling—had failed.[68]

The two men climbed back into Houghteling's old grey Chevrolet sedan and drove east nonstop to Delaware. The next contact, a man of ostentatious wealth, lived outside Wilmington. He led Houghteling and Wilson on a tour of his mansion and grounds. Every time Wilson tried to turn the conversation to the NSA, the industrialist interrupted and seemed bored. Chalk up another failure, Wilson thought, as he gaped at the opulence surrounding him and struggled at dinner with his first finger bowl. As the two men made the long return trip back to Madison, Houghteling kept reassuring a despondent Wilson, "You did fine."[69]

To Wilson's amazement, two $6,000 checks soon arrived at the NSA office. The identity of the two benefactors was concealed from most of the staff, but penciled notations on a document in the NSA archives make it possible to identify them as the Chicago lawyer Laird Bell and the Wilmington industrialist Thomas E. Brittingham, Jr. Both men were very wealthy and had impressive credentials in either governmental or philanthropic circles. Bell was a member of the CIA-created Committee for a Free Europe and a personal friend of Allen Dulles. Brittingham was a major donor to the University of Wisconsin.[70]

Seventeen years later, Houghteling confided the truth to Wilson, who quotes him as saying, "I played my part. You played yours. The difference was that I was in on the secret and you were not."[71] He also expressed his delight in obtaining CIA funding to a *New York Times* reporter: "I thought it was a great coup."[72] This charade suggests a major shift in channeling funds to NSA, since these funds appear to be the first to come from Frank Wisner's Office of Policy Coordination, the government's covert action unit, and not through the World Student Service Fund as more established philanthropies had done.

Frank Wisner's deputy in the clandestine OPC unit, Franklin Lindsay, confirmed during an interview that the office supplied the funds, even recalling the amount decades later. "We were just getting organized," Lindsay remembered, "and it wasn't a lot of money."[73]

Even by today's standards, the NSA summer project appears staggering in its scope and ambition. Twelve students, many of them undergraduates, fanned out to interview student leaders from the British Isles, Scandinavia, Belgium, Luxemburg, France, Germany, Switzerland, Austria, Yugoslavia, Italy, Greece, Turkey, the Near East, French North Africa, Nigeria, Central Africa, the West Indies, and Southeast Asia.[74] They were asked to explore the attitudes of foreign student leaders toward the IUS, without taking a position on the IUS or an alternative to it. Each received lengthy written instructions to guide his or her contacts and questioning. Each was asked to file a written report. Most undergraduates were thrilled for a chance to travel, and there is no evidence that anyone thought surveying student opinion was objectionable. Once again, the Harvard committee found men uniquely qualified for the sensitive assignments in Yugoslavia, the Middle East, and Southeast Asia. These men, who had expertise far beyond that of the undergraduates, were forerunners of future CIA-funded NSA international staff and overseas representatives.

William (Bill) Roe Polk, originally from Texas, traced his ancestry to an American president. On his résumé, he claimed fifteen years of experience in South America, "including work in the student movement at the University of Chile," and "a year and a half in the Middle East."[75] Polk would soon take over as HIACOM chair. Frank Fisher, the World War II veteran who had served on the Harvard committee since its inception, took the assignment to Yugoslavia.[76]

The Asian assignment went to a man with exceptional credentials. Harvard law student James P. (Jim) Grant was born in China, the son of American missionaries, and spoke fluent Mandarin. He spent World War II in the Burma-China Theater, and at the age of twenty-three accompanied General George Marshall on his historic 1945 mission to negotiate a peace pact between the warring armies of Mao Zedong and Chiang Kai-shek. Grant remained in China as a special assistant to Walter S. Robertson, an American diplomat charged with overseeing the truce. When the truce failed, Grant transferred to the United Nations Relief and Rehabilitation Administration in northern China, but a year later he left for another special assignment—to conduct negotiations with Zhou Enlai, prior to the collapse of Chiang Kai-shek's army.[77]

Grant periodically interrupted his law studies when the U.S. government needed him. In 1948–49, he took a year's leave of absence to establish the U.S.-China Aid Mission, the equivalent in Asia of the Marshall Plan in Europe, and a program that the Truman administration hoped might counter Mao's communist appeal. When Mao's forces overwhelmed those of Chiang Kai-shek in 1949, Grant moved the office to Canton (Guangdong); his wife escaped from the communist zone on the last plane out of Langzhou.[78]

In 1949–50 Grant squeezed in another year of law school before agreeing to close out the China aid program in Formosa (now Taiwan). Once in the region, he traveled for the NSA. The one credential Grant omitted from the résumé he submitted to the NSA was his military intelligence background—he probably belonged to the same military intelligence reserve unit in Boston as Farmer.[79] Grant continued to work with the NSA for several years.

No other Western national student union had the resources to travel so widely or the sophisticated personnel to gather the kind of intelligence the CIA wanted. The NSA gained unrivaled access to student opinion, and often had a chance to mold it. Even students who did not have a secret relationship with the CIA readily followed requests to submit detailed reports on their conversations to the new Paris office of the NSA, established that summer to handle travel arrangements.

Unaware of Houghteling's connection to the CIA, Erskine Childers expected to head the traveling international team. But as soon as he reached Europe, he received a steady flow of instructions from the Madison office. Increasingly irritated, he protested. President Kelly rebuffed him, then dealt the final blow: he ordered Childers home from Europe.[80]

Kelly's excuse was that Childers was needed in Ann Arbor, site of the forthcoming NSA Congress in August. Childers cared deeply about the NSA and did not want to engage in open conflict that might harm the still fledging organization. He returned as ordered. In the end, the large delegation envisioned by Childers to assess the Second World Student Congress in Prague dwindled to three observers. The trio was instructed to take no initiative and refrain from making any commitments on behalf of NSA.

On August 24, 1950, Olof Palme of the Swedish Student Federation flew into Prague to chair an informal caucus of European, Canadian, and American students.[81] Palme had hoped for an agreement on the need to establish both an alternative international organization *and* a permanent secretariat to administer projects conducted under its auspices. He found the student union leaders still sharply divided.[82] Finally, Palme persuaded them to convene again in Stockholm in December, subject to two major conditions: there would be no discussion of a new international organization and no discussion of political matters.[83]

It would have been difficult under any circumstances to create a pro-West rival to the IUS, since few student unions were clamoring for it. It would be even harder to build such an organization while publicly denying its Cold War raison d'être. Yet this was precisely what happened.

5

ALLARD LOWENSTEIN AND THE
INTERNATIONAL STUDENT CONFERENCE

AT THE SAME TIME that dissident student unions led by Olof Palme were meeting in Prague and plotting strategy against the International Union of Students, the NSA Congress was holding its annual meeting at the University of Michigan, at which the delegates elected one of the NSA's most famous, indeed controversial, presidents. Allard Lowenstein has been accused of establishing the connection between the NSA and the CIA,[1] but U.S. government documents and NSA archives reveal that he was in fact a thorn in the Agency's side and that the ties were developed in spite, rather than because, of his efforts. Within the NSA, he tried to win control over the international program, though without success. Overseas, his aggressive anticommunism nearly derailed two years of work by the Harvard group. However, he was no match for government officials, who found ways to circumscribe his role and routed clandestine funds through establishment channels that bypassed NSA headquarters.

Lowenstein, an Upper West Side New Yorker with an early passion for civil rights, peered out at the world from behind thick lenses. Socially awkward, often disheveled, Lowenstein upset his liberal family as a sixteen-year-old when he chose to attend the University of North Carolina, where as a freshman he fought Jim Crow laws while proudly sporting a Confederate Army hat.

Drawn to student politics, Lowenstein attended every NSA Congress from the organization's inception. In 1948, he considered running for president. In many ways, he was the quintessential heir to the original liberal anticommunists; in fact, he attended the successor to the Campobello Leadership Institute, the Encampment for Citizenship, in 1947, where he first met Eleanor Roosevelt, who hosted workshops at her Hyde Park home. He and Roosevelt became good friends. He also belonged to Americans for Democratic Action, the home of Roosevelt liberals. But Lowenstein's experiences within the NSA illustrate how liberals could be in general agreement over ends but fight fiercely over the means to achieve them.

Lowenstein displayed powerful rhetorical skills that one colleague likened to those of Winston Churchill.[2] During his campaign for NSA president in 1950, he roused delegates with an emotional assault on communism and Soviet control of the IUS, exhorting them to form a pro-Western alternative student alliance.[3] Lowenstein's passionate oratory put him at odds with the Harvard liberals who ran the international program. They argued for a nuanced approach: lay out the criteria for an alternative but don't advocate for it. The stance was tactical: major European student unions were not ready to oppose the IUS, and the NSA could not initiate action without allies. But Lowenstein tended to jump into situations. He worked on instinct not diplomatic tact.

The undergraduates at the 1950 Congress responded to Lowenstein's passion by electing him president. But for the important position of vice president of international affairs they chose an MIT senior backed by the Harvard group: Herbert Eisenberg, an aspiring architect who favored crew cuts and bow ties, was as circumspect in airing his opinions as Lowenstein was flamboyant.[4] The personal and political mismatch between the two officers resulted in a year of intense internal conflict.[5]

Eisenberg, in his Cambridge office, readily took direction from the Harvard group, while the Madison-based Lowenstein tried to assert his authority, arguing that the president should be "first among equals," even though the NSA Congress had granted vice presidents autonomy over their respective programs. Eisenberg resisted Lowenstein's pressure, although he initially tried to be accommodating. In the fall, Eisenberg loaded up his Studebaker with files and drove from Cambridge to Madison for a lengthy stint. But his patience thinned when Lowenstein decided to represent the NSA at the meeting of student union leaders in Stockholm. Eisenberg felt that he had been undercut, reduced to a technical expert.[6]

Lowenstein's decision to go to Sweden also dismayed former NSA officers, including Ted Harris and Bob Smith, who had both joined the Geneva staff of the International Student Service. Harris worried about

Lowenstein's desire to openly battle the IUS and tried to draw him out by letter. "I am very anxious to know your approach," he wrote to Lowenstein in November 1950. Did Lowenstein understand the importance and parameters of the meeting?[7]

Harris did not want to "risk offending by unnecessary advice or prying" but felt impelled to express his reservations. "I am concerned about the role that NSA will play in the Stockholm meetings, December 17 to 27th. You probably realize that these meetings are of great importance to the whole world student movement, and that we are now at some kind of crossroads. . . . I strongly urge you to try and talk with some people who have recently been in Europe and who have had an opportunity to learn the many psychological and political factors which are absolutely essential to . . . what may be done in Stockholm strategically and what should be done ideally."[8]

Harris may have been articulating Olof Palme's alarm as well, since the two men had recently met. Palme did not know Lowenstein and had reason to be concerned.[9] The stakes were very high for the Swedish leader. He had given his word to skeptical European student leaders about the nature of the conference, assuring them that "we do not want it to become a political crusade against the bad men in the Kremlin."[10]

The Stockholm invitation precipitated internal fights in several important student unions. In November, a knock-down, drag-out battle within the leadership of the British National Union of Students (BNUS) nearly split the organization in two.[11] If the British pulled out, the meeting would effectively be over before it began. From Prague came more dissension: in a hand-delivered letter to Stockholm delegates, Josef Grohman and Giovanni Berlinguer of the IUS accused the conference of being schismatic, a charge that normally carried great weight. They alleged that the delegates had "convened on the basis of non-cooperation with the IUS." The National Union of Czechoslovak Students, then firmly controlled by communists and led by Jiří Pelikán, the future head of the IUS, also protested by letter. Pelikán invoked the argument that had worked so effectively in the past: the Stockholm conference would divide "students into two isolated camps."[12] Some Western European unions agreed. The French denounced any attempt to shatter world unity.[13] Palme struggled to retain the meeting's nonpolitical focus: he attended the contentious BNUS executive committee session, and, as he later told Eisenberg, also spent hours "backing off the Swiss, the Austrians, the Germans, the Belgians, not to mentioned the Italians," who were "all running wild for a Western Union."[14]

The State Department also fretted. Secretary of State Dean Acheson sent a CIA-cleared cable to the U.S. Embassy in Stockholm, outlining his hopes for the meeting and instructing officials to remain behind the scenes. "Department interested in encouraging new organization." But "too overt a display of official interest might hamper rather than stimulate such action."[15]

When the conference opened on December 17, Eisenberg, Palme, and the senior cadre of former Harvard-NSA officials learned that they had been right to worry about Lowenstein. Despite briefings on the Stockholm conference ground rules—in late November, Eisenberg distributed a printed summary to all NSA officers and regional chairs—Lowenstein took the floor on the second day and launched into an anticommunist tirade.[16]

Lowenstein belittled the practical-projects approach favored by the Harvard group and Eisenberg. He called for an all-out fight against the IUS. "When the Communists say they want peace we know too well what peace they want, and why; . . . We will not be contributing to the attainment of peace . . . if in our deliberations we confine ourselves to . . . increased student exchange or better travel programs, in a world pushed to the brink . . . by the willful scheming of evil men bent on world domination for one nation."[17]

Lowenstein argued that for four long years the NSA had deferred to "the overall student unity," while the IUS was creating "a world structure cleverly designed to give to it a monopoly on programs for international student cooperation." As a result, "we are . . . four years behind . . . in those areas of the earth where communication is harder, democracy newer, and governments poorer, and where, with foresight and cunning, the IUS has laid a pattern to twist and undermine the legitimate aspirations of people long craving freedom." He ended his speech by calling for a new international union.

Eisenberg was aghast.[18] Lowenstein had just violated the two painfully negotiated conditions that made the Stockholm meeting possible: there would be no proposals for a new organization and no political discussion. One can also imagine Palme's distress, the panicked conversations among delegates, the late-night meetings, the heated arguments, as he and other delegates tried to salvage the situation.[19]

The delegates at Stockholm voted overwhelmingly to "regret" Lowenstein's speech, a step just shy of censure, though Lowenstein later claimed that many told him in private that they agreed with him.[20] This may have been the case, but they had ground rules to follow, which had been put in place in part to protect delegates under instruction from their respective student unions, and could not publicly go counter to them.

There is no evidence, as some have surmised, that Lowenstein's hardline speech was a ploy sanctioned by the Harvard group. On the contrary, the speech jeopardized Eisenberg's assignment for the NSA: to win the lead role in administering a practical-projects program. Prior to Stockholm, the Harvard group had developed projects tailored to Southeast Asia, the Middle East, and Latin America. On the plane to Europe, Eisenberg had suggested a title for the package, Students Mutual Assistance Program (SMAP).[21] But after Lowenstein's speech, conferees balked: Why reward the Americans with SMAP when the NSA president had just ridiculed its significance?[22]

Deft maneuvering behind the scenes, especially by Bob Smith and Stanley Jenkins from the BNUS, rescued Eisenberg's mission. Smith personally approached delegates, many of whom he knew. Privately the pair pushed the argument that the NSA alone had the resources to coordinate a new program. American Embassy officials were later effusive in their praise for Smith's work.[23]

Stockholm delegates finessed the question of whether to create a rival organization by voting to meet again as the International Student Conference, a name chosen to indicate its contingent nature. They stipulated that any future meeting required a majority vote.[24] This conceit, substituting *conference* for *organization*, would last until 1964.

When Eisenberg returned to the United States in mid-January, having remained in Europe to attend another conference, he discovered to his shock that Lowenstein was claiming credit for launching a new international organization. The NSA president distributed copies of his Stockholm speech to the executive committee in late December; when Eisenberg told the Madison staff that the delegates had voted to "regret" Lowenstein's speech, no one believed him.[25]

The executive committee had already voted to give "unequivocal support to the president's position."[26] Eisenberg became so incensed that he wrote to Olof Palme and begged him to verify in writing the reaction of the Stockholm delegates.[27] But it was too late. By the time a transcript arrived, the myth that Allard Lowenstein had achieved his dreams in Stockholm had taken hold at the NSA.[28]

In Europe, however, Robert Donhauser, a cultural attaché at the American Embassy in Stockholm (and probably a CIA operative), penned a scathing critique of Lowenstein's performance. Whatever brilliance Lowenstein had as a speaker, and Donhauser conceded that point, "he was looked upon as immature and as a somewhat abrasive element of the conference." Donhauser claimed that Palme and other Swedish student leaders shared his negative opinion. They had informed Donhauser that "Lowenstein had blighted all chances for the US delegation to assume a leadership position at the conference."[29]

Donhauser also found Eisenberg wanting, and issued a warning to his Washington superiors: "It is not felt that the present leaders of NSA are of sufficient caliber to carry through their part of the program with regard to its planning and implementation to the most advantageous extent." Given the "rising importance of international student activities," Donhauser concluded, "things must change."[30]

The Donhauser cable set the stage for new CIA interventions in the NSA. Elections for the international vice presidency would no longer be left to the vagaries of the democratic process, although as a practical matter no leadership change could occur until the NSA Congress convened in August 1951. The Harvard-NSA nexus that had worked so well now presented a problem. The HIACOM-planned projects were intended to showcase the NSA as an exemplar of international cooperation, but its planners had no rationale for representing the NSA abroad. The Harvard group was technically subordinate to the NSA's elected officers and could not assume their official status at international meetings.

Donhauser's reference to "their part of the program" should be underscored: it directly contradicts the later CIA contention that the Agency gave funds to the NSA solely to enable NSA officers to carry out activities devised by students. In reality, the projects planned by the Harvard group had been coordinated with CIA and State Department officials and were viewed as part of a larger CIA covert operation.

Six weeks after the Stockholm meeting, Allen Dulles, now deputy director of the CIA, and Harvard professor William Y. Elliott, a CIA consultant, made this cooperation explicit during a discussion of the NSA. Someone on behalf of the NSA had turned down an offer of a full financial subsidy for the organization. The unnamed person reportedly protested that "such a course of action would run counter to [the NSA's] basic principle of independent thought and action and would in a sense reduce it to the position of being a tool of its government."[31]

Dulles and Elliott agreed that the situation was "an extremely delicate one, particularly with reference to the laying on of any plans involving the passing of funds." A full subsidy did not seem "feasible, practicable, or desirable, in view of the facts hereinabove expressed." But as a memorandum of their conversation indicates, that delicacy did not rule out funding for individual projects that "require the use of the aegis of the National Student Association." Support could occur "through the penetration which we have made, . . ." (the next line and a half are blacked out). Dulles cited as an example the Southeast Asia project, "being prepared jointly by this office [CIA] and the [State Department's] Far East Division."[32]

That this discussion occurred at the highest level within the CIA, with its second-ranking official, and involved terms such as *aegis* and *penetration*, destroys the CIA's later argument that NSA officers, desperate for funds, came hat in hand to the U.S. government. It makes the opposite point: the CIA recognized that care must be taken not to "offend or arouse the suspicion of the National Student Association that the government is at all interested."[33]

Lowenstein had no hand in conceiving or preparing the projects discussed by Dulles and Elliott. He was not even briefed on the package of Harvard-prepared projects until after the Stockholm meeting, when he traveled to Cambridge. On the evening of January 16, 1951, Lowenstein joined the Harvard men at Cronin's bar and listened as Robert Fischelis (of the German project), Frank Fisher and Jim Grant (Southeast Asia project), William Polk (Middle East project), and newcomer Carl Sapers (HIACOM) briefed him on the omnibus package of regional seminars, conferences, and information bulletins.

Immediately afterward, the same evening, Fisher summarized their conversation in a letter to Lowenstein. He listed projects in Germany, Southeast Asia, and the Middle East, plus "information programs backing up these programs."[34] He cited a budget of $60,000, and reiterated the importance of creating a special entity to receive the funds, since the NSA would "need to show financial responsibility."[35]

What precisely Fisher told Lowenstein about the sources of the funding or knew himself is not clear; in his letter, Fisher stated, "These funds will come from philanthropic foundations and from a few individuals." The letter is sprinkled with references to Lowenstein's agreement on specific issues—"our present time table, as agreed with you." All the Harvard men present that evening signed Fisher's letter. Fischelis added a handwritten note: "We are all in agreement with what Frank has written."[36] It is hard not to draw the inference that if Lowenstein were to disagree with any planned project in the future, he would have to battle the entire HIACOM group.

His encounter with the would-be junior State Department notwithstanding, Lowenstein did not give up his efforts to sell a harder-line approach to the IUS. But gaining access to U.S. government officials was not easy for the interloper. At the beginning of his term, Lowenstein had tried to establish a liaison with the State Department independent of Eisenberg. Harry Seamans from the Division of Public Liaison had blocked the attempt, telephoning Eisenberg to reconfirm that the international vice president was the department's sole contact on international issues.[37]

Not long after the Harvard briefing, Lowenstein tried a different approach. He met with Senator Ralph Flanders, a Vermont Republican, and asked for assistance in obtaining entrée to the State Department. Flanders obliged. He contacted Assistant Secretary of State George C. McGhee, writing that Lowenstein had come to him "with a story of serious concern relating to the students in an International Student Organization of which they are members and delegates." Lowenstein had warned about the "inroads made by Communist agents."[38] Flanders confused the IUS with the ISC (the Stockholm-created International Student Conference), which suggests that the congressman did not quite grasp the issue, but he dutifully requested that someone at the policy-making level give Lowenstein a hearing.

What, if any, conversations Lowenstein had with State Department officials as a result of Flanders's letter are unknown. It is conceivable that Lowenstein is the unnamed person in the Dulles-Elliott memo who rejected financial assistance to the NSA. But even that offer is likely to have been represented as coming from U.S. government funds and not the CIA.

What is certain is that the CIA made no attempt to enlist Lowenstein further, either in the movement of funds or the coordination of HIACOM-NSA overseas projects. Instead, the Agency turned to a far more prestigious body to assist the Harvard group: between 1950 and 1952, the Council on Foreign Relations solidified the growing tie between the Harvard contingent and the OPC as part of its overall assistance to U.S. intelligence operations. The Council's role further demonstrates that the NSA was considered part of a larger operation to fight communist penetration abroad.

THE COUNCIL ON FOREIGN RELATIONS in New York was created in 1921 to analyze foreign policy issues, and soon became the most influential think tank in the country. Its standard approach to an issue was to create a study group of prominent individuals and hire a staff director. In February 1949, nearly a year before Dulles and Elliott discussed NSA funding, the CFR created Study Group 5152 to assist the State Department with "the expansion of existing government and private intelligence and research activities."[39] Part of its purpose was "to discover how the United States through educational exchange programs, technical assistance, and other similar means might best strengthen or promote the emergence of 'democratic leadership.'"[40]

The study group planned strategy in "critical areas"—shorthand for constituencies vulnerable to communist penetration, among them intellectuals, labor, and "organized students."[41] For each constituency, members identified organizational weaknesses, developed specific programs, raised funds when necessary, and monitored progress.[42] This was not new terrain for the CFR. A scholar who examined CFR records dating from 1945 to 1949 concluded that it was frequently used as "a clearing house for projects," and that by 1950 the Council had built "a substantial cohort of covert political activities."[43]

Senior, seasoned World War II intelligence veterans steered Study Group 5152. Chair Whitney H. Shepardson had been chief of secret intelligence in London, placing him atop OSS networks in Europe, North Africa, the Middle East, and Asia. Other OSS alumni included *Reader's Digest* head Harry H. Harper (Bulgaria), Carnegie Corporation director John Gardner (Washington), and James H. Mysbergh (Indonesia). Individuals who held government posts included Allen Dulles, Foy D. Kohler (of Voice of America), and Kenneth Holland (of International Exchange Activities). In 1950, Holland left his government position to become the director of the Institute of International Education (IIE), founded in 1919, which contracted with the State Department to administer student and cultural exchange programs, including the new Fulbright program for scholars. In his IIE role, Holland developed a program paralleling that of the study group called "Leaders of a Free World."[44]

The CFR staff director was Edmond Taylor, a journalist and psychological warfare expert. He initially handled contact with the Harvard NSA group. After leaving the *Chicago Tribune*, Taylor had trained with British intelligence early in World War II. When the war ended, enamored of the One World movement, Taylor worked with UNESCO in Paris until he became disillusioned with its bureaucracy. He returned to the United States ready, as he later wrote, "to apply Bolshevik standards and methods, if necessary, to defend the democratic revolution."[45] Taylor, sounding a bit like Joseph Lash during the Campobello training, argued that democracy could not survive "unless its leaders and elite groups . . . function . . . as combat cadres for the masses."[46] The position of CFR study group director offered him an opportunity to help create those cadres.

On March 13, 1951, Taylor reported to the study group that Melvin Conant of the Harvard group planned to conduct research on student activities in Southeast Asia.[47] Like other HIACOM personnel, the twenty-seven-year-old Conant (no relation to the university president) sported impressive credentials.[48] He had graduated from Harvard in 1949 and stayed on to earn a master's degree in Far Eastern studies.[49] Taylor briefed Conant on the study group activities and received assurances that Conant would share his reports with them. Many years later, Conant described the purpose of the Southeast Asian trip in hardhitting political terms: "to analyze Communist penetration in certain groups" and to recommend "counter action."[50] At the time, NSA headquarters understood Conant to be identifying Southeast Asian students who might participate in a regional seminar on self-government as a way of establishing relations with Asian students.

During this period, routing clandestine funds remained a problem. Frank Fisher at Harvard repeatedly urged the NSA to set up a "funds receiving corporation," but despite constant prodding by Fisher and Jim Grant, Lowenstein was slow to act.[51] In Conant's case, Taylor handled the finances. Grant, the Asia specialist who had identified Conant for the assignment, informed Lowenstein that he had "finally wangled a private contribution from a Harvard lawyer in the Washington area which should take care of Mel Conant's trip."[52] Fisher then informed both Eisenberg and the Madison staff that since the matter was urgent, given Conant's imminent departure, HIACOM would keep control of the funds.[53] (Whether intended or not, the fluidity of financial arrangements, the secrecy surrounding them, and the existence of two international offices in Cambridge made accountability difficult for NSA headquarters, even if it had been more rigorous in its reporting obligations.)

During Conant's absence, Taylor told the study group that he and Shepardson, acting "in a purely private capacity," a phrase that may have been intended to keep certain machinations out of the official minutes of the study group, had secured financial assistance for a Southeast Asian seminar.[54] The proposal had the "strong backing of the U.S. government," and would be resubmitted to a foundation that had previously turned it down, but this time a special ad-hoc committee would review the application.[55] During this period of domestic covert operations, lower-level program officers not privy to private agreements made by their superiors sometimes created temporary snafus by rejecting grant applications. Taylor alluded to, but did not identify by name, the Rockefeller Foundation, which had inadvertently rejected the same funding proposal. The relationship between Frank Wisner in OPC and John D. Rockefeller III was particularly close; Rockefeller even attended top-secret meetings of the covert action staff, giving him unusual access to covert plans.[56] The Rockefeller Foundation also openly supported programs desired by the U.S. government—for example, it granted funds for American participation in the German seminar.[57]

The Southeast Asian seminar, like the German seminar, had multiple objectives. On one level, it fostered contact and friendship among foreign student leaders. On another, the United States sought to create a regional caucus of politically reliable students in Asia. The region became a high priority for the U.S. government after Mao's victory in China in 1949 and the advent of the Korean War in June 1950. Fears were widespread that newly independent Asian countries would fall under communist influence. When Jim Grant traveled to the region in 1950, the summer before Conant, he had identified Indonesia, which had recently been liberated from Dutch control, as a potential seminar host.[58]

During this period, and somewhat ironically, Eisenberg complained bitterly about the absence of funds for Harvard-NSA projects. While he understood that the Council on Foreign Relations might assist the NSA, there is no indication that he ever realized that the burgeoning NSA international operations were nestled in a larger program of psychological and political warfare driven by U.S. intelligence. He trusted the more senior men at Harvard. When a British student leader asked him to overturn a HIACOM decision, Eisenberg forthrightly responded, "I cannot and do not wish to go over the heads of the Harvard people,"[59] hardly an appropriate attitude for the official elected by the NSA Congress to execute its international program.

IN THE SIX MONTHS BEFORE the August 1951 NSA Congress, Allard Lowenstein had dwindling contact with the Harvard group and virtually none with Eisenberg.[60] In July, Lowenstein's assistant, Shirley Neizer, who was charged with churning out reports, working papers, delegate mailings, and logistical information for the influx of eight hundred or so students, realized that the staff needed material on the international program. She wrote frantically to HIACOM (not Eisenberg), citing "an utter lack of knowledge," and asking, "Who has been on the committee, what has been accomplished, what problems have you run into during the year, recommendations, etc.?" She requested a copy of the Conant report. And she asked: "Who have been the donors for the projects?"[61]

At the Congress, held in Minneapolis, it was noteworthy that Carl Sapers, the new chair of HIACOM, gave the international program report to delegates, rather than Lowenstein or Eisenberg. Sapers surely angered both officers when he praised the prescience of the Harvard committee: the "NSA [by which he meant HIACOM] had anticipated the Student[s] Mutual Assistance Program by two years when it sent Tom Farmer to Germany in 1949 to do a report on student conditions." Sapers informed the plenary that Lowenstein "chose to delegate SMAP to Harvard, probably because of the success of Polk, Grant, Fisher and Fischelis." He underscored Lowenstein's support by citing the meeting in Cronin's bar.[62]

Sapers also praised the International Student Information Service (ISIS), originally announced in February 1947 by Douglass Cater, and

ther, the Congress's resolution required that prospective members "be willing to subordinate ideological differences in common service" through a program of practical activities.[68]

Lowenstein did not give up easily. He backed as a candidate for NSA president William (Bill) Dentzer, who shared his views on creating a forthrightly anticommunist international student organization. Dentzer, a clean-cut senior from Muskingum College, a small liberal arts school in eastern Ohio, edged out the liberal-caucus candidate Kenneth Kurtz from Swarthmore by just thirteen votes.[69] Dentzer, however, would soon modify his position, secretly cooperating with the CIA; in fact, he later joined the Agency as a career staff officer.

Lowenstein also backed his close friend Helen Jean Rogers for the office of international affairs vice president. As a student at the Catholic Mundelein College in Illinois, the beautiful and stylish Rogers was a member of the Chicago region's Catholic group before the 1947 NSA constitutional convention. In 1948, Rogers was elected NSA secretary.[70] Now in her fifth year with the NSA, she electrified the Congress with a tale of international intrigue at a recent conference she and Eisenberg had attended in Rio de Janeiro and her description of the tumult of Brazilian student politics.

Rogers told the hushed assembly about seeing bullet holes from recent battles between students and communists. She recounted the courageous, but futile, confrontation of Brazilian students with IUS official Giovanni Berlinguer, after his impassioned defense of the importance of the IUS. A few days later, the NSA delegates nominated Rogers for the international vice presidency. Lowenstein later estimated that she had the support of 80 percent of the delegates. He was sure that Rogers would win and carry on his agenda.

But the election quickly took a series of dizzying turns. Liberal-caucus member Galen Martin from Kentucky recalls challenging Rogers's credentials on the grounds she was not an enrolled student.[71] Another delegate remembers that a tearful Rogers inexplicably withdrew her candidacy and stood before the delegates "for what seemed a parliamentary eternity—ten or twelve minutes—crying." According to Barry Farber, a delegate from the University of North Carolina, "she wasn't weeping, she was crying as the mob urged her to accept this high honor and office." The nomination, Farber says, was hers by acclamation.[72] Instead, as an in-house NSA history later recounted, "Amid a protracted scene of mob hysterics," Rogers threw her support to her rival, Harvard graduate student Avrea Ingram.[73]

Ingram, a twenty-five-year-old graduate student who favored trench coats and carried his umbrella British style, like a cane—he reminded Eisenberg of Alfred Hitchcock—had the sophisticated credentials urged by Robert Donhauser, the American embassy official in Stockholm.[74] Born in 1927 and raised for the first fifteen years of his life in Texas, Ingram served in the U.S. Navy as a lieutenant (JG) during World War II. He graduated from Georgia Tech in 1947, then worked for the Southeastern U.S. Division of Shell Oil Company in sales, advertising, and public relations before enrolling at Harvard in 1949 for graduate school. He claimed fluency in Spanish and some French.[75] Delegate Barry Farber describes him as one of those "perpetually middle-aged men mature beyond his years."[76]

With no prior history in the NSA aside from a few months as a volunteer with the Harvard committee, after Rogers's withdrawal, Ingram nonetheless had the field to himself. Whipsawed by the emotion on the floor, restive delegates refused to crown his election by voting against acclamation by an astounding 40 percent, but they could not prevent his victory.[77]

Years later, by then a perennial NSA Congress-goer who had witnessed numerous elections, Lowenstein described the Ingram election as the most curious he had seen. His biographer David Harris quotes Lowenstein as saying that the one thing he knew for sure was that Ingram was not "the spontaneous choice of the congress voters."[78] If Rogers bowed out of the election at the CIA's request, she never told Lowenstein, though they later had a short-lived romance. Years later, however, he wondered.[79]

While it is speculation, Ingram may have been identified and recruited by Professor Elliott, who regularly tapped promising graduate students for CIA "P work," as he called it, shorthand for "psychological warfare." Ingram surfaced as a volunteer in the HIACOM office shortly after Elliott conferred with Dulles about NSA funding.[80] With Ingram's election, CIA funds flowed.

But the accusation that Lowenstein established the tie between NSA and CIA is a different matter. All the evidence is to the contrary. The Harvard liberals moved easily in elite circles—most were born into them—while Lowenstein, the outsider, had to bang on congressional doors to gain access. The historian William Chafe, a prominent Lowenstein biographer, reflected on the question in 1998: "Overall, I remain pretty well convinced that Lowenstein's personality was one that was inconsistent with his becoming an operative for the agency."[81]

Furthermore, the NSA was not tied to the CIA by a lone individual. NSA officers did not go to the U.S. government asking for funds; the government came to them. The relationship grew because of multiple factors: the legacy of the ISS-Roosevelt group, with its determination to create anticommunist American student leaders; the desire to project American leadership overseas in the postwar period; the influence of World War II intelligence veterans who were now students; and—most important—the NSA's interest in affiliating with the International Union of Students. Fear of the latter made every action the NSA took with regard to affiliation a matter of interest to intelligence officials.

The advent of clandestine OPC funds during the summer of 1950 represented a different operational level of cooperation with U.S. intelligence. Coincidentally, or perhaps not, another U.S. government agency closed its investigation on the NSA after Ingram was elected: on November 5, 1951, FBI director J. Edgar Hoover officially ended his five-year investigation of the NSA.[82] Over the next few years, the involvement of the NSA in CIA covert actions would grow in many directions, far beyond what its progenitors might have imagined. NSA covert operations would span five continents and reflect numerous government-defined objectives. The CIA would recruit and induct dozens of American students into the secret relationship, administer security oaths under the Espionage Act to ensure their silence, and assign them CIA case officers to enforce their fidelity to a covert agenda.

PART TWO

DENIAL OPERATIONS

6

THE COUNTEROFFENSIVE

WITH ALLARD LOWENSTEIN no longer an obstacle, the International Student Conference a reality, a reliable person in charge of NSA international programs, and the Council on Foreign Relations ready to assist, the CIA ramped up what former agents call "denial operations."[1] The aim: to counter Moscow-backed international organizations with pro-Western organizations that would offer an alternative to various constituencies—youth, students, labor, and intellectuals—by undermining claims that the communists alone spoke for these groups. *Denial operations* makes a larger point: the CIA did not merely subsidize the NSA with a few travel grants, as it later claimed; the CIA ran a covert operation through the NSA as part of its counteroffensive against Soviet-backed international organizations.

The CIA's objectives may have been straightforward, but their execution required both ingenuity and resources. The CIA had to manage its counteroffensives clandestinely, which meant finding ways to fund them without the majority of the participants realizing where the money came from. It had taken years to foster an alliance that could potentially challenge the International Union of Students. While Thomas Farmer, who had joined the CIA by 1951, and others in HIACOM had worked behind the scenes to achieve a successful meeting in Stockholm, the viability of a future ISC rested on publicly stated objectives, the leadership of talented students, and an agenda that could attract global members.

The International Student Conference began life with multiple obstacles, some self-imposed, such as the public denials by its organizers that it was an organization at all. Having rejected Cold War rhetoric as a viable way to sell the ISC to either Europeans or students from outside Europe, the ISC lacked a strong mobilizing pitch. Its emphasis on practical projects pitted technocratic language against the passionate rhetoric of communist ideology, with its pungent criticism of Western imperialism, racism, and colonialism, and its promise of a better future.

Further, the ISC would never be able to counter the influence of the Prague-based International Union of Students, with its roughly eighty member countries, unless it had an equivalent membership. In 1951, the participation of students from Asia, Africa, the Middle East, and Latin America in the ISC was an open question. If it became identified as a Western organization, the odds of its attracting students from out-side Europe decreased. Before NSA international affairs vice president Herbert Eisenberg left his post in August 1951, he outlined the dilemma following the Rio de Janeiro conference he attended with Helen Jean Rogers. He described the Cuban delegation as "anti-communist, anti-government, anti-vested interest, anti-dictatorship, and highly nation-alistic." But, he added, "I'm not so sure where they stand on practical projects."[2] Had Eisenberg not been so earnest a young officer, his com-ment might be mistaken for deadpan humor.

By contrast, the IUS had a natural constituency among student groups bound by common ideological commitments. Some were affiliated with their country's communist party. In China, students were required to join the large and powerful All China Students Federation. Soviet youth joined Komsomol, the All-Union Leninist Young Communist League. But the IUS also attracted organizations that ran counter to their repres-sive governments; South African students, for example, affiliated with the African National Congress, home of the young Nelson Mandela. In fact, when it was founded all but the most conservative European stu-dent unions joined the IUS. At the time, many European unions con-tained left-wing factions that were comfortable with its anti-imperialist worldview and did not object to its harsh anti-Western rhetoric. They readily joined chants of "Hands off Korea" or "Hands off Malaya" that rocked the rafters at IUS meetings.[3]

By 1951, the ad-hoc nature of the NSA-CIA relationship added to the difficulty of building a global student organization that could com-pete with the IUS. The CIA, needing to keep its role secret, had yet to establish a method for the routine delivery of funds. During delibera-tions of the Council on Foreign Relations, study group members dis-cussed making use of a buffer organization, which could disguise the government's hand and "be able to handle the problem of getting official money to students."[4] By the time of Avrea Ingram's election, that organization was being formed but was not yet operational.

Ingram's correspondence after he took office in September 1951 suggests that he not only knew where the money would be coming from but expected the problem of delivery to be resolved shortly. He wrote to president Bill Dentzer, who had relocated NSA headquarters to Boulder, Colorado, in a belt-tightening measure, about "a long-term, revenue-producing project. If it proves feasible . . . it will *eliminate* NSA financial problems in the future."[5] In October, Ingram told an NSA academic adviser that he had all the money he needed to operate a Latin America program, "just as we planned it."[6] He did not identify specific donors, although to a prospective NSA staff member, he indiscreetly described a "new hush-hush agency in the government" that would be able to finance the NSA.[7] In early November, he told a friend at Georgia Tech that he had found an angel.[8]

Ingram's immediate angel was none other than John Simons. The Catholic founding father had never returned to Fordham law school and had remained close to the NSA since his election in December 1946 as treasurer of the National Continuations Committee at the Chicago meeting. In September 1947, after the constitutional convention Simons volunteered to set up the first NSA accounts in Madison. Between then and 1950, he parlayed his work with the World Student Service Fund in New York into a full-time position with the International Student Service in Geneva in 1948–49. Simons first surfaced as a financial angel during the summer of 1951 when he offered Helen Jean Rogers and Herbert Eisenberg funds to attend the meeting in Rio. Until her death, Rogers swore the money for this travel came from Braniff Airlines, but archival letters indicate that she knew of Simons's involvement and had promised to keep it secret.[9]

With Dentzer and, especially, Ingram in charge of the NSA's international projects, Simons operated more openly. (Dentzer referred to him in correspondence with Ingram as the Simons Fund.) Dentzer now knew that the source of money actually lay elsewhere: he mentioned Simons's ability to "talk with money-bags" or to "touch money bags."[10] Simons discreetly used a Department of State address for mail, and today Dentzer vigorously denies knowing during his presidency that the funding came from the CIA.[11] But there is no doubt that he knew the money

came from the U.S. government. In November 1951, declassified documents reveal that Dentzer and Ingram submitted an omnibus funding
proposal to President Truman's new Psychological Strategy Board, a
group that was intended to coordinate psychological warfare projects
across government lines.[12] They acted after Gordon Gray, the director
the board, solicited a proposal.[13] The whole enterprise might have been
an example of crossed wires. Thomas Farmer was surprised to learn of
the submission, since the board had no funds to award; he speculated
that in its coordinating role the board wanted some sort of program review.[14]

Simons's status as a funder gave him new clout in the organization,
at home and overseas. Janet Welsh of Smith College, a member of the
NSA executive committee, was stunned to find Simons at the December
1951 meeting. She protested to Dentzer, and later recalled being told the
NSA could not jeopardize its funding by asking Simons to leave. After
she learned of the CIA involvement in 1967, Welsh expressed her sense
of betrayal. "American students had founded a real, democratic student
organization," she lamented, "consciously and deliberately independent
of the U.S. government, and in contrast to the Soviet Union."[15] But
Welsh was one of the few who objected to Simons's presence. As the
CIA's Farmer observed retrospectively, few recipients ever raised questions about the source of funds, regardless of whether they suspected a
government hand.[16]

Throughout the fall of 1951, Simons functioned as the key liaison for
Dentzer and Ingram as the three planned for the second International
Student Conference, scheduled for January 1952 in Edinburgh. Their
tasks were clear: they needed not only to increase the turnout of Europeans but broaden attendance from outside Europe. It was not clear how
they would manage the latter, although the extensive summer travel in
1950 had identified some prospects.

While the CIA had assisted HIACOM in mapping out for the NSA
regional strategies to reach Asian and Latin American students, none
had borne fruit. After the Council on Foreign Relations–facilitated trip
to Asia, for example, Melvin Conant cataloged the problems. In confidential reports to HIACOM, the NSA, and his CFR sponsors, he observed that the time lapse between Jim Grant's visit in 1950 and his arrival a year later had proved costly. "Student groups in Burma, Malaya,

Thailand, and Indonesia have been deeply disappointed in the National Student Association's total failure to follow up on Jim Grant's trip."[17]

More important, Conant warned, he found widespread suspicion of the NSA's motives. In Burma, his translator suspected "that I was out to organize an anti-Communist bloc in southern Asia and they wished no part in it." Conant finally persuaded the Burmese student otherwise, and cautioned his colleagues, "I am convinced that *none* of us realized the intensity of this problem. It is not enough that the NSA be sincere; it is necessary that the NSA prove its sincerity over a long period of time by concrete demonstration of its anxiety to have solid relations out here."[18]

In fact, HIACOM and the NSA did want to build a regional bloc of noncommunist students in Asia but they typically portrayed their motives as entirely altruistic. Jim Grant offered perhaps the clearest statement of this double-speak in February 1951: "In the long run it will be impossible to avoid being plagued abroad by the apparent inconsistency of saying for internal consumption that this is primarily a fight [against a] communism program while at the same time telling the Southeast Asian student that our primary motive is to help him. The two may be perfectly consistent to us; they are not to a Southeast Asian student that we are trying to help and win over to our side."[19]

Conant, who understood the tension between private agendas and public statements, also believed that key assumptions about the seminar strategy in Asia were wrong. "We felt certain . . . that Burmese students would 'be safe,' and hoped Indonesians would be also. But that was not necessarily so." Nor could the NSA hand-pick participants for a Southeast Asian seminar, Conant argued: "You just can't do it."[20] Invitations had to go to the head of a national union of students. He urged the group "to think deeply on [these points] and not dismiss them as things often gone over in the past." He informed Grant, who had left Harvard but continued to oversee the Asian program from Washington, "I agree completely, after my tour here[,] with the views of those officers of the Rockefeller Foundation that more time is required in order to make the seminar a success."[21]

With the Asia program stalled and the Edinburgh conference fast approaching, Simons used his CIA contacts to identify foreign students who might come as observers. But even this plan proved difficult. Two Indonesian students refused to accept American travel funds until

Simons found a way to route the plane tickets through the Indonesian Embassy in Washington.[22]

If NSA contact with Asians, who had little experience with the United States, sparked suspicion of American motives, the problem was magnified tenfold in Latin America. The NSA had to overcome long-standing hostility toward the colossus from the north. While President Franklin Roosevelt had adopted a Good Neighbor Policy in an attempt to build better relations, years of economic domination and the practice of sending in U. S. marines to resolve conflicts had left bitter memories.

In the summer of 1951, a breakthrough occurred when Brazilian students agreed to organize a Pan-American conference. If successful, the NSA (and its backers) would gain a toehold in Latin America. To boost the chances of success, Helen Jean Rogers had remained in Rio for a few weeks while Eisenberg returned to the United States.[23] She had offered administrative assistance to the Brazilians, although she fully understood, as she assured Eisenberg, that the NSA needed "to avoid the appearance that the Pan-Am conference is our show."[24]

Like Conant, Rogers discovered that the NSA had underestimated "the feeling that can be generated against us in other parts of this continent." As evidence, she reported a conversation with "unpleasant Venezuelan boys" who pressed her over whether the proposed conference would "be a Yankee affair."[25]

Scheduled dates for the Pan-American conference came and went, partly because the Brazilian organizers were consumed with an internal fight over IUS membership. At one point, the anti-IUS faction seemed to have the upper hand. Dentzer and Ingram's hopes soared. Dentzer enthused about bringing Latin American delegates to Scotland, assuming, that is, they were "favorably inclined toward USNSA."[26] If such were the case, "we can expect to go there with the support of nations from an under-developed area who are not afraid to denounce the IUS, knowing that they can hardly be called 'war-mongering imperialists.'" By December 1951, these hopes had faded, but Rogers argued that the delay might be a blessing. She had come to fear that the Pan-American Conference might devolve into an attack on U.S. imperialism. Encouraging large numbers of Latin American students to come to Edinburgh suddenly seemed risky. In the end, only Brazil's União Nacional dos Estudantes attended.[27]

In January 1952, when Ingram, Dentzer, and Simons arrived in Edinburgh, they encountered a damp, cold climate that chilled them to the bone. The Scottish castle where delegates assembled had no heat on Sundays, making the temperature almost unbearable, though outside the castle, political tempers generated plenty of heat. Pro-IUS pickets gathered to protest the meeting. Ingram described the "Communist press in England" as "very abusive of the conference."[28] Left-wing press charged that the meeting was "an attempt to divide the student community by setting up a rival organization," a statement uncomfortably close to the truth. But many delegates had come to Edinburgh, as they had to Stockholm, with mandates against the founding of a new international organization.[29]

Nonetheless, the Americans left Edinburgh with a string of victories. Complex negotiations and vote trading had resulted in a green light for a permanent secretariat, even though delegates reaffirmed that the ISC was not an organization. No one contested the idea of forming the secretariat; the discussion centered rather on its powers and composition. The Dutch offered space for the permanent secretariat in the university city of Leiden. In return, the Dutch agreed not to seek an administrative position within the secretariat.[30]

The NSA secured a seat on the five-member Supervision Commission, which oversaw the secretariat and made all personnel appointments. The inclusion of the other four members—France, Sweden, England, and the Netherlands—gave rise to charges that an Anglo-Scandinavian bloc controlled the ISC. Delegates reserved a seat for a Latin American but decided not to fill it until after the oft-postponed Pan American Conference convened. Once again, delegates awarded the NSA responsibility for program development, using the Stockholm terminology of SMAP, the Students Mutual Assistance Program.[31]

After the conference, Ingram left for a two-week stay in Paris to debrief CIA officials and plan for the future. Along with CIA headquarters in Washington, the Paris station would become a center of NSA operations, since the location of the ISC secretariat fell under the jurisdiction of the Western European division. Every summer, witting staff gathered in Paris to discuss programs and personnel assignments.[32]

As Ingram analyzed the Edinburgh meeting, he singled out the two Indonesian students that Simons had financed as hopeful prospects to help plan an Asian regional project. The president of the major Indonesian student union (PPMI), Dahlan, had come directly from Indonesia. The former president, Munadjat, traveled from the Netherlands, where he was studying. After the ISC, Ingram had journeyed by train from Edinburgh to London with the two and felt that he had broken through "the outer veneer of friendliness of Orientals and had them speak extremely frankly." Dahlan, he wrote, had praised the American delegation and its positions.[33]

Dahlan had agreed to host the long-sought regional seminar in Asia and to distribute the HIACOM-produced *International Information Bulletin* within Indonesia. While these objectives were "nothing new," Ingram wrote, "we had been unable to get over [to] these people either the sincerity of our work or its importance."[34] Simons did not share Ingram's optimism. In a phone call to the Harvard group's Frank Fisher, Simons confided that in most conversations he found Dahlan noncommittal.[35]

Whatever ambivalence the Indonesians had originally felt toward accepting American funds, once in Edinburgh they were more receptive. Ingram accompanied Dahlan and Munadjat to their hotel room, gave them cash supplements to the travel grants, and promised more when they left. Ingram later told Harvard's Carl Sapers that he had emphasized that the payments "did not mean that NSA held a stick over their head."[36] The cash awards of a hundred dollars might seem modest, but in today's dollars they would be roughly nine hundred dollars. Ingram also committed the NSA to paying postage costs to distribute the *Information Bulletin* throughout Asia.[37] These two acts established a precedent that became routine in NSA contact with foreign student leaders: discreet cash payments and public awards of technical assistance.

American largess did not go unnoticed at Edinburgh. Simons's ability to award global travel grants came under scrutiny by friends and enemies alike. In March, Fred Jarvis, the NSA-friendly deputy president of the British National Union of Students, alerted Dentzer to new IUS charges. "The NSA is coming in for a good deal of attention, the technique being to discredit you by suggesting that all your international activities are financed by mysterious 'outside sources' and that projects like the Edinburgh conference and SMAP are similarly financed and being used to further U.S. foreign policy." He urged Dentzer to dispel the notion.[38]

Dentzer issued a flat denial. "I can assure you that we have never received one cent from any agency or person in any way connected with the U.S. government." He agreed "wholeheartedly . . . that the IUS propaganda makes it much more imperative that we tell all students the fact of what we are doing."[39] But even as he was making his denials, Dentzer was scheming with Ingram to use U.S. government resources to place Dentzer inside the new Leiden-based secretariat.

The NSA was not after the top position in the new Coordinating Secretariat (COSEC). As a practical matter, too much anti-Americanism existed among European unions for the Americans to have a chance of winning. But too much visibility within the secretariat carried a risk. The combination of American leadership with American resources would brand COSEC as an American instrument. Still, the NSA needed someone on the inside. Simons, Dentzer, and Ingram concocted a plan. When his presidential term ended, Dentzer would announce that he had received a floating scholarship for research abroad. He would pick a topic that made Leiden a logical place to reside and volunteer half of his time to the secretariat. Ingram was tasked with convincing his colleagues on the Supervision Commission to accept Dentzer's offer.[40]

Dentzer prepared briefing material for Ingram that was unusually blunt about U.S. intentions. "The money argument. You know what cannot be said about the fact that Americans will not be able to contribute unless someone they know is there."[41] In the same letter, he reprised the argument: "If I go over, American $$$$$$ will follow and . . . if I don't, they won't."[42]

Ingram was worried. "Our proposal is somewhat a hard one to put without arousing suspicions of our motives or without appearing to be using our contribution as a lever." Fortunately, the Supervision Commission had authorized a budget that, in vague terms, included staff assistance. Ingram therefore "sought a solution within the scope of the budget."[43] The ploy succeeded at the Supervision Committee meeting in June 1952, but just as quickly threatened to unravel.

Ingram initially reported to Dentzer that it had been easy. "I simply announced when nominations were being taken for the Permanent Secretary that NSA had no interest but that we did have an application for the second position, which I would make as soon as the first place was filled." Ingram then pitched Dentzer as planned. Everyone agreed.[44]

In the ensuing weeks, however, British students revolted. John Thompson, who represented the BNUS on the Supervision Commission, returned to England to find his colleagues in an uproar. They protested against hiring someone who happened to be in the neighborhood and demanded that Thompson reverse his vote. Thompson notified Dentzer by letter that he would press for a reversal.[45]

In response, Ingram and Dentzer played good cop/bad cop. Ingram protested in high moral dudgeon. He told Thompson that Dentzer had been "hired for his qualifications" and argued that "how Mr. Dentzer had been able to arrange his personal affairs [is] of secondary importance."[46] In a three-page, often obsequious letter, Dentzer then described how upsetting it would be for an American who cared deeply about the international student movement to be barred from making a contribution. "I do not need to point out the obvious disadvantages in some areas of the world that are faced by one who is a citizen of the United States. There is no doubt that many students in certain countries doubt the sincerity of anyone from the United States, even those who may be as liberal and critical of my government as one such as I." Treating his appointment as a fait accompli, Dentzer wrote that he would be disappointed if he were forced to resign.[47]

The impasse remained until Helen Jean Rogers, then serving as a Latin American specialist for the NSA, used her considerable diplomatic skills to resolve the issue.[48] While in Europe for a meeting of World University Service (formerly the ISS, renamed in January 1951), she held informal conversations with several Supervision Commission members.[49] Rogers concluded that Dentzer faced stiff opposition. She suggested that he redefine his role in Leiden, dropping his title and describing his intention as providing assistance.[50] She thought this would help Thompson with his problem at home. At the same time, she warned that the British had the NSA over a barrel. A few months earlier, the CIA had intervened directly in the competition to lead the secretariat. The intervention had not only backfired; it made Thompson the chief candidate for the position.

The CIA had wanted Olof Palme to run COSEC, since the United States considered it essential that a delegate from a colonial power not be in charge of the secretariat. Yet as the May 1 deadline for applications approached, Palme had not applied. On April 29, a day before the deadline, and apparently without consulting the NSA, Secretary of State Dean Acheson had sent a secret security information cable to the U.S. Embassy in Stockholm. The cable described the Edinburgh meeting as "a major step forward in propaganda battle against INTERNATIONAL

Union of Students (IUS), one of the most important worldwide COMMIE front ORGS." Palme's leadership was "an essential element in success new Secretariat." The cable emphasized that since the ISC's "primary function is influence student groups in areas which now or recently under colonial rule, a SCAN student leader wld be best person lead Leiden Secretariat successfully."[51]

Use the Swedish Foreign Office as leverage, Washington urged, since "Info available DEPT indicates relationship between SFS and SWED GOVT very close, that Palme has been reporting for some YRS to SWED FONOFF on activities of IUS."[52]

While the Swedish Foreign Office supported the request that Palme apply for the position, Palme refused.[53] Not prepared to take no for an answer, the State Department made a second attempt, this time, suggesting that the U.S. embassy approach Palme directly.[54] Again, Palme refused. Three weeks after the application deadline but before the Supervision Commission met in June, American officials tried one last time. Embassy officials were to approach the Swedish Foreign Office and spell out in greater detail the advantages of Palme, which included "the possibilities of the position as source of intelligence for FONOFF."[55] Palme still refused, but the request shows that CIA officials understood the intelligence-gathering potential of the new ISC from its inception.[56]

Rumors of these actions circulated quietly among NSA insiders. Rogers railed to Ingram at length about the "Swedish fiasco" and the "bit of stupidity" emanating from "our friends to the south," using a common euphemism for the CIA. She closed her correspondence with Ingram, writing, "Best no more of this until we are in the same room." Rogers was keenly aware that if the fiasco became public, the student counteroffensive might be aborted. "If it ever breaks out in the NSA Congress it will certainly be damaging." Let's hope it is all a bad dream, she added.[57]

The Swedes offered a temporary rescue from the Palme situation. In negotiations with the five-member Supervision Commission, the former president of the Swedish Student Federation, Jarl Tranaeus, agreed to lead COSEC on an interim basis, though he was available for only a few months. Active in student politics since 1946, Tranaeus had participated in the German seminar and attended both the Stockholm and Edinburgh ISCs. Like Palme, he had close ties to the U.S. embassy.[58] As part of the informal agreement, after six months, Thompson, a British army veteran from Manchester, would replace Tranaeus as permanent secretary.[59]

The deal infuriated Dentzer, Ingram, and Rogers, but Thompson had the votes in the Supervision Commission. Ingram repeatedly argued that putting COSEC under British leadership sent the wrong signal to non-European students. Similarly, Rogers could not understand why the British "don't realize the situation . . . that a person from a major colonial power (and probably the most important colonial power) should not have the top position." How could he be effective in the "underdeveloped areas"? Despite these drawbacks, when Rogers realized that NSA opposition to Thompson would be seen as retaliation for British objections to Dentzer, she recommended that the NSA acquiesce for the time being.[60]

The Americans regrouped and decided to try to restrict Thompson's tenure to a few months by re-opening applications in early 1953. But by then, Thompson was entrenched within both COSEC and British intelligence. While the two intelligence services cooperated with each other, tensions often arose, and each delighted in scoring little victories over the other. Eventually, Ingram and Thompson developed a close personal bond, easing the tension within the secretariat, and leaving Thompson in charge of COSEC until 1957.[61]

By the end of Ingram's NSA term, permanent institutions had finally replaced the ad-hoc funding arrangements with the CIA. On August 1, 1952, the Simons Fund disappeared and Simons reappeared as the assistant director of the Foundation for Youth and Student Affairs (FYSA), based in New York City. Simons handled the student side while director David Davis, a former OSS official who had previously helped establish the Western alternative to the pro-Soviet World Federation of Democratic Youth, handled youth affairs.[62] From 1952 to 1967, FYSA supplied the lifeblood for NSA-CIA programs, although as the operation grew, additional CIA conduits were needed to give the appearance of diversified funding.[63]

FYSA tried to project itself as a traditional American philanthropy by placing wealthy and prestigious men on the board. Arthur Houghton, Jr., president of Steuben Glass, for example, hailed from one of the wealthiest families in America; he also served as a Rockefeller Foundation trustee. J. Garvin Cavanagh was vice president of Cavanagh Hats, a firm founded by his father and based in Norwalk, Connecticut.[64] Since communists believed that capitalists pulled the strings of American foreign policy, their presence was expected and helped to further deflect attention from the source of the funds.

A few FYSA board members played operational roles, helping to integrate student and youth operations with other projects in Frank Wisner's firmament. Michael Ross was the CIA's overseas man in the Congress of Industrial Organizations (CIO). A former communist from Britain, Ross was rapidly becoming central to trade union politics in Europe.[65] Another board member, Kenneth Holland, from the Council of Foreign Relations' Study Group 5152, was a long-time friend to American student organizations. As the director of the Institute of International Education and administrator of government cultural exchange programs, he possessed files on hundreds of foreign students. Holland's predecessor, Laurence Duggan, had denied the CIA access to IIE dossiers, but Holland had no such qualms.[66] As did other members of the study group, he freely offered his access.[67] One board member seemed an anomaly, given the need to protect FYSA from prying eyes. Frederick W. Hilles, a professor of English at Yale, had been chief of military intelligence in Britain during World War II.[68] Collectively, the men on the FYSA board had extensive networks and contacts that could be called upon to do discreet favors for the CIA.

Neither Davis nor Simons made key policy decisions; those were made by men like Thomas Farmer, who joined the CIA full time in 1951, initially as an assistant to Deputy Director Allen Dulles, then as a staff officer to the Eastern Europe division, and his superiors at CIA headquarters in Washington. By 1952, Wisner's free-wheeling empire of Mighty Wurlitzer projects, as they were known inside the CIA, had been corralled into a new division, International Organizations (IO), that included Farmer.[69] Division director Thomas Braden, a former OSS agent and later a Washington-based journalist, described the IO division as "a new weapon" and "the first centralized effort to combat Communist fronts."[70]

Not everyone in the CIA shared Braden's enthusiasm. In fact, the IO division had been opposed by all but one of the CIA division heads, men Farmer today dubs "the Dukes"—seasoned intelligence veterans who oversaw traditional spies and jealously guarded their fiefdoms.[71] The Dukes tended to disparage Wisner's operations, viewing his agents as cowboys and amateurs. But Braden had an ally in his old friend Allen

Dulles, who ignored both his friend Wisner and internal opposition to authorize the new division and fully integrate OPC covert activities into the CIA.

Before the IO division was formed, as Farmer noted in a later interview, the heads of the geographical divisions (the Western Hemisphere, Asia, etc.) were "hardly talking to each other—probably not at all—and liked it that way." Farmer personally experienced their hostility. He described going into Turkey and being "scared out of his wits" by the CIA station chief, who told him: "Okay, Mr. Farmer, you're such a smart ass. You're on your own, if the Turkish service picks you up." Generally, Farmer said, he had "a pretty free hand," thanks to Wisner's deputy, Franklin Lindsay in the Eastern Europe Division, who "ran interference with the venerable group, the spies that collected intelligence, and didn't want to foreclose a nice asset like Olof Palme."[72]

Farmer cited Palme as an example for a specific reason. Once, when forced to go through the Stockholm CIA chief to get a message to Palme, a practice he generally eschewed, Farmer recalls the chief saying of Palme, "Oh yes. Bright boy. We're thinking about recruiting him." Farmer pleaded with the man not to, saying that he feared Palme would never speak to him again. "We were both patriots," Farmer continued, "Why get into this whole business of who was running who."[73]

One newcomer to the IO division was Yale graduate Cord Meyer, Jr. Meyer would one day head the division, oversee youth and student operations, and, still later, direct all CIA covert operations. The World War II veteran, a chain smoker who had lost an eye to a Japanese grenade, had gained recognition at the founding of the United Nations as one of two wounded veterans chosen to serve as top aides. Long before he joined the CIA in 1951, Meyer had become a household name among NSA activists at Harvard. Meyer had won a prestigious Harvard Fellow, an honor that allowed him time to write and, as an expression of his early commitment to peace, to preside over the World Federalists, a private organization dedicated to a federated world government. Postwar confrontations with communist activists began to temper his views on world government.

In May 1946, Meyer had fought a legendary battle in Des Moines, Iowa, against communists in the newly formed American Veterans Committee. Working alongside several members of the Harvard NSA group, among them Frederick Houghteling and Frank Fisher, Meyer set up clandestine twenty four-hour stakeouts to identify left-wing students, used walkie-talkies for tactical communication, and successfully kept communists from winning leadership positions. These battles left a lasting mark. He evolved from an ardent advocate of world peace to a committed, if still liberal, anticommunist Cold Warrior, an evolution he later described in his memoir, *Facing Reality*.[74]

After Meyer joined the CIA, in 1951, he rose rapidly within the Agency. But he had to fight another battle on his way up, this time with J. Edgar Hoover. In general, the FBI director derided Wisner's operation and his "gang of weirdos," and he found Meyer's brand of liberalism suspiciously leftist.[75] Even though Meyer survived Hoover's attack, it left lasting scars, hardening his anticommunism and driving him further into alcohol.[76] After both Braden and Farmer left the CIA in 1954, Meyer took over the IO division.[77]

The integration of Mighty Wurlitzer projects into a new division and the establishment of FYSA, the funding conduit, overcame many of the difficulties that plagued the early years of denial operations. Witting NSA staff no longer had to run around the country conducting fundraising charades or sign security oaths on moonlit roads next to Wisconsin cornfields. By the end of his first term as vice president of international affairs, Ingram had also asserted more command over the Harvard subcommittee and its endless supply of Harvard students. He instituted a desk structure that paralleled the State Department and CIA geographical regions, and held regular meetings to coordinate projects in Latin America, Asia, and the Middle East. Ingram also made frequent trips to New York and Washington to confer with John Simons and Jim Grant, among others.

WHILE THE NSA AND CIA concentrated on the operational details of building the ISC, the International Union of Students was undergoing a shakeup. In the spring of 1952, Josef Grohman abruptly resigned as president. Since many Westerners viewed Grohman as Stalin's puppet, his replacement by another communist did not seem significant. What happened to Grohman between 1946 and his resignation in 1952 is a story little known in the West, and one that shows how blind anticommunists could be to the nuances of communist politics.

Grohman had joined the Czechoslovak Communist Party in 1945, at a time when most Czechs held the party in esteem for its resistance to the Nazis. The failure of the West to come to the nation's aid in 1939 when Hitler seized the Sudetenland, home to German-speaking Czechs, had created intense resentment. Emboldened, Hitler had gone on to occupy the entire nation, leaving Czechs feeling further abandoned by the West. Like others who joined the Communist Party after World War II, Grohman embraced socialism and rejected Western capitalism, which he felt ignored those on the economic bottom. But fidelity to communist ideology, admiration for the Soviet Union, and loyalty to Stalin were not one and the same.

In March 1952, Grohman left Prague to attend an IUS executive committee meeting in Budapest. His wife, Jarmila Maršálková, who also worked in the IUS secretariat, accompanied him, and later described these events. When they reached Budapest, Grohman discovered his old friend and former IUS vice president Aleksandr Shelepin had flown in from Moscow to see him. A rising star in Kremlin politics, later to become KGB director, Shelepin told Grohman, "You must leave Budapest: your life is in danger." Shelepin advised Grohman to protect himself and his family by resigning his IUS post.[78]

According to Maršálková, Grohman's first instinct was to refuse. Although they later divorced, she describes him today as a "man of principle." Throughout the night, he paced the gardens of the small villa where the committee met and agonized with Maršálková over the alternatives. By dawn, Grohman realized that he had no choice. The couple had left their two small children behind in Prague and understood the danger of defiance. Grohman resigned that morning, citing health reasons.[79]

Ralph Blumenau, a British student who worked with Palme and Farmer on the first phase of the German student project, wrote in his diary that he and his British colleagues believed that Grohman had been "given more important work to do."[80] In fact, he no longer had any job.

Grohman had become Stalin's victim. In 1949, after Yugoslavia challenged Soviet economic policy and was expelled from the Cominform, the Soviets tightened their grip over all of Eastern Europe. Purges, arrests, and show trials became common as an increasingly paranoid Stalin conjured conspiracies against his power.[81] He cut telephone contact between the Russian and Western sectors of Berlin and consolidated communist control of East Germany.[82]

Unlike communist takeovers in most East European countries, Czech communists had risen to power without the assistance of the Soviet army, making them less subservient to Moscow. In 1951, Stalin's hench men arrested the entire top echelon of the Czech Communist Party, including its general secretary, Rudolf Slánský, on charges of "an anti-government conspiracy." The communist official closest to Grohman, Benrich Geminder, who was in charge of foreign relations, was also arrested and later executed.[83]

Before Grohman's death in 1995, he and former IUS secretary general Thomas Madden, today a retired physician living in the United States, reunited and held lengthy postmortems on the early IUS years. Both Madden and Maršálková argue that before the 1948 Czech coup, Grohman had complete freedom to run the IUS. They point to the fact that neither Madden nor Grohman supported the Soviets' demand that the new IUS affiliate with the World Federation of Democratic Youth. They depict the Soviet student union as annoyingly slow to pay dues. Madden also insists that Grohman was blindsided in September 1948 by the Soviets' demand that the IUS oppose the Marshall Plan and worked frantically behind the scenes to engineer a compromise.[84]

Before the Czech coup, the Soviet Union held one seat on the IUS executive committee, the same as the United States. According to Maršálková, the Soviets took up posts within the IUS secretariat in 1949, changing the atmosphere in the office.[85] Her recollection squares with the date the Russians took up posts in several Czech state ministries. In October 1949, for example, Soviet agents pronounced the Czech State Security apparatus too lax to root out enemies and took over investigations, which led to the execution of prominent Czech communists.[86]

In retrospect, Madden believes that he and Grohman were naive about what was happening in Yugoslavia. Both men were close to many Yugoslav students, and they thought they could keep the IUS out of the conflict. But Soviet pressure grew intense and dangerous. In February 1950, Madden recalled sitting in disbelieving silence at an IUS executive committee meeting in London as Grohman delivered a diatribe against the Yugoslavs.[87] Ralph Blumenau, who was also present that day, described it as a display of communist fanaticism, writing in his diary, "Grohman's face during the early exchange was a study in itself. His rather handsome face was quite flushed and distorted with rage and hatred."[88] Neither Madden nor Blumenau knew that before the speech, Czech embassy officials in London had summoned Grohman and issued an ultimatum:

he must denounce the Yugoslavs or put his family in Prague at risk.[89] Grohman raged, yes, but not because of ideological passion.

By the time Shelepin warned Grohman of the danger he faced, Grohman had been accused of many crimes. His friendship with Yugoslav student leaders had been recast in a traitorous light as Titoism. Grohman also had openly opposed the purge of the Hungarian youth movement by the pro-Stalinist Hungarian Communist Party general secretary Mátyás Rákosi. Charges against Grohman included contact with foreign intelligence agencies, and Westerners more generally. The urgency of Shelepin's plea "to leave Budapest immediately," becomes understandable. Grohman told Madden during their postmortems that he didn't mind resigning and was relieved that he had not been imprisoned.[90]

Bernard Bereanu, a budding mathematical genius from Romania whose work later impressed President Richard Nixon, took over the IUS presidency; then he, too, became a purge victim.[91] Madden, who left the secretariat in 1951, was succeeded by Italian Communist Party student leader Giovanni Berlinguer. In 1952, Czech leader Jiří Pelikán, known then as an ultra hard-liner who ruthlessly purged politically suspect students from Charles University, rather than as the reformer he would become in the mid-1960s, became IUS president, a position he held for more than a decade.

The IUS was now entering its most doctrinaire period. But the West received an unexpected dividend from Stalin's crackdown: just as the CIA started an all-out push to build the International Student Conference, the IUS began losing members.

7

THE BATTLE FOR MEMBERS

FOR THE NEXT FEW YEARS, denial operations could be quantified by membership wins and losses. At its founding in 1946, the International Union of Students claimed a membership of six million students from seventy-eight countries. By 1952, it had lost about fifteen member student unions, mostly from Europe. In 1952, the Edinburgh International Student Conference hosted twenty-five countries, some of them observers. The lopsided numbers suggested that the ISC would have to fight to gain legitimacy as a representative worldwide organization. And unknown to most ISC members, the CIA would be fighting right along with them.

CIA headquarters celebrated every IUS loss, every ISC gain. Thomas Braden, the International Organizations division chief, described rejoicing the day "an agent came in with the news that four national student associations had broken away from the Communist International Union of Students and joined our student outfit instead."[1]

After the Edinburgh ISC, John Simons zeroed in on the Middle East as a possible location for a future conference, hopeful that it might attract the area's students and broaden the ISC base.[2] In June 1952, he deployed former NSA president Ted Harris to explore this possibility.[3] Months later, Harris's report was pessimistic: "The whole area [is] too unstable." To drive home the point, Harris described a scene in Beirut: "Just now, below my window Lord Mountbatten is emerging from a government office. A large crowd, thickly populated with young people[,] is being held back by police. Although the general attitude is sullen silence, I can hear cries in French and English . . . 'Go Home!'" He cautioned that the NSA "could do more harm than good" in the Middle East, since "only two groups locally would be interested, Arab nationalists and Communists."[4]

William Polk, who had surveyed student opinion in the Middle East for HIACOM in the summer of 1950, had already warned Simons that there was a new source of resentment in the Arab world: the U.S. government's recognition of the State of Israel. In an eerily prescient report, Polk wrote, "The West now seemed completely overwhelming. . . . Its movies and advertising posters had violated Moslem ethics; its techniques and industry had uprooted and revolutionized Arab handicrafts and social structure; its cars, trains, and planes had brought Damascus and Cairo close to Paris and London; and now, before the eyes of the terrified Moslem students, the West seemed to be taking root as the nation of Israel in the heart of the Fertile Crescent." These factors, Polk argued, were leading to "extremes, both Communism and Islam."[5]

The NSA also stepped up its efforts in Asia, where the strategy of holding a regional seminar to identify noncommunist students and promote interest in the ISC remained stalled. In early January, Frank Fisher took over the Southeast Asia program. After graduating in 1951 from Harvard Law School, he had returned to Winnetka, Illinois, to establish a law practice, but following what Avrea Ingram described to a colleague as "considerable pressure (both external and internal)," Fisher agreed to defer his practice and return to work with Ingram and HIACOM.[6] The strategy of employing consultants and temporary staff without student status had become accepted in the International Commission, since the NSA constitution was silent on the point. Fisher signed on for a six-month tour of Indonesia, Burma, the Philippines, Hong Kong, Malaya, Thailand, India, Pakistan, and Afghanistan.[7]

Before he left for Asia on April 8, Fisher conferred with John Simons, handled contacts with the Department of State, including W. Bradley Connors, the International Information Activities specialist for the Far East Division, and checked in with the Council on Foreign Relations, which passed along funds for his trip.[8] Despite his consultant role, Fisher exhibited no qualms about giving direction to Ingram, chastising him on one occasion for lax information procedures, "because of the grave risk they represent to the international program of NSA." He singled out work on Southeast Asia, where "there are several documents which should not be available for the sort of general distribution which assures their falling into the hands unfavorably disposed to NSA."[9]

Despite his seven years of service with HIACOM and other evidence of his insider status, Fisher vigorously denies being made witting by the CIA. In a contemporary interview he asserted, "They didn't have to. I was doing exactly what was called for." Fisher also insisted that his motives were entirely altruistic: "I just wanted to get the students educated."[10] But Fisher's résumé, left behind in the NSA archive, along with his reports from the 1952 trip, suggest a harder-nosed politics. In his résumé, written after the Southeast Asian excursion, he included as an area of expertise, "special attention to problems of communist infiltration in foreign student movements."[11]

In confidential reports written after his Asian trip, Fisher concluded that the Asian seminar idea was dead, or at least out of NSA hands.[12] He had met Indonesian student leaders in Jakarta and Bandung who talked about hosting a broad-based Arab-Asian conference. A dangerous plan, Fisher warned in his report to Ingram and HIACOM: such a gathering could become a "hot political conclave that will only train students to reckless political agitation."[13] He explained why. "If Arab states turn up strong, if Indian Communist-inclined students show up, if Communist China is invited and send[s] competent students, if some issue is then especially hot (Tunisia, Egypt-Sudan) such [agitation] could happen." And the IUS, Fisher felt, would be the beneficiary.[14]

In terms of regional objectives, the NSA had not neglected Latin America, since the continent had the potential to yield numerous ISC members. The oft-postponed Inter-American Conference finally convened in late January 1952, not long after the Edinburgh conference. The NSA sent a five-person delegation to Brazil, including Bill Dentzer, Helen Jean Rogers, and Avrea Ingram, but added two delegates to emphasize its racial and ethnic diversity. These were Barry Farber, a Jewish student from the University of North Carolina, and Herbert Wright, an African American representing the National Association for the Advancement of Colored People. Post-conference reports glowed with satisfaction at the way the delegation had surprised and impressed the Latin Americans.[15] Rogers noted that the Brazilians "didn't think there would be even one Negro in our NSA congress." The conference was judged successful, since the Cuban student federation had pledged to organize a second hemispheric conference that included the NSA.[16]

In the late summer, Rogers enrolled in the Harvard graduate program in government, at the same time becoming Ingram's special assistant for Latin America.[17] Dentzer, Ingram, and Rogers all wrestled with the question of how to confront the widespread anti-Americanism in Latin America. Rogers blamed it on lack of personal contact. She concluded that delegates at the Brazilian conference had "no understanding of life in the US." She reported, to her chagrin, that some students saw the United States and the Soviet Union as equal evils. She had repeatedly heard delegates claim that the United States was "subservient to the interests of the United Fruit Company, Standard Oil and other large interests." This affected the NSA, she pointed out, since "delegates at the January conference evinced skepticism that American students could take action independent of the State Department and against unreasonable economic exploitation."[18]

Rogers, Ingram, and Dentzer never argued that U.S. policy toward Latin America should change or that the NSA should protest that policy. Rather, they believed that the NSA had to change the perceptions of Latin Americans toward it. If diligence and persistence could have achieved that goal, Rogers alone might have succeeded. She interrupted her graduate studies on a daily basis to keep letters flowing to Latin American student leaders, most over Ingram's signature.[19]

The international office blanketed Central and South American student unions with copies of *La Vida Estudiantil*, a new magazine produced by the NSA-affiliated, CIA-supported International News Center in Atlanta. HIACOM also sent out batches of the *International Information Bulletin*, describing student projects in housing and literacy, as well as overseas travel opportunities.[20] Armed with a special FYSA grant of $20,000, Dentzer invited every Latin American student union that had attended the Brazil conference to the late-summer NSA Congress.[21] The equivalent figure today would be $175,000.

Above all, Dentzer, Ingram, and Rogers pursued the Cubans, since the fate of the future Pan-American conference rested with them. Ingram invited the head of the Federation of Cuban Students (FEU) to address the NSA Congress, in part to overcome the Cubans' skepticism of the NSA's motives. Havana-based students, preoccupied with overthrowing General Fulgencio Batista, the U.S.-backed dictator who had suspended the Cuban constitution, begged off. Dentzer responded with an expression of NSA support. "Our every sympathy is with you in your struggle for constitutional government, and the best interests of the university and the nation." To further demonstrate their bona fides, he pledged that the NSA would pass a resolution at the Congress condemning Batista.[22]

In the end, the NSA Congress heard from Marcelo Fernández, a Cuban engineering student enrolled in the summer program at MIT in Cambridge and a future stalwart of the Fidel Castro regime.[23] To the several hundred students gathered at the University of Indiana, Fernández described in dramatic detail the way Batista's police treated university students: unarmed students and professors were "jailed and beaten in the secret police headquarters."[24] Delegates gave Fernández a standing ovation, and, as Dentzer had promised, the Congress declared its "opposition to the actions of those dictatorships existing in some Latin American countries which have violated the traditional rights of students and interfered with the autonomy of the university."[25]

The Congress's action on Cuba illustrates how the NSA's international resolutions served regional agendas: they were not meant primarily to educate American students on foreign policy issues. The Cuban resolution, for example, would demonstrate to Latin Americans that the NSA could criticize Batista—and by extension other dictatorships—because it had no ties to the U.S. government, thereby addressing the chief source of suspicion of NSA motives. Deft phrasing enabled the international staff to link condemnation of the dictatorship with education, thereby conforming (barely) to the *students as students* requirement in the NSA constitution. The resolution curried favor with the Cuban student union by praising "its efforts to preserve student rights, academic freedom and the autonomy of the university which the dictatorship of General Batista has tried to destroy."[26]

While the Latin America strategy held the promise of a long-term payoff, the NSA was working against the pressure of the looming third International Student Conference, scheduled for Copenhagen in January 1953. An increase in attendance was imperative. Bill Polk, the Middle East specialist for HIACOM, earlier had suggested a strategy for increasing Middle East representation. He urged Ingram to work through the (CIA-supported) American Friends of the Middle East to identify Middle Eastern students studying in the United States.[27] Once they became acquainted with the NSA, he argued, selected individuals could be invited to the ISC. The plan was easy to execute, thanks to overlapping board membership—Kenneth Holland sat on the boards of both the

CIA funding conduit FYSA and American Friends of the Middle East. Holland identified ten Middle Eastern students to be invited to the 1952 NSA Congress, assuring Ingram that FYSA could offer financial support for their travel and board.[28]

The presence of foreign students in the United States now suggested a more general strategy. Between 1952 and 1954, the CIA encouraged and often subsidized new associations of foreign students in the United States. In rapid succession, the American Friends of the Middle East launched four separate organizations: the Organization of Arab Students (OAS), the Iranian Students of America, the Associated Students of Afghanistan (ASA), and the Pakistan Students Association.[29] The CIA-created Committee for a Free Asia, later renamed the Asia Foundation, also backstopped some of these projects. It circulated an English-language magazine, *The Asian Student*, as part of its program to combat communist influence throughout the region, and regularly featured news from the U.S. based associations.[30] The CIA also supported a similar organization of African students in the United States.[31]

As with many student projects underwritten by the CIA, the dollar amounts required to sustain the U.S.-based associations were relatively small; the ASA's annual budget was $10,000.[32] But small resources yielded large benefits. At a minimum, foreign students provided information on the political climate in their home countries and entrée to promising leaders since many, if not most, foreign students studying in the United States were destined to become governing elites after they returned home, which suggested the value of long-term investments.

Ingram turned to the new student associations to swell attendance in Copenhagen. At Ingram's request, the ISC secretariat (COSEC) extended an invitation to the new leader of Iranian Students of America, Houshang Pirnazar.[33] In his request to John Simons for a FYSA travel grant, Ingram portrayed Iran as having no student union. In fact, Iran did have a student union but of the wrong political flavor; it belonged to the IUS and had close ties with the pro-Soviet Iranian Tudeh Party.[34]

At the CIA, such seemingly inconsequential acts—inviting an Iranian student to the ISC—had a broader purpose than building ISC membership. More ambitious CIA objectives were at stake. In Iran, the CIA plotted to oust its president, Mohammad Mossadegh, who, although democratically elected, had provoked the West with his decision to nationalize the Iranian oil industry. Fearing that Mossadegh would not resist Soviet influence, British and American intelligence joined forces to overthrow him.[35] The installation in 1953 of a pro-West regime led by Mohammad Reza Pahlavi as the Shah of Iran ushered in a period of American dominance. Identifying pro-West Iranian students served the Agency's larger agenda of deepening ties between Iran and the United States. Sometimes witting personnel at the NSA were aware of these broader agendas; sometimes these agendas were obscured, protected by the highly compartmentalized world of intelligence.

In 1952, another coup overthrew the King Farouk monarchy in Egypt and installed Muhammad Naguib as president, an act that opened up similar opportunities for American influence in the Middle East. Ingram also brokered travel funds to Copenhagen for two Egyptian students from the new U.S.-based Organization of Arab Students.[36] Once again, in the formal request for FYSA funding, Ingram portrayed Egypt as having no organized student union. That claim was also false. The nationalist, but not communist, League of Egyptian Students belonged to the IUS. As a practical matter, Egyptian officials typically denied students passports to travel abroad, so the league was not a major player in the IUS.[37] But the United States hoped that the new Naguib regime would look favorably on both the NSA and the pro-West ISC.

Frank Fisher and Helen Jean Rogers also identified foreign students met during their respective travels in Asia and Latin America, and supplied names in confidence to COSEC. Fisher profiled Asian students on his tour through the region, while Rogers used Catholic networks in Latin America to scour for potential ISC invitees. Once Simons cleared the travel funds, Fisher acted as a broker. He cabled the hand-picked Asians: "Limited funds now available for travel grants to Copenhagen international student conference," suggesting they "contact COSEC Leiden, the Netherlands."[38] Rarely did a flattered student turn down the opportunity to travel.

The fiction that FYSA, the source of travel funds either directly or through COSEC, was a private American foundation gave director David Davis and assistant director John Simons a rationale for attending the ISC.[39] Thus, unknown to the foreign students gathered in Copenhagen, CIA career staff were observing their behavior, soliciting their political views during informal chats, and reporting the results to their superiors. As were the NSA witting staff. The NSA archival files contain reports on every aspect of the Copenhagen conference: a record of daily events, profiles by country, profiles by delegation, and individual delegate information.[40] A list of still-classified files at CIA headquarters protects the identity of students recruited during this time, but declassified indexes show that there were recruitments, again confirming that from its inception the CIA used the ISC for more than denial operations.[41]

All the frantic organizing prior to Copenhagen paid off, at least in NSA eyes. Ingram was ecstatic with the turnout.[42] More than a hundred observers and delegates from thirty-four countries came to Denmark. Thirty-one national unions of students requested and received delegate status. The Copenhagen ISC constituted, Ingram later wrote, "the largest student gathering of legitimate student federations in the world ever that has taken place."[43] The turnout, he raved, was "successful in excess of our most optimistic hopes."[44] In a letter to Frank Fisher, Ingram sounded the same theme and observed that the increased attendance, "for the first time, placed the balance of power outside the European Commonwealth countries and approach."[45]

State Department officials decided to take their own measure of its success. U.S. embassies in Asia were asked to survey press coverage of the Copenhagen meeting, "covertly to determine feasibility of forming a new international student organization."[46] Cables warned the overseas officials that the IUS, "realizing the potential power of COSEC, has used all available means of media to discredit it." The results of the survey were uniformly disappointing. New Delhi cabled back, "No comment in the press or from local students circles on this conference." A Bangkok official "found no discussions of the International Student Conference at Copenhagen." The Rangoon (Burma) cable read, "No reaction . . . has been observed."[47]

Not only was favorable publicity on the ISC scant, the IUS secretariat in Prague ginned up negative press, circulating a broadside under the provocative title "Glass Hats, US State Department, and the Leiden Secretariat (Or How They Came to Copenhagen)." It described how delegates compared notes on who had paid for their travel and discovered a common source. The delegates then raised questions on the plenary floor about the American foundation behind the largess. The IUS editors identified the men on the FYSA board by name, but focused on the industrialists.[48]

To the chagrin of the NSA, a delegate from Indonesia—the number one priority in Southeast Asia—publicly criticized the gathering.[49]

Busono, a student then at Charles University in Prague, and later imprisoned in Indonesia for anti-government activities, published an account of the Copenhagen conference in *IUS News*. He ridiculed the ISC's claim to be a genuinely representative international student body. "A whole afternoon and evening devoted to discussion on what exactly is a NUS [national union of students] resulted in a 100 word resolution."[50]

Busono asked rhetorically: "Why did the Iranian delegate come from New York? An Egyptian from California? Why were there no delegates from the two largest Asian countries, Japan (750,000 students) and China (3 million students)? Why did the Danish government deny the Burmese delegate a visa? Why did most Asian delegates come from European cities, for example, Paris, London or The Hague?"[51]

The Indonesian highlighted the larger problem for the ISC, its insistence on being apolitical. "This we altogether reject! In our country every organization has the struggle for national independence in its programme, because this is a pre-requisite for a democratic education and for better conditions of life and study." Busono then quoted Subroto, the new president of the Indonesian student federation (PPMI), who was thought by the NSA to be a solid ally, and said that he "confirmed" that "the only representative student union is IUS."[52] Americans had identified the Western-friendly Subroto as the person who might lead the PPMI out of the IUS.[53] Whether or not Subroto made the remarks ascribed to him, the public spotlight put him in a difficult position.

Ingram privately denounced Busono as an IUS plant, but the criticism struck a nerve, since not only NSA enemies were making it: an ISC member and NSA ally from the National Federation of Canadian University Students, Charles Taylor, had made similar comments after he observed an IUS meeting in Bucharest in September 1952. He had shared his report with the NSA and described the apoliticism of the ISC as the hardest charge to defend. "It is clear that in many parts of the world, notably many Asian countries, such a distinction is ludicrously unrealistic, and to an Asian[,] insistence on such a distinction can easily be interpreted as showing an attitude of little concern for his problem."[54]

Ingram's personal notes after the Copenhagen meeting show that he wrestled with the problem raised by Busono and Taylor. The NSA was caught between "Europeans—completely non-political" and "Latin Americans—completely political."[55] The Europeans, he wrote, were unprepared for the "impact of under-developed area participation." The eight Latin American delegations wanted the conference "to adopt a more political tone," seemed irritated with the emphasis on "practical projects and nothing else, and constantly threatened to withdraw."[56]

But the problem was broader and deeper than Ingram appeared to understand. In retrospect, it seems obvious that NSA strategies to expand the ISC would eventually exacerbate, not mitigate, the problem of political demands. The more successfully the conference attracted students from outside Europe, the more frequently such demands would arise. Similarly, it appears not to have occurred to the NSA-CIA team that with numerical growth would come new voting blocs and unpredictable alliances. In 1953, Ingram registered dismay that Yugoslavia tried (and failed) to gain a seat on the Supervision Committee by allying with a bloc of Latin American unions. Why would Latin American students cooperate, he wondered.[57]

Despite hints of trouble ahead, Ingram, Simons, Dentzer, and others continued their efforts to recruit new members. They did not abandon a practical-projects approach, but tried to modify it. The NSA experimented with a junior version of the U.S. foreign aid program known as Point Four, which emphasized technical-assistance grants and self-help.[58]

The suggestion had come from Harvard's Jim Grant, who had joined the Technical Cooperation Administration (TCA), which oversaw the Point Four program.[59] John Simons asked Bill Ellis, now a student at Harvard Law School, to test the feasibility of Grant's idea in Asia. Ellis, who did occasional contract work for Simons, set off for Burma, Indonesia, India, and Pakistan.[60]

The formal proposal for Ellis's trip captures the earnest if naive faith of the organizers that American know-how could replace politics. It depicts students from underdeveloped countries as prone to agitation and sets out the necessity of rerouting their energy. Asian students needed to move beyond the "outmoded tactics" used during independence movements, when their "major purpose was to create havoc and unrest for the Western power." If their energy could be redirected into national development goals, such as rural reconstruction projects, students could work with the West rather than against it.[61]

U.S. government cables notifying American embassies about Ellis's trip contain the same optimistic view of technical programs. They describe his mission: "to establish friendly relations between the university students in this area and students in the United States and other parts of the free world; to strengthen the moderate student movement; and to help make the student movements in the area positive assets for national development and reconstruction."[62] Prospective projects would "show the students that their governments are rendering constructive service to the people and that problems cannot be solved by simple panaceas as advocated by the Communists but required technical skills, time, money, and hard work."[63]

When Ellis reached Asia, he found much to confirm the stereotype of students as political agitators, but little to suggest the viability of technical-assistance programs. He arrived in Burma just after elections at the University of Rangoon, during which students had discovered the government's attempt to intervene against suspected communist influence. Amid demonstrations, protests, and general chaos, rival students set ballot boxes on fire.[64] Ellis narrowly escaped a police raid on a Rangoon dormitory. A rural reconstruction program at this time, he concluded with understatement, "would be most unwise."[65] In a letter to Ingram, Ellis added a caution that was ignored in practice: "In any case, we must not give the appearance that we have loads of money and that everyone can take us for suckers. I hate to say that, but it is in some ways unfortunately true."[66]

Moving on to India, Ellis was confronted with a complex student scene. When the IUS was founded, three Indian student federations had sought delegate status. Eventually, the pro-Soviet All India Student Federation won out. Although Jim Grant, Melvin Conant, and Frank Fisher had all visited India during their Asian trips, little had come of their work. U.S. embassy officials in New Delhi continued to identify promising Indian student leaders, and warn against those they believed to be communists.[67]

In 1950, the Congress Party under Prime Minister Jawaharlal Nehru had encouraged the founding of the National Union of Students India (NUSI), but it had weak campus roots and could not meet ISC criteria for membership. A further obstacle was A. J. Shelat, a Gujarati socialist and medical student, who had won the NUSI presidency by one vote. For months, Shelat had been on the warpath against the World University Service (as the International Student Service was now named) in Geneva, and by extension the United States, since Americans supplied the bulk of WUS funds. He bombarded the NSA with diatribes against the WUS India committee, accusing its leader, Virendra Agarwala, and his "batches of henchmen" of squandering "thousands of rupees."[68] How can it be democracy, Shelat demanded, if "Geneva nominates one person in India who in turn nominates all the rest?"[69] The conflict was most unusual. The NSA drew heavily on WUS country committees for trusted contacts in Europe and Asia, and the overlap between WUS and ISC activists (including John Thompson, Olof Palme, and Bill Ellis) was considerable. Not in India.

But Shelat was also anticommunist. He argued that with the right deployment of resources the "commies could be smashed."[70] When Ellis got to India, he tried to convince Shelat to end his opposition to the WUS and attend the next ISC meeting as an observer, following up after his return to the United States with further exhortations: "You have a definite obligation both to yourselves and foreign students to come to Istanbul"; it would be an opportunity "to express your point of view," especially since "you continually expressed your disappointment with the manner and superficial approach which has characterized the actions of the USNSA and other western student organizations."[71]

As a further inducement, Ellis proposed that Shelat "come armed with a specific proposal for the joint planning and implementation of a technical team of students who would travel and work with NUSI in India from May until September."[72] Most foreign students readily took this kind of bait, and Shelat did not disappoint. Sometime after the 1954 ISC in Istanbul, he obtained a FYSA grant.[73] Thus began a decade of U.S. subsidies, both open and clandestine, to Indian students, along with considerable meddling in their internal affairs.

The NSA soon scrapped a student Point Four program in favor of more direct approaches. ISC rules permitted recognition of national committees if they were representative and intended to become student unions. In 1953, the CIA poured resources into developing national committees in Egypt, Syria, Lebanon, Pakistan, Sierra Leone, and Jamaica. Over the years, such funding became a reliable way into a country's student politics, regardless of whether a national committee or a national student union ever materialized.

The approach in Egypt illustrates the CIA's technique. In the spring of 1953, Simons commissioned a Harvard student and Fulbright scholar, Frederick C. Thomas, to identify existing student groups in Egypt.[74] Notwithstanding Thomas's major finding, that "there are no non-political student organizations in Egypt," Simons and the NSA pushed ahead with plans to encourage the creation of an Egyptian national committee. Sometime before August, the NSA identified a potential organizer, Abdul Haz Shaaban, an Egyptian student studying at the University of Michigan, who was about to return to Egypt. Before he left the United States, Shaaban attended the 1953 NSA Congress.

At the Congress, Shaaban had brought tangible evidence that a new Egyptian-American alliance was in the making, reading a personal greeting from Egyptian president Muhammad Naguib. Newly elected NSA president James Edwards and international affairs vice president Leonard Bebchick thanked Shaaban for his message as a sign of "a spiritual bond between the students and peoples of this country and your nation which we hope has found root and will flourish."[75] A few months later, the two NSA officers traveled to Cairo and met with Naguib personally in his palace office. During this period of optimism, Simons awarded Shaaban funds for a National Egyptian Committee.[76]

To nudge developments along, the NSA hired a new coordinator for the Middle East, Robert Williams, who had worked previously with African students.[77] Williams enrolled in the African Studies program at Boston University and kept in touch with Shaaban on behalf of HIACOM.[78] In a typical letter, Williams might ask casually, "Have you had an opportunity to discuss the formation of an Egyptian National Union of Students with students from AUC [American University in Cairo], Al Alzar or Cairo University?"[79] Williams would then hint that the World University Service might establish a center in Cairo that could be headquarters for the Egyptian National Union. He could make such offers because the CIA had placed a witting American student on the WUS staff in Geneva to ensure coordination.[80]

One of Williams's more blatant suggestions was that a delegation from the U.S. Organization of Arab Students travel to Egypt "for the purpose of organizing a Pan-Arab student Conference to be held somewhere in the Arab world during the summer of 1954."[81] Within months, the NSA would come to abhor the idea of Pan-Arabism, but at the time it seemed like an expedient hook for corralling Middle Eastern students. Ted Harris, then in Egypt on a Fulbright, followed up on Williams's suggestion.

Harris reported that Shaaban was skeptical of the whole idea, and Shaaban himself bluntly wrote to Williams, "I do not believe that the sponsorship of such a conference from a group outside the area (such as North America or Paris) is a very wise way of ensuring support in this area. I would rather wait until we have our own national union."[82] In 1954, a military coup overthrew Naguib and ushered in the regime of Gamal Abdul Nasser, beginning an era of intense Egyptian nationalism. The NSA would try a second time before abandoning its effort.

Just before Naguib was deposed, the ISC met in the Middle East, or, rather, as close as regional politics made possible. The Istanbul locale would be remembered for several things: freezing temperatures, the presence of an IUS representative, many new observers and members, and most of all a compromise intended to loosen the strictures of *students as students* and accommodate the demand to debate political issues.

Bill Dentzer, then a Yale law student and still working with the CIA, joined the NSA delegation to Istanbul. During the conference, Dentzer brokered a deal between the Europeans and the more political of the unions. The result was a new vehicle called the Research and Investigation Commission (RIC). Delegates who wanted to condemn a dictator or call for the ouster of a colonial power could request an investigation of conditions in a particular country so long as the issue was linked to academic freedom or educational opportunity. If a majority of ISC delegates agreed, the commission would assemble an international team, conduct an investigation, and report back the following year. In this way, hot political topics would be removed from immediate debate and return as fact-laden briefs. At the time, it seemed like a brilliant solution to the problem of political demands.

The Americans—who justified the cost of RIC as a weapon to use against communist regimes—won backing at Istanbul for an investigation of East Germany. By contrast, non-Western ISC delegates, who had little interest in Cold War problems, voted to investigate educational conditions under the Perón dictatorship in Argentina and racial discrimination in South Africa, a harbinger of investigations to come, when RIC would be turned against the United States and its own racial policies.

Dentzer's high-profile role won him the RIC chairmanship. He enhanced his reputation by securing immediate funding for the commission and its first investigation of racial conditions in South Africa. He notified his colleagues that he had "personally secured a grant from Mr. C. V. Whitney, a sportsman and breeder of winning race horses."[83] By now adept at handling cover stories, Dentzer assured the others he had informed Whitney that "we could accept no funds if any strings were attached, and he fully understood and agreed with this procedure."[84] Dentzer and his immediate successors kept a tight rein on RIC, at least initially, by dint of a procedural detail. Unlike the Supervision Commission, which required candidates to have support from home student unions, RIC could nominate anyone to be an investigator. It could therefore hand-pick its personnel and prevent the appointment of firebrands.

The Istanbul conference drew student leaders from forty countries, a number high enough to justify a publicity campaign afterward. COSEC press releases made the bold claim that the only countries missing in Istanbul were those from the Iron Curtain and satellite countries.[85] Denial operations seemed to be heading for a smashing success, at least as long as no one looked too carefully at the composition of the delegations.

The ISC may have lacked a natural constituency, but CIA resources proved it could play the numbers game at least as effectively as the IUS. Whether the International Student Conference could inspire loyalty or win new friends for the West without generous material incentives remained to be seen.

8

OPENING THE SPIGOT

THE NSA-CIA OPERATION grew so rapidly between 1952 and 1954 that it is tempting to conclude that intelligence officials never met a student problem they couldn't solve with CIA resources. Those resources covered NSA international operations in the United States, activities related to the ISC and COSEC, including NSA dues, and other projects designed to impress foreign students. This funding was in addition to direct support for the ISC and COSEC overseas operations. Inevitably, the need for secrecy and supervision grew along with the outpouring of resources.

By mid-1954, a snapshot of expanded operations would include the following: The CIA funded the NSA International Commission administrative and staff expenses, including salaries for the international vice president, an assistant, desk officers (at hourly rates), overseas representatives, and short-term project staff.[1] At the annual NSA Congress, the CIA funded special sessions for student body presidents and campus newspaper editors, leaders who shaped campus opinion on international programs and policies.[2]

The CIA financed NSA publications aimed at overseas students, including the *International Information Bulletin*, a new Spanish-language magazine, and Spanish translations of NSA Congress proceedings. It funded travel for foreign students to attend the NSA Congresses: forty in 1954, up from twenty in 1952.[3] Separate grants covered hospitality for foreign guests at the Congress, and campus tours before and after it. The NSA international office, still located off-campus at Harvard, quietly routed administrative funds to NSA headquarters to equalize the

lauded the private group that awarded funds to run it, while refusing to disclose the funding source. "This kind of trust in American students is something of a novelty," he told delegates, "and burdens us with living up to the tremendous responsibilities of the trust." He described the unnamed donors as "lay and vocational experts in international affairs," who understand "the irrefutable logic of the NSA program."[63]

Who could refute Sapers's rendition? Not Eisenberg. Not Lowenstein. Not the Madison staff. Not the typical undergraduate from Buffalo or Houston or Los Angeles. The only people who knew enough to parse these exaggerations and distortions had no interest in doing so. Lowenstein had never delegated SMAP to HIACOM, as Sapers suggested. Lowenstein inherited an ongoing international program. If anything, the Stockholm delegates believed that *they* had delegated SMAP to the NSA, not to any specific group within it. And Lowenstein had had no hand in creating its component projects.

But SMAP was not the only issue confronting the Congress; there was also the question of NSA policy regarding the IUS. This was a matter on which Lowenstein could wield influence among the undergraduates. How he might use that influence at the Congress had worried Olof Palme throughout the spring and summer. Eisenberg's frequent letters to Palme had stoked these fears; in one he told Palme, "There is a great movement here to set up a new union at the next conference, spearheaded by you know who."[64]

In late July, Palme wrote urgently to Eisenberg, "It is an absolute prerequisite that nothing disastrous happens at the NSA Congress[.] If your people start running absolutely wild on the Lowenstein angle, I fear that the attitude of the British will stiffen and there will be no progress."[65] The British were not yet fully committed to the International Student Conference formed in Stockholm, and Palme feared they might step back farther if the NSA followed Lowenstein's lead. The key to success was "to move forward slowly and cautiously, and above all, in closed ranks."[66]

Closing ranks was not Lowenstein's style. But despite his oratorical skills, he failed to persuade a majority of delegates to support a Western Union of Students.[67] Rather, delegates chose the nuanced language preferred by the Harvard group; they voted for "an international organic framework for cooperation, provided it gain the support of students from Latin America, Asia, the Middle East, Africa, and Europe." Fur-

vast disparity in resources, providing roughly one-fourth of the NSA domestic budget, which hovered at around $12,000.[4]

The CIA funded NSA delegations to a number of overseas meetings, among them the International Student Conference and meetings of the World Assembly of Youth and the World University Service, as well as special meetings, such as the Japanese International Student Conference, which was actually a fledgling attempt to build a national student union in Japan, intended to counter the IUS-affiliated Zengakuren.[5] It paid the NSA's dues to the ISC, among the highest in the conference, since dues were calculated on the basis of students represented, and the NSA claimed 800,000 to one million students.[6] In the single month of May 1954, the NSA international office submitted fourteen separate proposals to FYSA, consisting of only one or two pages each, all of which had been secretly negotiated ahead of time and were assured of success.[7]

Internationally, CIA funds flowed in increasing amounts to the ISC and its Coordinating Secretariat (COSEC). They supported a growing COSEC staff and administrative expenses; supplied travel funds for Supervision Commission meetings, whose members expanded from five to nine countries; and funded a COSEC publications program in French, Spanish, and English that included informal bulletins, *The Student* magazine, and special reports.[8] In 1954, the Research and Investigation Commission joined the list.

Each year, David Davis and John Simons at FYSA held secret meetings outside Leiden to discuss future funding with John Thompson, the COSEC administrative head, and with the NSA representative, first Dentzer, then Ingram.[9] In some cases, FYSA contracted directly with foreign students to work within a region, as Simons did with Enrique Ibarra from Paraguay, a Pax Romana member and trusted confidant of Helen Jean Rogers.[10] In addition, FYSA supported projects related to the NSA agenda that were routed through COSEC.

By 1954, Simons had become vexed by the fact that by funding a single delegate per country he put control in the hands of one person to interpret the annual ISC after he or she returned home. FYSA therefore increased its travel budget for the next ISC in Istanbul, making two awards available per country, at a cost of $66,823.90 (today more than half a million dollars), triple what was spent for the Copenhagen ISC.[11]

The total cost probably ran higher: Simons often financed Latin American travel directly through the New York office of Pan American Airlines.[12] Although COSEC dispensed most ISC travel funds, Simons kept considerable discretion in his own hands. He created five categories of eligibility, with priority reserved for unions with a demonstrated interest in the ISC.[13] Within two years, the annual cost of an ISC in today's dollars exceeded a million dollars. These expenditures are a far cry from the later claim that the CIA gave only a few travel grants to American students.

FYSA also abandoned its policy of requiring European national unions of students to pay their own travel expenses to the ISC. As the ISC began to meet outside Europe, the distances created fears of lower turnout by even the stalwart European members. Simons included in his COSEC grant award increased money for European student unions to travel to an ISC. In between the now annual conferences, Simons awarded NSA funding to bring European students to the United States to meet with the NSA president and tour campuses, either as a reward to allies or to shore up lukewarm support for the ISC.[14]

With financial resources assured, Ingram and others worried far more about finding qualified personnel. By 1952, as World War II veterans left campus, few students even at the graduate level had the "sophistication" of Douglass Cater, Thomas Farmer, James Grant, or William Polk. Individual campuses had begun to protest the overreliance on Harvard students for international affairs assignments, putting the International Commission under pressure to cast a wider net for delegations and individual projects.

Had CIA funding really been aimed, as the Agency later maintained, at facilitating an agenda determined by the NSA, personnel would not have been an issue. Scores of American students were available for goodwill tours or to attend international conferences, regional seminars, work camps, and other joint ventures. One student body president, eager to attend the Istanbul conference, experienced a typical rebuff by the international vice president: "Istanbul is a very fluid and tricky affair, and we must be certain that our delegates are fully aware of the intricacies of the game."[15]

But prospective personnel needed to be screened, trained, tested, and able to pass background security checks. In 1953, the CIA established a recruiting vehicle, the International Student Relations Seminar. The ISRS (pronounced IS-RIS) offered a six-week summer course for selected students.[16] The CIA asked Ted Harris, then at Princeton University, to direct the seminar. Since his NSA presidency, Harris had worked for the ISS-WUS in Geneva, and for John Simons in the Middle East in the summer of 1952.

To assist Harris, the CIA selected Paul Sigmund, a Harvard graduate student in government. The twenty-three-year-old Sigmund was a smart, savvy man with a gift for argument. He explained his willingness to cooperate with the CIA in pragmatic terms: "It kept me out of Korea."[17] With the reinstitution of the military draft, CIA-engineered deferments became valuable commodities, although usually a student had to serve six months of basic training and agree to continue working with the CIA beyond his year in office.

Unlike many newcomers, Sigmund had prior experience with the NSA. As a Georgetown University undergraduate in 1948, he had moved in Catholic circles, campaigned for an NSA chapter on campus, and attended an NSA Congress. Before joining the ISRS staff, Sigmund worked as Ingram's assistant. He handled everything from an early German student-exchange program, openly financed by the U.S. Department of State to bring leaders of the new German student union, VDS, to the United States, to foreign student hospitality at the NSA congress.[18] In fact, after extensive discussions about personnel problems with Ingram and Simons, Sigmund crafted the proposal for the summer seminar.

The ISRS applicant pool included self-selected students and those who were tapped by the NSA old guard. Talent scouts included the CIA's "P source" (professors), who identified students suited for work in psychological warfare against the Soviets, campus administrators, and deans of students. Personal interviews were mandatory. As one NSA officer put it: "The interview is . . . the only way of uncovering personality difficulties as well as superficial thought processes."[19] Kenneth Holland and others on the FYSA board served as the selection committee. Occasionally, the NSA argued for the admission of a student to the seminar for political reasons whom it had no intention of recruiting.

The six-week ISRS session, initially held at Harvard, and later outside NSA headquarters in Philadelphia, gave the CIA time to conduct background security checks. Some students were excluded from future employment by their politics or personality. Others were rejected if their parents had politically suspect backgrounds (that is, too leftist) or had engaged in dubious business activities. Reluctant but talented recruits might be enticed to give up their summer in return for vague promises of future overseas postings. But such offers had to be kept indefinite until security investigations were complete and the students had been tested.

Students who enrolled expecting a general course on international relations found the curriculum disappointingly narrow. It emphasized IUS-ISC relations and specific national student unions, their politics, factions, and personalities. Seminar participants occasionally heard from academic specialists such as Harvard's China expert John Fairbank and German expert Carl Friedrich, but by and large professors were there simply to give the seminar a patina of academic respectability.[20]

For the most part NSA elders served as faculty.[21] John Simons taught the history of IUS-ISC relations. FYSA director David Davis lectured on the Soviets and youth activities. Helen Jean Rogers, Frank Fisher, Robert Williams, Paris-based David Duberman, and other NSA veterans handled various geographic areas, often lecturing on multiple countries and topics.[22] They imparted a distinctly NSA-centric perspective on such matters as IUS calls for unity meetings (invidious) or invitations to tour the Soviet Union (harmful). Harris and Sigmund used written essays, role-playing, and seminar discussions to determine whether a student strayed outside the preferred positions.

Of all the mechanisms created by the NSA-CIA team, the summer seminar was the most successful. Critics who argue over whether the CIA controlled the NSA miss the point of a sophisticated recruitment program. As both Allen Dulles and Thomas Farmer have emphasized, the most effective agents are those who share a community of interest: men and women who passionately support the same goals and objectives as the CIA.[23]

The critical question is rather who crossed the threshold into the NSA-CIA fraternity and who was excluded. Once candidates became part of an NSA-CIA operation, signed the security oath, and started reporting to a CIA case officer, the boundary between student organization and spy agency blurred. The longer a witting student stayed involved, and many logged five years in return for escaping the draft, the more thoroughly the boundary dissolved, making it impossible to determine where the NSA's interests stopped and the CIA's began.

As the operation grew, the CIA expanded its pool of recruits to include students studying overseas on Rhodes, Rotary, or Fulbright scholarships, and people who had a demonstrated interest in international affairs, expertise in a country or region, or valuable language skills. In 1958, the NSA obtained Fulbright applications from the Institute of International Education, which were to be kept secret, locked in a filing cabinet and returned.[24] The CIA eventually slipped young career staff officers who worked at headquarters, although not necessarily with youth and students, into the summer seminar to be educated in the nuances of ISC politics and prepared to represent NSA overseas.

As a condition of acceptance into ISRS, students were required to attend the late-summer NSA Congress after completing the course. They mingled with delegates and helped ensure that the Congress passed desired international resolutions. They also steered delegates toward CIA-preferred candidates for elective office. The ISRS graduates did not have to be witting; most readily deferred to signals from ISRS leadership. While the CIA identified preferred candidates, plans sometime went awry. In its first year, ISRS saved the day when it unexpectedly produced a back-up candidate.

Leonard Bebchick was the son of a tobacco distributor from New Bedford, Massachusetts, with no previous experience with the NSA. A graduate of Cornell University who originally majored in pre-med but quit after setting a record for the "highest glass breakage bill in freshman chemistry," Bebchick had devoted his extracurricular time to the student newspaper, *The Cornell Sun*, and the campus radio station rather than student government.[25] He became smitten with political science courses taught by Professors Mario Einaudi and Clinton Rossiter, and when he saw a flyer describing the summer seminar, Bebchick glimpsed an alternative to weeks spent in the gritty seaport of New Bedford. He applied, he remembered, primarily because "I wanted to travel abroad." After his ISRS acceptance, Bebchick simultaneously enrolled at Harvard University's summer school to pursue his new interest in international politics. A few weeks later, he ran for NSA office.[26]

Paul Sigmund recalls the circumstances.[27] At the last minute, the candidate backed by the CIA for international vice president could not run, and insiders cast about for an alternative. During the Congress, Bebchick had won kudos for advancing the NSA position on foreign student exchanges. The NSA opposed allowing short-term foreign student exchanges with members of the Soviet bloc, fearing that naive students would come away impressed with the communist system and not understand how tightly the Soviets controlled the agenda. (That the NSA offered foreign students the American equivalent of short-term exchanges by calling them campus tours seemed to escape everyone's attention.) In a heated committee session, Bebchick took on students from Swarthmore and Oberlin who argued that the NSA should support student exchanges regardless of their duration. Bebchick's passionate support for NSA policy signaled he was a team player and could advance the right arguments.

Today Bebchick is proud of his performance. "I confronted the argument bang on. I hit the ball out of the park." Another source of pride was going up against Allard Lowenstein, who sided with the students favoring short-term exchanges. After only "two or three months with NSA," Bebchick says, the CIA "thought my instincts were basically sound politically," and "they threw their weight to me." More humbly, Bebchick added that they were "sort of desperate."[28] Bebchick was elected vice president for international affairs.

Some time after Bebchick's election, Farmer invited him to the stately Mayflower Hotel, situated a few blocks from the White House. As Bebchick underwent the ritual of signing the security oath, he remembers Farmer stating that "each year we make two people witting, and they have the decision of whether or not they want to go along with it."[29]

Bebchick did not hesitate, he said in an interview, despite his total ignorance of the CIA. "I mean, they were as covert as anything could be in the Cold War." He recalls telling Farmer, "I'd studied with Hans Morgenthau and I'm all for this." (Morgenthau, a professor at the University of Chicago, was known for advocating realpolitik in international relations.) Bebchick today defends his participation: "We were doing God's work," he says, lightly pounding his fist on his law library table for emphasis. "We were not starry-eyed idealists; we were all pretty hardened people, all political types who had a realistic assessment of what the world was all about, and yet we felt we were doing God's work."[30] This mingling of religious fervor, a sense of a higher calling, the desire to fight communism, and a lack of moral qualms about working undercover, tied the students more firmly to the CIA than any security oath ever could.

At the Mayflower, Farmer told Bebchick that some in the CIA had resisted making him witting. "They went to Uncle Allen [Dulles], and he had to make the decision whether Bebchick should become witting or not," he said, speaking of himself in the third person. Bebchick speculated that his liberal positions on the *Cornell Sun*, where he argued in favor of China's admission to the U.N., among other issues, had created concern.[31]

The high-level reassurance from Dulles gave the liberal Bebchick a feeling of protection, as well as importance. "Here we were," says Bebchick, "out in international meetings condemning American policy being advocated by John Foster Dulles, the Republican secretary of state for Eisenhower and Allen Dulles's brother. We always felt comfortable about doing that because we knew our guy was Uncle Allen, and Uncle Allen would go and talk to brother John."[32]

The NSA needed more than secret protection from Uncle Allen to survive. It required bipartisan political support from top-level U.S. government officials to ward off attacks by right-wing conservatives and hard-line anticommunists, including Senator Joseph McCarthy, who was being fed information by J. Edgar Hoover, no fan of the CIA, which he felt infringed on his territory.[33] In the early 1950s, flamboyant McCarthy supporter Fulton Lewis, Jr., among others, picked up where Allen Crow from Detroit had left off in 1947, and accused the NSA of communist sympathies. On his weekday radio program, when Lewis wasn't advocating the impeachment of Harry Truman, declaring the U.N. a "colossal farce," or describing Europe as "full of Marxists and appeasers," he was ranting against the NSA.[34] Paradoxically, after years of wariness toward Catholics, NSA liberals began touting their prominence in the NSA as evidence that charges of communist penetration were false.[35] Key senators, congressmen, and even presidents credentialed the NSA by sending congratulatory telegrams to the annual congresses.[36]

During his term (1953–54), Bebchick also recalled Farmer telling him that the NSA "was presented to the National Security Council," or a similar body, as an example of "a highly successful CIA-controlled front in the American battle against communism."[37] While Bebchick's use of the phrase "CIA-controlled front" slips out effortlessly in conversation, this kind of language makes other NSA-CIA veterans cringe. Nothing is more vehemently denied than the notion that the CIA controlled the NSA or its international offspring. The report Bebchick referenced was most likely one to the Committee on International Information Activities, commissioned by President Eisenhower at the beginning of his term.[38]

Farmer misled Bebchick on one crucial point: that only two NSA officers were witting. While it was technically true that only two *elected* NSA officials were witting, Bebchick was stepping into an ongoing CIA operation, one with career opportunities and a well-established, if subtle, hierarchy. At a minimum, during Bebchick's term, the NSA-CIA team consisted of Cord Meyer, Jr., and Farmer, full-time career officers at CIA headquarters; Simons, a CIA career officer at FYSA; Ingram, who replaced Dentzer on COSEC; David Duberman, the NSA representative in Paris; and Ted Harris and Paul Sigmund of ISRS. Dentzer, Bill Ellis, Helen Jean Rogers, and other HIACOM desk officers also took specific CIA assignments.[39]

By the time Bebchick assumed office, the CIA had additional safeguards in place to ensure fidelity from elected officers. One was financial: Bebchick was told, as were all future NSA international vice presidents, that his salary was not guaranteed. The NSA would "carry me for six weeks," he related, "and then I would have to go out and raise money."[40] But he was not to worry because "there were places to look for money." On advice from Ingram, Bebchick contacted a "Mr. Smith" from Texas, who promptly agreed to fund his salary.[41] This provision made it appear to the uninitiated that the International Commission had to fund itself or go out of business. In practice, it further insulated the international program from prying eyes.

The other safeguard was a new position inside the International Commission. In early 1953, FYSA began funding an assistant to the international vice president. The first assistant, Edward Gable from the University of Southern California, was identified by one of his professors. Ingram traveled to California to interview Gable, who knew nothing about the NSA but accepted the offer. At the time, Ingram's secretary, Catherine (Kitty) Fischer, remembered feeling displaced. "I just couldn't understand why we needed another person."[42]

Gable might work for Ingram, but soon after he took the position, he received a reminder of who held the purse strings. In a written account, "The Day John Simons Was Here," Gable described Simons's thorough scrutiny of the international office. "I must admit that by the time we had gone through the rooms I was beginning to feel as if it were a congressional investigation," he told Ingram.[43] Simons also reviewed the activities of HIACOM, which was equally unexpected since technically HIACOM was a committee of the Harvard Student Council, and Simons funded individuals, not HIACOM per se.

The CIA relationship with the NSA also was solidified by the natural deference that students then exhibited to their seniors: freshmen to sophomore, junior to senior. Typically, top NSA officers were recent college graduates, but close enough in age to others on the NSA-CIA team to create an atmosphere of camaraderie. Bebchick noted that NSA veteran Helen Jean Rogers immediately took him under her wing. He regularly stopped by her apartment near campus, where they would have tea and "she would fill me in."[44]

During his term, Bebchick also deferred to former NSA president Bill Dentzer. Under normal circumstances, as the elected official in charge of the NSA international program, Bebchick could expect to lead the U.S. delegation to the ISC. Instead, he asked Dentzer whether he should attend.[45] While Dentzer answered in the affirmative, he informed Bebchick that other important decisions were to be in more senior hands. Bebchick, in turn, relayed these to Bill Ellis, writing, "You will be in charge of making all final decisions on administrative, financial matters." Rogers would be "more or less in charge of the policy end of the affair."[46]

Despite this deference, Bebchick insists today that he felt like a free agent. "We were given general guidelines and briefings, but basically they relied on our good judgment. I would take guidance. I would listen. I would generally go along. If I thought it was crazy, I would say no."[47] Asked if he could remember advice that he rejected, Bebchick could not. But he went on to contrast his year in office to his later experience with the CIA during the World Youth Festival in 1959 where policy control was more stringent.[48]

Within the NSA, Bebchick learned to be more secretive. After one meeting of the international advisory board, he told James Edwards, the president, that "Helen [Jean Rogers] and Bill [Dentzer] expressed extreme [underlined four times] displeasure over certain aspects of the consolidated financial statement.[49] Furthermore, "they were shocked to find the sources of income explicitly stated, including exact contributions from the Foundation for Youth and Student Affairs, the Committee for Free Asia, and William Smith." NSA policy, he reminded the also witting Edwards, was never "to make public the exact amount of the contribution."[50]

Bebchick also reported the "most serious slip": the identification of FYSA funds in the financial report. Rogers and Dentzer told him it was "unwise and dangerous to reveal the exact amount of support, particularly when such aid constitutes such a predominant portion of the IC's budget." Bebchick's watchdogs had pointed out the financial data were "exactly what the IUS has been dying to get their hands on for years. They now have the documentation to establish a close, if not organic, relationship between the Foundation [FYSA] and the IC [International Commission]." Rogers and Dentzer warned that the disclosures raised the "question of policy control" and could have "domestic repercussions, as well as disastrous international ones."[51]

These statements are particularly illuminating: they leave no doubt that Helen Jean Rogers and Bill Dentzer understood that the risks of public disclosure were not limited to IUS enemies in Prague or Moscow; they violated the NSA constitution.

How is it that no one noticed the burgeoning operation or the influx of so many new resources? Only one adult adviser, Dennis Trueblood, from the dean's office at the University of Indiana, who chaired the NSA Advisory Committee, ever officially questioned the financial arrangements. When he submitted his resignation after the 1952 Congress, he laid out five problem areas within the organization, topped by "international policy and fund control. Being a voluntary association of student governments, NSA has a policy of accepting funds with 'no strings attached.' However, when funds are accepted, and the source not published, there is immediate question as to the 'strings attached.'"[52]

Since Trueblood was sympathetic to the danger of the IUS, he suggested that external educators review all policies and funding sources. "Such a plan would enable the educational world to have representatives aware of NSA internal operations in this field and would at the same time provide for a certain amount of secrecy in the operation of certain phases of the international program."[53]

In response, Ingram appeared to strengthen the oversight of the international program by establishing a new International Advisory Board (IAB). In fact he further insulated it from scrutiny. Ingram made sure that old hands outnumbered non-witting appointees. When the (probably) unwitting IAB chair, Sylvia Bacon, prepared the 1954–55 fiscal repuit to the NSA Congress plenary session, it included the following statement: "The money received to finance the 1954–55 operation of the International Commission is not tainted. The Commission has not sold its soul to either right or left wing groups."[54] No one demanded evidence or even a financial accounting.

When nonwitting undergraduate veterans of the NSA looked back, many concluded that the one area the CIA could not manipulate was officer elections. But they pictured CIA agents as outsiders with no connection to the NSA. In some years, candidates for NSA office were witting *before* they announced their candidacies. In 1954, both top officers had been recruited beforehand.

That year the candidate for president was Harry Lunn, a brash, opinionated University of Michigan graduate, former editor of the *Michigan Daily*, with little NSA experience but a developing taste for travel and the good life. A few months before his graduation, Edwards and Bebchick tried to recruit Lunn for the ISRS summer seminar. Lunn wanted assurances of a foreign post afterward. Neither Edwards nor Bebchick could make that decision; they cabled Lunn that an overseas position was "contingent on summer performance."[55] On May 23, after another exchange of letters and phone calls, Lunn declined the offer.[56] A week later, he changed his mind. He later told a *New York Times* journalist that the CIA recruited him during this time, which explains his change of heart.[57]

John Simons had sweetened the NSA proposition. Knowing that Lunn needed to earn a living during the summer, Simons awarded him a grant to produce a booklet titled "How to Run a Campus International Program."[58] While it paid the bills, Lunn was far from enthusiastic. According to Bebchick, "Harry hated that assignment, just hated it."[59] Yet the project gave Lunn carte blanche to travel around the country and survey campus-based international projects. Presumably, it gave the CIA time to complete its security investigation, normally conducted during the ISRS seminar. By the end of the summer, the booklet was complete and Lunn—with CIA support and a mere three months of contact with the NSA—was elected president.

Still, Bebchick says Lunn came close to losing the election. One of his main opponents was a student from Southern California, Kay Wallace Longshore, a man whom Bebchick described as "open at the collar, rough and ready, independent-minded." During the first roll call, Lunn was trailing Longshore. Bebchick hustled over to Pete Weston from the Great Northwest region, "and I put my hand down around his shoulder . . . and I said it would make a great deal of difference to the future of our association" if he could get his delegation to support Lunn.[60]

Bebchick continued, "They caucused, and changed their vote. Harry won by the skin of his teeth, 4 or 5 votes, and that's what did it." Bebchick and Weston were not close friends, but Bebchick believes Weston responded favorably because "I was the leadership," and the leadership had asked him to switch candidates.[61]

Lunn rose rapidly on the CIA career ladder, eventually becoming a case officer and later FYSA director. His personality, which former colleagues at the *Michigan Daily* describe as one of not suffering fools gladly, or at all, evoked strong feelings from those who dealt with him. A few found him charismatic and charming; many found him arrogant, overbearing, and occasionally ruthless. A later NSA president considered him a snake. Friends say Lunn "loved the life of the spy."[62]

The year Lunn squeaked by as president, Paul Sigmund won the position of international affairs vice president. By then, Sigmund had been witting for several years, as Ingram's assistant (1952–53), ISRS assistant director (1953), and ISRS director (1954).[63] Over time, the CIA suffered a few defeats. But by then, other mechanisms were in place. These included the security oath, the absence of a guaranteed salary, an assistant who reported to the CIA, and the presence of a savvy overseas team that could bypass top officers.

While Lunn may have hated his summer assignment, the survey of existing programs shaped the signature achievement of his presidency. The resulting Foreign Student Leadership Project (FSLP) adopted a direct approach to grooming overseas leaders. The project brought to the United States hand-picked foreign students from Asia, Africa, Latin America, and the Middle East for a year of education, with paid tuition and living expenses.[64] On campus, the scholarship students were encouraged to participate in student government. The NSA hoped the students would return home and create a student union or take over an existing one.

The FSLP brought the CIA into dangerous territory. The 1947 statute authorizing the CIA placed strictures against operations within the United States. The project, located in Cambridge, was risky enough for the CIA to seek a bona-fide philanthropy as a partner. After a year of negotiations, the Ford Foundation agreed to help fund the project. John Simons became secretary of the FSLP board, and David Davis served ex-officio. Without any representation from the Ford Foundation, the FYSA board reviewed applicants submitted by witting staff.[65] The CIA promoted Ted Harris to direct the FSLP.

The program rarely worked as intended: few foreign students wanted to stay for a single year, fewer still became enamored of student government. Those who returned home typically had lost their political base. But the FSLP did bring dozens of talented students to the United States, and many of these later became prominent in their home countries or in international organizations, including a future U.N. secretary general.

Ironically, the CIA had to seek a presidential executive order to prevent other U.S. intelligence agencies from raiding this tempting pool of talent.[66] CIA career officers who dealt with FSLP acknowledge that the bar on recruitment of a foreign student while on U.S. soil did not apply after the student returned home, but they are coy about particulars.[67]

Before his term expired Sigmund visited Paris in June 1955 for an annual CIA-NSA discussion of personnel assignments, and then attended a lavish party for James Edwards, the former president, who was spending the year in France as an NSA representative. Sigmund gaped as he saw that every table "was equipped with its own faucet running wine—not water."[68] It was an apt metaphor. The CIA spigot flowed not with wine or water but with clandestine funds, and the result could be just as intoxicating. Only in retrospect would those involved in the NSA operation realize that these were halcyon days.

Stalin's death in 1953 unleashed new political forces in Eastern Europe. Two years later, nationalist leaders in Asia, the Middle East, Africa, and Latin America shook up the international system by refusing to choose sides in the Cold War. The problems faced by the NSA-CIA team became more difficult, and less subject to technical fixes, however generous the resources. The tendency to reduce problems to programs or projects persisted but proved inadequate to the challenge of combating powerful new political currents. The NSA's witting staff struggled to keep up with the changes.

9

THE SPIRIT OF BANDUNG

ON MAY 23, 1956, Harry Lunn boarded an Air India flight in Calcutta en route to Jakarta, the capital of Indonesia.[1] Lunn and other passengers were headed for the Asian-African Students Conference in Bandung, one of the country's most beautiful cities, hosted by the Indonesian student union. Lunn, who had completed his year as NSA president, carried journalist credentials from the *Christian Science Monitor,* but he still worked for the CIA.[2] His mission was not to report on the conference but to sabotage its aims. The hot political conclave that Frank Fisher had warned about in 1952 was about to take place, and it would shake up the student world.

The year before, on April 18, 1955, another Bandung conference had convened that was to change the dynamics of the Cold War, when the prime ministers of India, Pakistan, Ceylon, Indonesia, and Burma had hosted a week-long Asian-African Conference. Before then, no Asian (or African) leader would have dreamt of calling an international conference without a European sponsor. The display of independence transformed the region's understanding of itself and exhilarated racial minorities throughout the world.[3] The conference also marked the emergence of the Chinese on the foreign policy stage, although neither U.S. policy makers nor the CIA yet viewed their new visibility as a sign of a potential split with the Soviet Union.

At the conference President Sukarno of Indonesia, President Nasser of Egypt, Prime Minister Nehru of India, and Foreign Minister Zhou Enlai of China presented a new doctrine of nonalignment in the Cold War. Nehru told the assembled delegates, "We do not agree with the communist teachings, we do not agree with the anti-communist teachings, because they are both based on wrong principles."[4] He then asked how countries dividing into two blocs could make the world safer. Nehru urged the twenty-nine African and Asian nations in attendance to remain neutral in the confrontation between the Soviet Union and the United States.[5]

The declaration of principles adopted at the end of the conference included nonaggression, respect for national sovereignty, noninterference in internal affairs, racial equality, and peaceful coexistence. In what became known informally as "the spirit of Bandung" delegates issued a challenge to the West by denouncing colonialism and imperialism in all its manifestations, political, social, and economic.[6]

That first Bandung conference had thrown the United States into turmoil. Its mere announcement had frightened and angered the Eisenhower administration, though some State Department diplomats derided it as the Darktown Strutters Ball—a slur on both its racial composition and its regional ambitions.[7] Up to this point, foreign countries had been seen as either with or against the United States, a position made explicit by Secretary of State John Foster Dulles.[8] The secretary viewed neutrality as "immoral and short-sighted."[9] Both liberal and conservative Cold Warriors viewed nonalignment (neutrality) as a victory for the Soviets. A diplomatic journey to Moscow or Beijing by an Asian or African leader, often a display of newly won independence, risked the withdrawal of U.S. economic assistance or other sanctions.

The popular press had also whipped up public opinion against the 1955 Bandung conference.[10] On January 1, months before the meeting, *Newsweek* proclaimed that an "Afro-Asian combination turned [*sic*] by Communists was being contemplated" and must be stopped.[11] Another *Newsweek* article invoked fears of a "yellow peril," and asked, "Asia: Can the West Hold Back the Tides?"[12] Columnist Walter Lippmann warned that the conference meant to enforce the doctrine of Asia for Asians.[13] The danger that people of color would form an alliance against a minority white world triggered much of the hysteria.

If, in 1956, the student delegates aboard Air India seemed tense, it might have been because of the memory of what happened a year earlier. The flight from Hong Kong to Jakarta scheduled to carry Zhou Enlai to the conference blew up shortly after takeoff. A last-minute plane change enabled him to survive the assassination attempt. Two bombs, later found in the wreckage of the plane, killed sixteen passengers.[14] Though

CIA involvement in the bombing was suspected at the time, it was never proved, despite a boast by an agent who claimed to be complicit. An investigation by the U.S. Congress revealed that CIA station chiefs in Asia had recommended the assassination of an Asian leader in order to disrupt the Bandung conference, but top CIA officials allegedly rejected the suggestion.[15] But the mere fact that intelligence officials considered such an extreme measure reveals the depth of America's anxiety about the new alliance.

In the near term, the original Bandung conference had less impact than the administration had feared—the result, according to Eisenhower's psychological warfare adviser C. D. Jackson, of "heavy lifting by Allen Dulles' boys."[16] The United States had worked to undermine it through its closest allies in the region, especially Japan and the Philippines (Americans could observe the conference but not participate). The strategy involved diluting resolutions to make them more palatable to the West and insisting that Soviet aggression be condemned along with Western imperialism. Junior CIA operatives such as Harry Lunn intended to replicate this feat at what was being called the Little Bandung conference.

Lunn feared the conference would reposition the International Union of Students as "the only real friends of students in general and colonial students in particular."[17] If the conference created an Asian-African student federation affiliated with the IUS, corresponding defections from the International Student Conference could turn the ISC back into a strictly Western enterprise. Lunn also dreaded, as the Eisenhower administration did, the development of a "third force of neutralists in the student world."[18]

During the students' flight to Jakarta, an aura of suspicion and distrust hung over the plane.[19] NSA allies from India and the Philippines had been locked in a months-long battle for control of the conference. Some Bandung-bound delegations were internally divided, their polarized views contained under a thin veneer of civility. Infighting among Indian student groups reached such a pitch that Prime Minister Nehru had stepped in to allocate slots to contending groups, including the IUS-affiliated All India Students Federation.[20] Delegates en route to Bandung knew they were heading for a showdown.

The NSA-CIA team adapted strategies used at the first Bandung conference to sabotage the new one. The NSA publicly embraced conference goals, while working behind the scenes to disrupt the proceedings. Since neither the NSA nor the European unions had been invited, effective sabotage depended on the prowess of proxies.

Not all those proxies were adroit. British authorities in Hong Kong, citing security concerns, delayed for days the ship carrying the fifteen-person Chinese student delegation to Indonesia. The delegation finally returned to China and flew to Indonesia. The stalling tactics threw the Chinese delegation into chaos—no one met them at the airport at Jakarta, and new accommodations had to be found. According to one Southeast Asia specialist, by the time the Chinese students reached Bandung, they were "incensed with the British."[21]

Ironically, the NSA's recurrent efforts to cement ties with Indonesia student leaders in PPMI created some of the problems Lunn would face in Bandung. In 1953, Bill Ellis had recommended that the NSA invite PPMI leaders Aminuddin and Radjab to tour American campuses. Their presence in the United States from late 1954 to April 1955 removed both students from home just as the spirit of Bandung was galvanizing the region.[22] In their absence, left-wing students from Indonesia, Egypt, and China seized control of conference planning. Once Radjab and Aminuddin returned, they regained control of the Indonesia student union, but more militant students remained in charge of the international planning committee.[23]

Throughout the previous year, Lunn had scrambled to gather intelligence about the conference. After his presidency ended in September, he won a coveted spot on a COSEC-sponsored five-person team touring Asia. The delegation had a multiracial cast, and included participants from the Gold Coast (now Ghana), South Africa, Guatemala, and Italy, although a closer examination showed that it mirrored the Anglo-Scandinavian bloc that dominated the secretariat. The Ghanian student held British citizenship, and the representative from South Africa was white.[24] The Italian, Vittorio Bono, and the Guatemalan delegate, Eduardo Palomo, were Catholic activists trusted by the NSA.

The overt purpose of the eighteen-thousand-mile tour was to document educational conditions in nine countries: East Pakistan, Burma, Thailand, Vietnam, Hong Kong, the Philippines, Indonesia, Malaya, and Ceylon.[25] But the trip also permitted Lunn to gather intelligence on the upcoming conference. Which countries had received invitations? Who planned to attend? What were their politics? Overall, he hoped to assess the extent of these countries' independence from the West.

Both overt and covert missions paid propaganda dividends. Press conferences and press releases in each country announced the COSEC team's presence and touted the ISC's concern for educational opportunities. If Asian interlocutors raised the issue of Western imperialism, Lunn deflected them by pointing to Soviet imperialism in Eastern Europe, a line of attack also used by Western allies at the 1955 conference.[26] Frank Wisner's Mighty Wurlitzer reinforced the COSEC tour with a regional media campaign. For example, the CIA-funded Asian Students' News Service highlighted political bias in the committee planning.[27]

Just in case targeted audiences were not getting the message, more than six hundred articles on the team's travels were published in national and local student magazines, newsletters, and bulletins. Longer articles appeared in the COSEC publication *Student Mirror* and were widely reprinted and translated into French, Spanish, and Arabic. As usual, the CIA footed the bill for the paper blitz.[28]

After the Asian tour ended, Lunn worked frantically to complete an eighty-page report, "Independence and the Student," in time for Bandung's opening session on May 26. The report framed anticolonial issues from a *students as students* perspective.[29] On May 22, Osman Sid Ahmed Ismail, a COSEC associate secretary from Sudan, lugged the fresh propaganda arsenal on board an Air India flight from Paris to Jakarta. In Bandung, Ismail distributed his cargo and became a source of information for Lunn.[30]

When Lunn stepped off the plane into the tropical heat of Jakarta, he faced many unknowns, including who was heading the Chinese delegation. Lunn finally identified the leader as Chien Ta Wei, "an aging (probably over 35), balding," and, in his view, "sinister" figure.[31] Lunn presumed the Egyptian delegate would be a supporter of Nasser, one of the heroes of the senior Bandung conference, but he had no specific information. When a thirty-eight-year-old professor from Cairo University, Dr. Hassan Ashmawi, arrived with "a 10 June ticket to Peking in his pocket," Lunn concluded the Egyptian delegate was not about to upset the Chinese.[32] He chalked up another loss.

The NSA was not without friends. By the time Lunn arrived in

Jakarta, where the all-important credentials committee met to certify attendees, twenty-four-year-old Guillermo de Vega, president of the Student Council Association of the Philippines (SCAP), a conference participant and key NSA ally, was effectively throwing sand in its gears.[33] Days of wrangling ensued, as one delegation after another arrived to pick up credentials only to have its bona fides as a representative student union challenged by de Vega. Since the conference could not begin until the committee determined its membership, the scheduled opening day came and went while the credentials committee battled on.

The delay served Western interests. Had the Bandung conference begun as planned on May 26, pro-IUS delegations might have controlled the proceedings and created a new, IUS-affiliated regional organization since they were among the first to arrive. The NSA had to scramble to get sympathetic delegations to Bandung. On May 14, John Simons at FYSA authorized COSEC to make emergency travel grants to twenty ISC members.[34] The African list included East Africa (regional association), the Gold Coast, Senegal, Sudan, Sierra Leone, and South Africa. Asian unions included Burma, Ceylon, Hong Kong, India, the Philippines, and Vietnam. (Australia and New Zealand had also been invited.) The list for the Middle East and North Africa reflected the dearth of choices, but included the new Lebanese student union, Turkey, Tunisia, and Israel.[35] Quite a few delegations spurned the offer, however.

The need to swell conference ranks with friendly faces became so dire that the NSA began working its way through Middle Eastern and Asian foreign student associations based in the United States. How artfully the NSA used its public identity as a union that stood in solidarity with the aspirations of Asian and African students to cloak its sabotage agenda is illustrated by the case of Afghanistan.

Eleven days before the conference was scheduled to open, NSA international vice president Clive Gray contacted Mohammed Ghausi, president of the U.S.-based Associated Students of Afghanistan. Gray told Ghausi, then an engineering student at the University of California, Berkeley, that Harry Lunn had found "widespread enthusiasm" for the Asian-African Students Conference on his recent tour, and wanted to help spread the word. Some student unions, Gray dissembled, "have been inadvertently omitted from the invited list." He suggested that Ghausi might want to write for an invitation.[36]

Of course, neither Lunn nor Gray was excited about the conference and neither believed the lack of an invitation to be inadvertent. But it was a clever move. Afghanistan had no formal student union, so Ghausi could arrive in Bandung without having to ward off rivals.

Anticipating Ghausi's favorable response, Gray took the next step. "Harry Lunn said that he imagined the financial question would be a major one."[37] Perhaps Ghausi could approach his current financial backers; in addition, the NSA would assist. Thus did Ghausi, just days away from completing his undergraduate degree, find himself on a flight across the Pacific, excused from several final exams by accommodating Berkeley faculty.

Ghausi, a top science student who later became dean of engineering at the University of California, Davis, today describes himself in the mid-1950s as not at all political. He knew nothing of either COSEC or the IUS, but after he arrived in Bandung, he came to understand Western fears about the conference. Comfortably pro-West, Ghausi had no use for the Soviets, particularly since his grandfather, a general in the Afghan army, had died fighting the Russians near the Soviet-Afghan border. Ghausi said he needed no prompting on how to vote.[38]

What made Ghausi and other students contacted by Gray so effective was that, however anti-Soviet their outlook, they also spoke against colonialism and imperialism. In fact, both Ghausi and a similarly deployed Iranian were so convincing that the IUS representatives believed them to be against COSEC and the ISC as well. This erroneous perception caused considerable mirth for Simons, Gray, and Lunn. "Big joke," Gray wrote, ". . . since we were responsible for getting both delegates there."[39]

While pro-West delegates scrambled to reach the Bandung conference, Guillermo de Vega kept the credentials committee in turmoil. The conference newspaper, *Bandung Spirit*, finally lambasted de Vega publicly for his obstreperous behavior, and reported that he "demanded many small questions, in order to postpone any agreements; one day he demanded the minutes, another day a permanent girl secretary, and when all this was there, he said he could not participate in the meeting because he had another appointment."[40]

But de Vega's stalling tactics worked. The credentials committee finally threw up its hands and admitted to the conference all delegations that reached Bandung. A communiqué affirmed the nonpartisan nature of the conference, and renounced affiliation with any international student bloc.[41] An immensely pleased Lunn speculated, correctly, that the Indonesian government had played a decisive role in the capitulation.[42] The cost of providing for the idle delegates was roughly $7,000 a day.[43]

In fact, Indonesian president Sukarno was in the United States, on his first visit since Indonesia achieved independence in 1949, when all this was happening.[44] On May 17, Sukarno addressed a joint session of the U.S. Congress, stressing the similarity between the American and Indonesian wars of independence, and praising Paul Revere. His speech received widespread praise from politicians and the U.S. media.[45] Afterward, the Eisenhower administration promised Indonesia $25 million in development aid.[46] With money and prestige at stake, Sukarno had no interest in deliberately antagonizing the United States.

On May 30, the Asian-African Students Conference finally convened at Bandung Technical University. Twenty thousand people, including twenty-seven official delegations, crammed into the Varia Theatre to hear former Indonesian prime minister Ali Sastroamidjojo welcome the delegates. Sastroamidjojo, a leading organizer of the 1955 conference, recapitulated its themes and set the tone for the days ahead. He urged the students to break down "the remnants of colonialism," and stressed that Asians and Africans "must be allowed to find our own approach to the solutions of our problems."[47]

The Algerian student leader Mohammed Benyahia elaborated on these themes, reviewing the history of modern colonialism and tracing it to the 1884–85 Berlin Conference at which the European Great Powers had convened "to share out African and Asian countries among themselves."[48] As his chronological tour of history reached the first Bandung conference, his declarations elicited thunderous applause: "The European Empire is from now on an empty concept." It "is no longer entitled to take the leadership in the international sphere." The times "are gone when racial discrimination and oppression were the pillars of the world."

Benyahia could not resist a dig at the ISC *students as students* philosophy. "Allow me to say here that the only fruitful means of cooperating with Algerian or colonial students is to help them take off the colonial yoke."[49]

Soon afterward, the assembly buzzed with political demands. The Chinese wanted to debate their claim to Taiwan. Indian delegates wanted to raise the Kashmir border dispute with Pakistan. Others lobbied for China's right to a seat on the U.N. Security Council. A Syrian delegate took the floor and proclaimed, "The problem of Palestine is the world drama of the Twentieth Century." The result, according to one observer, was bedlam.[50] The opening session quickly adjourned.

When the delegates reconvened, de Vega gave a speech that Lunn viewed as the defining moment of the conference. "Are we still tied to the apron strings of our school masters?" de Vega thundered. If they opened the floor to political issues, "then we have to discuss the questions of North Korea, South Korea, North and South Vietnam, Red China, Taiwan, Kashmir, reparations, etc., etc." He asked the delegates to consider only those issues that bound them to one another. He then lobbed a rhetorical bomb. "Let us condemn colonialism, all right, but let us be wary that we should not fall prey to a more superb, more colossal and more gigantic colonial power of the East." He declared the meeting "a hoax and a farce" and walked out. Nine other delegations followed. All but de Vega returned.[51]

Mohammed Ghausi joined with the minority pro-Western group "to try and calm things down."[52] He told delegates, "[We may] belong to diverse cultures, different traditions, we speak different languages but one thing is common in us all — the desire to promote understanding, knowledge and friendship." Ghausi stressed the debt "we who are privileged" owe our societies and suggested a focus on economic development to achieve "freedom for all, racial equality and peace."[53]

While de Vega's histrionics gave the West a fresh round of publicity, how effective his antics were was questionable. The Philippines had the unlucky distinction of being a former U.S. colony, making it difficult for de Vega to shed his image as an obedient American mouthpiece. Even the *New York Times*, whose coverage emphasized anticommunist victories, felt compelled to report charges that de Vega was "under instruction of the United States State Department."[54] Lunn's maneuvering was so obvious that the same article also reported charges that "U.S. newspaper men covering the conference actually were a front."[55] The Indonesian communist newspaper reported a secret meeting of U.S. embassy officials and a Japanese and a Filipino delegate in Room 73 of the Savoy Homann Hotel.[56]

After de Vega stormed out of the meeting, an Indian delegate close to the U.S. embassy in New Delhi, Pran Nath Sabharwal, stepped in. Sabharwal represented the National Union of Students India (NUSI) and had traveled to Bandung on a COSEC grant.[57] He gave an eloquent speech praising Gandhi, Nehru, and other great anticolonial leaders. He advocated solidarity with the fight against colonialism. He then advanced ISC principles and urged student organizations to be nonpartisan and dedicate themselves to economic reconstruction and educational opportunities.[58]

Despite Sabharwal's entreaties, Lunn was unsure whether Western allies could prevent the creation of an Asian-African student federation.[59] In his opening remarks, the Egyptian delegate Hassan Ashmawi had laid out such a federation's goals and objectives. He emphasized cultural cooperation, and his remarks, at least on the surface, were indistinguishable from rhetoric that might be heard during an ISC meeting.[60]

Yet the proposal for the creation of a regional student federation never came to the plenary floor. Lunn concluded that the Chinese had retreated, perhaps because they sensed defeat or because they did not care as much about the Egyptian initiative as he had presumed. However the proposal died, its death gave the NSA and COSEC a much-heralded propaganda victory, regardless of whether they had anything to do with it. Lunn had made stopping the proposed federation *the* political test of the conference, and he intended to capitalize on its demise.

A last-minute bombshell nearly turned the Western victories into a defeat for the United States. A resolution surfaced that condemned racism "wherever it occurred" and linked racial segregation in South Africa and the United States.[61] However liberal Lunn and other NSA officers considered themselves on civil rights and issues of race, they found the parallel outrageous. After some frantic behind-the-scenes scrambling, the linkage was dropped.

Despite political differences, conference delegates adopted the final resolutions by acclamation. They overwhelmingly supported the Algerian national liberation movement against France, notwithstanding lobbying by the French. The students in Bandung stood with the Arabs on the question of Palestinian refugees' right of return to their lost territory. They unanimously opposed nuclear testing. Out of the public eye, in a form of consciousness-raising, delegates from disparate countries compared notes, discovered common—and debilitating—aspects of colonialism, and forged bonds that soon appeared in the form of new (or resurrected) ideologies of pan-Arabism and pan-Africanism.[62]

After the showdown in Bandung, both the Mighty Wurlitzer and bona-fide journalists churned out glowing accounts of the communists' defeat. An AP wire story headline declared, "Student Parley Becomes Donnybrook."[63] It reported, with gross exaggeration, that students from the Philippines, India, and Pakistan "out-shouted the Reds." An unsigned *New York Times* editorial praised Western success without identifying its architects. "Those who upset the communist plans at Bandung have rendered a service to honest student exchange of ideas by exposing the falsehood of a scheme that is neither honest nor 'student.'"[64] It described the conference as "the usual Communist attempt to capitalize on diatribes against 'colonialism' among persons whose countries have recently changed from a dependent status to an independent one."[65] Such condescension reflected a commonly held Western view that recently independent nations should be grateful for their freedom and cease complaining against their former colonial masters.

When Lunn returned to the United States, he continued the triumphal storyline with his *Christian Science Monitor* article, "Red Control Fails at Youth Parley." He described the failure to establish a regional federation and other measures as key blows to the communists' plan. At the same time, he downplayed any lasting significance of the Bandung conference and dismissed the delegates as "elites [who] undoubtedly feel they have achieved a successful meeting" merely by voicing "their dissatisfaction with the colonial past." He unabashedly listed as a major achievement "limiting mention of discrimination to Asia and Africa rather than including the United States." Lunn gave Sabharwal credit for many of the victories, introducing him to the *Monitor*'s readers as the "shrewd Indian leader who managed to control his own unruly delegation and outmaneuver the Communists at the same time."[66]

Soon, the NSA-CIA team would ensure that Sabharwal's version of the Bandung events would be widely read; his booklet "Little Bandung: A Report on the Asian African Students Conference," was subsidized by CIA funds and published by the University Press of Delhi.[67] Sabharwal assured his readers that COSEC had "no ulterior motive" in issuing travel grants, and praised its practical-projects programs.[68] After years of searching, it appeared that the NSA had finally found a cooperative and friendly student leader in India.

Lunn sounded a far less triumphal note in confidential documents, however. The victories in Bandung had been short-term and defensive. The Americans still lacked a coherent and active anticommunist alliance in the region. Noncommunists were "too few and too busy to establish

. . . widespread contacts and cooperation among themselves that would be of benefit to students in the area in the future." Despite the offer of free tickets to Bandung, several hoped-for allies—from the Gold Coast, Nigeria, Senegal, Sierra Leone, and South Africa—had turned down the invitation. Moreover, Lunn warned that ad-hoc alliances forged at the conference would bear bitter fruit for the Americans. He had intelligence that delegates from China, India (other than Sabharwal), and Japan had met with Hassan Ashmawi to plan a follow-up meeting in Cairo.[69]

Both Bandung conferences confronted the Eisenhower administration with a choice between lofty American rhetoric in favor of self-determination and the need to keep intact alliances with European colonial powers. After the 1955 conference, John Foster Dulles sought funding from the Rockefeller Foundation for a new Council on Foreign Relations study group, in partnership with the British, to consider questions of colonialism and self-determination. Then Eisenhower had a heart attack, British interest waned, and the initiative evaporated. While the U.S. government chose to stand with its European allies against Asian and African revolutionary movements, the gist of the study group idea—putting the United States in a position to champion decolonization—presaged heated debates inside the foreign policy establishment that would last for years.

The NSA faced similar choices. The need for NSA witting staff to take stronger positions on anticolonialism, imperialism, and racism, even at the risk of alienating some of their European allies, had been evident even before the conference. Bandung raised the stakes. But no one anticipated how quickly the spirit of Bandung would move inside the ISC and push the confederation to the left.

SHIFTING BATTLEFIELDS

THE ASIAN-AFRICAN STUDENTS CONFERENCE in Bandung decisively shifted the Cold War student battleground. While by the mid-50s the International Student Conference had won the numbers game—ISC attendance (delegates and observers) had climbed to between fifty and sixty countries, with a roughly equivalent loss in IUS European members—it was in danger of losing political relevance. The potent issues of colonialism, imperialism, and racism could no longer be dismissed as communist propaganda. They mobilized a constituency larger than any the Soviets could manufacture. Unless the ISC appealed to Latin American, Asian, and African students, it could not remain competitive. Denial operations had been a necessary but far from sufficient strategy to win the counteroffensive against the International Union of Students.

The next ISC was scheduled to meet in Ceylon (today's Sri Lanka), just three months after the Bandung conference. The necessity of competing with Bandung led to a summer of frantic organizing. But how far the NSA could push the ISC to speak out against colonialism without alienating key European members was uncertain. Even before Bandung raised the stakes, some Europeans were protesting the conference's growing political orientation.

The French walked out of two successive International Student Conferences, in Istanbul (1954) and Birmingham (1955), over colonial issues. The Swiss publicly "warned of the control of the Conference by the Arab-Asian bloc which was only interested in politics." During his year in Paris as an NSA representative, Paul Sigmund got an earful from Eastern European exiles. "The exiles were somewhat unhappy with the way ISC was dominated by Asians and Africans, neutralist in orientation." They were critical of the NSA delegation, "who they felt were inexperienced and irresolute—compromised too much and didn't keep the extremists in line."[1]

The NSA also had a domestic problem. If the international staff wanted to take more militant positions abroad, they needed authorization from the NSA Congress. But if the NSA moved too far left, rightwing anticommunists would gain new fodder for their perennial attacks. Moderate students also might protest.

The NSA Congresses had become less liberal and less interested in international questions. During the presidential election of 1952, many undergraduates preferred Republican Dwight Eisenhower to Democrat Adlai Stevenson.[2] While NSA foreign policy resolutions were carefully written to emphasize academic freedom and educational opportunity, the full Congress rarely held extended debate on them.[3]

This lack of attention was deliberate. The NSA executive committee voted on resolutions left undecided in plenary sessions if time ran out, and its members usually deferred to the expertise of top officers. Since incumbent officers chaired the plenary sessions, they could ensure that the clock ran out by reordering the agenda.

But there was one issue that elicited strong passions among NSA delegates: civil rights. While it was an article of faith inside the NSA that segregation was a southern problem, not representative of the entire country, officers did not want to risk losing southern members. In the logic of the Cold War, if the South disaffiliated, the NSA could no longer claim to speak for all American students, the basis of its legitimacy overseas. For years, this dynamic created pressure to compromise on racial issues.

A 1955 Congress resolution to support the 1954 U.S. Supreme Court decision in *Brown v. Board of Education* that segregated schools were inherently unequal precipitated so much conflict that it took all-night negotiations and the prowess of Texan Ray Farabee, a future state senator known for his liberal civil rights views, to craft a compromise. In the end, the resolution carried more cautious language than that used by the Supreme Court: "The USNSA reaffirms its acknowledgement of the concept of equality of opportunity for all people . . ." The resolution advocated education, "concerning the problem of integration and its possible solutions." It did not advocate any national action.[4]

At the same time, international staff understood the damage that racial discrimination in America caused overseas. In 1952, Frank Fisher had written, "Students in Southeast Asia are extremely interested in activity of NSA in connection with the Negro problem. They feel our good faith in dealing with all persons of different color at stake."[5] The NSA tried to disguise its own lack of racial diversity by including African Americans in its international delegations. The Bandung pairing of segregation in South Africa and the United States had unnerved the witting staff and underscored the international problem.

Developments in the United States had also put pressure on the NSA to speak more forcefully on race. In late August 1955 fourteen-year-old Emmett Till was brutally murdered for allegedly whistling at a white woman. The September 15 issue of *Jet* magazine featured a picture of Till's mutilated body at his open-casket funeral, which fueled world outrage. The criticism spread far beyond the communist press, affecting America's allies as well as its enemies. Then on December 1, Rosa Parks, a domestic in Montgomery, Alabama, refused to give up her seat in the whites-only section of a city bus, sparking a boycott of the city's segregated transportation system. The boycott's leader, a young minister named Martin Luther King, Jr., received significant press coverage overseas, much of it favorable. When King connected the civil rights movement at home with anticolonial movements abroad, the spirit of Bandung entered the American discourse.[6] But the NSA had remained silent.

Finally an incident of racial violence occurred on an American campus that the NSA could not ignore. On February 6, 1956, a young African American woman, Autherine Lucy, who had been inadvertently admitted to the University of Alabama, won a federal court order upholding her right to attend classes. When she arrived on campus, students pelted her with eggs, yelled racial epithets, and burned desegregation literature. Press articles described an unruly mob yelling, "There's Autherine, kill her!"[7] The atmosphere in Alabama was so explosive that NAACP litigator Thurgood Marshall, the future U.S. Supreme Court justice, feared for Lucy's life and brought her to stay with his family in New York.[8] School officials banned Lucy from the university for her own protection, an act most civil rights leaders regarded as an evasion.

News of the Lucy episode roared around the world.[9] Unless the NSA acted quickly to condemn the incident, it risked censure by friend and foe alike. Further, the prospect of the ISC, secretly supported by U.S.

government funds, condemning the United States threw overseas staff into a tizzy.

From London, Crawford Young, a Fulbright student and 1953 graduate of the University of Michigan, then serving as an NSA representative, warned, "The strength of the reaction to this thing over here perhaps cannot be enough stressed." Young feared that the British National Union of Students, one of the NSA's closest allies, would condemn the Lucy incident at its next meeting. He suggested that the NSA assemble a white paper to arm students "with some mitigating facts" and "at least channel any protests effectively."[10]

Young, who had attended the NSA Congress in the summer of 1952, acknowledged that there would be problems getting the members to agree on his proposal, but suggested that a report could be "delicately phrased" so as "not to inflame Southern opinion."[11] International affairs vice president Clive Gray, who knew well the temper of NSA Congresses, as Young did not, tried to explain the difficult line he walked. "There are those who feel we should tread softly in order not to aggravate the situation further and force the student government at Alabama to repudiate us, whereas there have been others who feel the important thing is to get out a strong statement for international consumption."[12] In an effort of appeasement, Gray sent out a letter in support of Lucy to the NAACP with copies to foreign student unions but did not circulate it in the United States.[13] For campus consumption, the international office prepared a more conciliatory memorandum.[14]

Nonetheless, Young's idea of a white paper took hold. After a few false starts, Helen Jean Rogers prepared the twenty-three-page "Letter About Racial Discrimination in the United States and Efforts for Its Elimination," which turned the volatile issue of racial violence into a fact-laden brief on the southern problem and the growing improvement of American race relations. Perhaps with an eye on the southern constituency, not a single incumbent NSA officer signed the letter. Rather, the letterhead featured former NSA officers, among them African Americans Bill Ellis and Ted Harris.[15]

White papers and Gray's actions did not lessen the need to get a strong civil rights resolution on record at the 1956 NSA Congress, especially after the public yoking of the United States and South Africa at Bandung. The urgency was driven home to Gray in July when he received a letter from the head of the Guatemalan student union requesting "all possible documentation on cases of racial discrimination in the United States." The request for material, Gray informed Avrea Ingram at CO-SEC, was timed for a Latin American Congress meeting, "so that he might present resolutions against racial discrimination in South Africa and North America."[16]

Gray had been right to worry. The attempt to use the Lucy incident to prepare the 1956 delegates for a stronger resolution on race turned the Congress into a melee. The NSA had invited both Lucy and Herbert Wright, the NAACP youth director, to address the delegates. At the last minute, NAACP officials worried that Lucy might adversely affect her court case by speaking publicly, so Wright spoke on her behalf while she sat near him on the stage. As Wright began to speak, the Alabama delegation rose up and began to sing "Dixie." James Forman from Roosevelt University in Chicago, one of the few African American student body presidents in the country, and others responded by belting out "The Star Spangled Banner," trying to drown out the southerners.[17] The meeting descended into chaos.

Nevertheless, despite the infighting, the Congress voted on a stronger resolution, to the relief of the international staff. Sigmund rejoiced when an Ivory Coast student said he was happy to learn "that American students were struggling for the elimination of racism and against colonialism."[18] From England, Young reported that the BNUS president, Frank Copplestone, had come around on the Lucy issue, and "felt he would have done the same thing [banning Lucy from the university] if he had been on the Board of Trustees."[19] Overall, Young thought, echoing the NSA line, most overseas students understood that the "Negro's plight in the Deep South is not characteristic of the entire country."[20]

Not everyone agreed. After the Congress, Forman, who later led the more activist Student Non-Violent Coordinating Committee (SNCC), concluded that the NSA was irrelevant to the black struggle. Not only was it too conservative, he wrote, but its leaders "saw themselves as moving in governmental circles."[21]

The international staff also needed the NSA to address colonialism and imperialism in advance of the Ceylon ISC. While the Congress might have been more willing to take a stronger stand on these issues than it did on race, the larger problem involved NSA allies. At the 1955 ISC in Birmingham, England, the NSA had backed a mild resolution that described national independence as "a prerequisite of full educational opportunities" and recognized "the desire of students in dependent and colonial areas to participate in a society as free and independent people."[22]

The Birmingham resolution unleashed a rancorous debate. Brazil led a fight over the word *desire* and tried to replace it with the "right to independence."[23] Great Britain and France argued against the entire resolution. A Malayan delegate asked the conference, If the British "do not want to hear about our practical problems, why do they invite us here?" The amendment substituting "right" for "desire" passed, 27–1 with 3 abstentions, but the low tally suggests that several unions left the floor to avoid a vote.[24] The final resolution, which expressed ISC solidarity with "students under colonial domination," passed by a similar margin, 26–3, with 6 abstentions.[25] The votes prompted the French to walk out for a second year in a row, saying, "Good luck everybody. Enjoy your little resolutions. We are going back to France to serve the true interests of French students."[26]

Then, at Bandung, students had enthusiastically embraced the Algerian student union, UGEMA, and its struggle against French colonialism, and UGEMA expected no less of the ISC in Ceylon. But UGEMA was hardly a typical student union. It served as the student arm of the Algerian Front de Libération Nationale (FLN), which on November 1, 1954, had launched its war of independence by setting off synchronized bombs in a number of Algerian cities.[27] The French government regarded the FLN as terrorists, though UGEMA had legal status in France because it qualified as a religious organization (in English, UGEMA would be translated as Algerian Union of Muslim Students).[28]

But while UGEMA might be technically legal, Algerian students in Paris and other French cities faced frequent arrest and detention, even assassination. Not long after the war began, the thirty-one-year-old vice president, Zeddour Belkacem, disappeared from Paris.[29] According to Paul Sigmund, Zeddour's body had been "put in a sack and dropped into the sea [and] later washed up on the shore."[30] At this point, it was easy for NSA staff to sympathize with the plight of the Algerians; most agreed with principles of self-determination and held no brief for French colonialism. But now they were called upon to act.

During Sigmund's year in Paris, UGEMA planned a one-day hunger strike for January 20, 1956, to commemorate Zeddour's assassination, but also to protest the murder and imprisonment of Algerian students held without trial in French and Algerian jails. Before television created a world audience for strikes and demonstrations, revolutionary leaders had to find dramatic ways to capture international attention.[31] A successful strike offered one avenue. Sigmund grew alarmed when he discovered that the East German student union had offered to mobilize support for the strike among IUS colleagues. "Can we get into this?" he asked.[32] The affirmative answer began a six-year relationship between NSA and the UGEMA revolutionaries.

The UGEMA strikes in Paris and other major French cities deepened divisions between French and Algerian students, and further complicated NSA relations with the French student union, UNEF. One of the Paris representative's tasks was to ensure smooth relations between the NSA and UNEF, a job most found difficult, if not impossible.

In June 1956, Sigmund warned his colleagues that UGEMA had an agenda for the Ceylon ISC beyond official recognition. He had heard that the Algerians intended to organize an Asian-African bloc within the ISC.[33] Edgardo Carvalho, a Uruguayan student leader who had come to Paris, told Sigmund bluntly that he was there to assure UGEMA of Latin American support.[34] With roughly twenty Latin American ISC members, the situation was grave. If the NSA did not support UGEMA it would lose influence to the more militant bloc. If, instead, the NSA championed Algerian independence, it might be able to win influence with both the Algerians and their supporters in the ISC.

The NSA had been currying favor with UGEMA since 1954, shortly after UGEMA's headquarters was established in Paris near the Sorbonne. (When Sigmund arrived in November 1955, he continued James Edwards's practice of dropping by the UGEMA office for casual chats with its president, Ahmed Taleb-Ibrahami, among others.) Now, notwithstanding the difficulty with the French, the NSA decided to signal its support to UGEMA in advance of Ceylon. Sigmund suggested that UGEMA get in touch with Clive Gray in the NSA international office for assistance with travel funds.[35] In turn, Gray approached the CIA-funded American Friends of the Middle East and lauded UGEMA in ways that exaggerated the Algerians' position on communism. "In rejecting extremes of political action, and refusing to engage in violence to express opposition to French actions, the UGEMA has also kept clear of Communists and openly denounces their international student front, the International Union of Students."[36]

In reality, the UGEMA leadership, though decidedly noncommunist, had not denounced the IUS. Indeed, after the Bandung conference, UGEMA officials sought and received recognition from the IUS.[37] The Algerians' main aim at all international meetings was to secure support for their cause—not to choose West over East. But Gray boasted that by "openly choosing" to come to Ceylon, the Algerians had turned to the "mode of cooperation which representative national unions of students through the world have turned to as an alternative to the IUS."[38] The CIA paid the Algerians' passage to the ISC so that it could use their attendance to stamp them as pro-West moderates.[39]

The decision to back the Algerians put the NSA in the unusual situation of being opposed to official U.S. foreign policy. In the early years of the NSA, CIA covert foreign policy objectives were congruent with official U.S. government containment policies. Denial operations, for example, checked Soviet expansion within major world organizations as part of a larger counteroffensive. But in 1956, Eisenhower continued to support the French against the Algerians, creating a disjunction between official policy and CIA covert action.

While the CIA is legally prohibited from making foreign policy, considerable evidence suggests that the liberals in the IO division tried to do so. In the summer of 1956, the various international constituencies it helped fund took stands in favor of Algerian independence within weeks of one another, among them labor (International Confederation of Free Trade Unions), youth (WAY), and students (ISC).[40] While many CIA liberals genuinely supported Algerian independence, they also believed that the Algerians would ultimately win, and that the United States needed to establish influence with them as early as possible.

The situation created a paradox. The more the NSA distanced itself from official U.S. foreign policy, the more it earned respect among overseas students. At the same time, CIA backing gave staff the courage to push the campus constituency beyond where they were inclined to go.

The same relationship between the NSA and the U.S. government applied to the issue of imperialism. In the early years, the NSA worked comfortably with students who lived under U.S.-backed dictatorships in countries such as Paraguay and Haiti. By the mid-1950s, international staff were engaged in intense debates over NSA policy toward Latin America. Rumors of a Latin American voting bloc in Ceylon made these discussions urgent.

The challenge to existing policy was begun by a young Harvard sophomore identified by Helen Jean Rogers, then in her fourth year of graduate work. Nineteen-year-old Luigi Einaudi, a blond, Nordic-looking Italian who later rose to top positions in the U.S. State Department and the Organization of American States, took over Latin American work from Rogers. He came to the NSA with impeccable family and political credentials.[41] He was the grandson and namesake of the postwar Italian president (1948–1955) Luigi Einaudi, an ardent anti-fascist closely allied with the Americans. His father, Mario, had fled Mussolini in 1933, immigrating to the United States, where he taught at Harvard and subsequently had a distinguished career at Cornell, pioneering courses in international relations.[42]

The younger Luigi, born in 1936, was schooled at Phillips Exeter before enrolling in Harvard. Today, he does not dispute that he became witting, but he downplays Rogers's influence and claims, "I recruited myself to NSA."[43] Einaudi became the first person on the international staff to focus on the harmful effects of U.S. foreign policies in Latin America, rather than on the transformation of negative opinions through student-to-student contact.

In October 1955, after completing ISRS training, Einaudi undertook his first assignment to Latin America. He attended a conference hosted by the Chilean committee of the Congress for Cultural Freedom, part of Frank Wisner's CIA-funded network of anticommunist liberals and social democrats. He bonded easily with a young Chilean Radical Party leader, Pedro Guglielmetti; they wandered the streets of Santiago late in the evening, reveling in full-throated singing of Italian military anthems. From Santiago, Einaudi made side trips to Argentina and Uruguay.[44] Even before he returned to the United States, his letters to the NSA contained a challenge to existing policy.

Einaudi argued against the view that anti-imperialist rhetoric was a cloak for communist sympathies. Latin American students were both anti-imperialist *and* anticommunist, he claimed.[45] He criticized the NSA's reliance on Catholic and conservative students in the region. "It has been underlined again and again that the right is with us anyway, that the left has the influence and that it is from the radical and socialist ranks that we should choose any exchange students."[46]

Upon his return to Harvard, Einaudi elaborated his beliefs. Pro-Yankee groups, he argued, "are generally too moderate in their positions and in some cases lacking in competent leadership"; they would be unable to convince left-wing students.[47] The NSA and COSEC should "cease to rely on the Catholic groups [and] work with the anti-Communist left of the sort he met at the Congress for Cultural Freedom."[48]

Einaudi honed his arguments throughout the academic year. In recommending students for the new Foreign Student Leadership Project, he acknowledged to director Ted Harris that students in Latin America could be considered leftist, and that "there is usually a majority which is willing to accept in part the Communist program, and especially the Communist explanation of imperialism."[49] But, he pointed out, only Ecuador belonged to the IUS. He speculated that the roughly three hundred students from Mexico, Brazil, Ecuador, and Chile who attended the Soviet-backed World Youth Festival in Warsaw in 1955 did so out of curiosity.[50]

Einaudi argued that the NSA needed to understand that Latin American students were "deeply and violently concerned about liberty," a concern that expressed itself in "opposition to dictatorships, and opposition to 'el imperialismo norteamerican,' which is believed to be at once aiding dictators, local monopolistic interests, and oppressing the people." If the NSA wanted to establish its bona fides with Latin American students, it needed to support their efforts to overthrow repressive dictators.[51]

A perfect opportunity lay at hand. In Cuba students were leading the movement to oust Batista. Einaudi had met some of the Cuban student leaders while traveling in Latin America. The head of the Cuban student union (FEU), José Antonio Echeverría, nicknamed Manzanita (Little Apple) or, less charitably, El Gordo (the Fat One) for his roly-poly physique, had a reputation as an anticommunist and a democrat. The NSA calculated, correctly, that Europeans in the ISC would not oppose a resolution that backed the overthrow of Batista since they did not care what happened in Latin America. Preparations were made to get Echeverría to Ceylon.

Despite his criticism of Latin America policy, Einaudi remained loyal to the overall goals of the NSA-CIA operation. On one occasion he warned Avrea Ingram that Juan Barros Barros, a Chilean who worked under COSEC auspices, did not appear sufficiently committed to CO-SEC. Barros had given Einaudi an earful about Harry Lunn's role in Bandung. He argued that for Lunn to switch hats so quickly, traveling to Asia with a COSEC-sponsored team and then reappearing in Bandung as a journalist, "gives excellent grounds for charging that Harry is an agent of the State Department and that State controls COSEC through him." Einaudi told Ingram, "The fact that he has said this both to me and to John Simons rather indiscriminately seems to indicate that he might not be adverse to repeating it also in Latin America. In turn, that could spell damage to COSEC interests in the region."[52]

As the tension built toward the Ceylon ISC, all available NSA hands were pressed into service. The Bandung conference had brought to the fore the question of which Asian student union might serve as an anchor in the region. Indonesian neutrality had dashed any hope that the PPMI could play that role. The Philippines also had to be ruled out because of its strong ties to the United States. Japan might seem a logical candidate, given the prolonged American occupation, but the large and powerful Zengakuren student association had a strong communist presence. Through the Asia Foundation, the CIA had devised a strategy to combat Zengakuren's influence by forming an alternative but thus far had had little success.[53]

Partly by default, and despite general U.S. suspicion that Prime Minister Nehru's neutral stance was a camouflage for pro-Sovietism, the NSA trained its sights on India. Helen Jean Rogers dropped everything in early June 1956 and rushed to Bombay. Robert C. Fisher, a Harvard and Columbia Law School graduate under consideration for an overseas position, joined her. Within weeks of their arrival in India, Rogers and Fisher filed separate reports on the National Union of Students India (NUSI), its history, current leadership, political factions, and future possibilities. The problem, Rogers concluded, remained its intransigent president, A. J. Shelat.[54] The FYSA award to Shelat after the 1954 Istanbul ISC had been intended to strengthen the student union by enabling it to hold a national conference, but the conference never materialized. The NUSI remained weak, and, as a stream of NSA visitors agreed, "not a national union in any sense save name."[55]

More encouraging, Rogers reported that the communist-led All India Students Federation had "suffered serious defeats at major universities." As important, Nehru's Congress Party showed signs of renewed interest in youth and student affairs.[56] Rogers believed that it was "a decisive moment for NUSI to revitalize itself and fill the vacuum." But, she warned, "Here Shelat stands in the way."[57]

Not for long, Rogers might have added. Harry Lunn arrived in Bombay, conferred with Rogers and Fisher, and suggested they split forces.[58] Fisher visited major campuses in Benares (today's Varanasi), Aligarh, and Calcutta to sample student sentiment for ousting Shelat. Rogers and others covered campuses in Bombay (Mumbai), New Delhi, Maharajah, Dacca, Lucknow, Hyderabad, and Madras and touched base with Pakistani student leaders in Lahore and Karachi. They were joined by Harold R. Sims, an African American, who impressed Fisher because he used a bicycle to make contact with ordinary Indians.[59] All reports led to one conclusion: Shelat must go.[60]

The antagonism toward Shelat served the interests of American favorite Pran Sabharwal, who had helped carry the day at Bandung. As an NUSI officer, Sabharwal had been working for months to oust Shelat. He initially benefited from Nehru's insistence on a diverse Indian delegation to Bandung but during the conference Sabharwal had edged out members he did not trust and suppressed dissent by insisting on a unit rule. The muzzled students returned to India enraged. Nehru, embarrassed, took to the Parliament floor and criticized the entire Indian delegation, an act that stoked further antagonism toward Sabharwal. Shelat retaliated by terminating Sabharwal's status as acting general secretary.[61]

The NSA continued to back Sabharwal, while acknowledging that his behavior in Bandung had been damaging to his support within India. Sabharwal's principal asset was that communist students viewed him as a threat. In the logic of the Cold War, success for Sabharwal equaled a defeat for the communists. For the moment, therefore, despite his flaws, he remained the Americans' choice to displace Shelat.[62]

It is not clear whether Sabharwal knowingly accepted financial assistance from the CIA before the Bandung conference or received it afterward as a reward for his performance. According to Clive Gray, Sabharwal received regular stipends from a CIA case officer who worked out of the American embassy in New Delhi, explosive information had it been known at the time.[63]

In the drive to oust Shelat, Gray counseled a Shelat opponent to use the unfulfilled terms of the FYSA grant against him: "If you give the impression that Shelat was an embezzler, which he was, you tend to discredit him and his supporters all the more."[64] The attempt by the NSA to oust Shelat proved costly in the short term: within the year, the Indian student union collapsed. Perhaps this would have happened without the meddling by Gray, Rogers, and others associated with the NSA—anger against Shelat had been building and opposition toward his leadership growing—but the Americans' interventions cannot be ruled out as a factor. Even Gray acknowledged that the NSA got itself into an "embarrassing mess."[65] Worse, not long after the collapse, the NSA soured on Sabharwal. Gray decided that he had "a bad case of OOGH (Our Own Great Hero)."[66] Disillusioned, Gray paid Sabharwal off with CIA funds in a New Delhi Hotel. "I had a suitcase full of cash," he reveals today.[67] He describes Sabharwal as bitter, but notes matter-of-factly, "We had to clear the old guard out of the way."[68]

While the Indian student union was floundering, the Americans continued to seek ways to promote the Ceylon ISC among Asians. Since it was imperative that the conference match the vibrancy of the Bandung conference, the CIA devised a way to increase regional turnout. Before the conference convened, John Simons offered funding through CO-SEC for a two-week seminar in Colombo, Ceylon's capital city. Sixty Asian students snapped up the offer of travel grants.[69] As Simons had calculated, many stayed on for the ISC, held on the nearby new Peradeniya campus of the University of Ceylon. Not only did the plan ensure a large Asian turnout but the seminar continued to bear fruit. It became an annual event, akin to the German seminar (which had been renamed the International Student Seminar).[70] Eventually, Simons funded a separate Asian Press Bureau.[71] The NSA had its regional anchor.

Thanks to a summer of intense preparation, the Ceylon ISC initially seemed to go well. Clive Gray remembers sitting with Paul Sigmund and saying, "This is great. We're really running the show."[72] The NSA staved off criticism on American segregation and won praise for its struggle against racism. Confident of further success, the NSA team trooped off to visit the Buddhist Temple of the Sacred Tooth. They returned to find a major crisis unfolding—Sigmund was unable to remember the details in a recent interview—but they all vowed never again to go off duty.[73] When the conference ended, Gray recalled making a more sober assessment: "Our job was to keep the ISC from blowing apart."[74]

The recognition of UGEMA and a resolution on Algerian independence contributed to the acrimonious atmosphere in Peradeniya. Once again, the French walked out of the conference: the Algerian and French positions were too far apart for compromise. Sigmund, Gray, James Edwards, and others tried to rewrite the Algerian resolution to satisfy other angry Europeans. They substituted "students rights" language for "national independence" and rammed it through a committee. But once the resolution reached the larger plenary, the ISC delegates voted to restore the original language desired by the Algerians. Seeing the handwriting on the wall, the NSA delegation voted with the majority, and the stronger resolution won on a 26–22 vote.[75] One of the NSA newcomers on the delegation, Harold Sims, afterward reported widespread disgust among British and European delegates at the Americans' maneuvering.[76]

Still, as predicted, the anti-Batista Cuban resolution inspired no opposition from Europeans. Einaudi took Echeverría under his wing and helped draft a strong resolution in support of the Cuban cause. It expressed "solidarity with the Cuban students who struggle for liberty and for university autonomy in their country."[77] By the time the conference was over, the CIA had spent, in today's money, more than a million dollars.[78]

THE CEYLON CONFERENCE signaled the end of denial operations. In 1956, forty of the fifty-nine ISC attendees (delegates and observers) came from outside Europe.[79] The battle for global legitimacy was over. The battle to win Asians and Africans to Western capitalism and democracy was just beginning.

The shift of emphasis could be seen in the NSA-CIA staff assignments. In order to develop closer ties with Indian student leaders (once they were identified), Gray agreed to settle for a year in New Delhi and represent the NSA. To enhance his credibility, he would enroll at the University of New Delhi and write a thesis on colonialism and economics. Robert Fisher, who had helped Helen Jean Rogers assess the Shelat problem, went to Japan. Crawford Young finished his Fulbright in London and took over the Paris job from Sigmund as NSA overseas representative, concentrating on African students.

After three long years in Leiden, in mid-October 1956, Ingram and his small puppy Paco sailed from the Netherlands to New York.[80] Ingram moved up the CIA ladder and joined John Simons at FYSA. Edwards took over the COSEC position. Einaudi turned over his Latin American duties to a young Fordham and Columbia graduate, Ralph Della Cava, who had worked with the Young Adult Council, an affiliate of the CIA-funded World Assembly of Youth.

Meanwhile, important shifts were taking place in the Soviet Union.

For much of 1956, the NSA witting staff basically ignored two major changes in Soviet policy: Khrushchev's new doctrine of peaceful co-existence with the West, first articulated in 1953 after Stalin's death and codified in a seven-hour speech at the 20th Party Congress in February 1956, and his denunciation of Stalin in a "secret speech" at a closed session of the same meeting. The NSA dismissed peaceful coexistence as window dressing. Gray summed up the prevalent view: "Although a new era of sweetness and light has set into the international picture, we feel that the Soviets are as determined as before to promote as effectively as possible the spread of the Communist system, oriented to Moscow."[81]

News of Khrushchev's condemnation of Stalin reached the West in June 1956, when the *New York Times* printed the heretofore top-secret document confirming the rumors.[82] But its meaning was not yet clear. Only after the consequences began to be seen in the disruption of Eastern European regimes, including riots in Poland and an uprising in Hungary, did both COSEC and the NSA revise their agendas.

PART THREE

COMPETITIVE COEXISTENCE

———————

HUNGARY AND THE STRUGGLE
AGAINST NONALIGNMENT

IN MID-OCTOBER 1956, Clive Gray, who continued his work with the CIA, was still in Cambridge, Massachusetts. He had agreed to travel to the Middle East and Southeast Asia before settling in New Delhi. In both regions, he would assess the aftermath of the Bandung and Ceylon conferences, and identify candidates for the Foreign Student Leadership Project. Suddenly, Gray's schedule was thrown into turmoil. An uprising in Budapest had caught the West by surprise, and television and press headlines were following the fast-paced developments.

On October 23, thousands of Hungarians, led by university students, jammed the streets of Budapest in protest against the Soviet-backed communist government. They shouted the battle call of the nineteenth-century poet and revolutionary Sándor Petőfi, "Stand up, Hungary, your country calls," and chanted, "Russians go home." They toppled a statue of Stalin in a Budapest city park, cutting it down just above the knees, and stuck a flagpole in the boots so that the Hungarian flag billowed atop the jagged metal.[1] An angry crowd armed with a few rifles and Molotov cocktails stormed the state radio station and broadcast demands to the government. The New York Times reported demonstrations across the country.[2]

The uprising had begun with events at Technical University in Budapest the day before. A routine assembly meeting called by DISZ, the communist youth organization, was thrown into confusion when a student from Szeged, Hungary's third-largest city, approached the auditorium stage and requested permission to speak. No one interrupted party youth meetings. Yet here was a student from a newly formed independent student organization, MEFESZ, insisting on the microphone.

An engineering student, Béla Lipták, who until that moment had been slumped in his seat in boredom, was astonished by the student's audacity, but his "heart stopped" when someone shouted to the soldiers who were already advancing on the student, "Let him speak." Lipták said to himself, "God, has he lost his marbles?"[3]

But then, Lipták recalls, someone began clapping. The applause started slowly, then "turned into a hurricane." Excited students surged toward the stage and formed a protective circle around the student from Szeged. He was finally allowed to speak to the assembly, and he told them that Polish exchange students at Szeged University had sent him to ask for support for their bid for freedom. At that very moment, he told the crowd, Soviet tanks surrounded Warsaw. When he finished, someone started singing the outlawed Hungarian national anthem.

After that, the energy in the auditorium was unstoppable. Students began drafting demands of the Hungarian government, including the withdrawal of Russian troops. They then planned a silent demonstration for the following day in support of the Polish people, intending to march from the university to the statue of General Bem, a Polish military officer who fought with the Hungarians in the revolution of 1848.

Lipták, a march organizer, later described the reaction of ordinary Budapest citizens as the students crossed the Margit Bridge over the Danube and reached the Pest side: an old woman fell to her knees and crossed herself; a janitor dropped his broom; people hung out of open windows; shopkeepers closed their stores; some joined the swelling crowd. Later estimates put the final size of the march at between 250,000 and a half-million Hungarians.

For nearly a week, citizens awakened to a power they had never known. Hungarian troops defected and joined the rebellion. Soviet troops and tanks rolled out of Budapest. Reformist Communist Party leader Imre Nagy returned to power, fulfilling one of the students' demands. For nine or ten days it seemed the Hungarian people had triumphed.

Then the images reaching the West changed.

Soviet tanks returned from the Hungarian border and thundered into Budapest. Ordinary people armed with rifles, handguns, or bombs made out of empty bottles and gasoline-soaked rags were no match for the heavy artillery. Some young, intrepid Hungarians tried to stop the tank assault by throwing themselves in their path and were mowed down. On November 4, newly installed Prime Minister Nagy sought refuge in the Yugoslav Embassy. Before he fled, Nagy broadcast a plea for his fellow Hungarians to leave the country rather than live under Soviet occupation. Over the next month or so, two hundred thousand refugees trekked through dark, muddy terrain, risking mined fields and Russian bullets to reach the border. Many poured into Austria, among them hundreds of students.[4]

The Soviet intervention in Hungary was a gift to Westerners looking for a psychological weapon against communism. (Vice President Richard Nixon had cynically foreseen such a possibility at a National Security Council meeting on July 12, when he mused, "It wouldn't be an unmixed evil, from the point of view of U.S. interest, if the Soviet iron fist were to come down again on the Soviet bloc.")[5] In response to the influx of refugees, the CIA deployed its existing assets to Vienna, including staff from Radio Free Europe, the World Assembly of Youth, the Free Europe Committee, the World University Service, the Congress for Cultural Freedom, COSEC, and the NSA.[6] Here was an opportunity to make sure the world knew the truth about Soviet imperialism, and to blunt nonalignment movements that had been sweeping Asia and Africa.

The prominence of Hungarian students in the uprising gave the NSA a rationale to act. As the newly elected international affairs vice president, Bruce Larkin, explained to Gray: "When the situation first broke, we were reluctant to take extreme action which could be cited as going beyond the point we would go for Paraguayans, Algerians, etc. But we soon lost that view, since the uniqueness of Hungary is that it is singularly and peculiarly the most brutal suppression of an entire country in recent history, and it is very much related to students as such."[7] (When later accused of inaction regarding the Suez crisis, the NSA took the pious position that no students were involved.)

In the United States, NSA officers stumped the campuses to raise funds for Hungarian refugees. On November 8, it co-sponsored with the International Rescue Committee a rally at Madison Square Garden in New York City that featured Anna Kéthly, a socialist leader in the Nagy cabinet, who had come to petition the United Nations for international assistance. Istvan Laszlo, a student leader of the uprising from Sopron University near the Hungarian-Austrian border, accompanied Kéthly.

But like all such operations within the NSA, the Hungarian campaign had a covert as well as a public purpose. After the rally, John Simons,

Gray, and others met with Laszlo, whose real name was Alpár Bujdosó (the pseudonym was to protect his family), until nearly 4 A.M. to persuade him to tour American campuses under NSA auspices.[8] Before the tour began, he testified before the U.S. Senate to atrocities committed by the Hungarian police. The diminutive Bujdosó tried to hide his distinctive ringlets under an orderly's white cap and wore a mask to further disguise his identity, although the next day, speaking at Harvard, he courageously disposed of the mask.[9]

Bujdosó crisscrossed the United States to the point of exhaustion.[10] He told riveted campus audiences that fellow students had elected him on October 23 to "take command of an army of 5,000 students, workers, peasants and Hungarian soldiers." He described how during the invasion, he had "defended a six-mile stretch on the Austro-Hungarian border against three Soviet tank attacks." This crucial corridor served as a safety-value through which thousands of Hungarians escaped.[11]

On the stump, presumably unaware of CIA funding that supported his tour and financed Radio Free Europe, he openly criticized the news organization for broadcasts that had led Hungarians to expect aid from the West.[12] His traveling companions, Ralph Della Cava (NSA) and an interpreter, turned a blind eye to Bujdosó's public pitch for armaments, though his appeal for scholarship funds kept small checks pouring into the international office in Cambridge—just enough to camouflage the infusion of CIA funds.[13] Meanwhile, his tour was giving a tremendous boost to the NSA's propaganda struggle with the IUS.

The international staff believed, correctly, that the International Union of Students in Prague would follow the Soviet line and depict the uprising as a counterrevolution. After a period of silence, the IUS issued a bulletin that urged medical and relief supplies be sent to Hungarian students but omitted any reference to the uprising. After years of carefully worded diplomatic exchanges between Cambridge and Prague, the NSA fired off blunt missives to IUS officials. One cable stated: "IN HUNGARIAN LETTER YOU SAY NOTHING REGARDING SOVIET INVASION OF HUNGARY AND SOVIET MASSACRE OF STUDENTS STOP ONE MIGHT CONCLUDE FROM YOUR LETTER THAT A HIGH WIND HAD STRUCK SOME HUNGARIAN UNIVERSITY STOP."[14] The chance to do some forthright needling must have been gratifying.

The campus tours, U.S. publicity campaign, and barrage of cables against IUS also camouflaged the CIA's covert agenda, whose principal aim was to find Hungarian students who could persuade neutralists in Asia to abandon nonalignment. Clive Gray put aside his scheduled travel and headed for Vienna. Gray had three goals: to find a Hungarian who could write a book about the uprising for Westerners; to identify a half-dozen or more Hungarians who could tour Asia and Latin America and talk about what happened; and to establish a Hungarian student federation before someone else did.[15] He was constantly looking over his shoulder, fearful that either IUS officials or the Russians would find out what he was doing and expose his activities.[16]

Gray established a base at the Regina Hotel in the University section. Vienna was in chaos, with students scattered all over the city, most of them unable to speak German. The few Hungarian translators in the city were in heavy demand. Refugees were dazed, tired, and fearful about their future. The situation improved for Gray when the Austrian student union (OH) received permission to use a Studenheim (hostel) on Pfeilgasse Street that could house three hundred students.[17]

Gray approached his search for Hungarian students like a theater producer holding auditions, seeking to cast the right combination of personality, maturity, firsthand experience, and acceptable politics. For the tour of Asia, he needed Hungarians "who had been in Budapest during the entire revolution, had experienced all the important events, and had taken active part in the fighting."[18] At the same time, they needed to be progressive on economic issues, or students in Asia and Latin America would tune them out. Further, he needed students who could "make a good impression on non-white students who might have something of an inferiority complex."[19]

After his first week in Vienna, Gray reported no progress on a student federation "except for a few eager beavers among the Hungarians themselves."[20] He rejected three students who had made it to Vienna after being released from Hungarian prisons, concluding they were "bitter anti-Communists" who lacked "tact," and thus were not "the right people to make an effective presentation."[21] Later, four students from Budapest arrived claiming a mandate from the Students Revolutionary Committee to organize a federation.[22] Gray ignored them.

By mid-December, a frustrated Gray had opted for a placeholder strategy. Relying on two brothers recommended by Bujdosó, Endre and Laszlo Lenches, and their friends from Sopron University, he notified COSEC of the creation of a new Federation of Refugee Hungarian Students. Associate Director James Edwards immediately issued a press release to announce "provisional recognition" of the federation. In the United States, Bruce Larkin also publicized the new federation.[23] He quoted Gray as if he had been a disinterested bystander: "We have queried our representative in Vienna and he describes the federation as 'representative and reliable.'"[24] Quick public recognition on both sides of the Atlantic made it difficult, if not impossible, for other Hungarian students, like the four from Budapest, to win international recognition, however authentic their mandate.

But Gray also understood the risks of the placeholder strategy. As the uprising faded into history, both the IUS and other Hungarians would challenge a federation that did not have a representative base.[25] He was also contending with leaders of older Hungarian exile organizations who had poured into Vienna, eager to find new roles for themselves. Gray regarded the Hungarians who had been exiled during World War II or the Soviet takeover of 1948 as bitter, often fanatical anticommunists. "The old exiles are all politically tarnished in the minds of the neutralists," he told Larkin. By contrast, Gray averred, students who had actually confronted Soviet tanks would give the new federation moral authority, and a credible claim to represent all Hungarian students. He just had to find the right Hungarians.[26]

The federation, even if flimsy, needed an agenda that could generate international publicity. But the Lenches kept rejecting Gray's ideas for action as possible violations of Austria's neutrality. At one point, their anxiety became so intense that they suggested a moratorium on *all* activities. In the end, Gray took matters into his own hands. He had heard rumors that the Soviets were deporting Hungarians to Russia. With time of the essence, it did not matter whether the rumors were true: the issue of deportations would be an ideal hook on which to hang a worldwide campaign.[27]

Gray decided that if the Algerians would co-sponsor a request for COSEC to launch a campaign against deportations, he could link African revolutionaries with Hungarian freedom fighters. The Algerians rejected the idea, as did other North African and Asian student leaders. Finally, in the absence of other signers, Gray made a mad dash to Geneva and pressured the Swiss student union into signing the request.[28]

A break occurred when Eugene Metz, who worked for the Free Europe Committee, introduced Gray to Bela Janko, an older exile who had returned to Budapest in the early days of the uprising. At first, Gray seemed uncertain; he described Janko as someone who "blew into Vienna with the idea of setting up a grand scheme for taking care of all the scholarship desires of Hungarian students." But after a while, he decided that Janko's energy "could be siphoned off into an organization . . . primarily devoted to telling Hungary's story to the outside student world."[29] It was a decision he later regretted.

After choosing his man, Gray had to convince Janko that a new organization was necessary, and at the same time convince the wary Lenches that Janko should take over the student federation.[30] As an incentive for Janko to cooperate with the Lenches brothers, Gray hinted that the old and new federations might later merge. His arguments did not persuade Endre Lenches, who resigned. Once again, Gray saw the student federation slipping away from him: "I began to have a desperate feeling that the committee project was going to flop unless drastic steps were taken."[31]

As they had so often in the past, CIA resources eased the impasse. Gray offered Janko generous assistance and a top position in the federation.[32] He prepared a list of founding members that included George Gömöri and András Sándor, two of the four students from the Student Revolutionary Committee, even though both men had left for England. (The other two returned to Budapest.) Gray publicly depicted the departing Endre Lenches as a founder who had "transferred his initiative to the new leaders."[33]

Gray worked quickly thereafter, since he needed to be in Warsaw before Christmas. Protests in Poland had helped spark the Hungarian uprising, and Gray was to explore possible contacts between the NSA and the Polish student union (ZSP).[34] He had heard tantalizing rumors that ZSP might withdraw from the IUS. Before he left Vienna, Gray found office space for the Hungarian student federation, a mimeograph machine, and other supplies. He drafted cables in the federation's name and requested financial assistance from other national unions of students for its activities.[35]

Ralph Della Cava replaced Gray in Vienna. When he arrived on December 18, he realized almost immediately the disparity between the glowing press releases put out by COSEC and the NSA and the reality. Della Cava counted exactly "two people whom we can count on to go on teams, one for office work and several others who will remain in

Vienna." He feared that the NSA could one day be left with squabbling factions of Hungarians, and the opportunity to convert neutral nations into Western allies would be squandered. He found the refugees not only at each other's throats but dispirited, their hopes of returning to a free Hungary declining.[36]

As the exiled Hungarians continued to fight among themselves. Della Cava finally moved the federation out of Vienna to Cologne, Germany, infuriating the German student union Verband Deutscher Studentenschaften. Then a representative from the adult-led Hungarian Revolutionary Council (HRC) turned up in Leiden, met with COSEC staff, and tried to quash the union, newly renamed the Union of Free Hungarian Students (UFHS).[37] Della Cava also fought continuously with Bela Janko, who chafed at the Americans' constraints on his leadership. In frustration Della Cava reported that he "went on a tirade." He told Janko that "he was a revolutionary and if he were to deny this [cooperation] he was also to deny the principles for which he fought—the freedom of his country."[38] Della Cava's "ace in the hole," he wrote forthrightly, was financial leverage. He had earlier threatened to return a $5,000 check to the NSA, if Janko did not shape up.[39] While Della Cava was devoted to the Hungarian cause—"they were my heroes," he said in an interview—his actions suggest that he never wavered from the CIA agenda.[40]

Hungarian refugees were also coming to the United States, and the NSA began evaluating them as candidates for various projects, including the proposed tours of Asia and Latin America. While the screening met one goal—a wider pool of Hungarian students—it thrust the NSA into a conflict between rival Hungarian student factions at Bard and Saint Michael's College. The opportunity to travel to Asia created further acrimony as students jockeyed for a place. The NSA began to rely on the judgment of Béla Lipták, who had witnessed the first stirrings of the uprising as a student at Technical University and was heading a committee of Hungarian students in the United States. Yet as soon as Lipták identified a candidate for the Asian tour, Janko would veto the choice.[41]

By mid-March, Della Cava realized that the original plan of sending two teams to Asia was "doomed, certainly dimmed." He blamed Janko. "Most prominent in this regard, has been the driving egoism, puritanical Catholicism, and political conservatism of one, Bela Janko."[42] Della

Cava, a Catholic himself, eliminated Janko from consideration for any of the tours, even though he still had to work with Janko as a federation official.

By the end of April 1957, the net result of all the frenetic activity on both sides of the Atlantic seemed to be an increase in the number of Hungarian student groups secretly supported by the CIA, either through FYSA or through private conduits that passed on CIA funds. The Catherwood Foundation, which earlier supplied a salary for the NSA international affairs vice president, supported the initial federation office in Vienna.[43] The San Jacinto Fund in Texas, another CIA conduit that occasionally funded the NSA and COSEC, awarded the UFHS secretariat in Germany a ten-thousand-dollar grant.[44] FYSA supported a meeting in Chicago of sixty-eight Hungarian students to form the American-Hungarian Students Association, led by Lipták. FYSA supported the UFHS Asia tour but nixed ambitious plans to target Latin American audiences.[45]

The Asia tour finally began on May 1, more than six months after the uprising. The internecine fussing of the previous months proved to be a dress rehearsal for the disarray that marked the tour. The delegation included thirty-year-old Charles Derecskey, who had fought in the Hungarian underground against the Nazis during World War II and acted as translator for Bujdosó's campus tour; Bujdosó himself; László Kiss, a Hungarian student in the United States chosen by Lipták—over the objections of Gray, who thought him a "parochial Roman Catholic, too conservative for India," and inflicted with an "overly aggressive temperament"—and Balázs Nagy, described by Gray as an ardent Marxist based in Paris, a member of the original Petőfi Circle of intellectuals that had formed in Budapest after Stalin's death.[46] The group's tour was to include Pakistan, India, Indonesia, Hong Kong, Malaysia, Thailand, the Philippines, and Japan.

The trouble started when India—a leader of the nonaligned movement and a target of the tour—denied the team visas. The reason? The visit violated India's policy of neutrality. A cable sent later to NSA headquarters explained, "Government of India did not wish to take sides for or against the USSR in regard to Hungary and therefore . . . desire to avoid controversy in India."[47] The Hungarians spent two days in Calcutta, where Gray met up with them, but he had no more sway with the Indian authorities than anyone else.[48] The team then split up, Buj-dosó and Derecskey heading for Indonesia, while Kiss and Nagy went to Japan.

Della Cava had been skeptical about the visit to Indonesia. "With all the revolution that's going on in that scattered dropplings of islands, you would imagine that they wouldn't be too happy about the arrival of Hungarian revolutionaries to tell them how it's really done!!!"[49] At the time, neither Gray nor Della Cava knew that a CIA hand lay behind the rebellion under way in Indonesia's outer islands, part of an attempt to topple President Sukarno.[50]

When Derecskey and Bujdosó arrived at the Jakarta airport, no one met them. After waiting until 3 A.M., they made their way into the city, where they found the streets lined with banners welcoming Kliment Voroshilov, the Soviet chief of state, who was arriving the following day for a two-week visit. The next morning, when the secretary general of PPMI surfaced, he denied inviting the Hungarians to Indonesia and asked them to remain secluded in the hotel during Voroshilov's visit. But Bujdosó and Derecskey saw a propaganda opportunity: during World War II, Voroshilov had been stationed in Budapest, and assisted the Russians to take over Hungary. At an improvised press conference in Jakarta, Derecskey and Bujdosó denounced the Soviets' suppression of the Hungarians. The resulting publicity was the high point of the tour: Jakarta papers carried the students' remarks on the front page along with the coverage of Voroshilov's visit.[51]

Buoyed by the publicity, Bujdosó and Derecskey left Jakarta to tour other Indonesian cities, hoping to find sympathetic students, if not in the PPMI, perhaps in Catholic organizations. But everywhere they went, they found fierce advocates of neutrality. The reception in Bandung was especially chilly. The two kept hearing unfavorable comments about Harry Lunn's behavior at the Asian-African Students Conference.[52]

In Thailand, Derecskey and Bujdosó had trouble making contact with students. When they did, they found more commitment to nonalignment. Even more disturbing, Thai students argued in favor of joining both student internationals, the IUS and the ISC.

In Japan, the Tokyo-based NSA overseas representative Robert Fisher had assured Della Cava that the Hungarian delegation would be welcome, though in an earlier letter, Fisher had warned that he was not on speaking terms with Zengakuren.[53] He apparently did not foresee the possibility that the left-wing Zengakuren would actively protest the Hungarian delegation: the students blocked Kiss and Nagy from speaking at the University of Tokyo. Kiss and Nagy finally found platforms in smaller venues, but the encounter left them dispirited over the lack of interest in the uprising among the Japanese.[54]

In a surprise move, and over the objections of Derecskey, Bujdosó and Kiss insisted on adding South Korea to their itinerary. The NSA saw no point, and considerable hazard, in visiting a country so firmly allied with the United States. But the Hungarians were insistent. When they arrived in Seoul, to everyone's chagrin, South Korean dictator Syngman Rhee engineered an impromptu photo opportunity with the Hungarians, himself, and a visitor from the United States, Republican New York governor Nelson Rockefeller. Rhee used the photo op to declare U.S., Korean, and Hungarian solidarity.[55] The fiasco went beyond Derecskey's worst fears. Not only were the Hungarians not making a dent in neutralist ideas, they had in effect declared themselves to be in the American camp. Hobnobbing with an American-backed Asian dictator was hardly the way to reach fierce Asian neutralists who were also fierce anticolonialists and anti-imperialists.

Paradoxically, the Hungarians received a warm reception from Korean students, eager to receive instruction on how to start a revolution and bring down a dictator.[56] Three years later, in April 1960, when South Korean students led the effort that toppled Rhee, some Hungarians believed that their visit had had an inspirational effect.[57]

But the propaganda bonanza envisioned by the CIA did not materialize. Neither publicity nor direct appeals convinced foreign students, let alone entire Asian countries, to abandon their commitment to nonalignment. John Simons, who originally supported a proposal for Hungarian teams to tour Latin America, cooled to the idea.

Nonetheless, almost everyone associated with the Hungarians' Asian tour declared it a success.[58] NSA publicity emphasized the importance of the tour, the heroism of the Hungarians, their high-level meetings in Korea and Ceylon, and the confrontation with the Soviet official in Indonesia. Derecskey declared himself "enthusiastic about the results."[59] But the NSA no longer expected publicity from the uprising to help stem the neutralist tide.

How did the Hungarians feel? Years later, their assessment is mixed. Some former officers argued the Asia trip put the new student union on the map, gave it legitimacy, and elevated its status within the ISC. But most acknowledged that being tied to the United States hurt their cause. For the delegation to have been credible with neutralists, said a former leader, the UFHS would have had to be free to "criticize the largest democracy in the world." This dilemma, wrote Julius Várallyay in his 1992 history of the UFHS, foreshadowed tensions within the organization that eventually led to its demise.[60]

Within a year of the Asian tour, Simons's support for Hungarian exiles had waned. He declined to fund UFHS chapters in Austria and Argentina.[61] He rejected a proposal to establish an Asian information bureau at UFHS headquarters (at a cost of $85,000), a request that had drawn his previous informal approval.[62] In late November 1957, Simons complained to the NSA that he still had not received a formal report on the Asia tour.[63] In three separate letters written on February 7, 1958, Simons questioned UFHS headquarters expenses and its proposed budget, and declined to commit funds for the October 1958 UFHS Congress, although he said he would entertain a proposal closer to the conference date.[64]

Over the next few years, the Hungarians gradually realized that their overreliance on the United States and Europeans was detrimental to their agenda. In order to win majority support for a Free Hungary in the United Nations, they needed votes from Asians, Africans, and Latin Americans. By 1962, federation leaders had decided to drop the word *free* from the name in an attempt to seem more neutral. In turn, John Simons cut off the remaining funds.[65]

The Hungarians turned to the NSA for help, noting that the NSA had made the first introductions to FYSA. In a memo to the files, an NSA officer claimed to have informed UFHS leader József Vizhányó that "he could not expect other Western national unions, who saw the Hungarian perspective from their own perspective and not from a Hungarian one, to actively take up the UFHS policy of forgetting about 1956, and talking about recent progress."[66] Simons's actions and the NSA's dismissive remarks surely had to do with ISC politics: if FYSA, the major funder of COSEC, was found supporting doctrines of neutrality, the rationale for continuing the ISC's fight against the IUS made no sense. The CIA-financed Free Europe Committee (based in New York), which did not share FYSA's relationship with the ISC, continued to support the federation, albeit with less generous funding.[67]

Despite these setbacks in influencing Asian and African neutralists, the CIA was not yet willing to abandon the strategy of spotlighting Soviet aggression in Hungary or trying to force neutralists to choose sides. When the CIA learned that the 1957 World Youth Festival would take place in Moscow, it decided to send evidence of Soviet tyranny right into Khrushchev's backyard.

12

DEBATING DEMOCRACY IN RED SQUARE

THE DECISION TO HOLD the 1957 World Youth Festival in Moscow so soon after the Soviets' invasion of Hungary struck the NSA-CIA team as audacious, a provocation that could not go unanswered. Since 1947, the festivals, sponsored by the World Federation of Democratic Youth and the International Union of Students, had vexed the CIA, especially since a left-wing youth group in the United States determined who would go to represent America. Intelligence officials sometimes encouraged a few political moderates to infiltrate the biennial festivals in Prague (1947), Berlin (1951), Budapest (1949, 1953), and Warsaw (1955) to observe and report back, but festival leaders usually discovered the interlopers.[1] At the 1951 festival in the German Democratic Republic, for example, the Harvard student Gerome Goodman crossed into East Berlin and was able to bunk with the American delegation until festival officials claimed they caught him writing down names on laundry bag tags and asked him to leave. His subsequent article, "I Crashed Stalin's Party," made for good publicity in the United States, but did little to deter the festival's attraction for thousands of young people.[2]

The NSA-CIA team believed that a festival in Moscow would give the Soviets a tremendous opportunity to capitalize on surging anticolonial sentiment and influence thousands of young people from Asia and Africa. NSA field reports reinforced this conclusion. African, Asian, and Latin American students planned to attend the festival in record numbers. In Santiago, Ralph Della Cava, who had resumed his Latin American duties after the Hungarians' tour of Asia, learned that Bolivia and Chile intended to send a hundred students each. If that figure were "duplicated throughout the continent," he calculated, "there very well could be more than 1,000 Latins at the Moscow Festival." He spoke for many in the NSA when he argued, "A strong pro-West voice will be [needed] to neutralize [Soviet influence] once they return."[3]

From New Delhi, Clive Gray warned that Asian students were "falling for the new openness" promoted by Soviet premier Nikita Khrushchev and his new policy of peaceful coexistence between East and West.[4] In addition, Khrushchev had promised freedom of movement for all festival participants, and the world's youth were flocking to Moscow.

What the NSA staff found particularly galling was that, as in the past, left-wing Americans would be representing the United States in Moscow, and the Soviets were touting their attendance and that of other Westerners as proof that the festival was not political. Gray spoke for many NSA overseas staff when he began shouting loudly through memos, cables, and reports, "SOMETHING HAS GOT TO BE DONE!!!!!!!!"[5]

But what? The NSA had always boycotted the festivals, a position that was unlikely to change. The rationale was fairly simple in Cold War terms: NSA attendance would legitimate the festival and hand the Soviets a propaganda victory. But this position was rarely stated openly, since the NSA scrupulously avoided Cold War rhetoric. Paris-based Crawford Young, who now spent most of his time with African and other foreign students, reported his frustration with trying to explain NSA policy in apolitical terms. "The long and short of it is that it is damn difficult to convince even non-Communist Africans of the reasons behind our non-participation in the Festival."[6]

Once again, the CIA provided an answer to the dilemma. The NSA would continue its boycott while the CIA sent a small group of politically reliable older American graduate students to Moscow, among them former NSA officials, who would claim that they were attending the festival out of curiosity. But once in Moscow they would look for opportunities to raise the Hungarian issue.

Richard Medalie, a twenty-eight-year-old former NSA officer (1949–50), then at Harvard Law, was one of those tapped for the assignment. "I met a man in Harvard Square," he said in a later interview, declining to identify his contact, "who handed me an airline ticket from Boston to Washington with a false identification card to match the name (Dr. Carlton) on the ticket." After briefings in Washington, Medalie agreed to go to Moscow and portray his decision as a spontaneous impulse. As a Carlton College undergraduate (hence the name on the ticket), Medalie had been involved with the NSA since 1948, when his delegation to the Congress "wanted nothing to do with" the International Union of Students.[7]

Medalie's experience with the NSA changed his outlook and his life. At the 1949 Congress, he roomed with an African American, an encounter that resulted in a lifelong commitment to civil rights. As important, that year he was elected NSA educational affairs vice president.[8] Toward the end of his term, in the summer of 1950, Medalie worked closely with Frederick Houghteling and the international team. He was one of the few men who knew the names of the secret donors, although there is no evidence that he was witting at that time.[9]

After the 1950 Congress, Medalie never returned to Carlton College. In rapid succession, he won a Fulbright to London and enrolled in graduate school at Harvard, where he studied under Zbigniew Brzezinski and wrote a thesis on the Soviets' takeover of Eastern Europe before entering law school. The son of Russian immigrants—his mother had escaped from the Soviet Union by boat across the Black Sea during Stalin's first five-year plan; his father had arrived earlier from Ukraine—Medalie had learned a smattering of Russian as a child. He became fluent at Harvard and also spoke Serbo-Croation.[10]

Medalie believes that Helen Jean Rogers identified him for the festival operation.[11] CIA officials had vetted his performance two years earlier when he represented the NSA at an IUS-sponsored conference in Dubrovnik. Paul Sigmund and Clive Gray, also in attendance, had given him stellar marks.[12] Particularly useful had been his ability to converse with his Yugoslav hosts.

For the Moscow assignment, Medalie recruited another Harvard law student, George Abrams, who subsequently became his brother-in-law. A former *Harvard Crimson* editor, Abrams later identified his recruiter simply as "a former NSA person" used to dealing with international matters.[13] Abrams recounted a similar meeting in Harvard Square, where he received a ticket under a phony name for an initial briefing in Washington. The CIA also recruited a handful of Rhodes Scholars, although several dropped out, fearful of violating U.S. prohibitions against travel to the Soviet Union.[14]

The first problem Medalie and Abrams faced was getting into the festival. The left-wing U.S. Committee for International Student Cooperation (CISC) controlled appointments to the American delegation, and was unlikely to credential them. Nor could they enter the Soviet

Union directly from the United States without violating the McCarran Act, which banned travel to Communist countries. Secretary of State John Foster Dulles publicly warned that U.S. travelers to Moscow risked having their passports revoked.[15] It was a classic CIA conundrum: covert action meant adhering to a cover story, even with top-ranking government officials. The Americans had to reach Moscow in a manner that would not later discredit their cover story as curiosity seekers. Medalie remembers that one after another option was explored and discarded.[16]

The solution they finally hit on was ingenious. During the Dubrovnik meeting, Medalie had established contact with leaders of the Polish student union, ZSP. Although at the time the Poles seemed quite hostile to him and to the West generally, after the Hungarian uprising—and partly as a result of Gray's work—relations between NSA and ZSP had thawed. Discussions were even under way for an NSA-ZSP exchange program. Medalie contacted his friends in ZSP, and they agreed to help the Americans secure visas through the Soviet embassy in Poland.[17]

Before leaving for Moscow, Medalie and Abrams returned to Washington for briefings, along with a short course on espionage techniques—how to detect and disable an eavesdropping device, how to avoid being followed. Abrams later said that he never fully grasped the risks they were facing until he returned to the United States. At the time, his excitement about "getting to peek behind the Iron Curtain" overrode his fears.[18]

A few weeks later, the two arrived in Moscow as members of the Polish delegation. Buried in their luggage were copies of the U.N. special report on the Hungarian uprising and its suppression by the Soviets. The report had not yet been formally approved by the General Assembly, but it challenged the Soviets' version of events, and the CIA calculated that Khrushchev would never permit it to circulate in the Soviet Union.[19] Intent on exposing both Khrushchev's peace offensive and neutralist doctrines as frauds, Medalie and Abrams looked for an opportunity to use the U.N. material.

Once they were inside Russia, Medalie and Abrams were not permitted to remain with the Polish delegation, as they had hoped to do. The festival host committee sorted arrivals by country, so Medalie and Abrams joined the 180 or so American delegates, who were crammed four to five to a room in a dormitory on the outskirts of Moscow.[20] Abrams later emphasized the contrast between accommodations for Westerners and those reserved for nonaligned delegations. "The dark-skinned and the Arab delegates . . . were given the red-carpet treatment. Instead of five to a room, the Indians and Africans and Arabs were put in rooms with two or three people. Instead of cafeteria-service meals, the Russians gave the delegates of uncommitted countries their own dining halls, with waiters and candlelight service." [21]

Festival organizers had adopted Pablo Picasso's iconic dove of peace as its symbol, and at the opening day parade two to three million people lined the route shouting "Peace and Friendship," the official slogan of the festival. The left-wing American delegation was crowded onto a decorated flatbed truck that sported a large American flag. All along the parade route, Russians waved small American flags at the delegation, made and distributed by the Soviets. One of the Americans on the truck, Robert Carl Cohen, who had earned a master's degree in filmmaking at UCLA and was studying for a doctorate at the Sorbonne, described the euphoria of the moment in film later posted on the Internet: "The first large U.S. group to enter Moscow since 1945 when the then-General Eisenhower joined with Dictator Stalin to honor Red Army soldiers after the Nazi defeat." [22]

Medalie and Abrams tried to avoid being seen or photographed with the left-wing American delegation, sometimes walking on opposite sides of the street. In a report to NSA staff Medalie described how troubling he found the four-hour parade. "It was frightening to realize that this shouting of peace and friendship was deeply sincere, and to know at the same time how much the Soviet political leaders had bent the meanings of these words to their own uses." [23]

Over the next two weeks, a packed schedule offered the thirty thousand delegates a blend of serious seminars and cultural events, film festivals, art exhibitions, poetry readings, jazz concerts, and a performance by the Bolshoi Ballet. Khrushchev hosted an international ball inside the Kremlin, giving twelve thousand foreign delegates a chance to have their picture taken with him. [24]

When they arrived, Medalie and Abrams had stopped by the American Embassy and explained that they had decided to visit the festival on a whim. They found the officials decidedly cool. The atmosphere was so chilly, Medalie recalled, that the embassy refused their requests for copies of U.S. publications. Unable to reveal that they had the imprimatur of the U.S. government, they were treated by American officials as leftists.

Undaunted, Medalie and Abrams looked for opportunities to stir up trouble wherever they went—proudly crashing a cocktail party thrown by Khrushchev, for example. But the event that became legendary in NSA-CIA circles and convinced the CIA to expand its counter-festival operations in the future occurred in Red Square, when Medalie and Abrams stood in front of Lenin's Tomb, right in front of the Kremlin, and debated democracy with a crowd of about a thousand spectators.[25] Curious Muscovites peppered them with questions. How many rooms does your house have? What is the average wage in America? How many children go to school in America? Tell us about the Ku Klux Klan. Tell us about discrimination in the United States. The encounter occasionally turned heated over issues of nuclear testing and disarmament: As part of his peaceful coexistence campaign, Khrushchev had urged a suspension of nuclear tests and a general reduction in the world's armaments. Medalie countered that the "issue isn't suspension itself but how to successfully control it."[26] Watchful police would periodically start to move in on the Americans, but according to Medalie, all either of them had to do was shout "festival" and the police would retreat.[27]

Pressed to explain why U.S. authorities had denied visas to festival-goers, Medalie explained that it was "a symbolic protest against the cruelty and illegal slaughter of [meaning "by"] Soviet troops in Hungary."[28] Here was the opening the two men sought. They began to read excerpts from the U.N. report on the Hungarian uprising.

It did not take long for the official Hungarian delegation to appear to contest the U.N. report's conclusions and defend the Soviets' action as necessary to suppress "fascist counter-revolutionary elements."[29] Medalie later observed that his Hungarian adversaries were so adept at arguing their case he had difficulty "parrying questions and contrasting statistics."[30] But filled with excitement for what they had pulled off, Medalie and Abrams returned to Red Square for several more nights to continue their thrust and parry.[31]

The Soviets were not pleased. While authorities refrained from interfering during the sessions, the official Communist Party newspaper *Izvestia* began to run attacks on Abrams, calling him an FBI spy, while another newspaper, *Sovetskaya Rossiya*, denounced him as a State Department plant. It also editorialized against Western newsmen who "report the Festival in a vicious anti-Soviet spirit, roaming the streets looking for incidents, and when impressions are inadequate resort to fantasy."[32]

Most delegates, however, could not read Russian and remained unaware of the accusations.

What mattered to the CIA was the propaganda bonanza generated by the men's actions. One UPI headline read, "Minnesotan Talks Reds to Stand Off." An interview with Medalie's mother in Minnesota prompted another headline, "Reds Won't Sway Son."[33]

Soviet authorities waited until the pair attempted to leave the country to make trouble. Medalie wanted to fly out. The Soviets argued, "If you come in by train, you leave by train."[34] Medalie got his way by screaming in Russian at the festival organizers. Abrams was detained at the Moscow airport for several hours in a solitary room and then refused permission to board a plane. He left by train for Paris. Abrams's brush with Soviet police prompted more dramatic headlines: "Red Blaster Safe in Newton [Massachusetts]."[35]

Both Abrams and Medalie were hailed as heroes. When Medalie landed at New York's Idlewild Airport, reporters and photographers swarmed the plane. Not yet aware that he was the focus of the media crush, Medalie scanned the passengers for a famous person. He realized what was happening when "someone grabbed me and scooted me away to a special room at the airport to do interviews."[36]

The public attention went on for days. Dave Garroway featured Medalie on the NBC's *Today* show. Senator Hubert Humphrey (D-Minn.) invited Medalie and Abrams to Washington to testify in closed session before the Senate Foreign Relations Committee. Medalie and Abrams stuck to their cover story: they were two intrepid Americans who had dared to confront Soviet communism in Red Square. Asked later how he felt about lying to the U.S. Senate, Medalie hesitated, then offered a common Cold Warrior refrain, "I guess I felt I served a higher purpose."[37]

Not every festival delegate from the United States received favorable publicity. Several dozen American delegates ran afoul of the Department of State when they accepted an invitation from the All Chinese Student Federation to visit China on their way home. Embassy officials in Moscow tried to frighten them out of going, while Acting Secretary of State Christian A. Herter sent out a "Dear Fellow Citizen" letter. "By traveling to Communist China at this time you will, in the considered view of your government, be acting as a willing tool of Communist propaganda intended, wherever possible, to subvert the foreign policy and the best interests of the U.S."[38] Forty-one Americans defied the warning and made the six-thousand-mile trip via Trans-Siberian railroad.[39] The filmmaker Robert Cohen wangled press credentials from NBC television and became the first American to film inside Mao's China.[40]

At least one American festival delegate who traveled abroad ran into political trouble later from a witting NSA representative. When Joanne Grant, a civil rights activist and one-time assistant to W. E. B. DuBois, arrived in New Delhi with a friend, Clive Gray used his access to the American embassy to get them kicked out of the country. Today, he rues the act: "I am not very proud of it."[41] But at the time, discrediting left-wing American students as tools of Soviet propaganda was as central to CIA strategy as trying to convince neutralists to abandon nonalignment—and about as effective.

After their return from Moscow, Medalie and Abrams spent two days in a Washington safe house being debriefed by a CIA Russian specialist and writing reports. Medalie thought that most of the American delegation were innocent idealists and described lead organizer Barbara Perry from Chicago as someone "who really believed that the Festival could produce peace." He reported that to his surprise many left-wing delegates had defended the United States, including the controversial requirement that visitors from the Soviet Union or Eastern bloc countries must be fingerprinted before entry. Medalie believed that there were "extreme left-wingers" in the delegation, but he found them "difficult to identify." [42]

But Medalie also challenged State Department and NSA policy. Making the same argument that Czech foreign minister Jan Masaryk had made in 1947, Medalie argued that refusing to send a diverse American delegation to the festival forfeited a major opportunity to challenge the Soviets. Abrams agreed and said so publicly. What was gained, he asked. "Most of the so-called neutralist countries were not influenced at all by the State Department position and sent representative delegations." Abrams called State Department policy "the ostrich approach"; it guaranteed that only left-wing Americans would represent the United States.[43] Abrams put forth a new proposition: "What seemed to me especially impressive in Moscow was the impact of the politically *unsophisticated* American youth, able to counter the false impressions held by the average Russian." He described how astonished Muscovites were to learn from a young blond student that she had a "Negro" college roommate.[44]

The CIA and State Department were unmoved by the arguments. Nor did the NSA change its boycott policy. It turned out that liberals were not the only voices weighing in on the Moscow festival.

What Medalie and Abrams did not realize was that there were other CIA eyes and ears at the festival, belonging to conservative young professionals who drew different conclusions. Among them was Raymond Garthoff, a newly minted Soviet specialist from the Rand Corporation, soon to join the CIA as a career officer. In his memoir, Garthoff described returning with valuable loot, including a classified Soviet military report.[45] Garthoff's traveling companion during the festival was Alexander Dallin, a young Soviet scholar from Columbia University who traveled to Moscow by attaching himself to the Swedish delegation. Dallin's father, David, had fought as a Menshevik in the Russian Revolution before being forced into exile.[46]

Both Garthoff and Dallin spoke Russian, and they conversed with hundreds of students in Moscow and nearby cities. They returned with dozens of photographs that included self-identified dissidents, along with a pictorial record of conditions in the Soviet Union. Garthoff warned that "the much-feted Africans and South Asians seemed tremendously and favorably impressed with Moscow, the Russians and what they were told was Communism."[47] His conclusions would have played on the CIA's worst fears.

The CIA view that the festivals were tightly controlled propaganda events, even if largely true, blinded the Agency to their subtle impacts. According to Russian and non-Russian sources alike, Khrushchev's Thaw was not a sham, even though some of the new openness was engineered for the festival and disappeared afterward.[48] But the festival itself did presage a new movement in the Soviet Union. The Russian poet Yevgeny Yevtushenko, who participated, later hailed it as the "great beginning of liberalization in Russia." His moment of personal freedom came when he "broke the Cold War rules" and kissed an American girl, later quipping, "My socialist lips touched so-called 'capitalist lips.'" He remembered the thrill of meeting foreigners from Africa and South America, a first for many Russians. The festival made him feel like "a part of humanity. . . . a humanity which was stolen from us."[49]

Yevtushenko was not alone. Young Russians from this period made up what later became known as the Gorbachev generation, and would embrace Mikhail Gorbachev's policies of glasnost and perestroika.[50] At Moscow State University, from which he had recently graduated, Gorbachev had been part of a circle of privileged students who detested Stalin, had grown skeptical of Soviet propaganda, and openly read and discussed Western literature.

In fact, the festival, in the opinion of two Russian scholars, was a crucial step in the Thaw. "Many witnesses of the festival would concur later that it was a historical landmark as important as Khrushchev's secret speech."[51] It was "a grassroots happening that paralyzed all attempts at spin control, as well as crowd control." The scholars also assert that "the appearance of young Americans, Europeans, Africans, Latins, and Asians in the streets of the Soviet capital shattered propagandist clichés."[52] In 2007, Russians celebrated the fiftieth anniversary of the festival as part of their cultural heritage, its significance independent of the Soviet regime that sponsored it.[53]

In retrospect, it seems clear that the CIA International Organizations division was like other bureaucracies: it measured success in terms of short-term operational goals. Thus defined, the Medalie-Abrams project succeeded. The men had denied left-wing American delegates an exclusive franchise. They had disrupted festival events and annoyed festival organizers, goading the Soviets into a public condemnation of their soapbox lectures on Hungary. They had obtained firsthand intelligence. Not least, their audacity had generated favorable publicity in the United States.

But the long-term dilemma for the NSA-CIA team was the growing power of the spirit of Bandung. Nationalists of every stripe in Asia, Africa, and Latin America were challenging the United States to live up to its principles of self-determination. By 1957, CIA liberals in the IO division, eager to compete with the Soviet Union and win favor with anticolonial revolutionaries, had begun to experiment with new and riskier strategies through private-sector groups. Since revolutions, by definition, require youth and energy, the NSA international operation was uniquely positioned to win the trust of young revolutionaries, or so it seemed. Even if they lost, the CIA stood to gain valuable information.

13

COURTING REVOLUTIONARIES

IN 1957, AFTER YEARS of building up the membership of the International Student Conference, the CIA-NSA group realized that the last thing the ISC needed was additional members from Africa, Asia, the Middle East, or Latin America. It had become clear that a continued influx of more militant students would further politicize the conference. The NSA was caught in a trap of its own making. Its very success had resulted in a shift of power inside the ISC, one that put the NSA and other European unions in a minority. After the Ceylon ISC, how long the NSA would be able to support and at the same time temper demands from anticolonial and anti-imperialist students was unclear.

After a visit to Egypt in January to probe post-Bandung attitudes, Clive Gray observed, "There should be a point at which enough is called enough, and that point is before we get to Egypt."[1] The ISC gradually became of secondary importance to the Americans. It remained a visible alternative to the IUS, and useful for conducting projects under CO-SEC auspices, but no longer the primary objective of counteroffensive strategies. The important battles between East and West were taking place in individual countries, and often in locations without established national unions of students.

Gray referred to this policy shift in his report, identifying Egypt as "a good place to test our new approach . . . striving toward bilateral contacts between American and other students outside the national and local union framework."[2] Witting staff looked for moderate, pro-Western students who had the potential to become leaders in their countries one day, regardless of their organizational affiliation.

Paul Sigmund's reports from Paris in 1955–56 had already begun to focus on individual leaders. "If[,] as many expect, Algeria will ultimately receive some sort of independence within or without the French union, the events of the past year will be important in forming the attitudes of those who will be called upon to lead the new nation, as their fellow North Africans are being called upon in Morocco and Tunisia."[3] At this point, the belief that educated elites would be the ones to govern after independence was a foregone conclusion, though things did not work out that way.

The pursuit of individual moderates created tensions within various NSA-CIA programs. The NSA, for example, wanted to control the selection process for the Foreign Student Leadership Project, to ensure that no foreign student union could dictate its choice for the scholarship. At the same time, staff had to avoid being too heavy-handed about it, lest their actions provoke hostility from top officials of the targeted union, whose goodwill they needed within the ISC. Frequently, the NSA would solicit multiple applications in the hope of getting its preferred selection.

In general, the annual ISCs were becoming a headache. The NSA delegation's maneuvering in Ceylon had annoyed many ISC members, especially Europeans. Crawford Young was tasked with doing further analysis on their reaction to the fact that "the Afro-Asian-Latin American group could carry any vote on which they presented a united front."[4] At the same time COSEC still served NSA-CIA objectives. COSEC could be used to reward friends (with staff positions, tours, projects), legitimate foreign student contacts, and ease the task of gathering intelligence.

The World Youth Festival in Moscow had left no doubt about the priority the Soviets placed on anticolonial students from Asia and Africa. For the witting team to compete with the Soviets, the NSA had to convince revolutionary student leaders that American students supported their goals. Over the next few years, the NSA concentrated on Cuba and Algeria, never guessing that the successful revolutions there would become iconic, inspiring militant revolutionaries throughout the world and leaving moderates out in the cold, or that Algeria and Cuba would join the enemy camp.

In the late 1950s, the NSA-CIA team placed outsized hopes on the success of these two movements. Overseas staff believed that support for Algerians could win the NSA friends across North Africa and the

Middle East. Messaoud Ait Chaalal, the UGEMA president, encouraged these hopes. He argued that an independent Algeria, aligned with Tunisia and Morocco, would influence both Middle Eastern and African politics. In the short term, he boasted, without UGEMA's affiliation, "the ISC would lose all of Africa."[5] The NSA similarly viewed support for Cuban revolutionaries as the key to winning influence throughout Latin America, especially in convincing students that the NSA opposed the U.S. government's support of right-wing dictators.

While it might seem an uphill climb for the NSA to convince the Algerians and Cubans of its leftist sympathies, the young revolutionary leaders had an incentive to build relationships with U.S. students. The Algerians viewed America's pressure on France as key to winning independence, while the Cubans needed Eisenhower to end his support of Batista and stop the flow of U.S. military aid to the island. Both Algerian and Cuban student leaders saw in the nearly one million American students that the NSA claimed to represent a small army, able to put pressure on their government. The NSA encouraged this illusion with constant talk of student solidarity. In private, the story was different. The NSA had no history of taking to the streets to protest U.S. foreign policy and no intention of doing so.

The fact that each side was motivated to cooperate did not mean these relationships were always amicable. Whether the NSA provided moral support (resolutions) or tangible resources (funds), it often expected a quid pro quo. Crawford Young made this explicit in November 1956 when UGEMA refused to back the deportation campaign instigated by Clive Gray on behalf of the Hungarians. "They won't lift a finger," Young complained.[6] "This annoys the hell out of me—I'm going to make it clear to them tomorrow that from a practical point of view if the average American student discovered that UGEMA took no interest in the plight of Hungarian students, he would be far less inclined to do anything for the Algerian students."[7] Young would have been hard-pressed to find American students who were even aware of the Algerian cause, let alone any who were annoyed with the Algerians' position on Hungary, but such threats became increasingly commonplace.

The Algerians' refusal to help the Hungarians stung especially because just a few days earlier, the new NSA president, Harald Bakken, had flown to Paris and offered UGEMA leaders assistance. Bakken, a midwesterner from the University of Minnesota, had postponed his junior year to run for president, making him one of the youngest elected to lead the NSA. Over a couscous dinner in Paris with Young and UGEMA leaders, Bakken offered to broker financial support from FYSA.[8]

Overseas staff finally grasped that UGEMA's refusal to cooperate was not due to indifference to the Hungarians' plight. Rather, the Algerians were furious over what was going on in the Middle East: the war over the Suez Canal, which had begun on October 29. While Great Britain, France, and Israel strafed targets in Egypt, the NSA and COSEC remained silent.

From the Algerians' standpoint, the NSA had linked Western colonialism and Soviet imperialism in its condemnation of deportations. Now it was refusing to stand by its own policy. If the attack on Egypt did not represent a clear-cut case of Western imperialism, what did? Even though the United States was not a partner in the Suez War (and Eisenhower had been nearly apoplectic over his allies' actions), the administration had never publicly condemned the military action. The NSA defended its own inaction with the claim the war did not involve students.[9]

North African students were not alone in their anger. Feelings ran high among students from Asia, elsewhere in Africa, and especially the Middle East, who also saw the NSA silence on Western aggression as hypocrisy and COSEC inaction as invidious, especially in light of the secretariat's all-out effort for Hungarian students. The NSA's representative in Japan explained that students were far more upset about the Suez, which fit into the dominant narrative about Western imperialism, than they were about Hungary.[10]

In practice, neither the NSA nor COSEC could ever really divorce itself from Western policies. Every twist and turn of U.S. policy toward France over the Algerian question, for example, influenced the NSA's relations with UGEMA. On February 13, 1957, the U.S. ambassador to the United Nations, Henry Cabot Lodge, Jr., blocked a strong General Assembly resolution favoring immediate negotiations with France for Algerian self-determination.[11] This did not help Crawford Young's job: the Algerians, he reported, feared "that the US, the only country in a position to bring the horrid thing to an end, is going to limit itself to pious declarations in favor of 'liberal' solutions."[12] At the same time, Young was not recommending that the NSA take a more activist approach: the NSA Congress, he wrote, "did not (and I don't think should) protest the pro-colonial activity."[13]

UGEMA leaders were not shy about pressing the NSA for tangible support, especially as their situation grew worse. By early 1957, the war for Algerian independence had entered an extremely bloody phase. French paratroopers in Algiers cordoned off the Muslim area of the city, known as the Kasbah, which served as an FLN sanctuary. Many Algerians died there or were later taken prisoner. The French also used torture techniques that included electrodes on genitals, dunking and drowning in bathtubs, brutal beatings, and summary executions.[14] The battle decimated the FLN leadership in Algiers, giving greater prominence to the young leaders in exile.[15]

Meanwhile, in Paris, the French police were taking the battle to UGEMA. They arrested, jailed, tortured, and in some cases executed Algerian students, including UGEMA's founding members. On March 1, the French arrested the founding secretary general of UGEMA, Ahmed Taleb-Ibrahimi, a medical student and FLN member, for "threatening the external security of the state."[16] By June, Young was reporting that the UGEMA executive committee had dwindled from fifteen members to four or five. The French government cut off scholarships to UGEMA students, leaving many stranded in France without any means of support. As French atrocities mounted, the need for financial assistance, especially scholarships, became a UGEMA priority.[17]

The NSA toyed with awarding one or two scholarships to Algerians under the Foreign Student Leadership Project, an option Young advocated.[18] Director Ted Harris responded with a cable: "Have place for best Algerian," but "prefer Tunisian." He counseled Young to be patient, promising that the NSA would try to bring in more North Africans "in the next year or two."[19] One can imagine the Algerians' reaction had they seen this cable, with its cavalier sentiment that was so at odds with both the urgency felt by UGEMA leaders and the NSA's assurances of solidarity.

At the end of his term in Paris, Young's despair over French-Algerian relations is evident in his reports and letters. The conflict, "this poisonous, moldering affair," was tearing French society apart. But he had also had it with French students, whose union, UNEF, had fractured over the conflict. "Perhaps one year of UNEF is as much as a normal human being can stand."[20]

For years, the NSA had used CIA funds to soothe ruffled feathers among the French (and other European) student leaders by subsidizing trips to the United States. NSA Paris representatives talked openly of this support as an investment. In 1954, the NSA representative, David Duberman, had claimed the credit when his preferred candidate agreed to run for UNEF president and won.[21] And Young, during his year in Paris, had become impressed with another UNEF leader who had unwittingly benefited from CIA funds, Pierre Cossé. He told Bruce Larkin, the international affairs vice president, "I don't know how much if any of this is due to his attending the USNSA Congress last year, but he seems to be the first really good UNEF investment in this regard."[22] But these investments rarely paid off, and relations remained difficult.

Just when Young's pessimism over the Algerian conflict was greatest, an indication came that U.S. policy might be about to change. On July 2, Senator John F. Kennedy (D-Mass.) delivered a speech to his colleagues on the Senate floor that challenged every facet of President Eisenhower's Algeria policy.[23] He argued that the current U.S. stance damaged not only Algeria's future but also America's interests on the entire African continent.

Kennedy asserted that "the most powerful single force in the world today is neither communism nor capitalism, neither the H-bomb nor the guided missile." It was "man's eternal desire to be free and independent" and "the single most important test of American foreign policy today is how we meet the challenge of imperialism, what we do to further man's desire to be free." Describing the Algerian FLN leadership as "pro-West moderates," he warned that lack of U.S. support could drive them into the arms of the Soviets. In arguing for freedom for the Algerian people, Kennedy was implicitly recognizing the legitimate aims of all nationalists who fought colonial power.[24]

The senator took on the comparison between Hungary and Algeria. "The great enemy of that tremendous force of freedom is called, for want of a more precise term, imperialism—and today that means Soviet imperialism and, whether we like it or not, and though they are not to be equated, Western imperialism."[25]

Kennedy's speech was so radical a departure from mainstream opinion that some prominent Democrats joined with Eisenhower Republicans—and most of the foreign policy establishment—in condemning it. Vice President Nixon dismissed the Kennedy speech as "brashly political."[26] Some saw it as appeasing the pro-Arab faction in the State Department. Secretary of State Dulles, even though he thought French policy toward Algeria might soon backfire, told the French ambassador that the two of them were "now in the same boat," both under fire from Kennedy. As reported in *Time*, "Kennedy set off a cannon cracker in the Senate that rattled the windows at the other end of Pennsylvania Avenue and burned an ally 3,800 miles away."[27]

Kennedy might as well have thrown a grenade at the Élysée Palace. The French government warned resident Americans to stay off the streets; just two days after the speech, on July 4, a literal bomb exploded outside the American embassy in Paris.[28]

Five days later, Kennedy tempered his remarks, explaining, "Of course the Soviet Union is guilty of far worse examples of imperialism." But he reiterated his belief that "the worldwide struggle against imperialism, the sweep of nationalism, is the most potent factor in foreign affairs today."[29] Restating the gist of his earlier speech, he warned that failure to support the current pro-West moderates would "inevitably" mean that "extremists, terrorists, and outside provocateurs" would take charge. Would moderates not turn to "Moscow, to Cairo, to Peiping [Beijing], the pretended champions of nationalism and independence?"[30] He could not have known how close he was to predicting the future or that he would preside over that shift.

Kennedy's speech exhilarated Algerians. On July 22, Young reported, "We are now once again in the good graces of the North Africans."[31] Relations also warmed between the NSA and the national unions of Morocco and Tunisia — countries that were friendly to the United States, but whose more militant student unions stood with the Algerian nationalists and were often to the left of their governments.[32] Traveling in Asia, Clive Gray reported being "overjoyed . . . because it seems to mark the beginning of enlightened participation in the Algerian question by responsible American leaders." He predicted, "Agitation will grow which will force this, or the succeeding administration, to put some pressure on the French."[33]

While Kennedy gave Algerian revolutionaries hope, the NSA remained trapped between Eisenhower's public support for France and UGEMA's demand for material support, which far out-stripped the NSA's capacity to deliver. To this point, the NSA had brokered modest CIA funds for UGEMA from FYSA and American Friends for the Middle East, but even the CIA had to be circumspect about damaging the U.S.-French alliance. Unable to give substantial financial support, the NSA looked for opportunities to demonstrate moral support. These were not hard to find.

In late 1957, the NSA went to bat for an Algerian student, UGEMA general secretary Mohamed Khemisti, whom Young once judged harshly as "fanatic and unreasonable."[34] On November 12, the French police arrested Khemisti and transported him to Algiers. His colleagues feared for his life. Young cabled the NSA that it was imperative to act quickly. "Otherwise people will say that USNSA does not like K. because he went off to Red China and North Korea."[35] A jailed fanatic posed little risk, so the NSA delivered a letter of protest at the French embassy in Washington and worked in tandem with Senator Kennedy's office to pressure French officials to give Khemisti a fair trial.[36]

COSEC also campaigned for Khemisti's release. Young later assured members of UGEMA: "We have protested against the arrest of M. Khemisti as vigorously as at the time of the Hungarian affair."[37] A stretch, to be sure, but NSA international staff on both sides of the Atlantic agreed that the action rescued COSEC's relations with UGEMA. Clement Moore, Young's successor in Paris, speculated that if COSEC had not acted, "UGEMA would not have attended another ISC."[38] However much the NSA wanted to avoid a more intense politicization of the ISC, UGEMA had to remain a member or the ISC would lose its ability to compete with the IUS on an issue—Algerian independence—that was galvanizing students around the world.

In addition to mending the relationship with UGEMA, the NSA later reaped further rewards for the Khemisti campaign. Although Khemisti spent two years in the notorious Algiers prison Maison Carrée, his life was spared. In 1962, he became the first foreign minister of the independent Algeria. At a White House reception, Khemisti praised the NSA and facilitated a private meeting with the new Algerian president, Ahmed Ben Bella.[39]

At the time of Khemisti's arrest, NSA overseas staff reports warned that UGEMA was losing patience with the West. Ali Lakhdari, an NSA favorite—educated, erudite, and diplomatic, a future Algerian ambassador to the United Nations—reportedly declared, "Only NSA in the West does anything, because basically in spite of pious declarations, the students of the West (with the exception of USNSA) do not really care about Algerian students."[40] Yet the criticism was subtly aimed at the NSA as well, since Lakhdari continually pressed Clement Moore about the NSA's unfulfilled promises to give Algerians scholarships to the United States.

The NSA's hands were still tied by official U.S. policy: to establish a scholarship program for Algerians in the United States with CIA funds, however well camouflaged, apparently went beyond what the CIA felt it could do. Bankrolling revolutionaries required more significant funds than those used to buy modest access. As an interim solution, the Ford Foundation granted funds for a scholarship program jointly sponsored by COSEC and the World University Service in Geneva. In an unusual move, the Ford Foundation deferred to the NSA in setting the terms of the grant, which suggests that someone with a higher rank than witting NSA personnel had approached the foundation.[41] But the Algerians pressed for more, invoking offers from the Eastern Bloc as leverage.

In 1958, Daniel Idzik, a former NSA officer, then the CIA's man at the WUS, reported a conversation with Messaoud Ait Chaalal, and warned the NSA: "The Algerians' backs are against the wall. Three NSA scholarships are considered to be a drop in the bucket—perhaps even less than a token."[42] By contrast, the East Germans had offered a hundred scholarships. More ominous, Idzik wrote, "The Chinese offered on the spot to match whatever figure Ait Chaalal could come up with."[43]

Idzik reminded his colleagues that Ait Chaalal had put his prestige on the line to defend the ISC, at the risk of jeopardizing his own position. "He now feels that the pressure is really on them [UGEMA's leadership], this coming from their own constituency which they have been holding back from taking up the scholarship offers made by the Eastern Europeans, and that unless something happens soon they may get tossed out of office."[44] If the NSA did not act quickly, the "Algerians will take up the scholarships available in [Iron] Curtain areas, and anything done during the past months will have gone down the drain."[45] Today Idzik is one of several who describe the Algerians as tough negotiators, not meek supplicants.[46]

CLEMENT MOORE, a graduate of Phillips Exeter Academy and Harvard with little NSA experience, had taken over the Paris post in the middle of the Algerian crisis. In early December 1958, Moore told Young that he found Paris to be just as Young predicted: "Many cups of coffee and a few riots for good measure."[47] What Young had not warned Moore about was the French police. Nor could he have—Young did not know until later that the French secret police had him under surveillance and had compiled a dossier on his activities.[48] Thus, after Moore gave a rousing speech at the UGEMA annual congress that December, he got a lesson in the darker side of Paris.

Before dawn on January 13, 1958, two Paris police agents roused Moore from his bed. They informed him that a technicality required his presence at the central police station and gave him fifteen minutes to dress. At the Préfecture of Police, Moore handed over his passport. As the shock wore off, he tried to figure out what he had done, finally deciding that the rumors he had heard might be true: those who "mixed themselves up in pro-Algerian student politics sometimes have to put up with little annoyances."[49]

After several hours, an official informed him that he had forty-eight hours to clear out of France "for reasons of national security," and handed him a signed document declaring him a threat to public order. The official referred to Moore's recent speech and reminded him that he was a "guest" in France who should have acted more courteously. How would Moore feel, he continued, "if a foreigner made speeches about racial segregation" while in the United States? After he was released, Moore packed his things and decamped for London.[50]

Except for one terse press release, the NSA gave no publicity to Moore's ouster. Larkin concluded that Moore's speech, liberally sprinkled with salutations such as "Comrade," went beyond NSA policy.[51] Moore had declared, "Just as the racists of Little Rock have lost, colonialism will succumb to the incomparable power of an independent Algeria."[52] Moore adamantly disputed that he exceeded NSA policy, but Larkin chose not to circulate Moore's speech in the United States.[53]

Paradoxically, what threatened the NSA at home strengthened its reputation abroad. From Asia, Gray reported that the Moore episode "makes excellent publicity for NSA out here."[54] Gray praised Moore's courage on behalf of Algerian students in letters to African and Asian student leaders.[55] Young, now at COSEC, received such an outpouring of praise for Moore's speech that he re-raised the question of giving it wider publicity.[56] Larkin reiterated the decision to bury Moore's speech.[57]

Privately, Young and Moore thought that the Algerians were placing unrealistic expectations on the NSA. "They think that a thousand foundations stand ready to leap forth with mammoth programs if only Bruce

Larkin claps three times and intones the magic words," Moore wrote after a difficult conversation with Lakhdari. He then went on to describe the Algerians' complaints against the West as the "usual materialistic neutralist line of blackmail."[58]

Moore eventually coined the more benign phrase *competitive coexistence* to capture the ability of the Algerians to play the West off against the East. He described Ait Chalaal, someone he liked, as "the most-pro-Western and the most sophisticated leader of UGEMA I have known," but also reported that Ait Chalaal had acknowledged that "he was happier to see the two blocs continue to throw brick bats at each other than merge into a student UN."[59]

Two weeks after Moore's deportation, French police stormed the offices of UGEMA, arrested the officers, and seized correspondence and other files. In a bolder move, they violated the traditional neutrality of the Cité Internationale Universitaire and arrested UGEMA president Ait Chalaal, vice president Chaib Taleb, and Mahfoud Aoufi, head of the Paris section. The government justified the raid by describing UGEMA as the "terrorist arm of the FLN."[60] It then banned the Algerian student organization altogether. Many students languished in jail without trials.[61]

UGEMA moved its base out of France to Tunis, which made it easier for the NSA to increase financial support without having to worry about the French government's scrutiny. But another year would pass before the NSA delivered what Algerians desired most: a major scholarship program. During that year, right-wing vigilantes terrorized Algerians in France, the French Fourth Republic fell, and World War II hero Charles de Gaulle returned to power. Soon afterward, Eisenhower informed de Gaulle that he could no longer support his policy in Algeria, because the United States "cannot abandon our old principles of supporting national freedom and self-determination, and we cannot support the colonists."[62]

In June 1959, the NSA announced the formation of the Algerian Student Leadership Project to bring twelve Algerians to study in the United States.[63] Within a year, the project had expanded to thirty-five persons. Over the next seven years, CIA case officers received a steady flow of intelligence on the Algerians' political orientation, personality traits, and future promise.[64] A yearly conference of all Algerians in the scholarship program permitted a greater number of NSA-CIA staff to make assessments.

By the early 1960s, CIA funds were being used to train a second tier of Algerian leaders: engineers, scientists, administrators, and others needed to run an independent country. In December 1960, Dan Idzik, then at Harvard Law School, contracted with the CIA to assist an NSA-sponsored conference of American-trained Algerians; Idzik remembers being close to tears when the group raised the Algerian flag. He felt, as others did in the NSA, that he stood with the future leaders of Algeria, and that he had had a part in their success.[65]

CLOSER TO HOME, the NSA attempted to court Cuban revolutionaries. With Cuba's proximity to the United States (just ninety miles away), Cuban revolutionaries, unlike the Algerians, had a constituency within the United States. A small but significant Cuban exile community in Miami was actively aiding anti-Batista dissidents. Carlos Prío Socarrás, the president ousted by Batista in 1952, provided financial support to José Antonio Echeverría, the head of the Cuban student federation (FEU), the NSA favorite who had received backing at the Ceylon ISC.

But Echeverría did not just lead the student union; he also headed the Directorio Revolucionario Estudiantil (DRE), a Havana-based paramilitary underground organization. As opposition to Batista grew, the DRE expanded its base beyond students.[66] In August 1956, just days before Echeverría came to the ISC in Ceylon, he traveled to Mexico City to confer with Fidel Castro, recently released from prison. After hours of intense negotiations, on September 1, Castro and Echeverría held a press conference to announce a pact.[67] They demanded that Batista call for elections and restore the Cuban constitution. The Mexico City Pact legitimated Castro with Cuban students and linked the guerrilla movement with the urban resistance, although some students questioned its wisdom.[68] A few months later, Castro left Mexico to begin his assault on the Batista regime. Within months of the Ceylon conference, Echeverría would be dead and the NSA would confront new questions of political violence.

DRE leaders never pretended to be either moderate or nonviolent. The students believed that the key to getting rid of Batista was a *golpear arriba*, a "strike at the top" or deathblow. Cut off the corrupt head of the Cuban government, and constitutional democracy could be restored. In 1956, DRE leaders plotted to kill Batista. The plan failed, although DRE member Rolando Cubela did assassinate the head of the Cuban police during a daring shoot-out in a Havana nightclub. Despite vigorous criticism from Castro over the students' precipitate actions, which did not accord with his strategy, the students continued their efforts to overthrow Batista in a single, decisive action.[69]

On the afternoon of March 13, 1957, DRE members stormed Batista's palace intending to kill the dictator. Confident of success, Echeverría headed out from the University of Havana in a separate car to commandeer the state-run Radio Reloj and announce Batista's demise. For a brief moment, Echeverría and his armed comrades believed that the DRE had triumphed: they broadcast the end of the Batista regime over the radio transmitter, although in Echeverría's haste he forgot to throw the main switch. No one heard him say, "People of Cuba! Rise up! Go out into the streets! Workers leave your place of employment and support the revolutionary struggle! Soldiers, sailors, policemen, join the struggle!"[70]

Batista escaped the assassination attempt and directed a counterattack from his desk on the fourth floor of the palace. The students at Radio Reloj finally realized their failure. They tore out of the station, climbed back into the car, and sped toward the University of Havana, by tradition a safe haven, since police had no jurisdiction on campus.[71]

They nearly made it. Within blocks of the campus, police surrounded the car. When the students tried to flee on foot, the police sprayed them with bullets. The twenty-four-year-old Echeverría and four others died on the spot. Police then charged the university and shot anyone who got in their way.[72] Within the month, police had tracked down and murdered many of the remaining student leaders, including Echeverría's friend and FEU vice president Fructuoso Rodríguez.[73] With Echeverría's death, Castro's main contender for leadership of the Cuban revolution, and a dedicated noncommunist, had been eliminated. His loss enabled the guerrilla leader to consolidate his influence over the urban resistance led mainly by students.

The violence created a dilemma. The NSA had been able to win support for the Cubans at the ISC in Ceylon in part because European members tended to ignore Latin American issues. COSEC, for example, acknowledged the deaths of the Cuban student leaders only with a terse paragraph in a routine circular, "We are sorry to inform you . . ."[74] When Ralph Della Cava attended a conference in Argentina, he discovered that the lack of attention had "raised tempers all over Latin

America."[75] Outraged students compared the situation in Cuba to that in Hungary. They contrasted the secretariat's matter-of-fact announcement of the murders with the all-out mobilization undertaken on behalf of Hungarian students. Was their martyrdom not equal?[76]

The implications for ISC, according to Della Cava, were serious. He warned that Latin American students were carving out a third position between Yanqui imperialism and Soviet communism, viewing both as "cancerous evils of the same order." It had not helped, he reported, that the COSEC delegation to the Latin American Student Congress was more interested in pursuing *las chicas* than in attending the proceedings.[77]

Della Cava struggled with what to do about the 1957 NSA Congress, scheduled for Ann Arbor in August. "For some of us, there may be a moral problem regarding the armed attempt of a few to assassinate 'president Battista.' In this fact, it differs distinctly from a justifiable revolution of an entire nation. Then again, who is to say that Echeverria's actions did not have the complete sympathy of his people, who may be more timid than he? These are just some hasty reflections on the problem for NSA to adopt a resolution regarding the Cuban events."[78]

Uncertain over how to proceed, the NSA initially remained silent on the killing of the Cuban student leaders. At the Congress, NSA staff offered an omnibus resolution against all dictators and their "dictatorial encroachment on the University and on academic freedom."[79] While it deemphasized Cuba, this was a strong political statement. As late as 1959, the *New York Times* could report: "President Eisenhower said today that allegations that the United States supported dictatorships were ridiculous."[80]

The NSA did not experience the same kind of pressure for resources from Cuban students as it had from Algerians, since many of the Cubans were already on the CIA payroll. Yet despite this clandestine support, most witting staff did not realize the extent to which the CIA was playing both sides of the street. They knew of course that Washington openly supported Batista, sent military aid to Cuba on a regular basis, and trained Batista's security forces at the Panama-based School of the Americas. But they did not know that during an Easter weekend in 1955, Director Allen Dulles had slipped quietly into Havana for a secret meeting with Batista at which he offered funds for a new agency, the Bureau of Repression of Communist Activities (BRAC).[81]

Dulles was said by a CIA colleague to have hoped Batista would use the bureau to root out communists.[82] BRAC instead became the symbol of the brutality of a regime that did not hesitate to arrest, torture, or murder its enemies. Fifty years later, old passions rise in Latin American specialist Luigi Einaudi's voice as he describes the depravity of Batista and BRAC: "He was very good at dismembering people. . . . literally dismembered." He "nailed their body parts to wood."[83] It was a far cry from Dulles's hope that BRAC would be a "step toward liberty."[84]

In 1957, the CIA inspector general, Lyman Kirkpatrick, paid a visit to U.S. ambassador Arthur Gardner in Havana, a man who interpreted U.S. support for Batista so literally that he forbade embassy personnel to have any contact with Batista's opponents. Gardner's position, Kirkpatrick later wrote, articulating the classic CIA rationale for establishing relations with all parties to a conflict, "made no sense whatsoever from an intelligence standpoint." [85] Kirkpatrick assured the ambassador that contact with the rebels in no way implied support, and that CIA men were trained to be "completely neutral."[86] Either Kirkpatrick did not know what was happening in his own agency or he was giving false assurances. Support for the Cuban rebels had grown so strong within the CIA that Robert Reynolds, head of the Caribbean desk, later claimed, "Me and my staff were all Fidelistas."[87]

Fidelistas were also emerging on American campuses. An Indiana group founded American Students for a Free Cuba. In May 1958, students at the University of Colorado, a school known more for its proximity to ski slopes and 3.2 beers than political fervor, hanged Batista in effigy.[88]

NSA international staff reacted warily to news that a heretofore quiescent subcommission on Latin America at the University of Miami in Coral Gables sprang back to life, fired up by an intrepid, well-connected woman named Lucille Dubois. Her father, Jules Dubois, a *Chicago Tribune* journalist, was one of the key reporters on Castro's movement.[89] While the veteran Latin America correspondent later changed his mind about the virtues of Fidel Castro, his initial enthusiasm for the guerrilla leader permeated his reporting. Lucille Dubois developed her own ties to the Cuban revolutionaries who fled Cuba and poured into Miami.

The NSA international staff had never before been confronted by amateurs, as Bruce Larkin described Dubois. As he reminded Luigi Einaudi in early 1957, "Our thinking at the close of the congress in Chicago was that this sub-commission could be eased out of existence by neglect, but it seems to be alive and kicking."[90] Dubois would not be discouraged. She sent a steady stream of letters to Larkin. In one exasperated but humorous note, she proposed that the NSA international office take a "good will tour" to Miami.[91] Larkin either ignored or deflected her ideas.

Finally, the diplomatic Ralph Della Cava took over and tried to explain NSA policy on Cuba. He told Dubois that she could express "solidarity with the Cuban students," while "avoiding direct support of political factions that are involved in what seems to be an impending revolution."[92] Not privy to the ISC meetings where the NSA professed vigorous support for the anti-Batista movement, Dubois thereafter stuck to the script; she rebuked one ardent Cuban student: "Since I am under NSA, as a part of the International Affairs Commission, I will not and cannot participate in any political demonstrations!"[93]

At the 1958 NSA Congress at Ohio Wesleyan University, campus support for Castro had grown so strong among American students that delegates sponsored a resolution to the left of what the international staff wanted. At issue was the flow of military hardware to Cuba. In 1958, as middle-class, professional, and other elite Cubans deserted Batista, the Eisenhower administration finally agreed to halt the sale of arms to Cuba. Yet in an apparent violation of the embargo, arms were still reaching the Batista regime. The State Department claimed that the arms were orders already in the pipeline. The NSA resolution condemned the United States for violating the embargo. The international staff drew the line at outright criticism of U.S. foreign policy, and watered down the resolution; an amendment changed condemnation into a request for an investigation of alleged violations.[94]

The investigation never took place. Four months later, on New Year's Day 1959, Fidel Castro began his triumphal sweep toward Havana. Alongside him on that journey, often riding on a jeep fender, was Jules Dubois, who approvingly quoted a *Tribune* colleague comparing Castro's arrival in Havana to the liberation of France after World War II.[95]

Newly elected NSA officers Robert (Bob) Kiley (of Notre Dame), president, and Willard Johnson (UCLA), the first African American international vice president, fired off a telegram to Cuban students: "USNSA shares your jubilation over the defeat of dictatorship in your homeland of Cuba."[96] The cable pointedly reminded the Cubans of past NSA support and pledged future cooperation. "USNSA would be honored to assist in any way possible to translate its sympathy for student aspirations in Cuba, which had been repeatedly expressed throughout the ordeal you have suffered." *NSA News* carried a banner headline, "Cuban Students Hailed on Castro Victory."[97]

At this point, as Kiley, who had been made witting by NSA founding father Martin McLaughlin, also a Notre Dame graduate, said in a later interview, he had no problem with Castro's political orientation; he knew there was debate inside the CIA over whether Castro was a communist. He did not think so, although he shared the CIA's antipathy toward Guevara: "he was trouble."[98] Support for Cuba represented a logical progression for Willard Johnson, whose interest in international affairs had awakened at a result of the 1955 Asian-African Conference. The NSA also hired its first Hispanic staff members, the brothers Manuel and Robert Aragon from El Centro, California. Both were ardent supporters of the revolution and social reform in Latin America.[99] In February, Kiley and Johnson headed to Havana, where the two NSA officers could be seen next to the Hilton Hotel swimming pool deep in conversation with Castro and Guevara. Once again, it appeared that the NSA was in on the ground floor of a successful revolution.[100]

At the 1959 NSA Congress, José Puente Blanco, who had succeeded Echeverría as head of the Cuban student union, announced Operation Amistad (Friendship), the funding of inexpensive flights from Miami to Havana to foster solidarity between the two countries.[101] Over the next year or so, hundreds of NSA members took advantage of the flights; most came back enthusiastic about the Cuban revolution.

What Kiley did not realize was that while American students were hobnobbing with Castro and Guevara, the highest and most secret body in the White House, the 5412 Committee, had directed the CIA to begin countering Castro's appeal among students throughout Latin America.[102]

The NSA could not turn its Cuban policy around overnight. In addition, the NSA still benefited within the ISC by having Cuba as a member. If anything, in 1960, Kiley, now associate secretary at COSEC, worried that the new Cuban student union leader, Rolando Cubela, might leave the ISC. Such a departure could start a landslide of withdrawals. The ISC was scheduled to convene in September 1960 at Klosters in the Swiss Alps. Latin Americanist Ralph Della Cava warned witting staff that "a new generation of Cubans might not be aware of NSA's past support," making disaffiliation more likely. [103]

Despite Eisenhower's directive, the NSA voted at the ISC for a strong pro-Cuba resolution. It described the revolution as "a victory of the students and the people" and held that "any imperialist attempt to dominate a country economically and politically is contrary to the development of higher education and national culture." [104] The resolution decried the recent action of the Organization of American States to impose sanctions against Cuba as interventionist, which was a direct slap at the United States since it dominated the OAS and had insisted on the action. [105]

At Klosters, Kiley met with Cubela, whom he describes today as "affable, a bon vivant, a hail-fellow-well-met kind of person." [106] Cubela had fled to Miami in 1956 after killing the Havana police chief, but he later returned to Cuba to become a colonel in Castro's army. After the revolution succeeded, Castro replaced José Puente Blanco with Cubela, whom *Time* magazine dubbed "Castro's gun-toting bully boy," as head of the Cuban student union.[107] (A Canadian delegate at Klosters remembers that Cubela upset the Swiss by bringing his gun into the plenary sessions.)[108] Cubela would soon begin a clandestine relationship with the CIA, though the witting NSA staff would not be told of it. [109] As in North Africa, by 1959 it looked as though the NSA had found a way to distance itself from the U.S. government and place it on the side of the revolutionaries.

Yet it seemed that for every gain the Americans made in demonstrating solidarity with revolutionary movements, the Soviets came up with new ways to counteract them.

14

GLORIA STEINEM AND
THE VIENNA OPERATION

THE FIRST TIME Clive Gray heard rumors that the 1959 World Youth Festival would be held in Vienna, he was incredulous.[1] Why would the Soviets risk losing control of the festival by allowing it to be held in a noncommunist country, and why would the Austrian government, with its policy of strict neutrality, agree to it? He felt that the mere discussion of a Western location handed the Soviets a propaganda victory: it suggested confidence and openness on the part of the communists. And if the past was any guide, twenty thousand young people were likely to descend on Vienna.

The CIA went on the offensive, developing ambitious goals to "smash" the festival, "take over" the left-wing American delegation, and, most important, identify and recruit friendly foreign nationals from Africa and Asia to tie them more closely to the West, a plan later approved by the U.S. National Security Council.[2] The CIA launched a multi-layered operation, each group often unaware of the others, including a contingent of nonwitting American students and handpicked young professionals with more specific assignments. One such recruit was a Smith College graduate named Gloria Steinem.

"Gloria was our leader," murmured Moscow festival veteran Richard Medalie when he recalled her role in the Vienna operation.[3] Long before Steinem became a feminist icon, she was one of the few women in the NSA-CIA club. Although Steinem, who knowingly cooperated with the CIA, is sensitive today about her work with the Agency, as NSA colleagues attest, her friend Clive Gray beams when he recounts recruiting her.[4]

Gray met Steinem in New Delhi, where she held a Chester Bowles

Fellowship after graduating Phi Beta Kappa from Smith. He recalls that his CIA case officer in New Delhi suggested he look up this "intelligent and attractive young woman." Steinem had made a favorable impression on prominent Indians, including Indira Gandhi and Congress Party leaders. By the time Gray met her, Steinem had developed an interest in international politics; she had wanted to go to the Moscow festival in 1957, but could not find travel funds.[5]

When CIA officials decided to create a front organization to handle the recruitment of ordinary American students for the festival, Gray submitted Steinem's name to Harry Lunn. Lunn, then using the Department of Defense as a cover, looked over Steinem's credentials — noting especially her time in India and her connection to Gandhi and other Congress Party members and told Gray, "This person looks interesting. What about her?"[6]

Steinem became the public face of the Independent Service for Information on the Vienna Youth Festival. Incorporators included former NSA officers Leonard Bebchick, who became Steinem's co-director, Gray (who had turned down an offer from Bill Dentzer to join the CIA full-time), and Paul Sigmund, and Moscow festival veterans Richard Medalie and George Abrams.[7] On February 5, 1959, the incorporation papers were amended to reflect a simpler name: Independent Research Service (IRS).[8]

Medalie later described Lunn as "our puppet master," although Steinem's immediate boss was Bebchick. After his term as international vice president Bebchick had left the NSA and attended Yale Law School, where he did what he called "occasional chores" for the CIA. After law school, Bebchick took a job with the Civil Aeronautics Board and thought his CIA service was over. He was surprised when officials contacted him, described the plan to sabotage the festival, and asked him to run the operation.[9]

The Steinem group used the fact that NSA had once more boycotted the festival as its public reason for recruiting American students: "The organizers . . . support the position of representative student and youth groups in the U.S and Austria, the host country, along with those in numerous other non-Communist countries who have decided to boycott the Festival and deny it any official prestige. . . . At the same time, they [the NSA] do expect that many intelligent and patriotic Americans will wish to attend in an individual and non-representative capacity." Thus, the IRS group would gather information that would "lessen the exploitation of their presence for propaganda purposes."[10]

Moscow festival veteran George Abrams explained in *Newsweek* how young undergraduates could be effective advocates for American values. "When a fluffy, wide-eyed American girl of 19 is surrounded by the curious and asked hundreds of questions, her natural approach is her greatest asset."[11]

While Steinem looked for wide-eyed volunteers on the nation's campuses, overseas NSA staff, in another prong of the attack, had been trying to force the festival out of Austria. The strategy was to spark protest demonstrations in Vienna in the hope that the festival planning committee would change the location. Witting staff envisioned a joint protest by Hungarian students in exile and the Austrian student union.

Clement Moore, cooling his heels in London after being expelled from France, was deployed to contact the Hungarians. In May 1958, he sought out Alpár Bujdosó, the Hungarian who had stumped U.S. campuses in 1956 under the pseudonym Istvan Laszlo and now led the Union of Free Hungarian Students. Bujdosó, then in Vienna, heard Moore out but argued that demonstrations might provoke counterdemonstrations: foreign students studying in Vienna might be in favor of the festival. He initially declined to be involved.[12] (Moore reported yet another problem to the plan: festival organizers had yet to open a headquarters in Vienna, so there was nothing to demonstrate in front of or to raid—an observation that suggests the NSA had other tricks in its repertoire.)[13]

Moore had also discussed festival tactics with the head of the Austrian student union (OH), Herbert Mauser. At first Moore found him uncooperative. Mauser argued that the NSA should stay away from the festival altogether. Like Bujdosó, he feared that "unpredictable Austrians" might cause "physical harm."[14] His position puzzled Moore, since by spring 1958, virtually every youth and student group in Austria (including OH), except the young communists, had announced its intention of boycotting the festival. Moore concluded that Mauser was just lazy, preferring "nightclubs and glasses of beer."[15] Bruce Larkin suggested to his colleagues that the NSA carry on a friendship campaign, using every opportunity to "hot box" Mauser, and "convince him that he is really loved." Larkin then suggested, "If necessary, [offer] some kind of incentive to play ball."[16]

Mauser finally came around, although the NSA may have had nothing to do with his change of heart. The OH, Catholic Youth, Boy Scouts, and other groups formed an action committee in Vienna, and Mauser assured the NSA that he could produce a demonstration of thirty thousand along the Ringstrasse.[17] When the demonstration led by Catholic Youth took place, on March 3, 1959, bands of ultranationalist Austrian youth opposed to the festival turned out for it just as Mauser had warned. Their reputation as "toughs" renewed fears of street violence during the festival.

The decision to permit the festival to be held in Vienna had caused internal dissension among top Austrian government officials. Chancellor Julius Raab, who made the initial decision, defended his position later: "Austria as a free and democratic state could not have acted otherwise."[18] But the decision incensed President Adolf Schärf and the state secretary, Bruno Kreisky, soon to be foreign minister. They felt that Raab was either appeasing or favoring the Soviets. Schärf and Kreisky decided to take matters into their own hands and create their own antifestival operation.[19] During the festival, for example, Bebchick was given a special phone number: "If you have a problem," he was told, "here's the person to call in the prime minister's office."[20]

Despite mounting opposition inside Austria, the WFDY-IUS festival planning committee held fast to the Vienna site. For Khrushchev, 1959 was a time of confident, almost cocky, overtures to the United States. According to his biographer, the year before the Vienna festival, Khrushchev sought every opportunity to press for a U.S. visit.[21] He challenged Western allies to resolve the question of a divided Berlin. He proposed an end to nuclear weapons tests. Whatever fears the Soviets had about holding the festival in the West, the prospect of a propaganda coup seemed to override them.

WHILE EUROPEANS DEBATED the festival location, Steinem encouraged undergraduates to apply to the left-wing U.S. Committee for International Student Cooperation, which still controlled the official delegate selection. Organizers on the New York committee were overtly hostile to anyone associated with Steinem, but the Chicago organizers proved more willing to accept applications from people she recruited. Steinem and her staff screened candidates, often young professionals, for financial support, forwarding the recommended applications to C. D. Jackson, Eisenhower's former chief psychological warfare adviser. Jackson had long-standing ties to covert intelligence operations, had helped found Radio Free Europe in the late 1940s, and constantly goaded Eisenhower to fight communism more aggressively.[22] As an establishment figure, now a speechwriter and consultant to the president, and a seasoned behind-the-scenes operator, Jackson helped Steinem find corporate sponsors and camouflage CIA funds.[23]

Steinem had encouraged an application from Michael Harrington, leader of the Young People's Socialist League (YPSL) and Bebchick's New York apartment mate.[24] In general, socialists could be counted upon to cause trouble. They despised communists, knew their Marx and Lenin, and were great ideological infighters. Harrington was a charismatic figure, good at oratory, and able to go toe to toe with hard-line festival organizers.[25]

Although eager to take his first trip to Europe and meet other young socialist leaders, Harrington felt uneasy about accepting Steinem's offer. He feared that the State Department might be behind the funds, so he put the question to YPSL colleagues. After a lengthy debate, Harrington told Steinem he would go under two conditions: he would not officially join the delegation and would remain free to attack American capitalism and foreign policy. Soon afterward, Steinem reported to Jackson that Harrington had withdrawn his application.[26] Presumably Steinem or her staff did not agree to his stipulations. Witting operatives could take provocative stances against U.S. policy—they knew the boundaries—but it was quite another thing for outsiders to do so.

The older NSA cadre, among them former president Richard Murphy (1952–53) and international specialists Paul Sigmund and Helen Jean Rogers, scouted for individuals who, once in Vienna, could be provocateurs, a role quite different from encouraging young students to sign up with the American delegation. In some cases, the recruiters reached back a decade to find Cold Warriors with a taste for combat. Jack Ransohoff, a thirty-one-year-old nuclear engineer, agreed to disrupt a festival seminar on atomic energy. Charles Bartlett of the *Chattanooga Times* and *News Focus* steered Walter Pincus, then a twenty-seven-year-old rookie reporter, toward the festival project. Pincus, today a veteran *Washington Post* journalist specializing in national security issues, in an interview described Bartlett euphemistically as "plugged in," alluding to his cooperation with the CIA.[27] Pincus, a Yale graduate, had other credentials, having served for two years with the U.S. Army counterintelligence corps, where he interrogated people to probe for communist affiliations.[28] He thought the festival "sounded like a good story," but today, like so many others, Pincus emphasizes his passion to fight communism. On Bartlett's advice, Pincus talked with the FBI both before and after his trip to protect himself from charges that he had attended a communist event. (When he returned, he received—but declined—an offer to join the CIA full-time.)[29] CIA officers Harry Lunn and Bill Dentzer also went to Vienna, where they plotted strategy, advised Steinem and Bebchick, and mingled with the delegates.

By mid-July, the Independent Research Service had reached its recruiting goals. Bebchick believes that the IRS found at least 100 of the roughly 350 Americans who eventually headed for Vienna.[30] The influx of IRS-identified students caused friction between the New York and Chicago festival organizers. Most had signed with the Chicago organizers. At first, the New York group refused to recognize the Chicago contingent. While it relented, the simmering conflict would erupt during the festival.

Right-wing anticommunists in the United States also organized young people to go to Vienna. Herbert Romerstein, a former Communist Party member (in his teens) turned professional anticommunist investigator, recruited conservative Catholics and other hard-liners to disrupt the festival.[31] Romerstein later attributed his ten-thousand-dollar budget as a gift from Alfred Kohlberg, head of the China Lobby, a powerful anticommunist organization opposed to Mao's China and supportive of Chiang Kai-shek.[32] Even if he did receive a private contribution for the Vienna festival, the sheer scale of Romerstein's activities in Vienna suggests U.S. government cooperation.

The Romerstein group excelled at dirty tricks. They arranged for literature and lapel pins to be printed in Germany and brought to Vienna. The material was written in the festival idiom of "peace and friendship" but contained anticommunist messages. Thousands of festival delegates snapped up the faux festival pins printed in Chinese, Russian, German, and English, only to find they contained the phrase "freedom fighters."[33] According to information later printed in the *Congressional Record*, the Romerstein group was also responsible for planes that flew over the festival grounds with banners that read, "Free Hungary" and "Free Tibet."

Others infiltrated the festival leadership. Charles Wiley, a Romerstein ally, bragged that since he knew "a little of Communist jargon, I passed myself off successfully as an American Communist."[34]

In essence, Romerstein ran a covert operation within a covert operation. Some of his conservative recruits finagled their way into the American delegation by lying on their applications. Stephen Unsino, a student from Fordham University, a Jesuit school, applied to the Chicago committee but pretended to be from the more liberal Columbia University. Fluent in Russian, Greek, French, and Italian, Unsino volunteered to act as an interpreter, giving him unique access to the American delegation, both the IRS-recruited and the left-wing students.[35]

One other group may have been recruited from the United States. Thomas Garrity, a Vienna festival attendee who had been active in the NSA during the late 1940s, recalls hearing that U.S. Army recruits based at Fort Leavenworth, Kansas, grew their hair long enough to pose as students and went over to disrupt the festival.[36] No evidence has emerged to support the rumor, but none of the witting staff who worked on the Vienna festival rule it out. If the CIA feared right-wing Austrian toughs were spoiling for physical fights, it might have decided to take out an insurance policy.

In Europe, CIA officials worked also with pro-West youth groups to organize anti-festival strategies, among them the International Union of Socialist Youth, the World Assembly of Youth, and Pax Romana.[37] British intelligence undertook a strategy parallel to the Americans: to disrupt both the leftist British delegation and the festival. Years later, a European scholar conducting research in the NATO archives stumbled on documents that indicate that NATO, too, organized counter-festival activities.[38]

These various operations required substantial funding, although an exact figure is impossible to calculate. Steinem drew on CIA funds from a "special account" managed by C. D. Jackson.[39] She also had assistance from the chair of Chase Manhattan Bank, John J. McCloy, who while high commissioner of occupied Germany had organized against the 1951 World Youth Festival in East Berlin by hosting a simultaneous festival in West Berlin. In his banking capacity, he was able to route funds to Swiss banks. According to McCloy's biographer Kai Bird, these funds were then transferred to Liechtenstein, picked up by car, and delivered to Vienna.[40] Richard Medalie today describes the availability of funds as wildly excessive: "I had money coming out my ears."[41]

AS THE AMERICAN DELEGATES gathered with the roughly seventeen thousand young people who had come to Vienna, Steinem's group pressured festival organizers to host a meeting of the rival factions from Chicago and New York. The organizers first resisted the request and then acquiesced, and the meeting took place on July 25, the day before the opening ceremonies. Among the anticommunist Americans who headed for the confrontation was Malcolm Rivkin, a Harvard and MIT graduate who was part of the IRS group. When he first heard about the festival, Rivkin thought it would be a lark.[42] He wholeheartedly agreed that the festival was a propaganda show, "a bunch of baddies dipping the flag to the Communists."[43] But since the IRS would pay his airfare, he decided to go to Vienna and laze around Europe a bit afterward.

Shortly after the meeting began, Rivkin became ticked off when festival organizers announced that Marvin Markman, head of the New York group and overtly hostile to the IRS-recruited delegates, would chair it. Rivkin decided to demand an election. To be heard, he jumped up on a table to address the crowd, which he later described in an interview as a spontaneous decision.[44]

What happened next is a source of dispute. Rivkin says someone from the leftist American delegation jumped him.[45] Other reports accuse a French festival official, Jean Garcias, of leaping on the table to shove Rifkin off.[46] Regardless of the cause, irate delegates started clubbing one another. Rivkin remembers Zbigniew Brzezinski, the future U.S. National Security Advisor, being hit over the head. Eventually, everyone cooled down. The dueling Americans realized that they weren't getting anywhere by beating people up.[47]

Steve Max, a seventeen-year-old member of the New York group, had watched the brawl unfold. By 1959, the young Max had logged more time at political meetings than most politicians do in a lifetime. His father, Alan Max, had been the managing editor of the *Daily Worker*. In the mid-1950s, the younger Max had been active in the teen section of the pro-Soviet Labor Youth League, though in 1959 he was no longer active. (Known then and now for his droll sense of humor, Max said later that he realized young communists were swimming against the tide when meetings consisted of monotone recitals of rock-and-roll lyrics, an exercise designed to highlight bourgeois decadence.)[48] Max was finding the IRS tactics incomprehensible. Its members kept demanding to see the Russians, he said, yet the five hundred–person Soviet delegation was visible to every one, since they wore identical suits. Max's group, which included Paul Robeson, Jr., kept telling Steinem's troops, "Go outside and see the blue suits."[49]

Max observed other disruptions that he presumed came from the Steinem group, though they may have come from the Romerstein group. In a tented beer garden, left-wing Americans and Cuban delegates had warily struck up a conversation. As they talked, they started relaxing, and amicable relations were being established when, according to Max, "all of a sudden comes an American nobody knew. He sits down and picks a fight—soon everybody is screaming at everybody else. Then he leaves."[50] All dialogue ended. Today, Max shakes his head over the small act of sabotage. Most people were there to have fun.

But not everyone. Raúl Castro, Fidel's older brother and a member of the Cuban Communist Party, returned from the Vienna youth festival determined to make Havana a haven for youth organizing, especially in the Western hemisphere.[51]

After they arrived in Vienna, the veterans of the Moscow festival realized that there had been a flaw in their planning. According to Richard Medalie, it had been easy in Moscow to talk to ordinary Russians on the street and get his message across. By contrast, the Vienna festival was in the tightly controlled Messegelände parade grounds. Festival organizers policed the entry and exit gates. Those without credentials, especially Steinem and her provocateurs, had to sneak in and out through a hole in the fence. Some foreign delegations, especially those from Eastern Europe and China, were not accessible outside the parade grounds. The Chinese stayed in private homes and were surrounded by guards. Hungarians were housed on a guarded barge on the Danube. Unlike Moscow, "There was no mandate to be open," Medalie explained.[52] Even if they could get inside the huge pavilion, without maps or guides the saboteurs were soon caught up in milling crowds; it was like an exceptionally crowded state fair.

The IRS found that the ideal spot to distribute pro-Western literature was along the campground fence, a sensitive area for festival organizers. While distributing pamphlets from the U.S. Department of Agriculture, an Ohio woman tussled with a festival official. Western media reported that she had been "slapped in the face by a festival guard." [53] In another incident, Bebchick described how a "wonderful pregnant girl from Iowa . . . got knocked to the ground," and then admitted, "We used her, and she used herself . . . on the front lines."[54] Press reports of these incidents, many of them deliberately provoked by the Steinem group, reinforced the Americans' message that festival officials were so threatened by free expression they resorted to physical violence.

Bebchick described Brzezinski as an "excellent agent provocateur": the Polish-born Harvard instructor stirred up trouble by exploiting the traditional animosity between Polish and Russian delegates. Medalie also remembered that he and Brzezinski "went to the East European compounds and pretended we were Soviet delegates. We acted boorishly and insulted everyone in Russian."[55]

Some provocations were uniquely American. Nothing disrupted formal sessions more than the New Orleans marching jazz band, whose trumpets, drums, and saxophones blared lively anthems like "When the Saints Go Marching In." The band performed admirably, Bebchick claimed: "Every time we wanted to break up a session, like the Pied Piper of Hamelin, we would send the marching band out and they would draw people away from the meetings to listen."[56] The Yale Russian Chorus was also pressed into service and performed the same function.[57]

Other American tactics were designed to spark anger against the festival organizers. The Americans sent out fancy invitations to phantom cocktail parties. When thirsty invitees showed up for the party, the theory held, their disappointment would turn into wrath, and they would blame the festival host committee—and therefore the Soviets—for incompetence. These tactics were first used at the 1951 festival in Berlin. Many years later, a congressional hearing found that the repertoire in 1951 included "forged invitations, false promises of free bed and board, false notices of cancellations," and, appallingly, "attacks on participants with explosives, firebombs, and tire-puncturing equipment."[58] If the more aggressive techniques were used in Vienna, no one has claimed credit for them.

Far and away the most heralded aspect of the anti-festival operation, then and later, was the publicity blitz. Steinem worked with Samuel Walker, Jr., a vice president of the Free Europe Press, associated with Radio Free Europe, to put out a daily newspaper in six languages. In deference to the Austrian government's sensitivity over the broadcaster's controversial role in the Hungarian uprising and lingering bitterness among refugees, Walker camouflaged his identity by creating a temporary front called the Publications Development Corporation.[59] Steinem also had recruited Clay Felker, a journalist from *Esquire* magazine, to help her put out the daily. The plan hit an initial snag: a propaganda blitz required a distribution system.

Denied easy access to the festival grounds, the small Steinem team improvised. Since no toilet paper had been supplied to the outhouses serving the delegates, someone thought up the idea of furnishing them with the daily newspaper to use as a substitute. Of course, no one knows whether the toilet user would be able to read the paper; did a Spanish-speaking delegate find a message in Spanish or was he or she forced to peruse an Arabic edition? Walter Pincus later defended the distribution as superior to having thousands of papers snatched up by festival organizers and put in the trash.[60]

Walker later crowed that "400,000 copies of a daily newspaper" had been published.[61] He also estimated that 36,000 books had been distributed to festivalgoers, including *1984* and other works by George Orwell, and books by Milovan Đjilas, a Yugoslav critic of Tito and author of *The New Class*.[62] The avalanche of anticommunist propaganda led Walker to write to C. D. Jackson afterward and claim, "Never before have so many Young Republicans distributed so much Socialist literature with such zeal."[63] Yet one wonders whether the greatest effect of the blitz was that it fulfilled a bureaucratic need inside the CIA to measure success. Counting the number of publications distributed was far easier than assessing American influence on the political opinions of festival participants.

Today Bebchick deems the anti-festival operation a success for its propaganda value. "I said at the time, and I still believe, that it doesn't matter what happens in Vienna. The only thing that matters is what the world thinks happened in Vienna."[64] The "icing on cake," he asserts, was the ability of Steinem's group to influence international press coverage. "We did a masterful job in controlling the press. We learned what lazy slobs they are. They will take whatever you feed them." The American embassy in Vienna sent Steinem and Bebchick daily press clips, which reinforced their cynical view. "There was one bastard that we couldn't control, and only one," Bebchick said with grudging admiration. "That was Abe Rosenthal [of the *New York Times*]. He went his own way. He reported things. He did not take a handout. He did his own analysis. He was the only true journalist."[65]

Tipped by Steinem's group to cover certain issue seminars, the compliant press focused on the actions and statements of the young professionals from the United States. "Anti-Reds invaded discussion seminars and forced Communist speakers into debate with embarrassing questions," read one article. [66] During another seminar, Pincus sparred with Paul Robeson, Jr., while CBS filmed their confrontation. Pincus said he strode to the microphone to challenge the nonsense he was hearing only to find it turned off. Pincus demanded that the seminar be opened up to everyone who wanted to speak. Robeson, he recalled, kept asking him in return, "Why are you here if you aren't committed to the ideals of the festival?"[67]

Paradoxically, the strategy of bringing naive and nonwitting students to Vienna dismayed the older cadre. "The kids treated it as a lark," Pincus complained; "we wanted substance."[68] Festival organizers would buy off the young Americans with free tickets to major events, such as performances of the Bolshoi ballet, although Bebchick confesses today that he sneaked off to see the Peking Opera. Still, Bebchick and others stole as many tickets to events as they could get their hands on to minimize the turnout, loot that today resides in Bebchick's basement.[69]

Fed up with the college-weekend atmosphere, Pincus, Bebchick, and Brzezinski decided to dramatize the West's message. The trio found some banners, tied them together, and cut out letters to spell "Freedom." In preparation for the final parade, they dragged a wooden plank up to the top of a building and lay in wait. At dusk, the plotters threw the plank across a gap between two buildings and unfurled the banner. As the lights in their building went out, they scrambled across the plank to the adjacent building, out of reach of the pursuing police.[70]

BEBCHICK ALSO ADMITS that the central objective of the whole operation—establishing contact with Asian and African students—was a failure.[71] Like many who worked with the CIA, he stresses the future importance of attracting these students: "These were students, two or three years after we met them, who were representing their countries at the U.N., became foreign ministers, etc." Witting participants had been instructed to "make contact" and "start a relationship," then turn the names over to the CIA for follow-up.[72]

Cliff Thompson, a Rhodes Scholar and former president of the Executive Board of the *Harvard Crimson*, later published an account of the festival in the paper. Thompson pointed out that it was unrealistic to fantasize about "repartee in a Vienna wine cellar" with students from Africa or Asia. He questioned the pursuit of delegates who came as athletes or performers, and quoted a fellow conspirator as saying, "There's no good in a PhD candidate talking politics with a 16-year-old banjo player."[73]

Clive Gray today scoffs at the idea that festivals were a place to recruit foreign nationals. He described the Indians who attended the Vienna festival as "total opportunists" and "absolute dregs," not worth anyone's pursuit.[74] The point of the countermeasures, as Gray viewed it then, was to "make a stand," and show the Soviets that Americans "were not taking it lying down."[75] He said one could have "fleeting contact" with Third World delegations but by and large "you didn't know who they were." But Gray has changed his view of the festival's importance. He now says that the United States "could have ignored the whole thing and it wouldn't have made much difference."[76]

CIA liberals regarded the counterfestival operation as a success, especially after the *New York Times* ran a headline that read, "Reds Displeased with Red Fete."[77] The article claimed that the Soviets had concluded that they had underestimated the intensity of Western opposition. In addition, Steinem received high marks for her work in the United States and Vienna. When planning began for the next anti-festival operation in Helsinki, Finland in 1962, Steinem was asked to reprise her role and agreed. By then, the CIA had acquired an enthusiastic backer of counterfestival operations in the person of Robert F. Kennedy, the president's brother and U.S. attorney general.[78] In Helsinki, the CIA set up its own nightclub and targeted Africans, who were thought to love jazz. The tactic was as dubious as expecting parlays in Vienna wine cellars to pay off, although it resulted in memorable images of Steinem parting the beaded curtains to enter the nightclub as if she were Mata Hari.[79]

In a little-known postscript to the Vienna festival, Gray remembered standing around chatting with the CIA's Bill Dentzer when the longtime head of the IUS, Jiří Pelikán, walked by. By then, Dentzer had spent eight years fighting the IUS as NSA president, COSEC associate secretary, and CIA career staff, yet he did not recognize Pelikán; Gray had to point him out. The long-standing NSA policy of refusing contact with the IUS lest it confer legitimacy on the organization meant that Americans never evaluated their opponents firsthand.[80]

The policy against all contact remained in place even after the Eisenhower administration decided to hold talks with the Soviet premier. In fact, on the eve of the Vienna World Youth Festival, Americans watched television coverage of a conversation in Moscow between Vice President Richard Nixon and Nikita Khrushchev. The riveting encounter, dubbed the Kitchen Debate since it occurred in a model Soviet kitchen, should have signaled to the NSA that a policy of no contact might be difficult to maintain. If the United States could engage in détente, what prevented Americans students from dialogue with the IUS?

In 1959, the political world again shifted in important ways. The Cuban revolution stirred the imagination of Latin Americans, who sought to duplicate Castro's feat. African countries won independence from European colonial powers in increasing numbers, and joined together in newfound solidarity.

Khrushchev revised Soviet policy toward liberation movements. In the years after the Bandung conference, the Chinese, rather than the Russians, had emerged as the more aggressive supporters of revolutionary movements. In response, the Kremlin gradually altered its orthodoxy on how revolutions should occur (with Soviet guidance) and who should lead them (the proletariat).[81]

At the same time, American students were developing their own ideas about revolution and the threat of communism. The constituency pressure at the 1958 NSA Congress for a hard-hitting arms embargo against Batista's Cuba had presaged the change. But a revival of campus interest in politics was not confined to liberal students. The NSA would soon be pushed and pulled in opposite directions by liberals and conservatives, leading to some of the most turbulent years in the organization's history, and ultimately challenging the CIA operation.

SOCIAL UPHEAVALS

FOR YEARS, THE NSA had two silent partners in its covert work, the CIA and student apathy. But by 1959, student apathy had turned into new political activism by left and right alike. Competing factions contended for the soul of the NSA and challenged U.S. foreign policy. Whatever consensus underlay Cold War politics had started to fracture by the late 1950s, long before the Vietnam War widened those divisions into unbridgeable chasms. A small incident at Harvard hinted at the feisty new politics from the right.

On April 15, 1959, the victorious Fidel Castro toured the United States, basking in the frequent shouts of "Viva Fidel!"[1] The news that Castro would speak on the Harvard campus enraged a burly freshman with a rough-hewn, argumentative style, Howard (Howie) Phillips, and he decided to protest. As Castro made his way through cheering crowds to the front door of the Harvard Faculty Club for a reception in his honor, Phillips joined the throng and elbowed his way forward. When he reached the revolutionary leader, Phillips thrust out his hand and yanked Castro's beard.[2]

Inside the club, NSA international affairs vice president Willard Johnson had been invited to present Castro with a plaque on behalf of American students. It honored José Antonio Echeverría and Fructuoso Rodríguez, martyrs of the 1957 palace attack who, declared Johnson, "gave their lives in the struggle, victorious under the leadership of Fidel Castro."[3]

NSA leaders did not yet know Phillips, but they soon would. Long before he became the bête noire of moderate Republicans, he was provoking the liberal establishment of the NSA.[4] Phillips grew up in a tough ethnic neighborhood of Boston, the son of Jewish immigrants; he later became a Catholic convert. He chaired the Massachusetts Young Republican Club but also represented a new breed of young activists who would soon become known as Goldwaterites.[5] As a group, they viewed Eisenhower's détente policies toward the Soviet Union as tantamount to treason. The young conservatives demanded victory over the Soviet regime, not accommodation to it. As the episode at the Faculty Club indicated, Phillips was willing to thumb his nose at propriety to score a political point.

Phillips also nursed ambitions to lead the Harvard Student Council; as a freshman, he decided to reach for the presidency. He had entered Harvard just as the campus was in revolt over its NSA affiliation. Two moderate Harvard Student Council members, Marc Leland and Tim Zagat (the future co-founder of Zagat's Restaurant Surveys), had turned in a critical report on the 1958 NSA Congress. They argued that NSA delegates "do not represent the views of their student bodies" and were "unqualified to vote on national and political issues."[6] Resolutions were slapdash, debate meaningless, outcomes frequently determined by mass emotion.[7] The Student Council voted to terminate its NSA membership, ignoring pleas from NSA supporters to study the issue further, though the council did agree to hold a campus-wide referendum vote.[8]

Students who debated the referendum in the *Harvard Crimson* concentrated on foreign policy. Senior Andrew Warshaw complained, "You may or may not favor Algerian independence, but the question deserves more than a one-minute debate before being overwhelmingly backed." Warshaw used the Khemisti campaign as an example: "Can it really be said that American students favor the release of some obscure Algerian student leader-rioter now in jail? Sure we are for freedom, but who is the guy? Maybe he threw a bomb."[9]

Harvard's action was part of an incipient uprising against the NSA that was spreading across the country. Brown University's student body president urged disaffiliation because the NSA was "a waste of time and money."[10] At the University of Miami in Coral Gables, Lucille Dubois reported a huge fight that ended with a campus referendum, which was won by the NSA.[11] On the West Coast, NSA allies beat back a disaffiliation campaign on the Berkeley campus. Rumors flew that a group of student body presidents was going to explore forming a new national organization.[12] If that occurred, the CIA would have a crisis on its hands.

The growing political ferment on campus was not confined to young conservatives. Campus-based political parties organized by liberals took up controversial issues and challenged the power of fraternities and sororities, which dominated student governments. At the University of California at Berkeley and Los Angeles, liberals formed SLATE and PLATFORM, respectively, which protested racial exclusion clauses in fraternity housing, apartheid in South Africa, and the presence of the military training program ROTC on campus. SLATE leaders derided student government for its sandbox politics, but they also tried to take it over.[13]

For the most part, the NSA international staff welcomed the new liberal energy. Here, at last, was a constituency that supported its general agenda—from anticolonial movements to civil rights, without appearing to challenge specific NSA foreign policies. The new liberals resurrected the tactics of the 1930s, leading demonstrations, marches, and rallies, often in defiance of campus or local government bans. In the spring of 1959, a thousand Harvard students marched in support of nuclear disarmament. Other campuses protested nuclear testing, the House Committee on Un-American Activities (HUAC), and federal loyalty oaths. The Student Peace Union, a new national organization, called for a broad-based program of societal reforms.

There were other signs that liberal activists might challenge the NSA's business as usual. At the 1959 Congress, Isabel Marcus from Barnard College ran an aggressive campaign for international vice president. She stumped from caucus to caucus, making the feminist argument that the top leadership should include at least one woman.[14] The clandestine CIA caucus of witting staff and CIA case officers opposed her and backed Peter Eckstein from the University of Michigan. Eckstein had a base of votes in the sprawling Big Ten region and directed the summer seminar (ISRS), whose graduates campaigned on his behalf. But delegates embraced Marcus. The CIA ensured that Eckstein stayed within the NSA family, working with foreign students and later taking a post at COSEC.

While Marcus later acknowledged that she signed the security oath and was witting, she was never an insider.[15] She recalls her year in office as painful; she was often cut out of decision making. The witting staff frequently worked around her. Her assistant, Richard Miller, used his home address for sensitive matters with overseas staff.[16] When her staff specialists disappeared, as they did at times, it was later joked that they could be found at meetings with CIA case officers. At the time, she ascribed her isolation to working in an all-male environment.[17]

The CIA could deal with Marcus during her one year in office because it had a reliable president. Donald Hoffman, a University of Wisconsin graduate, had clean-cut frat boy looks and a buttoned-down style; he exuded not a whiff of rebellion. His ISRS application reflected his moderate temperament and ambition: "to be devoted to helping my fellow man and to do God's will."[18] Hoffman, though friendly toward Marcus, privately viewed her with masculine condescension: "Could we keep Isabel quiet?" he asked, after one international meeting.[19]

Soon after Hoffman's election, former NSA president Bob Kiley summoned him to Washington. After he arrived, Bill Dentzer joined them to discuss how the NSA was able to carry out its various programs and projects. Hoffman said later, "I had tremendous respect for Bob Kiley and had heard great things about Dentzer." When they assured him that all the previous officers had cooperated with the CIA, he signed the security oath.[20] Unlike Marcus, Hoffman developed an affinity for CIA work, and continued his intelligence career for the next seven years.[21]

The reliability of top officers and staff was a critical matter in 1960, since that year the NSA international office in Cambridge merged with the NSA headquarters, located since 1952 in Philadelphia.[22] Putting the two together in a rundown townhouse on Chestnut Street increased the risk that the nonwitting NSA staff would discover what was going on. The international staff occupied the upper floors and kept to themselves.

When Hoffman and Marcus took office, it looked as if the NSA would be spending the year fighting disaffiliation battles. The Massachusetts Institute of Technology voted to withdraw. A conservative student told the student newspaper: "We really don't care how NSA votes on the atomic bomb tests, we just don't want them to vote."[23]

Then a new movement erupted in the South that transformed the NSA, fueled external political attacks on the association, and led J. Edgar Hoover to reopen his investigation. On February 1, 1960, a handful of black students sat down in the whites-only seats at the Woolworth lunch counter in Greensboro, North Carolina, and refused to move. When news reached NSA headquarters, national affairs vice president Curtis Gans contacted Timothy (Tim) Jenkins, an African American from Howard University who was on the NSA executive committee, and suggested they go to Greensboro.

Both men shared a passion for civil rights. Gans, who was white, had grown up in Kentucky and graduated from the University of North Carolina but had championed civil rights from an early age. As a seventh-grader, he said later, "I threw a four-day tantrum and locked myself in my room so I would not have to attend a segregated school."[24] Jenkins was enrolled at a historic black campus that had long emphasized international issues.[25] No one needed to teach him about the spirit of Bandung or African nationalism. Together Gans and Jenkins persuaded the NSA to throw its weight behind the sit-in.

Shortly after they arrived in Greensboro, Gans said, the two got the feeling that the sit-ins were signaling the birth of a movement.[26] They were right. By some estimates, up to seventy-five thousand people engaged in spontaneous sit-ins across the South. Gans and Jenkins returned to Philadelphia and lobbied President Hoffman to put the NSA at the service of the movement. Gans credits Hoffman with giving them "the green light," despite his nervousness, and with never wavering.[27] Jenkins agrees.[28] For the first time, the NSA embraced civil disobedience: Gans and Jenkins used funds from the Taconic and Field Foundation in New York to support demonstrations in support of southern student activists, and, more daringly, for bail money to release students who had been arrested.[29]

In mid-April 1960, Gans and Jenkins represented the NSA at the founding meeting of the Student Non-Violent Coordinating Committee (SNCC) in Raleigh, North Carolina.[30] While Martin Luther King, Jr., wanted to tie the new activists to the Southern Christian Leadership Conference, SNCC asserted its independence from adult control. The act marked a generational break with established civil rights leadership, and a turning point for student autonomy more generally. Constance (Connie) Curry, a white Agnes Scott graduate who headed a race relations project sponsored by the NSA in Atlanta, offered SNCC its first office space.[31]

In late April, the NSA sponsored a conference at All Souls Church in Washington. The audience of roughly 400 students was mostly white, came from 38 states, and represented 188 colleges and universities.[32] Gans exhorted the students: "Take the fight to your own backyard." That night, the Northern Students Movement was born, a historical event that both Gans and Jenkins feel has been underacknowledged in civil rights literature. Jenkins argues that the original vision — to change racial attitudes in the North — dissipated as northern students flocked to the South to aid voter registrations drives.[33] But both believe that without the NSA, northern students would not have made such an immediate link with southern civil rights activists.

The NSA's actions were alarming J. Edgar Hoover, never a fan of civil rights. On March 3, he wrote to a lieutenant, "I think we had better take another look at this outfit. It is inconceivable that a group with such parallel goals as communist front groups have can be so 'legitimate.'"[34] He also began eavesdropping and surveillance of SNCC members and other young civil rights leaders.[35]

The more aggressively the NSA supported civil rights, the louder the accusations of communist influence became. Young conservatives, the new John Birch Society, and Fulton (Buddy) Lewis III, son of the broadcaster who had attacked the NSA in the early 1950s and the research director for HUAC, led the charge. The embattled Hoffman faced down his accusers, resulting in news headlines like the *New York Post*'s "Student Leader Denies Reds Inspire Protests."[36] Hoffman defended the demonstrations as exemplifying the best democratic tradition, a statement that just a few years earlier would have been deemed too radical for the NSA. At the same time he tried to cast the NSA position in Cold War terms: American students were "too unalterably committed to freedom to be taken in by totalitarian ideologies from either the right or left."[37]

But civil rights was not the only issue that riled conservatives and the FBI. Liberals were protesting against loyalty oaths as a relic of Cold War hysteria and a violation of civil liberties. When on May 13 the House Committee on Un-American Activities scheduled a hearing in San Francisco, students marched on the stately City Hall. Although the demonstrators were dressed in suits and ties, the police blasted the protesters with fire hoses. A young reporter from KPFA radio station in Berkeley caught the episode on tape, and a nationwide audience heard the screams of students as their bodies thumped down the steps.[38] Incensed liberals and civil rights activists joined a campaign to abolish HUAC. Young conservatives responded by forming the National Student Committee for the Loyalty Oath.[39]

A few months later, in August 1960, the NSA Congress theme, "A World in Transition: Students in Action," sounded like an ironic understatement. Delegates gathered at the University of Minnesota heatedly debated the legitimacy of direct action, a new term to describe sit-ins and mass rallies. Conservatives tried to discredit direct action as criminal activity, charging that sit-ins violated property rights and depicting demonstrations as riots. Delegates wrestled with new questions: What was the obligation of individuals? Were they willing to be jailed for their beliefs?

Sandra Cason from the University of Texas, known as "Casey" to friends, gave her answer to a plenary session: "I cannot speak for the sit-ins or for white southerners. I consider this problem to be an ethical one for which there can be only a personal decision." She asked, "When an individual human being has been denied by the attitudes of his community the exercise of his rights as a human being, has he the right to peaceably protest? The answer to this simple question can only be yes." But what drew tears from many delegates was her story of Henry David Thoreau's conversation with his friend Ralph Waldo Emerson after Thoreau was jailed over his protest of slavery. When Emerson asked, "Henry David, what are you doing in there?" Thoreau responded, "Ralph Waldo, what are you doing out there?"[40]

Connie Curry, who today is honored as a civil rights heroine, said Cason's speech still makes her scalp tingle. She viewed it as a decisive moment, which solidified NSA support "for civil disobedience and the Freedom Movement."[41] That night, after defeating numerous amendments, a lengthy three-page resolution on civil rights passed unanimously, a stark contrast to past battles.[42]

But Cason's speech did not provide the only riveting moment. Conservative Howie Phillips, by then a Harvard sophomore, and liberal Tom Hayden from the University of Michigan faced off in debate. Phillips stressed the communist threat at home and defended HUAC and loyalty oaths. Hayden dismissed them. Phillips argued against direct action and charged that sit-ins disregarded private property.[43] Hayden, like Cason, spoke about moral imperatives. Neal Johnston, editor of the *Chicago Maroon* at the University of Chicago, who watched the debate, later expressed the loathing that liberals felt for Phillips. He described the hirsute conservative as "positively s-s-s-simian," drawing out the sibilant for emphasis.[44]

Despite these contending forces, in 1960 the CIA caucus regained its edge over NSA elections. In 1959, on a trip to Asia, Harry Lunn had identified James Scott, a Williams College graduate studying in Burma on a Rotary International Fellowship, as a likely recruit. Scott agreed to do some minor reporting for Lunn. When his fellowship ended, Scott was offered the coveted NSA Paris post, which he held from 1959 to 1960. At the August Congress, the CIA caucus cleared the field of other candidates, drawing on tactics usually reserved for overseas battles.

During the summer Hoffman had learned that Gary Weissman, a Wisconsin graduate then in Berkeley, might seek elective office, possibly international affairs vice president. Hoffman made a special trip to Berkeley and tantalized Weissman with the prospect of an overseas post instead.[45] Weissman was interested and stayed out of the election. After the Congress, Weissman returned to Berkeley, as instructed, to wait for the appointment. Someone at the NSA had hinted at an imminent departure and told him not to rent an apartment. The offer never materialized. When the electoral threat had been averted, the overseas position evaporated.[46]

Weissman was not the only threat. Howard University's Tim Jenkins, an NSA loyalist, ISRS graduate, and liaison to civil rights activists, sought the international affairs vice presidency. Shortly after he announced his candidacy, someone made a motion to elect Jenkins to a national position. Before Jenkins could protest or decline, the delegates elected him by acclamation. At an NSA reunion years later, Jenkins said, "I guess I wasn't the kind of international officer they had in mind."[47]

The NSA presidency went to Richard Rettig from the University of Washington, a known quantity who had served in a national position. Curtis Gans, who thought about running for president, watched in disgust as the senior leadership maneuvered until, in his view, they found "someone they could own."[48] He described Rettig today as a "technocrat" whom "no one wanted."[49] "In retrospect," Gans said, "the 1960 Congress was the most manipulated election of the four I knew about."[50]

At the close of that Congress, the co-chair of the Young Republican National Federation, Carol Dawson, conducted a survey of the delegates. She found that the average student was far less liberal than the NSA resolutions and projects would indicate; an estimated 60 percent intended to vote for Richard Nixon in the upcoming presidential election.[51] The poll heartened conservatives and spurred them to organize.

It reinforced the notion of a liberal NSA elite out of touch with its student constituency.

Shortly after the Congress, William F. Buckley, Jr., invited Phillips and other young conservatives to his estate in Sharon, Connecticut. As the editor of the *National Review,* Buckley raised an erudite voice for conservatism. The invitation list of more than eighty students drew heavily from the National Committee to Support the Loyalty Oath, the Young Republication National Federation, and Youth for Goldwater for Vice President. After a weekend of discussion and debate, the assembled group founded the Young Americans for Freedom (YAF). Wresting control of the NSA from the liberals topped the list of YAF priorities.[52] They had one year to organize.

Dawson and the YAF were not the only conservatives targeting the NSA. A young woman from Northwestern University, Kay Wonderlic, now entered the fray. She had attended her first Congress in Minnesota, partly to get information on student government issues: how to evaluate faculty performance, how to run a good meeting. Instead, she found herself in debates over Angola and Mozambique. She could not fathom why. Angry and annoyed, she marched over to the college bookstore, bought a map of Africa, unfurled it at one session and demanded. "Who can find Angola on the map?"[53]

When Wonderlic returned to her campus, she launched the Student Committee for National Reform, SCANR (pronounced "scanner"). She prepared a pamphlet on the NSA, "An Analysis of the Structural and Functional Aspects of the United States National Student Association." Its tone was dispassionate, even scholarly. It had none of the stridency of the YAF material. She cited experts in democratic process and showed how NSA meetings violated its precepts. She raised questions about NSA finances. (On this she could obtain little information, noting in a later interview that NSA headquarters stonewalled her.)[54]

During her research, Wonderlic stumbled on one of the CIA's main means of control, the fact that Congress delegates voted on only a small percentage of policy resolutions. If a Congress ended before all resolutions could be considered, the executive committee would consider and vote on the remainder immediately after the Congress.[55] In 1960, the full Congress debated and voted on thirteen of ninety-five resolutions, and the NSA executive committee considered the rest. Of those, it passed a whopping forty-two resolutions that dealt with international issues. Wonderlic calculated that since the forty-two resolutions consumed a total of fourteen hours of debate, the average length of debate per resolution was twenty minutes.

Wonderlic made a list of the hastily decided resolutions, which offers a glimpse of the far-flung NSA operation: "East-West Cultural Center, World Youth Forum, Cuba, South Korea-Turkey, Nuclear Testing, Algeria, South Africa, Totalitarianism, Student Exchange, Emergent Areas Exchange, Eastern European Exchange, Sudan, Round Table, Foreign Student Programming, American policy, Portuguese Africa, China, Point Four Youth Corps, World University Service, ETI (travel office) 1960 Programming, Foreign student program, Puerto Rico, Campus International Program, Japan, India, Germany, West Irian [West Papua or Western New Guinea], Okinawa, Hungary, Dictatorship in Latin America, UNEF (French student union), Ethiopia, Argentina, COFSA [Conference on Foreign Student Affairs], Program Vice President Mandate, Research and Information, Individual Campus Exchange, FEANF (North African students), Latin American Policy, Spain, and Foreign Student Conference."[56]

Wonderlic believed that the process violated the NSA constitution. She interviewed executive committee members about the resolutions. A resolution that upheld the right of Japanese students to nonviolently protest against the Japanese-American Security Treaty, for example, drew the following responses: "One denied it was passed, one said he didn't know if it had been, and the other said a resolution to that effect was passed but he couldn't recall specifics of it."[57]

During the academic year 1960–61, Wonderlic took her campaign to reform the NSA on the road, traveling especially to member schools in the Midwest. Student councils that sought someone to debate Wonderlic frequently settled on Tom Hayden. By this time, Hayden had joined Students for a Democratic Society (SDS), whose founder, Al Haber at the University of Michigan, was a close friend.

At this juncture, the SDS was filled with liberal, rather than radical, students. Haber had broken away from the Student League for Industrial Democracy, the one-time home of Joseph Lash and Molly Yard, partly because it remained fiercely anticommunist. Haber also chafed under adult control from the parent body, the League for Industrial

Democracy.[58] SDS leaders saw NSA liberals as potential recruits, not as antagonists. At the Minnesota Congress, Haber organized the Liberal Study Group, which questioned long-standing Cold War shibboleths.

WHETHER VIEWED IN TERMS of campus upheavals, the Cuban revolution, or the birth of new political organizations, the spirit of the 1960s arrived even before John F. Kennedy took office. No one in the NSA understood then how decisions made in the late Eisenhower period, many of them by top-ranking CIA officers, would cast their shadows over the Kennedy administration.

On March 17, 1960, President Eisenhower had approved a top-secret plan (restricted even within the CIA) to invade Cuba and overthrow Castro.[59] Witting NSA students had no inkling that planning was under way for an invasion. An exception was Luigi Einaudi, who continued on occasion to advise the NSA, and had been alerted in early December by his Latin American friends that Cuban exiles were being trained in Guatemala. "Once I got tipped off . . . it was very easy to follow," he said years later.[60] When Einaudi learned that Kennedy had tapped the dean of faculty at Harvard, McGeorge Bundy, for national security advisor, Einaudi sought him out.

Bundy acknowledged that the rumors were plausible but claimed to have no firsthand knowledge. He then explained to Einaudi that Cuba was about to undergo a civil war between communists and liberals. Einaudi was incredulous. "I was not capable of understanding the mind that might say that."[61] Bundy quickly ended the interview, dashing Einaudi's hope that a new administration would mean "that these stupid things begun under the Eisenhower administration would be revisited."[62]

NSA witting staff were—virtually to a person—idealists who believed in Kennedy's promise of a New Frontier. When Kennedy talked about the torch being passed to a new generation, they saw themselves reflected in its light. At the same time, at the dawn of the Kennedy era, they were about to enter a world of growing militancy at home and abroad. President Kennedy soon discovered the shadowy virtues of covert action, and the CIA spigot opened wider.

At home, the new activists might still wear coats and ties, as the anti-HUAC demonstrators did when blasted by water hoses, or they might walk a picket line in favor of civil rights in high-heeled white pumps, as Sandra Cason did in Austin, Texas, but campus activists, left and right, were determined to challenge the status quo.[63] YAF leader Robert Schuchman captured the rebellious spirit of the New Right in a *Time* interview. He explained that Richard Nixon was too liberal to win his support in the 1960 presidential contest, then added, "You feel the thrill of treason when you walk around with a Goldwater political button."[64]

As the 1960s dawned, the NSA-CIA team realized that it would have to work harder to keep control over its far-flung operations, ensure their secrecy, and keep rival domestic political factions from tearing the NSA apart and jeopardizing clandestine activities.

In 1939, First Lady Eleanor Roosevelt displayed her support for American Student Union leader Joseph Lash when he was summoned before the Dies Committee, a forerunner of the House Committee on Un-American Activities. During World War II, Lash worked with Roosevelt to found a noncommunist student organization. (Library of Congress, Prints and Photographs Division)

Pope Pius XII reviewed NSA policy on the International Union of Students and gave direction to American Catholics. (Reprinted with permission of AP Images)

Allard Lowenstein is often accused of beginning the relationship between the NSA and the CIA during his presidency. In fact, he was an obstacle to its operation. (Courtesy of the Allard Lowenstein Collection, Wilson Library, University of North Carolina, and Jennifer Littlefield)

The NSA delegation at the 1956 ISC in Ceylon: (*front, l. to r.*) Clive Gray, Luigi Einaudi, James Edwards, and Bruce Larkin. The NSA supported the cause of Cuban revolutionary José Antonio Echeverría (*clutching papers, back right*), who was killed in 1957 during an attack on the Cuban dictator Fulgencio Batista. (Courtesy of Luigi Einaudi)

Hungarian refugee Alpár Bujdosó testifying before the U.S. Congress in disguise, fearful of reprisals to his family. He toured American campuses for the NSA under the name of Istvan Laszlo. (Reprinted with permission of AP Images)

Students protest the entrance of Autherine Lucy to the University of Alabama. (Library of Congress, Prints and Photographs Division)

The left-wing American delegation to the 1957 Moscow World Youth Festival. The CIA sent a handful of American students to Moscow to disrupt the festival and challenge the Soviet line on Hungary. (Courtesy of Robert Carl Cohen)

Malcolm Rivkin, one of two hundred American students sent by the CIA-funded Independent Research Service to the 1959 Vienna World Youth Festival. Rivkin tried to take over a raucous meeting of rival American factions. (Reprinted with permission of AP Images)

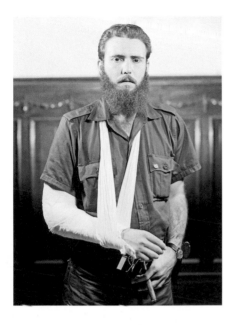

Rolando Cubela, head of the Cuban student union and dubbed by *Time* "Castro's gun-toting bully-boy," brought a gun to the 1960 ISC in Switzerland. It is uncertain whether Cubela was a double agent, working for both Castro and the CIA. (© Lester Cole/CORBIS)

The NSA helped build a constituency for the Cuban revolution by sending American students to Havana through Operation Amistad, a joint project with the Cuban student union. (Courtesy USNSA Collection, Hoover Institution Archives)

The first president of Algeria, Ben Bella (*center left*), and Foreign Minister Mohamed Khemisti (*second from right*) at a 1962 White House reception. Khemisti rewarded the NSA for its support of Algerian revolutionaries by arranging a private meeting with Ben Bella. (Reprinted with permission of AP Images)

ISC members (*l. to r.*) Jean Carriere and Jacques Gerin of Canada with incoming COSEC director Gwyn Morgan and outgoing COSEC director Jyoti Shankar Singh. Both Morgan and Singh presided over growing global student militancy that pushed the CIA-funded ISC to the left and ultimately destroyed it. (Courtesy of Paul Becker)

Philip Sherburne, who during his presidency (1965–66) single-handedly tried to oust the CIA from the NSA. (Courtesy of Philip Sherburne)

Former NSA president and CIA career agent Harry Lunn. (© Carol Harrison)

In 1967, NSA oversight board chair Sam Brown charged that students had been duped into signing security oaths. Brown later headed the moratorium against the Vietnam War. (© Bettmann/CORBIS)

Zybněk Vokrouhlický, pictured here in 2008, was one of three Czech communist presidents of the International Union of Students. In 1968, the Soviets expelled him for participation in the reform movement known as the Prague Spring. (Photo by the author)

Olof Palme (*c.*) protesting U.S. foreign policy in Vietnam with the ambassador from North Vietnam (*front left*), 1968. The anticommunist Palme had earlier been the CIA's choice to lead the ISC Secretariat, but he refused.

PART FOUR

LOSING CONTROL

16

SHOWDOWN IN MADISON

IN 1961, THE NATIONAL STUDENT ASSOCIATION became a political battleground, as both the disaffected new conservatives in the Young Americans for Freedom and the leftist Students for a Democratic Society, who saw it as fertile recruiting ground, plotted to take it over. The traditional liberals who led the association found themselves caught in the middle, trying to repel YAF initiatives and coopt SDS leaders.

Over the next few years, as the CIA caucus fought to retain control of the NSA, it focused on the threat from conservatives, whose aggressive anticommunism and insistent demands for a victory over the Soviets ran counter to everything the liberals believed would win friends for the West. For years, the NSA had insisted to foreign student leaders that it had no Cold War agenda, even when its actions belied the rhetoric. Witting staff had become skilled at the verbal acrobatics necessary to reconcile the tension between public pronouncements and private agendas. But in 1961, YAF demands for the NSA to take a more vocal anti-communist stand threatened to upset this balancing act.

In the face of the imminent YAF threat, the NSA-CIA team ignored the challenge from the left. Yet SDS members were organizing on numerous campuses. They opposed Kennedy's Cold War policies and ridiculed fervent anticommunism. They attacked the Cold War as a costly impediment to tackling problems at home of poverty, unemployment, and education. Despite vigorous fights with older liberals and socialists over the lessons of the 1930s popular fronts, the SDS defiantly refused to prohibit communist students from joining. Students across the country were developing a new interest in Marx and Hegel, reading the sociologist C. Wright Mills's *Listen Yankee* (a defense of the Cuban revolution), forming study groups, and churning out mimeographed critiques of U.S. foreign policy that were passed from campus to campus.[1]

Almost all the thousand-plus students who poured into Madison, Wisconsin, in late August 1961 for the NSA Congress expected a show-down between left and right. Years later, some of them understood they were bearing witness to the irreconcilable political forces that eventually would alter and polarize U.S. politics.

In anticipation of the 1961 congress, YAF member Howard Phillips, the intrepid Harvard conservative who in protest had grabbed Fidel Castro's beard, put together an ad-hoc Committee for a Responsive National Student Organization. Its list of leaders reads like a Who's Who of the new right: Carol Dawson Bauman, M. Stanton Evans, David Franke, Tom Huston, Fulton Lewis III, and Robert Schuchman. Phillips lobbied outgoing NSA president Richard Rettig to invite the conservative senator John G. Tower (R-Tex.) to speak at a plenary session, calling Tower a "living symbol of the rising conservative tide among American youth."[2] When Rettig chose a date that conflicted with Tower's Senate obligations, Phillips charged that the conflict was deliberate. Phillips also requested that conservative working papers be distributed at the Congress, but Rettig refused.[3]

The YAF prepared for battles over Cuba (against Castro), the House Committee on Un-American Activities (in favor), and the new Peace Corps proposed by Kennedy (against). By mid-August, conservative reform organizations had sprouted like weeds. Phillips's committee newsletter listed five groups no one had ever heard of before.

The NSA was not without allies. The Students for Democratic Action (SDA), the home of Roosevelt liberals, among them NSA veteran Allard Lowenstein, mobilized to ward off both the YAF challenge and separate threats coming from Kay Wonderlic. A liberal Harvard student and NSA loyalist, Barney Frank, formed Independent Student Action to offer alternative reforms.[4] Frank, quick-witted, brash, and fast-talking, frequently disarmed NSA opponents with his biting wit. The future congressman from Massachusetts hoped to defuse the conservative backlash against the NSA by appearing to lead a reform movement, albeit one that had the support of the NSA leadership.

Civil rights activist Curtis Gans returned to the Congress to direct the SDS-dominated Liberal Caucus. Gans cared deeply about the NSA, and like many liberals felt that the new conservatives threatened its very existence. The senior NSA leadership encouraged him, even though he was often to their left on positions. He later explained, "I probably pushed them beyond where they would like to be, but I wasn't crazy," referring to the heated rhetoric of the SDS.[5] Earlier in the summer, for example, SDS founder Al Haber had warned prospective NSA delegates that the YAF consorted with "racist, militarist, imperialist butchers."[6]

Delegates listened as keynote speakers tried to shape the upcoming debates. The governor of Wisconsin, Gaylord Nelson, an ardent New Deal liberal and Wisconsin progressive who had fought the right-wing anticommunism of Senator Joseph McCarthy, dismissed the new conservatives. "There is no conservative revival . . . merely a revival of the Know-Nothing spirit."[7] Former NSA president Richard Murphy reverted to an old cliché and told delegates that if they were attacked from both left and right, they were doing something right.[8] Richard Rettig accused the conservatives of hindering the ability of NSA officers to carry out Congress mandates.[9] In his longer report to the NSA executive committee, Rettig acknowledged a serious and growing gap between the campuses and the NSA officers.[10]

The two hundred Young Americans for Freedom who descended on Madison wore suspenders on the plenary floor so they could recognize one another. They tracked debates and votes via walkie-talkies.[11] Phillips was on academic probation at Harvard and could not be an official delegate, but he set up shop in the nearby Madison Inn with a battery of secretaries and staff and produced a flow of pamphlets and flyers, despite a behind-the-scenes fight over the high cost of the operation. The conservatives lived up to their advance billing, vocally opposing any remotely liberal measure, including support for the new Peace Corps, a centerpiece of the Kennedy administration.

In his role as chair of the Committee for an Effective Peace Corps, formed the previous spring, Phillips had called instead for a hard-hitting propaganda campaign against international communism. He suggested that the Peace Corps change its name to the Anti-Communist Freedom Corps.[12] He argued that volunteers should be trained in communist propaganda, undergo security clearances, and be prepared to combat socialist and Marxist ideas.[13] Liberals easily defeated the conservative minority and passed a resolution in full support of the Peace Corps.[14]

These were mere skirmishes compared to the fight over HUAC. The YAF maintained that the protest against HUAC earlier in the year in

San Francisco was communist inspired. In the previous months, conservatives had traveled the country to prove their charges by showing a HUAC-made movie, *Operation Abolition*, which portrayed communists as seeking to destroy the nation's security and as having duped the noncommunist liberals, tricking them into going against the forces of law and order.[15] Left and liberal delegates, incensed at what they perceived as either slander or poppycock, stepped up their demands that HUAC be abolished. That demand in turn frightened witting NSA officers and staff, who, despite their general antipathy toward HUAC, feared that such a position would leave the association open to charges of communist infiltration.

After heated debate, postponements, and parliamentary maneuvers, the vote to call for HUAC to be abolished succeeded, 269 to 156.[16] It appeared that the left had won a decisive victory. But the final resolution had been artfully amended by witting staff: it recognized the legitimacy of the U.S. Congress "to investigate acts of espionage, sabotage, and conspiracies to overthrow by force the Government of the United States" and recommended that "these functions be exercised by the Judiciary Committees of the House and Senate respectively."[17] In effect, the resolution enabled the NSA to argue that it did not advocate abolishing investigations into subversive activities—just the body that traditionally conducted them.

The trickiest issue for the international staff was Cuba. Two and a half years after Castro came to power, the NSA had not changed its position in support of the revolution, despite Eisenhower's mandates and growing reports of repression within the country. In the months before the Congress, NSA staff worked to ward off a YAF initiative to condemn Castro for atrocities as well as an SDS initiative to condemn the United States for actions against Cuba, while coping with internal pressure over the arrests of Cuban students who had once been close to the NSA.

One such student was Ramón Prendes, and Lucille Dubois, the irrepressible head of the Latin American subcommission in Miami, mounted a one-woman crusade on his behalf. Prendes, who had once plotted to kill Batista, had spoken at the 1958 Congress. Now he was under arrest in Havana, and in January 1961 Dubois pleaded with the NSA to take action, warning, "They [the exiles] know for sure Ramón will be shot."[18]

It fell to Latin America specialist Manuel Aragon to explain to Dubois why the NSA could not act on Prendes's behalf. In February he assured her that the NSA was "increasingly preoccupied about the situation in Cuba as more information on the repression of students has become available." But the question was "extremely delicate," he added, because the NSA had "cordial relations" with Roland Cubela, a Castro lieutenant and the gun-toting head of the Cuban student union.[19]

Then, four months before the Congress, the full import of Eisenhower's directives became clear, narrowing the NSA's options. Near midnight on April 14, the first American-backed Cuban teams trained in Guatemala departed from a Nicaraguan port to invade Cuba. (It seems that Phillips was not the only one obsessed with Castro's beard: the Nicaraguan dictator Luis Somoza, an American ally, requested souvenir hairs from it in return for his support.) As the disastrous Bay of Pigs invasion began, American officials from Secretary of State Dean Rusk to U.N. Ambassador Adlai Stevenson denied any U.S. involvement. The resulting debacle cost 200 lives; 1,197 invaders were captured, including Americans.[20]

Anyone who worked with Latin Americans knew that the invasion would put the entire region in an uproar. Even Cord Meyer, the students' ultimate overseer in the CIA, later confided in his diary that he regretted going along with Richard Bissell, head of clandestine operations and the invasion's principal architect.[21] Meyer blamed his acquiescence on the influence of his elders in the Georgetown social set who thought highly of Bissell.

Yet two months after the invasion, the NSA was still hedging its bets. Manuel Aragon told an NSA constituent that the International Commission had "not found it possible at this point to make a decision on the representative nature of FEU in Cuba now or on the representative nature of any of the exile groups."[22] To anyone in the know, it was jaw-dropping dissembling.

The truth was that not long after the revolution, Havana had begun to rival Prague as a center of militant activity. Raúl Castro had made good on his World Youth Festival promises, offering Havana to the International Union of Students and the World Federation of Democratic Youth as a base for reaching Latin American young people. Soon afterward, the Cubans hosted a Latin American Youth Congress and established a school to train revolutionaries.[23] The Cubans also hosted a Congress of Central American Students, wresting control of it from Guatemala.[24]

In June 1961, Havana hosted an IUS Council meeting and welcomed thirty-six delegations to the city.[25] The elaborate pageantry mimicked the World Youth Festivals. Welcome banners streamed from Havana buildings and President Osvaldo Dorticós and Prime Minister Castro mingled with the delegates. The Cuban National Theater produced special programs, including a beauty pageant. The FEU led tours to the Bay of Pigs. IUS president Jiří Pelikán made a pilgrimage to the grave-site of José Antonio Echeverría and placed a wreath on his tomb. The IUS then voted to condemn "aggression against the Republic of Cuba by the imperialist government of the United States" and to "denounce new plans for aggression hatched by those who wish to utilize the Organization of American States."[26]

Bob Kiley, by then on the COSEC staff, today describes the 1960–61 period, understatedly, as "one of rising tension" between NSA witting staff and CIA case officers.[27] The NSA friendship flights to Havana finally ended but the campus constituency created as a result of Operation Amistad fueled protests against the invasion. Within the ISC and COSEC, enthusiasm for the revolution remained high. Not only would the NSA be isolated if it condemned Castro at home or in the ISC but doing so would undermine claims of independence from U.S. foreign policy, the basis of the NSA's overseas legitimacy. Yet there seemed to be no middle ground.

At the 1961 Congress, both the YAF and the NSA used Cuban exiles to try to gain an advantage with delegates. The YAF had invited New York–based Lesmes Ruiz to dramatize Castro's crimes.[28] The Congress initially rejected a request for Ruiz to speak on the procedural grounds that he lacked delegate status, but after frantic consultations, international vice president Jim Scott moved that the rules be suspended.[29] Ruiz delivered an emotional brief against Castro. Then Robert Schuchman from the YAF demanded an investigation into charges of repression and proposed that a delegation be sent to Cuba.[30] Scott stepped in to squelch the idea, arguing that such a trip "might enrage rather than mollify Castro. It is in the best interests of NSA that YAF should play no part, not even a small part, in the Cuban business."[31]

Delegates then followed Scott's lead and agreed to hear from the NSA-preferred Cuban exile, Juan Manuel Salvat. The former head of Agrupción Católica at the University of Havana, Salvat had once belonged to Echeverría's revolutionary group Directorio Revolucionario

Estudiantil. Like many Catholics, Salvat had turned against Castro, and in 1960, Castro had arrested him for protesting a visit from the Soviet official Anastas Mikoyan. After his release from prison, Salvat fled Cuba to Miami and joined the Bay of Pigs operation.[32]

Salvat was among the young Cubans who slipped secretly onto the island ahead of the disastrous landing. He was caught, arrested, and released—probably because he operated under a false identity. A few months after he spoke to NSA delegates, Salvat would begin what the CIA called "boom and bang" operations—hit-and-run raids against the Castro regime. By then, the Kennedy administration had approved Operation Mongoose, a covert operation to harass Castro after the invasion failed.[33] (In his most famous exploit, in the summer of 1962 Salvat and his friends powered across the seas in a leaky dinghy from Florida to blow up the Havana hotel where Castro was entertaining a Russian delegation, but the bombs exploded after Castro and his entourage had left.)[34] And it would be Salvat and his fellow raiders who first identified the Russian-made missiles on the island of Cuba that led to the Kennedy-Khrushchev confrontation and took the world to the brink of nuclear war.[35]

The great irony in the NSA's decision to choose Salvat over Ruiz is that both were on the CIA payroll.[36] The CIA believed in funding all factions in a political conflict, although the CIA station chief in Miami, Ted Shackley, later wrote that he had warned his superiors that leaders of the new DRE (Directorio Revolucionario Estudiantil en el Exilio), including Salvat, resisted direction and treated U.S. policymakers with "contempt I repeat contempt."[37] That contempt would turn to hatred and accusations of betrayal after the missile crisis, when Kennedy cracked down on their boom and bang adventures and ended funding subsidies.[38]

At the Madison Congress, Salvat won the delegates' rapt attention when he described how Castro had arrested student leaders José Puente Blanco, founder of Operation Amistad, and Alberto Muller, a palace attack survivor. After the speech, the delegates agreed to send a protest telegram to Castro urging him to spare the lives of the students who had been arrested. Salvat later praised the NSA action, believing that it, along with similar protests in Latin America, saved Muller's life. "So great was our influence," Salvat wrote to Manuel Aragon afterward, "that Che [Guevara] himself went to the Oriente to forbid the court to impose a penalty of more than twenty years."[39]

Yet the international staff managed a sleight of hand to keep the cable to Castro separate from the NSA's resolution on Cuba. Having satisfied anti-Castro sentiment, the longer resolution on Cuba balanced praise for the revolution's achievements, such as Castro's literacy campaign, with concern for violations of academic freedom. It contained a mild protest against the Bay of Pigs invasion: "The attainment of a Cuban solution to the problems [of academic freedom] is jeopardized by such external interventions as the United States government involvement in the Cuban refugee invasion of April, 1961 and the Soviet arms shipment to the Cuban Government."[40] By pairing Soviet arms shipments with the U.S.-supported invasion, the NSA could argue that it was even-handed in its criticism. The only mandate for action involved "gathering information" on conditions in Cuba. Once again, the NSA international team had preserved its flexibility, avoiding an outright condemnation of the Bay of Pigs and keeping its overseas options open.

The NSA leadership had been prepared for the debates on HUAC, Cuba, and even the Peace Corps. What caught officers off guard was an inflammatory speech by *National Review* founder William F. Buckley. After the NSA refused to let a conservative give a major plenary speech, the YAF invited Buckley to the Congress to demonstrate that the NSA did not allow free speech. At the Madison Inn parking lot outside YAF headquarters, Buckley spoke to a large crowd one evening. He slammed NSA policy in Africa. "One of the great liberal fallacies is to assume that we can have freedom for Mau Mau, for Mozambique, and for Algeria." He called the NSA stands on Mozambique and Algeria geographically and anthropologically illiterate.[41]

Toward the end of his speech, Buckley took questions. A Ceylonese visitor asked why Buckley was critical of African independence movements when the United States itself had fought a revolution against a colonial power.[42] Buckley chastised the questioner: How dare he compare the "semi-savages of Africa to the American founding fathers."[43]

The crowd let out a collective gasp.

Infuriated by Buckley's statements, student guests to the Congress from Asia and Africa signed a petition against Buckley's remarks, while outgoing NSA national affairs vice president Tim Jenkins publicly condemned the remarks: "I think now we have unmasked in the final reality what exactly exists behind the face of the conservative imagination, because now we see the base, and the debased, colonial, repressive, slave-owning kind of mentality that can exist in a hard, fascist type of regime."[44] Jenkins's language in turn upset members of the NSA executive committee, which met through the night to decide whether to censure his remarks. Toward dawn they decided against censure, 30–0 with 3 abstentions, on the grounds that Jenkins had acted as an individual and not as an officer.[45]

Buckley later added fuel to the fire when he defended his remarks in the *National Review*, citing tribal wars in African countries as evidence of savagery, adding provocatively, "Some Africans have literally eaten their opponents."[46]

While Buckley was stirring up drama outside the formal sessions, exhausted delegates inside had to decide on another controversial issue: whether to invite the Student Non-Violent Coordinating Committee to affiliate with the NSA. James Forman, who after the 1956 NSA Congress had decided that the organization was too conservative a vehicle to fight for civil rights, attended the 1961 Congress as the new executive director of SNCC to plead the case. Jenkins and others in the NSA leadership had remained close to SNCC, hosting meetings and raising bail money for jailed students. A few months before the Congress, SNCC and the NSA had sought funds for a joint voter registration project, a plan intended to bring southern blacks to the polls that would later be recast by some black power and SDS militants as a diabolical Kennedy plot to coopt the radicalism of the civil rights movement. But the Congress rejected formal affiliation with SNCC, instead urging member campuses to cooperate with individual chapters.[47] It was a tepid gesture, and the new officers of the NSA scrambled to offset the damage to the NSA-SNCC partnership.[48]

The last act of the sleep-deprived delegates was the election of officers. Before the Congress, from his COSEC post in Leiden, Kiley had worried that a capable Notre Dame student, John Keegan, might run for NSA president and "attempt to make political capital of the mysterious NSA establishment's involvement in policy-making at the Congress."[49] He advised witting staff of this "potentially very dangerous tactic" and urged them to reduce the visibility of "overseas representatives, the International Advisory Board and 'old-hand' expert advice in crafting resolutions."[50]

That someone from the SDS left would run for office was a foregone conclusion; the question was who. The answer was Tom Hayden, who wrestled with the decision after trying to sort out his experiences with NSA officers. In his memoir, Hayden noted that the international staff had rejected his application to the prestigious summer seminar on the grounds that he was already "sufficiently knowledgeable about foreign policy."[51] Perhaps as a consolation prize, Rettig had hired Hayden to write a booklet on the civil rights movement, and then refused to publish it, without explaining why.[52]

Hayden was also uncertain whether the NSA offered him a national platform. He could pursue his passion for civil rights and organize northern students if he ran for the post of national affairs vice president, previously held by Gans and Jenkins, which still served as the nerve center of the NSA's civil rights organizing. He decided to run.

Hayden soon heard rumors that he was too militant. Then he found damaging evidence of opposition from the leadership: "On the last night of the Congress," he wrote years later, "a yellow pad was obtained from the office of the NSA president. It was an organizational chart of the convention's political forces. On one side was a box inscribed *Hayden-Haber*. On the other was a box labeled *YAF*. Lines were drawn upward from the two boxes to a circle at the top of the chart marked *Control Group*."[53]

Hayden was aware that there was an NSA establishment that tended to run things, but he was taken aback by the blatancy of the diagram. He withdrew his candidacy and threw his support to Paul Potter from Oberlin, a more temperate SDS colleague with closer ties to the NSA leadership who, unlike Hayden, had been accepted to the summer seminar. Potter had lost an earlier vote in the presidential race against Edward (Ed) Garvey, a University of Wisconsin graduate and former student body president, but he had enough support to win the national vice presidency.

Hayden did not go gently. On the plenary floor, he gave an angry speech in which he lambasted the "secretive NSA elite" for blocking his candidacy.[54] After the Congress Hayden left the NSA and committed himself to the civil rights movement, where he continued his transition from liberal to radical. But the thrust of his campaign, and especially his charge that a secretive elite ruled the NSA, took hold among undergraduates.

The new president, Ed Garvey, had been recruited by Matthew Iverson, a University of Wisconsin friend who was then the assistant director of the Foreign Student Leadership Project. Iverson presented Garvey to the NSA leadership as "a very astute and successful campus politician," whose main drawback was cynicism about the NSA.[55] Iverson thought that immersion in the summer ISRS might bring him around. The strategy was effective in the short term: Garvey became a trusted witting officer who worked with the CIA for five years, including a year at CIA headquarters. But he is now scathing in his criticism of the NSA-CIA relationship.[56]

At the time of his election, Garvey had no inkling that he had been recruited into a special fraternity until Kiley invited him to Washington, ostensibly for a football game but in reality for the oath signing. (After he was made witting he went home, crashed through the door of his apartment and announced to his wife, "You will never believe . . . ," thereby violating his security oath within hours of having signed it.)[57] His astonishment at learning the secret soon gave way to something approaching awe. A succession of thoughts went through his head: relief that the NSA was not a "commie pinko organization" as charged by conservatives, a swelling of pride – "Damn, we're that good!"[58] He worshiped the Kennedy family, and when Kiley told him that Bobby Kennedy backed their work and asked if he would like to have his picture taken with Bobby and President Kennedy, he was euphoric: "I felt I'd fallen asleep and awakened to a wonderful dream."[59]

The CIA also had a reliable pick in the victorious international affairs vice president, a previously vetted Princeton graduate named Donald K. (Don) Emmerson. After a few weeks in office, Emmerson described the NSA to a Princeton audience as "a magnificent opportunity to work myself to the bone doing something I believe is worthwhile."[60] Over the next year, the reliability of the top officers, the warm personal relationship between Garvey and Paul Potter, despite their differences, camouflaged the growing ideological gap between liberals and the SDS.

An objective observer might have asked how long the NSA could survive a membership whose political beliefs were diametrically opposed to each other. Yet the CIA's obsession with the conservatives made them oblivious to the challenge from the left. After the 1961 Congress, Kay Wonderlic, who advocated procedural reforms, not the abolition of the NSA, had an encounter with a friend who she knew worked for the CIA. "She warned me to be careful," Wonderlic recounted in an interview; "The CIA is worried about your activities."[61] The caution left her mystified. How could the CIA be afraid of "a naive North Shore Chicago girl, a Miss Goody-Two-Shoes?"[62] Over fifty years later, she still could not answer that question. At the time, the warning frightened her. After marrying a YAF activist, she left the student scene.

The warning had not been idle. A declassified CIA memo, "Right Wing Attacks Against the United States National Student Association," written after the 1961 Congress, devotes four pages to the conservatives' actions and singles out Wonderlic for special attention. Using the language of the clandestine world, the author describes Wonderlic as running a front: "She operated SCANR out of her home but apparently cooperated covertly with YAF."[63] Wonderlic (today Kathy Kolbe) scoffs at the notion she was a stalking horse for the YAF and describes its members as wackos.[64]

The declassified CIA memo is also illuminating for its description of the conservatives. They are depicted as ignorant and ill-informed, susceptible to a "a series of pat solutions to problems which fail to meet the test of realistic applicability to the modern world but which are simple and easily understood."[65] Conservatives appeal to "segments of the American public which have difficulty understanding domestic, economic, or international political questions." While the contemptuous language accurately conveys the smugness that liberals felt toward conservatives, the memo does not qualify as good intelligence reporting.

The CIA memo ended on a dire note: "What has traditionally been a minor irritant has now developed into a major headache." The unnamed author singled out the YAF-led disaffiliation campaigns as attacks that threatened to undermine the NSA "claim to represent American students" and that could "seriously hamper the USNSA international program."[66]

The memo ends with a multi-point action agenda to decrease the conservative threat. Fifty years later, that portion remains classified.

THE CIA HAD ALWAYS WORRIED about the stability of the NSA. One of the reasons it obtained draft deferments for officers and staff was to avoid a sudden decimation of the association if all were called for active duty. But stability also meant support from the campus members. As the campuses came alive politically, John Simons at FYSA proposed and funded a new program intended to solidify student support for NSA international objectives. It was an abject failure. His Regional International Relations Student Seminars, patterned after ISRS, exposed the gulf between a given topic and the knowledge of the average undergraduate. In one role-playing session, a young woman tapped to play an Algerian revolutionary took a pro-French position.[67]

CIA liberals realized too late that the success of covert operations with a domestic organization such as the NSA depended on an underlying consensus about the Cold War. Years later, it became fashionable to blame the Vietnam War for shattering that consensus. But even a cursory examination of campus politics between 1959 and 1961 shows rising activism and challenges to Cold War policies from both left and right that predate the Vietnam protests. Liberals did not have to join the SDS or see themselves as part of the new left to develop doubts about the invasion of Cuba or abhor the violence against civil rights activists in the South. Liberals were slowly moving to the left. As their campus ranks swelled, their clout inside the NSA also grew.

17

PRO-WEST MODERATE MILITANTS

THE GLOBAL RISE in student radicalism complicated the CIA's mission of winning friends for the West. Around the world, militant students were sparking demonstrations against U.S. foreign policy and helping to overthrow friendly regimes. Thousands of Japanese students, angry over a new U.S.-Japanese Security Treaty, took to the streets of Tokyo in 1960, forcing President Eisenhower to cancel his upcoming visit.[1] In the same year, Korean students—who in 1957 had listened raptly to the Hungarian delegation describe how to run a revolution—ousted the American-educated, anticommunist dictator Syngman Rhee, who fittingly fled Seoul on CIA transport.[2]

A new generation of nationalists and revolutionaries was emerging, more radical, fiery, and challenging to work with than the hardest-line communist. Nationalists threatened Western interests because they *might* turn toward Moscow or Beijing, because they *might* create fertile ground for communism, not because they *were* communists or *had* pro-Soviet sympathies. But because some of them really were communists, it was difficult to discern where one ideology stopped and another began, who was moderate or radical, friendly to the West or untrustworthy.

The rise of global militancy drove the International Student Conference farther to the left. Student unions flaunted their rejection of Cold War paradigms by joining both the ISC and the International Union of Students. After years of chipping away at the restrictive *students as students* clause in the ISC governing rules, the new nonwhite majority eliminated it. In 1960, State Department officials warned overseas embassies that the ISC was "vulnerable to mass defections," or, even more ominous, a merger with its archenemy in Prague.[3] In 1961, an unidenti-

256

fied NSA Latin American specialist wrote, "The increasing number of unions in Latin America opting for full membership in the International Union of Students (including many non-Marxist controlled unions) in dicates [that] a feeling exists that COSEC is a Western product, if not a U.S. tool."[4]

At the dawn of the Kennedy era, witting staff had to manage a home-grown conservative insurgency, ward off a broader campus movement to disaffiliate from the NSA, prevent an ISC-IUS merger, and keep control of COSEC. One objective often clashed with another. The NSA toler-ated anti-Western rhetoric within the ISC to show that it was not a tool of the West. But there were limits: the NSA could not become so toler-ant that membership in the ISC became a domestic issue.

The NSA continued to wield influence within COSEC. Its benign-sounding programs provided the CIA with access to foreign students on five continents. Yet as early as 1959, David Baad, a Michigan Uni-versity graduate and editor of COSEC's magazine *The Student*, warned, "We are in real danger of losing control of COSEC at the next ISC."[5] The 1959 summit between Khrushchev and Eisenhower had resulted in "a warmer peace," which had had a deleterious effect on Cold War loyalties even among European allies. "We fight," wrote Baad, "not only the Communists but also Germany, France, North Africa and most of South America."[6]

In addition, the COSEC staff of sixty had grown into an administra-tive leviathan, rife with ideological and personality conflicts. Associate secretaries for North America, Africa, Asia, Europe, and Latin America, who oversaw programs of seminars, conferences, goodwill tours, and technical assistance projects, learned how to use these programs to build political bases. The travel business generated by COSEC was so lucra-tive that Pan American airlines financed the purchase of a small manse to house the large staff in Oestgeest, a few miles from the University of Netherlands.[7]

Traditionally, the NSA wielded enough influence on the Supervi-sion Committee to ensure that its candidates were elected to COSEC leadership. But in the early 1960s, after rumors of vote buying and slush funds made the rounds, the United States did not always get its way. One American COSEC staff member who participated in stratagems to keep control later observed that the NSA spent more energy plotting against friends than it ever spent on IUS enemies.[8] John Thompson had stepped down as head of COSEC in late 1957, ending a five-year period of stability, and the NSA scrambled to find trusted replacements, sometimes offering support for a candidate and then withdrawing it.

Although the NSA had backed Thompson's replacement, the American-friendly Hans Dall of Denmark, it was only a few years before Baad and Young were plotting to get rid of him. Dall's political differences with the NSA were minor but Baad, and Young on the COSEC staff, among others, had developed a list of grievances over administrative matters. They encouraged him to accept a deferred scholarship in Denmark. As Young explained in a letter to a trusted NSA colleague, "The scheme is involved and must be handled very delicately. Hans must feel not that he is asked to leave but that his scholarship offer is too juicy to miss."[9] As an inducement to leave, Baad quietly offered to forgive a loan Dall had taken from COSEC funds (supplied by FYSA).[10]

The NSA then backed Norman Kingsbury of New Zealand to replace Dall, instantly regretted the decision, and forced him out nine months later. Kiley today says of Kingsbury's election, "It was a mistake. It never should have happened."[11] Asked how the Americans engineered Kingsbury's departure, Kiley responded with a rare admission of the fist inside the diplomatic glove. "We just told him it wasn't going to work. He wasn't happy and really didn't want to leave but he left."[12]

By design, the NSA never sought the top position in the secretariat. But after Kingsbury's resignation in 1960, Kiley took over as acting head of COSEC until a new NSA-backed candidate, Jyoti Shankar Singh from India, could be positioned. Singh's rise required the NSA to ease out an incumbent Asian associate secretary because having two high-ranking Asians would unbalance the staff. While plotting to achieve this goal, Baad and Kiley were overjoyed when the Asian, Eustace Mendis of Ceylon, decided to leave on his own.[13]

Singh represented one of the few successful investments the NSA made in a foreign student union. After Clive Gray had paid off former ally Pran Nath Sabharwal, whom he saw as the main obstacle to the NSA's work in India, Singh, from Benaras Hindu University, emerged as a talented leader. The NSA rewarded him for his cooperation with secret cash grants to study abroad. Today Singh acknowledges the payments, even ruefully noting that he had been promised a second year at Oxford before he was pressed into service on COSEC.[14]

Singh claims he never questioned the fact that the funds came from the NSA, although that stretches credulity. In an interview, he modified his statement to say that *if* he had been told of U.S. government support, he would not have been surprised. "I assume that's what governments do." He also acknowledges today that had it been known in India that he had received the cash grant it would have severely damaged his position. "Oh, I would have been persona non grata."[15] But as Thomas Farmer said at the beginning of the CIA-NSA relationship, people who enjoyed U.S. support usually did not ask questions.

After leading COSEC, Singh went on to head the CIA-funded World Assembly of Youth. He emphasizes today that he never did anything against his beliefs—"Well, maybe some minor favors." The protestations are somewhat beside the point: candidates were tapped and rewarded precisely because of shared beliefs. Reflecting on the revelations of CIA funding, Singh stated, "I find the whole subject distasteful." Although he has since been in touch with Kiley, Singh said they have never discussed the CIA relationship.[16]

WHILE LEADING COSEC, Kiley also co-chaired a FYSA-funded program that thrust him deeply into African revolutionary politics. The African program consisted of thirty-three educational seminars in East, West, and South Africa.[17] Neither Kiley nor the witting staff cared what topics were discussed. As Don Hoffman, then in the Paris post, observed to Jim Scott, the purpose of the seminars was to offer "a chance for NSA to further evaluate promising leaders."[18]

In a later interview Kiley stressed the importance of Africa. "New countries were being born virtually every week," he said. "Students were important people . . . in Asia and Latin America," but in Africa, they were "*the* key actors."[19] The COSEC program gave him unprecedented access to these actors. By the time he was thirty, Kiley told a *New Yorker* writer, he had visited eighty-seven countries.[20]

Witting staff tried to adapt existing strategies to Africa—backing new student unions where possible, identifying students for COSEC work, and giving Africans opportunities to travel outside their home country. A few Africans were invited to apply for the Foreign Student Leadership Project. But these traditional strategies did not work well on a continent seething with revolutionary discontent. In 1963, the NSA terminated the FLSP program in favor of more specialized programs.[21]

The choice of co-chair for the African program, Lovemore Mutambanengwe from Southern Rhodesia (today's Zimbabwe), illustrates some of the difficulties created by this revolutionary ferment. Mutambanengwe was an advocate of Pan-Africanism and African unity as articulated by Ghana's Kwame Nkrumah and Guinea's Sekou Toure, and he brought his aggressive nationalism into the secretariat. The NSA staff privately disparaged Pan-Africanism as too closely associated with the (radical) spirit of Bandung, but its appeal was sufficiently widespread to inhibit public criticism.[22] By contrast, Mutambanengwe's predecessor, Isaac Omolo of Kenya (which did not achieve its independence from Great Britain until 1963), had been a British-oriented political moderate. Baad, who worked closely with Omolo, observes today that the Kenyan, who aspired to further education in England, did not wish to offend either the British or the Americans.[23] Mutambanengwe's interests were centered in Africa, and despite his militancy, he brought COSEC advantages. He was a board member of the predominantly white National Union of South African Students (NUSAS), one of the few bastions of liberal anti-apartheid activism, and had studied at Fort Hare, where Nelson Mandela had been a student.

Not only Mutambanengwe but the entire African program exacerbated long-standing tensions between the British and the Americans within COSEC. For years, the NSA had chafed against claims by the British that they understood and could evaluate Africans better than Americans. Whenever an African student was needed for a tour or conference or project, the British were quick to find an accommodating colonial. The NSA strained for access to African students. A limited means was through the Association of African Students in the United States and Canada, whose founding at Howard University in 1953 was co-sponsored by the NSA and the CIA-funded Institute on Africa-American Relations, later renamed the African-American Institute.[24] But the British still had the advantage when it came to African students.

A former COSEC British official, Gwyn Morgan, cheerfully admits today that he enjoyed "trying to screw the Americans up in Africa."[25] He had far less tolerance for militant nationalism than Kiley, and he did not trust Mutambanengwe, whom he believed to be "flat out against the West."[26] Although a number of documented episodes support Morgan's claim, this statement riles Kiley.[27] "See now that's the classic example . . . of the Brits getting their noses out of joint because an African is being anti-imperial. What is Lovemore supposed to do? Kiss ass? It's either that or he isolates himself. If you're going to be effective as the African associate secretary in COSEC, you've got to be anti-British and to a considerable degree increasingly anti-American."[28]

The argument over whether to tolerate, if not trust, Mutambanengwe also reflected the larger problem of political assessment. In the early days of NSA reporting to the CIA, foreign students were identified as either pro-communist or pro-West. In the 1960s, NSA staff groped for new political indicators. A Cameroonian student was described favorably because he was "skeptical of extremism and communist influence," and judged to be "a genuine nationalist, though perhaps of the more revisionist moderate variety."[29] A Congolese student was identified as "the conservative, intelligent, French-speaking African people have been looking for."[30] But should the NSA back him for a COSEC position? Would he hold the line against an IUS merger? Jim Scott, then in Paris, was skeptical. "Particular care would have to be given to the development of his ISC line as his lack of background might make him susceptible initially to the wrong line on the unity question."[31] After further evaluations by old hands, among them Ted Harris, the NSA decided it was too risky.[32]

Paradoxically, some students fell out of favor with the NSA because they were judged too pro-West. In 1959, the NSA selected a moderate Ghanaian student for an FSLP scholarship with the hope that he would return to Ghana and lead students and someday the nation. The Ghanaian, Kofi Annan, spent two years at Macalester College in Minnesota.[33] Matthew Iverson, the FSLP official who regularly evaluated Annan, predicted that he was not likely to get very far in Ghanaian politics "because he is so Western-oriented."[34]

As a practical matter, however, Annan could not return to Ghana because he risked being jailed as an opponent of the Nkrumah regime. His plan, according to Iverson, was to attend the University of Geneva and "lay the groundwork for a viable opposition to Nkrumah." Iverson then reached this conclusion about the future secretary general of the United Nations: "He is certainly a washout as far as FSLP objectives are concerned and the only encouraging fact that I can report is that he will be leaving the country by the end of the summer."[35] Judging the future potential of young foreign students could be tricky.

No one on the witting staff apparently challenged the underlying presumption that an American education would produce Western-friendly students, although they understood the racial problems Africans would have when they got to the United States. Nothing could dissipate friendly feelings faster than being refused a haircut in a segregated barbershop or denied an apartment lease.

Nkrumah, the nationalist president of Ghana, might himself have served as a cautionary tale: he spent World War II at the historically black Lincoln University (for his B.A.) in Pennsylvania and the University of Pennsylvania (M.A.). Yet biographers note that it was during this time that he absorbed the radical ideas that made him a nonaligned Marxist socialist and leading advocate of Pan-Africanism.[36] Reflecting on the problem of turning African students toward the West, Baad quotes Guinea president Sekou Toure: "If he wanted to send a kid overseas to become a communist, he'd send him to the United States or Western Europe. If you wanted a kid to become an anti-Communist, he'd send him to Moscow."[37]

Growing evidence also suggested that picking moderate pro-West leaders in a revolutionary situation was difficult, since they almost always lost out to militants. Yet the international staff plunged into African liberation movements, if anything, more deeply than they had in Algeria or Cuba. Many in the CIA, including John Simons, amended the usual quip about students as future leaders to "the guerrilla leader of today is the leader of tomorrow." But it should be noted that the NSA immediately cut the potential pool in half. After scouring Africa in the spring of 1961 for future leaders, Kiley wrote, "In general, the selection of women from anywhere in Africa ought to be discouraged at this stage. The few who are active are not terribly bright, nor will women be playing any significant role in either E. or W. Africa for some years to come."[38]

The NSA singled out the Belgian Congo, Portuguese West Africa, and South Africa as the areas of concentration. A mildly worded NSA resolution at the 1960 Congress, "Colonialism in Angola and Mozambique," provided the authority for witting NSA members to become involved in two emerging revolutionary movements. It also raised NSA meddling to new heights.[39]

The situation in Angola evoked obvious parallels to the French-Algerian conflict. While the Kennedy administration made general pronouncements in favor of Angolan self-determination, the United States continued to support its NATO ally Portugal. America had an important naval base under Portuguese control in the Azores, and the Portuguese government let Washington know that any contact with the Angolan terrorists would spell the end of its base. While Kennedy viewed Portugal's threat as blackmail, he tempered his public statements on Angola, and the State Department repeatedly assured the government of Portugal of its continued support.[40]

While the State Department soothed the Portuguese, the CIA did its best to stir them up. Under Eisenhower's administration, the CIA had begun financial support to Holden Roberto, head of the Union of Peoples of Angola (UPA). The Portuguese identified Roberto as a terrorist before his troops fired a single shot.[41] In 1959, Roberto met with then-Senator Kennedy, and from that point forward counted as allies the future president and his brother Robert.[42]

In March 1961, Roberto's forces launched a guerrilla raid inside Angola, signaling the beginning of the war for liberation. The raid killed scores of white farmers and unnerved key American policy makers, among them Secretary of State Dean Rusk, who called for an end to Roberto's subsidy. In a top secret meeting in June, Rusk softened his position; he did not object to support for Roberto if it flowed through private organizations "with no connection to the US government."[43]

Unlike the Algerian situation, where revolutionaries submerged their differences to maintain a united front, Roberto had competition for his leadership of the liberation movement. His principal rival, the MPLA (Angolan People's Liberation Movement), founded in the mid-1950s, had a general Marxist orientation, and some of its leaders belonged to the Portuguese Communist Party. In August-September 1961, militant students formed the General Union of Students of Black Africa Under Portuguese Colonial Rule (UGEAN), aligned with the MPLA and opposed to Roberto.

In the fall and winter of 1961, the NSA executed a series of tactical moves, audacious in their duplicity. The students pretended to support the MPLA-aligned, Marxist-dominated UGEAN while secretly plotting to form a rival student organization that favored Roberto. In September, Donald Emmerson sent FYSA funds through COSEC to UGEAN leader Luís de Almeida so he could attend a conference in Rabat.[44]

Archival correspondence between Emmerson and Kiley makes it clear that the funding was intended to maintain access to a group, UGEAN, that had popular support, even if it was politically unacceptable. At one point, Emmerson reminded Kiley, "We must be careful not to cut ourselves out of a group whose authority will not be challenged."[45] The NSA also distributed scholarship applications equally to UGEAN and pro-Roberto students. Peter Eckstein, who had lost the election to Isabel Marcus in 1959 and been moved to the Foreign Student Leadership Project, called the practice "a good idea . . . even if it [the NSA] did not intend to select anyone from the Marxist group."[46]

During this period, the NSA chose Jonas Savimbi, a Roberto ally also on the CIA payroll, to help undermine the more militant UGEAN.[47] On December 8, 1961, the NSA gathered eighteen Angolans, two Mozambicans, and one Port Guinean resident in the United States for a Conference on the Portuguese Colonies in Africa.[48] Holden Roberto keynoted the meeting, held at Camp Green Lane in Philadelphia. This historic gathering included most of the future revolutionary leaders in Angola and Mozambique who were backed by the United States, including Jorge Valentim, Daniel Chipenda, and Eduardo Mondlane, most of whom would lose their lives in their struggles.

The conference also furthered the goal of creating a rival to leftist UGEAN. The NSA supported the founding of a U.S. chapter of Angolan students, even though in the beginning the chapter had no organization with which to affiliate. The strategy was to knit several chapters into one larger, international organization. On March 10–11, 1962, a total of eighteen Angolan students, who represented chapters in the United States and Europe, met in Lucerne and announced the formation of UNEA (National Union of Angolan Students). Roberto's allies controlled the leadership: Jonas Savimbi became the secretary general and Jorge Valentim, an NSA favorite who was studying at Temple University, became the international vice president.[49] The European chapters barely qualified as chapters; most had three or four members. Nevertheless, the Americans celebrated the meeting as a success. Emmerson sent the new UNEA officers "We Shall Overcome" buttons, distributed by the Student Non-Violent Coordinating Committee, as an "expression of NSA solidarity."[50]

The NSA also ran a publicity campaign in the United States, including a special insert on Angola in the March issue of *Current*, a public affairs magazine, edited by NSA adviser Sidney Hertzberg.[51] In June, the NSA made good on an earlier promise to provide "a voice for Angolan students in the United States" by arranging for FYSA support for UNEA to publish a free-standing Angolan student newsletter.[52]

International staff showed none of the skittishness over questions of political violence that had plagued an earlier NSA generation. Emmerson applauded a newspaper article that revealed Algerian military support for Roberto's forces. As he told Kiley, "I was extremely encouraged by the item in today's *New York Times* concerning UPA rebel training provided by the FLN [Algeria]. If the UPA can fill their current great need for arms and well-trained military cadres and can build up greater intellectual leadership they may be able to overshadow the MPLA in the long run."[53] A few months later, Edward (Ed) Garvey and Emmerson would have an opportunity to make a direct plea for military support to former FLN leader Ahmed Ben Bella in a private meeting during Ben Bella's first visit to the United States as president of Algeria.[54]

Like the Algerians, Angolans pressed the NSA hard for scholarships — the lifeblood of exiled revolutionaries waging the crucial battle for public opinion. Early in the summer of 1961, the UGEAN leader Deolinda de Almeida told Jim Scott, "Your moral support is very meaningful for us," and assured him that the NSA resolutions were "adequate," but that their "greatest need is scholarships for our students in Europe."[55] When the IUS offered Angolans ten scholarships, an Angolan student based in Germany told David Baad at COSEC that he "would prefer for these students to be studying in Western countries."[56] It all sounded familiar to NSA staff: the Angolan revolutionaries had learned to play East against West. Nevertheless, the NSA delivered.

In 1962, the NSA established a special Angolan Scholarship Program. The program helped sustain members of Roberto's newly founded government in exile (GRAE). Paul Touba represented GRAE before the United Nations and simultaneously attended the University of Pennsylvania.[57] As with every Angolan student monitored by NSA staff, Touba's views were reported on by a succession of NSA staff.[58] These reports included sensitive information such as the aliases used by Roberto and his whereabouts.

Paradoxically, the Angolans were able to turn the CIA-funded ISC and World Assembly of Youth to their own purposes. In a 1996 interview, Holden Roberto described how he gained crucial Scandinavian support through WAY.[59] Jorge Valentim, who with NSA backing parleyed his position in UNEA into a position on COSEC, used the ISC network to raise funds and win backers for the Angolan cause.[60] The original ISC mission to foster cooperation through practical projects had taken a decided turn away from its original conception.

Later on, Roberto, Savimbi, and others turned on one another in a murderous civil war. But in 1962 no one could foresee that war (fueled by CIA resources), which would follow an equally costly battle for independence won by the Marxist-oriented MPLA. At the time, the CIA-NSA team believed it had found its moderate pro-West revolutionaries. Men like Jorge Valentim, Jonas Savimbi, and Holden Roberto were multilingual and intellectual, educated in Western institutions, and seemingly unreceptive to communist overtures. In April 1961, a few months after Roberto's forces launched the first raid into Angolan territory, *Time* hailed him as "a determined, soft-spoken, exiled African Angolan."[61]

THE NSA PLAYED an equally tricky part in its relationship with the National Union of Southern African Students (NUSAS), which it supported financially starting in the mid-1950s with FYSA grants, funds that NUSAS president John Shingler (1959–60) called "absolutely central to its survival."[62] American funds also enabled NUSAS to send leaders to important international conferences.[63] Sometimes the funds were used to support the flight of black South Africans through the underground railroad, a loosely organized, often ad-hoc network that smuggled Africans across the border.[64] Shingler and others have riveting, often terrifying, tales to tell about these escapes.

In South Africa, the liberal anticommunist NUSAS stood in opposition to the more militant African National Congress (ANC), home of Nelson Mandela, Oliver Tambo, Thabo Mbeki, and other future leaders. In 1946, the ANC Youth League had affiliated with the IUS and welcomed alliances with the South African Communist Party, and was therefore unacceptable to liberals. The tension between NUSAS and the ANC was often personal and palpable: Shingler remembers the ANC's Joe Slovo, a Communist Party member, poking him in the chest at a party and telling him that liberals like Shingler would be shot after the revolution.[65] Shingler, who admires Mandela today, opposed him at the time. He explains that the Mandela of the 1950s was not the same man who later ruled South Africa.[66]

In 1960, after the demonstration in Sharpeville that led to the massacre of sixty-nine protesters by the South African police, the government banned the ANC, and many of its members went into exile. They established new bases of operation in London, Stockholm, and elsewhere in Europe. The fight against apartheid entered a new phase, led by black Africans.

The NSA kept tabs on the ANC exiles' activities, partly out of fear that they might challenge NUSAS and form a rival black-led student union. They also pressured NUSAS leaders to be more militant. In a letter of May 1960 marked "personal, private, and confidential," David Baad told Shingler that he was speaking to him bluntly as a friend about "the slow but mounting criticism of the NUSAS position in South Africa."[67] Yes, NUSAS had a "high reputation overseas as a union battling against racialism," Baad wrote, but Africans coming through Leiden were furious over its tepid response to the Sharpeville Massacre. Baad then quoted the ANC leader Oliver Tambo: "The battle for human rights in South Africa would from now on have to be conducted from overseas." Baad advised Shingler to consider NUSAS's "future effectiveness on the international scene."[68] With NUSAS dependent on outside support, such friendly advice carried an implicit warning. The NSA was seeking a nearly impossible political stance, pressuring moderates to compete with militants by becoming more militant—but not so militant as to threaten an alliance with the West.

Not long after the Sharpeville Massacre, Shingler fled South Africa to become the Liberal Party's representative in Europe. In 1962, he had an encounter with Baad that left him shaken. The former NUSAS president, Magnus Gunther, then on the COSEC staff, had given up on nonviolent strategies to fight apartheid. Gunther now backed the clandestine National Committee for Liberation–African Resistance Movement (NCL–ARM), dedicated to sabotaging the infrastructure of the South African regime.[69] Gunther, a white Afrikaner whose family came from Germany, had tried unsuccessfully to use the ISC network to raise funds for the NCL–ARM. He later speculated that his failure was due to the inability to prove its existence since it consisted of small, secret cell groups.[70]

Then, one day, Baad, who was especially close to Gunther—they were housemates in Leiden—offered to assist with the funding. He asked Gunther to draft a funding proposal and promised to send it to an unspecified source. Gunther and Shingler worked on the draft proposal to fund the public face of the NCL–ARM campaign.[71] According to Shingler, Baad continually pressed them for names of the members. Identifying individuals who belonged to NCL–ARM would put black South Africans, in particular, in considerable danger. Gunther and Shingler became suspicious. They began to wonder whether the funds were in fact coming from the U.S. government. It did not take them long to suspect that the CIA was the source. Shingler describes the moment as one of "the most chilling of my life."[72]

Despite the NCL–ARM's pledge not to harm or kill civilians, a bomb set off on July 24, 1964, killed one bystander and injured others at a Johannesburg train station.[73] South African police arrested members of the NCL–ARM, including former NUSAS president Adrian Leftwich. Under intense questioning, Leftwich succumbed to police torture and gave up the names of other members, among them former NUSAS and Liberal Party leaders.[74] Gunther later described the destruction of the NCL–ARM as devastating since it "gave the government a way to crush the non-communist opposition to apartheid."[75]

One might assume that the NSA fully supported the anti-apartheid cause at home, given Baad's eagerness to push NUSAS to be more militant. But until the mid-1960s, the NSA had a history of limiting anti-apartheid activism. Both Bruce Larkin and Willard Johnson had rejected requests from the American Committee on Africa to participate in joint projects against apartheid.[76] Larkin cited restrictions in the NSA constitution, Johnson the lack of funds. The real reason is surely to be found in the friendly relations between ANC leaders and the committee.

Behind the various machinations, a kind of logic may be found. All these actions were aimed at damaging the ANC because of its inclusion of communists. That inclusiveness is why the CIA helped set up the arrest on August 5, 1962, of Nelson Mandela that led to his twenty-seven years of incarceration.

To offer credible competition to the ANC, white and liberal anti-apartheid groups like NUSAS had to edge closer and closer to militancy. In 1964, the NSA overseas representatives considered tossing NUSAS overboard. Paris-based George Hazelrigg urged others in the NSA to "reassess" the association's support of "white NUSAS," and look for "moderate Black leadership."[77]

The NSA ultimately did not abandon NUSAS. NSA staff played a role in arranging the historic 1966 visit by Robert F. Kennedy to South Africa, when the senator defied the government and met with banned

NUSAS leader Ian Robertson. But fears of a black militant alternative were well placed. By 1968, the black leadership had rejected NUSAS in favor of a new group, the South African Student Organisation. Its founder, Stephen Biko, was later arrested and murdered by the South African regime.[78]

The examples of Angola and South Africa illustrate how little NSA operations had to do with the ISC-IUS battle. In fact, having to bring dozens of African, Asian, Latin American, and Middle Eastern students together for a large ISC tended to disrupt these ongoing NSA agendas. Witting staff had to stop and assess the NSA's relationship with each national union of students or individual leader in light of an upcoming ISC.

Kiley was unhappy when the site of the 1962 ISC was announced: Laval College in Quebec. This was ominously close to the United States. It would be necessary to ensure that no enterprising undergraduates found their way to Quebec, observed the ISC, and raised questions about NSA foreign policy. Jyoti Shankar Singh, who had visited the Laval campus, gave Kiley the impression —inaccurately as it turned out—that access could be controlled.[79]

A PYRRHIC VICTORY

THE BENEFIT TO the United States of a CIA-funded organization that inveighed against the West seemed increasingly dubious. For years, the NSA had justified the International Student Conference as a symbol of democracy, a place where foreign student leaders could experience free and open debate. By the early 1960s, some witting staff had grown skeptical that the ISC was achieving even this limited objective.

In 1962, David Baad, who had spent several years on the COSEC staff, was finding the experience more and more dubious. "I was sort of coming to the conclusion that, first of all, most of these revolutionaries . . . and those groups that had been in independence movements and were coming to power really weren't interested in democratic institutions," which "inhibited their ability to maintain control and push for the kinds of reforms we advocated. Basically, they [militants] were in it for their own personal interest."[1] Overseas staff had perfected the art of maintaining access to individual revolutionaries. Tolerating their growing dominance within the ISC required tactical dexterity, a polite way of describing a new tangle of lies, feints, and deceits.

Typical of the dilemma was the situation in Latin America. While the NSA delegation to the 1960 ISC still supported the Cuban revolution, witting NSA staff members were working against *Fidelismo*, Castro-inspired militancy in Latin America. When Uruguay had offered to host a Latin American Student Seminar in 1960, in part to challenge a regional group that took its cue from Havana, militant factions within the Uruguayan student union gained enough power that it had to be postponed. Then, after the Bay of Pigs fiasco, Robert Kiley realized that if the seminar went forward, even friendly student unions might condemn U.S. policies. Peter Eckstein, who had succeeded Baad as editor of *The Student* magazine, warned that it could be a "complete disaster," with "the interesting spectacle of a COSEC-sponsored event denouncing COSEC and all its works."[2] Topics for seminar discussion included "land reform, agrarian reform, oil problems, and the root causes of under-development."[3] Each would lead inevitably to a discussion of Yankee support for dictators or economic interests.

The upshot was that FYSA killed the funding for the seminar, but not before nonwitting COSEC staff members Sylvio Mutal of Turkey and Patricio Fernández of Chile had negotiated a new date and assured the Uruguayan leaders that funding would be available.[4] The action caught all but the Americans on COSEC by surprise, and humiliated Mutal and Fernandez. Not content with killing the seminar, witting NSA staff also sought to punish the Uruguayan student union (FEUU) for its leftist turn. Manuel Aragon recommended that the NSA encourage a rival Uruguayan student union—even if one did not currently exist—because "the benefits of a rival union outweigh having to absorb criticism."[5]

All these factors—an ISC that barely served Western interests, a witting international staff that schemed against pro-Castro militants, and the growth of NSA operations outside the ISC framework—made witting staff dread the ISC scheduled for the summer of 1962 in Quebec. No one had any doubt that Cuba would dominate the proceedings, and it was essential that this meeting end with a condemnation of Castro. Taking a page from the Kennedy administration playbook, the NSA-CIA team decided that the most effective criticism of Cuba would come from another Latin American country, and the ideal candidate would be the Dominican Republic, which the Kennedy administration had singled out for attention, seeking to make it a showcase for democracy.

Late in his term, President Eisenhower had finally acknowledged that U.S. support for Latin American dictators made it easier for Castro to export revolution to their countries. A case in point was Rafael Trujillo, president of the Dominican Republic. As Eisenhower concluded, "American public opinion won't condemn Castro until we have moved against Trujillo."[6] In December 1960, just weeks before Kennedy took office, the CIA sanctioned the shipment of arms to coup plotters intending to assassinate Trujillo. In a parallel operation, the NSA launched a search for anti-Trujillo Dominican student groups to support. Robert Aragon found exiles in Venezuela, Puerto Rico, and Cuba, but none seemed ideal. A COSEC team finally identified a group in Costa Rica called the Federation of Dominican Republic Students in Exile (FEDE).[7] The NSA envisioned a post-Trujillo era when FEDE would drop the "E" and become a full-fledged ISC member and NSA ally. They channeled funds for FEDE leaders to attend the 1960 ISC, even though Aragon privately reported that the exiles "didn't know much about the university scene."[8]

On May 30, 1961, Trujillo was assassinated on a deserted stretch of highway outside Santo Domingo.[9] The aftermath did not go as planned, as is frequently the case with externally encouraged revolts. Dominican plotters found themselves unable to seize power after Trujillo family members and supporters discovered the plan. The Dominican Republic entered a period of political upheaval. But President Kennedy did not give up the idea of building a democratic showcase in the Caribbean, and under the new Alliance for Progress foreign aid program, the administration poured resources into the small country. The NSA stepped up its work to find a Latin American counter to Fidelismo.

That fall, Joseph Love, a Stanford graduate student in Latin American affairs, joined the NSA international staff in Philadelphia. The CIA engineered a relationship between Love and a more seasoned CIA operative in Latin America, Sacha Volman. The Romanian-born socialist, who had worked against the Nazis in World War II and fled Romania after the communists took over after the war, specialized in labor affairs.[10] In 1959, Volman set up the Institute of Political Education in Costa Rica to train noncommunist social democratic leaders in Latin America. Among his trainees were exiled Dominican students.[11]

Love flew to Costa Rica and with Volman counseled several Dominicans on how to hold a national congress and establish a national student union.[12] In early February 1962, Volman reported that the students had held a successful meeting. More important, he wrote, the "predominant political tendency will be Catholic, with the moderates following next and the Communists least."[13]

FYSA issued a grant to the NSA for a "Leadership Seminar for Students of the Dominican Republic," which the NSA passed through the Venezuelan student union to downplay U.S. interest.[14] (At this point, Venezuela was a firm ally of the United States—Romulo Betancourt's government had permitted the CIA to establish training camps for Dominican exiles in the country.) Love might be a novice, but he followed the traditional NSA pattern of placing outsized hopes on small operations. He agreed that the new Dominican student union could challenge the Cuban delegation at the upcoming ISC. President Ed Garvey echoed his enthusiasm, telling the NSA executive committee that success in the Dominican Republic "might change the entire balance of power in LA."[15]

The Cuban situation turned out to be far more complicated than anyone on the witting staff knew at the time. In March 1961, Rolando Cubela, president of the Cuban student union and Castro's confidant, had walked into the American embassy in Mexico City and offered to assassinate Castro. His offer came at a time when the CIA Technical Services division was working overtime to find a poison that would kill Castro—or, failing that, make his beard fall out. Whatever they made of Cubela, at that point CIA officials urged the Cuban to return to Havana and maintain his position with Castro. They scheduled a second meeting with Cubela for July 1962, under cover of the World Youth Festival in Helsinki, an event that would take place a few weeks after the Quebec ISC.[16]

No one on the NSA witting staff knew of Cubela's CIA connection. Years later, CIA veteran Tony Smith, who accompanied the NSA delegation to Quebec, nearly levitated off his sofa when asked if he'd known about it: "Oh God, no."[17] He doubted that even Cord Meyer, chief of the newly reorganized Covert Action staff, knew about Cubela. Kiley, who eventually rose inside the CIA to become director Richard Helms's assistant, concurs, although Kiley believes it likely that top CIA officials queried Meyer in some way, if only obliquely, about his knowledge of the Cuban student leader.[18] In fact, the NSA delegation to Quebec was terrified of the Cubans. Smith recalled: "Rumors circulated that the Cubans had found the main light switch and planned to plunge the proceedings into darkness in order to beat up the NSA delegation. We were petrified."[19]

Consider, then: In July 1962, Rolando Cubela was a member in good standing of the CIA-funded ISC, which was on record as supporting the Cuban revolution. The NSA viewed Cubela as a Castro loyalist who might put the Americans in physical jeopardy. At the same time, the CIA was plotting with Cubela to kill Castro. Considering what he knows today, Kiley insists that the Cubela situation was not exceptional: one could "never ever know for sure who one was really dealing with."[20]

As if to underscore Kiley's point, to this day no one in or out of the CIA is completely sure whether Cubela was a genuine defector or a Castro double agent, a "dangle," in CIA terminology.[21] The CIA top covert operator, Desmond Fitzgerald, continued to deal with Cubela. It would be Fitzgerald who, on November 22, 1963, the day John F. Kennedy was assassinated, represented himself as Robert Kennedy's personal agent and met with Cubela in a Paris hotel room to give him a pen filled with the poison known as Black Leaf 44.[22] Kiley may be right that witting staff never really knew whom they were dealing with, but there are few cases as dramatic or enigmatic as that of Rolando Cubela.

Before arriving in Quebec, the NSA delegation had decided upon a hybrid strategy to deal with the Cuban issue. They blanketed delegates with a Spanish translation of the 1961 NSA resolution on Cuba, which even-handedly praised aspects of the revolution and criticized U.S. and Soviet interventions. They publicized a new José Echevarría Scholarship Fund in honor of the fallen student leader.[23] The NSA also quietly encouraged a handful of anti-Castro Cuban exiles on the CIA payroll to appear at Laval College, where the ISC was being held, with literature on Castro's repressive policies, although ISC delegates expelled them on the first day of the conference.

More important, the NSA found a way to make Cuba a secondary issue: it precipitated a crisis over Puerto Rico.[24] This was done with the full knowledge that an argument over Puerto Rico would enrage the most militant ISC members, and probably cause them to walk out. It was a strategy that can be understood only in light of the convolutions of Cold War logic, Kennedy administration policy, and the habit of pinning large geopolitical hopes on single individuals.

Puerto Rico was the little irritant that wouldn't go away. Its status as a United States commonwealth had permitted IUS critics to ridicule the NSA position that "Puerto Rico is a free associated state of the USA, as a result of free and democratic elections."[25] It sounded dangerously close to the imperialistic slogan of French politician Pierre Mendès France, "Algeria is France." In 1956, a student organization dedicated to winning independence for Puerto Rico, the Federation of Pro-Independence Students (Federación de Universitarios Pro-Independencia; FUPI), joined the International Union of Students.[26]

At the 1960 ISC in Switzerland, FUPI successfully sought membership; even the NSA voted for its admission. The NSA did not have the votes to challenge the Puerto Ricans' credentials without unleashing charges of neocolonialism against the United States, even though the Aragon brothers discovered that FUPI had opened an office in Havana and worked with Raúl Castro.[27] They settled for modest changes in the resolution advocating Puerto Rican independence, substituting *self-determination* for *independence*. The short-term tactic vastly complicated NSA options in Quebec. Having previously given its blessing, on what basis could the NSA now declare FUPI illegitimate? Kiley supplied the answer.

In December 1961, Kiley informed Don Hoffman in Paris, "It is absolutely imperative that there be an alternative organization, ghost or otherwise."[28] He wrote again in April to Don Emmerson that the NSA had to "muster a sufficient challenge to FUPI credentials to enable, at the very least, the ousting of FUPI as a national union of students and, at the very best, the seating of a rival national union."[29]

This strategy was also linked to the Kennedy administration's alliance with the governor of Puerto Rico. A memo, most likely by one of the Aragon brothers, argued that a successful Puerto Rican independence movement, "would be undermining Governor Muñoz Marín's important influence in Latin America and all over the under developed world."[30] The author went on to explain that it was crucial to retain Muñoz's support of U.S. policies against Castro within the Organization of American States. Support for Puerto Rican independence at the ISC might unleash an outpouring in favor of independence from the youth and student wings of "leading popular political parties in Latin America."[31] The witting team convinced itself that the fate of Latin American student politics rested on what could be done to undermine the Puerto Rican independence movement.

Although purportedly acting in Governor Muñoz's interest, the NSA first had to convince him "of the importance of forming such an opposition group."[32] Once again, the NSA turned to Sacha Volman to secure the governor's approval.

At first the strategy seemed viable. Volman spoke to "the top echelon of the *Partido Popular*" (Muñoz's Popular Democratic Party) and reported that they were "anxious to activate the student organizations which they have and which function outside of the university." Follow-up should include a discreet visit from Love to see Santiago Polanco Abreu, a high-ranking official in San Juan who advised Muñoz on international affairs.[33]

But by mid-April 1962, not a single NSA representative had yet visited Puerto Rico. Kiley railed at the lack of progress. Wasn't it understood that the NSA must ensure "the presence of progressive Puerto Rican elements outside the militant independence movement"?[34]

As panic set in, the CIA turned to a Cuban exile on its payroll.[35] José Antonio González Lanuza was a participant in Operation Quick Kick: nighttime hit-and-run raids on Cuba operated out of Puerto Rico. Despite warnings from intelligence analysts that almost no chance existed of an anti-Castro uprising on the island, plans to overthrow Castro—sanctioned by the Kennedy administration as part of Operation Mongoose—barreled ahead.[36] In early May, González Lanuza took time out from the midnight raids to help the NSA create a Puerto Rican ghost student union.

Shortly after he arrived in San Juan, González Lanuza reported that most students were taking exams and didn't much care about forming a new organization.[37] Finally, he found three students close to Muñoz's Popular Party who agreed to form a provisional committee and come to Quebec.[38] In such a fashion, a second Puerto Rican student union was born, its members surely unaware of how much the NSA had invested in its existence.

Archival letters and memos show that witting staff understood that if they launched a frontal challenge to FUPI they risked a walkout by the more radical Latin American unions. But cleansing the ISC of its most militant members appeared to be worth the cost. The alternative was worse. In Kiley's view, anger over the Bay of Pigs threatened to destroy the ISC altogether by stirring up "an emotional climate of pro-Castroism and anti-Yankee imperialism," which could "create a stampede that includes everyone but Europe and North America."[39]

SEVENTY-SIX FOREIGN STUDENT delegations assembled at Laval College on June 27, 1962. The manufactured crisis came early. The report of the credentials committee, always the first item of business, set off the fireworks. As it had in 1960, the pro-independence FUPI easily garnered a majority vote in the credentials committee for delegate status.

Uruguay and Venezuela, former NSA allies, moved and seconded the decision in the larger plenary, commending FUPI for "fighting for the independence of Puerto Rico from American domination." Brazil chimed in with pleasure over seeing "the students of Puerto Rico in the fight for the independence of their country from the imperialism and colonialism of the United States of America." Panama joined the praise.[40]

A British student in attendance, David Triesman, later described what ensued. "In a way which has never ceased to amaze onlookers," he wrote, "the Secretariat apparently seemed to find, overnight, a rival, non-political union, which claimed to represent the Puerto Rican students."[41] The rival Pro-Federación de Organizacións Universitarios declared itself the true representative of Puerto Rican students. Astonished, Triesman watched as the delegates spent a full thirteen hours debating the recognition of FUPI. He later wrote that most Latin American student unions felt that "the aims of FUPI were more important than the bickering about who it claimed to represent."[42] A West African union leader cut closer to the bone, at one point calling the FUPI rival "a phantom organization."[43]

Chile, South Africa, Nigeria, New Zealand, and long-time ally Costa Rica supported the NSA. Wahid Ali from the West Indies, who chaired most of the marathon meeting, also declared himself on the side of the NSA — which was no doubt the reason he was in the chair.[44] Jyoti Shankar Singh, who had just taken over at COSEC, admits that he "deferred to the Americans," even though he did not understand why the NSA had previously recognized the Puerto Rican union and now was challenging it.[45]

The Luxemburg delegation called repeatedly for moderation. Ghanaians declared themselves confused.

When the final vote was tallied, Uruguay's motion to accept FUPI had lost, 41–33, with 2 abstentions. The Americans had carried the day by 8 votes.

The response was dramatic and instantaneous: thirty-five unions left the hall, although a handful later returned. All but two Latin American unions departed. French-speaking African unions walked out, as did Indonesia. Their leaders declared that they would withdraw their membership in the ISC unless FUPI became a full member.[46]

The remaining delegates debated whether a quorum still existed, declaring two days later that it did and proceeding with the conference.

Before the delegates left Quebec, they formally resolved to invite all the unions that had walked out to the next ISC. No one wanted to shoulder the blame for destroying whatever unity remained. The NSA had wanted the ISC purged, not dissolved.[47]

The NSA's maneuverings failed on two fronts. The post-Trujillo student union, the Federación de Estudiantes Dominicanos, which was credentialed in Quebec, had dropped the word *exile* but turned out to be more radical than the Americans wanted. It joined the IUS, and the opportunity to showcase a democratic alternative in the Caribbean slipped away. And the so-called representative Puerto Rican union cobbled together at the last minute disappeared into oblivion.

Shortly after the Quebec meeting, a handful of ISC members, including NSA allies, traveled to Leningrad to observe the IUS Congress. Their conclusions were dispiriting. Several wrote reports about the vibrancy and strength of the IUS. One concluded that the IUS was no longer a front organization but "a real student movement."[48]

The NSA international staff tried to minimize the Quebec debacle. A few months later, Garvey claimed in an NSA executive committee meeting following the 1962 Congress that the NSA had "stood firmly behind the democratic bloc despite tremendous pressure."[49] Outgoing international vice president Don Emmerson similarly assured the executive committee that he was "fairly certain" the dissident unions would "continue to participate in the Conference set-up."[50]

From its inception in 1950, the International Student Conference had claimed to provide a framework for cooperation. But it had never had a natural constituency beyond the well-established European unions. No unifying ideology or passion animated its participants. Even the argument that the ISC stood for democracy and against totalitarianism evoked charges by members that it was perpetuating the Cold War. In 1962, the question of who would continue to cooperate with the ISC seemed very much in doubt.

Kiley insists today that he tried to get the CIA to terminate its support for the ISC.[51] Baad also remembers serious discussions about termination but said no one could figure out how to dismantle the ISC. "You have to pull the plug by removing the money. And everyone was concerned about what kind of questions this would raise. Everyone was sensitive at that point about the agency's hand being exposed."[52] Kiley is also clear that the possibility of shutting down the ISC-COSEC complex did not mean that he favored stopping its subsidiary operations.[53]

If anything, those subsidiary operations grew under the Kennedy administration, fueled in part by support from the president's brother. In February 1962, Robert Kennedy had taken a world tour, during which he was confronted with considerable anti-Americanism. (In Indonesia, a student pelted him with raw eggs.)[54] A few months later, at Kennedy's request, the NSA brought its most reliable foreign allies to a meeting in Aspen, Colorado, to discuss the subject of youthful anger. The president of UNEF, Dominique Wallon, later summarized the meeting: "Bobby very direct, very honest, and sometimes very wrong." Wallon cited Cuba as an example of Kennedy's misunderstanding.[55]

Despite Kennedy's anger at the CIA over the Bay of Pigs, he became an enthusiast of covert action.[56] In his biography of the attorney general, Arthur M. Schlesinger set forth the reasons: Kennedy concluded that the conduct of foreign relations was changing. In a memo to the president, he emphasized that "more and more the people themselves are determining their country's future and policies."[57] The attorney general placed labor leaders, intellectuals, and students at the top of his list of critical actors.[58] Following his tour, Kennedy persuaded the State Department to establish the Inter-Agency Youth Task Force. He personally recommended for its staff director CIA career officer Martin McLaughlin, the Catholic activist who had so effectively organized Catholic cell groups at the founding of the NSA.[59] Kennedy's enthusiasm helped ensure a steady flow of CIA resources to the NSA and its increasingly far-flung operations.[60]

THE PERSISTENT QUESTIONER

IN JULY 1962, UCLA sophomore Stephen Robbins attended the Quebec conference on his own and acquired his first taste of international student politics. Robbins's journey from neophyte observer to president two years later changed the course of NSA history. Inquisitive by nature, sometimes brash, and always intense, Robbins began to ponder some of the oddities in the operations of the NSA International Commission. He pushed his way into the inner circle, first as chair of the NSA oversight board, then as president. When Robbins finally gained access to the NSA's secret, his shock gave way to a determination to reduce the CIA's stranglehold on the association.

It began as a lark. In the summer of 1962, Robbins, the chair of the sprawling NSA California-Nevada-Hawaii region, and a friend, James Mahoney, decided to observe the ISC in Quebec.[1] Unaware that the NSA discouraged casual visitors, the two assumed they would be welcome. When they arrived at the Laval campus, Robbins remembers Paul Becker, the Canadian in charge of logistics, greeting them warmly, if warily, "like loose cannons."[2] The perception was not misplaced. Becker, who was sitting with NSA president Ed Garvey when the pair appeared in the doorway, can still recall Garvey's reaction: "He groaned."[3]

At the time, Robbins and Mahoney chalked up the chilly reception to the fact that they were interlopers. They moved on. Having heard about the World Youth Festival in Helsinki, they returned to New York and met with Gloria Steinem, hoping to travel with her group. But Steinem also turned them down. At this point, Robbins considered their experiences with the NSA merely a little odd.

Although he had lived abroad, before Quebec Robbins thought of himself as mainly interested in domestic affairs.[4] He cared about civil liberties, civil rights, and nuclear test-ban treaties. Quebec whetted his appetite to learn more about the international side of the NSA. When he arrived in Columbus, Ohio, for the 1962 August Congress, he absorbed the lectures given by old hands on NSA history, including information about the rupture with the International Union of Students in 1948 and the formation of the International Student Conference, and the current state of student politics in Latin America, Africa, Europe, the Middle East, and Asia. Well, thought Robbins, this is all pretty interesting.[5] And he began to formulate questions—lots of them.

Robbins observed the older former NSA men who hovered around the edges of the Congress, sat in on committee sessions, and struck up informal conversations with delegates. In his mind, the presence of former NSA officers added stature to the association; despite busy lives, they seemed to care enough to devote a week or more to the Congress. Still, he found it a little peculiar that they had remained so engaged.[6]

Since Robbins harbored ambitions to run for president, he paid close attention to the mechanics of the elections. He spotted more anomalies. The ISRS graduates dominated the debate on international issues, but as a group he found them apolitical. Few had ever served as student body president or editor of the campus newspaper. Most were older graduate students who specialized in Africa, Latin America, or Asia. But they intimidated undergraduate delegates with their superior knowledge.[7]

Robbins watched as the candidate for president sailed to victory. Dennis Shaul, a twenty-four-year-old Notre Dame graduate and Rhodes Scholar, was a veteran of two World Youth Festivals, in Vienna (1959) and then as co-director with Gloria Steinem at IRS in Helsinki, and, unbeknownst to Robbins, was a former recipient of CIA per diems. Shaul later told a friend that in the past he had refused overtures to run for office because of his ambivalence over the CIA's role.[8] In 1962 he succumbed.

Robbins found the election for international affairs vice president troubling. The contest pitted Donald Smith of the University of Texas against Robert Backoff of the University of Illinois. Smith appeared to have the inside track when the contest suddenly turned ugly. Whispered innuendos and rumors about Smith's sexuality rippled through the delegations. It was a smear campaign, decided Robbins, but by whom and why?[9]

When Smith squeaked to victory, Robbins realized that Smith, as a former student body president and incumbent officer, had a political base that enabled him to win without support from the ISRS graduates. Still, Robbins was not alone in his feeling that something was very wrong. Howard Abrams of the University of Michigan protested the election tactics in a letter to Shaul. In his response, Shaul acknowledged that manipulations had regrettably occurred in previous years, then cited Smith's victory over Backoff as proof that no manipulation occurred: it was "the greatest example of a failure in this regard."[10]

In fact, Smith's election signaled a rare victory over manipulation, not its absence. The smear campaign had been a panicked response by witting officers. Outgoing NSA president Garvey today acknowledges that the CIA caucus originally backed Smith until they heard rumors, "at the very last moment," that he was gay. (Garvey emphasized "at the ver-r-r-ry last moment.")[11] If true, Smith would not have been the first homosexual officer; Avrea Ingram, the 1952–54 international affairs vice president, had been gay, though not openly, a fact not widely known among his colleagues until his tragic death, a reported suicide, in 1957.[12] (In 1967, the *Los Angeles Times* reported that after Ingram's death Bill Dentzer swore an Ingram family member to secrecy, confided the nature of Ingram's work, and suggested that the Russians might have killed him. The story was a fabrication, but it was a way to imply that Ingram had died as a patriot.)[13] In general, according to Dan Idzik, the CIA had dealt graciously with previous (closeted) gay officers.[14] The crucial issue with Smith appeared to be one of timing.

Few outside the NSA knew how badly Smith fared over the next year. A traditional perk of the post of international vice president was overseas travel, beginning with a fall trip to Europe. Witting staff toyed with the idea of grounding Smith. Don Emmerson, who had moved from the NSA to COSEC, discussed the problem with Paris-based Don Hoffman: "It would be extremely difficult and messy to prevent him from coming [over]."[15] He suggested that instead they "send him off to obscure places; get Reiner [director of FYSA] to scare him off of financial commitments, take care of his wanderlust and get him out of the office."[16]

Albert Reiner, who took over student activities at the funding conduit FYSA, played to the script. In October, he informed Smith that the foundation would be "cutting back," that "over expenditures would not be picked up by the Foundation, that no—absolutely no—grants would be made within a few weeks before or after an event."[17] In disbelief, Smith wrote to Emmerson that Reiner "even said NSA and COSEC should not assume that the Foundation will honor all of the major part of its commitments."[18] In his correspondence, Emmerson evaded any discussion of NSA finances; no doubt because he knew that FYSA's crackdown on the NSA would last only so long as Smith was in office.[19]

Relying on private mailing addresses for witting staff, threatening to cut off funding, and maintaining onsite personnel who reported to the CIA enabled the CIA's work with the NSA and COSEC to continue unimpeded. Thomas Olson, a graduate of the University of Minnesota, managed day-to-day affairs for Smith. Like his predecessors, Olson maintained a post-office box in Philadelphia for sensitive communications. In turn, he sent confidential material for Emmerson in Leiden to a private address. The volume of correspondence was so high that Emmerson advised Olson to send some material to the secretariat so as not to arouse suspicion.[20] The CIA also funded a position for the losing candidate, Robert Backoff; he handled contacts with foreign student organizations in the United States. His presence kept Smith from access and ensured a continued flow of intelligence reporting. The CIA rewarded Backoff the following year with the coveted post in Paris.[21]

At the end of Smith's term, in 1963, an overseas post that he believed had been promised to him before he ran for office disappeared behind a veil of denials and obfuscations. The humiliating rejection left him bitter and puzzled.[22] When Smith's friends demanded an explanation, the new NSA president Gregory Gallo defended it as a series of misunderstandings, and implied the fault lay with Smith.[23] What truly rankled Smith were the appointments of Robert T. Francis and William C. McClaskey, two men with no experience with the NSA. Both were assigned to work in Africa, the field promised to Smith.[24]

Since in the early 1960s the NSA was under heavy political attack from the right, Robbins and other liberals were circumspect about publicly criticizing the organization. Not long after the 1962 Congress, Richard Viguerie, the executive secretary of the Young Americans for Freedom and the future pioneer of direct mail, outlined a fifty-state plan to challenge the NSA campus by campus. Denouncing the NSA as a "tool of the radical left," he labeled its claim to represent 1.3 million students a "fantastic fraud."[25] Having been unable to take over the leadership, the YAF hoped to destroy the NSA. In the ensuing campaign, Viguerie flipped the NSA slogan "The students of today are the leaders of tomorrow" on its head, declaring, "The leaders of *tomorrow* will be conservative if organizations such as YAF can reach them *today*."[26]

By the end of the 1962–63 academic year, the YAF had helped persuade thirty-three campuses to disaffiliate; dozens more colleges or universities had considered and rejected affiliation. The list of disaffiliations included New York University (Washington Square branch), Indiana University, Ohio State University, the University of Texas, Northwestern University (Wonderlic's alma mater), Denison University, the Universities of Missouri, Oklahoma, Nebraska, Kansas, New Hampshire, and Utah, Vanderbilt University, Xavier University, Fordham University, Tufts University, Texas Christian University, and Franklin and Marshall College, among others.[27] Howard Abrams remembers that at one point it appeared that every single one of the Big Ten schools might withdraw.[28]

Thus Robbins pursued his criticism in private, through long letters to Marc Roberts, chair of the NSA executive committee. He denounced the use of "so-called experts" on policy committees who "in the guise of teachers" gave "biased opinions."[29] Shaul did his best to deflect the criticism, and at one point thought he had succeeded. He wrote to Roberts that Robbins was "coming around," but they should "continue to develop him."[30]

But Robbins was not the only one with questions. In May 1963, Howard Abrams confronted Shaul over the secrecy of the International Commission's operations. Shaul admitted that there "was a great deal of truth" in the charge that the International Commission was a "self-perpetuating oligarchy," but pointed out that many NSA critics, among them members of the Students for a Democratic Society, had been invited to attend the summer seminar.[31] Abrams, who learned about the Quebec meeting at secondhand, pressed Shaul on policy issues. He wanted to know why the NSA had not stood with the progressive student unions that walked out. Why was it so tepid in its support for Third World issues? Shaul vigorously refuted the last charge. He pointed to the extremely liberal resolutions compiled in the NSA Codification of Policy, published after each student Congress.[32]

But Shaul also told Abrams that he was distressed to hear that a "small revolution" was brewing, aimed at the International Commission.[33] He was partially correct. Robbins, Abrams, and others decided to avoid a confrontation at the 1963 Congress, however, to focus on reforming the oversight mechanisms of the NSA. Their plan was to abolish the thirty-three-member National Executive Committee and substitute a smaller National Supervisory Board (NSB). The intention, Robbins explains today, was to permit genuine oversight, which was harder to do with a large committee. The proposal created four meta-regions (Far Western, Mid-Western, Northeastern, and Southeastern), which each had two or three representatives, depending on the number of member schools in the region.[34]

Shaul paid little attention to the reform package. He had his hands full trying to balance the left and right factions within the NSA. By the summer, sit-ins, pickets, and demonstrations were no longer being confined to soda counters or large corporations—protesters now were attacking policies of the Kennedy administration. Shaul had little interest in antagonizing administration officials, especially since he was hoping to persuade Robert F. Kennedy to address the Congress.[35]

Shaul's problems piled up. In early summer, a coalition of civil rights organizations announced a march on Washington for late August to pressure Congress to pass stalled civil rights legislation. At that point, the Kennedy administration was opposed to the march, fearing it might set back the legislation. Further complicating things for Shaul, the dates conflicted with the NSA Congress, ensuring a contentious debate over whether the NSA should support the march. In May, Indiana University—site of the August Congress—voted to withdraw from the NSA. Pre-signed contracts made it impossible to cancel the Congress, but it was an awkward situation.

In late July, Shaul took steps to defuse the tension. He invited SDS activist Paul Booth to discuss "how far the Association can go at this moment in its social action policies."[36] He also asked Booth to take charge of a Congress seminar on education and the Cold War.[37] Booth agreed. Shaul also sought to placate the right. Richard Meece, head of the Young Republican National Federation, had attacked Shaul for sitting on the liberal Americans for Democratic Action board while presiding over the NSA. In a *Washington Post* interview, Meece charged that the NSA was "not committed to open debate."[38] Shaul notified Meece that he had resigned from the ADA board and acknowledged that his acceptance of the position had been a mistake.[39]

At the 1963 Congress, Shaul tried to reconcile the left and right, tell-ing delegates, "We must restore the philosophy of student government; restore what it means to be a participant in democracy." He described American students as "politically powerless for too long," even using the leftist depiction of students as "downtrodden reserves in society." The key, he told delegates, was balance. The association was not afraid of direct action but must uphold principles of nonviolence. The national leadership of the NSA was "sensitive to the charge that the association is run by an elite," but changes would have to "come from within."[40]

The reform package proposed by Robbins and others to establish a ten-member National Supervisory Board passed without controversy, although it left intact the separate International Advisory Board. Rob-bins was elected chair. He was joined by liberals Howard Abrams and Mary Beth Norton from the University of Michigan. Norton, later a pioneering feminist historian, cooperated despite her frequent annoy-ance at her male colleagues. She says today of the NSA: "The worst sex-ism I ever encountered." During the Congress, she steamed when Rob-bins told her that "girls couldn't chair large meetings." But she put aside her personal feelings because like the others she cared about the NSA and did not want to play into the hands of the right wing.[41]

At the Congress, despite the usual fear of insurgent candidacies, the elections went smoothly for the CIA caucus. Gregory Gallo from the University of Wisconsin, an ISRS graduate and Catholic moderate, won the presidency.[42] The international position went to Harvard Univer-sity's Alex Korns, who had been groomed for the post since 1961, when he worked on an Algerian students' conference. He had since assisted foreign student delegations and served as assistant director of ISRS. Be-fore his election, Korns had even written his senior thesis using confi-dential NSA documents. The thesis itself was marked "confidential."[43]

After the Congress, Robbins returned to UCLA for his senior year. His new position as NSB chair gave him more clout for his persistent questioning of NSA operations. Now he focused on policy, starting with the NSA position on Iraq. In February 1963, Ba'athists in Iraq had spear-headed a coup against the ruling prime minister, General Abdul Karim Kassem. The NSA Congress, prodded by the international staff, had congratulated Iraqi students on the revolution and praised their role in it. A similar resolution hailed the Ba'athist-led revolution in Syria. What Robbins knew about the Ba'ath Party, he said in a later interview, "reeked of fascism."[44] But before confronting the NSA leadership about these resolutions, Robbins decided to seek out the opinion of Arab students on the UCLA campus. What he learned increased his doubts.

Robbins pressed Korns to explain why the NSA had given "unqualified support to the Ba'ath Party in Iraq." He pointed out that the regime seemed anything but democratic and submitted a list of particulars. Before the coup, for example, Iraq had twenty-six newspapers; now there were two. The "repression of civil liberties in Iraq and Syria," Robbins charged, had reached "severe proportions."[45]

Korns defended NSA policy, even though in the compartmentalized world of the CIA, he surely knew only part of the story. The CIA had worked for years to oust Kassem because he was deemed too tolerant of the Iraqi Communist Party. The agency scoffed at the argument that Kassem used communists to counter Nasser's Pan-Arabian appeal.[46] In fact, in 1958, the U.S. Senate had summoned CIA director Allen Dulles to explain the "intelligence failure" that allowed Kassem to come to power.[47]

The Iraqi Ba'ath Party became the CIA's chosen instrument to overthrow Kassem. Despite its socialist orientation, the United States believed that the Ba'ath could be a bulwark against Soviet penetration. In 1959, the CIA deployed a young Iraqi Ba'athist named Saddam Hussein to assassinate Kassem. He failed and had to flee to Cairo, where the CIA gave him ongoing financial support.[48]

In February 1963, after a successful CIA-backed coup, Kassem was killed by an Iraqi firing squad. James Critchfield, CIA chief of the Near East division, later called it a textbook example of a CIA operation: "We really had the t's crossed."[49] A Ba'ath leader also later acknowledged, "We came to power on a CIA train."[50] But the most serious aspect of the coup, with implications for the NSA, was the preparation by the CIA of a list of alleged communists and leftists targeted for elimination under the new regime.[51] The list included leading members of the IUS-affiliated General Union of Iraqi Students (GUSIR).

Before the coup, the NSA had done its part to oust Kassem by backing a new organization, the National Union of Iraqi Students (NUIS), formed in Baghdad on November 23, 1961, to challenge the pro-Soviet GUSIR.[52] The NSA gave NUIS broad press coverage and, through COSEC, urged ISC members to protest against Kassem.[53] At one point, the NSA used documents smuggled out of Iraq to prepare anti-GUSIR material.[54] U.S. embassy officials in Iraq tracked the progress of NUIS, and nudged it along.[55] NUIS officers were encouraged to move up the date of a scheduled congress so that a delegation would be able to attend the 1962 ISC in Quebec.[56]

Six months or so after Quebec, NUIS called for a student strike, which some historians say helped divert attention from other aspects of the coup.[57] When the predictable violence broke out, NUIS blamed Kassem. Once again, the NSA played a supporting role, publicly praising NUIS for being "at the core of a new effort to bring down the Kassem government."[58]

In the aftermath of the coup, NSA field staff reports glowed with satisfaction. Exiled Iraqi student Walid Khadduri at Michigan State University praised the NSA, writing to headquarters that he was "singularly pleased by the USNSA-COSEC commitment prior to the February 8 revolution."[59]

But the coup was followed by large-scale violence. By March 1963, the Ba'athists had arrested an estimated ten thousand Iraqis and executed an estimated five thousand.[60] The Soviet Union charged the United States with enabling a bloodbath. A senior U.S. official later observed, "We were frankly glad to be rid of them [the communists]."[61] No one has admitted to supplying student names to the new regime, but every year NSA staff turned in hundreds of reports that contained assessments of foreign students. It apparently never occurred to witting staff that the information might flow through their CIA case officers into a broader CIA pipeline, a fact that today haunts many of them. But the consequences of the killings for Iraq were serious: the former National Security Council adviser Roger Morris maintained that the arrests and murders decimated Iraqi elites.[62]

In his response to Robbins, Korns downplayed the violence. He relied on field staff reports to assure Robbins that the Ba'ath Party was "ably led" and had "a promising program."[63] He acknowledged that it was difficult to defend the Iraqi student union as democratic, but with the exception of the Lebanese union, Korns argued, no student union in the Middle East could be defended on civil libertarian grounds. "Nevertheless, I would defend a policy of close cooperation with the Ba'ath unions on the grounds that these unions are the most dynamic and significant in the Middle East."[64] He repeated the argument that NUIS had a broad base, "seems to enjoy the enthusiastic support of a large number of Iraqi students," and was at the "forefront of the Ba'ath movement."[65] He ignored reporting that showed that it had gained favor with the Chinese, who saw the IUS member GUSIR as pro-Soviet.[66]

Korns also confided to Robbins that the NSA expected the Iraqis to control five ISC votes, "Syria, Jordan, Libya, and perhaps Palestine," all countries where the Ba'ath Party was active. Further, he added, Iraqi "influence might extend to Morocco."[67] In NSA-CIA terms, that prospect spelled bonanza. The expectation continued the pattern of placing large hopes for an entire region on changes in one country.

Robbins did not buy Korns's explanation. "It seems to me that the resolution congratulated the Iraqui [sic] and Syrian students on their 'democratic revolution.' If this was not the case, then I would like to withdraw my comments."[68] Robbins knew perfectly well that the text read, "Recognizing the courageous effort of the National Union of Iraqi students in the successful revolution of 8 February 1963, against the dictatorial and brutal regime of General Kassem, USNSA congratulates NUIS as it begins its new role in striving to create a free and open society in Iraq."[69]

But Robbins also knew he had reached an impasse. The undergraduate from California could not compete with the International Commission no matter how much history he knew or how many Arabs he consulted. Robbins mentally filed the NSA's support for the Iraqi and Syria Ba'ath parties as another mystery.[70]

Robbins may have been too much of a neophyte to grasp the politics of the ISC in Quebec the year before, but he came to understand what the NSA had in store for the militant students who had walked out. Publicly, the NSA pledged fealty to the resolution to invite the dissidents to the next conference. Privately, the NSA-CIA team was discussing a "splitting strategy" to permanently force unfriendly members out of the ISC.[71]

How much Robbins knew about the strategy is unclear, but he suspected enough to call it a campaign of harassment and protest to Korns.[72] "I do not believe that the proposed plan to eliminate the extreme left from the ISC is sound. The recent coup in the Dom Rep will probably make the Lat American Unions even more restive, but I am inclined to believe that, even if you win, you will succeed only in gratifying the [International] Commission's lust for absolute control over all variables and the negative results could be disastrous. It seems to me that enough power exists now to control COSEC and I wish you would provide me with *concrete* evidence of programs or activities that would be improved or facilitated by eliminating this group from the Conference."[73]

After Quebec, Korns privately called the ISC an "artificial bucket of worms," so he either agreed with Robbins or had decided to placate him.[74] "Your misgivings about this idea are well founded," he wrote back, "and I am far from sure in my own mind as to what will have to be done at the next ISC."[75] He suggested that an answer might be to strengthen the secretariat. If COSEC were given the "normal powers and privileges of an executive, it [would] be in a much better position to defend itself and to counter disruptive tactics within the ISC."[76] Korns's suggestion reflected a growing consensus that the ISC-COSEC problems were structural and not the consequence of its membership.[77]

Rather than try to convince Robbins of the merit of individual policies, NSA president Gallo and Korns decided to coopt him. Not long after Robbins's letter about the Quebec ISC, the two officials invited Robbins to join an NSA delegation to Asia scheduled to depart in December 1963.[78] Robbins accepted.

Robbins went to Indonesia, the Philippines, Singapore, and Malaysia. "It was a fabulous experience," Robbins said later.[79] He met student counterparts and had audiences with top political leaders. The excursion also gave Robbins access to overseas international staff, whom he peppered with questions. Soon Korns was writing them frantic letters to find out what Robbins had learned, "so as to be prepared for his next onslaught."[80]

Korns sent one note to Paris-based George Hazelrigg, who had caught up with the NSA delegation in Manila, reminding him, "We have up to now denied all intent to 'exclude' national unions at the next ISC."[81] What had Hazelrigg divulged about Quebec? Korns suspected that the answer to his question was "too much," but blamed himself. "Don't feel too badly," he told Hazelrigg, "I should have warned you in advance."[82]

Throughout the spring of 1964, NSA headquarters continued to try to bring Robbins into the fold. Gallo and Korns urged him to apply for the summer seminar, and Robbins toyed with the idea; the Asia trip had spurred his interest in international affairs. But his concerns over the peculiarities in the international program kept mounting. He declined the invitation—a decision he now describes as among "the best I ever made."[83]

Just before graduation, Robbins had one more encounter with NSA headquarters that left him troubled. He was called into the UCLA chancellor's office to discuss a telegram from Gallo and Korns that protested the upcoming visit from the shah of Iran to receive an honorary degree from the university. Could Robbins explain the cable? He could not. While Robbins had no use for the shah and saw him as dictatorial and corrupt, the NSA cable struck him as inappropriate. He also wondered why, as the head of the NSA Supervisory Board, he would have been left in the dark about Gallo and Korns's intentions. He contacted NSA headquarters to ask for an explanation.[84]

Before long, the UCLA chancellor received a two-page letter of apology and an explanation of NSA policy from Gallo and Korns. They were concerned, they said, about the shah's repressive policies, and they saw only two viable options for a post-shah regime: a pro-communist government and the noncommunist National Front, heirs to former President Mossadegh, whom they called "a fierce national leader." Thus, NSA policy was "to shore up National Front elements among Iranian students and convince them that they have friends in the West and thereby help to insure that if the Shah is ever overthrown his place will be taken by democratic rather than Communist revolutionaries."[85] (Left unmentioned was Mossadegh's overthrow by the CIA in 1953 for being too nationalist and too lenient with communists.)

Unknown to Robbins—and most of the NSA constituency—the NSA had, through its witting members, become deeply involved with the anti-shah Iranian Student Association in the United States (ISAUS), assisting with funds but also filing extensive reports. This involvement was not simply another case of the CIA working both sides of the street. The shah was a firm ally of the United States, and the CIA was working closely with the Iranian secret police in SAVAK, a bureau that it had helped established. The support for the dissidents appears, on the basis of the evidence, to have been a matter rather of encouraging NSA staff to gain access to these students.[86]

Unlike student dissidents supported by the NSA in the past, in fact, the Iranian students in the United States were in a life-threatening situation. SAVAK agents, often attached to the Iranian Embassy, pursued them throughout the United States.[87] To allay the shah's suspicion that ISAUS was getting help from the U.S. government, the State Department asked the Justice Department to deport any Iranian students suspected of being communist. Back in Iran, the students faced the shah's firing squad.[88]

The ISAUS president, Ali Mohammed S. Fatemi, was among those who received deportation orders—and who had reason to fear the shah. His uncle Hassan Fatemi had been the foreign minister in the Mossadegh government; the two had intended to escape from Iran to the United States together, but on the eve of their departure, his uncle was arrested by the shah's agents and later executed.[89] Fearing that he faced a similar fate, Fatemi filed a lawsuit to prevent his deportation.[90] In his efforts he had the support of the attorney general of the United States, Robert F. Kennedy, who resisted State Department requests to enforce the deportation order. After Kennedy had ordered an FBI investigation of the Iranian dissidents, he told a friend, "The FBI report is in, and not a bloody one of these kids is a Communist, so I just told Rusk [Secretary of State] to go chase himself."[91]

By the time Robbins was asked to explain NSA policy on Iran, in May 1964, some of the Iranian students, including Fatemi, had given up on the possibility of peaceful change and had formed the Student Revolutionary Preparedness Committee.[92] Today, Fatemi renounces violence as "never legitimate," and seems embarrassed about this period of his life.[93] But according to NSA reports at the time, Fatemi's colleague Faraj Ardalan moved the committee's agenda ahead and slipped secretly into Algiers, where with the assistance of President Ben Bella, he planned "to establish a training school for Iranians who in the future would commence para-military anti-Iranian Government activities."[94] Ironically, the NSA dithered before offering this committee a small amount of funding, only to have its offer rejected. One staff member in contact with Fatemi and Ardalan observed in a later interview, "They didn't want us to know as much as we wanted to know."[95]

Even the witting NSA staff did not seem to understand the danger posed to Iranian students by their constant reporting on them, and the risk that SAVAK could get hold of the information. Fatemi today condemns the reporting as a betrayal of the Iranian students' secrets and adds, "Every one of us could have been killed."[96] Robbins, of course, was unaware of the gap between NSA policy as explained by Gallo and Korns and these dangerous games. But the whole episode made him more determined than ever to probe the secrets of the International Commission.

A few months later, in August, Robbins headed to his third NSA Congress, to be held at the University of Minnesota. Despite his unanswered questions, he had decided to run for president. He believed—correctly—that the NSA establishment would oppose him, but the witting staff had greater concerns. The electoral drama focused not on the presidential race but on the international contest. The small revolution that Dennis Shaul once worried about had made its appearance. On August 27, SDS activist Paul Booth from Swarthmore College took the stage and told delegates, "We need a year of close, critical scrutiny of the international affairs of this union of students." Booth was running for international vice president with a campaign platform that NSA constituents needed to have a "meaningful way" to affect the policy of the International Commission. In a reference to the Quebec ISC, he charged, "Delegates had no say in the critical issue of NSA relations within the ISC and its relations with radical unions of students in the underdeveloped world." He urged the delegates to break up the "monopoly of relevant information" that blocked full participation, stating, "There is no good reason why secrets should be kept from us."[97]

To the cheering and whistling crowd, Booth declared that if, within a year, access to information were not opened, "it may be necessary to propose the creation of an elected independent watchdog group—with access to all files and the job of sending out monthly reports to student governments." In a surprise move, Booth then withdrew from the race and endorsed his opponent, Norman Uphoff, a 1963 graduate of the University of Minnesota, then at the Woodrow Wilson School at Princeton, and called for a "unanimous election by acclamation."[98]

In a later interview, Booth explained his thinking. He had felt powerless to "affect the course of events, even after four years of being an active and loyal participant in NSA affairs." His campaign speech was motivated in part by his irritation at "the appearance of adults who ran around the place. If only," Booth joked, "we had known the concept of transparency."[99]

Absent transparency, Booth could not have known that Norman Uphoff had CIA backing. Uphoff, a tall, affable man, likes to remind people that his full name is Norman Thomas Uphoff, a reference to his godfather, Socialist Party leader Norman Thomas.[100] His parents were prominent Quaker activists in Wisconsin peace and labor circles, and at the University of Minnesota Uphoff had headed the Student Peace

Union and served as student body president. As a pacifist, he opposed the Vietnam War. In this respect, Uphoff's politics tacked close enough to the SDS to make his candidacy acceptable.

But Uphoff also held the traditional socialist antipathy toward communism that distinguished his politics from those of the SDS. In fact, the Steinem group had twice sent Uphoff and Student Peace Union activists abroad to cause trouble at Soviet-sponsored events. He attended the Helsinki World Festival of Youth in 1962, where he helped prepare a big banner for the final parade that read, "No Test, East or West." He says it got the desired reaction: "The Soviet delegation went nuts and tore the banner apart."[101]

Agency officials had approached Uphoff months before the Congress after rumors circulated that Jeffrey Greenfield, the outspoken editor of the *Daily Cardinal* at the University of Wisconsin, might run. Witting staff had had plenty of opportunity to test Greenfield, since he had traveled to Asia in the same delegation with Robbins. Today Greenfield scoffs at the notion that he was a threat. "If they had just asked."[102] Despite his very liberal politics, he disclaimed any affinity for the SDS, noting that as a New Yorker who grew up on the Upper West Side, he had long memories of the Stalin-Hitler Pact and popular front politics. But Greenfield was first and foremost a journalist, as inquisitive (and smart) as Robbins, and therefore perhaps not a welcome candidate.

At the same time, whether or not they identified with the SDS, Uphoff, Greenfield, and Robbins, along with other liberals, were moving to the left on a variety of issues. In fact, Greenfield wrote Robbins's campaign speech. Had the CIA been able to find a way to keep Robbins from knowing the NSA's secret, it surely would have done so. Everyone in the Agency knew that he took nothing on faith, questioned everything, and, by his own admission, rarely removed the bit from his teeth.

20

LIFTING THE VEIL

AS ONE OF HIS FIRST acts as president, Stephen Robbins demanded to see the association's financial records. Comptroller George Mugler tried to deflect his requests, but the more evasive Mugler became, the more determined Robbins was to get his hands on the accounts. "I was already after three or four tries getting at the testy level," he said in a later interview. "I was notorious for having a temper, as I still am. So Mugler knew it wasn't going to work."[1]

Then, out of the blue, Robbins got a call from his predecessor, Greg Gallo, known to this day for his "calm, facilitating skills."[2] Gallo had moved to New York to become the vice president of the CIA-funded United States Youth Council. Gallo suggested they get together in Washington. As Robbins boarded the train bound for Washington, he had a hunch that after years of tearing at the impenetrable NSA curtain, he was about to have his curiosity satisfied. In Washington, Robbins and Gallo went to the Intercontinental Hotel, where Ed Garvey was waiting for them. If Robbins had felt apprehensive, he relaxed. Garvey was someone he liked and trusted.[3]

Gallo left Robbins alone with Garvey, who administered the security oath. Garvey then described the NSA-CIA relationship in a way that Robbins later realized was incomplete at best. All Robbins had to do was "keep the secret." Everything was "voluntary." Robbins was "under no obligation to do anything he didn't feel was right."[4]

At first, Robbins said later, he couldn't absorb what he'd heard. Had it been the State Department financing the NSA, he would not have been surprised. But the CIA involvement left him "absolutely astonished, just

stunned." It didn't take long, he added, for his "nerve endings to quiver
. . . danger, danger." His mind ran over what he knew of the CIA—
the Bay of Pigs invasion, the overthrow of President Jacobo Árbenz in
Guatemala—yet here was Garvey, assuring him, "We're smarter than
the striped pants [State Department] guys."[5]

But for Robbins, everything fell into place. "Anyone who was really
familiar with the association knew there were mysteries," Robbins explains today. At the time, people talked about "they" and "them" but
thought in terms of a vague establishment.[6] Now he understood why
he and Mahoney had not been warmly received in Quebec. To have
a regional chair raise a substantive question about why the NSA supported one foreign union over another or why it adopted a particular
policy threatened the business of the International Commission. For
years, undergraduate apathy and the diversionary prowess of international staff had kept this threat at bay. It did not matter that American
students could not find Angola on the map, as critic Kay Wonderlic had
once demanded, so long as they went along with the experts.

The CIA tie also explained the absence of political acumen among
the ISRS graduates, and why prized recruits often came from graduate programs or geographical area specialties. It explained the seemingly innocuous resolutions that expressed fraternal greetings, pledged
solidarity, registered dismay, reproached a foreign government, or
condemned a violation of academic rights. All played a part in a larger
agenda. Support for the Ba'ath Party was part of the overall CIA strategy
in the Middle East, support for the anti-shah Iranian students part of an
attempt to gain access to dissident students, and perhaps future leaders.

The international vice president, most international staff, and the
overseas representatives worked for the CIA, as did the older former
NSA men who hovered around the Congresses. Now Robbins was being
asked to come up with a code name and told he had a case officer. He
chose the name "Wellor," but apparently no one caught the wordplay: an
anagram of "Orwell," the author of the dystopian novel *1984*, a cautionary tale about incipient totalitarianism and thought control.[7] Robbins
was assigned a seasoned case officer instead of Garvey, who might normally have been chosen. According to a witting colleague of Garvey's,
the Agency realized right off the bat that Robbins was too smart for
Garvey to handle.[8]

Once Robbins was witting, George Mugler shared the financial accounts with him. As he studied the books, Robbins was astonished to discover the magnitude of the NSA's financial dependency on the CIA. Both the international and domestic commissions needed CIA resources for their survival.[9]

Over the next few months, Robbins began to realize that the NSA president had little to do with decision making by the international team. "They don't work for me and it's *really* clear. And they don't work for Norm [Uphoff] either. Every one of those guys [staff and overseas reps] was dealing directly—all the time—with their counterparts [in the CIA]. That's just the way it was. Did they keep secrets from me? Sure they did. Did they keep them from Norm? They kept them from everybody. It's a need-to-know deal."[10]

Norman Uphoff, who had run for office at the CIA's urging, today agrees with Robbins. He ruefully notes that many of the NSA Congress resolutions on foreign policy were excellent, but after they were passed he wondered "to whom should he direct [copies of] them."[11] All such resolutions served an international agenda largely unknown to the student congress, although Robbins and Uphoff got glimpses from time to time when they attended operational meetings.

Such meetings took place at the Shoreham or the Statler-Hilton or other hotels in Washington, occasionally in New York. The atmosphere, Robbins stresses today, was collegial but it did not disguise the power structure. "It's not some quasi-military operation where people are barking orders or any of that stuff, but when you're sitting around the table, you all know who is playing."[12] Robbins realized that his instincts about the aftermath of Quebec were accurate. He learned that the NSA-CIA team had controlled the travel grants to the 1964 ISC in Christchurch, New Zealand, and had manipulated visa requests so that only friends and allies were able to attend.[13]

Robbins felt trapped. He could not seek the counsel of former NSA leaders, since old hands sanctioned and sustained the relationship. His security oath forbade him to seek an outside opinion. He described his gradual understanding of the scope and significance of the CIA's presence in the NSA: "The first thing you go through is you are just adjusting to the new reality, and you're kind of amazed that the government would actually put this money into your deal. Then, gradually, you discover that it isn't your deal. It's their deal. See, there's nothing about the making witting process—those three hours with Ed Garvey—nothing that prepares you for the relationship."[14]

Despite his anxiety, Robbins also got a taste of the pleasure that often accompanies being in the know, playing for high stakes, and feeling important. That his colleagues were brilliant, learned, and quick with a bon mot made the game that much more attractive. He enjoyed the envious look on others' faces when he announced he was off to Paris or other foreign capitals. After a Spartan undergraduate existence, having a company credit card was exhilarating. Others noticed dramatic changes in his dining habits. "Why was twenty-two-year-old Stephen Robbins known to every maître d' in Washington, D.C.?" asked the former NSA staff member and journalist Robert Walters rhetorically, as he ran through his own list of NSA anomalies.[15]

Dining at the best restaurants was fun, Robbins admits, but his conscience nagged him. As he tried to cope with his often contradictory emotions—"it was fun; it was wrong"—one fact seemed central: as NSA president, he was betraying his electorate, the NSA constitution, and his own sense of self. "Even if we make the 'right' decision, there's no democracy here. We sell these decisions to our constituency . . . they don't bubble up from them, and if we can't sell them, we hide them, or we blow a lot of smoke that makes everybody confused."[16]

One incident in particular incensed Robbins. At an ops meeting in early spring 1965, the CIA-NSA agenda included the upcoming World Youth Festival scheduled for Algiers and how it was to be sabotaged. Robbins got a firsthand look at the kind of dirty tricks the CIA had pulled the NSA into.

The venue of the festival was particularly distressing to U.S. officials because they had spent so many years trying—and failing—to ensure a friendly, pro-Western Algerian regime. Their joy when the Algerians had won their independence had turned sour in a matter of months. In October 1962, the new president, Ahmed Ben Bella, arrived in the United States for a state visit with President Kennedy. Flanked by his foreign secretary, Mohamed Khemisti, he was welcomed to the White House, while Kennedy extolled the Algerians' courage and likened them to the American founding fathers.[17] NSA officers, present for the White House reception, thrilled when a beaming Khemisti praised the NSA for its support. But a few days later, the Algerians flew to Havana, where

Ben Bella stood shoulder to shoulder with Fidel Castro, announced their joint support for worldwide liberation movements, and demanded that the United States close down Guantánamo army base and leave the island.[18]

Thereafter, relations between the NSA and the Algerians became complicated. Algerian students in the United States continued to enjoy support, and the Algerian scholarship program expanded.[19] In Algeria, relations with the renamed Union Nationale des Étudiants Algériens (UNEA) grew rocky as radical Algerians took over and opted to join the IUS. Paris-based Robert Backoff summed up the new direction of UNEA in Algiers: the students now had a "total identity with the IUS, Eastern European socialism, and [they were] mildly pro-Chinese on the question of national liberation."[20] In short, they had defected.

Ben Bella, eager to wield influence in Africa and the Middle East, welcomed the prospect of hosting the 1965 World Youth Festival. Back-off warned witting staff that if the festival were a success, the Algerians would "be unbearable to talk to," and their influence within the IUS would increase.[21]

Spurred to even greater heights of covert ingenuity, the top secret 303 Committee, consisting of representatives from the National Security Council, the CIA, and the Departments of State and Defense, approved on December 3, 1964, a "Program of Covert Counteraction against the 9th World Youth Festival Algiers, 1965/5."[22] Details of the CIA plan remain classified, but during the meeting, CIA director John McCone described the difficulties the Americans would have in Algiers when contrasted to "the relatively friendlier areas in Vienna and Helsinki." They could not count on a Western-friendly government to help their sabotage efforts. Before the meeting adjourned, National Security Advisor McGeorge Bundy praised the CIA for its past strategies, finding especially noteworthy the "useful by-product" of the Steinem-led Independent Research Service for its "educative impact on young Americans."[23]

By the time Robbins and other NSA-CIA staff met to plan further strategy to undermine the festival, rumors had circulated that SNCC might send a delegation to Algiers in a show of solidarity. Julius Glickman, a Texan who then staffed North African affairs at NSA headquarters, suggested that the NSA "give strong consideration to forming a private group to counteract the damage they could do."[24] His suggestion showed how effortlessly strategies long used overseas to undermine nationalists and militants could be turned against former friends and allies at home.

But the final straw for Robbins was yet to come. During a brainstorming session someone suggested that the Americans get hold of a worn-out Russian oil tanker and create an oil spill off the Algerian coast. It was classic Cold War thinking: an ecological disaster would demonstrate to festival delegates that the Soviets relied on outdated and hazardous equipment and lacked environmental sensitivity, which in turn could be attributed to their failed economic system. Furious, Robbins slapped his folder of material shut, excused himself from the table, and headed for a prolonged stay in the nearest restroom.[25] Discussions of the anti-festival operation continued without him.

Decades later, Robbins's feelings are still strong: "Dirty tricks. . . . Donald Segretti," he mutters, invoking the name of Richard Nixon's legendary dirty trickster. "I do not believe it is appropriate to do those things—to stop up toilets and arrange for oil spills on beaches. It's not just that it is pragmatically stupid, it's immoral. And I have no doubt that there were dozens of decisions like that during my year. Some of which I knew about, most of which I didn't."[26]

As Robbins's anger grew, his options dwindled. As he examined the NSA's finances, any fantasies he might have had about pulling the plug on the International Commission evaporated. He did not have enough time left in his presidency to free the association from its financial dependency on the CIA. The campaign being run by the Young Americans for Freedom to destroy the NSA via campus referendums served as a daily reminder that the association had powerful enemies. Robbins decided that his course of action would depend on who became the next NSA president.[27]

Robbins believed that the right person for the job was Philip Sherburne from the University of Oregon. Robbins had first met Sherburne at the 1963 Congress in Bloomington. He had come to admire the thoughtful and hardworking Sherburne, the first in his family to go to college.

Sherburne grew up on a dairy farm near Rainier, Oregon, a small village of approximately one hundred inhabitants. When he was fifteen, his father was killed in a farm accident, and he took over the farm's management. Despite his daily chores of milking cows and mending fences, Sherburne's leadership qualities stood out, and he won several scholarships to the University of Oregon. In order to accept them, he had to give up farming. Sherburne sold the animals and leased the land. Determined to get to his first NSA Congress in 1963, he drove a university car fifty-five straight hours from Eugene to Bloomington. (None of his three companions had a driver's license.) What he found thrilled him. "I had never been around people from other countries," he said later.[28] The NSA opened up vistas beyond the Eugene campus, and he returned brimming with ideas.

Robbins felt that Sherburne, who in 1964 had been elected the national affairs vice president, would react as he had to the revelation of the CIA's involvement in the NSA. He also believed that Sherburne shared his commitment to the NSA and would never do anything that might harm the association. But Robbins did not know about episodes in Sherburne's past that suggested a capacity to stand firm against a crowd, for example the time when Sherburne's fraternity brothers brought an illegal keg of beer into the house and he threatened to report the violation, explaining, "If you don't agree with the rules, then let's fight the rules, but I'm not going to sneak around." After a notorious rape occurred on campus Sherburne led a fight to have serious campus crimes tried under state law, against tremendous pressure from both alumni and the state legislature.[29]

In early May, several months before the 1965 Congress, Robbins urged his CIA contacts to make Sherburne witting. Despite the CIA's later contention that NSA officers signed the secrecy oath only after they were elected, many had become witting beforehand. Robbins's request seemed not to set off any particular alarms, despite the fact that the CIA rarely, if ever, made staff on the national commission witting.

On May 18, Robbins and Sherburne met Ed Garvey and Harry Lunn at the Marriott Hotel in Arlington, Virginia, where Garvey and Lunn made Sherburne witting, adhering to the standard line: knowledge of the CIA relationship was limited to the international staff and the president of the NSA. Sherburne, like Robbins, remembers the pitch framed in terms of "we good government guys (liberal/CIA) against bad government guys (State Department)." The CIA could support democratic movements around the world, he was told, while the State Department supported dictatorships.[30]

Garvey and Lunn then flattered Sherburne, telling him how impressed the Agency had been with his performance as a national officer and that they hoped he would run for NSA president at the August Congress. They confided that he had strengths that compensated for Robbins's weaknesses in administrative matters, and they needed his immediate assistance with a number of pressing projects, including dealing with the accumulated NSA debt and the pending headquarters move from Philadelphia to Washington. Those who had found Robbins difficult surely thought they glimpsed a more congenial future in the calm and competent Sherburne.[31]

After the meeting ended, Sherburne confronted Robbins. "You son of a bitch," Sherburne remembers saying.[32] Robbins tried to explain that he had felt hamstrung as president by not knowing what was going on in advance; once he knew, he had only months left in his term. He wanted time to strategize with Sherburne but didn't want to violate his security oath, and he had been hopeful that if Sherburne could be made witting early he would have more time than Robbins had to find a way out of the NSA's extreme financial dependency on the CIA without wrecking the association.[33]

All summer long, Sherburne and Robbins wrestled with what to do. Sherburne could not understand why every past officer had cooperated, and by the end of the summer he had made a quiet vow to terminate the relationship. He told no one, not even Robbins.[34]

Sherburne chose as his code name "Mr. Grants," to symbolize his determination to replace CIA funds with philanthropic funds. In addition to the need to raise annual operating expenses, a hidden deficit, sometimes estimated at more than $400,000, yoked the NSA to the CIA.[35] There seemed "no way," Sherburne said later, to "terminate the relationship without bankrupting the organization."[36]

Both Robbins and Sherburne saw an opportunity in the planned move of NSA headquarters. The NSA would occupy two adjacent townhouses off Dupont Circle. If the association could obtain title to this prime office space and let the buildings' value inflate for a time, perhaps their increased equity might be a source of funds. "If worst came to worst," Sherburne recalled saying, "We could sell them."[37]

Over the summer, the two officers decided to rob CIA Peter to pay CIA Paul. They scraped together funds from existing accounts and borrowed $40,000 from the National Savings and Trust Company against the purchase price of $110,000.[38] At this point, the Independence Foundation, a CIA conduit in Boston, appeared willing to back the NSA's ownership. The two NSA officers also negotiated with CIA conduits for an additional $15,000 in moving expenses and $50,000 for renovations to connect the two townhouses and transform them into office space.[39]

During these discussions, Sherburne remembers Robbins as cautious, never openly advocating severance.[40] Robbins confirms that he believed an abrupt termination would destroy the NSA, although he still excoriates himself for not "marching up to the third floor [where the international staff was housed] and cleaning it out"; "I just didn't have the balls."[41] In lieu of a grand but possibly fatal gesture, Robbins and Sherburne determined to lessen the association's dependency on CIA funds. The key to fundraising, they decided, was a development director, someone who could remain with the NSA longer than one year.[42]

Robbins and Sherburne offered a three-year contract to Michael Wood, a freckled-faced, red-headed graduate of Pomona College. Wood had impressed Robbins with his civil rights work in Watts, a poverty-stricken area of Los Angeles.[43] He was already on the NSA national staff, directing a tutoring program for inner-city kids. Pleased with their progress, Robbins and Sherburne turned their attention to the August Congress.

To make the strategy work, Sherburne still had to be elected NSA president, but by August a new factor had entered their calculations: the war in Vietnam. Since Kennedy's assassination, President Lyndon B. Johnson had gradually escalated the American troop presence in Vietnam. In February 1965, without fanfare or public announcement, Johnson began bombing the North Vietnamese. The nation's campuses erupted in protest. Robbins and Sherburne knew that the CIA would oppose any resolution that called for unconditional withdrawal, something students might support, although neither of them did. Thus, the Congress was likely to be tense, and the debate over Vietnam could affect officer elections in unknown ways. Neither man had any idea how worried the Johnson White House and the CIA had become—to the point of obsession—about the NSA's position on the war.

The CIA had begun planning for the Congress months earlier. The Agency contracted with Daniel Idzik, a former member of the NSA team, to visit Vietnam, meet with students there, and prepare a report that could head off an unfavorable resolution. Idzik, who had graduated from Harvard Law School and joined a big accounting firm, later called such gigs very lucrative financially.[44]

In his subsequent report, Idzik described the U.S.-backed regime of South Vietnam's Ngo Dinh Diem, who was assassinated in 1963, as "corrupt and oppressive," and explained that Vietnamese students played "a prominent role in his downfall."[45] Most important, he quoted Saigon-based students as favoring a continued U.S. presence: "We like and need the Americans. They can't leave, and we don't want them to. Our destinies are at stake." He left Vietnam with the belief that, "given time and understanding assistance, they [the students] will be able to play an important and constructive role in the development of their country."[46]

About the time Idzik was completing his report, a new form of campus dissent arose. On March 24, 1965, the University of Michigan held a "teach-in" on Vietnam during which professors and policy makers debated the merits of U.S. policy in Asia. Teach-ins spread to campuses around the country, fueled by growing anger over the expansion of the war and the bombing campaign against North Vietnam.

While their format reflected traditional academic conventions, teach-ins infuriated White House, Department of State, and Pentagon officials. President Johnson told his national security advisor McGeorge Bundy: "I am just against White House debating."[47] In mid-May, dozens of campuses held a same-day national teach-in. Johnson forced Bundy to cancel his scheduled appearance at the last moment. Thinking to calm the situation, Walt Rostow, who was soon to replace Bundy at the White House, in a broadcast piped into 100 campuses made the case for the administration, but all he did was generate new levels of outrage with his visible contempt for critics of the war.[48] By early summer, the CIA was looking for a high-level spokesman to defend administration policy at the NSA Congress.

Neither Robbins nor Uphoff remembers (or ever knew) who invited Vice President Hubert H. Humphrey to come to Madison. Uphoff says he did not, even though he was nominally in charge of the international program.[49] A declassified internal CIA memorandum suggests that the idea came from inside the Agency. At one point the head of clandestine operations, Desmond Fitzgerald, worried that the vice president might not carry enough weight. He urged CIA deputy director Richard Helms to consider inviting the president.[50]

In his brief to Helms, Fitzgerald summarized the history of "CIA [word blacked out] and support" for the NSA, and characterized the current problem: "A limited number of people belonging politically to the extremes of American political life . . . will undoubtedly raise United States policy in Vietnam as an issue and assert that USNSA should adopt a resolution highly critical of American policy there."[51] The Congress offered "an unusual opportunity to reach a critical audience of opinion-makers in most of the major university centers in this country." Fitzgerald assured Helms that the president would "receive a courteous response," and that Vietnam "will not occupy the main attention of the Congress delegates."[52]

While a CIA official could hardly improve his case by conjuring a boisterous crowd of student critics, his depiction of antiwar critics as extremists represented a profound misreading of the antiwar dissent. But it accurately reflected the Johnson administration's tendency to deny the legitimacy of the movement: Secretary of State Dean Rusk likened the protesters to Hitler appeasers of the 1930s.[53]

As a further hedge against student criticism, the CIA also contracted with former international vice president Donald Emmerson, at that time a Yale law student. Over the summer, Emmerson spent several months in Saigon before returning to the Congress as a so-called resource person.[54]

In retrospect, the CIA's preparation for the Vietnam debate was over-kill. No one in the NSA leadership believed that the radical position would prevail. Uphoff had assured Emmerson while in Saigon that "the 'left' will not be able to force a position of unconditional withdrawal."[55] Uphoff believed that the key issues would be whether the United States "should agree to (or initiate) a ceasefire" and whether it "should negotiate with the VC [Viet Cong]."[56] Yet the White House and the CIA continued to take an extreme view of what might happen at the Congress.

A week before the Congress began, administration officials panicked. On August 12, Charles Sweet, who was in Saigon working for the International Voluntary Service but also for the CIA, received an urgent message: could Sweet get to Madison immediately? As Sweet explained in a letter to his parents, Bundy's aide Chester Cooper "was worried about the National Student Conference, especially what position the students might take toward VN."[57] The Vietnam Task Force at the State Department offered to fund Sweet's trip if he could wangle an official invitation from the NSA.[58] Just hours before his twenty-three-hour flight to San Francisco, Sweet obtained an invitation. Yes, the NSA would welcome an observer from the International Voluntary Service.[59]

The Congress opened on August 17, on the beautiful Wisconsin campus set alongside Lake Mendota, where the NSA had held several conventions. The large terrace outside the student union beckoned delegates who preferred to spend their time in the sultry summer weather sipping beer and sampling bratwurst to debating political issues. But on the night of August 23, most flocked to hear the vice president of the United States. University officials, concerned about possible demonstrations, had relocated the evening's event at the last moment from the large stock pavilion (known as the Cow Palace), where delegates had been meeting, to the smaller, more manageable Wisconsin Union Theater.

The exhausted Charles Sweet arrived in time to hear Humphrey address the delegates. In his signature forthright style, Humphrey took on the issue of demonstrations. In his most famous putdown, he told the students, "The right to be heard . . . does not automatically include the right to be taken seriously." It depends "entirely on what is being said."[60]

Television footage from that evening shows a respectful audience, dressed in suits and ties, despite the sweltering August heat and humidity. I sat onstage behind Humphrey, clad in my high school graduation dress and pumps, my hair swept up into a beehive. A year later, television footage of an NSA Congress would show the world crowds of longhaired students dressed in T-shirts and jeans.[61]

Outside the glare of television cameras, participants could find many shades of opinion on Vietnam. Allard Lowenstein arrived in Madison to announce a new Vietnam Committee, headed by Yale's antiwar chaplain William Sloane Coffin and socialist leaders Norman Thomas and Michael Harrington.[62] Although not part of the CIA caucus, Lowenstein still had a tendency to jump into the center of action wherever he found it. By the summer of 1965, Lowenstein was engaged in a bitter battle with Robert Parris (later Robert Moses), the charismatic leader of the 1964 Mississippi Summer Project, a SNCC program that drew hundreds of northern white students to the South to register voters.[63]

In Madison, Lowenstein and Moses clashed in a debate that lasted well into the early morning hours.[64] Unlike more established civil rights groups that feared alienating President Johnson, whose support they needed to pass civil rights legislation, SNCC had taken a position against the war in Vietnam. But the showdown between Lowenstein and Moses involved far more than Vietnam policy. The simmering tension between the left and liberals like Lowenstein had begun to disrupt the traditional Democratic coalition of labor unions and ethnic minorities. At its core, the debate raised fundamental issues about how to change American policies. Although both groups opposed the war, Lowenstein urged the assembled students to work "within the system."[65]

The soft-spoken but more militant Moses, by contrast, drew connections between racism in the American South and the U.S. role in Vietnam and argued against "the system." Moses claimed that voter registration only made a black person a free slave. He had helped organize the unsuccessful challenge to the Mississippi delegation to the Democratic convention the previous summer in a now-historic episode that resulted in bitter feelings among many civil rights activists toward the Democratic Party. Lowenstein rebutted that the political system responded to protest and activism through elections. For everyone involved in these disputes, these questions were far from esoteric; they were deeply personal and often life changing. Once again, students asked themselves: Which side are you on?

As if to tweak the choice between system-accepting liberals and system-rejecting radicals, a new group appeared on the scene. Don Emmerson surfaced as the sole staff to a Radical Middle Caucus, suggesting that he had found a vehicle to get out his message on Vietnam. Ricki Radlo from Radcliffe, one of its few members, explained later why she was drawn to it: "We wanted something in the middle that was responsible and positive."[66] Radlo said she often agreed with the left position substantively but objected to its overheated, at times hysterical, rhetoric. Emmerson also had a quiet partner in the American Friends of Vietnam (AFVN), regarded as a White House "front," which may have had some modest CIA funding.[67] AFVN members Gilbert Jonas and Seymour Reisin arrived in Madison and blanketed the delegates with reports, draft resolutions, and other material.

News from Vietnam heightened the tension at the Congress. Six days before the plenary debate, a newspaper headline in the *Liberal Bulletin*, published for delegates, screamed, "U.S. Jets Bomb North Vietnam in Their Heaviest Raids So Far (500,000 lbs)."[68] The Vietnam debate began on the evening of August 31 and lasted until 5 A.M. Despite the emotional atmosphere, the Johnson administration and the CIA managed to win. Barely.

Pro-administration activists Jonas and Reisin wrote a confidential postmortem for AFVN that offers an interesting perspective on the debate, the politics of the NSA, and the subsequent officer elections. The two divided the Congress into four leadership subgroups: the Establishment, the Liberal Study Group (the SDS and its allies), the Radical Middle, and the Conservatives. They focused on the "stunning" abdication of "the establishment," and blamed Robbins, Uphoff, and Sherburne for "hardening NSA opposition to our current policy in Vietnam."[69]

Liberals Howard Abrams, Jeffrey Greenfield, Eugene Groves, and Edward Schwartz tried to delete from the resolution a positive reference to the U.S. role that read, "USNSA believes that the United States presence in South Vietnam is one of the elements necessary until other guarantees can be found to assure self-determination for the South Vietnamese people."[70] While the language stayed in, by a vote of 185–119, Jonas and Reisin were aghast that Sherburne supported the deletion. "It is unusual for an NSA presidential candidate to commit himself in the midst of plenary guerrilla in-fighting!" Still the AFVN members celebrated the amendment's defeat as "a major victory for the Administration." They praised the Radical Middle Caucus and Emmerson for their work.[71]

Whatever divisions existed over Vietnam at the Congress did not affect Sherburne's election. Despite the AFVN's criticism of the officers, he was in step with most Congress delegates, skeptical of administration policy but not a radical critic. He glided to victory unopposed, mostly because the NSA-CIA caucus had spent the summer quietly putting together an acceptable slate. In order to get Sherburne, Robbins acquiesced in the choice for international vice president, Carlton Stoiber, a Rhodes Scholar from the University of Colorado and 1964 ISRS graduate. Sherburne had roomed with Stoiber during the ISRS and looked favorably on his candidacy. He gambled that Stoiber would be supportive of his strategy to get the NSA away from the CIA, even though he knew Stoiber was running with Agency backing.[72] Robbins and Sherburne thus had a vested interest in the slate.

At the last moment insurgents challenged the handpicked candidates. Malcolm Kovacs, a Roosevelt University graduate who had worked off and on with the International Commission, ran against Stoiber. My husband, Michael (Mike) Enwall, a recent graduate of the University of Colorado and ISRS, challenged James A. Johnson from the University of

Minnesota for the position of national affairs vice president.[73] Neither Kovacs nor Enwall had intended to run when he arrived in Madison.

Robbins, who controlled the podium during the elections, admits today that when he sensed the political momentum shifting toward the insurgents, he "just ended it."[74] Robbins gaveled the elections closed, as delegations began to change their votes and more clamored for recognition.[75] Enwall, who lost by one vote, remembered Robbins's exact words as he slammed down the gavel. "If what I think is happening is happening . . ."[76] The rest of his words were lost to the roar of the delegates, pro and con, as Stoiber and Johnson were declared the winners.[77]

As Sherburne approached the podium in the Cow Palace to give the traditional incoming president's speech, he could see the older CIA men sitting far up in the gray bleachers, a group that included his case officer, Matt Iverson. He tried to send them a message: "I talked about the importance of independence of NSA and its democratic character, that it was always a struggle for us to do that." At the time, Sherburne remembers thinking, "People are not going to know what I mean, except for Matt Iverson."[78]

In that judgment, Sherburne calculated correctly. Despite political warning signs that ranged from the Vietnam debate to Sherburne's presidential speech, the CIA apparently expected the Sherburne regime to be business as usual.

PART FIVE

THE FLAP

21

PHILIP SHERBURNE
TAKES ON THE CIA

WHEN FACED WITH A CATASTROPHE, CIA officials typically call it a "flap" to render the problem less potent; the phrase suggests a short-term disruption rather than long-term damage. In the fall of 1965, CIA officials seem not to have seen that a flap was imminent in the NSA, despite evidence that the association's leftward drift was increasing the danger of exposure. After all, NSA presidents came and went, had little say about international operations, and faced prison terms if they revealed the secret relationship. The CIA still held the purse strings, and CIA case officers kept a close watch on their charges.

As soon as he took office, Sherburne ran up against the CIA's power. Someone in the Agency blocked the purchase of the Washington headquarters buildings. On October 26, Sherburne informed the NSA National Supervisory Board that the "Independence Foundation decided not to provide a down payment for the two buildings."[1] The $40,000 mortgage loan obtained in May had come due, but the NSA could not make the payment, giving the CIA an opportunity to prevent it from taking ownership of the S Street buildings. On October 20, the First National Bank of Washington executed a new property deed for the two buildings and identified the bank's role as "an intermediary for an undisclosed trust."[2]

Sherburne had wrung a concession for not fighting the transaction: the NSA would occupy the new headquarters off Dupont Circle rent-free for fifteen years.[3] As a consolation prize, this was not too bad. Or so Sherburne thought at the time. Later, when things got nasty, the CIA tried to renege on the deal and evict the students.

With one prong of his strategy to find a way to refinance the NSA thwarted, short-term fundraising became urgent. Sherburne had hoped that the CIA would make the new development director, Michael Wood, witting, a hope that now seems naive. In retrospect Sherburne surmises that the Agency viewed Wood as something of a radical and therefore unreliable.[4] But without Wood's knowledge, Sherburne's ability to build an inside team that understood and supported his strategy was limited. He could convey the urgency of fundraising to Wood but not the reason for that urgency.

As Wood settled into the development job, he found it strange that Sherburne placed a handful of foundation contacts off-limits, among them the Foundation for Youth and Student Affairs in New York and the Independence Foundation in Boston. As a fundraiser, Wood knew that a good prospect for increased support was existing donors. But he accepted Sherburne's direction.[5]

In the first several months of his presidency, Sherburne negotiated a number of deals with Covert Action 5, the CIA branch for youth and student affairs.[6] Director Robert Kiley and Assistant Director Matthew Iverson claimed that the NSA owed the CIA hundreds of thousands of dollars but, perhaps to foster a cooperative relationship, they agreed to forgive the debt.[7] They also seemed to acquiesce in Sherburne's proposal to treat all CIA conduits as if they were bona-fide philanthropies; he would submit proposals that reflected NSA priorities.[8] In essence, Sherburne proposed back to the CIA the same terms the Agency conveyed to each new set of elected NSA officers. At the Marriott Hotel, Edward Garvey had emphasized Sherburne's freedom to call the shots. At this point, Sherburne believed Kiley and Iverson viewed him as a sparring partner but not an adversary, an advocate for greater independence but not someone who might jeopardize the overall relationship.[9]

Kiley concurs. At the time he did not think that Sherburne's attitude warranted undue concern. "I can recall no NSA president when told about this thing who went, 'oh, that's really interesting,' including myself, so I'm not in a position to say that Phil just took it in stride."[10] But Kiley continued to believe that he need not worry about Sherburne past the point when he should have started worrying.

Sherburne expected opposition from the CIA but not from the new international vice president, Carlton Stoiber. He described Stoiber's views in retrospect as "the basic story line. . . . this [the NSA-CIA relationship] was a valuable thing, and . . . NSA's future would really be jeopardized in its ability to deal internationally" if it were threatened.[11] While accounts at the time and later support Sherburne's version, Stoiber disputes it. He insists today that he supported Sherburne's goals, just not his strategy, and felt that breaking with the CIA, if not negotiated properly, could do significant damage to the association.[12]

By early November, whatever the precise points of disagreement between Stoiber and Sherburne, their conflict had brought the International Commission to a standstill. Cables went unanswered. Mail stacked up. Program decisions languished. International staff describe Stoiber as spending limited time at NSA headquarters.[13] The dispute spilled over to other issues. In early November, Stoiber refused to sign a letter confirming NSA support for an antiwar march planned for Washington that month.[14]

Sherburne became so frustrated with the impasse that he contemplated asking the National Supervisory Board to impeach Stoiber. Instead, shortly before Thanksgiving, Sherburne had what he now describes as a "come to Jesus" meeting with Stoiber.[15] The confrontation ended with Stoiber's resignation.

As Sherburne cast about for a replacement, he toyed with the idea of asking Stephen Robbins to return. Robbins, then in graduate school at UCLA, had decided to enlist in the army, but Sherburne believed he would defer his plans if he could help carry out the strategy the two had devised. Sherburne—who remains a friend of Robbins—laughs when he recalls what stopped the plan. The CIA's reaction was unequivocal: "Not possible."[16] One year of the obstreperous Robbins had been enough.

Sherburne turned instead to a fellow Oregonian, Charles (Chuck) Goldmark, a tall, blond Reed College graduate, then serving as administrative assistant on the International Commission. The two knew each other from NSA activities in the Great Northwest region. While Goldmark was a graduate of ISRS, Sherburne believed him to be a trusted confidant. He was unaware that the position held by Goldmark had been tied to the CIA since 1953, when Ed Gable had been hired.[17]

Sherburne later described his assessment of Goldmark as half-right: "personally loyal but not always on board."[18] Goldmark, he said, agreed that the NSA needed to gain more control over the international program. His friend's mixed allegiances are difficult for Sherburne to discuss today, given subsequent events: a few months later a deranged right-wing anticommunist extremist broke into Goldmark's house and brutally murdered Goldmark, his wife, and their two children.[19]

But even if Sherburne had had Goldmark's unequivocal support for his program, it might not have made much difference. By mid-1965, the CIA had a considerable cadre of people overseas operating in the name of the NSA, and Sherburne gradually realized, just as Robbins had, that he had little control over them. He could not even obtain a simple travel schedule from Paris-based representatives Duncan Kennedy, Robert Francis, and Robert Witherspoon. In addition, Harry Lunn at FYSA directly funded some former NSA staff in overseas posts, among them Latin American specialist Robert Aragon, cutting the NSA out of the loop.[20]

Between November 1965 and March 1966, Sherburne felt the force of the CIA's power, which went far beyond budgetary battles. In the beginning he felt isolated and apprehensive. By spring, he was fearing for his life.

In late November, Sherburne approved travel for Latin American specialist Frederick (Fred) Berger to visit the Dominican Republic. The son of an Argentine mother and a German father, Berger grew up in South America, spoke several languages, and had attended Kenyon College in Ohio before enrolling at Columbia University. His politics trended left, certainly more left than previous Latin America specialists.[21] He often defined himself as "radical but democratic."[22]

Berger envisioned building alliances between the left in the United States and Latin America—an aspiration that bespoke his activist bent.[23] He vigorously condemned President Johnson in April 1965 for sending twenty thousand marines to the Dominican Republic on the dubious grounds of an imminent communist takeover. At a proposed teach-in on Dominican policy at Manhattanville College, Berger urged the organizer to make the question of U.S. unilateral intervention a focal point.[24]

But the idea for the Dominican Republic trip did not come from left-wing radicals. It grew out of Berger's discussions with State Department officials, who hoped to establish future student exchanges there.[25] Since the overthrow of the Trujillo dictatorship in May 1961, the prospect of a democratic showcase in the Caribbean had given way to military coups and political violence. Death squads roamed the streets of Santo Domingo, and right-wing generals were quick to shoot dissidents.

Left-wing radicals were equally quick to strike back. The university shut down after the coup that ousted President Juan Bosch, a onetime favorite of the CIA. In late 1965, after the American military intervention in the Dominican Republic, the new CIA director, Admiral William F. Raborn, Jr., privately summed up U.S. policy with two words: "a mess."[26]

When Berger accepted the invitation, new elections in the Dominican Republic were just months away. As usual, Dominican students were crucial to the election outcome and regime stability. The CIA was pouring millions of covert dollars into support for its latest preferred candidate, Joaquín Balaguer, a one-time protégé of the dictator Trujillo.[27] But the Agency was concerned that the left might win. In a common tactic to secure leverage over the victor, the CIA also channeled covert funds to former president Bosch, from whom it had withdrawn support in 1963.[28] True to form, the American embassy claimed that it was neutral.[29] In short, this was not a propitious time for someone with Berger's politics to visit the Dominican Republic. But Sherburne approved the trip, in part because the NSA wanted to maintain good relations with the State Department.

When Berger reached Santo Domingo, he spent time with different left-wing student factions, including Bosch supporters, socialists, Marxists, and communists. In his subsequent report, Berger acknowledged that the discourse was filled with terms such as "Imperialism, oppression, the Yanqui invaders, neo-fascist, reactionary, oligarchic, counter-revolutionary." But, he averred, "Listen carefully [and] you realize they are not speaking of a violent revolution but a peaceful democratic one respecting the 'dignity of man.'"[30] American embassies in Latin America complained regularly about NSA visits as unwelcome meddling. In this case, embassy officials in the Dominican Republic were livid over Berger's presence.

According to Sherburne, Kiley abruptly ordered Berger to leave the Dominican Republic immediately, go to Miami, and avoid contact with Sherburne. Berger obeyed the order to depart, but defiantly contacted Sherburne after he reached Miami.[31] The CIA, Berger reported, wanted him to terminate his entire Latin America trip, including planned stops in Uruguay and Argentina. Trying to assert his authority, Sherburne directed Berger to proceed.[32]

Sherburne then confronted Kiley and Iverson. Their interference ran contrary to all previous assurances. Why had they ordered Berger out of the Dominican Republic? The two refused to explain other than to claim it was for Berger's own good. Berger died in 1988, but for years afterward close friends claimed that Kiley had informed him that he was about to be killed by "our own people," a vague but menacing phrase that could have meant anything from a specific threat to generalized danger.[33] Berger later told Sherburne that he had met with a hostile CIA official in the embassy who had detailed information on Berger's activities, and who advised him to get out of the country.[34] Kiley professes not to recall the events.[35] Whatever the reason for the order, the episode reinforced a message to Sherburne: you are not calling the shots.

During Berger's absence, Sherburne grappled with a new threat. Long-standard draft deferments for NSA staff had disappeared. Throughout the fall of 1965, eleven staff members received notices that they had been reclassified 1-A, making them eligible for the draft.[36] When Sherburne confronted Kiley and Iverson, they shrugged and claimed they could not do anything.[37] Today, Kiley denies that he or the CIA used the draft to punish Sherburne: "It would have been a really dumb thing to do."[38] Nevertheless, the timing remains suspect.

The loss of draft deferments put tremendous pressure on Sherburne. He now felt that his actions carried life-and-death consequences. It was one thing to risk destroying the NSA by defying the CIA; he could also be sending his friends to die in Vietnam.[39] With the Johnson administration escalating the war, the possibility was very real. The NSA, wrote Chuck Goldmark to an overseas representative, could become "a one-way ticket to Vietnam."[40]

In desperation, Sherburne turned to top political officials for help. He contacted the president, the vice president, and Senator Robert F. Kennedy.[41] Finally, the White House stepped in. Humphrey arranged a meeting with General Lewis B. Hershey, director of the Selective Service. To Sherburne's surprise, Hershey seemed affable, even sympathetic, but he told Sherburne he could not give the organization a blanket deferment—that would be "indiscreet, if not impossible."[42] But Hershey told Sherburne not to worry. "If any of your boys get into trouble with the Presidential Review [Appeal] Board, just give me a call. We'll send for their files, and just sort of er ah sit on 'em."[43]

Despite the favorable outcome, Sherburne said he felt queasy about Hershey's assurances, viewing him as "a feeble, fossilized, perhaps absent-minded old man."[44] Fortunately for Sherburne, Hershey had suggested a follow-up meeting with his special assistant, Edwin Dentz. When that visit produced similar assurances, Sherburne felt more secure. But he did not breathe easily until the Presidential Review Board met in March and ruled in favor of individual NSA student deferments. As it turned out, Hershey was not quite as feeble as Sherburne thought. The following year, when the NSA decided to support the draft resistance movement, Hershey summoned Sherburne's successor to his office for a little tête-à-tête.[45] It would also not be the last time that Sherburne sought and received assistance from the vice president.

In early January, Harry Lunn began to squeeze the NSA financially.[46] At first, he made minor reductions to previously agreed-upon grant amounts. Then the cuts escalated. He requested additional budgetary details on new proposals. Despite an earlier agreement to forgive the NSA's debt, Lunn claimed that the association owed huge sums to FYSA. In addition, Lunn informed Sherburne: "We also plan to study the extent of duplication of content and audience coverage among the various publications we support since there are some indications of overlap." The coming year's support could "change considerably."[47]

The reductions stunned Sherburne. He already viewed Lunn as "a bit of a snake," but had trusted Kiley's word on the funding.[48] Kiley acknowledges today that Lunn could be very difficult—even Kiley had to work hard at getting along with him—and that Lunn was the wrong person to be dealing with Sherburne.[49] As the cuts continued, Sherburne finally threw up his hands. He asked Kiley and Iverson to let him know, quite apart from the debt, which he considered forgiven based on Kiley's commitments, "exactly how much they were going to cut off that year's funds so that I could decide how difficult a financial position NSA was going to be in."[50]

Lunn then claimed that the NSA had a whopping $70,000 operating deficit.[51] With six months left in his term, Sherburne's options seemed limited. He scrambled. He fired staff. He canceled the summer ISRS. He whittled the deficit down to $35,000.[52]

Today, both Robbins and Sherburne believe, along with other former witting staff, that the perennial deficit run by the NSA, often encouraged by FYSA officials, was deliberate. It gave the CIA additional leverage over any officer who made trouble. When cooperation prevailed,

FYSA routinely picked up administrative or project over-expenditures. When conflict arose, FYSA cracked down, as the earlier episode with Don Smith's election attests.[53]

Sherburne decided to lay his cards on the table. The next time he met with Kiley and Iverson, he told them that he wished to sever ties with the CIA. The NSA could not be assured independence as long as any relationship to the Agency existed.[54]

Later, when everything blew up, Cord Meyer claimed that a mutually agreed upon "quiet divorce" was under way.[55] For Philip Sherburne, the divorce was neither mutual nor quiet. And the worst was yet to come. In February and March, while he was dealing simultaneously with draft deferments and budget cuts, he had to square off with the CIA over Spain and Vietnam.

A single line in a 1965 NSA funding proposal to FYSA, "support for the Spanish student underground," hints at NSA involvement with anti-Franco forces.[56] For years the Franco dictatorship had controlled the major Spanish student union. Slowly, painfully, and secretly, an alternative student organization had gained momentum. A clandestine meeting was planned for early March at the University of Barcelona. Kiley and Iverson warned Fred Berger to stay out of Spain. But Berger—with Sherburne's blessing—ignored their directive.[57]

When the rector at the University of Barcelona discovered the students' plans, he refused permission for them to assemble. The leadership changed the meeting site to the Capuchin monastery of Sarria, near Barcelona, a location that was not disclosed to most participants until an hour before the meeting.[58]

Berger and Wilfred Rutz, a Swiss student who was active in CO-SEC, reached the monastery by car from southern France. They found it packed with more than four hundred students. Berger later described the atmosphere: "Everyone seems aware that he is present at a historic occasion. Thirty prominent Spanish intellectuals were present to witness the event. Intellectuals who did not dare to come sent messages of support."[59] Rutz addressed the body in French on behalf of COSEC. When it was Berger's turn, he rose to speak.

At that moment, a delegate grabbed the microphone from Berger's hands and announced, "The police have just arrived outside and are demanding that we abandon the monastery and surrender our identification papers."[60] An eerie calm settled over the crowd as those assembled considered their options. The Spanish police were brutal. Unlike the American civil rights movement, Spain had no tradition of peaceful or nonviolent civil disobedience.

To Berger's astonishment, the delegates began singing in English "We Shall Not Be Moved," one of the songs that gave courage to American civil rights activists. Even more stunning, the Capuchins refused to let Franco's police into the monastery, the first instance of open defiance since the Spanish Civil War. The monks prepared food for nearly five hundred people, and the meeting continued. The police retaliated by cutting off the monastery's telephones and electricity. And still they met. The Capuchin bishop sent in new supplies.[61]

The standoff went on for three days. The Spanish police finally forced their way into the monastery, where they bludgeoned and arrested many students. Dozens of students were subsequently banished for three years from their universities. Professors who stood in solidarity with the students were barred from teaching for two years.[62]

The Spanish police arrested Rutz and Berger and threw them out of Spain. While Kiley scoffs at the notion, Sherburne believed then and believes today that the CIA tipped off the Spanish authorities as a way of teaching Berger a lesson. A Marxist faction had organized the clandestine meeting, which gave Sherburne further grounds for his suspicion since the NSA had previously supported Christian Democrat students.[63] Undaunted, Berger spent the next few days in Paris trying to convince the Paris CIA station and NSA representatives to take the new anti-Franco movement seriously, regardless of the Marxists in its midst. He also traveled to Leiden and made the same pitch to COSEC.[64]

Back in Washington, NSA headquarters buzzed with news of Berger's arrest. Without knowledge of the machinations behind the scene, Berger's participation appeared to be a courageous act of civil disobedience against a fascist dictator. Only Sherburne and a handful of others knew that Berger had risked the wrath of his own government to be there. Berger's arrest had a lasting effect on Sherburne; it made him wonder just how far the CIA would go.

That same month, Sherburne accepted an invitation from the State Department Vietnam Task Force to visit Vietnam. The two-week tour offered a chance to meet with Vietnamese student leaders, get a first-

hand reading on the conflict, and prepare for another contentious debate over U.S. policy at the 1966 Congress, especially after Johnson's
escalation of the war.

The U.S. troop strength had grown to 197,000. Over Christmas,
President Johnson ordered a pause in the bombing of North Vietnam
but it ended on February 1. Negotiations were nowhere in sight. This
time a demand for unconditional withdrawal might gain a majority at
the Congress. As outgoing president, Sherburne would have an influential voice in the debate. He decided to take the opportunity to see conditions at first hand.

At first Kiley seemed supportive of the trip. But as the departure date
drew near, Sherburne became aware that Kiley was agitated and did not
want him to go.[65] After Berger's experience, Sherburne felt that he defied the CIA at some peril, but remained committed to the trip.

Sherburne had asked Charles Goldmark and the nonwitting Asian
specialist Greg Delin to accompany him. A few nights before their
scheduled departure, Sherburne and Goldmark were playing a game of
ping pong in the basement of their rented house in Silver Spring, Maryland, when Goldmark told Sherburne that the CIA had approached him.
"They've asked me to be the contact point on the trip over there to kind
of help control where you go, what you see, and let them know what
[you're] trying to do." Sherburne recalls Goldmark saying, "I feel completely caught here, I don't know what to do." Sherburne made an instant
decision: "That's easy," he said. "You're not going. I'm not going to put
you in that position."[66] No doubt relieved, Goldmark told colleagues
that he was canceling his trip because of work overload.[67] Sherburne
instead invited Africa specialist Malcolm Kovacs, who he believed—
incorrectly—was nonwitting. But it turned out to be a safe choice, since
Kovacs supported what he knew of Sherburne's efforts to reduce the
Agency's influence in the NSA.[68]

Before Sherburne left for Vietnam, he realized that he had to put out
one more fire. Michael Wood was noisily raising questions about NSA
finances. He had tried to answer Wood's probing queries without violating any confidences, but Wood was not satisfied. He grew obstreperous,
attracting attention of other staff. Sherburne began to worry about what
Wood might do in his absence.[69]

Two days before Sherburne left for Vietnam, Wood issued an ultimatum: "Either I was going to function as Director of Development and

assume total responsibility for the fund raising program or he was going to have to get a new Director of Development."[70]

If Wood resigned, Sherburne knew that he would not go quietly.

Wood later testified in a closed U.S. Senate hearing, "I complained incessantly." He did not understand the disparities in fundraising between the domestic and international commissions. The national staff labored for days over a grant proposal for an educational or a civil rights project, but almost never received a positive response. By contrast, the international staff turned in short, often sloppy, proposal letters and got money overnight. Something did not make sense, and he wanted answers.[71]

Sherburne reasoned that it might be better to tell Wood the truth. He could not afford to lose him with the remaining deficit still to retire. In mid-March, before he left for Vietnam, Sherburne booked a table at the Sirloin and Saddle restaurant on Connecticut Avenue and, over a prolonged and emotional lunch, Sherburne described the role of "certain government agencies" in the NSA.[72] Wood asked whether he meant the CIA. Sherburne nodded. Wood said later that at first he was "astounded" then "pissed off."[73] He felt the CIA's involvement to be "a basic perversion of the democratic processes of the organization."[74] Sherburne stressed the confidential nature of his disclosures.[75] At the time, Sherburne felt that placing confidence in Wood was worth the risk of violating his security oath. He had thwarted a potential explosion and gained an ally. Sherburne left the restaurant feeling that Wood would redouble his efforts to raise money for the NSA.[76] He turned his attention back to Vietnam.

Wood knew so little about the CIA that he spent the weeks while Sherburne was in Asia reading everything he could get his hands on.[77] In 1966, few sources existed for the general public. Wood found a copy of *The Invisible Government*, published in 1964 by David Wise and Thomas B. Ross, which the CIA had tried unsuccessfully to keep from the public. Wood described his growing reaction as one of "horror, indignation, feelings of personally being betrayed," and a "strange curiosity to know more about how we were being used."[78]

Secrets are usually a burden to those who hold them. Before long, Wood felt the need to tell someone. He confided the secret to his best friend—in strictest confidence, of course. And just as predictably, that confidant had to tell his best friend, again in strictest confidence. Within weeks, a new web of secret holders existed, none of them subject to the security oath.

On March 20, when Sherburne boarded the first leg of his flight to Los Angeles, he felt real fear. No matter how difficult the previous months, he had never worried about his personal safety. His concern had been saving the NSA, protecting his staff from the draft, and raising non-CIA funds. With the Berger episode fresh in his mind, he tried to understand why the conflict with the Agency had grown so bitter. He respected and even liked Kiley and Iverson. Why would they oppose this trip—after all, it was sponsored by the State Department, and the CIA had people on the Vietnam task force. But if the CIA wanted to hurt him, he realized that his traveling around a war zone would offer them a perfect chance. In Los Angeles, he stayed overnight with his brother and sister-in-law. He decided that, in case he didn't return, they should know the whole story as well.[79] Thus, within a period of days, he violated his security oath for a second time.

Soon after Sherburne arrived in Saigon, he learned the reason Kiley had been agitated. The tipoff came from General Edward Lansdale's aide Charles Sweet, who confided his CIA credentials to Sherburne, told him that the International Voluntary Service was a cover, and said that cables had come from CIA headquarters warning that Sherburne was emotionally unstable and not to be trusted.[80] The Agency, Sweet told him, believed that Sherburne intended to use what he learned on the trip to lead antiwar demonstrations upon his return. Sherburne recalled seeing copies of the cables, one of which described him as brilliant. "One of the few times they ever said anything nice about me," he quips today. Sweet, he said, had dismissed the cables, saying it was stupid of the Agency to be so paranoid.[81]

Today, Sweet does not remember showing the cables to Sherburne, but he confirmed in a contemporary interview that he got "a warning to watch out," that he was dealing with a "very sensitive political group," critical of U.S. foreign policy.[82] The warnings did not square with what Sweet knew about the NSA or Sherburne. Besides, the visit had the backing of the South Vietnamese government. General Nguyen Cao Ky, the prime minister and one of Sweet's principal contacts, had personally approved the tour and made decisions about the itinerary. Sweet summarized the schedule in a pithy letter to his parents: "Leave today for Hue and the student riots; Danang and the Marines; Qui Nhon and the refugees; and Dalat and the strawberries."[83]

Sweet explained the high-level attention Sherburne's trip received as "a general feeling in the mission that if we brought NSA to see what the youth are doing in this country, they could take it home."[84] His superiors believed that the time in Vietnam had "turned [Donald] Emmerson around" to support U.S. policy. And the U.S. Operations Mission in Vietnam had identified Vietnamese students as key to the war effort. In May 1965, Sweet told his parents the mission believed the United States could "win the war in the next five months if 'those students' are under control."[85]

As a result, Sweet worked closely with the Saigon Student Union. One of Sweet's first acts after he arrived in Vietnam was to raid a U.S. military depot in order to resupply the union with desks, chairs, typewriters, and mimeograph machines. He enrolled in Buddhist University to learn more about Vietnamese culture and establish relationships with Buddhist students, the most critical of all student constituencies.[86]

Sweet also started a Summer Youth Program that engaged thousands of Vietnamese students from many of South Vietnam's provinces in building schools and low-cost housing. He drew on roughly $3 million in local currency left over from a CIA-funded rural development program. Many Vietnamese students eagerly accepted these funds, said Sweet; they knew their source but rarely discussed it.[87]

In Saigon, Sherburne, Kovacs, and Delin met with General Lansdale as well as student leaders of all persuasions—Buddhist, Catholic, and a few who favored Ho Chi Minh's National Liberation Front. Afterward, Sherburne realized that the Sweet-Lansdale team represented a "kind of separate foreign policy," often at odds with others in the U.S. government.[88] He was enthusiastic about Sweet's programs, liking the philosophy of self-help that guided them. Sweet in turn recalled Sherburne as "really impressive."[89] Even today, he remembers the NSA delegation favorably as "trying to get good information, like newspaper reporters, to put together an objective picture."[90] As a result, Sweet concluded that the CIA warnings about the NSA president were misguided.[91]

Upon their return to the United States, Sherburne, Kovacs, and Delin prepared "A Report to the Constituency," which supports Sweet's memory. It factually describes what the trio found: widespread anti-

Americanism, fear that Vietnamese culture and values were being destroyed, and a simultaneous reluctance to see the Americans pull out. The delegation reported little support among Vietnamese students for the National Liberation Front or the Viet Cong.[92]

Sherburne distributed the report widely. This time there were no numbered copies, no tiered secrecy classifications, and no personality profiles of student leaders. He sent the same report that he sent to student government members to Vice President Humphrey. He sent it to Vietnamese student leaders. He invited readers in both countries to comment on its accuracy.[93]

The report's dispassionate language concealed the despair Sherburne felt after the trip, especially at the contrast between the bombing raids and Sweet's more humane approach. One image haunted him. The delegation had flown out of Hue in a military helicopter so laden it could barely lift off the ground. American officials desperate to leave clamored for a ride. The pilot literally placed his foot on the chest of a CIA man and pushed him to the ground before taking off. As a high wall loomed directly in front of them, Sherburne thought, "This is it."[94] While the risky take-off had nothing to do with Sherburne's politics or his confrontation with the CIA, the scene added to his sense of the horror unfolding in Vietnam.

But Sherburne's politics were liberal, not leftist. He did not favor either immediate or unilateral withdrawal. Early in his term, he told a Stanford friend that he was not "too concerned with providing an alternative to the Left on the college campuses, but only opening up all of those campuses to a reasoned and intelligent discussion about both the war in Vietnam, and the larger issues facing our entire policy in Vietnam."[95] He worried more about the civil liberty implications of those who charged that antiwar protests "sow[ed] the seeds of treason" or were instigated by the Communist Party.[96] Sherburne protested such charges in an open letter to Attorney General Nicholas Katzenbach, published in the *New York Times*.[97]

If the teach-ins first held in the spring of 1965 made administration officials angry, antiwar demonstrations drove them crazy. A view developed in the highest reaches of the White House, State Department, and the FBI that the antiwar movement could not possibly be homegrown; it therefore must be financed by foreign powers. When in December 1965 SDS activist Tom Hayden, Yale professor Staughton Lynd, and Marxist scholar and Communist Party member Herbert Aptheker traveled to Hanoi to further peace negotiations, the administration's conspiracy theory of external influences at work seemed confirmed.[98]

Seen in this context, CIA headquarters had reason to fear Sherburne if he decided to lead a campus-based antiwar movement. Sherburne would have been more dangerous than Hayden, whom policy makers could, and later did, dismiss as radical, unrepresentative, even treasonous. Sherburne could appeal to middle-American students and a broad constituency. His style was rational, calm, and cerebral, not emotional or ideological. His rhetoric—to the extent he used any—ran toward the Jeffersonian and never included references to Fidel Castro, Che Guevara, or the two leading theoreticians of revolution, Régis Debray and Frantz Fanon.[99] It is ironic that the idea of leading an antiwar movement never entered Sherburne's head. In fact, in June, as he contemplated accepting his twice deferred Harvard Law School scholarship, he wrote a long letter to Sweet in Saigon, asking if there might be a place for him in community development work, although he ultimately decided in favor of law school.[100]

After he returned from Vietnam, Sherburne tackled the question of his successor. He identified a University of Chicago graduate, Eugene (Gene) Groves, then on a Rhodes Scholarship to Oxford, as someone whose politics suggested he would help get the CIA out of the NSA. Groves, a member of the Student Peace Union, hewed left and opposed the war, but was not a firebrand. In May, Sherburne flew to London to see him, going and returning on the same day, "one of the craziest things I've ever done."[101] He did not tell Groves about the CIA dilemma. Groves seemed interested in running for president but noncommittal.

By July, with just two months left in his term, Sherburne had decided that he had developed a strong enough relationship with Vice President Humphrey to approach him about the NSA-CIA problem. He reasoned that the vice president was, in effect, the U.S. government, and that technically he would not be violating his security oath in confiding in him. His earlier violations haunted him, even though he thought each case warranted. He wrote to ask Humphrey for an appointment.[102]

When Sherburne signed in at the White House security gate, he believed that he had succeeded against all odds in freeing the NSA from the CIA. He took pride in his achievement. The NSA staff had not been drafted. The deficit had been cut. Clean money had been raised. He believed that he would have the support of the vice president of the United States.[103]

Humphrey's long-time aide Ted Van Dyke attended the meeting. He listened as Sherburne summarized the CIA's involvement with the NSA and his strategy for becoming financially independent, and asked for the vice president's assistance. Van Dyke remembers Humphrey catching his eye, visibly stunned, and is convinced that Humphrey had no previous knowledge of the CIA connection.[104] The vice president had little access to major decision making in intelligence. He did not attend the weekly top-secret 303 Committee meetings of the National Security Council, which, in theory, approved all new covert projects. In fact, the previous year, Humphrey had tried to get President Johnson to exercise more oversight of the CIA. Johnson bluntly informed Humphrey, "My presidential foreign intelligence advisory board is already doing it."[105] Humphrey told Sherburne that he was sympathetic but his hands were tied.[106]

What Humphrey could do, he told Sherburne, was assist the NSA with fundraising. The vice president offered to write his wealthy supporters and ask them to make a donation. In the quid-pro-quo atmosphere of political fundraising, Humphrey believed that his appeal would work. Sherburne said later, "I went out of there feeling very good. I thought Humphrey was really going to help."[107]

One by one, Humphrey's long-time political donors and corporate friends declined to support the NSA. "It was unprecedented," says Van Dyke today. Top donors did not spurn a request from a sitting vice president. Van Dyke became convinced that someone was talking to them after Humphrey did and asking them to change their minds, perhaps a secretary or some other aide. Years later, Van Dyke had other encounters with the CIA, episodes that left him more convinced than ever that the Agency had interfered with Humphrey's request.[108]

Soon after the meeting, Cord Meyer descended on Humphrey, irate. Since Meyer knew everything about what was going on, from Sherburne's visit to his strategy for independence, Van Dyke concluded that Meyer was tapping Sherburne's phone.[109] But in a chilling coda to the episode, Kiley today claims that Humphrey picked up the phone "three minutes after Sherburne left," and called him at CIA headquarters. "I knew everything that Sherburne was saying to Hubert Humphrey," boasts Kiley. He explained that his closeness to the vice president dated back to the days when Humphrey was mayor of Minneapolis, Kiley's hometown. And he says defiantly about that particular phone call, "There are aspects . . . I will not tell you today."[110]

Unaware that the CIA knew of his meeting with Humphrey, Sherburne remained optimistic about receiving new funds. He also got the good news that Eugene Groves would run for NSA president. Still concerned about his security oath violations, Sherburne said nothing to Groves, and Groves made his decision to run unaware of the CIA's involvement or the hope that Sherburne attached to his candidacy.[111]

In late summer, someone in the new chain of confidences created as a result of Sherburne's conversation with Wood decided to reveal the secret to Edward Schwartz, an intense and able orator from Oberlin College who planned to run for NSA national vice president at the upcoming Congress. According to Schwartz, one night while sitting in a car outside the NSA offices chewing over election strategy, his friend Roland Liebert began hinting that there was something Schwartz didn't know about the NSA. Finally, Schwartz exploded: either stop hinting or tell me. Liebert told him what he'd learned. Schwartz agreed to keep the information secret; as he said later, "I didn't really care about international stuff."[112]

At the eleventh hour, just before balloting for officers began, Schwartz broke his promise and told Groves.[113] Groves, who had just learned about the CIA connection a few days earlier from Sherburne, was conflicted, since he had already declared his candidacy. He vacillated; he didn't want to be "in the middle of such an ugly thing—I felt betrayed, and I didn't want to betray my friends by my own actions," he said later.[114] More philosopher than activist, he thought perhaps he should return to Oxford and "contemplate the meaning of 'ought.'"[115] Ultimately, he decided to run and help the NSA make a final break with the CIA.[116]

After the Congress, Sherburne left for Harvard Law School, unaware that Michael Wood's indiscretion had led to a new web of people who knew about the CIA and were not covered by security oaths.[117] Wood readied himself for a second year of fundraising, not knowing that his confidences had been betrayed or that they had been passed on to others. He believed, as Sherburne did, that together they had accomplished something unprecedented, freeing the NSA from its reliance on CIA funds. But he watched carefully for evidence to the contrary. And he found it.

22

THE GAME WITHIN THE GAME

DURING PHILIP SHERBURNE'S presidential term, NSA headquarters staff paid little attention to the upcoming International Student Conference, scheduled for August 17–27, 1966, in Nairobi, Kenya, whose dates overlapped those of the NSA Congress, August 21–September 1. As outgoing president, Sherburne had to be in Champaign-Urbana, the site of the Congress, and could not be a member of the NSA delegation. After his year-long battle with the CIA, he believed that the timing was deliberate, to keep him from gaining access to ISC delegates or otherwise causing trouble. What Sherburne did not know was that the image presented by Kiley of the ISC as an important pro-West organization that championed democracy did not match its current reality as a hotbed of radical politics. As the ISC had continued to grow more militant and unpredictable, coping with its political complexity led to new levels of deception among witting staff and CIA case officers. Nonetheless, though the ISC and COSEC had become of secondary importance to the CIA, the Agency, still its primary funder, strove to maintain as much control as possible, especially within COSEC, since the secretariat oversaw the day-to-day programs that often provided cover for individual projects.

Earlier in the spring, as part of his attempt to get the NSA out of the role of a conduit for FYSA funds, Sherburne had told Kiley that the association would no longer funnel funds to COSEC for third-party projects; the only money coming through FYSA from the NSA would be the annual dues. Kiley retorted that the decision was not Sherburne's to make. Thinking back over the absurdity of Kiley's statement today, the former NSA president quipped, "Whose decision was it? The NSA Congress?" Sherburne also had expressed his doubts to Kiley about the value of the ISC. "My own feeling was that if the ISC went away, it was not going to be any big loss. IUS was still there primarily because we were, I mean, the ISC was there, and that they both would just wither away." Kiley began sending old hands to convince Sherburne otherwise.[1]

At this point, Kiley must be seen as playing good soldier, since he is emphatic that after the 1962 ISC in Quebec, he had concluded that the ISC "doesn't work; it's dumb," and made the case to his CIA superiors for its termination. Why did they reject his advice? He speculates, "There was a kind of vested interest that had been built over time that was very hard to break." But he also acknowledges the country-to-country relationships built through COSEC programs had become a justification for reaching foreign students, even if "it wasn't a very efficient way."[2] That attitude could explain Kiley's strong reaction to Sherburne's refusal to serve as a conduit for routing these project funds. Of course Kiley would never have confided in Sherburne the crucial distinction between an out-of-control ISC, and a COSEC that still served U.S. interests through its myriad tours, seminars, and other projects.

Ironically, a few months earlier, at CIA headquarters, officials had requested that Edward Garvey seek the top position in COSEC, telling him that the ISC would soon be terminated. In April 1965, Secretary General Gwyn Morgan of Great Britain had resigned, leaving COSEC leaderless. A reluctant Garvey, then working at Langley, agreed to apply, mainly because the term would be short. (Witting students often remained with the NSA-CIA operation for five years and spent one of those years at CIA headquarters.) Today he is unsure whether his CIA superiors lied to him. "I have no clue whether [what they said was] true; there is no way to differentiate truth from fiction." Looking back, Garvey explained that an atmosphere of such intrigue prevailed inside the CIA that "you never knew the game within the game within the game."[3]

While the command to Garvey to run may have made sense to his superiors, incredulity over his candidacy prompted Jyoti Shankar Singh, one of the Americans' closest allies, to tell Garvey to his face that he was making a mistake.[4] Singh had ably run COSEC from 1962 to 1964 and was then directing the CIA-funded World Assembly of Youth. The incumbent Asian associate secretary at COSEC, Ram Labhaya Lakhina, also from India, went farther and declared his candidacy against Garvey. Lakhina, a graduate of the Foreign Student Leadership Project, had

been a one-time favorite of the NSA. But about this time, and for reasons that are not clear, the NSA's witting staff turned against him. Some
say he was too pro-Palestinian. Others disparage him as too compliant
and pro-British. Lakhina insists that he opposed Garvey "on principle,"
and spoke for those who felt that the United States already had "excessive influence."[5]

Garvey muscled his way to victory. He explained away his two-year
absence from involvement in either the ISC or COSEC by telling colleagues he had been in the army.[6] When Lakhina realized that Garvey
had the votes, he withdrew his application. But the Garvey-Lakhina
contest turned the secretariat into a virtual armed camp, divided between two strong but discordant personalities and exacerbated by policy
differences. Each suspected the other of using the travel budget to line
up votes for a future contest. The conflict would erupt into open warfare at the 1966 ISC in Nairobi.

If the CIA had needed further evidence that the time had come to
terminate the ISC, the Nairobi meeting provided it. *Hair-raising* was
the word Charles Goldmark chose to described it. "A *disaster*," said a
Swiss student leader friendly to the NSA.[7] No matter which geographical region the delegates came from, no matter how current or sophisticated NSA intelligence might be on individual delegations, the Americans went to Africa with few allies and a truckload of troublesome issues.

By 1966, most Latin American student unions had joined the IUS.
Membership in the ISC had dwindled to four Latin American countries:
Paraguay, Costa Rica, Chile, and Mexico.[8] President Johnson's policy of
"no more Cubas" had resulted in a wave of U.S.-backed military coups in
Central and South America that further angered the hemisphere's students. The 1965 U.S. military intervention in the Dominican Republic
made militants out of moderates and anti-Americans out of all of them.
The year before, several students had died in a protest over U.S. ownership in the Panama Canal Zone. The NSA dithered for over a week before issuing a terse press release, "Mourn deeply deaths of Panamanian
students," which served to increase the fury of the Latin Americans.[9]

Before the Nairobi meeting, Fred Berger warned Garvey, "Today
NSA is hardly known to the leaders of the Latin American student movement, and most of them would assume in any case that NSA is an arm
of the aggressors and imperialists, our protestation to the contrary."[10]
Berger could not think of more than two Latin American countries that

might consider ISC membership, Bolivia and Honduras. He put another twelve "firmly in the Marxist radical camp." Echoing comments made today by Kiley, Berger concluded that national unions of students were not a "stable building block" to build pro-West sentiment.[11]

Berger also warned Garvey to expect hostility from formerly friendly unions. Costa Rican leaders, previously reliable allies, had turned against the NSA. "They opposed you for Secretary General only because you were an American, but now they oppose you also on the grounds that you are dishonest and betray the ISC's best friends."[12] In fact, the charges of double-dealing were mostly true.

The situation was bad not simply on the Latin American front. Virtually all NSA-CIA strategies to win influence in the Middle East had failed. The dalliance with the Ba'ath parties in Iraq and Syria blew up six months after the coup in Iraq. Hard-line Ba'athists staged a second coup, after which they declared the National Union of Iraqi Students illegal. Within the year, NUIS officers closest to the Americans had been arrested and imprisoned.[13] In 1964, only two Middle Eastern unions in addition to Israel's received funding for the ISC in Christchurch: NUIS chapters in exile (London and Beirut) and the Lebanese union.[14] Not long before the Christchurch ISC, Lebanon had opted for membership in both the ISC and the IUS, "to express a neutral East-West policy."[15]

In the early 1960s, when the CIA was searching for a way to offset Nasser's influence in the region, it encouraged the NSA to support the Palestinian cause since it was galvanizing Arabs across national boundaries. An initial assessment by Paris-based William Lee, a Dartmouth graduate and newcomer to the NSA, concluded that an alliance with the Palestinians could "counter some of the IUS push in Cairo and the Middle East."[16]

Lee's report cast the leadership of the General Union of Palestinian Students (GUPS) in a favorable, if condescending, light. He found them to be "exceptionally rational, moderate, and informed about the student movement by Arab standards."[17] But international staff also knew that the ISC could not survive a debate over Palestine. The Israelis viewed GUPS as an illegitimate student union, more akin to a paramilitary group, dedicated to the destruction of Israel. Lee passed on advice from Kiley to NSA headquarters: "Kiley feels COSEC initiatives are fairly limited in possibility and that NSA must try and move in."[18]

The decision to develop a relationship with the Palestinians courted disaster abroad and conflict at home. Initial strategies followed conventional patterns. Lee recommended "organizing a section of GUPS in the United States" and informed the NSA that he "had already discussed this possibility with GUPS General Secretary Lutuf Ghantous."[19] He suggested the usual "trip to the United States" and "a little publicity on the Palestinian student situation" to solidify the relationship with Ghantous.[20] Lee also had recommended that the NSA establish a special scholarship program, as it had done for Algerian and Angolan students.[21]

In 1962, the NSA made a financial contribution to a work-camp project in Gaza, cabling the GUPS leader Hassan Hammam that the grant was "a symbol of solidarity with Palestine students."[22] As contact with the GUPS increased, Tony Smith, the CIA career officer on duty as one of three NSA representatives in Paris, almost touched off an international incident. Not long after the Cuban Missile Crisis of October 1962, the GUPS congress met in Gaza. Smith presented himself as a former Air Force veteran (to explain his lack of student status) and spoke about the crisis. He distinguished between offensive and defensive missiles, and condemned the Cuban missiles as offensive. Suddenly someone in the back of the room whom Smith could not see under the glare of klieg lights shouted, "I don't think you are who you say you are. I think you work for the CIA."[23]

Smith froze. And turned red. He prayed that the color in his face was not obvious to the delegates below the high stage. "I tried to protest but not too much," he says today. Years later, as the episode lost its sting, Smith played with the idea about writing a humorous essay "on blushing and espionage."[24] At the time, the unexpected and startling challenge underscored how careful he needed to be. He was treading on dangerous ground for other reasons: Smith's grandfather Judge Joseph M. Proskauer was a former head of the American Jewish Committee and deeply involved in the creation of Israel.[25] Smith had had unprecedented access to Israeli officials; he had met David Ben Gurion, the first prime minister, and other members of the founding generation as a child.[26]

Even without knowledge of Smith's CIA or Israeli ties, the Palestinians had reason to be suspicious of the Americans. The GUPS was a complicated organization, comprised of refugee students scattered across Middle Eastern and North African countries. Numerous political tendencies coalesced within it, from Ba'athists to Nasserists to Arab nationalists and independents.[27] But the GUPS also exercised significant clout in the region. The new Palestine Liberation Organization headed by Yasser Arafat funded the GUPS, although the union tried to preserve its autonomy by demanding agreed-upon objectives in writing.[28]

For the NSA, support for the GUPS was tricky not only because it created tension with the Israeli student union but also because the Palestinians received almost no assistance, even in the form of moral support, from European ISC members. In late March 1965, the NSA was one of two ISC delegations that attended a GUPS international seminar in Cairo whose purpose was to generate publicity for the Palestinian cause.[29] Paris-based Robert Witherspoon had carefully briefed an Israeli representative before the meeting and assured him that the NSA would not support any anti-Israel resolutions.[30] During the meeting in Cairo, his colleague Robert Backoff honored Witherspoon's promises. But international vice president Norman Uphoff, making one of his few overseas trips, made off-the-cuff remarks at the GUPS seminar that infuriated the Israelis: the NSA, he assured them, "resisted taking a pro-Zionist position on Israel."[31] For months afterward, the NSA deflected inquires about the speech and claimed not to have a copy of Uphoff's remarks, which had appeared in the Arab press.[32]

Uphoff's speech became a cause célèbre for Israeli student leaders.[33] Knowing how much trouble the speech could cause NSA domestically, the Israeli students played their hand craftily, periodically threatening to circulate press coverage of Uphoff's remarks.[34] In the summer of 1965, when the NSA invited Arab students to come to the United States for a special seminar, the Israeli student union did contact the American Jewish Committee, whose leaders began to pay closer attention to the association.[35]

Until then, and despite regular denials of bias, NSA policies were blatantly pro-Arab. Witherspoon articulated the rationale in a confidential memo: the association needed "to take a moderately pro-Arab position on the Palestine issue" if only to "compensate for ISC shortcomings."[36] In a later memo he argued that the GUPS seminar had "laid bare the scarcity of support or even interest in the Arab case on the part of Western student unions."[37] After the seminar, despite the controversy over Uphoff's remarks, the NSA decided it needed a strong resolution on Palestine, even if it precipitated a battle at the Congress. The fight would occur over the phrase "Palestinian people" since it involved the right of refugees to return to their homeland, something the Israelis would challenge at all costs.[38] Witherspoon is blunt in his guidance: the NSA should try to support the words "Palestinian people," as a "sop to the Arabs," unless Israeli pressure forced a compromise.[39]

In the summer of 1965, the NSA undertook elaborate preparations to guarantee a successful Palestinian resolution. The CIA funded a special seminar for Arab students. Afterward, the seminar's hand-picked participants were invited to the NSA Congress to mingle with the delegates.[40] With Middle East seminar participants in tow, the NSA witting staff managed a nearly impossible feat at the 1965 Congress: they crafted a resolution that delighted the Arabs, especially the Palestinians, and assuaged (barely) the Israelis, though not without considerable conflict, drama, and a threatened walkout by the Israelis.[41]

Over the next year, a policy shift in the Johnson administration, along with scrutiny by the American Jewish Committee, prompted the NSA to fashion a more balanced position. Staff began to describe the NSA role as that of a broker and peacemaker of the Israeli-Palestinian conflict. "Our task," Backoff amended, "is to keep the big powers from war there and find a peaceful solution."[42]

Charles Goldmark welcomed the policy change. "It is healthier for NSA to play a completely independent role in the Middle East rather than cottoning to the Arabs at every turn."[43] The international vice president also told Witherspoon in Paris, "We have dumped on the Israelis long enough and although we should not go overboard in that direction, some gesture to demonstrate our good faith is needed."[44] An opportunity presented itself in the spring of 1966, when the Israelis invited an NSA delegation for a visit, all expenses paid.[45]

By the time of the Nairobi ISC in August 1966, the GUPS was so fractured that the NSA speculated its leaders might not come. Nonetheless, the NSA believed that other delegations would take up the Palestinian cause. The collision course within the ISC that the NSA had hoped for so many years to avoid seemed inevitable, but it was one that the NSA itself had charted.

If NSA allies in Latin America and the Middle East were limited in number, witting staff could still count on a significant showing by Asian student unions friendly to the NSA.[46] Ever since the 1956 regional seminar in Colombo, the CIA had funded an annual Asian seminar, and a meeting for Asian student press, and in 1965 the Agency had established an Asian Press Bureau. The escalating war in Vietnam was now threatening to shake up the region's solidarity, but not in a way the NSA desired.

Several other ingredients contributed to the volatile mix of delegations heading toward Nairobi. In a gesture of goodwill, COSEC had invited the student unions that walked out of the Quebec meeting in 1962. COSEC had also invited the IUS to send a delegation. While the latter was standard practice, cooperative host governments had usually found a way to deny the visas of the IUS members. The Kenyan government appears not to have played along, since numerous IUS members reached Nairobi.[47]

On August 17, seventy-one delegations streamed into Nairobi University College for the ten-day conference. As expected, Europe and Africa produced the largest number of national unions of students, seventeen and thirteen, respectively. No one from Algeria, Morocco, or Tunisia attended. Two rival Angolan revolutionary groups sent representatives: Jorge Sangumba was aligned with Jonas Savimbi, who had broken away from Holden Roberto, and Carlos Octavio (Belli) Belo represented the Soviet-backed MPLA. Israel and four other Middle Eastern unions attended, but two were aligned with the IUS.[48] Khosrow Shakeri from the Confederation of Iranian Students in Paris was openly anti-American. Lebanon's representative came from the U.S.-based Organization of Arab Students. Only Kuwait's union could be counted a friend of the West.

The NSA delegation arrived early and included Duncan Kennedy (Paris), Thomas Olson (COSEC), Chuck Goldmark (NSA), Fred Berger (NSA), and an eleventh-hour addition—John Gerhart, a Harvard graduate then in Kampala, Uganda. NSA overseas representatives had had their eye on Gerhart for nearly a year, and decided to see how he performed at a large meeting.[49] Goldmark had given him instructions to meet and talk with Africans as soon as he reached Nairobi but to "steer the conversation away from internal ISC politics."[50] The reason soon became clear.

By tradition, the Supervision Commission would choose the new COSEC leadership before presenting the candidates for approval at the annual conference. Candidates who were not selected would usually gracefully withdraw before the final vote, thus allowing COSEC to present a united front to the ISC delegates. Not this time.

Garvey later tried to describe what turned out to be the nastiest and most convoluted election in COSEC history. "All of the student unions on the left were trying to get me to run [for reelection] against Ram [Labhaya Lakhina] because they saw him as a very conservative alternative."[51] Garvey realizes today that it is hard to believe that the left would support an American over an Indian, but he insists that this was the case. Garvey, eager to return to law school, declined to run again. Instead he caucused with European activists from France and Belgium and backed Wilfred Rutz from Switzerland. In Garvey's view, Rutz, who was present at the siege of the Capuchin monastery with Berger, was the radical. Complicating the issue was the question of CIA support. Garvey describes CIA insiders as furious with his decision to support Rutz.[52]

Despite the backstage politicking, the now eleven-member Supervision Commission voted in favor of Lakhina. Today Lakhina boasts that he was the first secretary general to represent "the Third World," a claim Garvey dismisses as ludicrous: Jyoti Shankar Singh, he insists, was "an incredibly effective voice from the Third World."[53] Lakhina also claims to be the first ISC secretary general candidate to win "without American support."[54] Again Garvey scoffs: "That's the conceit. Who were 'the Americans' in this situation? Just because he didn't have my support didn't mean he didn't have the support of . . ."[55] He did not complete the sentence. Tom Olson, then an experienced witting team member whose next position after Nairobi would be at FYSA with Harry Lunn, fills in Garvey's statement: Lakhina had the support of the CIA.[56]

Yet Duncan Kennedy, whose next assignment would be at CIA headquarters, recalls taking a perverse delight in Lakhina's victory precisely because Kennedy thought it was a *loss* for the Americans: "I took a ma-li-cious pleasure in it, mal-li-cious pleasure."[57] He explains his rebellion. "It was here," in Nairobi, the future Harvard theorist of critical legal studies recalls, that "I began to ask myself whether I might be on the wrong side of history." His doubts must be seen as indicating the continued fraying of the tattered liberal consensus.[58] Ronald J. J. Bell from Scotland, a Lakhina supporter, later summed up the antics of the NSA delegation: it exhibited "signs of anarchy."[59]

To top it off, when Lakhina's victory over Rutz was announced, most delegates saw it as a victory for the British and stood up to sing "God Save the Queen." Fernando Duran from Costa Rica, who was among the singers, notes today that it was obvious to him that the battle was between the imperialists, and the British had won.[60]

Such was the atmosphere in Nairobi when the IUS secretary general, Nouri Abdul Razzak Hussain, an Iraqi who was considered pro-Soviet by the Americans and who had fled Iraq at the time of the CIA-backed anti-Kassem coup in 1961, was granted permission to address the delegates.[61] The IUS chief emphasized many of the same themes Garvey had in his opening speech, especially the need to seek world student unity, with its implication that the IUS and the ISC should merge, and then he fielded questions. A few NSA allies raised issues stemming back to 1948, when the IUS had failed to condemn the Czech coup, but Hussain fielded them deftly. At the end of the session, delegates gave Hussain a standing ovation and then voted to cooperate with the IUS—a complete repudiation of the long-standing NSA and ISC position—and the clearest statement yet that the Cold War between the two student internationals was over.[62] A South African delegate later praised the "end to Cold War claptrap."[63]

The general secretary of the Palestinian GUPS had managed to get to Nairobi for the conference, and received a boisterous welcome and a favorable vote on the controversial refugee question. Predictably, the Israelis walked out. The fact that the bill for all this disaffection was being footed by the CIA adds to its surreal quality today.

The NSA still had to face a debate over Vietnam. The CIA tried to reprise a successful strategy developed for the 1965 NSA Congress, but the results bordered on farce. The centerpiece was to be a direct appeal from South Vietnamese students. In Saigon, General Lansdale and Charles Sweet had obtained the requisite clearances from the Vietnam government for a delegation, but infighting in the Saigon Students Union over who should go became so intense that the delegation arrived five days late and nearly missed the debate. (When they arrived, the delegation was misidentified as members of the National Liberation Front for South Vietnam, an identification with the Viet Cong that delegation member and Buddhist leader Nguyan Kim Khanh believed was deliberate.)[64] When delegate Nguyen Tan Thiet spoke, in barely decipherable English, even his colleagues agreed that he did not help the cause.[65]

It probably did not matter what Thiet argued on the floor. Most of the delegates, regardless of political ideology or partisan affiliation, opposed the U.S. presence in Vietnam. Costa Rica's Fernando Duran, although a noncommunist Social Democrat, said in an interview, "I will tell you bluntly we were sympathetic to the Viet Cong."[66] If the United States had lost the support of long-time friend Costa Rica, it had lost the war for public opinion inside the conference.

But it was the French who brought the proceedings to a standstill by suggesting the delegates send a telegram to President Johnson and demand that he "withdraw American soldiers from Vietnam."[67] It was one thing to pass resolutions highly critical of United States foreign policy; the CIA had learned to live with a certain amount of anti-Americanism because it enhanced the ISC image as an independent body. It was quite another thing for a CIA-funded organization to directly challenge the U.S. president on foreign policy.

Kiley says today that after Nairobi he knew it was "all over."[68] While there is no reason to doubt his exasperation, his actions after the ISC do not conform with this view. The now biennial International Student Conferences might be painful, but COSEC programs were still in place, and within these it was business as usual. Goldmark, who eked out one of the few NSA victories at Nairobi when he won election as an associate secretary to COSEC, made this explicit in his post-Nairobi report. "Political resolutions set the tone and spirit of the ISC, but bear little relationship to its normal day-to-day activities." In Nairobi, he continued, "most of the Association's suggestions for ISC programs were accepted . . . and perhaps most importantly, the Association's representatives were able to conduct a number of highly successful bilateral discussions on programs with other national unions."[69]

Kiley seems to have bided his time, waiting for Sherburne to leave. In mid-September, Kiley set up a meeting with the new NSA president, Eugene Groves. Over several meetings, as Groves later testified in a closed hearing, Kiley and Matt Iverson painted "a fairly congenial picture" of the past NSA-CIA relationship. Their report astonished Groves, who by then had conferred with Sherburne and had a different perspective on what was going on. Yet when Groves indicated his hesitation about continuing the relationship, he said that Kiley argued that a rupture between the NSA and the CIA "would destroy a lot of what they considered very good institutions."[70]

Never having attended an ISC, Groves was unable to assess Kiley and Iverson's report. Nor did he have access to a transcript from Nairobi. He needed time to think. "I postponed any sort of judgment in the hope of getting more details and fuller knowledge of exactly the extent of the relationship, of how valuable such institutions as the International Student

Conferences were, and how this relationship would develop."[71] Besides, he later admitted, "there was no point in antagonizing the CIA before I know how to fight them."[72]

By nature, Groves tended to weigh all sides of an issue. Trained in mathematics, he approached situations in a calm, reasoned manner. During the 1966 NSA Congress he had responded to an emotional frenzy on the plenary floor over the free speech movement with the unpopular argument that "college administrations had received the message and were opening doors to discussion of grievances without waiting for riots."[73]

At the same time, Groves's position on Vietnam and other issues hewed to the left. Like Uphoff, Groves belonged to the Student Peace Union. Unlike Uphoff, Groves did not have the socialist's animosity toward communism. Over the next few weeks, Kiley kept up the pressure on Groves to continue the CIA relationship. He resisted. Kiley pushed.

Groves later described the escalation of tension. "Some of the agents . . . frantically accused me of undermining all the free world institutions that had been so painstakingly created over the last 15 years."[74] He considered going public, but wondered who would believe him. "I would have been totally ineffective without a much more extensive personal knowledge of the relationship and a casebook of collaborating evidence."[75]

Groves, responsible for a staff of nearly fifty people, began to experience the isolation that had plagued Robbins and Sherburne. "I've never felt so alone in my life," he said later.[76] But he also had to make decisions. The NSA president officially appointed overseas representatives, even if he didn't recruit the majority of them. Sherburne had left these positions vacant when his year as president was over to help Groves gain more control over the appointments. The international staff at NSA headquarters understood that directives were to come from Groves, but few were forthcoming.[77]

Moreover, Groves faced financial problems. Despite Sherburne's budget-cutting measures and his belief that the deficit had been retired, Lunn informed Groves that the NSA still owed another $20,000 to make up its deficit to FYSA. In addition, Lunn told Groves that the accumulated debt stood at $375,585. Regardless of whether the debt actually existed, new officers did not have the information necessary to challenge the figure.[78]

At first, Groves had been reluctant to involve the new international vice president, Richard (Rick) Stearns. Someone had warned him that Stearns was "not really reliable, and might like to play the game."[79] Stearns's trajectory from the 1964 ISRS to overseas representative in Beirut to his election suggested to Groves that he might already be part of the NSA-CIA team. Stearns insisted during an interview that he had not been but emphasized that he was a committed Cold Warrior: "Fighting communism was something I believed in very strongly."[80]

After a few weeks of working together, Groves warmed to Stearns and decided to trust him.[81] Since Groves, like others, had a healthy respect for the twenty-year prison term attached to security oath violations, he decided not to approach Stearns directly. He asked Kiley to handle it, and the three of them met at Kiley's home in Georgetown, when the oath was administered and the secret revealed. Stearns reacted as many others had: sharing information with your own government was one thing. He didn't object to that. But the covert funding was quite another, especially "the extent to which we were the captive financially of this network of foundations."[82]

When they left Kiley's house, Stearns and Groves walked the mile or so from Georgetown to the NSA office. Stearns remembers telling Groves: "We've got to find a way out."[83] He did not have moral objections to the CIA as such, but he felt strongly that the NSA should represent students' interests, "and not the interests of the United States government directly."[84]

Like Sherburne, Groves and Stearns had lukewarm feelings about the ISC and COSEC, at least what little they knew of them. The methodical Groves proposed an evaluation to assess the organizations' strengths and weaknesses. That way, he and Stearns could reach a conclusion in an objective manner. Kiley nixed the idea.[85]

Pressure on the new officers also came from Goldmark, who had settled into his COSEC position in Leiden. Freed from his conflicting loyalties to Sherburne, Goldmark urged Groves to consider the CIA as "any other funding source." After all, Groves recalled him saying, "It's easier to get it from them than from the Ford Foundation."[86]

After weeks of sustained pressure, the two NSA officers began to relent. Faced with a looming budget crisis to pay for international commission staff and programs, and increasingly fearful they might destroy an international organization they knew little about, they conceded, as Groves put it later.[87]

After Kiley assured them that new funds would come without strings, Groves and Stearns accepted a FYSA grant for $56,000 (technically, two separate awards of $28,000).[88] Privately they dubbed it a "kiss-off" grant, the last they would ever accept from a CIA conduit.[89] But having been schooled by Sherburne, Groves spelled out the terms on which he would take the money. He demanded that the CIA reporting require-ments cease—no more profiling of foreign students or foreign student unions, no more contact with CIA case officers or career staff. All over-seas representatives must report to him and Stearns. Kiley appeared to consent.[90]

Neither Groves nor Stearns shared the decision to take CIA funds with Sherburne—an omission that later had major consequences for them all. They did tell Edward Schwartz, who was furious. But Schwartz's focus remained on American campuses, which were exploding in protest over the war. He agreed to remain quiet. In exchange, Schwartz says he ex-tracted a promise: neither Groves or Stearns nor the CIA must interfere with his campus activities.[91] The two officers readily agreed to some-thing over which they had little control, although by tradition the CIA rarely interfered with national staff.

With these negotiations complete, Groves and Stearns thought their secret was safe and tried to restore some semblance of normalcy at NSA headquarters. They never dreamed that a grant from the association's oldest funding source would mean anything in particular to Michael Wood.

HIDE-AND-SEEK

WHEN THE CHECK from the Foundation for Youth and Student Affairs arrived at the NSA office, Michael Wood drew the only conclusion that made sense to him: the Central Intelligence Agency had weaseled its way back inside the association. Unaware of the officers' intention of making this the final CIA grant, Wood concluded that Sherburne's work had been in vain. Six months earlier, he and Sherburne had sparred over this point: Wood felt the only way to get the CIA out of the NSA was to go public.[1] Sherburne said no. Now Wood felt that publicity was his only option. The question was, how to do it?

Unaware of Wood's dilemma, Gene Groves and Rick Stearns grew increasingly irritated at his behavior. Wood got into fights with other staff members. He spent an inordinate amount of time working—or so they thought—outside the office on the campaign to lower the voting age to eighteen. Stearns later said that they feared his activities might jeopardize the NSA's nonprofit tax-exempt status.[2] Ed Schwartz said simply, "He was a pain in the ass."[3] The three officers made a decision: they fired Wood.

But Wood did not leave the NSA empty-handed. Once he had made the decision to go public with what he knew about the CIA, he had begun ferrying out caches of documents, financial and otherwise. He then assessed a number of news outlets, and finally decided to approach *Ramparts*, a small San Francisco–based magazine that had been founded by Edward Keating, a liberal Catholic, but had become more radical, especially on Vietnam.[4] The February 1966 issue, for example, had featured an article by Donald Duncan, a former Green Beret who fought in Vietnam, in which the U.S. presence in Vietnam was compared to the Soviet invasion of Hungary. Duncan warned, "We aren't the free-dom fighters. We are the Russian tanks blasting the hopes of an Asian Hungary."[5]

What Wood did not know was that the CIA was already in hot pur-suit of the magazine and its reporters. According to the late journalist Angus Mackenzie, a quick search of existing CIA files in March 1966 yielded information on approximately half of *Ramparts*' fifty-five writers and editors, many of them freelance or episodic contributors.[6] Primary targets included editor Robert (Bob) Scheer and Stanley Sheinbaum, a Michigan State University professor and the source for an upcoming article that would expose the CIA's involvement in a university project. Sheinbaum oversaw a training program for South Vietnamese police forces. When he was drawn into a scheme to kill a Vietnamese leader, he asked himself what an economics professor was doing in the middle of an assassination plot.[7] Shortly thereafter he resigned from the $25 million project and gave his story to Scheer.[8] CIA director Raborn di-rected Chief of Security Howard J. Osborn to investigate further. Did *Ramparts* receive foreign funds? If so, a legal basis might exist to shut down the magazine.[9]

Citing Sheinbaum and Scheer by name, Raborn enlisted the FBI and the Internal Revenue Service in his assault on *Ramparts*. Raising the for-eign funding canard, Raborn warned J. Edgar Hoover that the magazine might be a subversive operation, and ordered copies of its tax returns from the IRS. In addition, Raborn authorized agents to put a plant in-side the magazine.[10]

Ramparts was not the only media outlet digging for information about the inscrutable CIA. A successful book on covert activities and a *New York Times* investigation had already laid bare some of the CIA's secrets, to the consternation of all within the Agency. Before then, CIA officials could count on sympathetic senators and congressmen and tight-lipped White House officials to protect them from public scrutiny. The first time many Americans even knew about the CIA was in 1961 after the botched Bay of Pigs invasion; even then, President Kennedy took full responsibility and avoided a congressional investigation.

Then in 1964 Random House published Wise and Ross's *Invisible Government*, which explored the CIA's role in Iran, Guatemala, Cuba, Indonesia, Laos, and Vietnam, and raised fundamental questions.[11] Did the CIA influence U.S. foreign policy? What were the links between the

CIA and the military-industrial-congressional complex? When some-one at Random House slipped a pre-publication copy to CIA officials, then-director John McCone summoned the two authors to Langley and demanded they make deletions. They refused.[12]

According to Wise, CIA officials considered buying up all the copies, but abandoned the idea when Random House chief Bennett Cerf pointed out that he could print a second edition. Instead, McCone formed a "special group" inside the Agency to sabotage the book. Its number 1 weapon: bad reviews written by CIA agents under code names and passed to cooperative journalists and publishers; among the fake re-viewers was E. Howard Hunt, later of Watergate burglary fame.[13]

Following that, in 1965, the *New York Times* decided to launch its own investigation of the CIA, triggered by a slip of the tongue by Congress-man Wright Patman (D-Tex.) the previous year. As chair of the House Banking Committee, Patman had convened hearings to explore whether foundations were being used as tax dodges. The congressman inadver-tently identified the J.M. Kaplan Fund as a CIA conduit, and named eight (phony) foundations that passed funds through it.[14] CIA officials rushed to Patman's office. The following day, Patman announced that the CIA had nothing to do with his hearings and declared the matter ended.[15]

But the episode caused the *Times'* managing editor, Turner Catledge, to pay more attention to CIA activity. On September 2, 1965, Catledge noticed an odd story coming out of Singapore. Prime Minister Lee Kuan Yew publicly revealed that five years earlier the CIA had offered him a $3.3 million bribe for the release of two CIA agents who had been arrested. Yew had demanded $35 million, but ended up taking nothing in return for their release. Details of the story were truly bizarre, but the prime minister had produced as evidence a letter of apology from Secre-tary of State Dean Rusk. *Times* journalist Harrison Salisbury remembers Catledge thundering, "For God's sake let's find out what they are doing. They are endangering all of us."[16] The *Times* Washington Bureau chief, Tom Wicker, drafted a survey to send to the newspaper's worldwide net-work of journalists asking what they knew about the CIA. What were their experiences with the agency?[17]

James Jesus Angleton, the CIA counterintelligence chief whose job was to look for Soviet moles, had a copy of the survey before the ink was dry. The legendary Angleton had grown steadily paranoid after decades of professionally suspecting everyone of pro-Moscow sympathies. According to Salisbury, Angleton regarded the journalistic survey as a KGB instrument; the very phrasing of the questions "betrayed the hand of Soviet operatives."[18] While Angleton's reaction might have seemed extreme, the response to the *Times* survey at CIA stations around the world was similar.

CIA media liaison Colonel Stanley Grogan sent a memo to McCone, "NEW YORK TIMES Threat to Safety of the Nation," in which he suggested using the CIA's "heaviest weapons," including White House pressure, to combat the *Times*.[19] Salisbury, who saw the memo, described it as a scream from outer space. "*Any* questions, *any* attempt to probe what the CIA was doing, how it operated, what its intentions might be was seen as hostile, dangerous and frightening, capable of destroying the agency."[20]

In late April 1966, in the midst of the CIA furor over the two *Ramparts* articles, the *Times* published the fruits of its investigation in a series of five articles. While listing some of the CIA accomplishments, the articles depicted the Agency as without oversight; seemingly the government had no control over its increasingly questionable behavior.[21] Richard Helms, then Raborn's deputy, moved quickly to contain the damage, successfully killing a planned book based on the articles. Most of all, Salisbury noted in his memoir, the CIA feared a permanent record, available and accessible to all. He and Wicker thought that the CIA response was hysterical in the extreme, but they could not persuade the higher-ups to publish the book.[22]

Personal tragedies were also taking a toll on the clandestine activities of the CIA. On October 29, 1965, Frank Wisner, the covert entrepreneur and father of Mighty Wurlitzer projects, killed himself after a long period of mental instability that apparently began after the Hungarian uprising.[23] Cord Meyer had moved up a notch, becoming deputy director for plans (covert operations). But by all accounts, including his own, Meyer was spinning out of control.

In 1965, Meyer confided to his diary that for the past three years he had been "drinking too much," which had led to "scenes of deliberate and provocative rudeness on my part."[24] The murder on October 12, 1964, of Meyer's former wife, Mary Pinchot Meyer, left him further distraught.[25] The *Times* Washington bureau chief was among those who felt Meyer's rage after the *Times* published its series on the Agency. Meyer poked his finger at Wicker's chest at a cocktail party and shouted that Moscow must be pleased with him.[26] Although he apologized afterward, the outburst presaged his rage toward anyone who challenged the CIA, a list that later included the vice president of the United States. Thus, by the time Michael Wood approached *Ramparts*, the entire top echelon of the CIA felt itself to be under siege from the American media, and from *Ramparts* in particular.

It is not clear when the two top officials of Covert Action 5, Bob Kiley and Matt Iverson, learned of Wood's approach to *Ramparts*. In September 1966, before Wood was fired, they knew that a leak had occurred. Iverson traveled around the country trying to identify the culprit. He concentrated on former witting NSA staff.

My husband and I, grateful to have survived our brush with the CIA, were back in Boulder, hoping that we would never see the CIA men again. Without warning—we both remember the incident vividly— Iverson, Mike's former case officer, rang the doorbell. Mike and Iverson disappeared into an unfinished basement area to talk. After Iverson left, Mike told me that someone had violated his security oath and Iverson wanted to know what he knew. Mike told Iverson truthfully that he knew nothing.[27]

Groves and Stearns did not know that Iverson had set out to find the leak. Nor did they know about Wood's actions. Stearns later said that they would "never, ever" have fired Wood had they realized that he knew about the CIA.[28] Stearns made that comment some thirty-five years after Wood's departure, unaware that Wood's decision to go public had occurred *before* he was fired, not *because* he was fired.

THROUGHOUT THE AUTUMN OF 1966, young activists and journalists began to get mysterious phone calls from *Ramparts* editors Bob Scheer and Sol Stern. Judith Coburn, a *Village Voice* columnist living in Washington, described her call from Scheer: "We need you to work on something, and somebody is going to call you."[29]

"What's all this about?" asked Coburn, thinking his call might lead to a big moment in her journalism career. It was difficult for women to break into the field, and the men who dominated radical journalism awed Coburn. Getting a call from Scheer was like "getting called by the big Hollywood producer."

"I can't tell you . . . it's a long story . . . hush, hush," Scheer responded.

Coburn remembers thinking, "Oh, for Pete's sake. Everyone on the left always thinks that his phones are tapped. I . . . thought it was sort of melodramatic and a way of dramatizing yourself to say that your phone is tapped." She pressed Scheer. "Oh come on."

"Nope. Somebody's going to call you."

In Boston, Michael Ansara, a nineteen-year-old Harvard student who was active in the SDS, received a similar phone call: "This is Sol from *Ramparts*. Bob Scheer says you're our man in Boston. I'm going to give you the names of two foundations in Boston. We need you to do some research."[30]

"What kind of research?" Ansara queried.

"I can't tell you," Stern said.

"What's it about?"

"I can't tell you."

"Can you give me a clue?"

"No."

Ansara remembers Stern saying before he hung up, "Don't call me. I will call you and I want whatever you get." Unlike Coburn, Ansara remembered to ask, "How much will you pay me?" Stern offered $500. "Done," said Ansara, who was "dead broke" at the time. He had no idea what Stern was talking about, but if someone wanted to pay him for something, that sounded okay to him.

In Washington, a *Ramparts* editor approached Lee Webb, the former national secretary of SDS, then working at the Institute for Policy Studies, which had been founded by Marcus Raskin and Richard Barnet, left-wing policy intellectuals who had broken with the Johnson administration over Vietnam. Raskin also served as part-time editor of *Ramparts*. He asked Webb if he'd like to do some research; then Scheer followed up by phone and disclosed that the research involved the National Student Association. Unlike Ansara and Coburn, Webb had attended NSA Congresses, and knew several former NSA-SDS activists well, including Paul Potter, Paul Booth, and Tom Hayden. Scheer had been vague, but the project sounded interesting. Webb was in.[31]

Coburn waited for several weeks for a follow-up to the phone call from Scheer. Finally, she got another late-night call. It was local. The caller refused to identify himself, but said, "I have to come and see you." Coburn, who did not want to invite a strange man over at midnight, repeated her question: "Well, who are you?"[32]

After a pause, the man responded, "The *Ramparts* people told me to come and see you."

"Who are you?"

"I can't say."

Coburn reluctantly agreed to let him come over, all the while thinking, "Great . . . it's the middle of the night and this guy is going to come over to my house. I tried to get him to meet me somewhere else, but he sounded so urgent: 'No, no, I have to come over to your place.'"

When she opened the door she breathed a sigh of relief. "He was a large, bearlike, very sixties-ish-looking person, a completely familiar type to me, and that reassured me immediately." Her visitor finally told her his name was Michael Wood and he was the treasurer of the National Student Association. [Coburn misremembered here: Wood was in fact the former director of development, not treasurer.] Then he said, "I think the CIA is running the National Student Association."

Coburn suppressed a laugh; "This is the big story?" It was ridiculous. But she responded to his fear, since he seemed "scared out of his wits."

Coburn was aware of the NSA, but she did not take it seriously. During her four years at Smith College, Coburn, the daughter of conservative Republican parents, had grown steadily more radical. By the time she graduated, in 1964, her political world consisted of the Student Non-Violent Coordinating Committee, the Liberation News Service, the American Friends Service Committee, the Student Peace Union, and Students for a Democratic Society. During college, she majored in African studies, demonstrated against the H-bomb, and fiercely opposed the first U.S. advisers who went to Vietnam.[33]

Unlike Wood, who had had to read up on the CIA after he learned what was going on, Coburn had a distinct view of the Agency: "Right-wing assassins." The images that swam before her eyes were of Guatemala's Arbenz [overthrown by the CIA], the Congo's Prime Minister Patrice Lumumba [assassinated, CIA suspected], and Cuba's Castro. Why would the CIA care about the NSA?[34]

It was "literally unbelievable," Coburn recalled. "Well, I mean, it would be like someone walks into your house and says, So I met this guy from Mars the other day, and he says he could take us back there if you felt like going for a vacation." The notion that the CIA would be involved in the NSA seemed "just about the craziest thing I'd ever heard."[35]

Nevertheless, Coburn found Wood's fear so compelling that she sat up with him most of the night. She said of the experience, "I was never the same person." In the next few months, as she pursued the story, she discovered that one after another of her heroes had worked for the CIA, including Yale chaplain William Sloane Coffin, an outspoken critic of the war in Vietnam, who lately—and courageously in Coburn's view— had been supporting resistance to the draft.[36]

Coburn decided to confront Coffin in person, and went up to New Haven. When she entered his office, Coburn blurted out, "Did you work for the CIA?" Coffin swiveled in his chair and kept his back to her. After a period of deliberation, he said yes.[37] Coburn was torn. She wanted to ask Coffin, "Are you a bad guy?" But she also started to worry about what she was doing. "This was the first moment when I thought: I'm an enemy of the state."[38]

Coburn speculates today that the reason she and other *Ramparts* investigators found the CIA tie to NSA so hard to comprehend was that they had no understanding of liberal anticommunism. Her political education came from the SDS's Port Huron Statement, the quintessential document of the new left that criticized the American political system, not from Roosevelt liberals. She had no experience with people who distinguished their anticommunism from conservative, McCarthy-style witch hunts. Most of the *Ramparts* reporters viewed anticommunism as an overheated policy response, antithetical to civil liberties at home and destructive to U.S. foreign policy abroad.[39]

Meanwhile, Michael Ansara had begun his research in Boston. He had been given two names by Stern, the Sidney and Esther Rabb Foundation and the Independence Foundation. "Now what?" he said to himself. He began free-associating: Foundations. Grants. Fundraising. Suddenly, he remembered the name of a business firm that did political and nonprofit fundraising. They might be able to help him. He made an appointment with one of the partners, George Sommaripa.[40]

Sommaripa explained to Ansara that all foundations were required to file state and federal income tax returns; one portion detailed their grant awards and was open for public inspection. He advised Ansara to examine the foundations' tax records.

Ansara's first try was unsuccessful. At the Boston IRS office, he encountered a surly clerk who refused him access. Stymied, he returned to Sommaripa. A Democratic Party operative in Massachusetts, Sommaripa knew how to pull strings. On Ansara's behalf, he contacted the regional IRS office and chewed out the clerk for withholding public documents. When Ansara made his second visit to the IRS office, the chastened clerk gave him access to public records, but inadvertently handed over the complete file for each foundation, including the portions that were strictly confidential.

Ansara had just hit the jackpot.

According to Ansara, the tax returns might as well have been a "neon sign, blinking Look, Look, Look." From the confidential information, he could see that some of the money flowing into the foundation did not come from a family trust. The additional income matched dollar for dollar the amount of outgoing grants. Ansara asked the now-affable clerk for the 990 form, the public portion of the return that revealed nonfamily contributors to the foundations. When he saw the list of contributors, their significance "was as transparent as night and day." Someone or some agency was using foundations as conduits.

In just two days, the nineteen-year-old Ansara, sent on the sketchiest of missions, had stumbled on the CIA's covert funding network, though he did not yet fully grasp what he had discovered. While the large sums of money flowing into the Rabb Foundation led Ansara to suspect a government agency, he had no idea which one or why it was using the foundation. "*Ramparts* thought I was a brilliant researcher," Ansara laughs. "It was blind, dumb luck."

Although Sol Stern had never uttered the words "National Student Association," when Ansara saw the NSA listed as a grantee, he knew instinctively he was on to something. Since these grants came from Massachusetts foundations, he went next to the state attorney general's office to examine incorporation papers for the foundations he identified.

As Ansara began to visit Boston-area addresses a pattern emerged. More often than not, he found himself in a law firm. Secretaries and attorneys alike were tight-lipped. Trust fund. Managed for a client. Can't divulge more. No public information. No brochure.

Ansara found a copy of Martindale-Hubbell, a nationwide directory of lawyers. It contained law firm profiles with short biographies of individual members. As he studied it, he asked himself, What do these firms have in common? Before long, he spotted the connection. All had at least one senior partner who had served in the OSS during World

War II. The answer to which government agency was using the foundations became clearer. The CIA emerged as the logical candidate.

Stern had instructed Ansara not to make phone contact with him or *Ramparts*, but, staggered by his findings, Ansara went back to Sommaripa. He knew that Sommaripa's partner, David Bird, had once worked for the CIA. Ansara laid out his findings for Bird. By now he had a list of forty to fifty funds and foundations. Like Coburn, he felt a tremor of fear. Still disbelieving, he asked Bird, "Could this be true?"

In response, Bird picked up the phone and made a call. Ansara heard him declare to the person on the other end, "I know someone who has an interesting study, and it's about you." Bird had just told someone at or connected to the CIA about Ansara's findings. As *Ramparts* editor Warren Hinckle later wrote, "The CIA knew we were onto their game before we had time to discover what it really was."[41]

But even as the *Ramparts* editors began to recognize the enormity of the story, they remained confused about its significance. When in January 1967 Hinckle eventually met Wood, he described him as a wreck, "fidgety and run-down, a psychological war refugee from himself after a year-long battle with his conscience."[42] Hinckle grasped that Wood was not just afraid of the CIA; he was also guilt-ridden over his betrayal of friends. But Hinckle was puzzled, "stumped by the confounding question of what the CIA would want with a bunch of left-wing longhairs."[43]

As the story grew to encompass Africa, Latin America, Asia, and Europe, the reporters knew they needed help. Scheer and Stern hit an investigative jackpot when they found three seasoned researchers in New York City, Fred Goff, Michael (Mike) Locker, and John Frappier, who had just founded the North American Congress of Latin America. The three had become critical of U.S. foreign policy, based largely on their discovery of what American corporations and the CIA were doing behind the scenes in Latin America.

Goff, a Stanford University graduate, was in political transition. A close friend of former NSA president Allard Lowenstein, whom he met on campus when Lowenstein was dean of students, Goff had spent many hours on Lowenstein projects. In 1966, Goff had agreed to participate in the Committee on Free Elections in the Dominican Republic, whose leaders included Lowenstein and Norman Thomas, the grand old man of the Socialist Party. Lowenstein, Thomas, and Goff were among the electoral observers who went to the Dominican Republic. There Goff witnessed widespread corruption, yet when Lowenstein and Thomas arrived back in the United States, Lowenstein stepped onto the tarmac and declared the Dominican elections "free and fair." Lowenstein's public pronouncement preempted a more considered response and destroyed Goff's trust in him.[44]

Goff had also become suspicious about Lowenstein's role in Dominican politics. Lowenstein told Goff that his trusted contact in the Dominican Republic was Sacha Volman.[45] At the time Goff knew nothing about Volman but thought something was off about him. Shortly after he returned to the United States, Goff read an article that fingered Volman as a CIA agent. Filled with questions about both Volman and his own experience, Goff decided he had to find out more about the author, Michael Locker, a sociology graduate student at the University of Michigan.[46]

Locker was interested in power structures and the military-industrial complex. After the U.S. invasion of the Dominican Republic in 1965, he spent many hours at the business school library, "a great treasure trove of material," where he educated himself on the connections between sugar interests and foreign policy.[47]

During his research, Locker stumbled on press reports about Congressman Wright Patman's hearings and his inadvertent mention of the J.M. Kaplan Fund. (Kaplan was known as the Molasses King.) When he discovered the Kaplan Fund supported Volman, Locker pursued the connection. By the time he finished his research, he had concluded that "the CIA was an arm of a much larger establishment structure, a conscious arm, the most conscious arm, the most powerful arm, and that it really manipulated an enormous amount that went on in this country and abroad."[48] Locker sent his paper to the *New Republic*, which declined to publish it. But the mimeographed paper made the rounds of radical and peace conferences, where Goff happened to see it.[49]

With no advance warning, Locker received a call from Goff, who told him, "I've just come back from the Dominican Republic and I'd love to meet you in Ann Arbor." Locker's immediate response was fear: "I was suspicious. I was convinced that somebody's coming to find out more about me." His suspicions were not allayed when Goff, the son of missionary parents, arrived looking "straight as an arrow." Locker cut to the chase, asking Goff: "I have just one question: Who is Sacha Volman, and who does he report to?"[50]

"Fred laughed," reported Locker in an interview. "A real laugh. He knew exactly. And we became lifelong friends." They decided to team up, along with Locker's roommate, John Frappier, to pursue their commitment to investigatory research and Latin America.[51]

When the *Ramparts* editors drafted Goff, Locker, and Frappier for their investigation, they acquired experienced, politically aware researchers, who were fueled by outrage. "The whole objective," explained Locker, today a New York labor lawyer, "I mean the Dominican Republic was classic, was to split the labor movement, create a pro-Western, anticommunist faction which would rival the communist, socialist factions, and weaken the labor movement as a consequence. Terribly weaken them." For Locker and others, the lack of a unified and powerful labor movement meant increasing the power of the oligarchies—landowners, the Catholic Church, and the military—that ruled most Latin American countries, thus ensuring that social reform would not come to Latin America.[52]

Like Ansara in Boston, Goff and Locker spent hours poring over 990 tax forms at the Foundation Center in New York to identify donors. They focused on interlocking connections, tracked down addresses, and knocked on doors. Locker remembered, "They looked like legitimate operations, but the places reeked of being front operations. They wouldn't give interviews. Some gave interviews, but you caught them up in all kinds of contradictions."[53] The two men decided to try the list of grantees instead.

Locker visited the American Institute for Free Labor Development. "I just walked right in, and said I'm doing an investigation and I want to interview some people about possible CIA money that's come to this organization. Is there anybody here?"[54] The staff all worked in cubicles, with walls too high to see over, but Locker remembered hearing a "tremendous crashing and banging behind them." Thomas Kahn, the director, reacted as many others had: "He was furious. I mean absolutely livid that anybody would question his integrity."[55]

Goff and Locker tried to work systematically. They sent periodic write-ups to Ansara in Boston or Coburn in Washington They learned how to organize data by punching holes in three by five cards, so that by using a knitting needle or pencil, they could pull up cards on the same subject. They had no photocopying machine. Every bit of data had to be retyped on carbon copies. Sometimes *Ramparts* paid them. Sometimes it didn't. The Presbyterians in the New York–based Interchurch Center awarded them small grants, but not enough to finance travel.[56]

The *Ramparts* editors, by contrast, periodically blew into New York from San Francisco. They booked rooms at the Algonquin Hotel, ordered take-out from Sardi's, and kept the liquor flowing, creating more mystique than support. Locker said later that he was both "fascinated and repelled" by all the "flashy hotels, alcohol, cigarettes, fast talk."[57] Both Locker and Goff were uncomfortable with the editors, who were full of bravado and a "certain machismo."[58] They disliked the phony security; they, like the other researchers, had been instructed to talk only on pay phones, which added to the disorganization. No one, noted Coburn, *ever* answered the designated pay phone at the appointed time.[59]

The sheer size of the story swamped any attempt by the editors to impose a division of labor. "We would all be crammed into one hotel room," remembered Coburn, "fifteen to twenty people . . . everyone talking at once. People would say, 'Well, now what have we got about Kaplan?' And someone else would say, 'Well, we talked to Patman . . . okay, now where's the list of who they gave money to' . . . and then someone would say, 'oh, I don't know. . . . it's here somewhere.' Boxes crammed full of documents and research notes were all over the place. Then someone would say, 'Well, okay, do you want to talk about the civil rights movement now,' or 'let's have some reports from people who are working on the labor movement. So in Africa' . . ."[60]

At one point, according to Coburn, when everyone was talking at once, Locker started "jumping up and down on one of the beds saying, 'OKAY, shut up everybody. We'll take Latin America. You take Africa. You [Coburn] take the Congress for Cultural Freedom.' We divided up every region, every institution. It was just mind-boggling."[61]

At the same time, the bigger the story got, the more the investigative team feared for its safety. Even Coburn, who found the security measures silly, succumbed. "I remember thinking people were following us. I hated the pay phone thing, because I always felt that someone could just drive by, or that I could just disappear." It was crazy, she said in hindsight, "all out of spy movies."[62]

Lee Webb echoes Coburn's fear. "I really thought I might be killed."

Every night he would photocopy the material he had found, then divide the copies into three envelopes, and mail one set to his mother, one to his brother, and one to his home in Andover.[63] John Frappier sent a copy of his reports to a bartender in California.[64]

Webb and Coburn had another reason to feel anxious. One cold night they waited outside the NSA office on S Street for the staff to leave. Near midnight, they crept down the alley behind the office and crawled over garbage cans and trash bags to reach the back door. Finding it unlocked, they slipped in.[65]

As the hours ticked by, they rummaged through NSA files and photocopied documents, unsure which to fear most—a dwindling supply of toner or the D.C. police. According to Coburn, they focused on financial files, proof of building ownership, and other "money stuff." (Years later, the original deeds to the S Street building turned up in the moldering *Ramparts* files.) "I remember being completely terrified," Coburn confessed today. "That's when I thought we would certainly be arrested."[66]

ED SCHWARTZ BELIEVES that he was the first NSA officer to hear about the *Ramparts* investigation, sometime around Thanksgiving.[67] He remembers immediately phoning President Eugene Groves. By this time, Groves had realized that a "no-strings deal" with the CIA was no deal at all. Once he allowed the CIA's foot inside the NSA door, Groves had a difficult time keeping CIA case officers and agents away from the international staff, just as Sherburne had. At the time of the call, Groves had already realized that his strategy to oust the CIA had failed.[68]

Groves passed along the news to Philip Sherburne, then at Harvard Law School. When he heard that *Ramparts* knew about the NSA-CIA relationship, Sherburne said later, his heart sank. "The first thought that jumped into my mind was, Where is Mike Wood?" Still worried about his earlier security oath violations, Sherburne did not tell Groves that he had a prime suspect for the leak.[69]

Sherburne made further phone calls and located Wood in Detroit, where he was working for the New Politics coalition, an organizational attempt to strengthen the left-liberal wing of the Democratic Party. Sherburne asked Wood to come to Cambridge, and Wood agreed. The two men paced the streets while Sherburne raged at Wood. "I was pissed off at him. . . . really upset that he had violated our agreement. I had considered him . . . a friend, and [I] could not believe he was doing it."[70]

Wood—who by then could hardly retract his actions—argued that Sherburne should cooperate with *Ramparts*. Sherburne refused. At an impasse, and after hours of argument, they parted. Sherburne's roommate Steven Arons, a former NSA civil rights project director, had been an observer of the encounter, occasionally participating in the often-tense arguments. "You don't see Phil Sherburne angry very often," Arons said later, reflecting on the legendary Sherburne temperament. Part of the reason he was so upset, Arons speculates, was his concern that *Ramparts* might sensationalize the story.[71]

BY EARLY FEBRUARY 1967, the *Ramparts* staff had become extremely nervous about the story. The journalist Adam Hochschild, who later co-founded *Mother Jones* magazine, worked periodically at *Ramparts*, though rarely on the NSA story. One evening he joined the staff as they worked late into the night. Suddenly they heard a series of explosions. Diving for the floor, Hochschild remembered thinking "they had come to get us." As it turned out, the explosions were not bombs set off by the CIA. The *Ramparts* office was located on the edge of Chinatown in San Francisco—revelers were celebrating the Chinese New Year.[72]

Had the staff at *Ramparts* known the extent of the CIA offensive against them, they might have been forgiven their paranoia. When Richard Helms succeeded Admiral Raborn as CIA director, he shifted the pursuit of *Ramparts* to a super-secret team and chose as its head Richard Ober, a counterintelligence veteran. Kiley describes Ober as "a bad guy." Former CIA officer Tony Smith agrees, and adds that Ober was "paranoid."[73]

Ober's activities were so secret that Kiley, Smith, and others in Covert Action 5 did not know about them at the time, even though Ober's first assignment was to squelch the NSA story.[74] Ober pursued the question of whether *Ramparts* had foreign funds. He had already requested a full IRS audit as well as audits of individual *Ramparts* financial contributors. The assistant commissioner for compliance at IRS had assured Ober he could call up the tax returns "without causing any particular notice in the respective IRS districts." Ober agreed not to make his requests formal, so that "the Commissioner will be in a position to deny our interest if questioned later by a member of congress or other competent authority."[75]

But the full story of the CIA's pursuit of *Ramparts* may never be known. Years later, Evan Thomas, former *Newsweek* Washington bureau chief, interviewed Edgar (Eddie) Applewhite, one of the agents charged with discrediting the magazine.[76] Applewhite told Thomas, "I had all sorts of dirty tricks to hurt their circulation and financing. The people running *Ramparts* were vulnerable to blackmail. We had awful things in mind, some of which we carried off. . . . We were not the least inhibited by the fact that the CIA had no internal security role in the United States."[77] Applewhite went on to describe a scene with his boss, Desmond Fitzgerald, head of clandestine operations. Fitzgerald listened to him recount his activities, then commented, "Oh, Eddie, you have a spot of blood on your pinafore." Despite Applewhite's hints of illegal activities, he refused to divulge further details to Thomas.[78]

And so for several months *Ramparts* and the CIA pursued each other. One team relied on a group of budding journalists, slightly more seasoned editors, radical activists, and graduate student researchers. The other team had access to lavish government resources, including full-time professionals, and a secret but extensive network of contacts in the United States and abroad. It also was not averse to using dirty tricks. The game of hide-and-seek would continue until the last hours before publication.

24

DO YOU WANT BLOOD
ON YOUR HANDS?

MOST NSA STAFF remained unaware of the brewing storm until the evening of December 31, 1966, when about a dozen of them were gathered at Groves's house to discuss an antiwar campaign. The three officers, Eugene Groves, Edward Schwartz, and Richard Stearns, had been working with Allard Lowenstein to organize a letter of protest signed by student body presidents. Lowenstein wanted to mobilize Peace Corps volunteers, and had discussed the project with Harris Wofford, the assistant director. A Corps speechwriter, Tom DeVries, was present for the discussion.

The group sat around the living room. At some point, DeVries remembers, Lowenstein made a "truly off-hand comment": "Oh, did you hear that *Ramparts* is writing a story: NSA, Stepchild of the CIA."[1]

"The image I have of Groves," DeVries said later, "is that he just disappeared into the cushions, like all his muscles were gone. Stearns turned pale." Soon after, DeVries heard someone vomiting in the bathroom.[2]

A veteran of numerous NSA Congresses, DeVries knew the NSA well. As the director of the United States Student Press Association from 1964 to 1965, an organization of college editors, he had shared office space at NSA headquarters in Philadelphia. "It was just the biggest Goddamn shock," DeVries says today. "NSA was something to which all of us had devoted huge amounts of our lives, and made us who we were. It had a bigger impact on me [than] losing a parent, since none of us had been through that yet."[3]

When Lowenstein left Groves's house, he told his driver, former Stanford student Ken Stevens, about the conversation, adding that it would be "the usual sloppy *Ramparts* piece, lots of flash, little substance." (It was "typical of Al," Stevens said in a later interview, "to drop . . . confidential tidbits to flunkies. It made you feel like an insider . . . close to power.")[4]

No one knew how much *Ramparts* had uncovered. Groves and Stearns decided to try to find out. In early January, Schwartz headed for Berkeley, where on behalf of the NSA he inserted himself as a mediator into a pitched battle between student radicals and student government during a student strike for educational reforms.[5] Groves and Stearns urged him to take a side trip to San Francisco to meet with the *Ramparts* editors. He agreed.[6]

Schwartz's meeting with Warren Hinckle and Bob Scheer was uncomfortable.[7] Hinckle, who wore a black patch over one eye, was (and is) a character—brilliant, witty, undisciplined, difficult, and at the time rarely sober. A dartboard was placed prominently in the living room of his apartment, where they met, and as the two editors laid out the details of the story, Hinckle rhythmically tossed darts.[8] Schwartz, who knew the least about the CIA relationship, might well have felt like the dartboard, as he sat passively, letting each new revelation pierce him.[9] All he could do was listen.

Schwartz told the editors that any comment on the record would have to come from Groves, the NSA president. He pleaded with them not to destroy the organization. At one point, Scheer and Hinckle offered to give Schwartz the *Ramparts* mailing list to help the NSA raise money. The offer later became a point of contention between the NSA and *Ramparts* when rumors circulated that the list had been offered as a quid pro quo for confirming the story and supplying details. In fact, the *Ramparts* files show that Wood suggested the idea to the editors much earlier in the fall, precisely because he did not want the NSA to be hurt financially.[10] Wood apparently believed it likely that Groves would cooperate with *Ramparts*, having no idea how frightened the NSA officers were or how much pressure they were under.

As Schwartz flew back to Washington, he mulled over the conversation with Hinckle and Scheer. The implications of the kiss-off grant from FYSA hit him hard. He had known instinctively the grant was a mistake when he first learned about it. Now he hated himself for not throwing "a truly major fit" over it.[11] If Groves and Stearns had refused the CIA funding, they could claim honestly that they had inherited a clean organization.[12] The new officers were now compromised. Schwartz said later that his failure to stop the funding was a decision "I will regret the rest of my life."[13]

After Philip Sherburne confronted Michael Wood in early December, Sherburne realized he might face a prison term for violating his security oath. He also heard rumors that the CIA was able to create phony psychiatric files to discredit targets. He decided to seek legal counsel. The secretary of Harvard Law School recommended Professor Roger Fisher.[14]

Fisher had had previous experience with national security cases, but his most memorable contact with the CIA had been personal. In the late 1950s, Fisher had joined neighbors concerned about a proposal to build a behemoth CIA headquarters in Langley, Virginia. He fought the preemption of land-use laws for "the biggest building ever built," testified before Congress, and witnessed firsthand how the CIA manipulated government commissions and agencies to get its way. One evening, when Fisher returned to his home in nearby Vienna, he found Allen Dulles sitting on his doorstep. Fisher said later that he had "absolutely no trouble" believing Sherburne's tale about the CIA funding or that the CIA had "tried to get back in."[15]

The CIA soon aimed its fire at Fisher. Langley officials began calling him and suggesting he not take Sherburne as a client. Had Fisher "not noticed that he [Sherburne] was unstable?"[16] Sherburne was "bringing this on himself"; he "had a distorted impression of the situation and was behaving irrationally." He "was excessively masochistic and psychologically disturbed and in need of help."[17]

One day Fisher found Cord Meyer cooling his heels outside his campus office, there to make a personal appeal to Fisher not to take Sherburne's case. According to Fisher, when he refused to cooperate, Meyer made threats against Fisher's brother, who worked for USAID in Colombia. "Things would go better for your brother in Bogota," Meyer told him.[18] Ironically, the brother was Frank Fisher, founder, with Douglass Cater, of the Harvard International Activities Committee, where World War II intelligence veterans first teamed up with the CIA on covert activities. Roger Fisher was unimpressed by the threat. "What were they going to do?" he asks rhetorically. "Frank had no family. What could they do to him?"[19]

Failing to dissuade Fisher from taking the case, CIA officials tried to get him to meet with them without Sherburne, alleging that Sherburne had "got his facts wrong."[20] Again, Fisher refused. If Sherburne would deny the CIA relationship, they countered, the *Ramparts* story would disappear in a day or so. Fisher dismissed that notion as ludicrous, but the CIA was intransigent. If Fisher had had any doubts about the basis of Sherburne's fear, they were dispelled by these encounters.[21]

In January, Sherburne flew to Washington, for the first of many encounters with Kiley, Iverson, and other CIA officials. Meeting in a series of hotel rooms, they argued that Sherburne should try to kill the story. If that failed, all he had to do was denounce the article when it was published. That would make the story go away. Sherburne remembered Kiley saying, "*Ramparts* [is] a rag—the story wouldn't last more than a day."[22]

Today Sherburne is still incredulous at their reasoning. "I thought it was totally nuts. I told Kiley that at the very moment [of publication], it is going to make so much sense to people that this, in fact, is what has been going on. There's going to be so much interest in it." Sherburne argued that there was a better response. "I just thought it was so much better if NSA could say that the relationship began during the postwar period, had served its usefulness, [and] not compromised NSA's independence, but that it no longer made sense from the NSA perspective or from theirs."[23] But this was an option that Kiley knew did not exist.

No one had told Sherburne about the kiss-off grant. "At that point I didn't realize that there had been the continuation of money beyond ISC (dues)." When he found out that Groves and Stearns had received a FYSA grant, Sherburne understood why they could not speak of the NSA-CIA relationship in the past tense. He also realized they would bear the brunt of the exposé.[24]

Sherburne shuttled back and forth between his Cambridge apartment and Washington hotel rooms, asking himself why he was enduring these torturous sessions. He decided it was because "I felt bad about the fact that I was the source and that this whole thing was going to blow." Kiley brought in various old hands to talk to him, among them former NSA president Richard Murphy (1952–53), known to witting insiders as having worked with the youth side of Covert Action 5.[25] Murphy pointed out how awful the consequences for foreign students would be if the

Ramparts story were confirmed. Sherburne understood that exposure would have repercussions, but he did not feel they would be as extreme as Murphy predicted.[26]

The pressure on Sherburne became so intense that his girlfriend, who lived in Washington, and his Cambridge roommate, Steve Arons, became frightened for his physical safety.[27] According to Arons, he and Sherburne worked out a code to disguise his movements from potential phone-tappers; whatever time Sherburne gave Arons on the phone for his arrival at Boston's Logan Airport, Arons would increase by one hour.[28]

In late January 1967, Sherburne flew down for what he later described as the penultimate meeting with CIA officials. They met in a guestroom at the Statler-Hilton Hotel on K Street, not far from the White House. This time Groves, Schwartz, and Stearns were present. Kiley wanted all the officers to agree that they would deny the *Ramparts* story. But by then Sherburne was leaning toward confirmation.

Allard Lowenstein now joined the group. His presence confused everyone. Sherburne assumed that Kiley had invited him, though he did not know why: Lowenstein had never been part of the witting crowd. Sherburne said later, "It created a lot of doubt in my mind about what Lowenstein's long-term role had been." Lowenstein advocated a "sort of non-denial denial," a phrase later popularized during the Watergate scandal. Then he hammered away at the idea that publicity would mean "blood on your hands." If Sherburne confirmed the story, Lowenstein stressed, "Many people would get killed." His arguments did not differ substantially from those used by Kiley, Murphy, and others, but the fact that they came from Lowenstein made them powerful, even to Sherburne, who explained later, "I had a lot of respect for Lowenstein, so it was really troubling to me." In particular he thought that Lowenstein would exert a powerful influence on Stearns.[29]

Today none of the NSA officers who were present can explain Lowenstein's involvement, and Schwartz admits that it still troubles him.[30] Years later Kiley finally shed some light on his attendance: "Lowenstein would always come in on one of these issues. He really cared about NSA and the people in it. I think he knew that resources came from the CIA and it didn't really matter very much to him, as long as key people maintained their independence."[31]

But Lowenstein was not the person who had the biggest impact on

Stearns. At 4 A.M. that morning he had gotten a phone call during which Richard Murphy had threatened him that if he did not remain silent, any future career in government was over.[32] But direct threats were not needed. The most powerful argument, according to Schwartz, was "the mortality thing. I didn't want to wake up one morning and read about twenty-five dead Lebanese." Schwartz described Stearns, who had once represented the NSA in the Middle East, as nearly hysterical over this possibility.[33]

At this juncture, Groves, by his own admission, was paralyzed, trying to weigh the options. On one hand, if he confirmed the relationship, "There would be damage to innocent people." He thought perhaps the NSA could continue Sherburne's strategy of slowly replacing CIA money with "clean" funding; it might take about a year and a half to do it. On the other, he felt that the CIA's presence "was an unjustified use of private organizations." He later acknowledged that at this meeting he "had made no decision in my mind on whether or not this ought to be something that should come out [in] the open in the end."[34]

Sherburne felt that he was up against a unified front: "The general feeling was that if only I played ball, we could avoid all this." Schwartz seemed to be marginally on his side, but Sherburne did not regard him as a central player. Roger Fisher had urged Sherburne to reveal as little as possible, but Sherburne did not see how he could appear before the NSA Supervisory Board, which he surely would have to do after the *Ramparts* exposé was published, and say just a little bit about the CIA-NSA relationship. "I was almost in tears when I walked out of there. I really felt like I was right, but it was just so hard for me to understand why everybody thought I was wrong."[35]

Sherburne decided he needed a reality check. "That's when I thought about who can I talk to? Who can give me some outside perspective on this?" The name that popped into his mind was Arthur Flemming, the president of the University of Oregon. When he was student body president, Sherburne had worked well with Flemming. In addition, Flemming was on the NSA advisory board, although advisers never met and served only to legitimate NSA. And finally, Flemming had ties with top officials in both Republican and Democratic administrations.[36]

Before he left the Statler-Hilton, Sherburne found a pay telephone in the lobby and called Flemming's office. To his amazement, a secretary informed him that Flemming was in Washington to attend a meeting of the U.S. Civil Rights Commission. Sherburne might find him at the Hay-Adams Hotel—just a block and a half away.[37]

By the time Sherburne reached Flemming's room, the ever steady, emotionally controlled Sherburne describes himself as a gusher. All the agony of the past two years poured out: his discovery of the CIA relationship, his attempt to negotiate with the Agency, and his decision to sever the ties. He told of his role in creating the leak that had led to the *Ramparts* investigation, the current threats, the possibility of prison, his frustration, and, finally, his sense of doubt about what he was doing. When he was through, Sherburne said Flemming reassured him. "I think you are doing the right thing. You have a lot of courage. And I'll do whatever I can to help you." Sherburne felt waves of relief. "It was what I needed to hear, because there wasn't anybody I had more respect for [than Flemming]." Sherburne also told Flemming about his relationship with Vice President Humphrey, and Flemming speculated that Humphrey might support Sherburne.[38]

After the meeting, Sherburne felt safer. If anything happened to him now, the "who" and the "why" would be obvious. He still faced the possibility of a prison term, but that paled beside the fear of being killed. He phoned Kiley at CIA headquarters and told him of his decision to confirm the *Ramparts* story. "So, that was it . . . It was finally done. I wasn't going to have any more conversation about it. I think Kiley accepted it at that point . . . that this was the reality."[39] Today Kiley concurs. There was nothing more he could do.[40]

Sherburne returned to Cambridge and tried to refocus on his law school classes. Within weeks, both Sherburne and his roommate Steve Arons received reclassification notices from their local draft boards— located at opposite ends of the country—informing them that they were now eligible for the draft.[41] Having lived through the draft scare the year before, Arons remembered thinking that the CIA "seemed hell bent on sending us to Vietnam," and for a while he was "dead sure that's where we'd end up."[42]

At the same time, Sherburne began to hear rumors about his psychological instability, statements similar to those Cord Meyer had made to his lawyer. Kiley maintains today that he did not participate in the smear campaign, but he is not surprised that Meyer ran one. "I don't think Cord was entirely sane toward the end of this period."[43] Even NSA officers who knew the rumors were untrue helped spread them;

Stearns later apologized to Sherburne for impugning his reputation.[44] The rumor campaign created new tensions among Groves, Schwartz, and Stearns, just as they had grasped that Sherburne's decision meant they would face a public storm.

Neither the NSA officers nor Kiley knew that Lowenstein had decided to use his insider information to alert President Johnson's advisers to the coming story. In mid-January Lowenstein met with Douglass Cater, the NSA founder, then special assistant to the president. When Lowenstein emerged approximately forty-five minutes later, according to his driver, Ken Stevens, he was jubilant. Lowenstein swore Stevens to secrecy and confided the details of his conversations: he had met with Cater as planned, but also with Walt Rostow, Johnson's national security advisor, who asked him to draft a reply to the *Ramparts* story for the president. What remains especially vivid in Stevens's mind is how invigorated Lowenstein felt after his White House visit. He had felt shut out of the NSA. Now he was relevant again.[45]

In early February, rumors of the story finally reached NSA headquarters. When the staff confronted Groves and Stearns over the allegations, the two officers denied them. When it later became clear that they had lied, tempers flew. But the officers were in a bind: if they prematurely confirmed the rumors, they would lose control over any public response. At this point, Groves and Stearns were working on a strategy to preempt the *Ramparts* revelations.[46]

It is not clear who suggested holding a press conference to get the story out first, except that it originated at CIA headquarters. Roger Fisher, in touch with both Cord Meyer and CIA general counsel Lawrence Houston, said he conveyed the suggestion to Sherburne.[47] In a 2001 memoir, William W. Turner, a former FBI agent and later *Ramparts* editor, claimed that the original idea came from Richard Ober, head of the top-secret operation that targeted *Ramparts*.[48] After Sherburne's decision not to lie about the *Ramparts* allegations, someone, perhaps Kiley, informed witting NSA officers and staff that they could also confirm the past relationship but give no details.[49]

When Groves, Stearns, and Kiley began working on a press statement, a host of new problems occurred to them. What did "no details" mean? How much could they say? At some point, all three realized that the NSA might have an even bigger problem: What if they admitted the relationship and the U.S. government "turned around and said these people are lunatics?"[50] Not even Kiley could answer that one. Groves later testified that Kiley placed repeated calls to Acting Secretary of State Nicholas Katzenbach's office, urging him to "openly acknowledge the fact that NSA had been subsidized by the CIA."[51] No assurances were forthcoming.

The NSA officers were also concerned about how the revelations would impact foreign students studying in the United States and American students abroad; this had been one of the main reasons for their initial inclination to deny the story. Groves and Stearns had been sending urgent cables to Roger Pulvers, an American studying at the University of Kraków on an NSA exchange program, but Pulvers had not responded. Pulvers had no ties to the CIA, but everyone was fearful of how the Polish government might react. On February 6, Groves flew to London, where he fired off an urgent cable to Pulvers, asking Pulvers to come to London immediately. When Pulvers reached London on February 11, Groves told him that he could not return to Kraków. He must leave all his belongings and research notes behind. Pulvers was in tears. Groves later wrote, "I think it was more difficult for me to tell him this story than it would have been to tell of a death in his family."[52]

After being assured of Pulvers's safety, Groves moved on to Leiden to brief COSEC secretary general Ram Labhaya Lakhina. Lakhina later claimed that Groves had been incoherent and that he never uttered the word "CIA," so Lakhina had no idea what he was talking about.[53] Groves returned home in time to prepare for the NSA press conference, scheduled for Valentine's Day, February 14.

By now both the NSA and *Ramparts* had moles in the other's camps. *Ramparts* learned about the preemption strategy, which put the editors in a bind, since the March issue was not ready to print. Determined not to be outwitted by the NSA, the editors made a decision: *Ramparts* would scoop itself and publish a full-page ad in the *New York Times* that divulged the CIA tie before the NSA could hold its press conference.[54]

Groves and Stearns also began to alert members of the NSA's National Supervisory Board. Chair Sam W. Brown, Jr., was poring over theological texts at the Harvard Divinity School library when someone summoned him to the telephone. When he heard the news, he dropped everything and flew to Washington to convene an emergency meeting of the board. "One day a student at Harvard Divinity School, the next day on *Meet the Press*," Brown later quipped, as he explained why he never returned to Harvard. At the time, his shock was magnified by the fact that a few weeks earlier, Groves had personally assured him that there was no truth to rumors of CIA funding. As a result, Brown had dismissed the stories as baseless.[55]

Brown was not the only NSB member who had received assurances that the rumors were false. When treasurer Steven Parliament was in Washington in the summer of 1966, Michael Wood had asked him repeatedly whether he understood "where NSA's money came from."[56] Parliament had been puzzled; Wood "knew perfectly well" that the grants came from foundations. But Wood kept pushing the point: Had Parliament ever tried to meet with any of the foundations?[57]

Parliament returned to Minnesota for graduate school that fall but he kept mulling over Wood's questions. He decided to contact the NSA's major funders. Often he could not find a telephone number. When he did make a call, the person he asked to speak to was never available. As treasurer, he became concerned and reported his experience to Wood, who took him to a secret meeting with a handful of *Ramparts* writers. Afterward, Parliament contacted Groves to ask if the story was true, and Groves said no.[58] By the time the NSB convened, the atmosphere crackled with anger, distrust, and a feeling that more of the story was being withheld.

On the evening of February 13, while Groves and Stearns prepared for their press conference, the phone rang in the NSA office. The *New York Times* reporter Neil Sheehan was on the other end, asking for a reaction to the *Ramparts* ad. From that moment, pandemonium reigned at NSA headquarters. It lasted for months.

25

— THE FIRESTORM —

IN HIS MEMOIR, former CIA director Richard Helms recalled February 13, 1967, as "one of my darkest days." Helms had just finished touring the nuclear labs at Los Alamos, New Mexico, and was about to settle into his hotel room in nearby Albuquerque, when "an agitated young communications officer rush[ed] along the hallway . . . with one heavily sealed message from the White House in his briefcase. It was eerily succinct: Return to Washington immediately."[1]

After he reached CIA headquarters, Helms paced for several hours until President Johnson returned his call. The president briefed him on the impending *Ramparts* article but gave him no instructions on how to pull the "scorched chestnuts away from the fire." Helms understood Johnson's message to mean that "it was an Agency problem from start to finish."[2]

Helms knew what was at stake. "Exposure," he wrote, "could affect the most important covert projects in existence for some two decades." As he mentally reviewed the potential fallout, he realized that "hundreds of Third World students" would be at risk.[3] (Helms later testified that in fiscal year 1967, the International Organizations division budget for students was roughly $3 million, the equivalent in 2012 of $20 million.)[4] It would not matter that some students had been recruited and some were innocent of the source of their funds; all would be suspect.

At CIA headquarters, Bob Kiley braced for the worst. "There was nothing I could do about it," he said later.[5] Paradoxically, on the day the story blew, the CIA received one piece of eagerly awaited news. The Internal Revenue Service had acted on Ober's top-secret request for

370

financial information about *Ramparts*, a critical element in the strategy to shut down the magazine.[6]

In London, CIA staff officer Tony Smith accompanied the station chief, whom he describes as "an old drunk," to a meeting to inform the British of the *Ramparts* bombshell.[7] Cord Meyer's deputy, Walpole (Tad) Davis, chaired the meeting, during which the American chief snoozed and occasionally snored. Smith was embarrassed, but he had a more delicate problem. Many people knew about his time with the NSA, and he feared that his presence in England might either implicate British students who worked with COSEC or jeopardize his current work. CIA headquarters agreed. Smith and his new bride, who also worked for the CIA, left the country under pseudonyms and took a prolonged honeymoon in Italy at taxpayer expense.[8]

On February 14, the *New York Times* hit the newsstands with the full-page ad purchased by *Ramparts*. It promised that the magazine's March issue would "document how CIA has infiltrated and subverted the world of American student leaders over the past fifteen years." The *Washington Post* carried a similar ad. Front-page reporting elaborated on a "case study in the corruption of youthful idealism."[9]

Wire services carried the story nationwide. Edward Schwartz was in the back seat of a taxicab in Oberlin, Ohio, when he heard a radio announcer read the wire story. "An out of body experience, like listening to your obituary," was how he later described it.[10]

Helms summoned CIA career staff from around the world to headquarters for damage control. So many left the London station that a young newcomer, Susan (Sue) A. McCloud, later exclaimed that she was "left holding the bag."[11] An internal CIA report later estimated the number of agents called home at around two hundred.[12]

Before the press disclosures, both NSA president Eugene Groves and Allard Lowenstein had briefed White House aide Douglass Cater, and now Cater tried to protect the president by announcing that Johnson "had never been informed about the student operation."[13] When the *Washington Post* reporter Richard Harwood printed the claim, no one, not even other Johnson aides, found it credible. The White House officials dropped the defense.[14]

Cater later said in an oral history that all he could do was ride out the crisis. While professing not to have known about the CIA funding,

Cater offered an analysis of its development over time. "It had grown to an extent that I thought it was a very unwise public policy. CIA had imposed no substantive obligations." He then asserted it "had grown up without the kind of supervision that it needed."[15] It is not clear how Cater could know about the nature and trajectory of the NSA-CIA relationship if he had been ignorant of its existence before January 1967. The claim is also doubtful given his intelligence background and critical role in establishing the NSA's international program. Cater worked with many OSS and CIA colleagues over a fourteen-year period at *The Reporter* magazine.[16] Twice in the early 1950s, he took a leave of absence to consult for the secretary of the army and the director of the Mutual Security Agency. Early in the Kennedy administration, Cater was tapped for a top-secret assignment to review psychological warfare operations across U.S. government agencies, an odd assignment for a life-long journalist, even one tuned into Washington politics.[17] He clearly knew more than he acknowledged.

Vice President Humphrey was wrapping up a speech to Stanford University students when someone asked about the *Ramparts* story. Humphrey responded that the episode was "one of the saddest times our government has had in terms of public policy." He added, "I regret that the CIA was involved in this. I think we ought to keep our democratic institutions free of government coercion."[18]

Rumors soon circulated among witting staff that an outraged LBJ called the vice president and commanded him to "get back to Washington and shut the fuck up."[19] Humphrey's aide Ted Van Dyke confirms the gist of Johnson's order — "he was not pleased" — but added, "Johnson didn't speak that crudely to Humphrey."[20]

According to Van Dyke, the person who was both crude and out of control was Cord Meyer. Before the story broke, Meyer tried to enlist the vice president in damage control. Humphrey balked, and Meyer became so agitated he began yelling. Van Dyke cut the meeting short.[21]

At the State Department, Secretary Rusk was out of town. The responsibility for handling the *Ramparts* matter fell to Acting Secretary Nicholas Katzenbach, who later remembered that his first instinct was "to deny everything." Upon reflection, however, he decided that "It was a can of worms and I didn't want to know what was in the can."[22] Katzenbach sent the first of several memos to President Johnson on February 13. State was working on a "bare bones admission," but wouldn't have a firmer strategy until "we have seen the morning papers." Katzenbach also told Johnson, "I am not absolutely confident that we are [in] possession of all the facts." He feared the NSA story might "open up for questioning related programs of CIA."[23]

Katzenbach's chief of staff, Jack Rosenthal, learned what was coming over the weekend when he fielded frantic phone calls from Kiley. Despite this advance warning, Rosenthal, a former journalist, was unprepared for the conflagration. "I was taken aback by how quickly this blew up into an inferno."[24] Rosenthal, who was the head of the New York Times Foundation when I interviewed him, has seen his share of media storms, but this was the first. "I was just astonished by the speed and temperature it reached in a hurry."[25]

On February 15, Rosenthal sent White House press secretary George Christian instructions on how to handle the publicity. The memo, "Subject: CIA-NSA Flap," was so confusing that even Rosenthal decided it needed clarifying. After writing that "we will discuss it *only* in response to official, responsible statements made by groups who have in fact received government financial support—and maybe not even then, depending on facts," he added, "In other words, volunteer nothing."[26]

Secretary of Health, Education, and Welfare John Gardner knew the revelations would affect the educational community, and he had definite opinions on the subject. He had worried about an eruption earlier in the fall. "I began to pick up little signs that there might be some things going on with the . . . Asian-Pacific Institute, the National Student Association, the African American Institute and the labor unions," Gardner later recounted. It was nothing very specific, "just tiny things, but if you knew the territory, you began to wonder." Gardner knew the territory. "I had been in the Office of Strategic Services, so I knew any number of people in the CIA. I knew how they functioned."[27] In fact, Gardner and Richard Helms had been desk mates in the OSS.

Gardner decided to approach Allen Dulles, who had now retired. But Dulles "patted me on the head" and said, "Oh John, it's nothing." Gardner noticed that Dulles "didn't deny it and he didn't acknowledge it," but "he let me know that I was worrying needlessly." Gardner still did not know whether the rumors about extensive CIA involvement in the private sector were true, but if they were, he thought the CIA was making "a *big* mistake," which, if exposed, "could hurt wonderful people doing good work throughout the world." He decided to warn President Johnson.[28]

"We were on a helicopter together," recounted Gardner, going to Baltimore for a Social Security Honor Awards ceremony. "I tried to convey my concern. But Johnson had a tendency to talk over you if he thought you were getting into a subject that he didn't want to talk about." Douglass Cater and Social Security commissioner Robert Ball were seated across from Gardner and tried to help. But the whir of the helicopter blades and Johnson's monologue defeated them. Seasoned politicians know that if you don't know something, you don't have to deal with it, and Johnson was a master politician. "A complete loss," said Gardner.[29]

On the day the story came out, Gardner dictated his own statement, bypassing the requirement that Cabinet Secretaries clear all press releases with the White House. He declared that it had been "a mistake for the CIA ever to entangle itself in covert activities close to the field of education or scholarship or the university."[30]

On Capitol Hill, CIA allies had trouble getting their stories straight. Members of the Senate Armed Services Committee contradicted one another about whether they had ever been briefed. Senator Mike Mansfield (D-Mont.) fumed that the CIA "had never told the Russell committee of its NSA secret subsidies."[31] Senator Richard Russell (D-Ga.), who chaired the Armed Services Committee, retorted, Oh yes it had.[32] Within a week, Senator Russell came out swinging on behalf of the CIA. He dismissed the argument that academic freedom had been damaged as "just a lot of hogwash."[33]

Eight congressmen, including George E. Brown, Jr. (D-Calif.), wrote to President Johnson to demand "an immediate investigation at the highest level."[34] Eugene McCarthy (D-Minn.) introduced a resolution that would require a congressional investigation.[35]

Amid the uproar, Congresswoman Edith Green (D-Ore.) tweaked those who had condemned the NSA as subversive. "The House Committee on Un-American Activities must be chagrined that left-leaning students and labor leaders who have so aroused its ire are representatives of organizations financed and perhaps guided by a government agency it previously considered an unimpeachable ally. It would be an amusing spectacle to see the House Committee on Un-American Activities and the Central Intelligence Agency investigate each other."[36]

Conservative senators, on the other hand, were not amused. Strom Thurmond (R-S.C.) thundered, "The CIA . . . was building socialism behind the backs of the American people." The Agency "had developed its own agenda, getting Americans to accept the glorious utopia promised by international socialist government."[37] Senator Barry Goldwater (R-Az.) and his protégés in the Young Americans for Freedom called for an immediate congressional investigation into the radical leftist NSA.[38]

For weeks, Cord Meyer had worked the Hill like a man possessed, visiting influential chairmen in the House and Senate. Meyer's nightmare scenario included public hearings and klieg lights. His biggest concern was Senator J. William Fulbright (D-Ark.), the powerful chair of the Senate Foreign Relations Committee and a growing critic of Johnson's policies in Vietnam. Meyer believed that Fulbright was the "key to damage control, even though he was not on the [CIA] oversight committee." After two meetings with Fulbright, Meyer concluded, "He did not entirely accept my explanation and clearly thought that a decision to terminate should have been made at an earlier date."[39]

In Leiden, COSEC general secretary Ram Labhaya Lakhina changed position a number of times. First he said he knew nothing about anything. When pressed to confirm that Groves had flown to Europe to brief him just days earlier, he acknowledged the visit but said that Groves had not explained what was going on. During a subsequent investigation by the Supervision Commission, he amended his statement: "Looking back, Groves did place [sic] some remarks indicating what was going to happen, but in such a vague manner, that only if I did know already, I would have understood that he knew too."[40]

Still protesting his ignorance, Lakhina defended the International Student Conference against all comers. He described the charges against the ISC and COSEC as "baseless and reckless." He condemned the CIA funding of the NSA as a "cynical betrayal of the ideals of American students as well as students in Africa, Asia, Latin America and Europe affiliated with the ISC." Finally, on behalf of COSEC, he condemned "the Government of the United States of America and its Central Intelligence Agency for the corruption of an apparently democratic student organization." He called for the suspension of the NSA from ISC membership.[41] If witting NSA operatives are correct that the CIA backed Lakhina's election to the position of secretary general, his performance can be considered audacious. Even if he was unaware of CIA support, his vigorous protest served CIA interests.

On February 15, President Johnson announced that he had requested the CIA "to cease all aid to youth and student programs and to review other agency-funded anti-Communist programs housed in nongovernmental organizations."[42] LBJ then washed his hands of the controversy by appointing a three-member commission (the Katzenbach Committee) to investigate: Cabinet Secretary John Gardner, CIA director Richard Helms, and Under Secretary of State Nicholas Katzenbach. He gave them just weeks to report.

Cord Meyer later acknowledged that the president's move had been crucial in warding off congressional hearings.[43] But Johnson's announcement gave Helms a jolt. It implied that there might be additional covert CIA projects which were not yet publicly disclosed.[44] Nor had Johnson taken responsibility for the NSA program. Two former presidents who might have borne some of the blame, Truman and Kennedy, were dead. The CIA was still in danger of being left out in the cold.

At NSA headquarters, exhausted and distraught officers faced a press onslaught. Reporters from the *Washington Post*, the *Washington Star*, the *Los Angeles Times*, and other major newspapers swarmed the office. In the middle of the chaos, the NSA National Supervisory Board convened in closed session at the nearby Dupont Hotel. Paranoia ran so high that notebooks were collected at the end of the day and put in safety-deposit boxes.[45]

When one board member said he had heard that electronic bugs could be embedded in ashtrays, the board changed hotels. On another occasion a briefcase was left unattended in a hotel hallway, and panic ensued.[46] A former nonwitting NSA National Affairs officer, James A. Johnson, then on the NSB, told friends that he feared "he might be shot dead on the street."[47] Robert Kuttner, also a nonwitting NSA staff member who handled foreign student exchanges under Groves, said in a later interview, "We scared ourselves silly."[48]

Philip Sherburne appeared before the Board and tried to answer questions without violating the "no details" pledge negotiated by his lawyer. Groves and Stearns knew the least but filled in what they could. Recalling those frantic days, NSB member Jean Hoefer Toal faults herself for not being more astute. "We should have figured out something was wrong," if for no other reason than because of "all these older men, wearing clothes from the middle '50s who came to the [NSA] Congress." Toal, today chief justice of the South Carolina Supreme Court, found the revelations "horrifying," especially "the way they scared you to death if you told," referring to the security oaths.[49]

Ricki Radlo, one of the youngest NSB members, battled feelings of shock and betrayal.[50] As a freshman at the 1965 NSA Congress, she had unwittingly served the CIA's Vietnam agenda as a member of the Radical Middle Caucus led by Donald Emmerson. In retrospect, she understood how easily students could be manipulated. In an interview she groped for words to describe how these events affected her. She went from being an idealistic "good government type" to having "an incredible feeling of unease" and then to "a sense of surrealism."[51] When Radlo tried to describe the situation to adult outsiders, "They thought I was absolutely nuts." Yet with the press clamoring for a response, "we had to pull ourselves together."[52]

On Friday, February 17, NSB chair Sam Brown issued a statement on behalf of the board that read, in part, "We are shocked at the ethical trap into which young men of great integrity have been placed by covert actions of the CIA."[53] He asserted that students had been duped into signing the security oath. He called for a congressional inquiry. He described the NSA staff as engaged in spying.[54]

Brown did not stop there. Traveling from campus to campus, he condemned the CIA-NSA relationship to anyone who would listen. Assistant U.S. Postmaster Richard Murphy, the former NSA president who had threatened Richard Stearns, was so furious that he took a leave of absence and followed Brown around the country, making sure CIA defenders countered Brown's assertions. Finally, someone in the top echelon of the Johnson administration demanded that Murphy stop and return to Washington.[55]

Meanwhile, behind the scenes at the White House and State Department, aides scrambled to find evidence that a president had authorized the CIA-NSA operations. National Security Advisor Walt Rostow scoured the files from the top-secret 303 Committee going back to its antecedent 5412 Committee under Eisenhower.[56] He could not find any document before February 25, 1959, that might indicate White House approval. The last entry, for December 3, 1964, concerned the counter-festival program against the scheduled 1965 World Youth Festival in Algiers. In a classified memo to President Johnson, Rostow defended the absence of documentation, describing the limited role of the 303 Committee as being "to examine new programs."[57]

The State Department searched its own 303 Committee files and put a different spin on the missing authorizations. The NSA relationship exemplified "a trend by CIA officers to bypass . . . the Department to clear operations on a piecemeal basis with Country Directors or Assistant Secretaries." Therefore, the department lacked "adequate detail on how certain programs are to be carried out."[58]

The CIA offered a third explanation. Invoking the authority from a 1947 National Security Council directive, officials told the White House that "many of CIA's continuing covert action projects and programs were therefore begun when responsibility for policy conformity rested with the DCI [Director of Central Intelligence] in accordance with existing NSC directives." Under the Truman administration, between 1949 and 1952, the CIA director had approved eighty-one covert actions on internal authority. The unidentified writer of this top-secret memo, perhaps Cord Meyer, explained that the decision on whether to brief the president resided with the CIA director.[59]

In other words, this CIA document, not declassified until 1999, more than thirty years after the fact, reveals that Allen Dulles (or his predecessor) alone approved covert projects, and that Dulles alone decided whether a sitting president needed to know about them.[60] The Katzenbach Committee could not make this admission public without adding to the mess. Since no one could find anything definitive on presidential authorization, the White House remained silent on the issue.

On February 17, Helms switched tactics. He tried to persuade long-serving congressmen to attest that the president had authorized the operations. He met in closed session with legislators well known for their ability to deflect criticism aimed at the CIA—Congressman L. Mendel Rivers (D-S.C.), chair of the House Armed Services Subcommittee, and ranking member William H. Bates (R-Mass.). After the session, Rivers and Bates greeted reporters and praised the CIA. They piously declared that their committee would have "failed in its duty" had it not enabled the NSA to fight communist penetration.[61] Then they asserted that the NSA-CIA connection had been known to every administration since 1952, and to the Armed Forces Subcommittee "for several years."[62]

The *Washington Post* quoted Rivers as saying that he "could see no reason to apologize for helping send students to international conferences as voices of the free world."[63] Rivers denied Sam Brown's assertion that spying took place. "Espionage was not involved—the survival of freedom was."[64] Thus, the lie that the CIA had merely slipped a few travel dollars to American students so they could attend international meetings began its march around the world before, in the words of the old adage, truth had time to put on its pants.

On February 21, Senator Robert F. Kennedy finally pulled Helms's smoldering chestnuts out of the fire. He announced publicly that it was unfair for the CIA to "take the rap" for funding the NSA. He asserted that Presidents Eisenhower, Kennedy, and Johnson had all approved the operations.[65]

A CIA colleague of Kiley's, who requested anonymity, confided the inside story of how Kennedy came to make this statement. Helms allegedly called Kiley with a long-winded hypothetical about a senator, say one from New York, who might even be a former attorney general, who might defend the CIA-NSA operations. What would Kiley suggest the senator say? Kiley, the story continues, put his feet up on the desk while talking to Helms and started talking. Helms asked to have the extemporaneous speech in writing. Kiley agreed and dashed for the elevator. When the doors opened on the seventh floor, the director's level, he found Helms pacing in front of them. When Kiley returned to his office, he casually suggested to his colleagues that they check out the TV monitor at noon for an announcement by Senator Kennedy from New York.[66]

In his memoir, Cord Meyer was still thankful. One of "the most damning lines of attack," he acknowledged, was the lack of policy approval. "I was grateful to Kennedy for his timely intervention but not surprised, since I had personally briefed him when he was attorney general on these programs on a number of occasions and received his enthusiastic encouragement to expand our activity in this field."[67] No one questioned Kennedy's knowledge of what former administrations might have done. No one pursued Cater's earlier claim that Johnson did not know about the relationship. With this single statement, the press ceased to ask questions about presidential authorization, and the issue disappeared.

Little by little, the CIA began to stifle the public outrage. A covert action operation of significant breadth and depth was reduced to a few travel grants. Decisions made largely by Allen Dulles and other CIA officials were attributed to Eisenhower, Kennedy, and Johnson. But other lines of attack still needed to be addressed. Among the more serious charges: the CIA had compromised the independence of a private organization. Who better to ward off these charges than witting participants?

Twelve former NSA presidents, all signers of the security oath, issued a press release on February 25: "Allegations that we were 'trapped' or 'duped' are arrant nonsense." They scoffed at the idea that the CIA had interfered with the NSA's activities: "Attempts at control would not have been tolerated." They trotted out the well-worn argument that NSA policies and programs were "consistently independent of and often in conflict with the positions of the government." They repeated the lie that each year only two officers were informed of the relationship. Conspicuously absent from the signatories were Allard Lowenstein, Stephen Robbins, Philip Sherburne, and Eugene Groves.[68] The signers included CIA career agents William Dentzer, Harry H. Lunn, Jr., and Robert P. Kiley. All three had administered the security oath to others, acted as CIA case officers, and given direction to new inductees. The other signers, James Edwards, Stanford L. Glass, Harald C. Bakken, K. Ray Farabee, Donald A. Hoffman, Richard A. Rettig, Edward Garvey, W. Dennis Shaul, and Gregory M. Gallo, worked for the CIA beyond their presidential year (with the exception of Farabee), several for five or more years.[69] Edwards, by then a Wall Street lawyer, gave a rare interview and came up with a quip that gained currency in the defense of CIA: "Actually we thought NSA was running CIA rather than the other way around."[70]

The CIA scored another victory when Gloria Steinem emerged as a prominent defender. She told *Newsweek:* "In the CIA, I finally found a group of people who understood how important it was to represent the diversity of our government's ideas at Communist festivals. If I had the choice, I would do it again."[71]

Three elements of a canonical CIA narrative were now in the public domain: the CIA's support for the NSA consisted of a few travel grants; top government officials approved the relationship; and the CIA never exercised control over the association or damaged its independence. Dentzer took this to extremes during a 1980 interview when he dismissed the significance of the whole operation: "Oh, someone must have called up Allen Dulles and said 'Give these people a few bucks.'"[72]

Public reaction to the CIA activities in the United States polarized quickly; there were CIA defenders and CIA critics. There was also a larger category of people who had no idea what it was all about. As NSB member Steven Parliament traveled around the country, trying to convince member schools to remain loyal, he had the same experience as Radlo: people were confused. "It didn't sound real." Some asked, "What on earth do they want of us?" Others asked, "What did they get?" No one could really answer.[73]

IN EARLY MARCH 1967, the Senate Foreign Relations Committee, chaired by J. William Fulbright, heard testimony that challenged the CIA's version of events on every score. But the testimony was closed to the public. Only a handful of senators attended, and the transcript remained classified until 1997.[74]

On March 6, Michael Wood told the senators that the CIA claims were lies. One by one, he addressed the Agency's contentions. One of the "most distressing things" was the State Department's assertion that "only two people each had been involved" in a given year. He challenged the scope of the operation, telling the senators the students did commit espionage for the CIA, and that the international agenda was determined by the CIA.[75]

Wood explained the difference between a subsidy and an operation: "The last and gravest misrepresentation was to represent the relationship as a subsidy."[76] He described it as "an integral relationship in which staff of NSA . . . became junior bureaucrats in Covert Action No. 5 or the Plans Divisions of the CIA." He pointed out that programs were approved by the CIA bureaucracy, not the NSA constituency.[77]

But the senators, away from the cameras and assured of secrecy, were in a playful mood. Senators Eugene McCarthy, Clifford Case (R-N.J.), and Fulbright teased one another about their reported complicity in organizations alleged in the press to be receiving CIA subsidies. Senator McCarthy quipped, "I found that I am a director of at least eight of these organizations at this point."[78] Senator Case referred to the *Ramparts* article and teased, "Are you a pipe, a conduit?" Chairman Fulbright chimed in, "You are?" McCarthy chortled, "I am. Do you want me to leave the room?" Senator Claiborne Pell (D-R. I.) joined the repartee with the news he was on "that Cuban Freedom Committee." The all-in-fun exchange ended in laughter.[79]

Ten days later, on March 16, Eugene Groves and Richard Stearns entered Room 116 of the Capitol to explain what they knew of the NSA-CIA relationship. This time the closed session consisted of only four senators—John Sparkman (D-Ala.), Albert Gore, Sr. (D-Tenn.), Case, and Fulbright.

According to the declassified transcript, on March 6, Senator Fulbright had told his colleagues in private, "The thing that disturbed me very much when I first read the report about this case in *The Washington Post*, well, my first reaction was, what is the Senate for? I guess we are serving as a front to make people think we have a democracy for the boys who really run the country, who are the very people that are described in this article, who have the foundations and who control the CIA and all the other agencies." Senator Joseph S. Clark (D-Penn.) supported him, saying, "I felt that ever since I came here."[80]

But by the time Fulbright spoke publicly, in an article for the *New York Times Magazine*, his tone was measured: "The fair evaluation of any human act requires that due account be taken of the time and circumstances in which the act took place."[81] Cord Meyer, who had been at odds with Fulbright over Vietnam, later called his public remarks "restrained," noting that "his attitude was important in moderating the congressional reaction."[82] Fulbright's mildly critical piece, "We Must Not Fight Fire with Fire," presented the NSA-CIA relationship as "a clear case of cold-war expediency." But Fulbright said he did not understand why it continued "when communism is no longer a threat."[83]

In a 1982 oral history interview, Richard Helms praised the damage control effort. He singled out statements from Senators Russell and Kennedy as crucial. "The fact that Senator Russell spoke up publicly and said that he had known about the agency's support of the National Student Association, followed by the public statement by Robert Kennedy that he had also known about this and had approved it, turned off the firestorm that was about to begin over this."[84]

President Johnson had given the Katzenbach Committee six weeks to complete its work. The investigation, such as it was, fell largely to one man, Katzenbach's aide Jack Rosenthal. After some negotiation, Helms agreed to let Rosenthal view original documents held at the CIA headquarters. For several days, a chauffeur-driven car picked up the young aide and drove him to Langley. Upon entering the CIA building, Rosenthal would be escorted into a small, windowless room, where he waited for a man to bring in a locked metal case. The CIA employee would carefully unlock the case, lift out a stack of documents, and sit outside the closed door. At the end of each day, he would return, scoop up the documents, and lock them back inside the metal case.[85]

Rosenthal could not believe what he read. "There were literally hundreds of organizations." He tried to approach the task as a journalist and organize the material in categories. "Some were quaint or outdated or of no consequence"; some he could not understand; a handful required a policy judgment. He tried to visualize concentric circles with the outer circle containing projects that could be made public. A second ring contained projects with limited disclosure. The inner ring, projects that were too difficult to deal with quickly, which could be sent to a future commission or "be kicked upstairs."[86] Once he came up with a system, he called it drudge work.

Rosenthal describes his encounters with Meyer as surprisingly cordial. He had heard of Meyer's harsh reputation, yet Meyer, rather than trying to browbeat him, tried to explain the rationale behind the operations. Meyer argued that the CIA wanted to work with liberals who were unable to obtain congressional funding, yet another explanation for the covert nature of the funding that soon gained currency.[87]

Meyer may have been pleasant to Rosenthal, but privately he was in a rage. He blamed the American public, the treachery of students, and the media. On March 10, he confided to his diary that, while it would take some time for him to understand what happened and why, he was certain of three things: "1) There is in this country a widespread conviction that 'the Cold War' was at best a struggle peculiar to the 1950s and at worst a confrontation that we ourselves provoked against an innocent Stalin. 2) Many of the most intelligent youth believe that if the means are pure the end will be good and that the survival of democratic institutions can only be insured by making them totally open, no matter what. 3) The N.Y. Times and the Washington Post are committed to the proposition that the CIA is a worse danger to American democracy than any conceivable external enemy and must be exposed as such."[88]

Throughout February and March, reporters from major newspapers around the country found evidence of CIA connections to more organizations. On February 18, the *Washington Post* carried three separate stories that identified additional foundations and organizations linked to the CIA.[89] Reporters retraced *Ramparts* investigator Michael Ansara's steps and discovered that funds given to these conduits corresponded dollar for dollar to awarded grants. The *Los Angeles Times* identified at least twenty-one conduits and foundations and more than fifty grantees.[90] One *Washington Post* headline read, "O What a Tangled Web the CIA Wove," and the article detailed CIA recruitment of "intellectuals, students, educators, trade unionists, journalists, and professional men."[91]

Despite the extensive reporting, a chorus of denial rose along the eastern seaboard. George Meany, head of the AFL-CIO, called charges of CIA involvement in labor "a damned lie." He brazenly asserted, "Not one penny of CIA money has ever come in to the AFL or the CIO to my knowledge over the last twenty years."[92] A few months later, former CIA agent Tom Braden undercut Meany's sweeping denials when he published a defense of the CIA's domestic programs in the *Saturday Evening Post*, and described the Agency's passing cash to the AFL-CIO's chief international operative, Jay Lovestone.[93] Allen Dulles and Braden never spoke again. Despite Braden's revelations, both Meany and Lovestone continued to deny the accusations. The pattern continued with the American Newspaper Guild, the American Fund for Free Jurists, the National Council of Churches, and numerous others.

Of all the identified recipients of CIA largess, the United States Youth Council (USYC) had the trickiest problem. It received 90 percent of its funding from FYSA, publicly identified by *Ramparts* as a CIA conduit.[94] Second, former NSA officers and staff held top positions in the USYC and had already acknowledged the CIA-NSA relationship, among them Gregory Gallo, who had led Stephen Robbins to his CIA induction ceremony.[95] Since it was impossible to claim complete ignorance, the USYC conducted a brief investigation, which largely consisted of paying a visit to CIA paymaster Harry Lunn. The subsequent report took the non-denial denial defense to new levels: USYC officials found no evidence to suggest that FYSA was a conduit.[96]

Lakhina's vigorous defense of COSEC did not survive the April 1967 Supervision Commission meeting.[97] Lakhina had solicited statements in advance from former British and American student officers attesting to the independence of the secretariat. The responses, available in the ISC archives, are almost comically identical. Most arrived on the same day. Edward Garvey, who reluctantly came to COSEC on orders from CIA headquarters, wrote, "During my term of office with the ISC Secretariat I had absolutely no reason to suspect that any relationship existed between the CIA and the ISC nor do I believe that any such relationship existed."[98] George Foulkes and Gwyn Morgan from Britain similarly said there was "no reason to suspect" any relationship. Jyoti Shankar Singh, then head of the CIA-funded World Assembly of Youth, varied his response slightly: "There was no reason or evidence to believe that any of the money provided to ISC originated from any secret agency."[99] Former COSEC directors John M. Thompson and Hans Dall took up another common refrain: whatever the source of funding, there were "no strings attached."[100]

The strategy did not work. The Supervision Commission members, meeting in Leiden, voted not to accept any new grants from FYSA or the San Jacinto Fund. By the third day of the meeting, everyone realized that the survival of the ISC was at stake. Numerous student unions had already resigned in protest. The Supervision Commission ordered a full investigation, unaware of the irony that it was CIA funds that had enabled them to convene.[101]

The investigation was doomed from the beginning. The British representatives, who like the NSA had a stake in preventing the disclosure of intelligence involvement, led the investigation.[102] Harry Lunn stonewalled. He called the request to view FYSA records an "invasion of privacy" of board member Amory Houghton's business affairs. Investigators pressed Lunn on the contradiction between his acknowledged role as NSA president, and his denial that FYSA was a conduit. Lunn gave three answers, all lies. First, he claimed that "FYSA was not involved in this relationship during his term of [NSA] office." Then he portrayed Houghton as "most upset" over allegations that FYSA was a conduit, since the charge was "totally untrue." Finally, he denied that FYSA was a Cold War instrument, going so far as to state that it had made funds available to communist students but they "had not been collected."[103]

Despite the fact that CIA-funded recipients remained under siege, Cord Meyer evinced optimism about the Agency's ability to continue covert operations. On March 20, he wrote to his deputy Tad Davis that he had seen the Katzenbach Committee report in draft. "Although we will be severely restricted in our contacts with domestic institutions, they are trying to give us leeway in which to operate."[104] A few days later, on March 29, the formal report was submitted to President Johnson, who subsequently announced an executive order prohibiting CIA use of private-sector organizations. Despite the apparent blanket prohibition, Meyer wrote to another CIA lieutenant, "New ground rules will be restrictive but not prohibitive."[105]

The damage control measures might have pleased CIA officials but not those who wished to see a full investigation. Even NSA president Groves characterized the Katzenbach Committee report as a whitewash.[106] For his part, Douglass Cater lambasted Groves for divulging details of the NSA-CIA relationship, and also for revealing that the two had spoken before the *Ramparts* article was published. Groves apologized to Cater for "compromising his position," and tried to explain his actions. He defended the phrase "ethical trap" used in the NSA press release, pointing out that it had replaced even sharper language.[107]

Groves tried to put his actions in a larger context. "A large portion of our mail has exhibited condemnation of past officers who, in the constituents minds, have sold out a generation of young Americans." He suggested that Cater see this anger "as a manifestation of a growing disaffection, not simply with the current administration, but with the processes of national government itself." Groves pointed to the war, the draft, and disappointment with progress on civil rights. There is a feeling, he told Cater, that "government is inherently dishonest."[108]

Groves was not alone in his criticism of the Katzenbach Committee. NSA veteran Curtis Gans, then staff director for Americans for Democratic Action, organized a protest petition that called for an impartial investigation. It was signed by Groves along with fifty former NSA staff and officers.[109] The petition also praised Sherburne and Groves's actions against the more inflammatory charges by left-wing critics.

The protests came to naught. The CIA, the State Department, the White House, and most of Congress had no interest in further investigation. The flap had been contained. In May, Cord Meyer received one of three medals he was to be awarded for distinguished service.[110] Soon after, Helms appointed him chief of station in London. Kiley rose within the CIA to become Helms's assistant.

During the summer of 1967, former NSA president Dennis Shaul stopped off in London to see Eden Lipson, a University of California graduate who had been active in the association. During a long evening, Shaul tried to justify the CIA relationship. According to Lipson's notes made immediately afterward, Shaul averred, "The big fish are still under water."[111]

THE ENEMY AT HOME

THE CIA BARELY TOOK A breath before it shifted into domestic sur-veillance of the NSA. Before the August 1967 Congress, CIA director Helms ordered agents to monitor and report on the sessions.[1] But even before the *Ramparts* article was published, the Agency had embarked on a campaign of petty harassment and reprisals.

Philip Sherburne and Steven Arons were not the only people whose draft status was reclassified. In February 1967, the Presidential Appeal Board denied draft deferments for five NSA staff members. At that time, deferments for Groves and Stearns also remained uncertain.[2] The NSA might survive the firestorm of publicity if member schools rallied round. It could not survive the wholesale draft of officers and staff.

In desperation, Groves and Stearns turned for help to former NSA vice president Leonard Bebchick, then practicing law in Washington. On March 9, Bebchick wrote a "personal and confidential" letter to Nicholas Katzenbach in which he pointed out the obvious: denial of the deferments would "spell the demise of the Association." He also ap-pealed to the administration's self-interest: "I am equally distressed over the repercussions to the President, the Administration and the Agency which may flow from the change in position of the Presidential Appeal Board." The issue would be "exploited by the press," which might infer that past deferments were "favoritism due to covert ties."[3]

In addition, CIA officials tried to evict the students from NSA head-quarters on S Street.[4] The National Supervisory Board had voted to terminate the fifteen-year rent-free lease negotiated by Sherburne, and urged Groves and Stearns to assume the mortgage for the NSA. CIA officials threatened to engage in a new form of a shell game: bankrupt the dummy foundation that held title to the property in order to clear the way for a possible foreclosure of the mortgage.[5] The NSA countered with a threat to disclose more details about the relationship with the CIA. Negotiations came to a halt. The NSA turned to veteran civil liberties lawyer Joseph L. Rauh, Jr., for further assistance as the stalemate persisted.

In August, Director Helms stepped in. He consulted the top-secret 303 Committee. The subsequent "divorce agreement," as it became known, enabled the NSA to assume the mortgage of $65,000.[6] Rauh further negotiated a hold-harmless clause to protect the NSA against any financial liability incurred by the relationship. Helms described the agreement as an "efficacious egress" from an awkward situation.[7] On August 22, just days before the Congress was to convene, Helms, Cord Meyer, and Kiley met with Groves, Stearns, and attorney Rauh to review the final agreement.[8]

Few of the fifteen hundred students who traveled to the University of Maryland in a display of support for the NSA knew of these machinations beyond the threat of eviction, which had made the newspapers in part because the *Washington Evening Star* reporter Bob Walters had an inside line on information. Walters had once worked for the NSA as an administrative assistant, and had extensive contact with former officers, remaining on friendly terms with both Sherburne and Kiley.[9]

Nor did the largely undergraduate crowd at Maryland know that the CIA was monitoring their debates.[10] Agents surely got an earful. At one major plenary, Allard Lowenstein appeared before the delegates and spoke passionately against the war in Vietnam. That evening he proposed a campaign to prevent the reelection of President Johnson. Curtis Gans and Sam Brown, present for the plenary session, had already signed on to the "Dump Johnson" movement, which drew NSA students in droves. Delegates also voted to support resistance to the draft and called for an all-volunteer army.[11] Ed Schwartz narrowly defeated Sam Brown, the NSB chair, for president.

Helms sent the collected intelligence on the Congress to National Security Advisor Walt Rostow, acknowledging its illegality: "The agency should not be reporting at all on domestic matters of this sort."[12] Nonetheless, Helms continued the practice under President Nixon, sending reports to National Security Advisor Henry A. Kissinger.[13]

Helms also resorted to darker psychological warfare measures through the Mighty Wurlitzer stable of journalists. Helms put a new story into circulation: the *Ramparts* revelations were part of a KGB plot, executed in Prague, fostered by a mole in COSEC, and carried out by complicit left-wing American journalists. These charges would be risible had Helms not repeated them in his 2003 memoir, where he wrote that after his conversation with President Johnson on February 13, 1967, he was not "entirely surprised" about the forthcoming revelations because he had a copy of a KGB gray letter.[14] The document, which Helms claimed was a KGB forgery, listed charges of CIA influence within COSEC. The forgery, he wrote, "alerted us to the presence of a Soviet sympathizer or, perhaps, agent within the [COSEC] secretariat."[15]

When they were informed during interviews that Helms had repeated these charges in his memoir, both Tony Smith and Robert Kiley blanched. Smith, who read the book before publication, lamented his laxity: "I should have caught that."[16] Kiley was more withering about his former boss. He suggested that Helms, who had assistance writing his memoir, "forgot to read that section."[17] But in 1967, a CIA-friendly columnist, Carl Rowan, dutifully put the rumors of a Soviet plot into public circulation.[18]

Long-time journalist and editor David Lawrence of *U.S. News and World Report*, a close friend of Allen Dulles and a proponent of the Vietnam War, also publicized the notion of a communist conspiracy.[19] In a widely circulated column, Lawrence wrote, "Both the Russians and the Red Chinese have infiltrated student organizations in the United States, which are fomenting discord and starting demonstrations to help turn public opinion against the American government." Any investigation, he continued, should be aimed at groups in the United States, "who operate in the interest of the Communist Party."[20]

While there is little evidence that the American public took seriously the accusation of a Soviet plot, the CIA and the FBI did. Both agencies were convinced that students had become part of a larger conspiracy to undermine the United States. On August 15, just days before the NSA Congress, James Jesus Angleton authorized Richard Ober, who had been running the anti-*Ramparts* operation, to "disrupt the enemy at home." The new mandate went beyond intelligence gathering, and included "the entire anti-war press and some 500 newspapers." The operation, code-named MH/CHAOS, did not stop at the water's edge: "MH" indicated that it was worldwide.[21]

Even before Ober received the expanded authority, on April 4, 1967, he had given Helms a report on 127 reporters, writers, and editors associated with *Ramparts*, along with details on 200 others with a contact at or a relationship with the magazine.[22] The report's conclusions and recommendations are still classified, but the journalist Angus Mackenzie interviewed Louis Dube, a CIA official who had read the report, and Dube pronounced it "heady shit." In August, Ober moved his operation of twelve-plus staff into special vaults in the basement of Langley, and expanded the number of suspect antiwar newspapers to 500.[23]

The breadth of Angleton's new charge stunned even Ober. "I can still vividly remember saying to myself at that moment, as I walked back to my office, that I had a bear by the tail. I was convinced then that the project would ultimately leak with explosive results."[24] Angleton had originally considered Cord Meyer for the task, thus leaving a choice — according to CIA insiders — between a man "not entirely sane" (Meyer) and one who was "paranoid" and "truly evil" (Ober).[25] Meyer declined the job. Before long, the NSA was in Ober's crosshairs. Declassified files from the CIA and FBI between 1967 and 1975 contain numerous documents on the association.[26]

The Dump Johnson movement elevated the visibility of Lowenstein, Gans, and Brown as targets. After Johnson bowed out of the 1968 election, scores of former NSA students could be found campaigning for the antiwar candidate Eugene McCarthy, and later for Robert F. Kennedy. Brown went on to lead the Vietnam Moratorium, organizing communities across the nation to light candles and march for peace. The more radical New Mobilization Against the War drew heavily on early SDS members active in the NSA, among them Paul Potter, Paul Booth, and Tom Hayden.[27] The list of former NSA people who led protest movements over the next decade is long and largely outside the scope of this book. One particularly egregious report, "Restless Youth," was sent by Helms to the White House; a summary of it survives today on the Internet, a fact that makes Kiley wince in disbelief.[28] He recalled the report as scurrilous and remembers advising Helms "to take a match to it."[29]

The CIA operation that began with a vendetta against *Ramparts* and expanded to include antiwar groups had significant long-term consequences. It set in motion an even larger catastrophe for the CIA. One may draw a straight line from the *Ramparts* exposures in 1967 to the 1975 congressional hearings on CIA activities and the revelation of the so-called Family Jewels, a collection of documents containing the deepest Agency secrets, including its part in assassinations. Many say the Agency never recovered.

In an oral history conducted after his retirement, Helms cited "the *Ramparts* business" as one of two factors precipitating the hearings. The other was the 1972 break-in at the Watergate Hotel when several "burglars" caught in the offices of the Democratic Party headquarters were revealed to have CIA backgrounds.[30] Nowhere does Helms acknowledge the common denominator of his pursuit of *Ramparts*, the Ober operation, and the motives of the Watergate burglars: all were attempts to prove foreign involvement in the antiwar movement.

The 1975 hearings were conducted by the Senate Foreign Relations Committee, led by chair Frank Church (D-Idaho). The committee peeled backed another layer of the NSA onion of secrets, but by no means revealed the core of the operation. In 2004, the staff director of the Church hearings, F. A. O. Schwarz, Jr., said he had no understanding then that the NSA activities included extensive reporting to the CIA on foreign students, a practice he calls "very serious indeed."[31] Despite fervent denials at the time, witting students *were* involved in espionage, as I have documented in this volume.

In 1977, the NSA changed its name to the United States Student Association. Since then, it has focused primarily on domestic student issues, lobbying for Pell grants and protesting the cost of higher education. This ironic return to the *students as students* mandate of 1947 was not entirely by choice. Several former USSA presidents argue that lingering suspicions about the CIA made it impossible to conduct overseas activities.[32]

The CIA has sought to prevent the USSA from finding out the truth about its history. In the early 1980s, the USSA engaged two pro bono attorneys to file a Freedom of Information lawsuit, a process that took many years. A federal judge supported the CIA in its request to withhold many documents in the name of national security but the Agency was forced to produce what is known as a Vaughn Index, a listing of denied documents by date and title.

David Sobel, one of the attorneys, spent hours working with the vast NSA international collection at the Hoover Institution, correlating Vaughn Index entries with archival material. One day the documents added to the Vaughn Index began appearing without dates, preventing him from making any further correlations. According to Sobel, a Justice Department official told him, "We know what you are doing."[33]

Now that a historical record exists, questions that remained unanswered in 1967 can be answered. For the first time, witting participants have gone on record and discussed the deeper issues raised by their activities: Were the counteroffensive strategies effective? Did the CIA help win the student Cold War? And who was the real "enemy at home"?

AFTER ALLEN DULLES RETIRED, the director bragged about the NSA operation. "We got everything we wanted. I think what we did was worth every penny. If we turned back the communists and made them milder and easier to live with, it was because we stopped them in certain areas, and the student area was one of them."[34]

Cord Meyer focused on the downside, viewing the demise of the operation in apocalyptic terms: "In retrospect, the decision taken by default not to replace the termination of CIA funding by some method of reliable open government support was an act of unilateral disarmament in the face of a continuing Soviet threat." Meyer cited the campaign against the production of a neutron bomb in 1977 as an example of a Soviet victory, once again suggesting that such protests could not be homegrown.[35]

In assessing these sweeping claims, we need to distinguish the original CIA objectives from those that came later. In the late 1940s and early 1950s, the CIA had straightforward goals: to deny the Soviets a monopoly position among the world's students, to build goodwill with foreign students, and to win adherents to democratic values.

Former COSEC and FYSA official David Baad agrees in part with Dulles. He believes that the early denial operations were successful: "We did stop the IUS in its tracks." He argues that in the mid-to-late 1950s, "the IUS had almost no noncommunist members."[36] Baad speculates that the mere existence of the ISC and COSEC prevented the IUS from fully using its "professional capability" and limited the ability of a KGB cadre to operate within the IUS.[37]

But as the years wore on and the objectives multiplied, those who understand the NSA-CIA relationship best offer more nuanced, often negative, assessments. The candid views of Baad, Tony Smith, and Robert Kiley, all career agents, and of Edward Garvey, Thomas Olson, Ronald Story, Duncan Kennedy, and others who spent several years or more with the CIA, are remarkable when one considers how passionately they felt about fighting the Cold War.

"A lot of things we had set out to do just did not work," says Baad. "As I look back at the ISC, and COSEC in particular, the preponderance of people from the Third World were there because they saw it as a step towards a career outside their country." Most COSEC staff never returned home. Many went on to careers in international organizations.[38]

Baad is also skeptical about the efficacy of scholarship programs and cultural exchanges as Cold War weapons. He thinks most students in NSA-sponsored programs left the United States "with mixed feelings." They were upset by the racism, he said, although that was not the only problem. He cites factors that ranged from language difficulty to feelings of isolation and even cold weather. He searches for a way to mitigate his negative assessment. "Maybe if they thought back on it, fifteen to twenty years later, they'd have a different view."[39]

Smith believes there were residual positive effects of the NSA's backing of the Algerian revolutionaries: for example, the American hostages freed by Iran at the beginning of the Reagan administration were transported to Algiers. But he readily admits he may be blinded by his intense feelings: "I was a real believer in Algerian independence, and I so fiercely wanted it to succeed."[40]

By contrast, Kiley does not see any lasting effect to the support of Algerian revolutionaries. "None of those people are of any account whatever in Algeria," he says. "It just didn't add up to a hill of beans . . . that's the real lesson of that entire period of time."[41] But in defense of the CIA operation, Kiley points out, "It was all a gamble. It was like playing pin the tail on the donkey in the dark." He is quick to say that he does not mean that it was a game, but that the people involved "really didn't know any better" because "there weren't that many tools available."[42]

Clement Moore, who today goes by the name Clement M. Henry, makes a broader point about projecting the ability of educated elites to lead newly independent nations. After studying Algerian students who led UGEMA, he concluded that "educated leadership could not serve as the effective representative of a complex and changing society."[43]

Opinion is sharply divided among the witting officers on whether the NSA should have relaxed its policy of having no contact between the

ISC and the IUS. Crawford Young believes there was no point in modifying the policy because the IUS was "nothing more than a docile instrument in Moscow's hands."[44] Baad basically agrees, even though he acknowledges that the IUS changed in the early 1960s. He admits that IUS leader Jiří Pelikán "might resist instruction occasionally," but sees no evidence that the IUS ever did anything contrary to Soviet interests.[45]

But Baad argues that an important principle was at stake. "One of our main messages was to distinguish ourselves from what IUS was all about—Soviet control and the promotion of totalitarian government institutions." Contact with the IUS would negate "our raison d'être."[46] Few NSA staff defied the ban. Overseas representative James Scott remembers his case officer's anger when he traveled to Prague on his own, visiting with the secretariat and meeting with Pelikán: "I got slapped around for that."[47]

Today Kiley argues that the no-contact policy was "a serious mistake," something he came to feel "more and more strongly" as time passed. Even at the time, he argued to his superiors in the CIA that "it was stupid" to refuse contact. Their fear, as Kiley recalled it, was that "the Third World types would not be able to resist the line coming from the bad guys." Today he calls this reasoning "truly ludicrous." If students were that susceptible, "we might as well find out now and not waste money and time." Looking back, he describes the CIA's intransigence as representing "a certain truly paranoid and narrow view of the world."[48]

Although no one has systematically studied the careers of those who played leadership roles in the ISC or the IUS, anecdotal evidence suggests that the ones who later rose to governmental positions in their countries were as likely to have been affiliated with the IUS as the ISC.

Asked why he thought militants as well as moderates had risen to national positions, Young, who became a specialist on Africa at the University of Wisconsin, pointed to the "shallowness of their ideological commitments." He said that his experience "once in the field as a professional" led him to conclude that African students studying in Europe often had a narrow view of the world. When they returned home, they had to confront reality and deal with African masses who did not use Marxist-Leninist language. "Militants especially," he said, "moderated their stances."[49] What is ironic about Young's statements is that psychological warfare aims to strengthen the hand of moderates against extremists; no one on the NSA-CIA team ever suggested that, under changed circumstances, militants might moderate themselves.

It is worth pausing to consider that all three major heads of the IUS, Josef Grohman, Jiří Pelikán, and Zybněk Vokrouhlický, emerged as leaders of the reform movement in Czechoslovakia known as the Prague Spring. All three faced down state power. Vokrouhlický, the only one still living in 2008, said that the three IUS leaders met frequently during the Prague Spring, and that all believed that contact with the West was central to their political development. Today Vokrouhlický views the rule of law, rather than democratic principles per se, as the sine qua non of a just society and a guarantor against arbitrary power. He counseled his daughter to study law.[50]

From the opposite side of the Cold War, Clement Henry came to a similar conclusion. Based on his study of revolutionary Algerian students, he wrote: "It is not so much democracy as the rule of law that Algeria most needs to develop its human potential and the civil society that UGEMA once promised."[51] These conclusions should give pause to contemporary advocates of psychological warfare, especially those who believe that the kind of Cold War operations documented in this book should be replicated to fight radical Islam.

THE NSA COLD WARRIORS share something else in common with their ideological counterparts. Tony Smith elaborates: "Eric Hoffer destroyed the utility of the phrase *true believer*, but we did all believe in what we were doing, no matter whether you came in the [CIA] staff route as I did or every other way right up to the Sherburne fork in the road." They were "looking for people who you knew once they understood what was going on would feel totally comfortable in terms of their own Weltanschauung. They were going out and doing something positive and beneficial and significant and important."[52] Clive Gray echoes Smith and other participants: "We did what we did out of conviction."[53]

Those who charge that the CIA controlled NSA officers or staff as a puppeteer a puppet miss the point of ideological commitment and a good recruitment program. When a student—often an older graduate student—signed the security oath and was made witting, he or she was initiated into what Allen Dulles called "a community of interest."[54]

The recruited students shared the same passions and objectives as their CIA case officers. In this sense, it is understandable that witting students would later insist upon their independence. Sharing a common agenda, they felt themselves to be free agents. But that is a very different question from whether the CIA operation compromised *organizational* independence.

At its best, the United States National Student Association was an exercise in democratic self-government. But no delegate of his or her own volition drafted resolutions in support of the Iraqi Ba'ath Party or protested educational conditions in Tunisia or crafted a position on the Rikuyu Islands. No undergraduate thought it important to shore up Puerto Rican governor Muñoz's position within the Organization of American States. No NSA delegate suggested giving Jyoti Shankar Singh cash to attend a university of his choosing.

Perhaps the best evidence of the power of a shared Weltanschauung is what happened when Philip Sherburne disrupted it. When he tried to establish boundaries between the NSA and the CIA—the very boundaries that Garvey insisted were already present—the CIA came down on him with all its power. As Philip Werdell, who was part of Sherburne's staff, later put it: "When outside forces have the secret power to imprison the officer and bankrupt his organization, the constituency is clearly at a disadvantage in the day to day decision-making process if not the ultimate fight for the officer's loyalties."[55]

Today, virtually all witting participants have given up the pretense that the NSA set the international agenda. Former international affairs vice president Bruce Larkin echoes Leonard Bebchick, acknowledging, "The older guys did policy." Scott puts it more graphically: "The tail wagged the dog."[56]

In 1967, Dennis Shaul tried to reconcile the disparity between those who set the NSA international agenda and the students who were supposed to do so. He offered this explanation to Eden Lipson: the resolutions, he said, "reflected the positions we felt the Congress would take if the members in fact knew anything about the situation, which they didn't."[57]

Clive Gray partially agrees, and cites the position on civil rights as an example: delegates were "broadly supportive" of fighting segregation but not ready to take action. Left to their own devices, student governments "were not going to antagonize the Eisenhower administration." But he adds today that he was "uncomfortable that pressure from a secret government agency did affect the decisions taken by NSA."[58]

Even CIA historian Michael Warner, who had access to still-classified material when writing an article on the NSA, concluded, "There is no question that the CIA indirectly influenced NSA offices and positions in domestic as well as international affairs, and it did so—as *Ramparts* magazine and other observers noted—on some of the most explosive issues of the day, including civil rights and Vietnam."[59]

A few insiders have also acknowledged that a legal line may have been crossed, since the CIA charter prohibited domestic activity. Tony Smith recalls his shock when he transferred within the CIA to Covert Action 5. After reading numerous files to prepare for his stint with the NSA, he queried his boss, former NSA president William Dentzer, about the legality of the operation. "I found him defensive," Smith remembered. Today Smith characterizes the CIA role in NSA legislation as "definitely a gray area."[60]

Decades later, Katzenbach Committee member John Gardner offered his perspective. "The thing that strikes me is that so many of these people are good people, well motivated, and well-intentioned people, who had come out of a tough war into another very tough Cold War and had a recognition that sometimes you had to play hardball. It's understandable that a lot of them made this terrible mistake, and I do think it was a terrible mistake." Gardner said he did not oppose secrecy per se, "but the fact is that when you get into deep secrecy, and deeply secret operations, you're involved in a very risky thing." So much that was beneficial, he added, was undercut and discredited.[61]

One of the prevalent justifications for the clandestine relationship put into circulation along with overt lies and distortions in 1967 was that liberal groups like the NSA could not obtain open U.S. government funding because Congress was in the grip of right-wing McCarthyism. Tom Braden first put this explanation into the public domain in the *Saturday Evening Post:* "The idea that Congress would have approved many of our projects was about as likely as the John Birch Society's approving Medicare."[62] While Braden's statement accurately describes the chilling effect of McCarthy's anticommunist attacks on liberal policy agendas and organizations, the question is whether McCarthyism compelled the NSA to accept clandestine funding.

Although alternative historical paths are difficult to argue, consider the implications of direct congressional funding to the NSA. How many foreign students would have openly accepted U.S. government funds? In 1952, the two Indonesians en route to Edinburgh were reluctant to take American funds from *private* sources. When asked for his views on this question, Bebchick, an ardent defender of the NSA-CIA relationship, exclaimed, "Can you imagine what our credibility would have been in dealing with student leaders of Indonesia or of Africa, if we arrived as people who were financed by money from the United States government? We would have no credibility and no entrée."[63] The clout of the NSA depended on its purported independence from U.S. foreign policy.

Cord Meyer, perhaps inadvertently, undermined the argument in his 1985 memoir. He wrote: "The open receipt of official government funds would have damaged the reputation for independence that the NSA had found so valuable in dealing with foreign students."[64] Other top CIA officials, with perhaps less to protect than Meyer, have made the point more bluntly. CIA director Stansfield Turner (1977–81) used intelligence jargon to describe NSA as "a classic cutout," an intermediary designed "to protect foreign recipients from accusations of associating with the CIA or being puppets of the United States."[65]

Michael Warner also touched on the problem of open funding in his article, although he put the onus of *rejecting* government financial support on the students: "At the height of the Cold War, officers of the National Student Association felt they could not openly accept funds from any U.S. government sources without compromising their moral authority and their entree with foreign student groups and leaders."[66] This kind of reasoning infuriates critics: If you compromise your moral authority by taking government funding, how do you maintain your moral authority by taking secret government funding? The pragmatic answer is: Only if you are not caught.

But a more serious issue exists for these witting participants, a concern that goes far beyond whether particular Cold War strategies were effective, whether NSA autonomy was violated, or whether the CIA overstepped its charter. What were the consequences of their intelligence gathering?

In general, the NSA's access to foreign students gave the United States firsthand information that might not have been available to American embassies or CIA officials. Over time, witting staff reported on thousands of foreign students' political tendencies, personality traits, and future aspirations. They submitted detailed analyses of political dynamics within foreign student unions and countries. Thomas Olson, who spent five years in various NSA and CIA positions, noted that NSA staff were rewarded for speed and accuracy. As he reviewed his experience, he found himself wondering whether the entire operation existed solely for the purpose of intelligence gathering.[67]

Considerable reporting focused on the International Student Conference and may therefore have been of limited utility. Duncan Kennedy, who worked at CIA headquarters in 1966–67, observed that the NSA "dumped a lot of information into the system that it didn't particularly want."[68] Yet Kennedy is among those who now worries about the information pipeline inside the agency. Edward Garvey, who also worked at CIA headquarters, puts it more dramatically: "My God, did we finger people for the Shah?"[69]

The NSA had unique access to Iranian dissidents in the United States, especially during the years that Ali Fatemi was in charge of the Iranian student union ISAUS. Surviving reports give intimate detail on internal ISAUS politics and on individual Iranians. The NSA was even privy to the formation of the Students Revolutionary Committee and their plans to obtain arms from the Algerians. As Fatemi emphasizes today, every member of the committee could have been killed if SAVAK agents had gained access to those reports.[70]

Stephen Robbins, despite his limited CIA involvement during his year as president, echoes Garvey's concern: "It's South Africa that keeps me up at night."[71] Did the NSA supply names of those who fought the apartheid regime to the South African government? Recall the moments of sheer terror described by exiled South African leader John Shingler when he and Magnus Gunther confided the top-secret activities of the African Resistance Movement to David Baad, and Baad pressed them for names.[72] Again, there is no evidence that NSA reports were involved in the arrests of ARM leaders, but we cannot be sure they were not.

Baad, who has the most long-term experience with CIA covert operations, distinguishes between the Iranian and South African situations. In the Iranian case, "it's possible" that intelligence was shared because "the Shah was our ally." He is skeptical about whether this happened in South Africa because "most people in the Agency didn't like the regime."[73] Yet as the record shows, the CIA never supported only one side of a political battle; in 1962, CIA officials helped facilitate the arrest of Nelson Mandela.

Asked today about these two situations, Kiley insists that protecting sources is "cardinal rule number one." In all likelihood, "a source is someone who would be used over and over again, so there would be a very high premium attached to protecting the person, almost at any cost." The thought that anyone in the CIA would "betray a source" to a foreign government is something, he argues, that "just doesn't happen": "the whole house of cards would come down if word got out."[74]

But the problem is not just protecting friendly sources. NSA reports included information on unfriendly nationalists, militants, and communist students. Even Smith says, "I assumed that, yeah, we might pass on the names of pro-Soviet Iranians in the Tudeh Party, and I wouldn't feel too badly about the names we identified." But Smith, too, seems chagrined that he did not consider this problem at the time. "I'm a career staff officer and I never thought about it."[75] During an interview, Bebchick, who served in an earlier era and did very little reporting, returned to the question of what happened to all the reports: "You raise an important point. I have never thought about it."[76]

Kiley, Baad, and Smith all acknowledge that counterintelligence chief James Jesus Angleton was the logical recipient for NSA reports. The mole-searcher's job was to make sure that foreign students who came to the United States were not communist agents. Still, Baad argues it is just as likely that general reporting went into "a black hole" inside the Agency.[77]

While it is tempting to charge Kiley, Baad, and Smith (and others) with willful blindness, something more powerful appears to be at work, something that returns us to the concept of Weltanschauung. These men shared a worldview: they hated communism and trusted the CIA. Good and evil seemed self-evident. They still speak of "good guys" and "bad guys." Those who knew them in the early 1960s remember them—in their trench coat uniforms, with their bulging briefcases, portable typewriters, and the appointment books they called "success diaries"—as supremely confident men, not given to self-doubt. Most did not question the CIA's methods or motives until they gained some distance from the experience. It is not surprising that the witting participants most troubled by the question of intelligence reports served during a time when characterizing foreign students was difficult: when they were reporting on a wide variety of nationalists, radicals, socialists, militants, Maoists, and Fidelistas. The danger of mischaracterization rose accordingly.

But even if we grant the NSA-CIA cadre shared ideals, noble goals, and altruistic motives, none of these in itself offers enough justification for covert action. It also must be judged in terms of consequences and outcomes. In light of the record offered here, Meyer's overwrought conclusions about unilateral disarmament are clearly not warranted. Nor does Allen Dulles's boast hold up. What, then, were the contributions of CIA domestic covert operations to the Cold War? This research suggests that we look more closely at specific objectives and specific goals before drawing any final conclusions.

What is striking about this record is that witting participants are mostly, though not entirely, in agreement about the successes and failures of the covert project. Whether the goal was instilling democratic values, fostering a commitment to democratic institutions, grooming students to be pro-West, or winning the allegiance of revolutionaries, the record is mixed at best and frequently dismal: the only success they all agree on is that the NSA-CIA operation denied the Soviets an exclusive franchise among students in the early period of the Cold War.

Still, paradoxes abound: there is no evidence that the ISC, in its role as an exemplar of democracy, ever persuaded anyone not of like mind to abandon communist doctrine. All three Czech communist leaders of the IUS agree that contact with the West was crucial to reshaping their allegiances and values, yet the CIA never modified its no-contact policy with the IUS. Perhaps it is appropriate to return to Eleanor Roosevelt's admonition of the early 1940s: the problem with hidden allegiances is that they close off a critical element of democracy, persuasion and debate, and to recognize that they carry an even more dangerous risk for a free society—the suppression of dissent and the pursuit of the dissenters.

CAST OF CHARACTERS

The following list is not intended to be exhaustive; rather, it contains figures of importance throughout the story I tell here. For an understanding of the term witting, *see the CIA Glossary, available at CIA.gov, which defines an* asset *as "a person with a formal relationship characterized by a witting agreement and a degree of commitment and control and who provides information or services."*

Manuel Aragon, Jr. Air Force, 1951–55; ISRS graduate, 1957; staff, NSA Latin American specialist, 1959–60; traveled to Cuba for NSA, 1959; NSA Latin American specialist, 1960–61; NSA delegate to ISCs in Lima, 1959, Klosters, 1960, Quebec, 1962. Witting.

Robert J. Aragon In military intelligence reserve; ISRS graduate, 1959; NSA Latin American specialist, September–December, 1959; January 1960–September 1962; NSA delegate to ISC in Lima, 1959; Quebec, 1962; held FYSA-funded position in Santiago, Chile. Witting.

David Baad COSEC press relations, 1958–59; editor, COSEC publication *The Student*, 1959–61; staff, CIA-funded WAY, 1962–63; FYSA staff; career agent. Witting.

Robert Backoff Special assistant, NSA International Commission, 1962–63; NSA representative in Paris, 1963–65. Witting.

Harald C. Bakken President, NSA, 1956–57; director, FSLP, 1958–59; director, ISRS, 1960 and 1961. Witting. (Deceased, 1998.)

Leonard Bebchick ISRS graduate, 1953; president, NSA, 1953–54; NSA delegate to ISC in Istanbul, 1954; director, ISRS, 1955; co-director, the IRS counteroffensive to the Vienna World Youth Festival, 1958–59. Witting.

Thomas Braden Staff officer, CIA International Organizations, 1950–54. (Deceased, 2009.)

Sam W. Brown ISRS graduate, 1965; chair, NSA National Supervisory Board, 1966–67. Not witting.

Sally Cassidy Ridgely Manor trainee, 1946; U.S. Catholic bishops' representative in Paris to monitor European student activities, briefed Vatican officials, and reported to Martin McLaughlin, 1946–47; exercised proxy vote for McLaughlin at IUS Council meeting, 1947; advised American Catholics on strategy for NSA Constitutional Convention, 1947. Witting status unknown or unverified. (Deceased, 2012.)

Douglass S. Cater OSS, Russian Section, 1943–45; delegate, Prague 25, 1946; founder, HIACOM, 1946; member, National Student Organization Continuations Committee, 1946–47; spearheaded HIACOM international projects, 1947; journalist,

Reporter magazine, 1950–64; special assistant to the secretary, U.S. Army, 1951; consultant to director, Mutual Security Agency, 1952; consultant to Department of State, 1961; author of secret report, now declassified, "Coordination and Overall Supervision of All U.S. Resources in the Propaganda-Political Warfare Field"; Special Assistant to President Lyndon Baines Johnson, 1964–1968. Witting status unknown or unverified. (Deceased, 1995.)

Erskine Childers Vice president, NSA International Affairs, 1949–50; opposed State Department interference in NSA affairs. Not witting. (Deceased, 1996.)

Melvin Conant Staff, HIACOM, 1951; undertook Southeast Asia tour for NSA and HIACOM, 1951. Witting status unknown or unverified. (Deceased, 2003.)

Ralph Della Cava ISRS graduate, 1954; NSA Latin American specialist, 1956–59; accompanied Hungarian students on U.S. tour for NSA, 1956; special assignment with Hungarian UFHS, 1957. Witting.

William Dentzer President, NSA, 1951–52; associate secretary, COSEC, 1952–53; NSA delegate to ISCs in Edinburgh, 1952, Copenhagen, 1953, Istanbul, 1954; chair, CIA-funded Research and Investigation Commission, 1954–55; career CIA agent in Youth and Student Affairs. Witting.

Lucille Dubois Directed NSA Latin American Subcommission, University of Miami, Cora Gables, 1956–59. Not witting.

Allen Dulles OSS, 1942–45; member, CFR, 1927–69; deputy director, CIA Plans division, 1950–52; director, CIA, 1953–61. (Deceased, 1969.)

Peter Eckstein ISRS graduate, 1957; took part in NSA–Soviet editors exchange, 1958; assistant director, ISRS, 1958–59; staff, NSA International Commission, 1959–60; editor, COSEC publication *The Student*, 1962–63. Witting status unknown or unverified.

James Edwards President, NSA, 1953–54; NSA representative in Paris, 1954–55; NSA delegate to ISCs in Istanbul, 1954, Birmingham, 1955, Ceylon, 1956, Lima, 1959, Klosters, 1960; associate secretary, COSEC, 1956–57; director, ISRS 1958; Witting. (Deceased, 2000.)

Luigi Einaudi ISRS graduate, 1955; oversaw Latin American affairs for NSA, 1955–56; member, ISC delegation to Central and South America, 1957; NSA delegate to ISCs in Birmingham, 1955, Ceylon, 1956. Witting.

Herbert Eisenberg Vice president, NSA International Affairs, 1950–51. Witting status unknown or unverified.

William Ellis NICC delegate with Prague 25, 1946; vice president, IUS, 1946; NSA delegate to ISC in Istanbul, 1954; worked as occasional FYSA-funded consultant to NSA, 1953–54. Witting status unknown or unverified.

Donald K. Emmerson ISRS graduate, 1961; vice president NSA International Affairs, 1961–62; NSA delegate to ISC in Quebec, 1962; associate secretary, COSEC, 1963–64; leader of Radical Middle Caucus at NSA Congress, 1965. Witting.

Michael Enwall ISRS graduate, 1965; NSA Middle East desk, 1965–66. My former husband. Witting.

Thomas L. Farmer In military intelligence; directed NSA German survey project, 1949; drafted proposal for German Seminar, 1949; co-director, German Seminar, 1950; member, Military Intelligence Reserve Unit, Boston; joined CIA as assistant to Allen Dulles, circa 1951; later worked for Frank Wisner and Thomas Braden. Witting.

Frank Fisher Vice chair, HIACOM, 1946; chair, HIACOM, 1947; adviser to NSA, 1946–52; traveled as NSA representative to Southeast Asia, 1952. Witting status unknown or unverified.

Roger Fisher Harvard law professor; lawyer for Philip Sherburne, 1967.

Edward Gable Assistant to president, NSA, 1952–53; assistant director, FSLP, 1956–57; director, FSLP, 1957–February 1958; CIA career. Witting.

Gregory Gallo ISRS graduate, 1962; president, NSA, 1963–64. Witting.

Curtis Gans ISRS graduate, 1959; NSA National Affairs vice president, 1959–60; staffed Liberal Caucus, NSA Congress, 1961. Not witting.

Edward Garvey ISRS graduate, 1961; president, NSA, 1961–62; delegate to ISCs in Quebec, 1962; Christchurch, 1964; Nairobi, 1966. NSA representative in Paris, 1962–63; CIA headquarters staff, 1964–65; secretary general, COSEC, 1965–66. Witting.

Charles Goldmark ISRS graduate, 1965; assistant to the NSA International Commission, 1965; vice president, NSA International Affairs, 1965–66; NSA delegate to ISC, in Nairobi; associate secretary, COSEC, 1966–67. Witting. (Deceased, 1986.)

James P. Grant In military intelligence; conducted NSA Southeast survey, 1950; developed HIACOM projects, 1950–51; Adviser to witting NSA staff, 1951–54. Witting status unknown or unverified. (Deceased, 1995.)

Clive Gray ISRS graduate, 1954; vice president, NSA International Affairs, 1955–56; NSA delegate to ISCs in Birmingham, 1955, Ceylon, 1956, Ibadan, 1957, Lima, 1959; NSA representative in Vienna to organize Hungarian refugees, 1956; NSA representative in India, 1957–58. Witting.

Josef Grohman In Czech resistance during World War II; chair, World Student Congress, Prague, 1946; president, IUS, 1946–52; resigned from IUS under Soviet pressure, 1952. (Deceased, 1995.)

Eugene Groves President, NSA, 1966–67. Witting.

James T. (Ted) Harris President, NSA, 1948–49; conducted Middle East survey for NSA, 1952; director, ISRS, 1953; NSA delegate to ISC in Istanbul, 1954; director, FLSP, 1955–56. Witting. (Deceased, 1989.)

George Hazelrigg ISRS graduate, 1959; FSLP, 1962–63; NSA representative in Paris, 1963–64; CIA career staff. Witting.

Richard Helms OSS, 1942–45; CIA career staff, 1947–73; Chief, CIA Plans division, 1963–66; director, CIA, 1966–73; negotiated NSA-CIA "divorce decree." (Deceased, 2002.)

Donald Hoffman ISRS graduate, 1959; president, NSA, 1959–60; NSA representative in Paris, 1960–61; worked with CIA, 1961–67. Witting. (Deceased, 2012.)

Kenneth Holland Assistant director, Office of International Information and Cultural Affairs, U.S. Department of State, 1946–48; U.S. representative to UNESCO, 1948–50; president, Institute for International Education, 1950–73; member, CFR

Study Group 5152, 1949–52; board member, FYSA, 1952–67; represented IIE on board of FSLP, 1956–63. Cooperated with CIA. (Deceased, 1996.)

Frederick Delano Houghteling Delegate, NSA Constitutional Convention, 1947; staff, HIACOM, 1947–50; executive secretary, NSA, 1950; obtained covert funds for NSA summer project, 1950. Witting. (Deceased, 1986.)

Daniel Idzik ISRS graduate, 1956; executive officer NSA, 1956–57; worked with CIA while a member of the WUS staff, Geneva, 1958–60; assisted NSA-sponsored Algerian student leaders conference, 1960; conducted Vietnam survey and report, 1965. Witting.

Avrea Ingram Vice president, NSA International Affairs, 1951–53; NSA delegate to ISCs in Edinburgh, 1952, Copenhagen, 1953; staff, COSEC, 1953–56; staff, FYSA, 1956–57. Witting. (Deceased, 1957.)

Timothy Jenkins ISRS graduate, 1959; vice president, NSA National Affairs, 1960–61. Not witting.

Willard Johnson ISRS graduate, 1957; vice president, NSA Educational Affairs, 1957–58; vice president, NSA International Affairs, 1958–59; NSA delegate to ISC in Lima, 1959. Witting.

Robert Kiley Vice president, NSA National Affairs, 1957–58; president, NSA, 1958–59; associate secretary, COSEC, 1960–62; NSA delegate to ISCs in Ibadan, 1957, Lima, 1959, Klosters, 1960, Quebec, 1962; staff, CIA career, 1962–70: director, Covert Action 5, youth and students; assistant to CIA director Richard Helms. Witting.

Wilmer Kitchens Executive secretary, WSSF, 1946–ca. 64; supported travel to found a national student organization, 1946; funded NSA International Affairs Vice President Robert Smith, 1947–49; sponsored NSA projects; openly co-operated with U.S. government officials, 1946–64. Witting status unknown or unverified. (Deceased, 1981.)

Alex Korns ISRS graduate, 1960; staff assistance to NSA-sponsored Algerian student leaders conference, 1960; assistant director, ISRS, 1961; NSA representative in Paris, 1962–63; vice president, NSA International Affairs, 1963–64; NSA delegate to ISC in Christchurch, 1964. Witting.

Ram Labhaya Lakhina NSA-FSLP funded student, University of Minnesota, 1961–63; NCUSI delegate to ISC in Quebec, 1962; member, COSEC Research and Investigation Committee, 1963–64; associate secretary, COSEC, 1964–66; secretary general, COSEC, 1966–68. Witting status unknown or unverified.

Bruce Larkin ISRS graduate, 1955; vice president, NSA International Affairs, 1957–58; NSA representative in Paris, 1958–59; associate secretary, COSEC, 1959–60. Witting.

Joseph Lash Executive secretary, American Student Union, 1936–39; staff director, U.S. ISS Committee, 1941–42. (Deceased, 1987.)

Allard Lowenstein President, NSA, 1950–51. Witting status unknown or unverified. (Deceased, 1980.)

Harry Lunn President, NSA, 1954–55; NSA delegate to ISC in Birmingham, 1955; member, COSEC delegation to Southeast Asia, 1955; CIA career officer, including director, FYSA, 1965–67. (Deceased, 1998.)

Thomas Madden British, secretary general, IUS, 1946–51.

Isabel Marcus ISRS graduate, 1958; vice president, NSA International Affairs, 1959–60; NSA delegate to ISC in Klosters, 1960. Witting.

Martin M. McLaughlin Military intelligence, 1944–46; delegate, Prague 25, 1946; director, JCSA, 1946–47; helped draft NSA Constitution, 1947; selected for NSA summer delegation to Prague, 1948 (did not participate); worked for U.S. government, including CIA, 1951–73; executive secretary to Robert F. Kennedy's Interagency Youth Committee, 1962; deputy assistant secretary of state for education and cultural affairs, 1964–65. Witting. (Deceased, 2007.)

Richard Medalie Vice president, NSA Educational Affairs, 1949–50; NSA representative, IUS, Dubrovnik, 1956; attended the World Youth Congresses in Moscow, 1957, and Vienna, 1959, at the request of the CIA. Witting.

Cord Meyer, Jr. Staff, CIA International Organizations division, overseeing youth and students, 1951; director, IO, 1954; chief, covert action staff, directorate of plans, 1962–1967; assistant deputy director, directorate of plans, 1967–73; station chief, London, 1973–76. (Deceased, 2001.)

Clement Henry Moore (today Clement M. Henry) ISRS graduate, 1957; NSA representative in Paris, 1957–58; NSA representative in London, 1958–59. Witting status unknown or unverified.

Louis Nemzer Chief, Social and Educational Affairs Branch in the Bureau of Intelligence and Research in the U.S. Department of State, 1947–49; briefed Catholics in NSA, 1947–48; oversaw intelligence studies of international youth and students' organizations, 1948–49. (Deceased, 1976.)

Thomas Olson ISRS graduate, 1962; assistant to NSA International Affairs vice president, 1962–63; NSA representative in Paris, 1963–64; delegate to ISCs in Christchurch, 1964, Nairobi, 1966; associate secretary, COSEC, 1964–66; staff, FYSA, 1966–67. Witting.

Olof Palme Member and president, Swedish Federation of Students, 1951–52; participant in NSA German survey project, 1949. rejected U.S. government overtures to direct COSEC, 1952; Relationship with Swedish intelligence. (Deceased, 1986.)

William Roe Polk Conducted NSA survey of Middle East students, 1950; desk officer, HIACOM, 1950–51. Witting status unknown or unverified.

Richard Rettig President, NSA, 1960–61; NSA representative in Paris, 1961–62. Witting.

Stephen Robbins Chair, NSA National Supervisory Board, 1963–64; president, NSA, 1964–65. Witting.

Helen Jean Rogers Member of JCSA Chicago group, 1946–47; secretary-treasurer, NSA, 1948–49; NSA specialist on Latin America, 1950–1952; adviser to NSA International Affairs vice president, 1952–55; delegate to ISC in Copenhagen, 1953; conducted survey of Indian students, 1956; Witting status unknown or unverified. (Deceased, 1998.)

Edward Schwartz Vice president, NSA National Affairs, 1966–67; president, NSA, 1967–68; learned about the NSA's CIA involvement from nonwitting source.

James Scott ISRS graduate, 1958; NSA representative in Paris, 1959–60; vice president,

NSA International Affairs, 1960–61; delegate to ISC in Christchurch, 1964. Witting.

Dennis Shaul Co-director, IRS, at Helsinki World Youth Festival, 1962; president, NSA, 1962–63. Witting.

Philip Sherburne ISRS graduate, 1964; vice president, NSA National Affairs, 1964–65; president, NSA, 1965–66. Witting.

Paul Sigmund Assistant to Avrea Ingram, 1952–54; director, ISRS, 1954; vice president, NSA International Affairs, 1954–55; NSA representative in Paris, 1955–56; NSA delegate to ISCs in Birmingham, 1955, Ceylon, 1956. Witting. (Deceased, 2014.)

John J. Simons Secretary-treasurer, National Student Organization Continuations Committee, 1946–47; director, Simons Fund, 1949–52; associate director, FYSA, 1952–61; CIA career officer. (Deceased, 2002.)

James W. Smith Delegate, Prague 25, 1946; president, National Student Organization Continuations Committee, 1946–47; NSA appointee to temporarily replace Bill Ellis in the IUS Secretariat, 1947; resigned IUS position, 1948. Not witting.

Robert Solwin Smith ISS delegate, 1947; vice president, NSA International Affairs, 1947–48; NSA representative to U.S. Committee for UNESCO, 1947–48; staff, ISS/World University Service in Geneva, April 1950-May 1951; Witting status unknown or unverified. (Deceased, 2013.)

Tony Smith NSA overseas representative, 1962–64; CIA Career officer. Witting.

Richard Stearns ISRS graduate, 1964, NSA representative in the Middle East, 1965–66; directed NSA Arab seminar, 1965; vice president, NSA International Affairs, 1965–66; Witting.

Gloria Steinem Co-director, CIA-funded Independent Research Service, sending delegation to World Youth Festival in Vienna, 1958–59; co-director, IRS, World Youth Festival, Helsinki, 1961–62. Witting.

Carlton Stoiber ISRS graduate, 1964; vice president, NSA International Affairs, 1965. Witting.

John M. Thompson President, BNUS, 1951–52; administrative secretary, COSEC, 1952–57. Cooperated with British Intelligence. (Deceased.)

Norman Uphoff ISRS graduate, 1963; vice president, NSA International Affairs, 1964–65; Witting.

William Welsh President, NSA, 1947–48; Not witting.

Frank G. Wisner OSS, 1942–45; director, Office of Policy Coordination, 1948–52; deputy director, CIA Plans division, 1952–58. (Deceased, 1965.)

Michael Wood Development director, NSA, 1965–66; exposed NSA-CIA relationship to *Ramparts*, 1966.

Crawford Young NSA delegate, ISC in Birmingham, 1955; NSA representative in England, 1955–56; assistant press officer, COSEC, 1956; NSA representative in Paris, 1956–57; associate secretary, COSEC, 1957–58; chair, Research and Investigation Commission, 1960–61. Witting.

CHRONOLOGY

1939   August 23: Stalin-Hitler nonaggression pact signed.

1941   July: Eleanor Roosevelt hosts the first Campobello Leadership Institute at her home on Campobello Island.

1942   July: Second Campobello Leadership Institute.

September 2–5: International Student Assembly at American University, Washington.

1945   October 29–November 10: World Youth Conference, London.

November 10: World Federation of Democratic Youth founded.

November 11: International Preparatory Commission formed in London to plan World Student Congress.

1946   January 25: American Preparatory Commission formed to select delegation to the World Student Congress.

August 18–27: World Student Congress held in Prague at which the International Union of Students is founded.

November 13: Public announcement of the creation of the Harvard International Activities Committee by World War II veterans.

December 28–30: American student convention held in Chicago: students vote to form a national student organization (the NSA) and elect a committee to prepare for its Constitutional Convention.

1947   August 30–September 7: Constitutional Convention of the U.S. National Student Association held in Madison, Wisconsin.

September: Central Intelligence Agency created.

1948   February 25: Communists take over Czechoslovakia, placing IUS in the Soviet sphere of influence.

June: The Office of Policy Coordination (covert action) established within the U.S. Department of State.

1949   August 24–September 4: The CIA tries to intervene in the NSA officer elections at the Congress.

1950   October–December: HIACOM coordinates major international programs with CIA regional divisions.

June: The CIA administers security oaths to Frederick Delano Houghteling, an NSA officer.

July–August: The CIA secretly funds an NSA global fact-finding trip to counter the IUS.

December 17–27: First meeting of pro-West International Student Conference in Stockholm.

1951   February 13: HIACOM publicly announces large-scale Students Mutual Assistance Program (SMAP).

February 17: Allen Dulles of the CIA and William Y. Elliott of Harvard discuss NSA programs and secret funding.

March 13: The Council on Foreign Relations Study Group 5152 agrees to assist HIACOM.

March 27: HIACOM notifies NSA of a new entity, Educational Projects, Inc., to receive individual and foundation funds for NSA international projects.

April 18: The CFR Study Group 5152 recommends the creation of a buffer organization to route secret funds to students.

August 20–29: HIACOM reports to the NSA Congress on substantial fundraising, donor names withheld.

September: The NSA national office moves to Boulder, Colorado.

November 10: Ingram and Dentzer submit NSA international prospectus to U.S. government Psychological Strategy Board with a budget of $100,000.

1952   January 3–8: Second International Student Conference, in Edinburgh, Scotland, establishes COSEC (ISC Coordinating Secretariat), to be located in Leiden, the Netherlands.

January 25–February 5: First Inter-American Student Congress held in Rio de Janeiro.

February 7: HIACOM and the CFR discuss future funding requirements.

May: U.S. State Department asks Olof Palme to lead COSEC. Palme refuses.

June 10–12: The ISC Supervision Commission meets in Leiden, selects first COSEC staff.

August 1: The CIA launches the funding conduit Foundation for Youth and Student Affairs (FYSA), which supports the NSA, the ISC, and COSEC.

September 1: COSEC begins operations in Leiden.

September: The NSA national office moves to Philadelphia; Gimbel Brothers donates office space. An adult adviser to NSA resigns, protesting the secrecy of International Commission funding.

1953   January 12–18: Third International Student Conference, Copenhagen.

January 20: Inauguration of Dwight D. Eisenhower as president.

February 15: *IUS News* attacks American funding of Copenhagen ISC.

March 5: Soviet premier Joseph Stalin dies.

July 20: The CIA funds the International Student Relations Seminar (ISRS) to recruit and screen international staff.

August 31: Senator Joseph McCarthy accuses Cord Meyer, Jr., of the CIA International Organizations division, of being a communist; Meyer placed on leave of absence.

October: Avrea Ingram becomes COSEC associate secretary in Leiden.

November: Cord Meyer reinstated.

December: CIA doubles its budget for the fourth International Student Conference.

1954   January 8–16: Fourth International Student Conference, in Istanbul, establishes the Research and Investigation Commission.

April 18: Gamal Abdel Nasser becomes president of Egypt.

October 31: The Algerian revolution against French rule begins.

1955 June 2: The Ford Foundation awards funding for the Foreign Student Leadership Project.

July 1–16: Fifth International Student Conference, Birmingham, England.

1956 May 30: African-Asian Students Conference opens in Bandung, Indonesia.

September 11–21: Sixth International Student Conference, Peradeniya, Ceylon (Sri Lanka).

October 23: Hungarian uprising begins.

October 29: British, French, and Israeli troops attack Egypt over Suez Canal.

November 10: Soviet tanks suppress Hungarian uprising.

1957 March 13: Cuban student leader José Antonio Echevarría killed in palace attack against Batista.

July 2: Senator John F. Kennedy gives precedent-setting speech on Algeria.

July 28–August 11: World Youth Festival, Moscow.

September 11–21: Seventh International Student Conference, Ibadan, Nigeria.

1958 January 13: NSA representative expelled from France over Algerian policy.

November 16: Independent Research Service founded to undermine the World Youth Festival in Vienna.

1959 January: NSA cables congratulations to revolutionary leader Fidel Castro on his victory in Cuba.

February 15–25: International Student Conference, Lima, Peru.

June: CIA funds the NSA-Algerian Leadership Project.

July 26–August 4: World Youth Festival, Vienna.

August 24–September 3: At the NSA Congress, a Cuban student leader announces the creation of Operation Amistad (Friendship), invites American students to Havana.

1960 February 1: Sit-ins begin in Greensboro, North Carolina, against segregation.

March 3: The FBI director reopens the investigation of the NSA.

April 17: The Student Non-Violent Coordinating Committee is formed; the NSA in Atlanta donates office space.

April 22–23: The NSA launches the Northern Student Movement at Washington, D.C., meeting.

May 13: San Francisco police turn hoses on anti-HUAC demonstrators at City Hall.

August 21–September 1: International Student Conference, Klosters, Switzerland.

September: Young Americans for Freedom founded; attacks NSA as left wing.

1961 January 20: Inauguration of John F. Kennedy as president.

March 15: Angolan revolutionaries launch guerrilla raids against Portuguese control.

April 17: Failed Bay of Pigs invasion to overthrow Cuban president Fidel Castro.

May 30: Dominican Republic dictator Rafael Trujillo assassinated.

August 23: William F. Buckley gives incendiary speech at the NSA Congress, Ohio State University.

November 3: President Kennedy authorizes Operation Mongoose to undermine Castro.

December 8–10: NSA conference on the Portuguese colonies in Africa at Camp Green Lane, Philadelphia.

1962 January: YAF leads disaffiliation campaigns against the NSA.

February: Attorney General Robert F. Kennedy takes global goodwill tour.

February 8: CIA plans action against conservative student critics of the NSA.

March: Cord Meyer becomes CIA chief, Directorate of Plans; oversees the merger of the International Organization division with Covert Action.

June 27–July 10: At the International Student Conference in Quebec, radical student unions walk out.

July 5: Algeria wins independence.

August: The NSA co-hosts the Aspen Institute where Robert F. Kennedy meets foreign student leaders.

October 14–28: Cuban missile crisis.

1963 January: The CIA funds the NSA's Angolan scholarship program.

February 8: President Kennedy imposes ban on travel to Cuba.

February 9: The Iraqi premier overthrown in coup.

April 11: Algerian foreign minister Khemisti assassinated.

August 28: Civil rights groups sponsor the March on Washington.

November 22: President Kennedy is assassinated in Dallas, Texas.

1964 June 22–July 1: International Student Conference, Christchurch, New Zealand.

August 27: At the NSA Congress, an SDS member publicly challenges the secrecy and information monopoly of the NSA International Commission.

December 3: The National Security Council considers covert counteraction for the upcoming World Youth Festival in Algiers.

1965 March: President Lyndon Johnson escalates the war in Vietnam.

March 24: First teach-in on the Vietnam War held at the University of Michigan.

July: The NSA convenes an Arab student seminar.

August 23: The CIA suggests that Vice President Hubert Humphrey attend the NSA Congress to sell Vietnam policy to students.

December 2–7: The CIA demands that the NSA specialist leave the Dominican Republic.

1966 August 17–27: International Student Conference, Nairobi.

October: *Ramparts* magazine launches investigation of the NSA's CIA ties.

1967 February 14: *Ramparts* places a full-page ad in the *New York Times* revealing the CIA financing of the NSA.

February 15: President Johnson appoints a three-member committee to investigate the *Ramparts* charges.

March 6 and 16: U.S. Senate holds closed hearings on the CIA-NSA relationship.

August 15: The CIA director expands the top-secret MH/CHAOS program against Vietnam War dissenters.

August 22: CIA director Helms agrees to a "divorce agreement" with NSA.

August 13–26: The CIA infiltrates the National Student Congress at the University of Maryland.

NOTES

Unless otherwise indicated, all interviews are with the author.
The Patriotic Betrayal (PB) Web site can be found at patrioticbetrayal.com.

Archives

I consulted these archives over a period of several years, and some have since
been reorganized. I note this in the list below. In my notes, I have given as full
information as possible to enable researchers to locate the documents.

CFR   Council on Foreign Relations Records, 1918–2011, Public Policy Papers, Department of Rare Books and Special Collections, Princeton University Library, Princeton, N.J.

Elliott   William Y. Elliott papers, Hoover Institution, Stanford University, Palo Alto, Calif.

FDR   Franklin Delano Roosevelt Library, Hyde Park, N.Y.

Flynn   Father Vincent J. Flynn Presidential Records, 1923–56, Series 2: Organizations and Associations, University of St. Thomas Archives and Manuscript Collections, St. Paul, Minn.

FRUS   Foreign Relations of the United States. Official documents of major foreign policy decisions, declassified and edited by the U.S. Department of State, Office of the Historian (Washington, D.C.: United States Government Printing Office). Volumes are also available at http://history.state.gov/historicaldocuments.

Fulbright   Executive Session of the Senate Foreign Relations Committee, hearings, vols. 1 and 2, March 6 and 16, 1967, chaired by J. William Fulbright. Declassified February 11, 1998, after a request from former NSA president William Welsh, who supplied the record to the author. For further information, contact the Office of the Historian. U.S. Senate.

H/NSA   United States National Students Association International Commission Collection, Hoover Institution, Stanford University, Palo Alto, Calif.

IISH ISC   International Student Conference Archives, Institute of International Social History, Amsterdam, the Netherlands.

JFK   John F. Kennedy Presidential Library and Museum, Boston, Mass.

Kotschnig   Walter Maria Kotschnig Papers, Special Collections, State University of New York, Albany. These papers have been reorganized since I consulted them.

LBJ   Lyndon B. Johnson Presidential Library and Museum, Austin, Tex.

Lowenstein Allard K. Lowenstein Papers, 1924–1995, Southern Historical Collection, Louis Round Wilson Special Collections Library, University of North Carolina, Chapel Hill.

McCloy John J. McCloy Papers, 1897–1989, Amherst Archives and Special Collections, Amherst College, Amherst, Mass.

Meyer Cord Meyer, Jr., Papers, Manuscript Division, Library of Congress, Washington, D.C.

Murray The Rev. John Courtney Murray, S.J., Papers, Special Collections Research Center, Georgetown University Library, Washington, D.C.

NARA National Archives and Records Administration, College Park, Md.

NCWC National Catholic Welfare Conference, United States Conference of Bishops, American History Research Center and University Archives, Catholic University of America, Washington, D.C.

NICC National Intercollegiate Christian Council, YMCA-Student Division records, 1886–1967, Yale Divinity School Library, New Haven, Conn.

Sweet Charles F. Sweet Collection, 1953–1990, Division of Rare and Manuscript Collections, Cornell University Library, Ithaca, N.Y.

W/NSA United States National Student Association/United States Student Association papers, Wisconsin State Historical Society, Madison.

Private Papers

Blumenau Ralph Blumenau unpublished diary

FOIA (CIA) Freedom of Information Act Files, Central Intelligence Agency

FOIA (FBI) Freedom of Information Act Files, Federal Bureau of Investigation

FOIA (State) Freedom of Information Act Files, U.S. Department of State

Murray letters Letters of the Rev. John Courtney Murray, S.J, courtesy of Murray's biographer Joseph Komonchak

Ansara Files Michael Ansara files on *Ramparts* investigation

Paget Files NSA pamphlets, newspapers, and reports sent to me by former NSA officials

Welsh Files NSA material from William Welsh

Chapter 1. A Fighting Faith

1. Joseph Lash, *Eleanor Roosevelt: A Friend's Memoir* (New York: Doubleday, 1964).
2. Information on the history of the American Student Union can be found at "Student Activism in the 1930s," http://newdeal.feri.org/students/index.htm. See especially "The Student Movement of the 1930s: Joseph P. Lash Interview," at http://newdeal.feri.org/students/lash.htm#26.
3. "At FDR's Summer Home Students Prepare to be Young Leaders," *PM's Weekly*, July 27, 1941. This article contains six pages of photos from the Campobello session by Mary Morris, of the PM staff.
4. "By 1949, she would (never again) compromise [with communists] (even on words)," Joseph Lash, *Eleanor: The Years Alone* (New York: Norton, 1972), 106.

5. Nelson Lichtenstein, *Walter Reuther: The Most Dangerous Man in Detroit* (Champaign: University of Illinois Press, 1997), 155.

6. Staff member Trude Pratt, who served on the ISS board and was close to Eleanor Roosevelt, referred to them this way. See FDR (Lash), Box 10, January 12, 1943, Lash letter to Lou Harris, for Pratt's views on the U.S. Committee.

7. Lash, *Eleanor Roosevelt*, 221.

8. Ibid., 232.

9. State Department officials tended to identify Lash and Yard as communists because of their prominence in the American Student Union. This confusion lasted into the postwar period, when the noncommunist United States Students Assembly was misidentified in a State Department memo as the American Student Assembly led by Molly Yard, and "almost certainly a CP front" (NARA RG 59, 250, June 18, 1946, "Miss Alice Horton and the coming International Students Conference in Prague," Memo from Harry Pierson, Act. Asst. Cf., Division of International Exchange of Persons, to Oliver J. Caldwell in his division).

10. "Education: To Act with Restraint," *Time*, September 23, 1940.

11. Lash, *Eleanor Roosevelt*, 221.

12. See FDR, Lash Papers, Box 26, ISS pamphlet.

13. See Kotschnig, Box 4 (Folder 17), September 4, 1941, Lash report on Student Leadership Institute.

14. Lash, *Eleanor Roosevelt*, 244.

15. Eleanor Roosevelt, "My Day," July 10, 1941.

16. See Louis Fischer essay in *The God That Failed*, ed. Richard Crossman (New York: Harper, 1949), 196–228.

17. Lash, *Eleanor Roosevelt*, 226.

18. Kotschnig, Box 4 (Folder 9), Camp-ISS-Bello Newsletter, July–August, 1941.

19. Lash, *Eleanor Roosevelt*, 245–46.

20. Ibid., 246.

21. Ibid., 245.

22. Ibid., 246.

23. Arthur M. Schlesinger, Jr., *The Vital Center: The Politics of Freedom* (Boston: Houghton Mifflin, 1949). See Peter Beinart, "An Argument for a New Liberalism," *New Republic*, December 2, 2004. Beinart revived the phrase "fighting faith" and argued for the parallels between liberal anticommunism and attitudes toward Islam after September 11, 2001.

24. "Education: Camp-ISS-Bello Vistas," *Time*, August 18, 1941. *PM's Weekly* also featured the concept of fighting faith; see "At FDR's Summer Home Students Prepare to be Young Leaders."

25. The Commission to Study the Organization of Peace (CSOP) led the planning for the United Nations. ISS members of CSOP included Clyde Eagleton, Frank Graham, William Allan Nielson, James T. Shotwell (Chair), George Shuster, Payson Wild, and Arnold Wolfers. For a complete list of ISS U.S. Committee members, see the PB Web site.

26. Kotschnig, Box 4, has extensive documentation detailing wartime relations with the Division of Cultural Relations, U.S. Department of State.

27. Kotschnig, Box 2, August 7, 1942, Kotschnig to Hans Kohn.
28. Delegate information on Luzzatto is from Kotschnig, Box 4 (Folder 9), International Assembly Report on Delegates and Observers; Information on Bruno Luzzatto also supplied by the Luzzatto family. Lash's views are expressed in Kotschnig, Box 4 (Folder 9), International Student Service, Minutes of the Executive Committee Meeting, September 23, 1942, p. 4. Photographs of conference members can be found at International Student Assembly, September 1942, Office of War information photos, Library of Congress, Washington, D.C., available at www.loc.gov/pictures/item/2004667424.
29. Eleanor Roosevelt, "My Day," September 2, 1942.
30. "President Franklin D. Roosevelt Broadcast to International Student Assembly," September 3, 1942, available at http://www.presidency.ucsb.edu/ws/?pid=16300. On FDR's intentions, see Lash, *Eleanor: The Years Alone*, 34.
31. H/NSA, Box 280, Description of Louis Harris and the International Student Assembly, September 2–5, 1942. See in the same box the "Declaration of the International Student Assembly," 1942.
32. Delegates pictured conducting short-wave broadcasts can be accessed at www.loc.gov/pictures/item/2004667433/. See also pictures taken during the International Student Assembly at www.loc.gov/pictures/item/2004667424. Information on Louise Morley in Kotschnig, Box 7 (Folder ISS): ISS bulletin, n.d., reported Morley departed for London in November 14, 1942.
33. William Allan Neilson, ed., *Proceedings of the International Student Assembly, Held at the American University, Washington, D.C., 2–5 September 1942* (London: Oxford University Press, 1944). See also Kotschnig, Box 4 (Folder 9), September 20, 1942, John Coleman to ISS General Secretary Andre de Blonay (Geneva), objecting to not locating the international assembly in Geneva.
34. Neilson, *Proceedings*.
35. Kotschnig, Boxes 2 and 4, contain extensive detail on the conflict within the U.S. ISS Committee. See, for example, Box 4 (Folder 17), several letters in draft by Clyde Eagleton and Walter Kotschnig explaining to ISS Geneva headquarters what had happened over the previous two years within the U.S. Committee. In Box 2 (Folder 25), Kotschnig describes cutting loose from soapbox orators. For a different view on the International Student Assembly, and its aftermath, see Margie Campbell, National Student Director, Young Communist League, "Two Obituaries and a Sermon," in the YCL magazine *Weekly Review*, March 16, 1943.
36. Kotschnig, Box 4 (Folder 9), n.d., Eagleton statement.
37. FDR: Joseph Lash Papers, Box 7 (Louis Harris); see especially November 15, 1942, Harris to Lash re the conflict, and February 11, 1943, Harris to Lash re developments after the split.
38. See Kotschnig, Box 4 (Folder 9), December 7, 1942, exchange between ISS committee members Alfred E. Cohn, Rockefeller Institute for Medical Research, and William Neilson, Smith College president.
39. Lash, *Eleanor Roosevelt*, 221. For further information on donors, see Kotschnig, Box 4, and the PB Web site.

40. Mary Lou Rogers Munts, "Origins of the United States Student Assembly (1943-1947)," in *American Students Organize: Founding the National Student Association After World War II*, ed. Eugene G. Schwartz ([Westport, Conn.]: American Council on Education/Praeger, 2006), 34–39. This edited volume was produced by the USNSA Anthology Project Committee, consisting of former NSA officers and staff.

41. See Kotschnig, Box 4 (Folder 15), September 10, 1943, SSA incorporation papers.

42. Ibid. On February 27, 1943, Kotschnig wrote to the World Student Service Fund proclaiming the Student Service of America a legal continuation of the ISS in the United States.

43. See Kotschnig, Box 8 (Folder 4), February 25–26, 1944, for example, Minutes of the Meeting of the Committee on International Education and Cultural Relations, U.S. Department of State. These minutes contain discussions on postwar student exchange programs. Several formal and ad-hoc committees at the State Department were similarly engaged in discussion of postwar programs.

44. See the extensive materials on postwar student exchange programs in Kotschnig, Box 2, General Advisory Committee of the Cultural Relations Division, U.S. Department of State.

45. Kotschnig, Box 7 (SSA), April 23, 1943, SSA minutes.

46. NARA, RG 800.4089/7-1945, July 7, 1945, Cable to Sec/State from U.S. Ambassador Winant/London.

47. Material about the Conference of Southern Students and copy of March 16, 1980, interviews with Douglass Hunt and Jimmy Wallace, courtesy of Richard Cummings, author of *The Pied Piper: Allard Lowenstein and the Liberal Dream* (Boston: Grove, 1985).

48. Interview with Mollie Lieber West, Los Angeles, February 23, 2001. Lieber West spent several hours with me poring over photo albums of the WFDY founding. See also Joël Kotek, *Students and the Cold War*, trans. Ralph Blumenau (New York: St. Martin's, 1996), esp. chap. 5, "The Creation of the World Federation of Democratic Youth," 62–86.

Chapter 2. Apostolic Catholics

1. See *Quanta Cura* (1864) and *Divini Redemptoris* (1937) at Papal Encyclicals Online, www. papalencyclicals.net.

2. John Courtney Murray, "Operation University," *America*, April 13, 1946, 28–29.

3. Martin Marty in Donald Pelotte, *John Courtney Murray: Theologian in Conflict* (New York: Paulist Press, 1976), ix–x.

4. Murray, "Operation University."

5. See NCWC, 91/6 (Social Action: Youth), May 14, 1947, Father Bermingham letter to Howard Carroll, NCWC General Secretary, re Cushing contribution in the summer of 1946.

6. See FOIA (FBI), 3/33, July 7, 1947, Jacobson's views on including communist groups.

7. Interview with Mollie Lieber West, Los Angeles, February 23, 2001.
8. H/NSA, Box 36, Draft NSA history, January 25, 1946, American Preparatory Committee meeting, YWCA; telephone interview with Alice Horton Tibbetts, Madison, Wisc., December 11, 2000.
9. A list of the Prague Delegation can be found in Eugene G. Schwartz, ed., *American Students Organize: Founding the National Student Association After World War II* ([Westport, Conn.]: American Council on Education/Praeger, 2006), 103. On Proctor's role in the Conference of Southern Students, see Charles Proctor, "A Great Vision of the Future," in Schwartz, *American Students Organize*, 969.
10. NICC, Box 198 (Administrative), June 4, 1946, Jacobson to Wilmena (Billie) Rowland.
11. Ibid., March 22, 1946, Minutes.
12. NCWC, 77/10 (Orgs: Pax), August 1, 1947, Edward Kirchner memo on Pax Romana history.
13. Kotschnig, Box 4 (Folder 9), September 29, 1942, European Student Relief meeting in New York.
14. Ibid. (Folder 14), June 17, 1943, Robert C. Mackie (ISS) letter describing Kirchner's role in raising relief funds.
15. Telephone interview with Alice Horton. Delegate selection ranged from campus-wide elections to self-identification. See Schwartz, *American Students Organize*, for memoirs of Prague 25 participants and others involved during this period.
16. Father John Courtney Murray, letter to his superior, Francis A. McQuade, S.J., May 8, 1946; Murray's biographer Joseph A. Komonchak supplied me with a typed copy of Murray's letter on April 10, 1999.
17. Briefing for Catholic educators on postwar plans, Fordham University, October 26, 1945, reported in "Catholic Intellectual Solidarity," *America*, November 10, 1945, 143.
18. Detail on Catholic students is in Martin M. McLaughlin, "On a Threshold," *America*, June 29, 1946, 263. See also H/NSA, Box 318 (JCSA), Operation University reports.
19. Pictures of both Eislers before HUAC on February 6, 1947, in *Life*, February 17, 1947, 99–100, available at http://oldlifemagazines.com/february-17-1947-life-magazine.html.
20. H/NSA, Box 318 (JSCA), Operation University reports.
21. Murray, "Operation University," 34–35.
22. Quoted in Edward J. Kirchner, "Preparing the Catholic Delegation," in Schwartz, *American Students Organize*, 77. An early version included the sentiment about fighting evil.
23. Murray letter to McQuade, May 8, 1946.
24. Obituary of Martin M. McLaughlin, *Washington Post*, November 29, 2007. McLaughlin's obituary does not specifically cite his membership in the CIA but dates his U.S. government service from 1951 to 1973. My interviews with former NSA witting staff confirm his status, however. McLaughlin occasionally administered the security oath to NSA officers.

25. II/NSA, Box 36, n.d. [ca. 1955], Bill Ellis notes for NSA history.
26. The curriculum vitae in Henry W. Briefs's thesis, #1221 (1954), in the George-town University Library indicates a three-year gap between 1943 and 1946. A *Washington Post* obituary dated April 27, 1999, identified the period as time spent serving in army intelligence.
27. Richard Cummings, interview with Jimmy Wallace, undated transcript courtesy of Richard Cummings.
28. Interview with Miriam Haskell Berlin, Cambridge, Mass., October 14, 1997.
29. McLaughlin had been a member of a Catholic Action cell at Notre Dame under the guidance of Father Louis Putz, who accompanied the Catholics to Europe in the summer of 1946. An obituary, "Rest in Peace: Martin McLaughlin (1918–2007)," describes McLaughlin as a member of one of the first Catholic Action groups as a graduate student of Father Putz. It is available at www.catholiclabor.org/NCL%20Inititiative/Feb%2008.pdf.
30. See Thomas Hughson, S.J., *The Believer as Citizen: John Courtney Murray in a New Context* (Mahwah, N.J.: Paulist, 1993).
31. "Prague Delegates Reach Decision on Much-Discussed Policy Reports," *Harvard Crimson*, July 23, 1946.
32. See, e.g., James Loeb, "Progressive and Communists," *New Republic*, May 13, 1946; see also articles in the May 20, May 27, and June 17, 1946 issues.
33. H/NSA, Box 318 (JCSA), January 31, 1947, Martin McLaughlin and Henry Briefs, eds., "Operation University," 5; two delegates were identified as communist (9).
34. H/NSA, Box 127 (Int'l Team), December 1947, Martin McLaughlin application letter.
35. LBJ, E-transcript, David G. McComb, Interview with S. Douglass Cater, no. 1, April 29, 1969, 4–5.
36. "Cater Selected as Harvard Delegate to Prague Parley," *Harvard Crimson*, May 25, 1946.
37. I was aware of the speculation in 1967. As I was conducting the research for this book, nonwitting sources continued to speculate about the origins of USNSA.
38. "Seven Prague Delegates Sail Early; Other Members to Follow in Week," *Harvard Crimson*, July 19, 1946.
39. Interview with Miriam Haskell Berlin.
40. Douglass Cater made the same point in "New York Session of Delegation to Prague Created Orderly Program," *Harvard Crimson*, October 7, 1946.
41. Martin McLaughlin, "Student Congress in Prague," *America*, December 14, 1946, 291–93.
42. NICC, Box 198 (Admin), Minutes of May 3, 1946, discussion on Negro representation; for comments on Catholics, see also Minutes of November 8, 1946, and n.d., Bill Ellis and Joyce Roberts, "Report on the Prague Conference."
43. Ibid., November 8, 1946, "Report on the Prague Conference."
44. William Yandell Elliott Papers, Box 3, Hoover Institution Archives, Stanford University; Godfrey Briefs's January 3, 1947, letter to Elliott refers to supply-

ing him previously with information on the IUS to use as ammunition against Cater; Briefs, Henry's brother, disparaged Cater as a "subaltern."

45. Henry Briefs spoke for the American Catholics, as quoted in "New Student Body Declared Leftist," *New York Times*, August 29, 1946.

46. Interview with Ralph Blumenau, London, July 2, 2003. Blumenau was a British delegate to the IUS.

47. NICC, Box 30, September 1946, Ellis to Mother and Dad.

48. NICC, Box 198 (Admin), November 8, 1946, Minutes.

49. Interview with Thomas Madden, Skokie, Ill., June 29–30, 2004.

50. Richard Helms, *A Look over My Shoulder* (New York: Random House, 2003), 348.

51. NARA, RG 59 250 (542), September 16, 1946, Steinhardt report to the secretary of state.

52. Interview with Bernard Lown, Newton, Mass., January 23, 2008. Douglass Cater also decried the "war is here" attitude; see "Cater Hits European 'War Is Here' Attitude, Calls for Student Exchange to Keep Peace," *Harvard Crimson*, October 25, 1946.

53. McLaughlin received his Ph.D. in 1948 for his dissertation on the formation of U.S. National Student Association: "Political Processes in American National Student Organization," University of Notre Dame, 1948.

54. NCWC, Box 84 (Organizations: Student), October 13, 1946, Minutes. See also H/NSA, Box 283 (JCSA), pamphlet "JCSA . . . What Is It?"

55. "JCSA . . . What Is It?" For information on Catholic cells, see Steven M. Avella, *This Confident Church, 1940–1961* (Notre Dame, Ind.: University of Notre Dame Press, 2005).

56. NCWC, 9/16 (Social Action: Youth), November 18, 1946, Bermingham to Stritch.

57. Ibid. Bermingham frequently invoked wartime intelligence experience to reassure wary priests; see Flynn, Box 13, August 7, 1946, Bermingham letter to Daniel A. Lord, S.J., St. Louis, editor, *The Queen's Work* magazine.

58. "JCSA . . . What Is It?"

59. McLaughlin, "Student Congress in Prague," 293.

60. William V. D'Antonio, *American Catholics: Gender, Generation, and Commitment* (Lanham, Md.: Alta Mira, 2001), 6.

61. See Patrick J. Hayes, *A Catholic Brain Trust: The History of the Catholic Commission on Intellectual and Cultural Affairs: 1945–1965* (Notre Dame, Ind.: University of Notre Dame Press, 2011).

62. See Philip Gleason, *Contending with Modernity: Catholic Higher Education in the Twentieth Century* (New York: Oxford University Press, 1995), 240–44.

63. Norman Weyand, S.J., "Report on Operation University," *Jesuit Educational Journal* (January 1948): 139.

64. Ruby Cooper, "Students Lay Plans for National Organization," *Daily Worker*, January 1, 1947. Lee Marsh singled out the Young Peoples Socialist League, arch-enemies of American Youth for Democracy.

65. H/NSA, Box 318 (JCSA), January 31, 1947, McLaughlin and Briefs, eds., "Operation University."
66. NICC, Box 198 (Admin), n.d., Ellis and Roberts, "Report on the Prague Conference."
67. Cater outlined his views in a series of five articles in the *Harvard Crimson*, October 7, 9, 11, 17, and 21, 1946; quotation on majority backing is from the October 21 article; the need for international cooperation is from "December 28 Chicago Parley Will Plan Students Organization," November 18, 1946.
68. H/NSA, Box 299 (WSSF 47–48), December 2, 1946, Wilmer Kitchen, letter to Jonathan Silverstone at HIACOM re funding for Ellis travel. For information on New England regional organization, see "Twenty Colleges Invited Here for Meeting Monday," *Harvard Crimson*, December 13, 1946.
69. "Board Will Take Applications for Chicago Meeting," *Harvard Crimson*, December 6, 1946.
70. "PBH Convention Draws Delegates of Seven Schools," *Harvard Crimson*, December 3, 1946, report on first, failed December 2 meeting. Report on second, successful meeting is "25 Delegates Make Plans in Meeting Here," *Harvard Crimson*, December 21, 1946.
71. "Communism Is Charged, Flays Liberals' Naivete," *Harvard Crimson*, December 19, 1946.
72. Elliott Papers, Box 3, Godfrey Briefs, letter of January 3, 1947, to Elliott.
73. "Elliott's Charges Scorned by Conference Delegate," *Harvard Crimson*, December 20, 1946. Cater blamed Henry Briefs by name for giving Elliott biased information.
74. NCWC, Box 84 (Organizations: Students), September 9, 1947, Bermingham to Monsignor Carroll.
75. Martin M. McLaughlin, "Conference in Chicago," *America*, March 29, 1947, 711–14. See also the essays in section 3: "The 1946 Chicago Student Conference," in Schwartz, *American Students Organize*, 109–26.
76. FOIA (FBI), 8/33, September 30, 1947, Milwaukee, Wisc., August 30–September 7, 1947, Report on NSA congress, author's name redacted.
77. Elliott Papers, Box 3, Godfrey Briefs, letter of January 3, 1947, to Elliot.
78. Samuel Cardinal Stritch Personal Papers, Box 2980, AAC "S," 6–7, January 6, 1947, Charles J. Marhoefer, "Report on the Activities of JCSA," Archdiocese of Chicago Archives and Records, Chicago, Ill.
79. Ibid.
80. Selig S. Harrison, "Parley Delegations Reconcile Differences," *Harvard Crimson*, January 7, 1947.
81. Ruby Cooper, "Students Lay Plans for National Organization," *Daily Worker*, January 1, 1947.

Chapter 3. Behind the Scenes

1. Material on these attitudes can be found in documents available at the Avalon Project of the Yale Law School, http://avalon.law.yale.edu/.
2. FOIA (FBI), 1/33. Chicago was designated the lead office; declassified documents contain hundreds of heavily redacted papers.
3. Ibid., January 22, 1947, FBI interview with William Y. Elliott.
4. Ibid., July 7, 1947, interviews with YMCA Student Division and YWCA Student Division officials, Student Federalists members, and numerous others.
5. Ibid. See, for example, the September 20, 1946, report from Legal Attaché from the American Embassy, London to Hoover.
6. NARA, RG 800.4089/11-1445, information on the World Youth Conference in London (November 1945), distributed to Navy Department, Washington, D.C.; Assistant Chief of Staff, G-2, War Department; Reading Panel, Military Intelligence Service; and Frederick B. Lyon, Chief, Division of Foreign Correlation, Department of State, whose job included coordination of intelligence reports.
7. Louis Nemzer, State Department Biographic Register, 1946: 344. See also H/NSA, Box 283 (JCSA), November 28–30, 1947, meeting; Nemzer warned Catholics "not to underestimate the effect of WFDY, IUS, on world politics."
8. George Kenneth Holland, State Department Biographic Register, 1946: 270.
9. For information on the student ships, see *Department of State Bulletin* 16, no. 2 (January 5–June 29, 1947): 392–417. Holland is quoted in Harry Hascall Moore, *Survival or Suicide: A Summons to Old and Young to Build a United Peaceful World* (New York: Harper, 1948), 100.
10. See Selig S. Harrison, "Parley Delegations Reconcile Differences," *Harvard Crimson*, January 7, 1947, on Cater's not running for president of the interim committee.
11. "Committee on International Affairs Participates in U.S. Student Union," *Harvard Crimson*, November 7, 1946.
12. "Council Body Will Circulate Global Paper," *Harvard Crimson*, February 6, 1947.
13. Ibid. See also H/NSA, Box 299 (WSSF 47–48).
14. Kotschnig, Box 4 (Folder 15), October 22, 1945, Gideonse to Kotschnig.
15. Kotschnig, Box 4, Minutes of SSA meetings, October 29, 1945, and November 20, 1945. OSS members included Malcolm Davis, a Harvard educator and top executive of the Carnegie Endowment for International Peace (Paris office), and Walter C. Langsam, historian and president of Staten Island College.
16. Ibid., March 19, 1946, SSA Minutes.
17. Ibid.
18. H/NSA, Box 299 (WSSF 47–48), April 11, 1947, WSSF memo on board expansion.
19. "University to Run Salzburg Class," *Harvard Crimson*, February 21, 1947.
20. Ibid.
21. Wilmer J. Kitchen had been the secretary of the Student Christian Movement in

New England. Information on this movement and Kitchen's role can be found at Manuscripts and Archives, Divinity School Library, Yale University, Record Group 57.

22. For details on the Salzburg Seminar, and other projects, see the PB Web site.

23. A list of board members is at the PB Web site.

24. H/NSA, Box 299 (WSSF 47–48), December 2, 1946, Wilmer Kitchen, letter to Jonathan Silverstone at HIACOM.

25. NARA, RG 59 800. 4089/6-647, June 6, 1947. Assistant Secretary William Benton disclosed that the request for the screenings came directly from the White House; see also 800.4089.6-2047, June 20, 1947, Secretary Marshall instruction to consular officials to deny return passage to those who reached Prague by other means.

26. H/NSA, Box 299 (WSSF 47–48), May 21, 1947, Harvard's William J. Richard, Jr., to Wilmer Kitchen, thanking him for the donation to support the information bulletin.

27. NARA, RG 59 800.4089/8-1447, August 14, 1947, Lovett to American Ambassador, Prague.

28. FOIA (FBI), 5/33, n.d., William S. Ellis, "Progress Report on the International Union of Students."

29. Philip Gleason, *Contending with Modernity: Catholic Higher Education in the Twentieth Century* (New York: Oxford University Press, 1995), 391. McLaughlin described the briefing in a letter to Gleason dated September 3, 1990.

30. NCWC, 84 (Organizations: Students), July 17, 1947, Apostolic Delegate A. G. Cicognani to Monsignor Howard J. Carroll.

31. Ibid., September 7, 1947, Father Bermingham memo summarizing strategy for the NSA constitutional convention to Monsignor Carroll.

32. Interview with Sally Cassidy, Newton, Mass., January 22, 1999.

33. Ibid. See also NCWC, Box 91/6 (Social Action: Youth), June 18, 1947, Father Bermingham re contact with Sally Cassidy; the declassified State Department Office of Intelligence Research report no. 5256, "*World Assembly of Youth,*" cites material from Cassidy.

34. Interview with Cassidy. The Vatican's Montini worked with the OSS during the war and apparently later received direct subsidies from the CIA; see Kevin A. O'Brien, "Interfering with Civil Society: CIA and KGB Covert Political Action During the Cold War," *International Journal of Intelligence and Counterintelligence* 8, no. 4 (Winter 1995): 431–56.

35. NCWC, 84 (Organizations: Students), September 7, 1947, Bermingham memo to Carroll summarizing strategy.

36. Samuel Cardinal Stritch Personal Papers, "S" Box 2980, AAC, October 21, 1947, Philip DesMarais, "Confidential Summary Report on the Constitutional Convention," Archdiocese of Chicago Archives and Records, Chicago, Ill.

37. Interview with Lee Marsh, Berkeley, Calif., April 13, 2001. In July 1946, Marsh had not yet renewed his Communist Party membership. Marsh quotation from FOIA (FBI), 5/33 coverage of the NSA Constitutional Convention.

38. H/NSA, Box 66 (International Reports), n.d., "International Affairs of

USNSA": Robert Smith gives this figure for the vote. See also Cardinal Stritch Personal Papers, October 21, 1947, DesMarais, "Confidential Summary Report," in which he credits Catholics with these and other victories.

39. Welsh Files, *The NSA News*, September 3, 1947.

40. NCWC, 84 (Organizations: Students), January 9, 1948, Apostolic Delegate A. G. Cicognani to Rt. Rev. Msgr. Howard J. Carroll with attached memo from Vatican Cardinal Secretary of State, Domenico Tardini, re submissions to Pope Pius XII.

41. Ibid., January 19, 1948, nine-page copy of a draft memorandum from Paul Tanner, Assistant General Secretary, to His Holiness and the Secretariat of State re the affiliation of NSA to the IUS. See also January 23, 1948, Archbishop Cushing to Tanner approving the draft memorandum, and February 20, 1948, Howard Carroll, General Secretary, to Your Excellency, formally responding to the Vatican.

42. Welsh Files, *The NSA News*.

43. Interview with William Welsh, New Brunswick, Maine, October 22, 1991; Welsh and I also had numerous telephone conversations and e-mail exchanges between 1997 and 2007.

44. Ruby Cooper, "Student Parley Debates World Affiliation," *Daily Worker*, September 7, 1947, reported the vote and the Catholic support for Welsh's opponent William Birenbaum.

45. The first NSA officers are pictured in *The NSA News*, October 1947, copy courtesy of former NSA president William Welsh.

46. National Self-Government Committee, Manuscripts Division, New York Public Library, Box 55, September 26, 1947, Smith to Sophia Pollack, Secretary, National Self-Government Committee.

47. H/NSA, Box 280 (ISS), October 1, 1947, Smith to Jack Peter, ISS Geneva.

48. H/NSA, Box 299 (WSSF 47–48), notes made by Smith for WSSF speech on November 4, 1947.

49. NARA, RG 800.4089/5-647, May 6, 1947, confidential cable from Ambassador Steinhardt, Prague, to Sec. State; May 6, 1947, secret telegram response from Central European division (CE) to Sec. State.

50. NARA, RG 800.4089/7-2947, July 29, 1947, Ambassador Steinhardt, Prague, report on the American delegation.

51. NARA, RG 800.4089/7-1847, July 19, 1947, Sec State cable to OMGUS, Youth Activities Branch, Berlin (Raymond Murphy, EUR/X); RG 800.4089/4-1847, April 18, 1947, from Ambassador Steinhardt, Prague.

52. Interview with Spurgeon Keeny, Jr., Washington, D.C., December 11, 1998.

53. H/NSA, Box 294 (U.S. Government), November 24, 1947, Robert Smith to Paul Lewand, U.S. Embassy, Prague.

54. NCWC, 84 (Organizations: Students), September 7, 1947, Father Bermingham to Monsignor Carroll.

55. Interview with Cassidy.

56. H/NSA, Box 280 (ISS), October 1, 1947, Smith to Peter.

57. Ibid.

58. Robert Solwin Smith, "Establishing the NSA International Affairs Office," in
    *American Students Organize: Founding the National Student Association after World
    War II*, ed. Eugene G. Schwartz ([Westport, Conn.]: American Council on
    Education/Praeger, 2006), 505.

59. H/NSA, Box 299 (WSSF 47-48), October 1947, Nancy Morehouse (ISS) to Bob
    Smith. State Department Biographic Registers for 1947 and 1948 list Doerr as
    assistant attaché, American Embassy in Berlin, a position often used as cover for
    intelligence work.

60. Interview with Welsh.

61. H/NSA, Box 299 (WSSF 47-48), n.d. [ca. November 1947], Treasurer's report,
    Appendix B. Resolution EC 47-42 authorizes a salary for Robert Smith.

62. H/NSA, Box 297 (UNESCO), April 13, 1949, WSSF Personnel Committee
    noted request from Bob Smith to terminate his official service after a month's
    notice and vacation. Smith left office at the end of August 1948.

63. H/NSA, Box 29 (Corres.), September 19, 1947, Smith to NSA Madison staff.

64. Ibid., October 2, 15-16, November 10, 1947, Smith letters to Madison staff.

65. Ibid., November 17, 1947, Smith to Welsh regarding external funds.

66. Ibid., November 12, 1947, Welsh to Smith.

67. FOIA (FBI), 6/33, October 1, 1947, Allen B. Crow, "Challenging Questions
    Which Have Been Thrust upon Our Colleges and Universities by the Organiz-
    ing Convention of the United States National Student Association."

68. H/NSA, Box 29 (Corres.), September 16, 1947. Welsh reported Crow's phone
    calls to Smith.

69. Ibid.

70. Interview with Welsh.

71. Ibid.

72. Ibid.

73. H/NSA, Box 295 (UNESCO 1947-1951), October 14, 1947, Welsh telegram to
    Smith re UNESCO appointment.

74. Interview with Welsh.

75. H/NSA, Box 293 (UNESCO Nat'l Commission), n.d., Harry D. Gideonse,
    "Report of the Committee on Youth Organizations," describing the decision to
    appoint representatives of three youth organizations at the March 26-27, 1947,
    meeting of the U.S. National Commission for UNESCO. Gideonse had identi-
    fied the future NSA as one of three student organizations.

76. Ibid., April 30, 1947; Charles Thomson, UNESCO secretariat, U.S. Depart-
    ment of State informed Jim Smith, president of the National Continuations
    Committee, that the appointment must be deferred until organization existed.

77. NARA, RG 59 800.4089-12-1047, December 12, 1947, Secretary of State
    responded to a December 10, 1947 request from Coulter D. Huyler, Jr., in the
    American Embassy in The Hague for information on the new USNSA. If the
    NSA was judged leftist, Huyler feared its influence on the Dutch student union.
    Huyler had served with OSS during World War II, then with the CIA.

78. FOIA (FBI), 7/33, April 23, 1948, Attorney General Tom Clark to FBI Director
    Hoover.

79. See the 1948 campaign documents in the Henry A. Wallace Collection, available at wallace.lib.uiowa.edu.

80. Alice Cox, "The Rainey Affair" (Ph.D. diss., University of Denver, 1970).

81. H/NSA, Box 29 (Corres.), December 13, 1947, Bob Smith to Madison staff with excerpts from Jim Smith letter.

82. Ibid.

83. Interview with Welsh; see also Stanley R. Greenfield, "Publicizing the New Organization," in Schwartz, *American Student Organize*, 157.

84. Welsh Files, NSA Executive Committee Minutes, December 27-29, 1947.

85. NCWC, 84 (Organizations: Students), Philip DesMarais, "Report on the Meeting of the Executive Committee of the National Student Association," December 27-30, 1947.

86. Interview with Welsh.

87. NICC, Box 30 (Bill Ellis Fund), December 9, 1947, Ellis letter urging the NICC to keep the IUS appointment in its hands and force NSA to cooperate. See also H/NSA Box 286 (NICC 47-48, 50), February 19, 1948, Muriel Jacobson letter to Robert Smith, stating that the NICC would be unable to officially appoint Jim Smith in place of Ellis.

88. H/NSA Box 29 (Corres.), January 13, 1948; Bob Smith informed the Madison staff that he was sending Spurgeon Keeny to Prague to observe the IUS Council meeting as an NSA observer. Whether the Madison staff understood that Keeny was to report on Jim Smith is unclear.

89. Interview with Keeny. Keeny supplied me with a copy of the original report; an abbreviated version is available at H/NSA, Box 29.

90. Interview with Keeny.

91. H/NSA, Box 29 (Corres.), July 12, 1948, Bob Smith to Madison staff (ellipsis substituted for misplaced comma).

92. Letter from Jim Smith to Aunt Alta, dated February 10, 1948, courtesy of Smith's sons Philip and Michael; see also H/NSA, Box 29 (Corres.), January 13, 1948, Bob Smith to Madison staff re Jim Smith's intent to resign.

Chapter 4. Enter the CIA

1. H/NSA, Box 29 (Corres.), n.d., Mimeograph, Jim Smith's eyewitness account of events in Prague.

2. Karel Kaplan, *The Short March: The Communist Takeover in Czechoslovakia, 1945-58* (London: Hurst, 1987); see also Bradley Abrams, *The Struggle for the Soul of the Nation* (Cambridge: Harvard University Press, 2005).

3. H/NSA, Box 29 (Corres.), n.d., Smith's eyewitness account.

4. Ibid.

5. Ibid.

6. Ibid.

7. Despite numerous claims and investigations, the suicide or murder verdict remains unsettled. Masaryk's private secretary, Antonín Sum, maintains that Masaryk jumped to his death, despondent after the communist takeover. See

interview with Sum, October 11, 1998, National Security Archive, available at http://www2.gwu.edu/~nsarchiv/coldwar/interviews/. For more recent information on the dispute, see David Blair, "Mystery of Jan Masaryk's Cold War 'Suicide' Deepens," *The Telegraph*, January 7, 2004, which reports a Czech official's claim that it was murder.

8. Interview with William Welsh, New Brunswick, Maine, October 22, 1991; see also Ellis's five-page letter, listing his substantive disagreements with IUS actions, H/NSA, Box 26, March 1, 1948. See also the report of resignations in "Americans Quit Student Union in Prague; Red-Dominated Group Silent on Beatings," *New York Times*, March 4, 1948.

9. "Americans Quit Student Union in Prague."

10. H/NSA, Box 29 (Corres.), March 6, 1948, Bob Smith to Madison staff.

11. Ibid., March 2, 1948, Bob Smith to Madison staff.

12. Ibid., February 20, 1948, Bob Smith memo, "NSA-IUS Negotiating Delegates, Communication No. 2."

13. Ibid., February 2, 1948, Bob Smith to Madison staff. Information on Nemzer's attendance is in H/NSA, Box 283 (JCSA), February 6, 1948, Philip DesMarais memo about the evening to Father Flynn.

14. H/NSA, Box 29 (Corres.), March 2, 1948, Bob Smith to Madison staff.

15. Ibid.

16. Ibid.

17. FRUS, Retrospective Volume: Emergence of the Intelligence Establishment, 1945–50, Document 241, Memorandum from the General Counsel of the Central Intelligence Agency (Houston) to Director of Central Intelligence Hillenkoetter, re the absence of authority for covert action, September 25, 1947.

18. Peter Grose, *Gentleman Spy: The Life of Allen Dulles* (Amherst: University of Massachusetts Press, 1994), 282. For more on Wisner and the evolution of covert action see also Evan Thomas, *The Very Best Men: Four Who Dared; the Early Years of the CIA* (New York: Simon and Schuster, 1995), and John Ranelagh, *The Agency: The Rise and Decline of the CIA* (New York: Simon and Schuster, 1986).

19. "Note on U.S. Covert Action Programs," *Foreign Relations of the United States, 1964–68*, vol. 12, Western Europe (April 16, 2001): xxxi–xxxv, available at www.fas.org/sgp/advisory/state/covert.html.

20. FRUS, Retrospective Volume: The Emergence of the Intelligence Establishment, 1945–50, Psychological and Political Warfare, Document 298, Memorandum of Conversation and Understanding, Implementation of 10/2, August 6, 1948.

21. Anthony Carew, "The American Labor Movement in Fizzland: The Free Trade Union Committee and the CIA," *Labor History* (February 1998): 25–42. Carew also documents tension between labor officials and the Ivy Leaguers in the CIA.

22. Ibid.

23. NARA, State Department Secret OIR Report No. 4507.1, "The WFDY: The Central Organization, Opposing Groups and Affiliates," April 1, 1948. Declassi-

fied under the twenty-five-year rule, reclassified in 2001, and declassified in June 2012 by author's request submitted in 2003.

24. Joël Kotek, *Students and the Cold War* (New York: St. Martin's, 1996), 73–74. This history is also covered in NARA, State Department Secret OIR Report No. 5256, "The World Assembly of Youth: International Organization of Non-Communist Youth," August 10, 1950. Declassified under the twenty-five-year rule; reclassified in 2001; and declassified in June 2012 by author's request submitted in 2003.

25. Box 47 (YAC 48–49). Undated history is contained in a twenty-two-page report on Young Adult Council, previously called Association of Youth Serving Organizations, United States Youth Council Papers, National Social Welfare Assembly, University of Minnesota, Minneapolis. See also NICC, Box 198 (Admin), December 14, 1945, Minutes.

26. NICC, Box 198 (Admin), November 8, 1946, Minutes.

27. NARA, RG 800.4089/3-248, American Embassy, Moscow to Secretary of State.

28. NARA, RG 800.4089/10-2047, October 20, 1947. Attached to these records is a November 25, 1947, memo from Raymond Murphy, EUR/X, to Howard Trivers, C[entral] E[urope], on the need for the IUS study.

29. Interview with Paul Bouchet and Pierre Rostini, Paris, October 18, 2004; Rostini made similar comments. Rostini and Bouchet were founding IUS members.

30. W. Bonney Rust, "Students in Czechoslovak Crisis," *Focus*, Summer 1948. *Focus* was a magazine put out by the British National Union of Students.

31. W/NSA, Box 103 (Brussels Conference). Roy Voegeli and Norman Holmes, observers at the August 1948 International Youth Conference in London on behalf of the NSA, also attended a September 3 meeting in Brussels of dissident national unions of students who wished to discuss the IUS issues before going to Paris to observe the September 8 IUS Council meeting. Voegeli's undated notes about the hostility directed toward the NSA were made after the IUS Council meeting and in discussions with Bob Smith, who was also in Paris.

32. NARA, RG 800.4089/1-1948, March 22, 1948, Secretary of State to London Embassy in response to a series of January cables.

33. NARA, RG 800. 4089/7-948, July 9, 1948, Secretary of State to American Embassies (Athens, Brussels, Copenhagen, London, Oslo, Paris, Praha [Prague], Stockholm, the Hague, Warsaw, Rome), predicting more bilateral cooperation.

34. Flynn, Box 13 (NFCCS), April 21, 1948, Martin Haley to Flynn, re NSA executive committee; see also May 13, 1948, confidential note from Haley to Flynn re John Simons's plan for an alternative union.

35. H/NSA, Box 66 (Internat'l Reports), n.d., Mimeo, "Report of the Year (1947–48) International Activities of the NSA."

36. H/NSA, Box 29 (Corres.), March 2, 1948, Bob Smith to Madison staff.

37. William M. Birenbaum, "From the University of Chicago to Prague's Polytech," in *American Students Organize: Founding the National Student Association after World War II*, ed. Eugene G. Schwartz ([Westport, Conn.]: American Council

on Education/Praeger, 2006), 581–89. Additional insight on the views of Lawrence Jaffa and William Birenbaum may be found in Box 127 (International
Team, Applications 1947).

38. H/NSA, Box 29 (Corres.), March 2, 1948, Bob Smith to Madison staff.

39. Peter Jones, as abridged by Pat Wohlgemuth Blair, "NSA's Relations with the
International Union of Students," in Schwartz, *American Students Organize*, 539.

40. Flynn, Box 16 (NSA), March 8, 1949, Joseph Scheider (Youth Department) to
Flynn.

41. Ibid., March 12, 1949, Michael J. Rubino (Catholic University) to Secretary of
State Dean Acheson.

42. In a story by Stuart Loory, "Student to Agent: Mystery Death Hides CIA Ties,"
Los Angeles Times, February 26, 1967, West was described by an NSA colleague
as very upset over the *Ramparts* disclosures.

43. See H/NSA, Box 33 (Corres.), January 15, 1949, Harris letter to West, and January 28, 1949, West response to Harris, for evidence of the tension between the
two officers.

44. H/NSA, Box 101 (German Project), Farmer's résumé (January 1949); interview
with Thomas Farmer, Washington, D.C., April 16, 1999.

45. H/NSA, Box 33 (Corres.), April 14, 1949, Rob West to Madison staff.

46. Interview with Farmer.

47. H/NSA, Box 29 (Corres.), May 28, 1949, West report to Harris on U.S. Army
grant. See also Boxes 101, 125, and 126 for more on the German project.

48. Interview with Farmer.

49. Ibid.

50. Ibid.; Wisner description came up in my interview with Franklin Lindsay, Cambridge, Mass., January 26, 1999.

51. H/NSA, Box 11 (Int'l Student Seminar). The name change occurred in 1952.

52. H/NSA, Box 101 (German Project), August 18, 1949, Farmer to West.

53. H/NSA, Box 33 (Corres.), October 13, 1949, Erskine Childers to National Staff.

54. Ibid.

55. For information on Voegeli's CIA service, see biographical material on Royal J.
Voegeli in Schwartz, *American Students Organize*, 153.

56. Conversation with Norman Holmes, Washington, D.C., April 7, 1997. See
also information about Colgate's approach in Norman L. Holmes, "Innocence
Abroad," in Schwartz, *American Students Organize*, 554.

57. FOIA (FBI), 12/33. Includes a fifty-five-page report on 1949 NSA Congress,
mostly redacted.

58. H/NSA, Box 33 (Corres.), October 13, 1949, Childers to National Staff.

59. Eugene G. Schwartz, "From Urbana to Ann Arbor," in Schwartz, *American Students Organize*, 237.

60. Flynn, Box 16 (NSA), March 8, 1949, Flynn to Scheider, Youth Department re
Robert Kelly pledge to reverse his vote.

61. H/NSA, Box 33 (Corres.), October 17, 1949, Childers to Kelly.

62. H/NSA, Box 304 (WSSF), February 19, 1950, Brock to Childers.

63. Flynn, Box 13 (NFCCS), May 15, 1950, DesMarais to Flynn.
64. Material courtesy of Craig Wilson, April 20, 1998. In May 1997, Wilson wrote a draft article based on his experiences with Houghteling, "My Brush with History," and shared it with me.
65. Roy Reed, "Ex-Student Describes Intrigue in Getting C.I.A. Loan in '50," *New York Times*, February 17, 1967.
66. Wilson, "My Brush with History."
67. Ibid.
68. Ibid.
69. Ibid.
70. H/NSA, Box 127 (Internat'l Team), summer 1950, Financial Statement; the scratched out names are Laird Bell, Chicago, and Thomas E. Brittingham, Jr., Delaware. Bell served on the National Committee for Free Europe, Allen Dulles, Chair. See his entry in Wikipedia at http://en.wikipedia.org/wiki/Laird _Bell. The philanthropist Thomas Brittingham, Jr., also donated funds to bring Scandinavian students to the University of Wisconsin.
71. Wilson, "My Brush with History."
72. Houghteling told his story to Roy Reed; see Reed, "Ex-Student Describes Intrigue in Getting C.I.A. Loan."
73. Interview with Lindsay.
74. Interview with James D. Garst, New York, May 31, 2004. See also H/NSA, Box 255 (Sweden), Garst report on Scandinavia. See PB Web site.
75. H/NSA, Box 66 (SEAsia '50), copy of William Polk résumé.
76. H/NSA, Box 27 (Fisher), n.d. Fisher served the last six months of his service in Hawaii, at the Armed Forces Institute, Central Pacific Branch.
77. H/NSA, Box 28 (Corres.), copy of James P. Grant résumé in January 10, 1951, letter sent to NSA staff member Jim Zucker.
78. Ibid.
79. Paget Files: James P. Grant Biographical History (1922–1995), attached to Ihsan Dogramaci, "A Tribute," *International Pediatric Association Journal* 6, no. 3.
80. H/NSA, Box 127 (Internat'l Team), August 4, 1950, Kelly letter to Childers.
81. Ibid., August 1950, Rob West Prague diary. Palme's biographer Kjell Osterberg told the author that Palme submitted a report about the IUS Congress that implied a longer stay but later observed that Palme's report was virtually identical to West's diary account.
82. H/NSA, Box 52 (British IUS Relations), November 13, 1950, Curtis Farrar to Herbert Eisenberg after conversations with Palme.
83. H/NSA, Box 127 (Internat'l Team), August 1950, Robert L. West, "Report to American Students on IUS World Student Congress."

Chapter 5. Allard Lowenstein and the International Student Conference

1. Hendrik Hertzberg, "The Second Assassination of Al Lowenstein," *New York Review of Books*, October 10, 1985. Hertzberg addressed the CIA allegations made

by Richard Cummings in a review of *The Pied Piper: Allard K. Lowenstein and the Liberal Dream* (New York: Grove, 1985).

2. H/NSA, Box 102 (HIACOM), April 13, 1951, Jim Grant to Herb Eisenberg re Lowenstein's oratorical skills.

3. Dennis Trueblood and Gordon Klopf, "A Report on the 1950 National Student Association Congress," *School and Society*, November 25, 1950, 340-41. Copy courtesy of Eugene G. Schwartz.

4. For background on Eisenberg, see Herbert W. Eisenberg, "NSA's 1950-1951 International Program," in *American Students Organize: Founding the National Student Association After World War II*, ed. Eugene G. Schwartz ([Westport, Conn.]:American Council on Education/Praeger, 2006), 520-24.

5. Ibid., 525. See also Kenneth R. Kurtz, "Candid Reflections of a Candidate," in Schwartz, *American Students Organize*, 307.

6. Eisenberg, "NSA's 1950-1951 International Program," 522.

7. H/NSA, Box 28 (Corres. '50-'56), November 3, 1950, Harris to Lowenstein.

8. Ibid.

9. H/NSA, Box 1 (ISC), October 12, 1950, Palme to West.

10. Ibid.

11. H/NSA, Box 52 (Farrar), October 31, 1950, Eisenberg to Curtis Farrar, Prague 25 member, requesting attendance at BNUS Council meeting. See ibid. (BNUS) for the Farrar report in a November 13, 1950, letter to Eisenberg.

12. H/NSA, Box 34 (IUS Corres. 1949-50), copy of undated hand-delivered letter from IUS officials. See also Box 1 (ISC), December 12, 1950, letter from National Union of Czechoslovak Students.

13. H/NSA, Box 2 (ISC), December 17-27, 1950, Transcript of the Stockholm proceedings.

14. H/NSA, Box 252 (Sweden), November 20, 1950, Palme letter to Eisenberg after BNUS meeting.

15. NARA, RG 59 800.4614/11-2750, December 12, 1950, Confidential telegram Sec State Acheson to Am Emb Stockholm, attached to copy of November 27, 1950, correspondence.

16. H/NSA, Box 1 (ISC), November 28, 1950, Eisenberg draft of Stockholm meeting objectives.

17. Ibid., December 18, 1950, Copy of Lowenstein's speech, "This Conference Must Make a Contribution to Peace in the World." The speech is also reprinted in Schwartz, *American Students Organize*, 562-64.

18. Conversation with Eisenberg, Madison, Wisconsin, July 25, 1997, at an NSA alumni reunion.

19. After Eisenberg read my "From Stockholm to Leiden" in *Intelligence and National Security* 18, no. 2 (June 2003): 134-67, which discussed the Stockholm events, he speculated in a letter to Eugene Schwartz (who sent me a copy) that one of Palme's colleagues had blocked his attendance at strategy meetings.

20. Conversation with Eisenberg (on vote); telephone interview with Joan Long Lynch, August 13, 1998 (on Lowenstein's claims). Lynch made the same point in

her "From Ann Arbor to Minneapolis," in Schwartz, *American Students Organize*, 273.

21. Conversation with Eisenberg. See also H/NSA, Box 1 (ISC), December 24, 1950, Eisenberg memo to the NSA executive committee, written while in Sweden, describing SMAP objectives and noting that after Lowenstein's speech, "we almost didn't put it across."

22. NARA RG 800.4614/1-2251, January 22, 1951, Robert Donhauser, American Embassy, Stockholm, to Secretary of State, citing confidential comments by Olof Palme and an unidentified former NSA officer, most likely Robert Smith.

23. Ibid.

24. H/NSA Box 2 (ISC), December 17–27, 1950, Transcript of Stockholm proceedings.

25. H/NSA, Box 1 (ISC), December 24, 1950, Eisenberg memo to the NSA Executive Committee.

26. Flynn, Box 13, April 17, 1951, Philip DesMarais report; see also Paget Files: *The NSA News*, August 19, 1951.

27. H/NSA, Box 255 (Sweden), February 9, 1951, Eisenberg to Palme.

28. William Chafe, *Never Stop Running: Allard Lowenstein and the Struggle to Save American Liberalism* (Princeton, N.J.: Princeton University Press, 1998), 107–8.

29. NARA, RG 800.4614/1-2251, Donhauser to Secretary of State. Palme also supplied a written report on the Stockholm meeting to the American Embassy.

30. Ibid. American officials gave firsthand assessments of both Lowenstein and Eisenberg, after talking with them during a lunch at the Embassy.

31. A memorandum of Elliott and Dulles's conversation was sent to Lewis S. Thompson, chief, Special Projects division, of OPC: see Milton W. Buffington to CSP [Lewis S. Thompson], "United States National Student Association, February 17, 1951," in Michael Warner, ed., *CIA Cold War Records: The CIA Under Harry Truman*, prepared by the History Staff, Center for the Study of Intelligence, Central Intelligence Agency, Washington, D.C., 1994. Available at NARA and online at https://www.cia.gov/library/center-for-the-study-of -intelligence/csi-publications/books-and-monographs/the-cia-under-harry -truman/index.html; reprinted in "Attachment 1: The CIA Considers NSA in 1951," in Schwartz, *American Students Organize*, 569.

32. Ibid.

33. Ibid.

34. H/NSA, Box 102 (HIACOM), January 16, 1951, Frank D. Fisher to Allard Lowenstein.

35. Ibid.

36. Ibid.

37. H/NSA, Box 294 (U.S. Government), November 1950, Eisenberg memo on State Department call.

38. NARA, RG 800.4614/1-2551, January 25, 1951, Flanders to George McGhee, Assistant Secretary of State, re meeting with Lowenstein.

39. CFR Study Group 5152, "The Role of Leadership in the Defence [*sic*] of the

Free World," November 15, 1950, minutes. For a list of study group attendees, see PB Web site.

40. Ibid. See also Edmond Taylor, *Awakening from History* (Boston: Gambit, 1969), 414.

41. CFR Study Group 5152, "Role of Leadership" minutes.

42. Ibid. See also the April 18, 1951, minutes, which report a second year of Carnegie Corporation funding for the study group.

43. Sallie Pisani, *The CIA and the Marshall Plan* (Lawrence: University Press of Kansas, 1991), 41.

44. CFR Study Group 5152, November 15, 1950, minutes; Donald Shank from IIE also joined the study group.

45. Taylor, *Awakening from History*, 393–95.

46. Ibid., 414.

47. CFR Study Group 5152, March 13, 1951, Minutes.

48. H/NSA, Box 102 (HIACOM), February 10, 1951, Frank Fisher, Memorandum on Foreign Seminar Proposals; Box 102 also contains biographical information on Melvin Conant.

49. Conant eventually became an oil expert with Exxon Corporation in East Africa, the Far East, and Australia from 1961 to 1973. There is a ten-year gap in his résumé between 1951 and 1961, a frequent indicator of intelligence work. He later taught at the U.S. War College. See Melvin A. Conant, Jr., résumé, Box 21 (Folder 18), White House Special Files Collection, Richard Nixon Presidential Library. Available online at http://www.nixonlibrary.gov/virtuallibrary/docu ments/whsfreturned/WHSF_Box_21/WHSF21-18.pdf.

50. Ibid.

51. See, e.g., H/NSA, Box 102 (HIACOM), January 16, 1951, Francis D. Fisher to Allard Lowenstein; March 7, 1951, Jim Grant to Lowenstein; March 11, 1951, Frank Fisher to Lowenstein; July 14, 1951, Carl Sapers to Shirley Neizer, Madison.

52. Ibid., March 7, 1951, Grant to Lowenstein.

53. Ibid., March 11, 1951 Fisher to Eisenberg and Neizer.

54. CFR Study Group 5152, April 18, 1951, minutes.

55. Ibid.

56. Pisani, *CIA and the Marshall Plan*, 48.

57. H/NSA, Box 66 (IC Reports), unsigned letter re Rockefeller Foundation funds for German Seminar, the second phase of the German project conceived by Tom Farmer in 1949. See also Box 283 (Orgs), May 18, 1950, Erskine Childers's memo on Rockefeller grant.

58. H/NSA, Box 66 (IC Reports), James P. Grant, "Southeast Asia Report 1950," 1–125.

59. H/NSA, Box 126 (German Seminar), April 16, 1951, Eisenberg to British NUS.

60. Eisenberg, "NSA's 1950–1951 International Program," 524. Eisenberg blamed Lowenstein for the lack of communication.

61. H/NSA, Box 102 (HIACOM), July 26, 1951, Shirley Neizer to William Ayers.

62. Ibid. n.d., Sapers's mimeographed report prepared for the 1951 NSA Congress.
63. Ibid. Sapers's report cited the figure of $5,000.
64. H/NSA, Box 255 (Sweden), February 13, 1951, Eisenberg to Palme.
65. Ibid., July 31, 1951, Palme to Eisenberg.
66. Ibid.
67. William T. Dentzer, "From Minneapolis to Bloomington," in Schwartz, *American Students Organize*, 542. Dentzer discussed the 1951 Congress and his and Lowenstein's views on the ISC.
68. Ibid.
69. Barry Keating, mimeo, "A History of the Student Government Movement in America" (New York: Students for Democratic Action, 1953), 35.
70. Chafe, *Never Stop Running*, 119.
71. Telephone interview with Galen Martin, Louisville, Ky., October 7, 1997.
72. Barry Farber, "Travels to Zagreb, 1951," in Schwartz, *American Students Organize*, 592.
73. Keating, "History of the Student Government Movement," 35.
74. Eisenberg, "NSA's 1950–1951 International Program," 525.
75. H/NSA Box, 16 (COSEC), Ingram résumé.
76. Farber, "Travels to Zagreb, 1951," 592.
77. Keating, "History of the Student Government Movement," 35.
78. David Victor Harris, *Dreams Die Hard: Three Men's Journeys Through the '60s* (New York: St. Martin's, 1982), 169.
79. Ibid.
80. H/NSA, Box 126 (German Seminar), February 8, 1951, Eisenberg to German Seminar co-director, Robert Fischelis, re Ingram's participation in an upcoming meeting.
81. William Chafe, correspondence with me, January 7, 1998.
82. FOIA (FBI), 18/33. An August 21, 1952, confidential FBI report cites the date that Hoover ended his investigation as November 19, 1951. Also in this volume of documents is information that the FBI withheld a 270-page report on the NSA dated October 1952 at the request of an unspecified government agency. FBI declassified documents Series 19 to 33 indicate that Hoover continued his coverage of NSA Congresses but relied mainly on printed material rather than reports from special agents.

Chapter 6. The Counteroffensive

1. Interview with David Baad, Saddlebrooke, Az., January 13, 2009.
2. H/NSA, Box 189 (Cuba), Eisenberg report on Brazil conference, July 28–August 5, 1951. See also Box 171 (Brazil 47–52), for further detail on the Brazil conference.
3. For a view of the early IUS, see Joël Kotek, *Students and the Cold War*, trans. Ralph Blumenau (New York: St. Martin's, 1996), esp. chap. 6, "The Creation of the International Union of Students," 86–106.
4. CFR Study Group 5152, April 18, 1951, minutes.

5. H/NSA, Box 67 (Staff Reports), September 20, 1951, Ingram to Dentzer.

6. H/NSA, Box 74 (NAC '47–56), October 20, 1952, Ingram to Harold Taylor, president of Sarah Lawrence College.

7. H/NSA, Box 104 (INC), November 20, 1951, Ingram to Lewis Levenson of Georgia Tech.

8. Ibid., November 6, 1951, Jim Grant (not to be confused with James P. Grant of Harvard, the Southeast Asia specialist) to Ingram.

9. H/NSA, Box 171 (Brazil 47–52), July 15, 1951, Rogers to Eisenberg.

10. H/NSA, Box 29 (Corres.), February 17, 1952, Dentzer to Ingram; see also Box 102 (Indonesia), February 27, 1952, Dentzer to Ingram.

11. Dentzer has insisted that he was not made witting by the CIA until September 1952, after his presidency. He repeated this in an article co-written with Norman Holmes, Richard J. Medalie, Richard G. Heggie, and William Welsh, "Covert U.S. Government Funding of NSA International Programs," in *American Students Organize: Founding the National Student Association After World War II*, ed, Eugene G. Schwartz ([Westport, Conn.]: American Council on Education/ Praeger, 2006), 567. In the same article, he asserted that he later found out that the funding began in November 1951.

12. Psychological Strategy Board Files, declassified documents: October 13, 1951, Ingram to Gordon Gray; October 19, 1951, John Sherman memo to CIA [name withheld]; November 10, 1951, Dentzer-Ingram proposal to Sherman; December 7, 1951, Sherman letter to Dentzer and Ingram assigning new liaison, William A. Korns; December 12, 1951, Sherman letter to CIA. All in Harry S. Truman Papers, Harry S. Truman Library and Museum, Independence, Mo. See also H/NSA, Box 104 (INC), December 19, 1951, Ingram report on December meeting with Korns in a letter to Bill Dentzer.

13. Ingram referenced Gray's invitation to submit a proposal in his October 13, 1951, letter to Gray, Psychological Strategy Board Files.

14. Interview with Thomas Farmer, Washington, D.C., April 16, 1999.

15. Janet Welsh, "Student Rights, Academic Freedom, and NSA," in Schwartz, *American Students Organize*, 386; interview with Janet Welsh Brown, Washington, D.C., October 26, 1998.

16. Interview with Farmer.

17. H/NSA, Box 67, July 29, 1951, Confidential Conant Report to HIACOM.

18. Ibid.

19. H/NSA, Box 102 (HIACOM), February 12, 1951, Grant, letter to Lowenstein, with suggested revisions to his statements on NSA, which Grant found too explicitly anticommunist.

20. H/NSA, Box 67, July 29, 1951, Confidential Conant Report to HIACOM.

21. H/NSA, Box 140 (SEAsia), June 18, 1951, Conant to Grant and Fisher.

22. H/NSA, Box 102 (Indonesia), December 20, 1951, Ingram to Soedarpo Sastrosatomo via the U.S. State Department.

23. H/NSA, Box 32 (Rogers), August 13, 1951, confidential letter from Rogers to Herbert Eisenberg.

24. Ibid.

25. Ibid.
26. H/NSA, Box 29 (Corres.), November 8, 1951, Dentzer to Ingram.
27. Ibid., December 19, 1951, Ingram letter to Dentzer.
28. H/NSA, Box 104 (ISIS), January 13, 1952, Ingram memo written in Paris to Carl Sapers, Harvard, after the January 3–8 Edinburgh ISC.
29. Ibid. See also H/NSA, Box 2 (ISC), for detail on the Edinburgh conference.
30. IISH ISC, Box 740, January 1952, Supervision Commission report; see also H/NSA, Box 104 (ISIS), January 13, 1952, Ingram to Sapers.
31. IISH ISC, Box 740, January 1952, Supervision Commission report.
32. Interview with Franklin Lindsay, Cambridge, Mass., January 26, 1999. See also H/NSA, Box 29 (Corres. 55–56), which contains an example of material from a 1955 summer meeting in Paris by an unidentified author, "Confidential Memorandum on Personnel, Not to Be Shown to Any Unauthorized Persons," followed by the admonition "Please do not leave this lying around where it is generally available." Page 2 is headed, "Strictly Confidential Top Secret in Fact." Copies went to Harry Lunn, Leonard Bebchick, and Helen Jean Rogers. Despite these admonitions, the document was left in the archival files.
33. H/NSA, Box 104 (ISIS), January 13, 1952, Ingram report on Edinburgh to Sapers identifying Indonesian students; January 14, 1952, Ingram to Fisher.
34. Ibid., January 13, 1952, letter from Ingram to Sapers.
35. H/NSA, Box 37 (IUS Corres.), January 22, 1952, Fisher memo on Simons conversation.
36. H/NSA, Box 104 (ISIS), January 13, 1952, Ingram to Sapers.
37. Ibid., January 14, 1952, Ingram to Fisher.
38. H/NSA, Box 52 (British IUS Relations), March 20, 1952, Fred Jarvis (BNUS) to Dentzer.
39. Ibid., March 25, 1952, Dentzer to Jarvis.
40. H/NSA, Box 32 (Rogers), June 30, 1952, Dentzer to Rogers with explanation of strategy.
41. H/NSA, Box 29 (Corres.), May 26, 1952, Dentzer to Ingram.
42. Ibid.
43. H/NSA, Box 32 (Rogers), June 1, 1952, Dentzer to Rogers.
44. IISH ISC, Box 1223 (Sup Com Meetings), draft minutes from June 9–10, 1952, later edited to exclude this remark. See the PB Web site.
45. H/NSA, Box 52 (British-IUS Relations), July 15, 1952, Thompson to Dentzer.
46. Ibid., July 21, 1952, Ingram to Thompson.
47. H/NSA, Box 12 (COSEC), July 31, 1952, Dentzer to Thompson and Jarvis.
48. H/NSA, Box 32 (Rogers), Spring 1952. Rogers, then enrolled at Catholic University in Washington, D.C., oversaw the Latin America program throughout the spring of 1952. See March 13, 1952, Top Secret draft, Helen Jean Rogers's proposed Latin American program, with a price tag of $37,500. On April 23, 1952, Rogers conveyed her optimism to Ingram in a letter citing prospective funding from "my family's friend."
49. H/NSA, Box 16 (COSEC), July 16, 1952; members of the ISC who also belonged

to the WUS included Jean Sarvonat (France), John Thompson (Great Britain), and Karl Tranaeus (Sweden).

50. Ibid. (SupCom '52–'53), July 29, 1952, confidential Rogers memo re personnel of the Leiden Secretariat.

51. NARA, RG 800.4614/4-2952, April 29, 1952, Acheson cable to American Embassy, Stockholm.

52. Ibid.

53. NARA, RG 800.4614/5-752 May 5, 1952, American Embassy Stockholm to Sec State re Swedish Foreign Office cooperation; 800.4614/5-1652, American Embassy Stockholm to Sec State re Palme refusal.

54. NARA, RG 59, 800. 4616/5-1652, May 15, 1962, Acting Sec State Bruce to American Embassy Stockholm.

55. NARA, 800.4614/5-1652, May 16, 1952, Sec State to American Embassy Stockholm.

56. NARA, 800.4614/5-2953, May 29, 1952, American Embassy Stockholm to Sec State.

57. H/NSA, Box 32 (Rogers), June 23, 1952, Rogers to Dentzer.

58. NARA RG 800.4614/1-2251, January 22, 1951, Robert Donhauser, American Embassy, Stockholm, to Secretary of State. Donhauser stated that Olof Palme, Bertil Ostergren, Jarl Tranaeus "have been known personally to officers of the embassy for some time and have cooperated in every way possible."

59. H/NSA, Box 16 (Sup Com '52–'53), July 29, 1952, Confidential memo from Rogers to Ingram and Dentzer.

60. Ibid.

61. Ibid., January 18–19, 1953, Minutes. Multiple sources have confirmed the involvement of British intelligence in the ISC and COSEC, including Gwyn Morgan, former British COSEC secretary general: interview with Gwyn Morgan, London, October 11, 2006. According to former International Affairs vice president Clive Gray, during this period COSEC American and British staff sometimes met together with their respective case officers. Interview with Clive Gray, Greensboro Vt., September 1 and 2, 2005.

62. NARA, RG 800.4614/4-451, D. M. Davis to Jessie MacKnight, Assistant Secretary of State, discussing the fact that his affiliation is hidden from other State Department contacts. Davis organized a meeting of the new World Assembly of Youth at Cornell during the summer of 1952.

63. Kotek, *Students and the Cold War,* 206. Kotek interviewed Thomas Braden, director of the International Division, who told him, "We used many foundations!" Additional conduits will be covered in later chapters.

64. In 1960, Amory "Amo" Houghton, Jr. (Harvard '50), CEO of Corning Glass, joined the FYSA board; Houghton had worked with Frederick Houghteling on HIACOM during the 1948–50 period. He later became a U.S. congressman.

65. Ted Morgan, *A Covert Life: Communist, Anti-Communist, and Spymaster* (New York: Random House, 1999), 287. Ross ran the CIO International Committee and later became international affairs director of the AFL-CIO.

66. A. M. Sperber, *Murrow: His Life and Times* (New York: Fordham University Press, 1999), 305. Murrow was a member of the IIE executive committee and backed Duggan's decision.

67. CFR Study Group 5152, October 24, 1951, Minutes.

68. Robin Winks, *Cloak and Gown: Scholars in the Secret War, 1939–1961* (New York: William Morrow, 1987), 275–76.

69. For an overview, see Hugh Wilford, *The Mighty Wurlitzer: How the CIA Played America* (Cambridge: Harvard University Press, 2009).

70. Thomas Braden, "I'm Glad the CIA is 'Immoral,'" *Saturday Evening Post*, May 20, 1967, 10–14.

71. Interview with Thomas Farmer, Washington, D.C., April 16, 1999.

72. Ibid.

73. Ibid.

74. Cord Meyer, Jr., *Facing Reality: From World Federalism to the CIA* (New York: Harper and Row, 1980), 51–55.

75. Evan Thomas, *The Very Best Men: Four Who Dared; The Early Years of the CIA* (New York: Simon and Schuster, 1995), 138.

76. Meyer, Box 5, Diary. See, for example, the entry of March 21, 1963, re drinking, "unused talents," and "wasted opportunities."

77. Ibid., entry of November 6, 1954, re CIA promotion.

78. Interview with Jarmila Maršálková, Velka Bukova, Czech Republic, September 8, 2008.

79. Ibid.

80. Blumenau, chap. 16, p. 172.

81. For an overview see George Herman Hodos, *Purge Trials: Stalinist Purges in Eastern Europe, 1948–1954* (New York: Praeger, 1987).

82. For postwar Germany, see Norman M. Naimark, *The Russians in Germany: A History of the Soviet Zone of Occupation, 1945–1949* (Cambridge: Harvard University Press, 1989).

83. Hodos, *Purge Trials*. For a personal view, see Heda Margolius-Kovály, *Under a Cruel Star: A Life in Prague, 1941–1968* (London: Holmes and Meier, 1997). Her husband, Rudolf Margolius, was executed with Slánský and others.

84. Interviews with Thomas Madden, Skokie, Ill., June 29–30, 2004, and with Maršálková.

85. Interview with Maršálková.

86. Karel Kaplan, *Report on the Murder of the General Secretary* (London: Tauris, 1990), 53–55.

87. Interview with Madden.

88. Blumenau, chap. 14, p. 130.

89. Interview with Maršálková.

90. Interview with Madden.

91. Bernard Bereanu later published "Self-Activation of the World's Nuclear Weapons System," *Journal of Peace Research* 20, no. 1 (1983), demonstrating the statistical inevitability of nuclear destruction.

Chapter 7. The Battle for Members

1. Thomas Braden, "I'm Glad the CIA is 'Immoral,'" *Saturday Evening Post*, May 20, 1967, 13.
2. H/NSA Box 37 (IUS Corres.), January 22, 1952, Frank Fisher memo on telephone conversation with Simons.
3. H/NSA, Box 28 (Harris), June 24, 1952, Dentzer cable to Ingram in Paris confirming Ted Harris's work for the Simons Fund.
4. H/NSA, Box 230 (Lebanon), July 31, 1952, Harris letter to Ingram.
5. H/NSA, Box 233 (Middle East), January 1951, William Polk report to HIACOM on his summer 1950 findings.
6. H/NSA, Box 104 (ISIS), January 13, 1952, Ingram to Sapers.
7. H/NSA, Box 140 (Fisher: SEAsia Trip), n.d. [ca. September–October 1952], Confidential Report Copy No. 1 Frank Fisher, Southeast Asia trip report.
8. H/NSA, Box 102 (Indonesia), January 25, 1952, Fisher to Ingram; February 27, 1952, Fisher prospectus to George Franklin, Jr. (CFR). See also Box 29 (Corres.), March 6, 1952, HIACOM letter informing Dentzer's office of CFR check for Fisher.
9. H/NSA, Box 102 (Indonesia), February 27, 1952, Fisher memo to Ingram, "Discretion in Handling Information Within NSA."
10. Interview with Frank Fisher, Austin, Tex., May 14, 2009.
11. H/NSA, Box 27 (Fisher), Handwritten notation on résumé.
12. H/NSA, Box 67 (IC Reports), n.d. [ca. September–October 1952], Fisher report, "NSA Policy in Indonesia."
13. Ibid.
14. Ibid. See also H/NSA, Box 140 (Fisher: SEAsia Trip), n.d., Confidential Report Copy No. 1.
15. H/NSA, Box 140 (SEAsia 51–52), Misfiled, Rogers, Report of the First Inter-American Student Congress in Rio, January 25–February 5, 1952.
16. H/NSA, Box 32 (Rogers), April 23, 1952, Rogers confidential letter to Ingram.
17. H/NSA, Box 227 (Latin America), contains extensive reports on Rogers's activities in Latin America. Harvard originally refused her admission, then reversed its decision; see Box 32 (Rogers), June 23, 1952, Rogers to Dentzer.
18. H/NSA, Box 140 (SEAsia 51–52), misfiled Rogers report.
19. H/NSA, Box 217 (India), December 2, 1952, Rogers, letter to Frank Fisher on her correspondence for the NSA: "as usual, I am forging Avrea's signature."
20. FOIA, Naval Institute, August 1952, NSA Student Congress, Ingram working papers. Why the Naval Institute had an interest in NSA is not clear, although Ingram was a Navy veteran. The Freedom of Information request was government-wide and resulted in material from the Naval Institute.
21. H/NSA, Box 29 (Corres.), March 27, 1952, Dentzer to Ingram.
22. H/NSA, Box 189 (Cuba), July 9, 1952, Dentzer, letter to Señor Alvaro Barba Machado, FEU.
23. Ibid., August 1952, copy of Fernández speech at the NSA Congress. For details

on Fernández, see Mario Llerena, *The Unsuspected Revolution: The Birth and Rise of Castroism* (New York: Ardent Media, 1978), 23.

24. H/NSA, Box 189 (Cuba), August 1952, Fernández speech.

25. Ibid., August 1952, copy of NSA Congress Cuba resolution.

26. Ibid.

27. H/NSA, Box 233 (Middle East), January 1951, Polk report, which had recommended working with Middle Eastern students studying in the United States. For information on the relationship between the CIA and the American Friends of the Middle East, see Hugh Wilford, *America's Great Game: The CIA's Secret Arabists and the Shaping of the Modern Middle East* (New York: Basic, 2013).

28. H/NSA, Box 277 (IIE), July 31, 1952, Ingram to Holland; Holland letter attached; August 6, 1952, Holland to Ingram.

29. H/NSA, Box 265 (Afghanistan), n.d. [ca. July 1954], Harry Lunn report on his role in the Afghanistan meeting of June 24–26, 1954, and attendance at the Pakistan Student Association in mid-June 1954. See also Box 268 (AFME), Iranian Student Convention, Denver, Colorado, September 1952. Box 268 also contains a report from AFME on these meetings.

30. FRUS, vol. 10: National Security Policy, Document 132, "Memorandum from the Central Intelligence Agency to the 303 Committee," re the Asia Foundation and Proposed Improvements in Funding Procedures, June 22, 1966. This memo refers to the 1954 funding; however the Asia Foundation grew out of the earlier Committee for a Free Asia, established in California on March, 12, 1951. See also Richard H. Cummings, *Radio Free Europe's "Crusade for Freedom": Rallying Americans Behind Cold War Broadcasting, 1950–1960* (Jefferson, N.C.: McFarland, 2010), 48. H/NSA, Box 165 (NUS: Asia), contains an example of *The Asian Student*, January 1953, published by the Asia Foundation.

31. H/NSA, Box 88 (African Scholarships), Ingram correspondence re the formation of the Association of African Students in America, June 11–13, 1953. The CIA's role in Latin American student associations has not been documented.

32. The ASA budget was confirmed in an interview with Mohammed Ghausi, Bolinas, Calif., October 7, 2005.

33. H/NSA, Box 220 (Iran), Ingram and Pirnazar correspondence.

34. The Organization of Tehran Students held a seat on the IUS Council. See Afshin Matin-Asgari, *Iranian Student Opposition to the Shah* (Costa Mesa, Calif.: Mazda, 2002), 175. See also Ervand Abrahamian, *Iran Between Two Revolutions* (Princeton: Princeton University Press, 1982), 332–33.

35. Stephen Kinzer, *All the Shah's Men: An American Coup and the Roots of Middle East Terror* (Hoboken, N.J.: Wiley, 2003). See also declassified documents in Electronic Briefing Book No. 28, *The Secret CIA History of the Iran Coup, 1953*, published November 29, 2000, at the National Security Archive of George Washington University, gwu.edu/~nsarchiv/NSAEBB/NSAEBB28/.

36. H/NSA, Box 3 (ISC), January 8–16, List of ISC participants, which identifies OAS representatives Bahgat el Tawil (no address) and Kamal Shair (Yale).

37. H/NSA, Box 197 (Egypt), July 1947, IUS circular, Information on League of

Egyptian Students. See also the League's letters to NSA, October 11 and 20, 1947, requesting assistance for food and textbooks.

38. II/NSA, Box 295 (Orgs: UNESCO), December 1952, Fisher cables to Singapore and New Delhi.

39. IISH ISC (FYSA), 180/2 (628), January 6, 1953, Davis (FYSA) to Thompson (COSEC) re meeting after the ISC.

40. H/NSA, Box 2 (ISC), January 4–8, 1952, Copenhagen reports.

41. FOIA (CIA), Vaughan Index, a computer printout of withheld CIA documents numbering in the thousands. See PB Web site for further details.

42. H/NSA, Box 28 (Ingram), January, 1953, Ingram's confidential notes on Copenhagen ISC.

43. Ibid., December 1952–February 1953, Progress report by Ingram.

44. Ibid.

45. H/NSA, Box 27 (Fisher), February 26, 1953, Ingram to Fisher.

46. NARA, 800.4614/-CO/1-1453, Confidential Security Information from Sec/State, tracing history of conference. Sent to Bangkok, Colombo, Djakarta [Jakarta], Karachi, Manila, New Delhi Missions, and Bombay, Calcutta, Kuala Lumpur, and Singapore Consulates.

47. Ibid., reactions attached.

48. H/NSA, Box 12 (COSEC Corres.), "Glass Hats, US State Department, and the Leiden Secretariat (Or How They Came to Copenhagen)," in Around the World, *IUS News*, February 1953.

49. H/NSA, Box 305 (Corres.), June 11, 1953, Ingram to Paul Denise (WSSF).

50. IISH ISC (FYSA), 180/1, Copy of Busono Wiwoho, "Travel Notes of an Indonesian Observer," *IUS News*, February 1953.

51. Ibid.

52. Ibid.

53. On Subroto's relations with the NSA, see the PB Web site.

54. H/NSA, Box 41 (NFCUS), Charles Taylor (Canada) report on the IUS meeting in Bucharest, September 1–3, 1952.

55. H/NSA, Box 28 (Ingram), January 1953, Ingram handwritten notes re Copenhagen ISC.

56. Ibid.

57. Ibid. See also H/NSA, Box 2 (ISC), Confidential reports; handwritten notes identify FYSA grants to Costa Rica, Honduras, Guatemala, Mexico, and Nicaragua (Central America), and to Argentina, Paraguay, and Uruguay (South America), a substantial increase in attendance from the year before at the ISC Edinburgh when only Brazil attended.

58. President Truman announced the Point Four program in 1949, but like many programs, its roots can be found earlier. See Truman Library, Oral history online interview with the administrator, Stanley Andrews (1952-30). www.trumanlibrary.org/oralhist/andrewss.htm.

59. H/NSA, Box 140 (SEAsia), May 1952, "Report to Advisory Committee Southeast Asia," states that Grant was with the State Department. See also ibid.

(SEAsia: Ellis), July 1952, Report of Bill Ellis meetings in Washington, D.C., with TCA officials, including Jim Grant, who was also associated with the law firm of Covington and Burling.

60. Ibid. (SEAsia: Ellis), July 10, 1953, Simons notification to Ingram of $3,000 grant for Ellis's Southeast Asian trip.

61. Ibid., Ellis funding proposal.

62. Ibid., Mid-July 1953, Copy of TCA memo to South and Southeast Asia Missions re Ellis trip.

63. Ibid.

64. Ibid., n.d., Ellis report on Burma.

65. Ibid.

66. H/NSA, Box 139 (SEAsia: Ellis '52–'53), September 6, 1953. Ellis to Ingram.

67. H/NSA, Box 217 (India). See, for example, November 24, 1952, Ruth Wright, American Embassy Education Officer in New Delhi, "personal restricted" letter to Frank Fisher re a pro-communist student leader; and June 4, 1954, Frank Parker, foreign aid adviser to the American Ambassador, to Paul Sigmund re names of Indian student leaders.

68. Ibid., October 1952, Shelat to Ingram.

69. Ibid.

70. Ibid.

71. Ibid., October 21, 1953, Ellis to Shelat.

72. Ibid.

73. The date of the FYSA grant is circa spring 1954; it later became a bone of contention between the FYSA, the NSA, and Shelat: see H/NSA Box 28 (Gray), September 1, 1957, Clive Gray to Indian student leader C. B. Tripathi. Box 3 (ISC), List of participants to the ISC Istanbul, January 8–16, 1954, confirms Shelat's attendance.

74. H/NSA, Box 33 (Thomas), April 7, 1953, Thomas to Ingram re confusion over reporting requirements; see also Box 27 (Fisher), May 21, 1953, Fisher response to Ingram re Thomas.

75. H/NSA, Box 197 (Egypt), September 9, 1953, Edwards and Bebchick letter of thanks to Major General Muhammad Naguib.

76. See, for example, IISH ISC (FYSA), 180, December 23, 1953, Simons to COSEC (Thompson) re Egyptian grant approval.

77. Williams, a Yale graduate with experience in the Middle East, helped establish the Association of African Students in the United States and Canada at Howard University on June 11–13, 1953, co-sponsored by the NSA and the Institute on African-American Relations. See the PB Web site.

78. W/NSA, Box 103 (FYSA), October 19, 1953, Williams is listed as a HIACOM area specialist and desk chief, although he was enrolled at Boston University.

79. H/NSA, Box 197 (Egypt), October 21, 1953, Williams to Shaaban.

80. American staff in Geneva WUS/ISS before 1953 included John Simons (1948–49), Ted Harris (1950–51), and Bob Smith (1950).

81. H/NSA, Box 197 (Egypt), October 21, 1953, Williams to Shaaban.

82. Ibid., November 20, 1953, Shaaban to Williams on a Pan-Arab conference and Ted Harris's frequent visits.
83. IISH ISC, Box 1235 (Sup Com: 1952–61), May 19, 1955, Dentzer letter to the Supervision Commission reporting a C. V. Whitney $4,500 grant for the South African investigation.
84. Ibid.
85. H/NSA, Box 29 (Corres.), n.d. [after the January 5–12, 1954, Istanbul ISC], Confidential memo from Len Bebchick to NSA advisory boards, pledging full report by March.

Chapter 8. Opening the Spigot

1. W/NSA, Box 103 (FYSA), January 5, 1954, Simons to Bebchick re quarterly funds. See also October 19, 1953, IC administrative budget, $30,640, September 1, 1953–September 1, 1954.
2. W/NSA, Box 2, July 26, 1953, Richard J. Murphy letter informing Gordon Klopf (NSA adviser) of the special sessions, citing a new FYSA grant for that purpose.
3. W/NSA, Box 103 (FYSA), June 7, 1954, Funding request.
4. Ibid., May 5, 1954, John J. Simons letter to Leonard Bebchick, with attached budget, showing that $3,000 was allocated to NSA headquarters, a practice that increased the national office's dependency on CIA funds.
5. Ibid., May 26, 1954, Bebchick letter to Simons confirming Istanbul ISC delegation expenses as $3,919.79; May 20, 1954, Prospectus to FYSA for WAY delegation to Singapore, $5,600; May 21, 1954, Prospectus to FYSA for WUS delegation to Oxford, England, $1,000; May 21, 1954, Japanese International Student Conference delegation, $3,800.
6. Ibid., April 30, 1954, Prospectus to FYSA for COSEC dues, $5,263.15 ($45,000 in today's dollars).
7. W/NSA, Box 103 (FYSA), contains copies of proposals listed above, as well as others.
8. IISH ISC (FYSA), 180. The archive has preserved the voluminous correspondence between COSEC and FYSA arranged chronologically. In one case, when Thompson was slow to request funds, Simons initiated the discussion: 180/2, January 13, 1953, Simons letter to Dentzer (COSEC), asking if he was wondering about the coming year, "and nothing in the COSEC jeans."
9. IISH ISC (FYSA), 180/1 (628), August 12, 1953, David Davis, FYSA, letter to Thompson, COSEC, about proposed meeting with Ingram in either Munich or Zurich. See also August 18, 1953, Thompson letter to Davis confirming September 25–26 meeting in Zurich. On September 4, 1953, Thompson changed the meeting location to Munich.
10. H/NSA, Box 12 (COSEC), August 11, 1953, Enrique Ibarra funding proposal; see also IISH ISC (FYSA), 180/2 (629), August 11, 1953, re Ibarra travel award and itinerary.
11. H/NSA, Box 12 (COSEC), October 23, 1953, original proposal for Istanbul ISC.

12. IISH ISC (FYSA), 180/1 (628), December 12, 1952. Simons's letter to Thompson re contact with Pan Am.

13. Ibid., 180/2 (629), December 3, 1953, Simons letter to Thompson re his categories for travel grants, which include 1) previous attendance, desire to cooperate; 2) previous observer; 3) European unions; December 4, 1953, Thompson and Ingram to Simons, listing possible attendees in the last two categories: 4) never attended; 5) has no recognized NUS [national union of students].

14. H/NSA, Box 26 (Duberman), June 8, 1954, Duberman recommended a tour for French leader Jacques Balland; Box 12 (COSEC) has a copy of Balland's six-page memo, a critique of the ISC.

15. H/NSA, Box 12 (COSEC), October 26, 1953, Len Bebchick to Chuck Seashore, University of Colorado student body president.

16. H/NSA, Box 27 (Fisher), May 11, 1953, Ingram to Frank Fisher conveying FYSA approval for the summer International Student Relations Seminar.

17. Interview with Paul Sigmund, Princeton, N.J., October 31, 2005.

18. Ibid. See also Henry J. Kellermann, *Cultural Relations as an Instrument of U.S. Foreign Policy: The Educational Exchange Program Between the United States and Germany, 1945–1954* (Washington D.C.: U.S. Department of State, 1974).

19. H/NSA, Box 105, October 10, 1955, Bebchick to Simons.

20. Ibid.

21. H/NSA, Box 103 (IC Project), copy of 1954 program and speakers.

22. Ibid. In 1954, Helen Jean Rogers alone covered COSEC, ISC, the Research and Investigation Commission, Germany, Italy, Scandinavia, South America, Spain, and Yugoslavia.

23. Peter Grose, *Gentleman Spy: The Life of Allen Dulles* (Amherst: University of Massachusetts Press, 1994), 230; interview with Thomas Farmer, Washington, D.C., April 16, 1999.

24. H/NSA, Box 101 (I.C. Project: Fulbright Scholars Recommended), March 25, 1958, Bruce Larkin memo to NSA President Stan Glass and Ralph Della Cava on secrecy of Fulbright applications loaned to NSA. Some Fulbright applications remain in the NSA archives.

25. Interview with Leonard Bebchick, Washington, D.C., April 27, 2000.

26. Ibid.

27. Interview with Sigmund.

28. Interview with Bebchick.

29. Ibid.

30. Ibid.

31. Ibid.

32. Ibid.

33. Cord Meyer, Jr., *Facing Reality: From World Federalism to the CIA* (New York: Harper and Row, 1980), 79.

34. Fulton Lewis, Jr., was a nightly radio broadcaster on the Mutual Broadcast Network; for content of his broadcasts see Fulton Lewis Jr., Papers at Syracuse University, http://library.syr.edu/digital/guides/l/lewis_f_jr.htm.

35. Frederick Houghteling, quoted in "Charges of Reds in NSA Are False," *Harvard Crimson*, June 5, 1951.

36. See, for example, August 23, 1950, "A Message from President Truman," to the NSA Congress, reprinted in Eugene G. Schwartz, ed., *American Students Organize: Founding the National Student Association After World War II* ([Westport, Conn.]: American Council on Education/Praeger, 2006), 258.

37. Interview with Bebchick.

38. The June 30, 1953, TOP SECRET Report to the President's Committee on International Information Activities, heavily redacted, is available at www.foia .cia.gov. See also NARA, RG 59 PPS 1953, Box 72, re financing by the CIA.

39. H/NSA, Box 26 (Ellis), October 22, 1953, Minutes, list of desk officers.

40. Interview with Bebchick.

41. H/NSA, Box 14 (COSEC), September 14, 1953, Bebchick was advised in a letter from Avrea Ingram at COSEC that funding was probable, and that Bebchick should contact as an intermediary in Texas one Herman Neusch, a World War II navy veteran who was active in Catholic youth circles and a delegate to the International Youth Conference (the forerunner of the CIA-financed World Assembly of Youth) in 1948 and the National Newman Club Federation international vice president in 1950. See also Box 32 (Helen Jean Rogers), August 13, 1951, Rogers letter to Eisenberg re Herman Neusch of Texas as a broker for securing Latin American program funds; Box 104 (International News Center). Neusch's position in 1953 is unknown.

42. Telephone conversation with Edward Gable, Pebble Beach, Calif., October 18, 1998; interview with Catherine Fischer McLean, Berkeley, California, March 17, 1999.

43. H/NSA, Box 36 (IUS), March 20, 1953, misfiled memo from Gable to Ingram.

44. Interview with Bebchick.

45. H/NSA, Box 36, October 27, 1953, Bebchick to Dentzer re ISC delegation.

46. H/NSA, Box 26 (Ellis), n.d. [ca. November 1953], Bebchick to Ellis.

47. Interview with Bebchick.

48. Ibid.

49. H/NSA, Box 29 (Corres.), March 2, 1954, Bebchick to James Edwards.

50. Ibid.

51. Ibid.

52. W/NSA, Box 103, n.d., Dennis Trueblood, "Observations of the 1952 Congress."

53. Ibid.

54. H/NSA, Box 74, August 8, 1955, Sylvia Bacon IAB report.

55. H/NSA, Box 90 (Campus Int'l Admin), March 20, 1954, Lunn to Bebchick re overseas post; April 5, 1954, Lunn to Bebchick re overseas post; undated response from Bebchick to Lunn, after receiving Lunn's May 6, 1954, telegram, rejecting the NSA offer.

56. Ibid., May 23, 1954, Lunn to Bebchick, rejecting ISRS offer.

57. Margarett Loke, "Harry Lunn, Jr., 65, Art Dealer Who Championed Photography," obituary, August 24, 1998, *New York Times*; telephone interview with

Margarett Loke, November 1, 1999, to confirm information in obituary. Loke, a *Times* staff arts writer, interviewed Lunn before his death. He discussed the timing of his recruitment. See also H/NSA, Box 90 (Campus Int'l Administrator), May 30, 1954, Lunn telegram to Bebchick to accept position of Campus International Administrator.

58. H/NSA, Box 90 (Campus International Awareness), May 24, 1954, Bebchick handwritten note on Lunn salary of $3,500.

59. Interview with Bebchick.

60. Ibid.

61. Ibid.

62. Mark Haworth-Booth, "Obituary: Harry Lunn, *The Independent*, September 8, 1998, available at http://www.independent.co.uk/arts-entertainment/obituary -harry-lunn-1196714.html.

63. H/NSA, Box 74 (IAB), November 1, 1959, International Activities Board Minutes, in which Sigmund's salary was reported retrospectively as having been granted by the Cummins Catherwood Foundation of Philadelphia.

64. H/NSA, Box 29 (Corres.), 1955–56, contains extensive correspondence on the origin and funding of the Foreign Student Leadership Project. See, for example, March 2, 1955, Paul Sigmund, summary of his meeting with Mel Fox at the Ford Foundation; April 12, 1955, Lunn letter to Sigmund, which includes the FLSP prospectus and issues of accountability.

65. H/NSA, Box 30 (Corres.), n.d. FSLP Board members included John J. Simons (FYSA), James T. Harris, Jr. (FLSP), and Donald J. Shank, Institute of International Education. See the PB Web site for complete list.

66. Interview with Robert Kiley, Cambridge, Mass., January 22, 2008. Kiley confirmed that the CIA had to go to the White House to get the executive order.

67. Ibid.; interview with Tony Smith, New York, N.Y., November 7 and 9, 2007; telephone conversation with Gable, who described recruitment as "the point" of the FLSP program.

68. H/NSA, Box 26 (Sigmund), June 3, 1955, Sigmund description of Paris party to student Janet Cooper.

Chapter 9. The Spirit of Bandung

1. H/NSA, Box 31 (Lunn), n.d., Confidential report on the Asian-African Students Conference.

2. The *Christian Science Monitor* editor Joseph Harrison later acknowledged the CIA relationship. See Stuart H. Loory, "The CIA's Use of the Press: A Mighty Wurlitzer," *Columbia Journalism Review* (September–October 1974): 9–18.

3. George McTurnan Kahin, *The Asian-African Conference: Bandung, Indonesia, April 1955* (Ithaca: Cornell University Press, 1955). For an African American perspective, see Richard Wright, *The Color Curtain* (Jackson: University Press of Mississippi, 1995). Wright's book on his attendance at the Bandung conference, originally published in 1956 by World Publishing, has been reissued.

4. Nehru's speech can be found at the Modern History Source Book site of Ford-

ham University, at http://www.fordham.edu/halsall/mod/1955nehru-bandung2
.html.

5. For a Chinese perspective, see Kuo Kang Shao, *Zhou Enlai and the Foundations of Chinese Foreign Policy* (London: Palgrave Macmillan, 1996).

6. See, for example, Jason C. Parker, "Small Victory, Missed Chance: The Eisenhower Administration, the Bandung Conference, and the Turning of the Cold War," in *The Eisenhower Administration, the Third World, and the Globalization of the Cold War*, ed. Kathryn C. Statler and Andrew L. Jones (Lanham, Md.: Rowan and Littlefield, 2006), 153–74; David Kimche, *The Afro-Asian Movement: Ideology and Foreign Policy of the Third World* (Jerusalem: Israel Universities Press, 1973). Additional sources can be found at the PB Web site.

7. Evan Thomas, *The Very Best Men: Four Who Dared; the Early Years of the CIA* (New York: Simon and Schuster, 1995), 157.

8. Paul F. Gardner, *Shared Hopes, Separate Fears: Fifty Years of U.S.-Indonesia Relations* (Boulder, Colo.: Westview Press, 1997), 128.

9. John Foster Dulles, Iowa State College speech, June 9, 1955, cited on the Arlington National Cemetery Web site, www.Arlingtoncemetery.net/jfdulles.html.

10. Cary Fraser, "Race and Realpolitik in the American Response to the Bandung Conference 1955," in *Window on Freedom: Race, Civil Rights and Foreign Affairs, 1945–1988*, ed. Brenda Gayle Plummer (Chapel Hill: University of North Carolina Press, 2003).

11. *Newsweek*, January 1, 1955, quoted in Wright, *Color Curtain*, 190.

12. Matthew Jones, "Segregated Asia? Race, the Bandung Conference, and Pan-Asianist Fears in American Thought and Policy, 1954-55," *Diplomatic History* 29, no. 5 (2005): 841–68.

13. Ibid.

14. Steve Tsang, "Target Zhou Enlai: The 'Kashmir Princess' Incident of 1955," *China Quarterly* 139 (September 1994): 766–82.

15. William Corson, *Armies of Ignorance: The Rise of the American Intelligence Empire* (New York: Dial, 1977), 366.

16. Quoted in H. W. Brands, *The Specter of Neutralism* (New York: Columbia University Press, 1990), 115; see also Department of State, Intelligence Reports, "Results of the Bandung Conference: A Preliminary Analysis," April 27, 1955, NARA, R & A Reports, IR, No. 6903.

17. H/NSA, Box 31 (Lunn), n.d., Confidential Report on the Asian-African Students Conference.

18. Ibid.

19. Ibid.

20. H/NSA, Box 218 (India), n.d. [ca. 1958], Clive Gray report, "Recent Developments in the Indian Student Movements," 13.

21. Willard A. Hanna, "The Little Bandung Conference," July 5, 1956, available at the Institute of Current World Affairs Web site, http://www.icwa.org/Former Articles.asp?vIni=WAH&vName=Willard%20A.%20Hanna. Hanna worked for the U.S. Information Agency in Jakarta.

22. W/NSA, Box 103 (Indonesian Student Hospitality Nov. '54–Feb. '55). The

prospectus from the NSA to FYSA is undated but circa November 1954, and includes itinerary and budget. See also H/NSA, Box 102 (Indonesian Student Tour 54–55), for extensive detail on the tour.

23. H/NSA Box 31 (Lunn), n.d., Confidential Report on the Asian-African Students Conference.

24. IISH ISC, Box 1235 (1955), Ref. 406/1, Appointments of de Graft Johnson (Ghana) and John Didcott (South Africa); IISH ISC (FYSA), 180/27 (628), 1955–56 Asian Delegation Prospectus; see also H/NSA, Box 16 (COSEC), for additional information on Asian tour.

25. IISH ISC (FYSA), 180/27 (628), 1955–56 Asian Delegation prospectus.

26. The U.S. government began using the phrase "Soviet imperialism" in the early 1950s, especially in guidance to Radio Free Europe. See Lazlo Borhi, "Containment: Rollback, Liberation or Inaction? The United States and Hungary in the 1950s," *Journal of Cold War Studies* 1, no. 3 (1999): 67–108.

27. H/NSA, Box 165 (Asia), October 19, 1955, press release.

28. IISH ISC (FYSA), 180/43 (630), May 22, 1956, International Student Delegation to Asia 1955–56, Report to John Simons.

29. H/NSA, Box 165 (Asia), COSEC report prepared prior to the Bandung conference, "Independence and the Student" (1956), 1–80.

30. IISH ISC (FYSA), 180/42 (630), May 14, 1956, FYSA grant to COSEC to cover Ismail's expenses. See ibid., August 29, 1956, letter from Thompson to Simons elaborating on Ismail's role at the conference.

31. H/NSA, Box 31 (Lunn), n.d., Confidential Report on the Asian-African Students Conference.

32. Ibid.

33. Greg MacGregor, "Filipinos leave Bandung Session," *New York Times*, June 5, 1956; see also *New York Times*, June 4, 1956, on charges of collusion with U.S. intelligence.

34. IISH ISC (FYSA), 180/42 (630), May 14, 1956, grant authorized up to sixteen thousand dollars. See also ibid., John Simons, May 7, 1956, cable to John Thompson on willingness to make emergency grants.

35. Ibid., May 14, 1956, grant.

36. H/NSA, Box 314 (Asian-African Students Conference), May 15, 1956, Gray to Ghausi.

37. Ibid.

38. Interview with Mohammed Ghausi, Bolinas, Calif., October 7, 2005.

39. H/NSA, Box 32 (Sigmund), July 17, 1956, Gray to Sigmund.

40. H/NSA, Box 314 (Asian-African Students Conference), *Bandung Spirit*.

41. "Blow for Bandung Reds, Neutralism Triumphs" in the *Singapore Free Press*, May 30, 1956, typified Asian anticommunist press headlines in support of perceived pro-West victories, especially the failure to establish an IUS-affiliated regional organization.

42. Greg MacGregor, "Indonesia Wary of Youth Parley," *New York Times*, June 4, 1956, re the Indonesia government's decision to withhold funds.

43. Lunn's estimate is in H/NSA, Box 31 (Lunn), n.d., Confidential Report on the

Asian-African Students Conference. See also Hanna, "Little Bandung Conference."

44. Sukarno unilaterally declared independence on August 17, 1945. Negotiations
with the Dutch, assisted by the United States, lasted three years, and stalled over
issues of territory and commerce. See the PB Web site.

45. "U.S. and Sukarno Benefit by Visit," *New York Times*, June 5, 1956, was representative of the positive press.

46. Denis Lacorne and Tony Judt, *With Us or Against Us: Studies in Global Anti-
Americanism* (New York: Macmillan, 2005), 215.

47. Quoted in, "Asia-Africa Session On: Students Convene in Bandung—Hear
Colonialism Scorned," *New York Times*, May 31, 1956.

48. Ibid.

49. Ibid.

50. Hanna, "Little Bandung Conference."

51. Quoted in Greg MacGregor, "Indonesia Wary of Youth Parley," *New York Times*,
June 6, 1956. Lunn's view can be found in H/NSA, Box 31 (Lunn), n.d., Confidential Report on the Asian-African Students Conference.

52. Interview with Ghausi.

53. H/NSA, Box 314 (Bandung), quoted in the Conference newspaper, *Bandung
Spirit*.

54. Greg MacGregor, "Walkout Filipino Explains Stand," *New York Times*, June 7,
1956.

55. Ibid.

56. H/NSA, Box 31 (Lunn), n.d., Confidential Report on the Asian-African Students Conference.

57. Ibid.

58. H/NSA, Box 165 (Asian-African Conference), Pran Sabharwal, "Little Bandung:
A Report on Asian African Students Conference (May–June 1956)" (New Delhi:
University Press, 1956). IISH ISC (FYSA), 180 (630), May 7, 1956, Thompson
(COSEC) prospectus to Simons (FYSA) contains a history of events that led to
the Asian-African Students Conference.

59. Greg MacGregor, "Youth Unit Urged for Asia, Africa; Egyptians at Bandung
Seek Federation with Purpose of Ending Colonialism," *New York Times*, June 5,
1956.

60. H/NSA, Box 314 (Asian-African Students Conference), COSEC-collected
material passed on to the NSA.

61. H/NSA, Box 31 (Lunn), n.d., Confidential Report on the Asian-African Students Conference.

62. Manoj Das (India) later described these conversations in "Forging an Asian
Identity," *The Hindu*, January 7, 2001, available at www.hindu.com/2001/01/07
/stories/1307017j.htm.

63. H/NSA, Box 314 (Bandung), clipping, "Student Parley Becomes Donnybrook,"
New York Herald Tribune, June 12, 1956.

64. "Student Conference," *New York Times* editorial, June 8, 1956.

65. Ibid.

66. Harry H. Lunn, Jr., "Red Control Fails at Youth Parley," *Christian Science Monitor*, June 27, 1956.
67. H/NSA, Box 165 (Asian-African Conference), Sabharwal, "Little Bandung."
68. Ibid.
69. H/NSA, Box 31 (Lunn), n.d., Confidential Report on the Asian-African Students Conference.

Chapter 10. Shifting Battlefields

1. H/NSA, Box 32 (Sigmund), January 6, 1956, Sigmund, letter to Clive Gray, conveying information from Ingram about the Swiss.
2. On support for Eisenhower, see Barry Keating, "How Its Own Cold War Influenced Liberal Student Activism," in *American Students Organize: Founding the National Student Association After World War II*, ed. Eugene G. Schwartz ([Westport, Conn.]: American Council on Education/Praeger, 2006), 812.
3. The NSA executive committee frequently considered and voted upon resolutions not taken up in plenary sessions.
4. Portions of the resolution on segregation are reprinted in Schwartz, *American Students Organize*, 451.
5. H/NSA, Box 67 (Staff Reports), August 1952, Frank Fisher, SEA report.
6. Richard Glen Lentz and Karla K. Gower, *The Opinions of Mankind: Racial Issues, Press, and Propaganda in the Cold War* (Columbia: University of Missouri Press, 2010). The impact of Bandung is described in Hazel Rowley, *Richard Wright: The Life and Times* (Chicago: University of Chicago Press, 2008), 471.
7. A picture of University of Alabama students burning desegregation signs can be viewed at the America's Story Web site of the Library of Congress, http://www.americaslibrary.gov/aa/marshallthrgd/aa_marshallthrgd_lucy_2_e.html.
8. Tillman Durdin, "Miss Lucy Flies Here for a Rest," *New York Times*, March 2, 1956.
9. NARA, RG 306, Box 4, July 24, 1956, "Opinion About U.S. Treatment of Negroes," USIA Public Opinion Barometer Reports.
10. H/NSA, Box 88 (Alabama Case), February 17, 1956, Young to Gray; see also Box 29 (Corres.), for Young's résumé.
11. H/NSA, Box 88 (Alabama Case), February 17, 1956, Young to Gray.
12. H/NSA, Box 33 (Young), February 28, 1956, Gray to Young.
13. H/NSA, Box 29 (Corres.), March 6, 1956, Gray to Lucy, c/o NAACP.
14. H/NSA, Box 88 (Alabama), July 23, 1956, copy of campus letter.
15. H/NSA, Box 29 (Corres.), July 1956, "A Letter About Racial Discrimination in the United States and Efforts for Its Elimination."
16. H/NSA, Box 14 (COSEC), July 10, 1956, Gray to Ingram.
17. James Forman, *The Making of Black Revolutionaries* (Seattle: University of Washington Press, 1972), 90.
18. H/NSA, Box 32 (Sigmund), June 19, 1956, Sigmund memo from Paris to Gray, reporting on conversations pertaining to the upcoming ISC.
19. H/NSA, Box 33 (Young), March 11, 1956, Young, letter to Gray.

20. Ibid.

21. Forman, *Making of Black Revolutionaries*, 91.

22. W/NSA, Box 103, July 15, 1955, partial transcript of the ISC Birmingham in "The Political Versus Practical Controversy at the International Student Conference," a confidential working paper prepared for ISRS participants.

23. Ibid.

24. Ibid. COSEC documents put the number in attendance at fifty countries but not all had voting privileges.

25. Ibid.

26. Ibid.

27. Clement Moore Henry argues that UGEMA retained its autonomy and did not take direction from the FLN. See his *Combat et Solidarité: Témoignages de L'UGEMA, 1955–62* (Algiers: Editions Casbah, 2010) (published under the name Clement Henri Moore). I also spoke with Henry on the issue. At the time, NSA had little doubt that UGEMA was the student wing of the FLN.

28. The UGEMA history (*U.G.E.M.A.: The Students of Algeria Are Fighting*, published by the "Press and Information Department of the International Union of Students") can be found in an eighty-two-page booklet available at http://bu.univ-alger.dz/UGEMA/Theses%20et%20Articles/UGEMA.The %20students%20of%20Algeria%20are%20fighting.pdf. See also, Yahia Zoubir, "US and Soviet Policy Toward France's Struggle with Anticolonial Nationalism in North Africa," *Canadian Journal of History* 30, no. 3 (December 1995): 58–84.

29. More information on UGEMA leader Zeddour Belkacem can be found at zeddour.commandant-moussa.com.

30. H/NSA, Box 32 (Sigmund), January 29, 1956, Sigmund to Gray. Zeddour's body was found on November 30, 1954.

31. Alistair Horne, *A Savage War of Peace: Algeria, 1954–1962* (New York: Macmillan, 1977), covers both the Bandung students conference and repeated United Nations resolutions.

32. H/NSA, Box 32 (Sigmund), January 6, 1956, Sigmund to Gray.

33. Ibid., June 19, 1956, Sigmund memo on Carvalho conversation.

34. Ibid.

35. H/NSA, Box 156 (Algeria '56–'57), August 21, 1956, Sigmund cable to Gray.

36. Ibid., August 28, 1956, Gray to Clifford Gurney, AFME.

37. Ibid., n.d., Sigmund report on UNEF and Algeria.

38. Ibid., August 28, 1956, Gray to Clifford Gurney, AFME.

39. Ibid., August 11, 1956, Gray cable to UGEMA offering financial assistance for one representative to Ceylon, and additional funds if UGEMA accepted the invitation to the NSA Congress.

40. Recognition of the Algerian cause was adopted by the CIA-funded International Confederation of Free Trade Unions (July) and the World Assembly of Youth (August).

41. Einaudi's biography is available at the Organization of American States Web site, www.oas.org/documents/eng/biography_sga.asp.

42. Mario Einaudi was an émigré scholar supported by the Rockefeller Foundation. He subsequently founded the Center for International Studies at Cornell University.

43. Interview with Luigi Einaudi, Washington, D.C., December 7, 2007.

44. Ibid. Einaudi remembers the Chileans paying for his trip, but at the time, he reported that the funding came through the Congress for Industrial Organization in Washington; see H/NSA, Box 29 (Corres.), Summary of Oral Report, Latin American Trip, October 9–21, 1955.

45. H/NSA, Box 183 (Chile), October 15, 1955, Einaudi to Sigmund and Gray.

46. Ibid.

47. H/NSA, Box 29 ('55–'57), October 9–21, 1955, Summary of Oral Report by Luigi Einaudi.

48. Ibid.

49. H/NSA, Box 28 (Harris), n.d., Einaudi to Harris, "Some FSLP Possibilities in Latin America."

50. Ibid.

51. Ibid.

52. H/NSA, Box 14 (Ingram), June 23, 1956, Einaudi to Avrea Ingram at COSEC.

53. Interview with Richard Heggie, Orinda, Calif., November 9, 2005. Heggie, a former NSA national officer (1948–49), went to work for the Asian Foundation (initially the Committee for a Free Asia), which funded the alternative to Zengakuren. He was assigned to Japan until 1956. See also H/NSA, Box 224 (Japan), for further information on the American effort, including an undated report from the International Seminar, held August 8–13, 1952, at Kobe College; and Box 32 (Sigmund), January 6, 1956, letter to Clive Gray, reporting that Heggie recommended giving up working at the national level in Japan and concentrating on individual student governments.

54. H/NSA, Box 89 (Asian Team '55–'56), July 19, 1956, Helen Jean Rogers to Clive Gray and others.

55. Ibid. See also Box 217 (India), Reports from Frank Fisher (1952), Bill Ellis (1953), Fulbright scholar Merrill Freed (1955).

56. H/NSA, Box 89 (Asian Team '55–'56), July 19, 1956, Rogers to Gray and others. The NSA also had important information from a young Indian leader, Hiralal Bose, who was close to Nehru. Bose attended Henry Kissinger's seminar for young foreign leaders at Harvard, and conveyed to Clive Gray that Nehru was disgusted with Shelat's inaction. See also July 31, 1956, Gray letter to Rogers.

57. Ibid., July 19, 1956, Rogers to Gray.

58. H/NSA, Box 27 (Fisher), July 16, 1956, Fisher to Gray re Lunn's instructions.

59. Ibid.

60. Ibid., August 3, 1956, Fisher to Gray.

61. H/NSA, Box 218 (India), n.d., Clive Gray, "Recent Developments in the Indian Student Movements," 13–15.

62. Ibid.

63. Interview with Clive Gray, Greensboro, Vt., September 1 and 2, 2005.

64. H/NSA, Box 28 (Gray), September 1, 1957, Gray to Indian leader C. B. Tripathi.

65. Ibid., March 2, 1957, Gray to Ted Harris.

66. Ibid., March 28, 1957, Gray to Bruce Larkin.

67. Interview with Gray.

68. Ibid.

69. IISH ISC (FYSA), 180 (630), August 10, 1956, grant submission.

70. H/NSA, Box 18 (Finances), December 8, 1958, Asian Seminar funding.

71. IISH ISC (FYSA), 180 (634), May 5, 1967, COSEC to FYSA re 1966-67 funding for the Asian Press Bureau. In 1967, Chandra Mohan Gulhati, director of the Asian Press Bureau, vigorously denied that the ISC had anything to do with the Cold War, asserting that charges of CIA funding sources were baseless; see "Asian Press Director Disturbed by Article," *Salient: Victory University Students' Paper* 30, no. 5 (1967): 11, available at http://nzetc.victoria.ac.nz/tm/scholarly/tei-Salient30051967-t1-body-d41.html.

72. Interview with Gray.

73. Interview with Sigmund.

74. Interview with Gray.

75. IISH ISC, Box 1089 (Algeria 1956-59), Crawford Young speech to UGEMA, December 1957.

76. H/NSA, Box 5 (COSEC: VI ISC Ceylon), undated typewritten copy of a Sunday *Times* of London correspondent's depiction of NSA behavior at Ceylon as "opportunist mano[e]uvr[ing]" and "clumsy." See also Box 166 (Asian-African Student Conference), Harold Sims's undated report after the Ceylon ISC, which describes the NSA as caught between two fires, the West accusing NSA of "expeditious folly, hoary imperialism and shifting imperialism and shifting alliances," and the East accusing it of "European favoritism, unlived principles, partisanship, political control and expeditious diplomacy."

77. H/NSA, Box 5 (COSEC: VI ISC Ceylon), Working Papers of the Sixth International Student Conference, held in Ceylon, September 11-21, 1956; Box 16 (COSEC), April 9, 1957, press release on Cuban resolution passed at sixth ISC.

78. H/NSA, Box 17 (COSEC Financial), June 8, 1956, Thompson letter to FYSA, with initial budget figure for ISC Ceylon, $121,815.80.

79. H/NSA, Box 12 (COSEC), October 5, 1956, Press release on sixth ISC.

80. IISH ISC (RIC), 1169, November 5, 1956, John Thompson letter to Swedish student leader informing him of Ingram's departure in October and making a joke about his dog, Paco.

81. H/NSA, Box 26 (Gray), June 6, 1956, Gray letter to Barry Farber re secret funding for Farber's trip to Soviet Union.

82. See Warren Lerner, "The Historical Origins of the Soviet Doctrine of Peaceful Coexistence," http://scholarship.law.duke.edu/cgi/viewcontent.cgi?article=3028&context=lcp The full text of the 20th Party Congress secret speech is in "Khrushchev on Stalin," *New York Times*, June 5, 1956.

Chapter 11. Hungary and the Struggle Against Nonalignment

1. The American Hungarian Federation Web site is an excellent source for photos. See http://www.americanhungarianfederation.org/1956/photos.htm.
2. Media coverage included wire services, network television, and numerous articles in the *New York Times*. See also the Radio Free Europe digital index on world press coverage at www.osaarchivum.org/digitalarchive/rferl_mc/index .html.
3. I originally found Béla Lipták's account, "Testament of Revolution," online at www.mefesz.hu, but it seems to have been removed. The account is also available in paperback of the same name published by Texas A & M University Press in 2007.
4. Victor Sebestyen, *Twelve Days: The Story of the 1956 Hungarian Uprising* (New York: Pantheon, 2006); see the PB Web site for more sources.
5. Minutes of 290th National Security Council meeting, July 12, 1956, available at www.gwu.edu/~nsarchiv/NSAEBB/NSAEBB76/doc2.pdf.
6. According to correspondence of Clive Gray between November 1956 and January 1957, those present in Vienna included Frank Ferrari, WAY; Eugene Metz, Free Europe Committee; Mike Iovenko, WUS; Shepard Stone, International Association for Cultural Freedom; Crawford Young, COSEC; and Clive Gray, NSA. See H/NSA, Box 211 (Hungary), December 9, 1956, twenty-three page report to Larkin for information on WAY, RFE, WUS, and COSEC. See also, January 23, 1957, Gray's ten-page report to Larkin asking for information on Stone.
7. H/NSA, Box 213 (Hungary), December 23, 1956, Larkin to Gray.
8. The NSA was a co-sponsor of this event, along with the International Rescue Committee. See Box 211 (Hungary), November 9, 1956, confidential memo from Harold Bakken to Bruce Larkin re meeting with Bujdosó afterward. Clive Gray and John Simons from FYSA were also in attendance.
9. See "Laszlo Calls upon Public Opinion to Save Hungary," *Harvard Crimson*, November 16, 1956. An AP photo of "Laszlo" giving testimony is in the plates section of this volume.
10. See H/NSA, Box 211 (Hungary), November 27, 1956, a scathing letter from Marian Lowe to NSA officers in Cambridge, accusing them of treating Laszlo (Bujdosó) like a circus animal.
11. Quoted in "Hungarian Says Leaders Need Help," *Greensboro Daily News*, November 29, 1956.
12. Ibid. See the PB Web site for Radio Free Europe funding sources.
13. American campuses held spontaneously rallies in support of the Hungarian uprising. The NSA requested that funds go to the New York office of the World University Service (formerly the World Student Service Fund). See, for example, "Students Rush Aid to Hungary," *Clarion*, November 30, 1956, the newspaper of Brevard Methodist College, which reported that Yale, Hunter, Stanford, and the California Institute of Technology had raised over ten thousand dollars. Some checks came directly to the NSA: see H/NSA, Box 211 (Hun-

gary), March 10, 1957, Allan Janger, NSA publications staff letter, to Ralph Della Cava re composition of support.

14. H/NSA, Box 37 (IUS Corres), November 21, 1956, cable to IUS Prague.

15. H/NSA, Box 211 (Hungary), contains Gray's voluminous letters and reports.

16. Interview with Clive Gray, Greensboro, Vt., September 1 and 2, 2005.

17. IISH ISC, Box 483, Hostel photo.

18. H/NSA, Box 28 (Gray), November 17, 1956, Gray, report on Vienna activities.

19. Ibid.

20. Ibid., November 19, 1956, Gray, Report on Vienna activities.

21. Ibid.

22. Ibid., December 9, 1956, Gray to Larkin.

23. H/NSA, Box 26 (Edwards), Edwards's résumé; information on COSEC release, Box 211 (Hungary), December 20, 1956, Larkin reporting Gray's assurance to National Executive Committee representative Jim Greene (Minnesota-Dakotas region).

24. H/NSA, Box 211 (Hungary), December 20, 1956, Larkin to Greene.

25. H/NSA, Box 28 (Gray), November 19, 1956, Gray to Larkin.

26. Ibid., December 9, 1956, Gray, twenty-three-page report to Larkin on events in Vienna.

27. Ibid.

28. Ibid.

29. Ibid.

30. Ibid.

31. Ibid.

32. Ibid.

33. Ibid.

34. H/NSA, Box 211 (Hungary), December 10, 1956, Gray to Niels Thygesen, Danish student leader.

35. Ibid., January 23, 1957, Gray to Larkin. Gray returned to Vienna after the Polish trip and remained until January 16, 1957.

36. H/NSA, Box 25 (Della Cava), December 22, 1956, Vienna report.

37. IISH ISC, Box 441 (Hungary), January 24, 1957, Edwards memo re conversation with Ferenc Molnar.

38. H/NSA, Box 212 (UFHS), March 15, 1957, Della Cava to Clive Gray and Robert Fisher (NSA Japan).

39. H/NSA, Box 213, February 3, 1957, Della Cava report.

40. Interview with Ralph Della Cava, New York, November 1, 2005.

41. See H/NSA, Boxes 211–15, for hundreds of reports and letters detailing the infighting and difficulties that the NSA faced in Vienna and New York when trying to put together a federation and select Hungarian student leaders for tours. For an example of Janko's decisions, see Box 211, March 6, 1957, NSA cable reporting that Janko had accused a potential nominee for the Asian trip of immorality and warning of dire consequences if the NSA didn't stop interfering in the selection process. See Box 212, March 15, 1957, Della Cava letter to Clive Gray and Robert Fisher (Japan) on these issues.

42. H/NSA, Box 212 (Hungary), March 15, 1957, Della Cava to Gray and Fisher.

43. H/NSA, Box 211 (Hungary), n.d. [ca. January 1957], Notice of Catherwood Foundation grant by Helen C. Whittemore, Secretary.

44. Ibid., February 8, 1957, notification of grant award from William A. Smith, San Jacinto Fund.

45. W/NSA, Box 103 (FYSA); see also H/NSA, Box 213 (Hungary), n.d., Memo to University Travel for round-trip transportation to Chicago for sixty-eight Hungarian students to form an American federation of Hungarian Students in June 1957, later called the American-Hungarian Students Association. See also H/NSA, Box 215 (Hungary), undated memo (no author), following the Asian tour, recommending that a UFHS delegation attend a scheduled meeting of the Latin American Student Congress rather than conduct a separate tour.

46. H/NSA, Box 213 (Hungary), n.d. Gray cable to Della Cava.

47. H/NSA, Box 211 (Hungary), July 26, 1957, cable to NSA Headquarters. The ellipsis replaces a comma.

48. H/NSA, Box 28 (Gray), May 23, 1957, Gray to Larkin.

49. H/NSA, Box 212 (UFHS), March 15, 1957, Della Cava to Fisher and Gray.

50. Interview with Gray.

51. H/NSA, Box 214 (UFHS), December 18, 1957, UFHS team transcript.

52. Ibid.

53. H/NSA, Box 213 (Hungary), February 2, 1957, Fisher to Ralph Della Cava.

54. Ibid.

55. Gyula Várallyay, *Tanulmány-Úton: Az Emigráns Magyar Diákmozgalom 1956 után* (Budapest: Századvég Kiadó, 1992), 173. I am grateful to Clive Gray for loaning me a copy of the volume and to Julia Kocz for translating it.

56. Ibid. 172.

57. Ibid.

58. H/NSA, Box 217 (Hungary), September 16, 1957, "Discussions with Charles Derecskey at Ibadan."

59. Ibid.

60. Várallyay, *Tanulmány-Úton*, 180-81.

61. H/NSA, Box 217, February 7, 1958, John Simons to UFHS President Aladár Meréyni.

62. H/NSA, Box 211 (Hungary), November 17, 1957, Ralph Della Cava to Derecskey re rejection of grant request.

63. Ibid. Della Cava conveyed Simon's complaint about the lack of reports and suggested a strategy for gaining FYSA's approval for additional funds. In this instance, Della Cava is fully in favor of the Hungarian students' agenda.

64. H/NSA, Box 217 (Hungary), February 7, 1958, Simons to Meréyni re three separate grant requests.

65. H/NSA, Box 213 (Hungary), April 10, 1962, UFHS president George Hursan to Donald Emmerson, NSA international vice president, expressing upset over grant denial.

66. Ibid., December 7-8, 1962, Unidentified author, most likely Donald Emmerson,

Report on two-day UFHS Congress in Leysin, Switzerland, noting his response to UFHS officers' anger over FYSA actions.

67. The Hungarians continued to receive some funding from Eugene Metz of the Free Europe Committee. See Várallyay, *Tanulmány-Úton*, 252.

Chapter 12. Debating Democracy in Red Square

1. NARA, RG 800.4089/8-1849; RG 800.4089/8-2449; RG 59 800.4614/8-1751; 800.4614/10-1751. More detail on U.S. government actions re the 1949 and 1951 World Youth Festivals may be found at the PB Web site.

2. Gerome Goodman, "I Crashed Stalin's Party," *Collier's Weekly*, November 10, 1951, 26–27. Although at the time Goodman denied taking down individual names, he turned a list over to American authorities in Berlin: see NARA, RG 800.4614/8-1751, August 1951, from Bryant Buckingham, American Consul, Berlin to Sec/State. Buckingham reported that Goodman sorted the names into wolves ("real communists") and sheep ("festival is for peace"). He also supplied photographs.

3. H/NSA, Box 25 (Della Cava), June 30, 1957, Della Cava report to unknown recipients.

4. H/NSA, Box 28 (Gray), April 30, 1957, Gray to Larkin.

5. Ibid.

6. H/NSA, Box 33 (Young), March 14, 1957, Young to Larkin.

7. Interview with Richard Medalie, Washington, D.C., June 10, 2005.

8. Ibid.

9. H/NSA, Box 127 (International Team Corres.), July 1, 1950, Medalie memo to NSA president Robert Kelly confirming that the donation from Brittingham (identifying him by name) had arrived.

10. Interview with Medalie.

11. Ibid.

12. H/NSA, Box 32 (Sigmund), July 17, 1956, Gray to Sigmund.

13. Sydney Ladensohn Stern, taped interview with George Abrams, courtesy of Stern. Stern interviewed Abrams for her biography *Gloria Steinem: Her Passions, Politics, and Mystique* (Secaucus, N.J.: Birch Lane Press, 1997).

14. Interview with Medalie.

15. George Abrams, "Talking with Russians," *New Republic*, October 14, 1957, 13–16.

16. Interview with Medalie.

17. Ibid.

18. Stern interview with Abrams.

19. The report, "United Nations Report on the Hungarian Uprising, 1956," can be accessed at libcom.org, http://libcom.org/history/united-nations-report-hungarian-uprising-1956.

20. Interview with Medalie.

21. Abrams, "Talking with Russians," 13.

22. Robert Carl Cohen, "Forbidden Journey, Part 1: America–Moscow, 1957," 2009,

Radical Films, http://radfilms.com/America_Moscow.html; the quotation is the caption to the still "Moscow, Lenin Stadium—July 1957" at http://radfilms.com /1957_forbidden_journey_moscow_stadium.htm.

23. H/NSA, Box 107 (ISRS), August 14, 1957, Medalie Confidential Report.

24. Pia Koivunen, "The 1957 Moscow Youth Festival," in *Soviet State and Society Under Nikita Khrushchev*, ed. Melanic Ilic (London: Routledge, 2009), 54.

25. The UPI report put the figure at a hundred instead of a thousand.

26. H/NSA, Box 107 (ISRS), August 14, 1957, Medalie Confidential Report.

27. Ibid.

28. Ibid.

29. Ibid.

30. Ibid.

31. Max Frankel, "Polyglot Youth in Moscow Debate," *New York Times*, August 2, 1957.

32. "Soviet Chides U.S. Youth," *New York Times*, August 9, 1957.

33. H/NSA, Box 298 (WFDY), press clippings.

34. Interview with Medalie.

35. H/NSA, Box 155 (World Youth Festival), press clippings.

36. Interview with Medalie.

37. Ibid.

38. "Americans Abroad: The Mis-Guided Tour," *Time*, August 26, 1957, 9.

39. Max Frankel, "41 Defy Warning, Set off for China," *New York Times*, August 14, 1957.

40. Robert Carl Cohen, "Inside Red China," 1957, Radical Films, Radfilms.com/ china.html.

41. Interview with Clive Gray, Greensboro, Vt., September 1 and 2, 2005. For information on Joanne Grant, see her obituary in the *New York Times*, January 15, 2005.

42. H/NSA, 106 (5th ISRS), summer 1958. Medalie excerpted some of his report on the festival in a mimeographed handout when he briefed ISRS delegates on NSA festival policy issues.

43. Abrams, "Talking with Russians," 14.

44. Ibid.

45. Raymond Garthoff, *A Journey Through the Cold War* (Washington, D.C.: Brookings Institution, 2001), 36.

46. For information on David and Alexander Dallin, see "Alexander Dallin Dies: Precise Historian of Russia," *New York Times*, July 27, 2000.

47. Harry Rositzke, *The CIA's Secret Operations: Espionage, Counterespionage, and Covert Action* (Boulder, Colo.: Westview, 1988), 163.

48. Richard Stites, *Russian Popular Culture: Entertainment and Society Since 1990* (Cambridge: Cambridge University Press, 1992), 132. Stites describes the Moscow festival as constituting a "great cultural turning point." See also Yale Richmond, *Cultural Exchange and the Cold War: Raising the Iron Curtain* (University Park, Md.: Pennsylvania State University Press, 2003).

49. Interview with Yevgeni Yevtushenko, *Red Spring*, episode 14, at http://www2
    .gwu.edu/~nsarchiv/coldwar/interviews/episode-14/yevtushenko1.html.
50. Richmond, *Cultural Exchange and the Cold War*, 12.
51. Vladislav Zubok and Constantine Pleshakov, *Inside the Kremlin's Cold War from
    Stalin to Khrushchev* (Cambridge: Harvard University Press, 1996), 175.
52. Ibid.
53. Koivunen, "The 1957 Moscow Youth Festival," 60.

Chapter 13. Courting Revolutionaries

1. H/NSA, Box 197 (Egypt), January 29–February 2, 1957, Clive Gray report,
   "Egyptian Student Movement," 36.
2. Ibid. 37.
3. H/NSA, Box 156 (Algeria '56–'57), n.d., Paul Sigmund, "Report on UNEF and
   Algeria."
4. H/NSA, Box 33 (Young), January 1957, Crawford Young report, "The Student
   Movement in Europe," 1.
5. H/NSA, Box 32 (Moore), April 17–18, 1958, Moore, "Algerian conference in
   England."
6. H/NSA, Box 33 (Young), November 7, 1956, Young to Larkin.
7. Ibid.
8. H/NSA, Box 156 (Algeria '56–'57), November 6, 1956, Bakken to UGEMA
   leaders.
9. H/NSA, Box 213 (Hungary), December 23, 1956, Larkin to Gray re remaining
   silent on the Suez crisis.
10. H/NSA, Box 27 (Fisher), November 26, 1956, Robert C. Fisher, first report to
    Larkin as an NSA representative in Japan.
11. Alistair Horne, *A Savage War of Peace: Algeria, 1954–1962* (New York: Macmil-
    lan, 1977), 247; see also Matthew Connelly, *A Diplomatic Revolution: Algeria's
    Fight for Independence and the Origins of the Post-Cold War Era* (New York: Oxford
    University Press, 2002), 130.
12. H/NSA, Box 33 (Young), March 1, 1957, Young to Larkin.
13. Ibid.
14. Horne, "The Battle of Algiers, January–March 1957," in *A Savage War of Peace*,
    183–207. The film *Battle for Algiers*, a fictionalized depiction of the siege, remains
    a classic in urban guerrilla warfare.
15. Paul Aussaresses, *Special Services, Algeria, 1955–1957* (Paris: Parrin: 2001).
16. H/NSA, Box 33 (Young), March 1, 1957, Young to Larkin.
17. On UGEMA arrests and the need for scholarships, see, for example, ibid., Janu-
    ary 25, 1957, Young to Larkin; March 14, 1957, Young to Larkin; November 10,
    1957, Young to Richard Beck.
18. Ibid., March 3, 1957, Young to Harris.
19. H/NSA, Box 157 (Algeria 1957–58), March 26, 1957, Harris cable to Young.
20. H/NSA, Box 33 (Young), July 22, 1957, Young to Larkin.

21. H/NSA, Box 26 (Duberman), June 8, 1954, Duberman letter to Bebchick re the need for funds to bring French critics of ISC to the United States.
22. H/NSA, Box 33 (Young), June 1, 1957, Crawford Young to Bruce Larkin.
23. John F. Kennedy, "Imperialism—Enemy of Freedom," *Congressional Record* CIII, Part 8, July 2, 1957, 10783–84, available at http://www.jfklink.com/speeches/jfk/congress/jfk020757_imperialism.html.
24. Ibid.
25. Ibid.
26. Jim DiEugenio, "Dodd and Dulles vs. Kennedy in Africa," *Probe* 6, no. 2 (January–February 1999), quoting *Los Angeles Herald Express* of July 5, 1957, available at http://www.ctka.net/pr199-africa.html.
27. Dulles quoted in Connelly, *Diplomatic Revolution*, 145. Kennedy's speech was characterized in "Foreign Relations: Burned Hands Across the Sea," *Time*, July 15, 1957.
28. Connelly, *Diplomatic Revolution*, 145.
29. John F. Kennedy in *Congressional Record* CIII, Part 8, July 8, 1957.
30. Ibid.
31. H/NSA, Box 33 (Young), July 22, 1957, Young to Larkin.
32. Ibid.
33. H/NSA, Box 28 (Gray), August 6, 1957, Gray, letter to Larkin.
34. H/NSA, Box 33 (Young), June 1, 1957, Young to Larkin.
35. H/NSA, Box 156 (Algeria '56–'57), November 21, 1957, Young to Larkin.
36. Ibid., February 4, 1958, Larkin to Senator Kennedy.
37. IISH ISC, Box 1089 (Algeria '56–'59), Circular No. 18/1957–58 on the arrest of Khemisti. See also H/NSA, Box 156 (Algeria).
38. H/NSA, Box 32 (Moore), December 2, 1957, Moore to Larkin.
39. H/NSA, Box 26 (Emmerson), October 17, 1962, Don Smith report to Don Emmerson on the White House reception with Ben Bella and the private meeting. See the photograph of Ben Bella and Khemisti in the plates section of this volume.
40. Ibid., November 10, 1957, Moore to international assistant Richard Beck.
41. H/NSA, Box 88 (Algerian Scholarships), October 5, 1958, Idzik to Willard Johnson.
42. Ibid.
43. Ibid.
44. Ibid.
45. Ibid.
46. Interview with Daniel Idzik, Otis, Mass., August 29, 2005.
47. H/NSA, Box 32 (Moore), December 2, 1957, Moore to Larkin.
48. Interview with Crawford Young, Madison, Wisc., October 17, 2005. He discovered the existence of this dossier the year after he left Paris, when he returned to testify on behalf on UGEMA leaders who were on trial. For months he darted in and out of Paris, often leaving minutes ahead of the French police.
49. H/NSA, Box 32 (Moore), Clement Moore, "J'Accuse," an undated account of his January 13, 1958, arrest.

50. Ibid.

51. Ibid., January 28, 1958, Larkin to Moore, reiterating earlier statements.

52. H/NSA, Box 156 (Algeria '56 '57), December 26, 1957, Moore's speech; see also Box 32 (Moore), December 27, 1957, French translation in *Le Monde*.

53. H/NSA, Box 32 (Moore), January 17, 1958, Moore to Larkin.

54. H/NSA, Box 28 (Gray), March 11, 1958, Gray to Larkin.

55. Ibid., February 11, 1958, Gray to Indonesian Nugroho Notosusanto.

56. IISH ISC, Box 1089 (Algeria '57-'58), February 28, 1958, Young to Larkin.

57. Ibid., February 17, 1958, Young rejects request for Moore speech; see also H/NSA, Box 33 (Young), February 15, 1958, Young to Larkin.

58. H/NSA, Box 32 (Moore), November 10, 1957, Moore to Richard Beck.

59. H/NSA, Box 32 (Moore), April 17-18, 1958, Moore report on the Algerian conference in England.

60. H/NSA, Box 158 (Algeria), newspaper clippings; see also IISH ISC, Box 1089 (Algeria '57-'58).

61. IISH ISC, Box 1089 (Algeria '57-'58), February 15, 1958, Crawford Young to Yugoslav student officials.

62. Stephen E. Ambrose, *Eisenhower: Soldier and President* (New York: Simon and Schuster, 1991), 539.

63. H/NSA, Box 157 (Algeria '59-'60), June 1, 1959, Scholarship program announcement.

64. For scholarship information, see the PB Web site.

65. Interview with Idzik; see also H/NSA, Box 30 (Correspondence), December 19-23, 1960, conference transcript.

66. Julia Sweig, *Inside the Cuban Revolution: Fidel Castro and the Urban Underground* (Cambridge: Harvard University Press, 2002).

67. Ramón L. Bonachea and Marta San Martín, *The Cuban Insurrection, 1952-1959* (New Brunswick, N.J.: Transaction, 1974), 69-70.

68. Ibid. 71.

69. Ibid. 107. Echeverría physically assaulted Castro's letter carrier, Faustino Pérez, when he discovered that Castro had accused Echeverría of treason and betrayal.

70. Bonachea and Martín, *Cuban Insurrection*, 116.

71. Ibid., 60.

72. Ibid., 119.

73. Ibid. 129.

74. H/NSA, Box 16 (COSEC), April 9, 1957, Circular 42/1956-57, Reference 110/Cuba.

75. H/NSA, Box 25 (Della Cava), June 1, 1957, Della Cava to Larkin.

76. Ibid.

77. Ibid., June 30, 1957, Della Cava to Larkin.

78. Ibid., June 19, 1957, Della Cava to Larkin.

79. H/NSA, Box 59 (10th Congress), copy of the August 1957 NSA Congress resolution on Cuba.

80. "Latin Aid Queried," *New York Times*, March 1, 1959.

81. Peter Grose, *Gentleman Spy: The Life of Allen Dulles* (Amherst: University of Massachusetts Press, 1994), 412.

82. Ibid.

83. Interview with Luigi Einaudi, Washington, D.C., December 7, 2007.

84. Enrique Cirules, *The Mafia in Havana* (New York: Ocean Press, 2004). See also, Thomas G. Paterson, *Contesting Castro: The United States and the Cuban Revolution* (Oxford: Oxford University Press, 1995), 63.

85. Lyman Kirkpatrick, *The Real CIA* (New York: Macmillan, 1968), 162.

86. Ibid., 159.

87. Tim Weiner, *Legacy of Ashes: The History of the CIA* (New York: Doubleday, 2007), 179.

88. H/NSA, Box 189 (Cuba), April 24, 1958, Robert K. Brown to Lucille Dubois, NSA subcommission; Box 73, July 15, 1958, Dubois to Larkin.

89. Sweig, *Inside the Cuban Revolution*, 70-71.

90. H/NSA, Box 26 (Einaudi), January 14, 1957, Larkin to Einaudi.

91. H/NSA, Box 228 (Latin America), April 14, 1958, Dubois to Larkin. See also Boxes 73, 227.

92. H/NSA, Box 63 (Int'l Commission Reports), March 21, 1958, Della Cava to Dubois.

93. H/NSA, Box 189 (Cuba), April 29, 1958, Dubois to Robert K. Brown.

94. H/NSA, Box 59 (11th NSA Congress), August 1958, Copy of resolution on arms embargo.

95. Jules Dubois, *Fidel Castro: Rebel, Liberator or Dictator?* (Indianapolis: Bobbs-Merrill, 1959), 363.

96. H/NSA, Box 63 (*NSA News*), reported in the February 1959 NSA newsletter.

97. Ibid.

98. Interview with Robert Kiley, Cambridge, Mass., January 22, 2008.

99. H/NSA, Box 32 (Marcus), 1959-60, copies of Robert and Manuel Aragon biographical information.

100. Interview with Kiley; see also H/NSA, Box 189 (Cuba 59-60), February 2-3, 1959, on the trip to Havana. Robert Kiley and Bruce Larkin were guests of Reynaldo Corpion, then an aide to Juan Nuiry Sánchez, a participant in the palace attack (1957) and described in 1959 as the "number three man in the army."

101. H/NSA, Box 191 (Cuba), September 1959, NSA Congress, José Puente Blanco speech.

102. Stephen E. Ambrose, *Eisenhower: The President* (New York: Simon and Schuster, 1984), 507.

103. H/NSA, Box 228 (Latin America), January 16, 1960, Della Cava letter to Bruce Larkin (COSEC).

104. Paget Files: "Ninth International Student Conference, Resolutions," 91.

105. Ibid.

106. Interview with Kiley.

107. "Cuba: Caning the Students," *Time*, March 18, 1966.

108. Telephone interview with Paul Becker, Toronto, Canada, August 14, 2006.
109. Interview with Tony Smith, New York, November 7 and 9, 2007. See Chapter 18, below, for more on Cuba.

Chapter 14. Gloria Steinem and the Vienna Operation

1. H/NSA, Box 28 (Gray), May 26, 1958, Gray to Larkin.
2. H/NSA, Box 299 (WFDY, 59-63), December 1, 1958, Bruce Larkin to Willard Johnson; "Memorandum of Discussion of the 415th Meeting of the National Security Council" (July 30, 1959), *Foreign Relations of the United States, 1958-1960*, vol. 3: *National Security Policy: Arms Control and Disarmament, Document 69*, available at U.S. Department of State Office of the Historian Web site, http://history.state.gov/historicaldocuments/frus1958-60v03/d69.
3. Interview with Richard Medalie, Washington, D.C., June 10, 2005.
4. Interview with Clive Gray, Cambridge, Mass., January 19, 2000. For attacks on Steinem by radical feminists, see Sydney Ladensohn Stern, "The Redstockings, Gloria, and the CIA," in her *Gloria Steinem: Her Passions, Politics, and Mystique* (Secaucus, N.J.: Birch Lane Press, 1997), 291-306.
5. Interview with Gray.
6. Ibid.
7. Ibid. See also H/NSA, Box 63 (Internat'l Student News), November 16, 1958, for a complete list of IRS incorporators. It includes Clement Moore, William J. Spinny, Prescott Evans, John Voll, Hull Daniels.
8. Ansara Files (IRS), Typed compilation of incorporation dates/names.
9. Interview with Leonard Bebchick, Washington, D.C., April 27, 2000.
10. H/NSA, Box 63 (Internat'l Student News), February 1958, Independent Service for Information on the Vienna Youth Festival, and the position of the U.S. Department of State.
11. Abrams quoted in "Our 400 and the Reds," *Newsweek*, July 6, 1959.
12. H/NSA, Box 55 (WYF), May 8, 1958, Clement Moore report, "Vienna Trip, May 5-8."
13. Ibid.
14. Ibid. See also H/NSA, Box 299 (WFDY, 59-63), December 1, 1958, Larkin letter to Johnson re the same fear of demonstrators.
15. H/NSA, Box 55 (WYF), May 8, 1958, Clement Moore report.
16. H/NSA, Box 299 (WFDY, 59-63), December 1, 1958, Larkin to Johnson.
17. Ibid.
18. For an overview, see "The Vienna Youth Festival," July 15, 1958, Background report, Archival I.D.: HU OSA 300-8-3-13174, Records of Radio Free Europe/Radio Liberty Institute at Open Society Archives at www.osaarchivum.org.
19. Oliver Rathkolb, "Austria Between Neutrality and Non-Alliance, 1953-2000," *Journal of European Integration History* 7, no. 2 (2001):103-26.
20. Interview with Bebchick.
21. William Taubman, *Khrushchev: The Man and His Era* (New York: Norton, 2003).

See especially chapter 15, "The Berlin Crisis and the American Trip: 1958–1959," 396–441.

22. Biographical data on C. D. Jackson can be found at the Web site of the Dwight D. Eisenhower Presidential Library, www.eisenhower.archives.gov.

23. Kai Bird, *The Chairman: John J. McCloy—the Making of the American Establishment* (New York: Simon and Schuster, 1992), 483–84.

24. Interview with Bebchick.

25. Harrington's commitment to the underprivileged later led him to publish his landmark study *The Other America* (1962), which put poverty on the American political agenda. See Maurice Isserman, *The Other American: The Life of Michael Harrington* (New York: Perseus, 2001).

26. Isserman, *Other American*, 171.

27. Interview with Walter Pincus, Washington, D.C., March 24, 2006.

28. Ibid.

29. Ibid. Pincus recounted that Bill Dentzer invited him to dinner and Cord Meyer suddenly "jumped out of the shadows."

30. Interview with Bebchick.

31. Romerstein worked for the New York State Legislature and frequently testified about "subversive" activities. See Paul Kengor, "Remembering Herb Romerstein," *American Spectator*, May 10, 2013, at www.spectator.org/archives.

32. Joseph Keeley, *Alfred Kohlberg: The China Lobby Man* (New Rochelle, N.Y.: Arlington House, 1969), 245.

33. Ibid.

34. Ibid. See also *Congressional Record*, 86th Congress, Charles Wiley HUAC testimony, February 4, 1960.

35. Stephen Unsino, as told to Phil Santora, "Diary of a 'Red' Delegate, *Daily News Special Feature*, August 12, 1959; Charles Wiley testified before Congress that he infiltrated the New York group: *Congressional Record*, Wiley HUAC testimony.

36. Interview with Thomas Garrity, Boulder, Colo., September 24, 1998.

37. H/NSA, Box 299 (WFDY 59–63), n.d. [early 1959], John Simons's handwritten notes re festival plans.

38. Giles Scott-Smith, e-mail communication with the author re NATO archives, March 4, 2004; see also H/NSA, Box 32 (Moore), July 11, 1958, Moore to Larkin re NATO involvement.

39. Bird, *The Chairman*, 484.

40. Ibid., 485.

41. Interview with Medalie.

42. Interview with Malcolm Rivkin, Bethesda, Md., May 5, 2000.

43. Ibid.

44. Ibid.

45. Ibid. See also AP photo, *Boston Traveler*, July 30, 1959.

46. Charles Wiley, part of the Romerstein group, named Jean Garcias: see *Congressional Record*, Wiley HUAC testimony.

47. Interview with Rivkin.
48. Interview with Steve Max, New York, May 3, 2000.
49. Ibid.
50. Ibid.
51. Ramón L. Bonachea and Marta San Martín, *The Cuban Insurrection, 1952-1959* (New Brunswick, N.J.: Transaction, 1974), 351.
52. Interview with Medalie.
53. Interview with Bebchick.
54. Ibid.
55. Interviews with Bebchick and Medalie.
56. Interview with Bebchick.
57. Raymond L. Garthoff, *A Journey Through the Cold War* (Washington, D.C., Brookings Institution Press, 2001), 35.
58. William Blum, *Killing Hope* (London: Zed, 2003), 61.
59. Bird, *The Chairman*, 484.
60. Interview with Pincus.
61. Bird, *The Chairman*, 484.
62. Ibid.
63. Ibid.
64. Interview with Bebchick.
65. Ibid.
66. *New York Times*, July 29, 1959.
67. Interview with Pincus.
68. Ibid.
69. Interview with Bebchick.
70. Interviews with Pincus and Bebchick. Pincus remembers sheets being tied together; Bebchick called them banners.
71. Interview with Bebchick.
72. Ibid.
73. Cliff F. Thompson, "Vienna Festival Chants 'Peace, Friendship," *Harvard Crimson*, October 14, 1959.
74. Sydney Ladensohn Stern, taped interview with Clive Gray, courtesy of Stern. Stern interviewed Gray for *Gloria Steinem*.
75. Ibid.
76. Interview with Clive Gray, Greensboro, Vt., September 1-2, 2005.
77. "Reds Displeased with Red Fete," *New York Times*, October 26, 1959.
78. Kennedy met with witting NSA students who opposed the 1962 Helsinki Festival. See Cord Meyer, Jr., *Facing Reality: From World Federalism to the CIA* (New York: Harper and Row, 1980), 103.
79. Stuart Weisberg, *Barney Frank: The Story of America's Only Left-Handed, Gay, Jewish Congressman* (Boston: University of Massachusetts Press, 2009), 50. Frank, who went to Helsinki with the Steinem group, wrote that more Finns than Africans came to the nightclub.

80. Interview with Gray, September 1–2, 2005.

81. O. Igho Natufe, *Soviet Policy in Africa: From Lenin to Brezhnev* (Bloomington, Ind.: iUniverse, 2011).

Chapter 15. Social Upheavals

1. Aleksandr Fursenko and Timothy Naftali, *One Hell of a Gamble: Khrushchev, Castro, and Kennedy: 1958–1964* (New York: Norton, 1997), 5–11.

2. Daniel Flynn, interview with Howard Phillips, April 17, 2005, Conservative USA, at www.conservativeusa.org, part 3, and at www.flynnfiles.com/blog /phillips/phillips3.htm.

3. H/NSA, Box 189 (Cuba 1958–60), April 25, 1959, NSA press release.

4. Phillips founded the Conservative Caucus in 1974; see his Web site: Conservative USA (www.conservativeusa.org).

5. Flynn interview of Phillips, part 3.

6. Richard E. Ashcraft and Peter J. Rothenberg, "Lonely Men of Harvard," *Harvard Crimson*, September 30, 1958; see also FOIA (CIA), #1250, Harvard report on the NSA.

7. FOIA (CIA), #1250, Harvard report on the NSA.

8. Peter J. Rothenberg, "Council Refuses Request for Discussion on NSA," *Harvard Crimson*, September 25, 1958; Richard E. Ashcraft, "Council Defeats Motion to Study NSA Decision," *Harvard Crimson*, September 30, 1958; "Students Report Petition for NSA Vote Complete," *Harvard Crimson*, October 3, 1958.

9. Andrew Warshaw, letter to the editor, "NSA: Rationale for Leaving," *Harvard Crimson*, October 11, 1958.

10. Reported in "Controversy Arises over NSA Decision," *Harvard Crimson*, September 24, 1958.

11. H/NSA, Box 73 (LA Sub-commission), July 15, 1958, Dubois to Larkin.

12. H/NSA, Box 24 (M. Aragon), December 4, 1958, Manuel Aragon to Willard Johnson.

13. SLATE's history can be found online at SLATE Archives, slatearchives.org/history.htm.

14. Interview with Isabel Marcus, Buffalo, N.Y., August 26, 1999.

15. Ibid.

16. H/NSA, Box 24 (Baad). See, for example, a document of December 23, 1959, in which Miller outlined a strategy in a letter to David Baad at COSEC to remove a Marcus letter from COSEC files.

17. Interview with Marcus. I heard jokes about staff members and their case officers during the year my husband was with the NSA.

18. H/NSA, Box 108 (ISRS), Spring 1959, Don Hoffman application for ISRS.

19. H/NSA, Box 28 (Hoffman), September 19, 1960, Hoffman to NSA president Richard Rettig re Dubrovnik meeting.

20. Interview with Donald Hoffman, Madison, Wisc., July 25, 1997.

21. Ibid. During the interview Hoffman confirmed his witting status and subse-

quent work with the CIA. The seven-year career figure is also contained in his obituary, "Donald Hoffman, Former New Orleans City Attorney, Dies at Age 76," *Times-Picayune*, May 25, 2012. His last post/cover was with the U.S. Mission to European Regional Organizations in Paris. Not long before he died, Hoffman bragged to a former NSA colleague, Robert Walters, about how many agents he had run while in Paris (Walters, e-mail to me, December 8, 2012).

22. FOIA (CIA), #3, December 3, 1958, declassified memo on office integration re security concerns, particularly the problem of financial accounting.

23. Jerry Glaser, "MIT Disaffiliates with NSA: Kaplan Proposes Alternate Group," *The Tech*, November 9, 1959.

24. Interview with Curtis Gans, Washington, D.C., May 5, 2000.

25. Interview with Timothy Jenkins, Washington, D.C., December 5, 2007.

26. Interview with Gans.

27. Ibid.

28. Interview with Jenkins.

29. The Taconic and Field Foundations were leading civil rights funders. Taconic, an early supporter of Martin Luther King, funded the NSA-sponsored meeting of April 22–23, 1960, on the sit-in movement, publicizing its support in campus newspapers. See, for example, Mary Frances Barone, "Gordon Roberts, Jim Walters Attend National Conference," *Wilkes College Beacon*, April 29, 1960. The Field Foundation supported another NSA project, the Southern Student Human Relations Seminar in Atlanta, directed by Constance Curry, who wrote about re-directing funds to support the civil rights movement in 1960 without objection by Field. See Constance Curry, "NSA's Southern Civil Rights Initiatives," in *American Students Organize: Founding the National Student Association after World War II*, ed. Eugene G. Schwartz ([Westport, Conn.]: American Council on Education/Praeger, 2006), 447.

30. John Lewis, *Walking with the Wind: A Memoir of the Movement* (New York: Harcourt, 1998).

31. Constance Curry, "Wild Geese to the Past," in Constance Curry et. al., *Deep in Our Hearts: Nine White Women in the Freedom Movement* (Athens: University of Georgia Press, 2002), 14.

32. FOIA (FBI), Press clipping, T. R. Bassett, "Students from 38 States Map South Sitdown Aid," *Wall Street Journal*, May 1, 1960.

33. Interview with Jenkins.

34. FOIA (FBI), May 10, 1960, A. H. Belmont to D. J. Parsons; attached is a March 3, 1960, memo from Hoover.

35. See Taylor Branch's seminal histories *Pillar of Fire: America in the King Years, 1963–1965* (New York: Simon and Schuster, 1999) and *At Canaan's Edge: America in the King Years, 1965–1968* (New York: Simon and Schuster, 2006).

36. FOIA (FBI), Press clipping, "Student Leader Denies Reds Inspire Protests," *New York Post*, July, 19, 1960.

37. Ibid.

38. The KPFA archives contain recordings of the HUAC hearings and interviews with demonstrators: www.kpfa.org/history.info/huac_home.html. See also tele-

vision footage excerpted from *Berkeley in the Sixties, a Documentary*, by Mark Kitchell at http://www.youtube.com/results?search_query=berkeley+in+the +sixties+documentary.

39. John A. Andrew III, *The Other Side of the Sixties: Young Americans for Freedom and the Rise of Conservative Politics* (New Brunswick, N.J.: Rutgers University Press, 1997), 26.

40. Tom Hayden reprints Cason's speech in his memoir, *Reunion* (New York: Random House, 1998), 40-42.

41. Curry, "Wild Geese to the Past," 19. See also David Barber, *A Hard Rain Fell: SDS and Why It Failed* (Jackson: University Press of Mississippi, 2008), 99-100.

42. FOIA (FBI), Press clipping. The final vote was reported in "Students in Action," *Daily Worker*, September 18, 1960.

43. H/NSA, Box 35 (Misc. corres.), August 1961, "Inside NSA" (copy in file); the essay contains Phillips's views.

44. Interview with Neal Johnston, New York, June 25, 2005.

45. H/NSA Box 28 (Hoffman), September 19, 1960, re Hoffman special mission to see Weissman.

46. Interview with Gary Weissman, Minneapolis, August 11, 2003.

47. Conversation with Jenkins at the NSA reunion, Madison, Wisc., July 26, 1997; Jenkins repeated his observation during his later interview.

48. Interview with Gans.

49. Ibid.

50. Ibid.

51. Gregory L. Schneider, *Cadres for Conservatism: Young Americans for Freedom and the Rise of the Contemporary Right* (New York: New York University Press, 1998), 60-61.

52. Andrew, *Other Side of the Sixties*, 125.

53. Telephone interview with Kay Wonderlic Kolbe, Phoenix, Az., June 8, 2006.

54. Paget Files: copy of Kay Wonderlic's report, "An Analysis of the Structural and Functional Aspects of the United States National Student Association."

55. M. Stanton Evans, "The Battle Against NSA," in *Revolt on Campus* (New York: Regnery, 1961), 156.

56. Wonderlic, "Analysis," 17. The Conference on Foreign Student Affairs was the name given at the 1959 and 1960 NSA Congresses to a group meeting for all foreign students in attendance.

57. Evans, "Battle Against NSA," 156.

58. For an overview of Al Haber, Tom Hayden, and the early SDS, see Kirkpatrick Sale, *SDS: The Rise and Development of Students for a Democratic Society* (New York: Vintage, 1973). See also Hayden's memoir, *Reunion*.

59. National Security Archives, a private nonprofit at George Washington University, has a special collection of declassified documents on the U.S. government actions re Cuba leading up to the Bay of Pigs and after at http://www2.gwu .edu/~nsarchiv/.

60. Interview with Luigi Einaudi, Washington, D.C., December 7, 2007.

61. Ibid.

62. Ibid.
63. Casey Hayden [Sandra Cason], "Fields of Blue," in Curry et al., *Deep in Our Hearts,* 310
64. "Education: Campus Conservatives," *Time,* February 10, 1961.

Chapter 16. Showdown in Madison

1. *Studies on the Left,* a journal published by Madison activists, is available in most university libraries. See also C. Wright Mills, *Listen Yankee: The Revolution in Cuba* (New York: Ballantine, 1961).
2. H/NSA, Box 35 (Misc. Corres.), David Duval, editor, Committee for a Responsive National Student Organization Newsletter, vol. 1, no. 1 (August 7, 1961).
3. Ibid.
4. Ibid., "Liberal Reform Group Started" (report on Barney Frank's activities).
5. Interview with Curtis Gans, Washington, D.C., May 5, 2000.
6. John A. Andrew III, *The Other Side of the Sixties: Young Americans for Freedom and the Rise of Conservative Politics* (New Brunswick, N.J.: Rutgers University Press, 1997), 98.
7. FOIA (FBI), SAC [Special Agent in Charge], heavily redacted coverage of NSA Congress, Milwaukee, September 13, 1961.
8. Ibid.
9. H/NSA, Box 35 (Misc. Corres.), copy of Rettig's August 1961 speech to the fourteenth NSA Congress.
10. Ibid., Rettig mimeographed report to the NEC, August 1961.
11. Rick Perlstein, *Before the Storm: Barry Goldwater and the Unmaking of the American Consensus* (New York: Nation, 2009), 155.
12. Ibid., 109.
13. Andrew, *Other Side of the Sixties,* 84.
14. Paget Files: Copy of NSA Codification of Policy, 1961. This booklet contains resolutions passed by the 1961 NSA Congress.
15. *Operation Abolition* can be seen on YouTube: http://www.youtube.com/watch?v= MeiW63M3bcI.
16. Robert M. Schuchman, "Charge of the Light Brigade," *National Review* 11, no. 10 (September 9, 1961): 161; see also Richard Merbaum, "The Right at NSA," *New University Thought* 2 (Autumn 1961): 29.
17. Paget Files: NSA Codification of Policy 1961.
18. H/NSA, Box 190 (Cuba '60-'61), n.d. [ca. January 1961], Dubois to James Scott.
19. Ibid., February 2, 1961, Manuel Aragon to Dubois.
20. A Bay of Pigs chronology is available at the National Security Archive Web site: "Bay of Pigs: 40 Years After," www2.gwu.edu/~nsarchiv/bayofpigs/chron.html.
21. Meyer, Box 5, Diary, entry of November 21, 1961.
22. H/NSA, Box 24 (M Aragon), June 20, 1961, Manuel Aragon to Tom Patton, Catholic University student body president.
23. FRUS, 1961-63, vol. 11: Cuba, Document 349, Office of Current Intelligence detail on student activity, July 3, 1962.

24. H/NSA, Box 24 (M Aragon), December 21, 1960, Aragon to Richard Miller.

25. H/NSA, Box 41 (IUS-Havana), Report of the IUS Executive Committee meeting, May 23–June 2, 1961.

26. Ansara Files: copy of May 23–June 2, 1961, IUS Executive Committee, General Resolution on Cuba, Record of Proceedings, 70.

27. Interview with Robert Kiley, Cambridge, Mass., January 22, 2008.

28. FOIA (FBI), 1/36 (15–17), *St. Louis Dispatch* clipping.

29. "Liberal Control," *Time*, September 1, 1961.

30. Schuchman, "YAF and the New Conservatism," *New Guard*, cited in Andrew, *Other Side of the Sixties*, 98.

31. Ibid., Schuchman quoting Scott. See also Austin C. Wehrwein, "Students Appeal for Cuban Youths," *New York Times*, August 21, 1961.

32. Jefferson Morley, interview with Manuel Salvat, *Miami New Times*, April 12, 2001.

33. FRUS, 1961–63, vol. 11: Cuba, Document 173, Memorandum from President Kennedy, November 30, 1961.

34. DRE students were happy to claim credit for the raid; see *Newsweek*, August 27, 1962. See also H/NSA, Box 191 (Cuba '60–'61), "Complete Information on the raid of Castro's Cuba by members of the Cuban Student Directorate," *The Cuban Report* (DRE: 1962).

35. Van Gosse, *Where the Boys Are: Cuba, Cold War America, and the Making of a New Left* (New York: Verso, 1993), 122.

36. For more detail on key members of the exile DRE, see the PB Web site.

37. Shackley photo and quote in Morley, interview with Salvat.

38. Ibid.

39. H/NSA, Box 191 (Cuba), August 29, 1961, Salvat to Manuel Aragon. For information on Muller and Puente Blanco, see PB Web site.

40. Paget Files: NSA Codification of Policy 1961.

41. FOIA (FBI), September 13, 1961, SAC Milwaukee to Hoover, heavily redacted.

42. Interview with James Scott, Palo Alto, Calif., November 10, 1998. Scott identified the Ceylonese (Sri Lankan) questioner as Eustace Mendis, a former member of the COSEC staff.

43. *NSA News* release, August 22, 1961, courtesy of Tim Jenkins.

44. Ibid.

45. Ibid.

46. Austin C. Wehrwein, "Talk by Buckley Angers Students," *New York Times*, August 23, 1961. FOIA (FBI), 1a/36, September 27, 1961, SAC Chicago to Hoover, includes a copy of Buckley's defense in the *National Review*.

47. Information on SNCC affiliation vote is in Austin C. Wehrwein, "Students' Vote Favors Abolition of Un-American Activities Unit," *New York Times*, August 29, 1961.

48. H/NSA, Box 78 (Memoranda), March–April 1962, Ed Garvey report to NEC.

49. H/NSA, Box 30 (Kiley), March 31, 1961, Kiley to Jim Scott.

50. Ibid.

51. Tom Hayden, *Reunion: A Memoir* (New York: Random House, 1998), 50.

52. Ibid., 49.
53. Ibid., 51.
54. Ibid.
55. H/NSA, Box 30 (Corres. 1956–60), November 21, 1960, Matthew Iverson to Files re his views on Garvey.
56. Interview with Edward Garvey, Madison, Wisc., October 17, 2005.
57. Interview with Edward Garvey, Madison, Wisc., July 26, 1997.
58. Interview with Edward Garvey, Madison, Wisc., July 7, 1992.
59. Interview with Garvey, October 17.
60. Scott Kirkpatrick, "Emmerson, VP of NSA Finds Job Worthwhile," *The Daily Princeton*, October 17, 1961.
61. Telephone interview with Kay Wonderlic Kolbe, Phoenix, Az., June 8, 2006.
62. Ibid.
63. FOIA (CIA), #489, declassified memo, February 8, 1962.
64. Telephone interview with Wonderlic Kolbe; Wonderlic later divorced YAF member James Kolbe, who became a U.S. congressman from Arizona.
65. FOIA (CIA), #489.
66. Ibid.
67. H/NSA, Box 123 (ISRS Regional), February 8, 1960, Gary Weissman to Gary Glenn.

Chapter 17. Pro-West Moderate Militants

1. "The Expendable Premier," *Time*, June 27, 1960.
2. Quee-Young Kim, *The Fall of Syngman Rhee* (Berkeley: University of California East Asian Institute, February 1983).
3. NARA, RG 511.00/6-2460, Herter to All American Diplomatic and Consular Posts, World Youth Forum, Moscow—July and August, 1961.
4. H/NSA, Box 228 (Latin American—General), n.d. [ca. 1961], "Some Thoughts on Yesterday's Meeting," a conference of Catholic students affiliated with the Chilean-based ORMEU (Office of Relations of University Student Movements) in Santiago; the author is most likely Manuel or Robert Aragon.
5. H/NSA, Box 24 (Baad), December 6–8, 1959, Baad to Peter Hornsby (British representative on COSEC).
6. Ibid.
7. Interview with Ram Labhaya Lakhina, Leiden, the Netherlands, October 9, 2004. Lakhina, the last director of COSEC, showed me the location of the former offices and discussed the Pan American purchase.
8. Interview with Ronald Story, Amherst, Mass., August 30, 2005.
9. H/NSA, Box 33 (Young), July 14, 1959, Young to Johnson suggesting strategy to remove Hans Dall.
10. Interviews with Hans Dall, Gilleleje, Denmark, October 7–8, 2006, and with David Baad, Saddlebrooke, Ariz., January 13, 2009. Dall could never understand why the loan was forgiven.
11. Interview with Robert Kiley, Cambridge, Mass., January 22, 2008.

12. Ibid.

13. H/NSA, Box 30 (Kiley), September 9, 1960, Kiley to Jim Scott, suggesting strategy to remove Eustace Mendis.

14. Interview with Jyoti Shankar Singh, New York, August 22, 2006.

15. Ibid.

16. Ibid.

17. IISH ISC, Box 1221 (SupCom 1962), March 12, 1962, John J. Simons to COSEC Supervision Commission re seminar programs.

18. H/NSA, Box 28 (Hoffman), June 5, 1960, Hoffman to Scott.

19. Interview with Kiley.

20. William Finnegan, "Underground Man," *New Yorker*, February 9, 2004.

21. H/NSA, Box 100 (FLSP), n.d. [ca. 1963], James Hendrick, FSLP history.

22. H/NSA, Box 31 (R Miller), December 26, 1959, James Scott, nineteen-page report on the FEANF (North African students) Congress, which includes a long discussion of Pan-Africanism. Scott suggested supporting it in public or principle but undermining specific applications.

23. Interview with David Baad, Saddlebrooke, Az., January 13, 2009.

24. H/NSA, Box 88 (African Scholarship), documentation on the NSA role at the Howard University conference, June 11–13, 1953.

25. Interview with Gwyn Morgan, London, October 11, 2006.

26. Ibid.

27. On Mutambanengwe's anti-Western attitude, see H/NSA, Box 237 (Nigeria), September 23, 1963, Tony Smith, confidential report on the NUNS [National Union of Nigerian Students] congress, and Box 77 (IAB), sixteen-page confidential report by Alex Korns to International Advisory Board, February 10, 1964. The NSA suspected that Mutambanengwe had inspired criticism of the NUSAS for its lack of black members.

28. Interview with Kiley.

29. H/NSA, Box 32 (Moore), January 6, 1958, Clement Moore to Bruce Larkin.

30. H/NSA, Box 187 (Congo), June 15, 1961, James Scott, evaluation of N'Goya, also spelled N'Goie.

31. Ibid.

32. Ibid., n.d., late spring 1961, N'Goie to Scott, asking for scholarship assistance; June 14, 1961, Scott to N'Goie stating lack of scholarship opportunities (which suggests a loss of interest in him).

33. Kofi Annan never identifies the FSLP or NSA, citing a Ford Foundation scholarship. See, for example, Kofi Annan (with Nader Mousavizadeh), *Interventions: A Life in War and Peace* (New York: Penguin, 2012), 12–13, where he mentions a Ford Foundation talent scout at a conference in Sierra Leone. However, the Ford Foundation funded but never actively participated in FSLP. The timing of the conference suggests that Annan encountered Crawford Young, the NSA representative for Africa, who visited West Africa, including a meeting with the Ghanaian National Union of Students, in 1958. See H/NSA, Box 106 (5th ISRS), Crawford Young's confidential report on his visit to Ghana and Kumasi, July 16–18, 1958, during a more general African tour.

34. H/NSA, Box 78 (Memoranda '60-'61), April 8, 1961, Matthew Iverson, memorandum to files, "Assessment after March 15, 1961 campus visit." In an earlier assessment, of November 22, 1960, Iverson described Annan as "an amazing politician and knows virtually everybody of importance on the campus." See also Box 13 (COSEC gen '57-'59), April 28, 1959: a Kenyan, Isaac Omolo, then the associate director for Africa on the COSEC staff, recommended Annan to Harald Bakken, director of the Foreign Student Leadership Project.

35. Ibid.

36. Nkrumah, who came to power in 1957, ruled Ghana until he was ousted in a 1966 coup. See FRUS, 1964-68: Africa, for U.S. role in the overthrow of Nkrumah.

37. Interview with Baad.

38. H/NSA, Box 237 (Nigeria), April 23, 1961 Kiley, to Don Clifford, FLSP director.

39. Paget Files: Copy of NSA Codification of Policy 1961.

40. Luís Nuno Rodrigues, "A New African Policy? JFK and the Crisis in Portuguese Africa," available at http://www.academia.edu/1691582.

41. George Wright, *The Destruction of a Nation: U.S. Policy Towards Angola Since 1945* (London: Pluto, 1997), 36; Wright places the first contact between U.S. officials and Roberto in 1959.

42. Fernando Andresen Guimarães, *The United States and the Decolonization of Angola: The Origins of A Failed Policy* (Instituto Português de Relações Internacionais, 2004), available at www.ipri.pt/artigos/artigo.php?ida=5.

43. FRUS, vol. 21: Africa, Document 350, Rusk to Deputy Undersecretary for Political Affairs (Alexis Johnson), June 18, 1961.

44. H/NSA, Box 160 (Angola), September 15, 1961, Emmerson to COSEC re NSA travel grant of $500.

45. H/NSA, Box 30 (Kiley), December 18, 1961, Emmerson to Kiley.

46. Ibid., December 18, 1961, Peter Eckstein to Kiley re distribution of applications to UPA and MPLA.

47. H/NSA, Box 160 (Angola), September 15, 1961, Emmerson to Kiley re $500 funding for UGEAN meeting in Rabat.

48. Ibid., December 8-10, 1961, Report on Conference held at Camp Green Lane, Pennsylvania.

49. Ibid., Detail on formation of UNEA and Jonas Savimbi. Savimbi also served as secretary general of Roberto's Union of Peoples of Northern Angola.

50. Ibid., March 30, 1962, Emmerson letter to Joaquim Lourenco Mateus Neto, UNEA.

51. Ibid., "The Role of Angola's Students," *Current*, March 1962.

52. H/NSA, Box 33 (Tony Smith), February 7, 1963, Copy No. 1 of UNEA newsletter. See also Box 160 (Angola), December 22, 1961, Tomas Turner to Johnny Eduardo in Leopoldville re opportunity to be the voice of the Angolan students.

53. H/NSA, Box 30 (Kiley), December 18, 1961, Emmerson to Kiley.

54. Interview with Ed Garvey, Madison, Wisc., October 17, 2005.

55. H/NSA, Box 160 (Angola), June 10, 1961, Deolinda de Almeida to Scott.

56. Ibid., January 4, 1961, Magnus Gunther to Jim Scott.

57. Ibid., July 3, 1962, George Hazelrigg to Johnny Eduardo, Deputy Foreign Minister, GRAE.

58. The NSA staff members who dealt closely with Angola include Robert Kiley, Donald Emmerson (1961–62), Thomas Turner (1961–62), Tony Smith (1962–64), George Hazelrigg (1962–63), James Hendrick (1963–64), Julius Glickman (1964–65), Norman Uphoff (1964–65), Robert Backoff (1964–65), and Robert Witherspoon (1964–65).

59. Tor Sellstrom, *Sweden and National Liberation in South Africa* (Uppsala: Nordic African Institute, 1999), 395.

60. Ibid., 403.

61. "Portugal: Soothing with Bullets," *Time*, April 28, 1961.

62. Interview with John Shingler, Montreal, October 25–27, 2007.

63. H/NSA, Box 30 (Kiley), March 30, 1961, list of South Africans traveling to a meeting in Tunisia.

64. Ibid., December 21, 1960, Kiley to Dick Beck re Billy Modise.

65. Interview with Shingler.

66. Ibid. See also Jonathan Mirsky, "Murdoch and Mandela," *Prospect*, April 20, 1998. Mirsky confronted Mandela over his reluctance to condemn human rights violations in China. A Mandela aide made it clear to Mirsky that Mandela had refrained from criticism since the Chinese communists had been unequivocally on the side of the ANC.

67. H/NSA, Box 24 (Baad), May 18, 1960, Baad to John (Shingler); Baad requested that Shingler tear the letter up after reading it.

68. Ibid.

69. Magnus Gunther, "The National Committee of Liberal (NCL)/African Resistance Movement (ARM)," in *The Road to Democracy in South Africa*, vol. 1: *1960–70* (South African Democracy Education Trust, 2005). For information on the SADET series of publications, see www.sadet.co.za/road_democracy.html.

70. Ibid., 189.

71. Interview with Shingler.

72. Ibid.

73. Gunther, "National Committee of Liberal (NCL)/African Resistance Movement (ARM)," 693.

74. Adrian Leftwich, "I Gave the Names," *Granta* (Summer 2002), 9–31.

75. Gunther, "National Committee of Liberal (NCL)/African Resistance Movement (ARM)," 249.

76. H/NSA, Box 266 (American Committee on Africa), October 17, 1957, Bruce Larkin to Gil Jonas, fundraiser for ACOA; January 19, 1959, Willard Johnson to George Houser, chair of ACOA.

77. H/NSA, Box 251 (S. Africa '62–'64), February 1964, George Hazelrigg to Alex Korns.

78. Donald Woods, *Biko* (New York: Holt, 1991).

79. H/NSA, Box 30 (Kiley), February 19, 1962, letter to Kiley (COSEC) from unidentified NSA officer (most likely Donald Emmerson) who visited Laval

College and found that pedestrian access would have to be restricted; he suggested issuing badges.

Chapter 18. A Pyrrhic Victory

1. Interview with David Baad, Saddlebrooke, Az., January 13, 2009.
2. H/NSA, Box 229 (Latin America), November 27, 1961, Peter Eckstein to Don Emmerson.
3. IISH ISC (FYSA) 180 (634), July 21, 1961, COSEC proposal to FYSA, "Study Seminar on Social and Economic Integration for Latin-American Students."
4. IISH ISC, Box 1220, April 3, 1961, Albert Reiner FYSA to Silvio Mutal.
5. H/NSA, Box 30 (Kiley), April 25, 1961, Manuel Aragon to Bob Kiley.
6. William Blum, *Killing Hope: U.S. Military and CIA Interventions Since WWII* (Monroe, Maine: Common Courage Press, 1995), 195; see also Jonathan Hartlyn, *The Struggle for Democratic Politics in the Dominican Republic* (Chapel Hill: University of North Carolina Press, 1998).
7. H/NSA, Box 24 (R. Aragon), January 19, 1960, Robert Aragon to Bruce Larkin.
8. Ibid.
9. Tim Mansel, interview with General Antonio Imbert, "I Shot the Cruellest Dictator in the Americas," BBC, May 27, 2011; available at www.bbc.co.uk/news/world-latin-america-13560512.
10. Volman had a flair for the flamboyant. See Georgie Anne Geyer, "Sacha Volman: Classic Original and Latin American Legend," March 16, 2001; available at http://www.uexpress.com/georgieannegeyer/index.html?uc_full_date=20010316.
11. H/NSA, Box 229 (LA '60-'65), Institute of Political Education, Newsletter, August 15, 1960.
12. H/NSA, Box 195 (DR), November 5-18, 1961, Love report on the Dominican Republic.
13. H/NSA, Box 245 (Puerto Rico), February 9, 1962, Volman to Love.
14. FOIA (CIA), #464, Prospectus for Leadership Seminar, Dominican Republic.
15. H/NSA, Box 78 (NEC), December 4, 1961, Garvey report.
16. Declassified CIA Inspector General's Report on Plots to Assassinate Fidel Castro, available at NARA 104-10213-10101, House Select Committee on Assassinations (HSCA), segregated CIA collection. Also reprinted in Fabián Escalante, *The CIA Targets Fidel: The Secret Assassination Report* (Melbourne: Ocean Press, 2002).
17. Interview with Tony Smith, New York, November 7 and 9, 2007.
18. Interview with Robert Kiley, Cambridge, Mass., January 22, 2008.
19. Interview with Tony Smith.
20. Interview with Kiley.
21. Brian Latell, *Castro's Secrets: Cuban Intelligence, the CIA, and the Assassination of John F. Kennedy* (London: Palgrave Macmillan, 2013), 190-95. Latell, a former CIA officer, insists that Cubela was a double agent; Cubela's case officer argues to the contrary.

22. NARA (HSCA), JFK Assassination Records, available at http://www.archives
.gov/research/jfk/select-committee-report/part-1c.html, contains 335 separate
documents on Cubela. See, for example, no. 161 (CIA), Information Report:
Possible Defection of Major Rolando Cubela. See also PB Web site.

23. Paget Files: Copy of NSA Codification of Policy 1961, Cuba, 129–131.

24. Interviews with Tony Smith, Kiley, and Edward Garvey (Madison, Wisc., October 17, 2005).

25. IISH ISC, Box 158, S. Babak, *Report of the IUS Delegation on the VIII ISC*, Lima,
Peru, February 15–29, 1959.

26. H/NSA, Box 229 (Latin America), n.d., The University Situation in Puerto
Rico, USNSA Latin American Team Report.

27. H/NSA, Box 36, n.d. [ca. April 1960], Robert Aragon memo.

28. H/NSA, Box 229, December 22, 1961, Kiley to Hoffman.

29. H/NSA, Box 30 (Kiley), April 2, 1962, Kiley to Emmerson.

30. H/NSA, Box 245 (Puerto Rico), 1960–62, anonymous memo on Puerto Rico.

31. Ibid.

32. Ibid.

33. Ibid., February 9, 1962, Sacha Volman to Joe Love.

34. H/NSA, Box 30 (Kiley), April 2, 1962, Kiley to Don Emmerson.

35. H/NSA, Box 16 (COSEC), May 29, 1962, Kiley to American Embassy official
G. F. Williams, Leopoldville, the Congo, re panic over ISC.

36. FRUS, 1961–63, vol. 11: Cuba Document 291, Program Review by Chief of
Operations, Operation Mongoose (Lansdale), January 18, 1962; includes the use
of sabotage squads.

37. H/NSA, Box 245 (Puerto Rico '60–'62), May 7, 1962, Jose Antonio G[onzález].
Lanuza to Love.

38. Ibid., May 24, 1962, [González] Lanuza to Love.

39. H/NSA, Box 30 (Kiley), April 2, 1962, Kiley, letter to Emmerson.

40. H/NSA, Box 9 (10th ISC Quebec), n.d., Proceedings of the 10th ISC, transcript.

41. David Triesman, "The CIA and Student Politics," in *The Student Internationals*, ed. Philip G. Altbach and Norman T. Uphoff (Metuchen, N.J.: Scarecrow,
1973), 180.

42. Ibid.

43. H/NSA, Box 9 (10th ISC Quebec), n.d., Proceedings.

44. Ibid.

45. Interview with Jyoti Shankar Singh, New York, August 22, 2006.

46. H/NSA, Box 9 (10th ISC Quebec), n.d., Proceedings.

47. Ibid.

48. H/NSA, Box 14 (COSEC), October 11, 1962, Don Emmerson, ISC, summary to
Don Smith.

49. H/NSA, Box 61 (14th Student Congress), Garvey report to the National Executive Committee at the August 1962 Congress.

50. Ibid., Emmerson report to National Executive Committee, August 1962.

51. Interview with Kiley.

52. Interview with Baad.

53. Interview with Kiley.

54. Associated Press, "Atty. General Able to Duck Cold Fried Egg In Indonesia," *Daily Mail*, February 14, 1962. For more on Kennedy's world tour, see http://rfkcenter.org/reassuring-an-anxious-world.

55. H/NSA Box 33 (Smith), October 1, 1962, Tony Smith reporting on the Aspen meeting in a letter to Don Smith.

56. Arthur M. Schlesinger, Jr., *Robert Kennedy and His Times* (Boston: Houghton Mifflin, 1978), 439.

57. Ibid.

58. Ibid.

59. McLaughlin served in Berlin, Paris, and Washington before becoming special assistant for youth activities to the assistant secretary of state. In that post, he continued his relationship with NSA leaders. See, for example, W/NSA, December 24, 1964, Norman Uphoff, Report on Majid Anouz and Ali Sahli (UNEA, U.S. Section) re January meeting with NSA's Julius Glickman and Martin McLaughlin re continuing Algerian scholarships.

60. Interview with Garvey, October 17, 2005. CIA officials emphasized RFK's support.

Chapter 19. The Persistent Questioner

1. Interviews with Stephen Robbins, Emeryville, Calif., March 30, 2005, and, Sacramento, Calif., May 31, 2005.

2. Interview with Robbins, March 30, 2005.

3. Telephone interview with Paul Becker, Toronto, Canada, August 14, 2006.

4. Interviews with Robbins.

5. Ibid.

6. Ibid.

7. Ibid.

8. Eden Lipson, notes on conversation with Shaul in 1967, courtesy of Lipson.

9. Interviews with Robbins.

10. W/NSA, Box 22 (Shaul Dayfile), May 27, 1963, Shaul to Abrams.

11. Interview with Edward Garvey, Madison, Wisc., October 17, 2005.

12. Avrea Ingram died on February 13, 1957, shortly after he returned to New York to work for FYSA. His body was found in the Gramercy Park Hotel and ruled death by strangulation. Though at the time it was assumed to be a suicide, witting staff now believe the cause was autoerotic asphyxiation. Dan Idzik, who was scheduled to have dinner with Ingram the night before he died, is among those who believe that Ingram was not alone. Interview with Daniel Idzik, Otis, Mass., August 29, 2005.

13. Stuart H. Loory, "Mystery Death Hides CIA Ties," *Los Angeles Times*, February 26, 1967.

14. Interview with Idzik.
15. H/NSA, Box 160 (UGEMA Post-Independence), November 26, 1962, Emmerson to Hoffman re Don Smith travel.
16. Ibid.
17. H/NSA, Box 26 (Emmerson), October 17, 1962, Smith to Emmerson re cutbacks.
18. Ibid.
19. See H/NSA, Box 14 (COSEC Corres.). What is striking is the absence of concern expressed by Emmerson in letters to Smith over Reiner's financial threats, presumably because he partly suggested the strategy; see above, note 15.
20. Ibid., October 15, 1962, Emmerson to Olson.
21. H/NSA, Box 78 (NEC Memos), November 22, 1963, Alex Korns memo on Backoff's overseas post.
22. H/NSA, Box 32 (Smith), January 19, 1964, Smith to Gallo, citing irreparable academic costs.
23. Ibid., January 24, 1964, Mary Beth Norton to Alex Korns.
24. Ibid., January 19, 1964, Smith to Gallo. The appointees were older than Smith: William C. McClaskey graduated from Brown University in 1961 (*Brown Alumni Monthly*, July 1968); Robert T. Francis graduated from Williams College in 1960 (http://www.zsrlaw.com/attorneys-government-affairs-staff/robert-francis).
25. John A. Andrew III, *The Other Side of the Sixties: Young Americans for Freedom and the Rise of Conservative Politics* (New Brunswick, N.J.: Rutgers University Press, 1997), 171; see also Fred Turner, "National Student Association Described as Left-Leaning," *Buffalo Evening News*, June 11, 1963.
26. Andrew, *Other Side of the Sixties*, 171.
27. FOIA (FBI), May 21, 1963, Fulton Lewis, Jr., *Washington Report*.
28. Telephone interview with Howard Abrams, Detroit, Mich., June 1, 2006.
29. H/NSA, Box 35 (Miscellany '61–'62), October 25 and December 1, 1962, Robbins letters to NEC chair Marc Roberts, expressing dissatisfaction with the NSA executive committee and oversight of NSA.
30. Ibid., February 12, 1963, Dennis Shaul to Marc Roberts.
31. W/NSA, Box 22 (Shaul Dayfile), May 27, 1963, Shaul to Abrams.
32. Ibid.
33. Ibid.
34. Interviews with Robbins.
35. W/NSA, Box 22 (Shaul Dayfile), July 5, 1963. Shaul letters to enlist the aid of former NSA elders Martin McLaughlin and Richard Murphy to approach Kennedy.
36. W/NSA, Box 22 (Shaul Dayfile), July 24, 1963, Shaul to Paul Booth, SDS.
37. Ibid.
38. Ibid. August 2, 1963, Shaul to Meece, Young Republican National Federation.
39. Ibid.
40. FOIA (FBI), August 31, 1963, Shaul speech, NSA Congress News; also in W/NSA, Box 10.
41. Telephone interview with Mary Beth Norton, Ithaca, N.Y., October 18, 1999.

42. FOIA (FBI), 27/36, September 26, 1963, confidential report to FBI Director Hoover.

43. H/NSA, Box 36, March 15, 1962, Alex Korns, "A History of the International Student Conference 1950-1960," senior thesis, Harvard University, marked "confidential."

44. Interview with Robbins, May 31, 2005.

45. H/NSA, Box 77 (International Affairs Bureau Reports), October 2, 1963, Robbins to Korns.

46. See, for example, Stephen Walt, *The Origins of Alliances* (Ithaca: Cornell University Press, 1987), and Hanna Batatu, *Old Social Classes and Revolutionary Movements* (Princeton: Princeton University Press, 1978).

47. Roby Barrett, "Intervention in Iraq, 1958-1959," *Middle East Institute Policy Brief* 11 (April 2008), 1-14.

48. Adel Darwish and Gregory Alexander, *Unholy Babylon: The Secret History of Saddam's War* (New York: St. Martin's, 1991), 22-23.

49. Lloyd C. Gardner, *Three Kings: The Rise of an American Empire in the Middle East* (New York: New Press, 2009), 290.

50. Patrick Coburn and Alexander Coburn, *Saddam Hussein: An American Obsession* (New York: Verso, 2000), 74.

51. Roger Morris, "A Tyrant 40 Years in the Making," *New York Times*, March 14, 2003.

52. H/NSA, Box 14 (Emmerson), January 21, 1963, Don Smith to Emmerson.

53. Ibid. See also Report on Iraqi Walid Khadduri, then at Michigan State University, which includes a discussion of the NSA's role prior to the February coup.

54. Ibid. Report on smuggled documents.

55. FOIA (State), A-1005, April 27, 1963, U.S. Embassy in Baghdad re Iraqi Student Congress.

56. Ibid.

57. Bob Feldman, "A People's History of Iraq: 1950 to November 1963," at Toward Freedom, www.towardfreedom.com.

58. H/NSA, Box 16 (COSEC), March 12, 1963, Smith to Emmerson re Walid Khadduri.

59. Ibid.

60. Said K. Aburish, *A Brutal Friendship: The West and the Arab Elite* (New York: St. Martin's, 1998).

61. Quoted in Richard Sale, "Exclusive: Saddam Key in Early CIA Plot," UPI, April 10, 2003. See www.upi.com/Business_News/Security-Industry/2003/04/10/Exclusive-Saddam-key-in-early-CIA-plot/UPI-65571050017416/.

62. Morris, "Tyrant 40 Years in the Making."

63. H/NSA, Box 30 (Korns), October 9, 1963, Korns to Robbins.

64. Ibid.

65. Ibid.

66. Ibid., Box 39 (Algeria), June 2, 1963, Tony Smith report describing a purloined IUS report on the Iraqi situation to Ed Garvey, Paris.

67. H/NSA, Box 30 (Korns), October 9, 1963, Korns to Robbins.

68. Ibid., October 25, 1963. Robbins to Korns.
69. Copy of resolution, courtesy of Stephen Robbins.
70. Interviews with Robbins.
71. See, for example, Box 25 (Olson), December 23, 1963, Olson to Korns re splitting strategy for next ISC, including the denial of travel grants, visas, and stringent enforcement of unpaid dues. It is unclear how Robbins knew about the strategy; he may have guessed or inferred it.
72. H/NSA, Box 77 (NEC Reports), October 2, 1963, Robbins to Korns.
73. Ibid.
74. H/NSA, Box 69 (Field Reports), April 6-9, 1964, Korns pre-ISC report on Chilean student union (UFUCH).
75. H/NSA, Box 30 (Korns), October 9, 1963, Korns to Robbins.
76. Ibid.
77. Ibid.
78. Interviews with Robbins.
79. Ibid.
80. H/NSA, Box 30 (Korns), February, 10, 1963, Korns to Hazelrigg.
81. Ibid.
82. Ibid.
83. Interview with Robbins, March 30, 2005.
84. Interviews with Robbins.
85. Letter from Gregory Gallo and Alexander Korns to Frank Murphy, Chancellor, UCLA, May 14, 1964; copy courtesy of Stephen Robbins.
86. M. J. Gasiorowski, *U.S. Foreign Policy and the Shah: Building a Client State in Iran* (Ithaca, NY: Cornell University Press, 1991).
87. H/NSA, Box 220 (Iran '61-'62), August 2, 1961, unidentified author, Memorandum of conversation with ISAUS president Ali Mohammed S. Fatemi. Fatemi claimed there were roughly 110 SAVAK agents attached to the Iranian Embassy and focused on the Iranian students.
88. On the deportation of Iranian students, see for example, FRUS, vol. 22: Iran, Document 21, Action Memo from Talbot to Harriman, re request to RFK to enforce deportation order, May 21, 1964.
89. Interview with Ali Fatemi, Paris, October 16, 2006.
90. H/NSA, Box 220 (Iran '63-'64), April 16, 1964, unsigned letter to Fatemi's lawyer Lawrence Moore indicating that the NSA had helped pay some of Fatemi's legal costs.
91. Arthur Schlesinger, Jr., *Robert Kennedy and His Times* (Boston: Houghton-Mifflin, 1978), 436.
92. H/NSA, Box 220 (Iran '63-'64), January 10, 1964, Ron Story memo, Student Revolutionary Preparedness Committee, based on a conversation with Fatemi.
93. Interview with Fatemi.
94. H/NSA Box 220 (Iran '63-64), Robert Backoff, "Conversations with Faraj Ardalan: Algiers, 10-13 May, 1964."
95. Interview with Ron Story, Amherst, Mass., August 30, 2005.
96. Interview with Fatemi.

97. Ansara Files (General International), Paul Booth speech to NSA Congress, August 27, 1964.

98. Ibid.

99. Interview with Paul Booth, Washington, D.C., March 24, 2006.

100. In 1948, Walter Uphoff, Norman's father, of the Socialist Party ran against Joseph McCarthy for the U.S. Senate. For more information on the Uphoff family, see Walter and Mary Jo Uphoff Collected Papers, Swarthmore College Peace Collection, Swarthmore, Penn.

101. Interview with Norman Uphoff, Ithaca, N.Y., August 18, 2006.

102. Interview with Jeffrey Greenfield, New York, April 23, 2009.

Chapter 20. Lifting the Veil

1. Interview with Stephen Robbins, Emeryville, Calif., March 30, 2005.

2. Profile of Gregory M. Gallo, DLA Piper Web site, www.dlapiper.com/greg _gallo/(accessed 2/10/14).

3. Interview with Stephen Robbins, Sacramento, Calif., May 31, 2005.

4. Ibid.

5. Ibid.

6. Ibid.

7. Ibid.

8. Skype interview with Thomas Olson, Cairo, February 3, 2009; also conversation with Olson, New York, September 11, 2009.

9. Interview with Robbins, March 30, 2005.

10. Ibid.

11. Interview with Norman Uphoff, Ithaca, N.Y., August 18, 2006.

12. Interview with Robbins, March 30, 2005.

13. Ibid., May 31, 2005. See also H/NSA, Box 239 (Palestine), January 29, 1965, Memo written by an unidentified NSA international staff re discussions with the IUS editor of *World Student News*, Mazem Husseini [Mazin Al Husseini], denied a visa by New Zealand; he protested as absurd the rationale for denial that "some of the IUS delegates had criminal records." See also H/NSA Box 10 (11th ISC Christchurch), June 22–July 1, 1964, for Alex Korns report, which includes a brief history of conferences from 1952 to 1964.

14. Interview with Robbins, March 30, 2005.

15. Interview with Robert Walters, Washington, D.C., October 24, 1998.

16. Interview with Robbins, March 30, 2005.

17. JFK, John F. Kennedy statement on Algerian independence, July 3, 1962, Speech Files.

18. Pierre Salinger, *With Kennedy* (New York: Avon, 1967), 249–50.

19. W/NSA, Box 99 (Ali Sahli), December 24, 1965, Norman Uphoff memo re $1,700 for the UNEA-US section.

20. H/NSA, Box 25 (Backoff), September 12, 1964, Backoff to Uphoff.

21. Ibid.

22. FRUS, Department of State, Johnson Administration, 1964–68, vol. 10:

National Security Policy, Document 171 Memorandum from the President's Special Assistant (Rostow) to President Johnson, February 18, 1967, Chronology of Briefings on Youth and Student Activities, Attachment g: Department of State, INR/IL Files, #134, Minutes of 303 Committee, December 3, 1964.

23. Ibid.

24. H/NSA, Box 157 (Algeria), January 12, 1965, Julius Glickman, confidential report on Mohamed Aberkane, Algerian Embassy, a former Algerian scholarship program participant.

25. Interviews with Robbins.

26. Interview with Robbins, March 30, 2005. The "stopped-up toilets" reference is to a tactic rumored to have been used at the 1962 Helsinki World Youth Festival.

27. Ibid., May 31, 2005.

28. Interview with Philip Sherburne, Santa Barbara, Calif., May 15-16, 2000.

29. Ibid.

30. Ibid.

31. Ibid.

32. Ibid.

33. Interview with Robbins, May 31, 2005.

34. Interview with Sherburne.

35. The debt figure varied from year to year. The $400,000 figure is from Fulbright, vol. 1, March 6, 1967, Sherburne testimony, 56. In a subsequent interview, Sherburne put the debt figure at $800,000. Debt figures are distinct from the 1965-66 operating deficit cited in the text.

36. Interview with Sherburne.

37. Ibid.

38. Ansara Files, S Street property deeds, executed on May 17, 1964.

39. H/NSA, Box 78 (NSB), November 25, 1965, Sherburne report to the National Supervisory Board on a grant of $15,000 from the Independence Foundation re renovations.

40. Interview with Sherburne.

41. Interview with Robbins, May 31, 2005.

42. Interviews with Robbins and Sherburne.

43. Ibid.

44. Interview with Daniel Idzik, Otis, Mass., August 29, 2005.

45. H/NSA, Box 62 (18th NSA Congress), copy of Idzik report on Vietnam, February 1965.

46. Ibid.

47. Taylor Branch, *At Canaan's Edge: America in the King Years, 1965-1968* (New York: Simon and Schuster, 2006), 243.

48. Kai Bird, *The Color of Truth: McGeorge Bundy and William Bundy, Brothers in Arms* (New York: Simon and Schuster, 1998), 321-22. LBJ was so upset at Bundy's actions that he asked aide Bill Moyers to fire Bundy. Moyers stalled.

49. Interview with Uphoff.

50. FOIA (CIA), #288, August 13, 1965, Desmond Fitzgerald Deputy Director for Plans, "Decision by Vice President Hubert H. Humphrey to address the US

National Student Association's National Student Congress and the possibility of an address by President Lyndon B. Johnson."

51. Ibid.

52. Ibid.

53. Rhodri Jeffreys-Jones, *Peace Now! American Society and the Ending of the Vietnam War* (New Haven: Yale University Press, 1999), 54.

54. H/NSA, Box 26 (Emmerson), June 23, 1965, Uphoff to Emmerson c/o U.S. Embassy in Saigon.

55. Ibid.

56. Ibid.

57. Sweet, August 22, 1965, Sweet to his parents.

58. Ibid. For more information on the Vietnam Task Force, see Chester Cooper, *The Lost Crusade: America in Vietnam* (New York: Dodd, Mead, 1970).

59. Telephone interview with Charles F. Sweet, Charlotte, N.C., August 25, 2006.

60. Donald Janson, "Humphrey Chides Antiwar Pickets," *New York Times*, August 24, 1965; copy of speech available in the Hubert Humphrey collection at the Minnesota Historical Society History Center at mnhs.org/library.

61. This shift in student zeitgeist is documented in the film *The War at Home*, a 1979 documentary by directors Glenn Silber and Barry Alexander Brown that follows the antiwar movement on the Wisconsin campus and includes footage of Humphrey's 1965 speech.

62. FOIA (CIA), #28, Liberal Caucus Bulletin, August 25, 1965.

63. William H. Chafe, *Never Stop Running: Allard Lowenstein and the Struggle to Save American Liberalism* (Princeton: Princeton University Press, 1998), details Lowenstein's conflict with Moses and SNCC.

64. FOIA (CIA), #28 *Congress News*, August 28, 1965.

65. Ibid.

66. Telephone interview with Ricki Radlo Lieberman, New York, January 11, 2010.

67. Joseph G. Morgan, *The Vietnam Lobby: The American Friends of Vietnam, 1955–1975* (Chapel Hill: University of North Carolina Press, 1997).

68. FOIA #28, *Liberal Bulletin*.

69. Gilbert Jonas and Seymour Reisin, September 7, 1965, "Report on the National Student Association Convention," courtesy of Eugene G. Schwartz.

70. Ibid.

71. Ibid.

72. Telephone conversation with Carlton Stoiber, Washington, D.C., March 25, 2005. Stoiber declined to be formally interviewed. The material in the text draws on my interview with Sherburne and my own memory of these events.

73. I was sitting onstage behind the podium taking notes during the elections. Michael Enwall was my husband at the time and Malcolm Kovacs a friend. Stoiber cast the deciding vote against Mike's election, although he and Mike remained friendly afterward.

74. Interview with Robbins, May 31, 2005.

75. Ibid.

76. Telephone interview with Michael Enwall, Lyons, Colo., August 30, 2006.

77. I recall that Stoiber actually cast two votes, his and a proxy vote.
78. Interview with Sherburne.

Chapter 21. Philip Sherburne Takes on the CIA

1. H/NSA, Box 78 (Reports), November 26-28, 1965, Sherburne to National Supervisory Board.
2. Ansara Files, S Street property deeds.
3. Nancy Moran, "Student Unit Moves into a Rent-Free, Plush Office Here," *Washington Post*, October 10, 1965.
4. Interview with Philip Sherburne, Santa Barbara, Calif., May 15-16, 2000.
5. Fulbright, vol. 1, March 6, 1967, Wood testimony, 8.
6. Fulbright, vol. 1, March 6, 1967, Sherburne testimony, 60-61. Sherburne and Lunn had agreed to approximately $320,000 in FYSA awards for FY1965-66, a little more than half the NSA budget.
7. Interview with Sherburne.
8. Ibid.
9. Ibid.
10. Interview with Robert Kiley, Cambridge, Mass., January 22, 2008.
11. Interview with Sherburne.
12. Telephone conversation with Carlton Stoiber, Washington, D.C., March 25, 2005. Stoiber declined to be formally interviewed.
13. H/NSA, Box 12 (COSEC 52-65), December 6, 1965, Gil Kulick (a nonwitting African specialist on the NSA staff), letter to Ed Garvey discussing Stoiber's inaction.
14. Greg Delin (not witting), of the Asia desk, signed the letter of support. Telephone interview with Greg Delin, Chicago, Ill., January 5, 2005.
15. Interview with Sherburne.
16. Ibid.
17. Those who held Gable's NSA position and continued to work with the CIA include Richard Miller (1960-61) and Tom Olson (1962-63). Miller and Olson also worked for FYSA.
18. Interview with Sherburne.
19. "Drifter Found Guilty of Killing Seattle Family," *New York Times*, June 6, 1986.
20. Robert Aragon, for example, worked for FYSA and opened an office in Santiago, Chile. Reported in "Playing It Straight: Who Did What and Why for CIA?" the editors, *New Republic*, March 4, 1967.
21. H/NSA, Box 25 (IC Corres.), December 8 and 10, 1962, Joe Love interview and assessment of Fred Berger.
22. Ibid., January 11, 1966, Berger, letter to David Langsam, a friend from Columbia University, spelling out his politics.
23. Ibid. In the same letter, Berger regretted that an alliance was no longer possible.
24. Ibid., October 25, 1965, Berger to Diana Dillon, Manhattanville College, who was setting up a teach-in on the invasion.
25. H/NSA, Box 195 (DR), November 7, 1965, Dennis Foianini memo to Carlton

Stoiber, with confidential background on Berger trip. See also Box 27, October 28, 1965, confidential proposal to Stoiber.

26. FRUS, Department of State, Johnson Administration, 1964-68, vol. 32: Dominican Republic, Document 129, Memorandum of Conversation between CIA officials and the White House, September 1, 1965.

27. Tim Weiner, *Enemies: A History of the FBI* (New York: Random House, 2012), 495n23, cites a lengthy memo from Desmond Fitzgerald claiming President Johnson wanted Balaguer to win.

28. Juan Bosch, *The Unfinished Experience: Democracy in the Dominican Republic* (New York: Pall Mall, 1966).

29. Giancarlo Soler Torrijos, *In the Shadow of the United States* (Boca Raton, Fla.: Brown Walker Press, 2008), 75.

30. H/NSA, Box 195 (DR), December 2-7, 1965, Berger preliminary report.

31. Interview with Sherburne.

32. Ibid.

33. After Berger returned, these claims circulated among witting staff, where I heard them. I also discussed them during my interview with Sherburne.

34. Fulbright, vol. 1, March 6, 1967, Sherburne testimony, 71-73. Sherburne also testified that the Agency man in the American embassy with whom Berger met knew which individuals Berger had contacted and the substance of their conversations.

35. Interview with Kiley.

36. W/NSA, Box 22 (Uphoff), December 17, 1965, Charles Goldmark, letter to Bob Francis in Paris, misfiled under Uphoff.

37. Interview with Sherburne.

38. Interview with Kiley.

39. Interview with Sherburne.

40. W/NSA, Box 22 (Uphoff), December 17, 1965, Goldmark to Francis.

41. W/NSA, Box 21 (Sherburne), January 5, 1966, Sherburne to Vice President Hubert H. Humphrey. See also January 7, 1966, Sherburne to Wes Barthelmes in Senator Robert F. Kennedy's office; January 5, 1966, Sherburne to The Honorable Lyndon B. Johnson.

42. Interview with Sherburne.

43. Ibid. See also W/NSA, Box 21 (Sherburne Dayfile), March 2, 1966, Sherburne letter of thanks to Vice President Humphrey.

44. Interview with Sherburne.

45. Fulbright, vol. 2, March 16, 1967, Eugene Groves testimony, 156-58.

46. Fulbright, vol. 1, March 6, 1967, Sherburne testimony, 66.

47. Ansara Files (Financial), January 17, 1966, Lunn to Sherburne.

48. Interview with Sherburne.

49. Interview with Kiley.

50. Fulbright, vol. 1, March 6, 1967, Sherburne testimony, 67.

51. Deficit figures vary. See H/NSA, Box 78 (NEC), March 17, 1964, President Greg Gallo, memo to the executive committee; Gallo had referred to a $50,000 deficit during his year, but here he cited successful fundraising that retired it.

Sherburne used the $70,000 figure for 1965–66 in Fulbright, vol. 1, March 6, 1967, Sherburne testimony, 67.

52. By July 1966, Sherburne had whittled the deficit down even farther, to $19,108.33. Ansara Files: Copy of Ten-Month Financial Statement ending July 31, 1966.

53. I discussed the deficits and cumulative debt in my interviews with Stephen Robbins, Emeryville, March 30, 2005, and Sacramento, Calif., May 31, 2005, and with Sherburne.

54. Interview with Sherburne.

55. Cord Meyer, Jr., *Facing Reality: From World Federalism to the CIA* (New York: Harper and Row, 1980), 105.

56. W/NSA, Box 21 (Sherburne), February 11, 1966, Sherburne to Harry Lunn, which contains a list of travel and technical assistance projects.

57. Fulbright, vol. 1, March 6, 1967, Sherburne testimony, 72–73. Sherburne testified that there was conflict within the CIA over Berger's trip. The CIA station in Madrid encouraged Berger to attend the meeting in Barcelona, whereas Kiley tried to prevent his attendance. I also discussed this issue in my interview with Sherburne.

58. H/NSA, Box 229 ('61–'65), Frederick E. Berger, "Special Report from a Spanish Monastery," *The Student* (Washington, D.C.: USNSA, 1966), 22.

59. Ibid.

60. Ibid.

61. Ibid.

62. See articles by Tad Szulc in the *New York Times*, March 11, 12, 13, 1966.

63. Interview with Kiley, who dismissed Sherburne's suspicions about Berger in Spain; interview with Sherburne.

64. H/NSA, Box 25 (IC Corres.), April 5, 1966, Berger letter to Dennis Foianini, a former Latin American specialist on the NSA international staff.

65. Interview with Sherburne.

66. Ibid.

67. W/NSA, Box 22, March 19, 1966, Goldmark to Eugene Groves.

68. Kovacs discussed the CIA issue numerous times with me and my former husband. In 1967, Kovacs—who was committed to ending the CIA relationship with the NSA—participated in discussions with Sherburne, his successor, Eugene Groves, and Bob Kiley.

69. Interview with Sherburne.

70. Ansara Files (General International), Michael Wood memo to *Ramparts* editors; interview with Sherburne. Sherburne's and Wood's accounts agree on most particulars.

71. Fulbright, vol. 1, March 6, 1967, Wood testimony on dissatisfaction and threatened resignation (7); on the nature of international staff fundraising proposals (25).

72. Interview with Sherburne.

73. Fulbright, vol. 1, March 6, 1967, Wood testimony, 8.

74. Ibid.
75. Interview with Sherburne.
76. Ibid.
77. Fulbright, vol. 1, March 6, 1967, Wood testimony, 8.
78. Ibid.
79. Interview with Sherburne.
80. Ibid.
81. Ibid.
82. Telephone interview with Charles F. Sweet, Charlotte, N.C., August 25, 2006.
83. Sweet, March 25, 1965, Sweet to parents, describing his trip with the "NSA boys."
84. Ibid. Sweet arrived in Saigon in 1964 about the time that students were teaming up with Buddhist monks to overthrow General Nguyen Khanh, head of the South Vietnamese government.
85. Sweet, May 10, 1965, Sweet to family.
86. Ibid.
87. Telephone interview with Sweet.
88. Interview with Sherburne.
89. Telephone interview with Sweet.
90. Ibid.
91. Ibid.
92. Paget Files. Philip Sherburne, Malcolm Kovacs, and Gregory Delin, "United States National Student Association Delegation to Vietnam: A Report to the Constituency," March 21–April 5, 1966.
93. Ibid. Sherburne sent the report to Vietnamese students through Charles Sweet: see W/NSA, Box 21 (Sherburne), June 21, 1966.
94. Interview with Sherburne.
95. W/NSA, Box 21 (Sherburne), October 20, 1965, Sherburne to Richard Stearns.
96. Ibid.
97. Ibid., October 20, 1965, Sherburne draft letter to Attorney General Katzenbach. The NSA joined with other organizations to protest the attorney general's remarks. See Robert J. Richard, "Katzenbach Is Assailed on Critics of Viet-Nam," *New York Times*, October 24, 1965.
98. John Dumbrell, *President Lyndon Johnson and Soviet Communism* (Manchester, U.K.: Manchester University Press, 2004), p. 116. Johnson called antiwar U.S. Senators "crackpots, who have been just plain taken in," and asserted that "the Russians are behind the whole thing." See also Robert Dallek, *Lyndon B. Johnson: Portrait of a President* (New York: Oxford University Press, 2004), 314, on LBJ's use of intelligence agencies to go after antiwar activists.
99. See Régis Debray, *Revolution in the Revolution? Armed Struggle and Political Struggle in Latin America*, trans. Bobbye S. Ortiz (Harmondsworth, U.K.: Penguin, 1967); Frantz Fanon, *The Wretched of the Earth*, trans. Constance Farrington (New York: Grove Weidenfeld, 1963).
100. W/NSA, Box 21 (Sherburne), June 21, 1966, Sherburne to Sweet.

101. Interview with Sherburne.
102. I typed the letter of request for an appointment with Vice President Humphrey while working as a secretarial temp at a Washington, D.C., law firm.
103. Interview with Sherburne.
104. Telephone interview with Ted Van Dyke, Los Angeles, October 19, 1998. Van Dyke subsequently wrote about these events in *Heroes, Hacks and Food: A Memoir from the Political Inside* (Seattle: University of Washington Press, 2007), 117-18.
105. FRUS, Department of State, Johnson Administration, 1964-68, vol. 33: Organization and Management of Foreign Policy, Document 219, Letter from President Johnson to Vice President Humphrey, January 22, 1965.
106. Interview with Sherburne. My then-husband, on the NSA Middle East desk, told me about Humphrey's reaction sometime in July 1966.
107. Interview with Sherburne.
108. Interview with Van Dyke. See also the list of Humphrey contacts in W/NSA, Box 22 (Sherburne Daybook), September 23, 1966, Sherburne memo to Eugene Groves: David Rockefeller, United States Steel, First National City Bank, Ford Motor Company, Chicago and Northwestern Railway, and Walter Reuther (UAW). Only the president of Chicago and Northwestern Railway made a contribution, which Groves later attributed to his friendship with the executive's son.
109. Van Dyke, *Heroes, Hacks and Fools*, 118.
110. Interview with Kiley.
111. H/NSA, Box 62 (20th NSA Congress), August 1967, President's Report, 1. Groves's speech, written for the 1967 NSA Congress held August 13-26 at the University of Maryland, states that Sherburne told him "shortly before the 19th congress." See also Fulbright, vol. 2, March 16, 1967, Groves testimony, 134-35, re discussions with Sherburne after the 1966 Congress.
112. Interview with Edward Schwartz, Philadelphia, May 2, 2000.
113. Ibid.
114. H/NSA, Box 62 (20th NSA Congress), August 1967, President's Report, 3.
115. Ibid.
116. Ibid.
117. One person who obtained the information from an intermediary, and not from Wood, was Edward Schwartz from Oberlin: interview with Schwartz.

Chapter 22. The Game Within the Game

1. Interview with Philip Sherburne, Santa Barbara, Calif., May 15-16, 2000.
2. Interview with Robert Kiley, Cambridge, Mass., January 22, 2008.
3. Interview with Edward Garvey, Madison, Wisc., October 17, 2005.
4. Interview with Jyoti Shankar Singh, New York City, August 22, 2006.
5. Interview with Ram Labhaya Lakhina, Leiden, the Netherlands, October 9 and 12, 2004.
6. Interview with Garvey, October, 17, 2005.

7. IISH ISC (File: CIA Connection), copy of October 13, 1966, Wilfred Rutz letter to the Supervision Commission re the Twelfth ISC in Nairobi.
8. H/NSA, Box 78 (Memos), January 1966, Fred Berger to Goldmark and Sherburne.
9. H/NSA, Box 77 (IAB), February 10, 1964, Alex Korns, Confidential Report No. 2. Press release language included in report to the International Advisory Board.
10. H/NSA, Box 25 (IC Corres.), January 10, 1966, Berger to Garvey.
11. Ibid.
12. Ibid.
13. Ibid. (Backoff), June 15, 1964, Backoff to Korns and Scott.
14. Ibid., April 18, 1964, Backoff memo on Middle East ISC delegations.
15. H/NSA, Box 233 (Middle East), February 7, 1964, Backoff reported Lebanon's action in a report on a proposed Middle Eastern Confederation of Students.
16. Ibid., February 19, 1961, Lee to Scott.
17. H/NSA, Box 238 (Palestine), January 4, 1961, Lee to Scott.
18. Ibid.
19. H/NSA, Box 233, February 19, 1961, Lee to Scott.
20. Ibid.
21. H/NSA, Box 238, January 4, 1961, Lee to Scott.
22. H/NSA, Box 239 (Palestine), n.d., USNSA cable to Hassan Hammam.
23. Interview with Tony Smith, New York, November 7 and 9, 2007.
24. Ibid.
25. Ibid.
26. Ibid.
27. H/NSA, Box 233 (Middle East), March 9, 1964, Backoff to Frank Crump, NSA travel office.
28. Laurie Brand, *Palestinians in the Arab World: Institution Building and the Search for State* (New York: Columbia University Press, 1988), 73, 75.
29. H/NSA, Box 25 (Backoff), March 1, 1965, Backoff to Uphoff re March 31–April 4, 1965, Palestine seminar.
30. H/NSA, Box 30 (Kovacs), May 29, 1965, Robert Witherspoon, memo to Confidential Files re conversation with Israeli Simha Salpeter.
31. Ibid.
32. Ibid. Uphoff's remarks were printed in the newspaper *Al Akhbar* on April 4, 1965.
33. Ibid. Salpeter obtained a copy of *Al Akhbar* from Israeli friends in Paris.
34. Interview with Norman Uphoff, Ithaca, N.Y., August 2006.
35. H/NSA, Box 233 (Middle East), August 10, 1965, Richard Stearns, letter to Robert Witherspoon, re Stearns's father's conversation with Simon Segal of the American Jewish Committee, who, based on information from Israeli students, was worried about the upcoming NSA Congress. See also August 12, 1965, Witherspoon, letter of reassurance to Segal.
36. H/NSA, Box 30 (Kovacs), May 29, 1965, Witherspoon memo to confidential files.

37. H/NSA, Box 233 (Middle East), September 10, 1965, Robert Witherspoon, memo on North Africa and Middle East strategy at NSA Congress.

38. Ibid.

39. Ibid.

40. Ibid.

41. H/NSA, Box 233 (Middle East), September 10, 1965, Witherspoon memo.

42. H/NSA, Box 25 (Backoff), March 1, 1965, Backoff to Uphoff.

43. H/NSA, Box 33 (Witherspoon), February 4, 1966, Goldmark to Witherspoon.

44. Ibid.

45. H/NSA, Box 25 (IC Correspondence), April 4, 1966, Fred Berger to Dennis Foianini. The delegates were Witherspoon, Richard Stearns (of Stanford University), Michael Enwall (Middle East Desk), and Steven Arons (Civil Rights Desk).

46. H/NSA, Box 30 (Korns), February 10, 1964, Korns, overview to the International Advisory Board, describing Asia as "the strongest region outside Europe for ISC."

47. H/NSA, Box 10 (11th ISC), undated newspaper clipping from ISC in Christchurch, "No Visas for IUS." By inference, the Kenyan government did not prevent IUS delegates from reaching the conference.

48. H/NSA, Box 10 (12th ISC), List of attendees who attended the Nairobi, Kenya, ISC, August 17-27, 1966.

49. H/NSA, Box 33 (Witherspoon), March 21, 1965, Witherspoon, in a memo to files, reports on a dinner with Gerhart and Alex Korns. Gerhart was characterized as "very impressive" and an "excellent contact." Gerhart had taught for a year in Tanzania in 1964-65. In 1966, he was about to spend an academic year at Makerere University in Uganda.

50. H/NSA, Box 10 (12th ISC), July 26, 1966, Chuck Goldmark, letter to John Gerhart.

51. Interview with Garvey, October 17, 2005.

52. Ibid.

53. Interviews with Lakhina and Garvey (October 17, 2005).

54. Interview with Lakhina.

55. Interview with Garvey, October 17, 2005.

56. Skype interview with Thomas Olson, Cairo, February 3, 2009; the issue was discussed more fully during conversation with Olson, New York, September 11, 2009.

57. Interview with Duncan Kennedy, Cambridge, Mass., September 7, 2005.

58. Ibid.

59. Ansara Files: Martin Abein and Edward Bomhoff, Interview with Ronald J. J. Bell, August 18, 1967, Appendix VI, *International Student Conference Report* (Amsterdam: Dutch Student Trade Union, 1968).

60. Telephone interview with Fernando Duran, San José, Costa Rica, January 21, 2009.

61. As of 2010, Nouri A. R. Hussain held the position of secretary general of the

Cairo-based Afro-Asian Peoples' Solidarity Conference. See the organizations Web page at UNESCO: http://ngo-db.unesco.org/r/or/en/1100062827.

62. H/NSA, Box 10 (12th ISC), detailed report on Nairobi ISC, August 17–27, 1966, including Hussain's speech. Presumably the NSA abstained from voting.

63. Robert McDonald, "The Arrogance of Ability: A Report on the Twelfth International Student Conference," *New African* 5, no. 10 (December 1966): 211–12, available at Digital Innovation South Africa at http://www.disa.ukzn.ac.za/new african/content/new-african-volume-5-number-10-december-1966. McDonald hailed the IUS-ISC resolution on cooperation as the major achievement of the meeting.

64. FOIA (State), secret airgram, October 25, 1966, American Embassy, Saigon to Sec/State described the ISC in Nairobi in detail, including Khanh's charge that the Iranian delegate deliberately identified the group with the NLF.

65. Ibid. The airgram summarized, "The Vietnamese delegations [another had been sent to the 1966 NSA Congress and the World Assembly of Youth] failed to perform effectively," and noted that the Mission Youth Committee was "reviewing the entire question of Vietnamese participation at international youth and students gatherings."

66. Interview with Duran.

67. FOIA (State), secret airgram, October 25, 1966. Khanh described the suggestion by the French.

68. Interview with Kiley.

69. H/NSA, Box 9 (12th ISC), copy of Goldmark's report on the 12th ISC, 17–27 August, Nairobi, Kenya, 10.

70. Fulbright, vol. 2, March 16, 1967, Eugene Groves testimony, 135, 136.

71. Ibid., 136.

72. H/NSA, Box 62 (20th NSA Congress), August 1967, President's Report, 3. Groves's speech was delivered to the 1967 NSA Congress held August 13–26 at the University of Maryland.

73. Groves quoted in Donald Janson, "Student Congress Emphasizes Political Activism," *New York Times*, September 4, 1965.

74. H/NSA, Box 62 (20th NSA Congress), August 1967, President's Report, 3.

75. Ibid., 2.

76. W/NSA (Groves), n.d. Groves's file contains a nine-page mimeographed report, "NSA and the CIA: On People and Power (Second Thoughts After the Storm)," in which he describes his feelings before and after the disclosures; quotation on p. 8.

77. Fulbright, vol. 2, March 16, 1967, Groves testimony, 136–37.

78. H/NSA, Box 62 (20th NSA Congress), August 1967, President's Report, 6.

79. Ibid.

80. Interview with Richard Stearns, Cambridge, Mass., February 1, 1993.

81. H/NSA Box 62 (20th NSA Congress), August 1967, President's Report, 6.

82. Interview with Stearns. For details of Stearns's security oath, see also Fulbright, vol. 2, March 16, 1967, Stearns testimony, 242. Stearns testified that the oath was

given under false pretenses, as a condition of a grant from the Agency for International Development.

83. Interview with Stearns.
84. Ibid.
85. H/NSA Box 62 (20th NSA Congress), August 1967, President's Report, 4-5.
86. Ibid.
87. Fulbright, vol. 2, March 16, 1967, Groves testimony, 136.
88. H/NSA, Box 62 (20th NSA congress), August 1967, President's Report, 7.
89. Interview with Edward Schwartz, Philadelphia, May 2, 2000.
90. Fulbright, vol. 2, March 16, 1967, Groves testimony, 137.
91. Interview with Schwartz.

Chapter 23. Hide-and-Seek

1. Fulbright, vol. 1, March 6, 1967, Michael Wood testimony, p. 6.
2. Interview with Richard Stearns, Cambridge, Mass., February 1, 1993.
3. Interview with Edward Schwartz, Philadelphia, May 2, 2000.
4. Peter Richardson, *A Bomb in Every Issue: How the Short, Unruly Life of "Ramparts" Magazine Changed America* (New York: New Press, 2009).
5. Donald Duncan, "The Whole Thing Was a Lie," *Ramparts* (February 1966), 12-24, quotation on p. 23.
6. Angus Mackenzie, *Secrets: The CIA's War at Home* (Berkeley: University of California Press, 1997), 17.
7. Ibid., 16.
8. John Ernst, *Forging a Fateful Alliance: Michigan State University and the Vietnam War* (Lansing: Michigan State University Press, 1998). My appreciation to Stanley Sheinbaum for sending me a copy.
9. Mackenzie, *Secrets*, 17.
10. Ibid., 19.
11. David Wise and Thomas B. Ross, *The Invisible Government* (New York: Random House, 1964).
12. David Wise, *The American Police State: The Government Against the People* (New York: Random House, 1976), 199-200. See also David Binder's interview with Wise in "Washington Talk: Intelligence; Measuring the Years in Terms of CIA Directors," *New York Times*, August 10, 1988.
13. Joseph Burkholder Smith, *Portrait of a Cold Warrior* (New York: Putnam, 1976), 432.
14. "Patman Attacks 'Secret' C.I.A. Link," *New York Times*, September 1, 1964. Foundations identified by Congressman Patman included Gotham, Michigan, Andrew Hamilton, Borden, Price, Edsel, Beacon, and Kentfield.
15. FRUS, 1964-68, vol. 10: National Security Policy, Document 49, Memorandum for the Record by Director of Central Intelligence, September 1, 1964. McCone had gone to the president about Patman's disclosures, which he attributed to "over aggressiveness" by congressional staff. He emphasized the "great damage" that had been done.

16. Harrison Salisbury, *Without Fear or Favor: An Uncompromising Look at the New York Times* (New York: Times Books, 1980), 514.

17. Ibid., 516-517.

18. Ibid., 517.

19. Ibid., 519-20.

20. Ibid., 521.

21. Reported by a *Times* team led by Tom Wicker, the articles were published on April 25, 26, 27, 28, and 29, 1966. Salisbury, *Without Fear or Favor*, 522-28, describes in detail CIA director John McCone's review of the articles prior to publication and his requests for changes.

22. Salisbury, *Without Fear or Favor*, 527.

23. Evan Thomas, *The Very Best Men: Four Who Dared; the Early Years of the CIA* (New York: Simon and Schuster, 1995). Wisner is one of the four men profiled.

24. Meyer, Box 5, Diary, March 21, 1963.

25. Nina Burleigh, *A Very Private Woman: The Life and Unsolved Murder of Presidential Mistress Mary Meyer* (New York: Bantam, 1998).

26. Salisbury, *Without Fear or Favor*, 525; see also Burleigh, *Very Private Woman*, 204.

27. In addition to my own recollection I draw on my telephone interview with Michael Enwall, Lyons, Colo., August 30, 2006.

28. Interview with Stearns.

29. Interview with Judith Coburn, Albany, Calif., December 3, 1999. The conversation that follows is from this interview.

30. Interview with Michael Ansara, Cambridge, Mass., January 20, 2000. The conversation that follows is from this interview.

31. Interview with Lee Webb, New York City, November 1, 2000.

32. Interview with Coburn. The conversation that follows is from this interview.

33. Ibid.

34. Ibid.

35. Ibid.

36. Ibid.

37. Ibid. For Coffin's work with the CIA, see Warren Goldstein, *William Sloane Coffin, Jr.: A Holy Impatience* (New Haven: Yale University Press, 2006), 71-82.

38. Interview with Coburn.

39. Ibid.

40. Interview with Ansara. The narrative that follows of Ansara's pursuit of the story is all from this interview.

41. Warren Hinckle, *If You Have a Lemon, Make Lemonade* (New York: Norton, 1973), 174. See also Richardson, *Bomb in Every Issue*, 74-81.

42. Hinckle, *If You Have a Lemon*, 172. Wood worked with other *Ramparts* staff before he met Hinckle.

43. Ibid., 173.

44. Interview with Fred Goff, Oakland, Calif., July 9, 2000.

45. Sacha Volman had worked with the NSA before the ISC in Quebec; see Chapter 18, above. See also Eric Thomas Chester, *Rag-Tags, Scum, Riff-Raff, and Commies* (New York: Monthly Review Press, 2001).

46. Interview with Goff.
47. Interview with Michael Locker, New York City, July 14, 2000.
48. Ibid.
49. Interview with Goff.
50. Interview with Locker.
51. Ibid.
52. Ibid.
53. Ibid.
54. Ibid.
55. Ibid.
56. Interviews with Goff and Locker.
57. Interview with Locker.
58. Interviews with Locker and Goff.
59. Interview with Coburn.
60. Ibid.
61. Ibid.
62. Ibid.
63. Interview with Lee Webb.
64. Interview with John Frappier, Pacifica, Calif., December 11, 2000.
65. Interview with Coburn.
66. Ibid.
67. Interview with Schwartz.
68. Fulbright, vol. 2, March 16, 1967, Eugene Groves testimony, 147–48.
69. Interview with Philip Sherburne, Santa Barbara, Calif., May 16, 2000.
70. Ibid.
71. Interview with Steven Arons, Amherst, Mass., September 5, 2005.
72. Interview with Adam Hochschild, Berkeley, Calif., February 10, 2000. The Chinese New Year began on February 7, 1967.
73. Interviews with Robert Kiley, Cambridge, Mass., January 22, 2008, and Tony Smith, New York, November 7 and 9, 2007.
74. Interview with Kiley.
75. CIA memorandum, Subject: IRS Briefing on Ramparts, February 2, 1967, Book 3: Supplemental Detailed Staff Reports on Intelligence Activities and the Rights of Americans, 422–23: United States Senate Select Committee to Study Government Operations with Respect to Intelligence Operations (Church Committee), 1975.
76. Thomas, *Very Best Men*, 330.
77. Ibid.
78. Ibid.

Chapter 24. Do You Want Blood on Your Hands?

1. Interview with Tom DeVries, Mariposa, Calif., August 12, 2000. Groves remembers the occasion similarly; see H/NSA, Box 62 (20th NSA Congress), August

1967, President's Report, prepared for the NSA Congress at the University of Maryland.

2. Interview with DeVries.

3. Ibid.

4. Telephone interview with Ken Stevens, New York City, August 24, 2000.

5. W/NSA, Box 21 (Schwartz), January 16, 1967, Schwartz, letter to Mal Kovacs on his Berkeley activities. See also January 31, 1967, Schwartz, second letter to Kovacs after he returned from California with more detail on his activities.

6. Interview with Edward Schwartz, Philadelphia, May 2, 2000.

7. Ibid.

8. Ibid. See also Warren Hinckle, *If You Have a Lemon, Make Lemonade* (New York: Norton, 1973), 178.

9. Interview with Schwartz.

10. Ansara Files: Michael Wood, n.d., memo on fundraising assistance in "Sequence of Research Activities."

11. Interview with Schwartz.

12. The officers were not aware that some sources responding to Sherburne's solicitations also received CIA funds, such as the Asia Foundation. FRUS, Department of State, Johnson Administration, 1964–68, vol. 10: National Security Policy, Document 132, Memorandum from the Central Intelligence Agency to the 303 Committee, June 22, 1966 defines the Asia Foundation as a CIA "proprietary," and discusses improvement in funding procedures; available at www .state.gov/r/pa/ho/frus/johnsonlb/x/9062.htm.

13. Interview with Schwartz.

14. Interview with Philip Sherburne, Santa Barbara, Calif., May 16, 2000.

15. Interview with Roger Fisher, Cambridge, Mass., January 27, 2003.

16. Fulbright, vol. 2, March 16, 1967, Roger Fisher letter of March 15, 1967, attached to declassified Fulbright hearing record.

17. Ibid.

18. Interview with Roger Fisher. Fisher identified Cord Meyer by indirection and not by name.

19. Ibid. Interview with Frank Fisher, Austin, Tex., May 14, 2009. Frank confirmed his brother's encounter with Meyer and the threat.

20. Fulbright, vol. 2, March 16, 1967, Fisher letter.

21. Interview with Roger Fisher.

22. Interview with Sherburne.

23. Ibid.

24. Ibid.

25. Obituary of Richard J. Murphy, *Washington Post*, August 19, 2006.

26. Interview with Sherburne.

27. Interview with Steven Arons, Amherst, Mass., September 5, 2005.

28. Interviews with Arons and Sherburne.

29. Interview with Sherburne.

30. Interview with Schwartz.

31. Interview with Robert Kiley, Cambridge, Mass., January 22, 2008.

32. H/NSA, Box 62 (20th NSA congress), August 1967, President's Report, recounts this information. Stearns's roommate, Steven Bookshester, heard the phone ring and witnessed Stearns's reaction: "He turned absolutely white, white as a ghost"; interview with Steven Bookshester, Washington, D.C., October 22, 1991.

33. Interview with Schwartz.

34. Fulbright, vol. 2, March 16, 1967, Eugene Groves testimony, 145–47. See also H/NSA, Box 62 (20th NSA Congress), August 1967, President's Report. Groves made similar points.

35. Interview with Sherburne.

36. Ibid.

37. Ibid.

38. Ibid.

39. Ibid.

40. Interview with Kiley.

41. Interview with Arons.

42. Ibid. See also Fulbright, vol. 2, March 16, 1967, Groves testimony, 157–58.

43. Interview with Kiley.

44. Interview with Sherburne.

45. Telephone interview with Stevens.

46. H/NSA, Box 62 (20th NSA Congress), August 1967, President's Report, 6.

47. Interview with Roger Fisher.

48. William W. Turner, *Rearview Mirror: Looking Back at the FBI, the CIA and Other Tails* (Roseville, Calif.: Penmarin, 2001).

49. Interview with Sherburne.

50. Interview with Richard Stearns, Cambridge, Mass., February 1, 1993.

51. Fulbright, vol. 2, March 16, 1967, Groves testimony, 160.

52. H/NSA, Box 62 (20th NSA Congress), August 1967, President's Report, 6.

53. IISH ISC, Box 1232, contains extensive material on the aftermath of *Ramparts*, including the ISC investigation and transcript of Lakhina's remarks.

54. Hinckle, *If You Have a Lemon*, 179.

55. Interview with Sam W. Brown, Jr., Berkeley, Calif., November 10, 1992.

56. Telephone interview with Steve Parliament, River Falls, Wisc., June 22, 2003.

57. Ibid.

58. Ibid.

Chapter 25. The Firestorm

1. Richard Helms, *A Look over My Shoulder: A Life in the Central Intelligence Agency* (New York: Random House, 2003), 343.

2. Ibid., 345.

3. Ibid.

4. Helms testimony, September 12, 1975, United States Senate Select Committee to Study Government Operations with Respect to Intelligence Operations

(Church Committee), vol. 10: The Domestic Impact of Foreign Clandestine Operations, 182.

5. Interview with Robert Kiley, Cambridge, Mass., January 22, 2008.

6. Angus Mackenzie, *Secrets: The CIA's War at Home* (Berkeley: University of California Press, 1997), 22.

7. Interview with Tony Smith, New York, November 7 and 9, 2007.

8. Ibid.

9. *Ramparts* ad, announcing March issue in the *New York Times* and *Washington Post*, February 14, 1967.

10. Interview with Edward Schwartz, Philadelphia, May 2, 2000.

11. Telephone conversation with Susan A. McCloud, Carmel, Calif., March 19, 2004.

12. Michael Warner, "Sophisticated Spies: CIA's Links to Liberal Anti-Communists, 1949-1967," *International Journal of Intelligence and Counterintelligence* 9, no. 4 (Winter 1996-97): 425.

13. Richard Harwood, "LBJ Called Unaware of Subsidy," *Washington Post*, February 17, 1967.

14. The claim might have been true, however; see R. Jack Smith, Interview with Richard Helms, June 3, 1982, Richard Helms Collection, CIA Center for the Study of Intelligence, 25, available at the CIA Freedom of Information Act Electronic Reading Room, www.foia.cia.gov.

15. LBJ, E-transcript, David G. McComb, Interview with S. Douglass Cater, no. 2, April 29, 1969, 4. For further information on Cater, see *Who's Who*, vol. 72-73, p. 526.

16. Elke Van Cassel, "In Search of a Clear and Overarching American Policy: *The Reporter* Magazine (1949-1968)," in *The U.S. Government, Citizens Groups, and the Cold War: The State-Private Network*, ed. Helen Laville and Hugh Wilford (Oxford: Routledge, 2005), 116-40. It is also noteworthy that *The Reporter* stopped publishing shortly after the 1967 disclosures. In addition, according to a conversation with Elke Van Cassel, all of its financial records have been destroyed.

17. NARA, 511.00/9-2861, September 28, 1961, U. Alexis Johnson to Under Secretary Chester Bowles, re proposed hiring of Cater; see also NARA, 511.00/10-1661, October 16, 1961, Luke Battle to Secretary of State, Reports and Operations, re Cater reported for duty.

18. Robert Walters, "Humphrey Unhappy over CIA Incident," *Washington Evening Star*, February 21, 1967.

19. Both Philip Sherburne and I remember hearing the pithy version (interview with Philip Sherburne, Santa Barbara, Calif., May 16, 2000).

20. Telephone interview with Ted Van Dyke, Los Angeles, October 19, 1998. Van Dyke's memoir covers the same ground. See *Heroes, Hacks and Fools: Memoir from the Political Inside* (Seattle: University of Washington Press, 1997).

21. Telephone interview with Van Dyke.

22. Interview with Nicholas Katzenbach, Princeton, N.J., June 24, 2005.

23. LBJ, Box 44 National Security Files, February 13, 1967, declassified Katzenbach memorandum.
24. Interview with Jack Rosenthal, New York City, November 2, 2005.
25. Ibid.
26. LBJ, Box 44, National Security Files, February 15, 1967, declassified memo, Rosenthal to Christian.
27. Interview with John Gardner, Palo Alto, Calif., September 13, 2000.
28. Ibid.
29. Ibid. Gardner spoke to Johnson on October 12, 1966.
30. Ibid.
31. Rhodri Jeffreys-Jones, *The CIA and American Democracy* (New Haven: Yale University Press, 1989), 159.
32. Ibid.
33. Richard Harwood, "CIA Reported Ending Aid to Some Groups," *Washington Post*, February 22, 1967.
34. LBJ, CIA National Security Files, *Ramparts*-NSA-CIA Folder.
35. Reported in Richard Harwood, "LBJ Called Unaware of Subsidies," *Washington Post*, February 17, 1967.
36. Edith Green, quoted in the *Congressional Record*, 90th Congress, vol. 113, part 31, p. 1662.
37. "The Cultural Revolution, U.S.A.," *New Guard*, Summer 1967. The *New Guard* was a magazine published by the Young Americans for Freedom.
38. "CIA/NSA: The Central Issue," *New Guard*, April 1967.
39. Cord Meyer, Jr., *Facing Reality: From World Federalism to the CIA* (New York: Harper and Row, 1980), 87.
40. IISH ISC, Box 1232 (CIA Connection), December 21, 1967, Sup Com interview with Lakhina.
41. H/NSA, Box 69 (Staff Reports), COSEC press statement, February 17, 1967.
42. Helms, *Look over My Shoulder*, 345.
43. Meyer, *Facing Reality*, 91.
44. Helms, *Look Over My Shoulder*, 345.
45. Interview with Sam Brown, Berkeley, Calif., November 10, 1992, and telephone interview with Steve Parliament, River Falls, Wisc., June 22, 2003. See also Philip R. Werdell, "Fun Birthday Surprise All for You," *Moderator*, April 1967. *Moderator* was, according to its cover tagline, "a magazine for leading college students" published in Philadelphia.
46. Telephone interview with Jean Hoefer Toal, Columbia, S.C., September 6, 2006.
47. James A. Johnson's fear was mentioned later by NSA president Eugene W. Groves; see H/NSA, Box 62 (20th NSA congress), August 1967, President's Report.
48. Informal conversations over several years with Robert Kuttner, Boston.
49. Telephone interview with Toal.
50. Telephone interview with Ricki Radlo Lieberman, New York, January 11, 2010.
51. Ibid.

52. Ibid.
53. Ansara Files, February 17, 1967, Statement of the National Supervisory Board.
54. Gerald Grant, "CIA Used NSA Staff for Spying," *Washington Post*, February 18, 1967.
55. Former NSA president William Welsh, who in 1967 served as an aide to Vice President Humphrey, conveyed this information in a conversation with me.
56. FRUS, Department of State, Johnson Administration, 1964–68, vol. 10: National Security Policy, Secret, Eyes Only, Memorandum from the President's Special Assistant (Rostow) to the President, February 18, 1967, 171.
57. Ibid. Rostow identified a total of seven dates.
58. FRUS, Department of State, Johnson Administration, 1964–68, vol. 10:, National Security Policy, State-CIA Relations with Respect to Clandestine Activities, Memorandum from the Deputy Director of the Bureau of Intelligence and Research (Denny) to Deputy Under Secretary of State for Political Affairs (Kohler), February 15, 1967, 261.
59. LBJ, FG 11-2 (CIA), Box 193, declassified CIA memo, Coordination and Policy Approval of Covert Operations, with appendixes, February 23, 1967.
60. Ibid.
61. Grant, "CIA Used NSA Staff for Spying."
62. Ibid.
63. Ibid.
64. Ibid.
65. Senator Kennedy's statement was widely reported. See, e.g., *Washington Evening Star* and UPI (United Press International) wire service, February 21, 1967.
66. Kiley's colleague asked that the story be off the record. In my interview with Kiley, Kiley claimed that he ran into Kennedy by accident and they discussed the situation but did not deny his role in Kennedy's statement.
67. Meyer, *Facing Reality*, 89. See also page 103 for his discussions with Kennedy about the World Youth Festival.
68. Robert Walters, "12 NSA Ex-Presidents Defend CIA Subsidies," *Washington Evening Star*, February 26, 1967.
69. Some NSA presidents worked with the CIA only for the year they held office.
70. James Edward, quoted in Stuart H. Loory, "Mystery Death Hides CIA Ties," *Los Angeles Times*, February 26, 1967.
71. "The CIA and 'The Kiddies,'" *Newsweek*, February 27, 1967. Steinem's defense is also featured in Robert G. Kaiser, "Work of CIA with Youths at Festivals Is Defended," *Washington Post*, February 18, 1967.
72. Richard Cummings, *The Pied Piper* (New York: Grove, 1985), 46.
73. Interview with Parliament.
74. Fulbright, hearing record, vols. 1 and 2, March 6 and 16, 1967.
75. Fulbright, vol. 1, March 6, 1967, Michael Wood testimony, 18.
76. Ibid., 20.
77. Ibid., 20-21.
78. Ibid., 15. Quips made on the record during Wood's testimony.
79. Ibid., 16.

80. Fulbright, vol. 1, March 6, 1967, 46, off-the-record discussion.
81. J. W. Fulbright, "We Must Not Fight Fire with Fire," *New York Times Magazine*, April 23, 1967.
82. Meyer, *Facing Reality*, 87.
83. Fulbright, "We Must Not Fight Fire with Fire."
84. Jack Smith, Interview with Helms.
85. Interview with Rosenthal.
86. Ibid.
87. Ibid.
88. Meyer, Box 5, Diary, March 10, 1967.
89. Kaiser, "Work of CIA with Youths at Festivals Is Defended," Grant, "CIA Used NSA Staff for Spying," and Richard Harwood, "Business Leaders Are Tied to CIA's Covert Operations."
90. Don Irwin and Vincent J. Burke, "21 Foundations, Union Got Money from CIA," *Los Angeles Times*, February 26, 1967.
91. Richard Harwood, "O What a Tangled Web the CIA Wove," *Washington Post*, February 26, 1967.
92. Meany's denials were cited in Richard Harwood, "New CIA Financial Aide," *Washington Post*, May 9, 1967.
93. Tom Braden, "I'm Glad the CIA is 'Immoral,'" *Saturday Evening Post*, May 20, 1967, 10–14.
94. Neil Sheehan, "Foundations Linked to CIA are Found to Subsidize 4 Other Youth Organizations," *New York Times*, February 16, 1967.
95. In 1967, two former NSA witting staff, Reed Martin and James Fowler, worked for Gallo.
96. Tim Wheeler, "National Student Assn Quits CIA-Tied Council," *The Worker*, May 14, 1967.
97. IISH ISC, Box 1232, Supervision Commission minutes, April 21–24, 1967.
98. Ibid., Garvey cable, April 14, 1967.
99. Ibid., 1967 cables from George Foulkes (n.d.), Gwyn Morgan (April 17), and Jyoti Singh (April 14).
100. Ibid., 1967 cables from John M. Thompson (April 18) and Hans Dall (April 17).
101. Ibid., Supervision Commission minutes, April 21–24, 1967.
102. Ibid. The British leaders included Ronald J. J. Bell from the National Union of Students.
103. Ibid., August 14, 1967, transcript of interview with Harry Lunn, director of the Foundation for Youth and Student Affairs.
104. Meyer, Box 1 (Correspondence), March 20, 1967, Meyer to Tad Davis.
105. Ibid., May 5, 1967, Meyer to Lew Lapham in Saigon. The text of the Katzenbach Committee findings can be found in *American Foreign Policy: Current Documents, 1967* (Washington, D.C.: U.S. Government, Department of State), 1214–16.
106. Robert Walters, "Ex-Student Aides Say White House Dodges CIA Issues," *Washington Evening Star*, March 30, 1967.
107. LBJ, White House, Central Files, Gen FG 11-1, March 23, 1967, Groves letter to Cater.

108. Ibid.

109. Ansara Files: "Statement of Former NSA Officers and Staff on NSA-CIA Controversy and the Katzenbach Report, March 29, 1967. See also Walters, "Ex-Student Aides Say White House Dodges CIA Issues."

110. Meyer, Box 1 (Correspondence), May 25, 1967, Sherman Kent, letter to Meyer, congratulating him on his award.

111. Eden Lipson, memo of 1967 conversation with Dennis Shaul, courtesy of Eden Lipson.

Chapter 26. The Enemy at Home

1. Jo Thomas, "C.I.A. Reported on Student Group After Cutting off Financial Help," *New York Times*, November 30, 1977. The report on the 1967 NSA Congress commissioned by Helms was disclosed to the *Times* by Morton Halperin and John Marks, who obtained numerous documents through a Freedom of Information Request.

2. Fulbright, vol. 2, March 16, 1967, Eugene Groves testimony, 151–59.

3. LBJ, FG 11–2, Leonard Bebchick to Nicholas Katzenbach, March 9, 1967.

4. Herbert Denton, "CIA Tries to Oust Student Tenants from Rent-Free Headquarters," *Washington Post*, June 14, 1967; Robert Walters, "Student Group Faces Cash, Rent Troubles," *Washington Evening Star*, July 10, 1967.

5. H/NSA, Box 62 (20th NSA Congress), August 1967, President's Report.

6. Robert Walters, "CIA Transfers Title of Building to Students," *Washington Evening Star*, August 11, 1967.

7. FRUS, Department of State, Johnson Administration, 1964–68, vol. 10: National Security Policy, Document 186. Secret, Eyes Only (Peter Jessup) Minutes of the Meeting of the 303 Committee, August 7, 1967.

8. FOIA (CIA), #206, August 22, 2967, Helms authorized a settlement; #200–201, papers signed on August 30, 1967, by newly elected NSA president Edward Schwartz.

9. Interview with Robert Walters, Washington, D.C., October 24, 1998.

10. Helms's directive reported in Thomas, "C.I.A. Reported on Student Group After Cutting off Financial Help."

11. Richard Blumenthal, "NSA Votes to Organize Resistance to the Draft," *Washington Post*, August 21, 1967.

12. Thomas, "C.I.A. Reported on Student Group After Cutting off Financial Help."

13. A summary of Helms's June 1970 report to Kissinger, "Restless Youth," is available at DocStoc, www.docstoc.com. A previous version of "Restless Youth" was sent by Helms to Walt W. Rostow in September 1968, available at LBJ, National Security Files (Intelligence File).

14. Richard Helms, *A Look over My Shoulder: A Life in the Central Intelligence Agency* (New York: Random House, 2003), 344.

15. Ibid.

16. Interview with Tony Smith, New York, November 7 and 9, 2007.

17. Interview with Robert Kiley, Cambridge, Mass., January 22, 2008.
18. Angus Mackenzie, *Secrets: The CIA's War at Home* (Berkeley: University of California Press, 1997), 23.
19. For information on Lawrence, see Alex Kingsbury, "David Lawrence: A Profile," *U.S. News and World Report*, May 16, 2008, available at www.usnews.com.
20. David Lawrence, "The CIA-Students Controversy," *Washington Sunday Star*, February 16, 1967.
21. Mackenzie, *Secrets*, 27. A recent book, written by a CIA officer who worked inside MH/CHAOS, defends the operation: Frank J. Rafalko, *MH/CHAOS: The CIA's Campaign Against the Radical New Left and the Black Panthers* (Annapolis, Md.: Naval Institute Press, 2011). Yet Rafalko confirms that the origins of the operations reside in the search for foreign influence, citing the August 15, 1967, meeting on page 15.
22. Mackenzie, *Secrets*, 24.
23. Ibid.
24. Ibid., 27.
25. Interviews with Kiley and Tony Smith.
26. FOIA, Declassified files from 1967 to 1975 contain many documents on the NSA; the latest date in the Vaughn Index of withheld documents is 1981, about the time the lawsuit was filed. The Index, which comprises hundreds of pages of computer printouts, will be added to the USNSA collection at the Hoover Institution at the completion of this project.
27. Sam Brown headed Youth for McCarthy before he and David Hawk, another former NSA staff member, founded the Moratorium Against the Vietnam War. For an overview of the antiwar movement, including the Moratorium and the role of Tom Hayden and others in the New Mobilization Against the Vietnam War, see Tom Wells, *The War Within: America's Battle over Vietnam*, Author's Guild Backprint.com edition, iUniverse, Inc.
28. See "Restless Youth" at DocStoc, www.docstoc.com.
29. Interview with Kiley.
30. Interview with Richard Helms, February 2, 1988, at "Oral History: Reflections of DCI Colby and Helms on the CIA's 'Time of Troubles,'" CIA Center for the Study of Intelligence Web site, cia.gov./library/center-for-the-story-of intelligence.
31. Interview with F. A. O. Schwarz, Jr., New York City, May 26, 2004.
32. Casual conversation with former USSA presidents Janice Fine (1981–83) and Tom Swan (1985–87).
33. I am grateful to David Sobel for numerous FOIA documents. In 1982 or 1983, as the director of the Youth Project, a philanthropy headquartered in Washington, I awarded a small grant to Sobel to obtain additional FOIA documents. Between 1998 and 2013, we had several conversations about the FOIA lawsuit, in which he described his experiences in the USNSA archives at the Hoover Institution.
34. Wayne G. Jackson, *Allen Welsh Dulles as Director of Central Intelligence, 26 February 1953–29 November 1961*; History Staff, CIA, printed in 1973, released

with redactions, 1994. Available at NARA, Records of the Central Intelligence Agency, RG 263.2.2.

35. Cord Meyer, *Facing Reality: From World Federalism to the CIA* (New York: Harper and Row, 1980), 106.

36. Interview with David Baad, Saddlebrooke, Az., January 13, 2009.

37. Ibid.

38. Ibid. According to Baad, an exception was Musa Bin Hitam, who held the position of associate secretary for Asia at COSEC and became deputy prime minister of Malaysia.

39. Ibid.

40. Interview with Tony Smith, New York, November 7 and 9, 2007.

41. Interview with Robert Kiley, Cambridge, Mass., January 22, 2008.

42. Ibid.

43. My thanks to Clement M. Henry (formerly Clement Moore) for a copy of his article on UGEMA, "Combat et Solidarité: Témoignages de l'UGEMA (1955–1962)."

44. Interview with Crawford Young, Madison, Wisc., October 17, 2005.

45. Interview with Baad.

46. Ibid.

47. Interview with James Scott, Palo Alto, Calif., November 10, 1998.

48. Interview with Kiley.

49. Interview with Young.

50. Interview with Zybněk Vokrouhlický, Prague, September 5, 2008.

51. Paget Files: Clement M. Henry article on UGEMA.

52. Interview with Tony Smith.

53. Interview with Clive Gray, Greensboro Vt., September 1 and 2, 2005.

54. Peter Grose, *Gentleman Spy: The Life of Allen Dulles* (Amherst: University of Massachusetts Press, 1994), 230.

55. Philip R. Werdell, "Fun Birthday Surprise All for You," *Moderator*, April 1967.

56. Interviews with Bruce Larkin, Santa Cruz, Calif., April 25, 1999, and Scott.

57. Eden Lipson, memo of 1967 conversation with Dennis Shaul, courtesy of Eden Lipson.

58. Interview with Gray.

59. Michael Warner, "Sophisticated Spies," *International Journal of Intelligence and Counterintelligence* 9, no. 4 (Winter 1996–97): 432.

60. Interview with Tony Smith.

61. Interview with John Gardner, Palo Alto, Calif., September 13, 2000.

62. Tom Braden, "I'm Glad the CIA is 'Immoral,'" *Saturday Evening Post* (May 20, 1967), 10–14.

63. Interview with Bebchick.

64. Meyer, *Facing Reality*, 101.

65. Stansfield Turner, *Secrecy and Democracy: The CIA in Transition* (Boston: Houghton Mifflin, 1985), 76–77.

66. Warner, "Sophisticated Spies."

67. Conversation with Thomas Olson, New York, September 11, 2009.
68. Interview with Duncan Kennedy, Cambridge, Mass., September 7, 2005.
69. Edward Garvey made this remark at an NSA-USSA alumni discussion, Madison, Wisconsin, July 1997.
70. Interview with Ali Fatemi, Paris, October 16, 2006.
71. Robbins's statement was made during an NSA-USSA alumni discussion, Madison, Wisconsin, July 1997.
72. See Chapter 17.
73. Interview with Baad.
74. Interview with Kiley.
75. Interview with Tony Smith.
76. Interview with Leonard Bebchick, Washington, D.C., April 27, 2000.
77. Interview with Baad.

ABBREVIATIONS AND ACRONYMS

ADA	Americans for Democratic Action
AFL	American Federation of Labor
AFME	American Friends of the Middle East
AFVN	American Friends of Vietnam
AID	Agency for International Development
AIMS	American Internists and Medical Students
ANC	African National Congress
ASA	Associated Students of Afghanistan (U.S.)
ASU	American Student Union
AYD	American Youth for Democracy, formerly Young Communist League
BNUS	British National Union of Students
CFR	Council on Foreign Relations
CIA	Central Intelligence Agency
CIO	Congress of Industrial Organizations
CISC	Committee on International Student Cooperation (U.S.)
COSEC	Coordinating Secretariat (ISC; Leiden)
DRE	Directorio Revolucionario Estudiantil (Cuba); Directorio Revolucionario Estudiantil en el Exilio (Miami)
EUR/X	Intelligence division of the U.S. Department of State, based in Berlin
FBI	Federal Bureau of Investigation
FEDE	Federation of Dominican Republic Students in Exile
FEU	Federación Estudiantíl Universitaria (Federation of Cuban Students)
FEUU	Federación de Estudiantes Universitarios del Uruguay (Federation of Uruguayan Students)
FLN	Front de Libération Nationale (Algérie) (National Liberation Movement [Algeria])
FSLP	Foreign Student Leadership Project (USNSA)
FUPI	Federación de Universitarios Pro-Independencia (Federation of Pro-Independence Students; Puerto Rico)
FYSA	Foundation for Youth and Student Affairs (CIA conduit)
GUPS	General Union of Palestinian Students
GUSIR	General Union of Iraqi Students
HIACOM	Harvard International Activities Committee (USNSA)
HUAC	House Committee on Un-American Activities (U.S. Congress)
IAB	International Advisory Board (USNSA)
IC	International Commission (USNSA)

IIE	Institute of International Education
IO	International Organization division (CIA)
IRS	Independent Research Service (CIA); Internal Revenue Service (U.S. government)
ISA	International Student Assembly
ISAUS	Iranian Students Association in the United States
ISC	International Student Conference (Leiden)
ISIS	International Student Information Service (USNSA)
ISRS	International Student Relations Seminar (USNSA)
ISS	International Student Service (Geneva)
IUS	International Union of Students (Prague)
JCSA	Joint Committee for Student Action (U.S.; Catholic)
MPLA	Movimento Popular de Libertação de Angola (Angolan People's Liberation Movement)
NAACP	National Association for the Advancement of Colored People
NCL–ARM	National Committee for Liberation–African Resistance Movement
NCUSI	National Council of University Students of India
NCWC	National Catholic Welfare Council
NEC	National Executive Committee (USNSA)
NFCCS	National Federation of Catholic College Students
NICC	National Intercollegiate Christian Council (YMCA/YWCA)
NSA	National Student Association; *also* USNSA
NSB	National Supervisory Board (USNSA)
NUIS	National Union of Iraqi Students; National Union of Israeli Students
NUSI	National Union of Students India
NUSAS	National Union of South African Students
OAS	Organization of Arab Students
OH	Österreichischen Hochschülerschaft (Austrian Students Organization)
OPC	Office of Policy Coordination (Covert action unit of U.S. government)
OSS	Office of Strategic Services
PPMI	Persatuan Pelajar Mahasiswa Indonesia (Indonesian Student Association)
RIC	Research and Investigation Commission (ISC)
SCAP	Student Council Association of the Philippines
SDA	Students for Democratic Action
SDS	Students for a Democractic Society
SMAP	Students Mutual Assistance Program (NSA)
SNCC	Student Non-Violent Coordinating Committee
SSA	Student Service of America, Inc.
UFHS	Union of Free Hungarian Students
UGEAN	Union Générale des Étudiants d'Afrique Noire (sous domination coloniale portugaise) (General Union of Students from Black Africa [under Portuguese Colonial Domination])
UGEMA	Union Générale des Étudiants Musulmans Algériens (Algerian Student Union)

UNE   União Nacional dos Estudantes/National Student Union (Brazil)
UNEA   Union Nationale des Étudiants Algériens (National Union of Algerian
         Students); União Nacional dos Estudantes Angola (National Union of
         Angolan Students)
UNEF   Union Nationale des Étudiants de France (French Student Union)
UNESCO   United Nations Educational, Scientific and Cultural Organization
UPA   União das Populações de Angola (Union of Peoples of Angola)
USNSA   United States National Student Association
USSA   United States Student Assembly (1943); United States Student Association
         (1977)
USYC   United States Youth Council
WAY   World Assembly of Youth
WFDY   World Federation of Democratic Youth
WFTU   World Federation of Trade Unions
WSSF   World Student Service Fund
WUS   World University Service (formerly International Student Service)
YAF   Young Americans for Freedom
YMCA   Young Men's Christian Association
YPSL   Young People's Socialist League
YCL   Young Communist League (U.S.)
YWCA   Young Women's Christian Association
ZSP   Zrzeszenie Studentów Polskich (Polish Student Union)

ACKNOWLEDGMENTS

A fifteen-year book project may begin with a single step but is sustained by a thousand acts of kindness from family, friends, donors, archivists, and obliging sources. I was blessed by the generosity of old friends and new acquaintances (on several continents) and more than my fair share of serendipity. It is painful not to acknowledge the hundreds of people who donated everything from guest bedrooms and couches to their services in what became known as the Great Typo Hunt, but their names would fill another book.

An Open Society Institute Fellowship made the first step possible. I thank Deborah Harding, Aryeh Neier, Gara LeMarche, and Gail Goodman for their leap of faith, and Tamera Luzzatto for opening the door. Individual donors and foundation colleagues sustained me at crucial junctures. My deepest appreciation to Stanley Sheinbaum, Anne Bartley, Ethel Klein, Cora Weiss (Reuben), Tim Enwall, Alan Rabinowitz (Tides), and Chuck Shuford (Needmor). I thank the Journalism Committee of the Fund for Constitutional Government for its donation, and the Fund's director, Conrad Martin, for years of sponsorship and expedited checks. Ann Idzik provided incomparable hospitality during the long years of research in the Hoover Archives at Stanford University. Alice Chasen gave generously of her editorial skills to midwife what we now affectionately call the "unabridged edition" of the manuscript. Ethel Klein and Ed Krugman insisted we mark each phase of the book with a celebration.

If I could create a heaven for archivists, I would do so; they are very special people who often go above and beyond what their positions require. Elena S. Danielson (Hoover Institution), Elaine D. Engst (Cornell University), and Mieke Ijzermans (International Institute of Social History) exemplified those traits.

Many people entrusted documents and files to me, most importantly, David Sobel, the pro bono attorney who spent years extracting classified material from the U.S. government through a Freedom of Information lawsuit. The first National Student Association president, William Welsh, patiently pursued and obtained declassification of the 1967 Senate hearings. Michael Ansara searched in his barn and unearthed his work for *Ramparts*. John Frappier similarly parted with his investigative papers.

As every author knows, sharing drafts with readers is risky business; an unkind cut can be devastating. Fortunately, in Bob Kuttner, Pamela Jensen, Marian Quartly, Terri Shuck, Tom DeVries, Glenna Matthews, and Susan Calkins I had ideal readers who gave me the benefit of their penetrating intelligence *and* left me elevated.

Finally, my appreciation to Marge Tabankin, a friend from the Carter administration and the first woman president of the NSA after the *Ramparts* disclosures, who insisted I meet "the perfect agent" for this project and introduced me to Steve Wasserman, just as he was making the transition from agent to Yale University Press executive editor at large. Steve became a tireless champion of this book, insisting that it was one of the most important he had ever brought to market. His advocacy and his unparalleled patience and kindness through the illness and death of my parents saw me through a very difficult period. I was equally blessed by having the gifted Susan Laity as my manuscript editor: she possesses superb editing skills, an uncanny ability to find my intent in tangled prose, and an enthusiasm for the manuscript that touched me deeply. My gratitude to the entire Yale family, especially to Steve's assistant, the exemplary Erica Hanson, for her immediate attention to my questions, to the reviewers who recommended publication, and to all the staff that have brought me to the end of my journey. My debts are infinite.

INDEX